EU Antitrust Enforcement

Law, Economics, History, Policy & Practice

Wouter P. J. Wils

106 West 32nd Street, Suite 144, New York, NY 10001, USA
www.concurrences.com
books@concurrences.com

First Printing, February 2024
978-1-939007-65-0 (Hardcover)
Library of Congress Control Number: 2024931608

Cover: Yves Buliard, www.yvesbuliard.fr
Book design and layout implementation: Nord Compo

Concurrences Books

Tributes

James F. Rill, *P. Lugard, J. Taladay (eds.), Forthcoming 2024*

Eleanor M. Fox – Antitrust Ambassador to the World, *2021*

Herbert Hovenkamp – The Dean of American Antitrust Law, *2021*

Frédéric Jenny – Standing Up for Convergence and Relevance in Antitrust, (Vol. I & II), *2019 & 2021*

Albert Foer – A Consumer Voice in the Antitrust Arena, *2020*

Richard Whish – Taking Competition Law Outside the Box, *2020*

Douglas H. Ginsburg – An Antitrust Professor on the Bench (Vol. I & II), *2018 & 2020*

Wang Xiaoye – The Pioneer of Competition Law in China, *A. Emch, W. Ng (eds.), 2019*

Ian S. Forrester – A Scot without Borders (Vol. I & II), *A. Komninos (eds.), 2015*

William E. Kovacic – An Antitrust Tribute (Vol. I & II), *2013 & 2014*

Practical Books

Competition Inspections in 25 Jurisdictions – A Practitioner's Guide – 2nd edition, *N. Jalabert-Doury (ed.), Forthcoming 2024*

The 2023 U.S. Merger Guidelines – A Review, *S. Sullivan (ed.), Forthcoming 2024 (in collaboration with the CCIA)*

The DMA and more – Future application and margin of manoeuvre for national jurisdictions, *G. Muscolo & A. Massolo (eds.), Forthcoming 2024*

State Aid & National Enforcement, *J. Derenne, D. Jouve, C. Lemaire, F. Martucci (eds.), Forthcoming 2024*

The EU Foreign Subsidies Regulation, *Andreas Reindl, Isabelle Van Damme, 2024*

Compendium of Antitrust Damages Action – International Chamber of Commerce (ICC) – 2nd edition, *J.W.H. Denton AO, F. Brunet, S. Williams, C. Inthavisay (eds.), 2023*

Pharmaceutical Antitrust: An Analysis of US and EU Law, *M. Thill-Tayara, G. Gordon (eds.), 2023*

Innovation Paradox in Merger Control, *G. Gurkaynak, 2023*

Antitrust and the Digital Economy, *Y. Katsoulacos (ed.), 2023 (in collaboration with CRESSE)*

Judicial Review of Competition Cases, *D. Ginsburg, T. Eicke (eds.), 2023*

Competition Law Treatment of Joint Ventures, *B. Bleicher, N. Campbell, A. Hamilton, N. Hukkinen, A. Khan, A. Mordaunt (eds.), 2022 (in collaboration with the IBA)*

Information Exchange & Related Risks, *Z. Marosi, M. Soares (eds.), 2022 (in collaboration with the IBA)*

Rulemaking Authority of the US Federal Trade Commission, *D. Crane (ed.), 2022*

The International Competition Network at Twenty, *D. Anderson & P. Lugard (eds.), 2022*

Competition Case Law Digest – 5th Edition, *F. Jenny, N. Charbit (eds.), 2022*

Competition Inspections in 21 Jurisdictions – A Practitioner's Guide, *N. Jalabert-Doury (ed.), 2022*

Perspectives on Antitrust Compliance, *A. Riley, A. Stephan, A. Tubbs (eds.), 2022 (in collaboration with the ICC)*

Turkish Competition Law, *G. Gürkaynak, 2021*

Competition Law – Climate Change & Environmental Sustainability, *S. Holmes, D. Middelschulte, M. Snoep (eds.), 2021*

Merger Control in Latin America – A Jurisdictional Guide, *P. Burnier da Silveira, P. Sittenfeld (eds.), 2020*

Competition Inspections under EU Law – A Practitioner's Guide, *N. Jalabert-Doury, 2020*

Gun Jumping in Merger Control – A Jurisdictional Guide, *C. Hatton, Y. Comtois, A. Hamilton (eds.), 2019 (in collaboration with the IBA)*

Choice – A New Standard for Competition Analysis? *P. Nihoul (ed.), 2016*

PhD Theses

The Economics of Digital Markets – Essays in Theoretical and Empirical Industrial Organization, *E. Arnoud-Joufray, Forthcoming 2024*

Abuse of Platform Power, *F. Bostoen, 2023*

Reform of Chinese State-Owned Enterprises, *X. Bai, 2023*

Competition & Regulation in Network Industries – Essays in Industrial Organization, *J-M. Zogheib, 2021*

The Role of Media Pluralism in the Enforcement of EU Competition Law, *K. Bania, 2019*

Buyer Power, *I. Herrera Anchustegui, 2017*

General Interest

Why Competition? Voices from the Antitrust Community and Beyond, *D. Crane, D. Gerard, R. Tritell (eds.), Forthcoming 2024*

Global Dictionary of Competition Law, *D. Healey, W. Kovacic, P. Trevisan, R. Whish (eds.), Forthcoming 2024*

Great Antitrust Enforcers, *W. E. Kovacic, 2023*

Competition – How to Speak Like an Expert, *E. Combe , 2023*

Women and Antitrust – Voices from the Field (Vol I & II), *E. Kurgonaite & K. Nordlander, 2020*

INTRODUCTION AND ACKNOWLEDGMENTS

EU antitrust enforcement has been radically transformed in the past thirty years. Following the decentralisation brought about by Regulation 1/2003, the European Commission now shares the public enforcement of Articles 101 and 102 TFEU with the competition authorities of the EU Member States. Indeed, the national competition authorities have in quantitative terms become the primary public enforcers of Articles 101 and 102 TFEU, adopting 90% of all decisions. Public enforcement has furthermore changed through the use of leniency, settlements and prioritisation. Following the EU Court of Justice's judgment in *Courage and Crehan* and the Damages Directive 2014/104, private antitrust enforcement, in particular in the form of follow-on actions for damages in cartel cases, has also significantly increased, raising delicate questions as to the optimal balance and interaction between public and private enforcement. Not surprisingly, increased antitrust enforcement has also brought renewed attention to the procedural rights of defendants and third parties in public antitrust enforcement, and the compatibility of the existing enforcement system and practices with the European Convention on Human Rights and the EU Charter of Fundamental Rights. Numerous judgments of the EU Courts, as well as of the European Court of Human Rights, have dealt with these issues.

Blending legal and economic analysis, and drawing on decades of practical experience, this book analyses the main questions of law and policy raised by this historical transformation of EU antitrust enforcement and by its current state.

The eighteen chapters of this book are each based on one or more papers published in the past fifteen years, which have been adapted and updated, often extensively, to take into account intervening developments, and to ensure a coherent whole.

Chapter I provides an overview of the genesis of Regulation 1/2003, its objectives, and its main results, as apparent twenty years later. It finds that the decentralisation to the national competition authorities, cooperating with the European Commission and each other in the European Competition Network, has been a major success, beyond expectations. On the other hand, the prediction that the reform would lead to a significant increase in the number of prohibition decisions adopted by the European Commission has turned out to be too optimistic. Ten possible explanations for this lack of increase in the number of prohibition decisions are tentatively examined. This chapter is based on a paper written for the conference *20 Years of Regulation 1/2003* at the Mannheim Centre for Competition and Innovation in November 2022 and published in (2023) *World Competition* 3, in (2023) *Neue Zeitschrift für Kartellrecht* 123 and in *Concurrences* no 4-2022.

Chapter II deals with Article 3 of Regulation 1/2003, which obliges the competition authorities of the EU Member States to apply Articles 101 and 102 TFEU whenever they apply national competition law to conduct falling within the scope of EU antitrust law. It examines the content and rationale of this provision, and the legal consequences in case of non-respect of this provision, using as an example the Facebook Decision of 6 February 2019 of the Bundeskartellamt (German Federal Competition Authority). This chapter is based on a paper published in *Concurrences* no 3-2019.

Chapter III gives an overview of the independence guarantees in EU law for the European Commission and the national competition authorities, when applying Articles 101 and 102 TFEU, and discusses more in general the notion of independence of competition authorities and its rationale. This chapter is based on a paper published in (2019) *World Competition* 149 and in *Concurrences* no 3-2019, as well as on a paper prepared for the 8th New Frontiers of Antitrust conference in Paris in June 2017 and published in *Concurrences* no 3-2017 and in *Kilpailuoikeudellinen Vuosikirja / Competition Law Yearbook 2017* (Finnish Competition Law Association 2018).

Chapter IV discusses discretion and prioritisation in public antitrust enforcement, in particular in the enforcement of EU antitrust law by the European Commission. It defines the notion of discretion and discusses the rationale of discretion, examines the enforcement of Articles 101 and 102 TFEU by the European Commission, and sets out various reasons for allowing competition authorities discretion to set priorities as to which cases of suspected or alleged infringements of the antitrust prohibitions they investigate and pursue, as well as a number of risks related to prioritisation. This chapter is based on a paper published in (2011) *World Competition* 353 and in *Concurrences* no 3-2011.

Chapter V deals with the European Commission's and the national competition authorities' leniency programmes, under which companies cooperating with their cartel investigations can obtain immunity from fines or a reduction of fines. It discusses the conditions and historical development of these leniency programmes, and assesses the positive effects and the possible negative effects of leniency, in the light of more than twenty years of experience. This chapter is based on a paper presented at King's College London Centre of European Law in June 2016 and published in (2016) *World Competition* 327 and in *Concurrences* no 1-2017 and reprinted in S. B. Farmer (ed.) *International Library of Comparative Laws – Comparative Competition Law* (Edgar Elgar 2020).

Chapter VI discusses two general questions concerning the use of settlements in public antitrust enforcement – namely, under which conditions the use of settlements contributes to optimal antitrust enforcement, and under which conditions self-incrimination and waivers of procedural rights by settlement candidates are compatible with fundamental rights of defence. The discussion of these general questions is illustrated with the specific example of two settlement procedures for the enforcement by the European Commission of Articles 101 and 102 TFEU – namely, the commitment procedure under Article 9 of Regulation 1/2003, and the settlement procedure in cartel cases. This chapter is based on a paper presented at the 13th Annual EU Competition Law and Policy Workshop at the European University Institute in Florence in June 2008, and published in (2008) *World Competition* 335, in *Concurrences* no 3-2008 and in C.-D. Ehlermann and M. Marquis (eds.) *European Competition Law Annual 2008* (Hart 2010).

Chapter VII discusses the place of compliance programmes in optimal antitrust enforcement, on the basis of an analysis of the nature of antitrust infringements, the rationale of company liability for antitrust infringements, and the possible positive and possible negative effects of compliance programmes. This chapter is based on a paper published in (2013) *Journal of Antitrust Enforcement* 52 and in *Concurrences* no 3-2013.

Chapter VIII discusses, from a legal and economic perspective, the problem of recidivism in EU antitrust enforcement. It first clarifies the concept of recidivism and then analyses the treatment of recidivism as an aggravating circumstance in setting the amount of fines, the interplay between recidivism and leniency, and the difficulty of drawing conclusions as to the overall effectiveness of EU antitrust enforcement from the observed incidence of recidivism. This chapter is based on a paper published in (2012) *World Competition* 5 and in *Concurrences* no 1-2012 and reprinted in S. B. Farmer (ed.) *International Library of Comparative Laws – Comparative Competition Law* (Edgar Elgar 2020).

Chapter IX discusses the compatibility with fundamental rights of the EU antitrust system in which the European Commission acts both as investigator and as first-instance decision-maker. This chapter is based on a paper prepared for the *7. Luxenburger Expertenforum zur Entwicklung des Unionsrecht* at the EU Court of Justice in December 2013 and published in (2014) *World Competition* 5 and in *Concurrences* no 2-2014, as well as an earlier paper prepared for the *17th St Gallen International Competition Law Forum* in 2010 and published in (2010) *World Competition* 5, in *Concurrences* no 2-2010 and in C. Baudenbacher (ed.), *Current Developments in European and International Competition Law – 17th St Gallen International Competition Law Forum 2010* (Helbig & Lichtenhahn 2011).

Chapter X deals with the fundamental procedural rights of companies that are targeted in the enforcement of Articles 101 and 102 TFEU by the European Commission or the competition authorities of the EU Member States. The chapter first provides a (non-exhaustive) list of such rights as applicable to the enforcement of Articles 101 and 102 TFEU by the European Commission, and explains the source of these fundamental rights in the EU legal order. It then examines the relationship between fundamental procedural rights and effective enforcement of Articles 101 and 102 TFEU. Finally, it examines the question whether or to what extent EU Member States can, for the enforcement of Articles 101 and 102 TFEU by their national competition authorities, provide for a lower or a higher level of procedural rights than the level of fundamental procedural rights applicable to the enforcement of Articles 101 and 102 TFEU by the European Commission. This chapter is based on a paper presented at the Institut für Kartellrecht of the Heinrich Heine University in Düsseldorf in September 2019 and at the Portuguese Competition Authority in October 2019, and published in (2020) *World Competition* 5 and in *Concurrences* no 2-2020, and an earlier paper presented at the 2nd New Frontiers of Antitrust Conference in Paris in February 2011 and published in (2011) *World Competition* 189 and in *Concurrences* no 2-2011.

Chapter XI deals with the role of the Hearing Officer in proceedings conducted by the European Commission for the enforcement of Articles 101 and 102 TFEU. After a brief discussion of the history and status of the Hearing Officer, this chapter examines the various powers and tasks of the Hearing Officer (other than the organisation and conduct of the oral hearing, which is discussed in the following chapter). This chapter is based on a paper published in (2012) *World Competition* 431 and in E. Rousseva (ed.) *EU Antitrust procedure* (Oxford 202), and a second paper published in K. Dekeyser,

C. Gauer, J. Laitenberger, N. Wahl, W. Wils and L. Prete (eds.), *Regulation 1/2003 and EU Antitrust Enforcement – A Systematic Guide* (Wolters Kluwer 2022).

Chapter XII deals with the oral hearing in proceedings conducted by the European Commission for the enforcement of Articles 101 and 102 TFEU. It analyses the legal basis and the nature and purpose of the oral hearing, examines who can request an oral hearing, and who can attend and speak at the oral hearing, compares the oral hearing with state of play meetings, and provides some general observations as to what factors may make addressees of a statement of objections decide in favour or against requesting an oral hearing. This paper is based on a paper published in (2012) *World Competition* 397.

Chapter XIII discusses the law, policy and procedure of legal professional privilege in EU antitrust enforcement. It focuses primarily on the enforcement of Articles 101 and 102 TFEU by the European Commission, but also touches briefly on the enforcement of EU antitrust law by the competition authorities of the EU Member States (addressing in particular the question whether those EU Member States that extend legal professional privilege to in-house lawyers are in breach of EU law), as well as on private enforcement. This chapter is based on a paper prepared for the OECD Competition Committee Roundtable on the Treatment of Privileged Information in Competition Proceedings in November 2018 and published in (2019) *World Competition* 21 and in *Concurrences* no 1-2019.

Chapter XIV provides a systematic overview of the procedural rights and obligations of third parties in investigations and proceedings conducted by the European Commission for the enforcement of Articles 101 and 102 TFEU. It examines (i) the possibilities for third parties to inform the European Commission about a suspected infringement and to trigger an investigation by the European Commission; (ii) the obligations and rights of third parties when responding to requests for information sent to them by the European Commission, when participating in interviews, and when submitting to inspections conducted by the European Commission; (iii) the possibilities for third parties to obtain information about pending proceedings and to express their views in them; the rules on the use of languages; and (iv) the protection of business secrets and other confidential information, and the restrictions on the use of information obtained by third parties through their participation in the European Commission's proceedings. This chapter is based on a paper published in (2022) *World Competition* 5 and in *Concurrences* no 2-2022.

Chapter XV deals with the publication by the European Commission of its decisions adopted in the enforcement of the competition rules laid down in Articles 101 and 102 TFEU. It examines (i) the legal basis of such publication and the interests justifying publication; (ii) what content of the decision must be published, may be published and cannot be published; (iii) the procedure and timing of the publication; and (iv) the relationship with public access to documents. This chapter is based on a paper published in *Concurrences* no 4-2020.

Chapter XVI deals with the re-adoption by the European Commission of decisions imposing fines on undertakings found to have participated in cartels in violation of Article 101 TFEU following the annulment of those decisions by the EU Courts on procedural grounds. It gives an overview of cases in which such re-adoption has taken place and analyses the applicable legal principles and policy considerations. This chapter is based on a paper published in *Concurrences* no 3-2021.

Chapter XVII contains a history of private enforcement of EU antitrust law and its relationship with public enforcement, from the 1957 EEC Treaty over Regulation 17 and Regulation 1/2003 until Directive 2014/104 and the current outlook. This chapter is based on a paper presented at the Law and Economics Conference on Cartel Damages in Europe at the Mannheim Centre for Competition and Innovation in 2016 and published in (2017) *World Competition* 3 and in *Concurrences* no 2-2017, as well as an earlier paper presented at the UK Association for European Law (UKAEL) Conference 'Competition and Private Enforcement: The Next Steps' in London in 2008 and published in (2009) *World Competition* 3.

Finally, chapter XVIII discusses the recent proposal of the German Monopolies Commission (Monopolkommission) to revise the Damages Directive 2014/104 to grant companies that have received immunity from fines under the competition authorities' leniency programmes also immunity from damages. It analyses the development of follow-on actions for damages, discusses the question of the optimal number of leniency applications, takes a closer look at the figures, examines the possible and likely causes of the observed evolution of the number of leniency applications, and argues that it would be unwise to grant immunity recipients full protection from damages, because this would be unjust, would harm public anti-cartel enforcement and would increase market concentration. This chapter is based on a paper published in (2023) *Wirtschaft und Wettbewerb* and in *Concurrences* no 3-2023.

I am grateful to Margaret Bloom, Claus-Dieter Ehlermann, Jens-Uwe Franck, Laurence Idot, Frédéric Jenny, Christian Kersting, Margarida Matos Rosa, Rupprecht Podszun, Heike Schweitzer, Philippa Watson and Richard Whish for having invited me to the conferences and lectures which prompted me to write the papers on which this book is based, to Henry Abbott, Michael Adam, Sven Albaek, Michael Albers, Elisavet Arsenidou, David Bailey, Eric Barbier de La Serre, Margaret Bloom, William Blumenthal, André Bouquet, James Bourke, Ingrid Breit, Claire Carrega, Fernando Castillo de la Torre, Theofanis Christoforou, Conor Clyne, John Connor, Dorothe Dalheimer, Anthony Dawes, Thomas Deisenhofer, Kris Dekeyser, Eddy De Smijter, Vittorio Di Bucci, Daniel Dittert, Jan Eijsbouts, Barbara Ernst, John Fingleton, Chiara Galiffa, Céline Gauer, Eric Gippini Fournier, Maribel Glogowski, Karl Hammarlund, Andreas Heinemann, Laurence Idot, Maria Jaspers, Jérémie Jourdan, Alison Jones, Manuel Kellerbauer, Šarūnas Keserauskas, Nicholas Khan, Assimakis Komninos, Hannes Krämer, Xavier Lewis, Frank Maier-Rigaud, Robert Marschall, Gero Meeßen, Bernard Mongin, Kirtikumar Mehta, Okeoghene Odudu, Siún O'Keeffe, Peter Oliver, Konrad Ost, Christine Parker, Xandra Reintjes, Anne Riley, José Rivas, Felix Ronkes Agerbeek, Peter Roth, Lorenzo Ruocco, Shahrzad Sadjadi, Géraud Sajust de Bergues, Ewoud Sakkers, Ralf Sauer, Maarten Pieter Schinkel, Ulrich Schwalbe, Enrique Sepúlveda García, Ailsa Sinclair, Daniel Sokol, Andreas Stephan, Sophia Stephanou, Joos Stragier, Mariana Tavares, Jonathan Tomkin, Vanessa Turner, Dirk Van Erps, Piet Van Nuffel, Freya van Schaik, Christian Vollrath, Anna Vernet, Florian Wagner-von Papp, Gregory Werden, Richard Whish, Geert Wils and Fabien Zivy for their stimulating comments on earlier versions of those papers, and to José Rivas and Kluwer Law International, editor and publisher of *World Competition*, as well as to all the editors and publishers of the journals and books in which those papers have been published, for having allowed me to use (updated versions of) these papers for this book, and to

Nicolas Charbit, Johannes Laitenberger and Ben Smulders for having encouraged me to adapt and update those papers and turn them into this book. All views expressed in this book are strictly personal and should not be construed as reflecting the opinion of the European Commission, its Legal Service, or any of the persons mentioned above. Comments are always welcome at Wouter.Wils@ec.europa.eu.

Wouter P. J. Wils
Brussels, 15 August 2023

TABLE OF CONTENTS

I. Regulation 1/2003: An Assessment after Twenty Years

A. Introduction

Regulation 1/2003[1] brought about a radical change in the way in which the EU antitrust prohibitions contained in Articles 101 and 102 of the Treaty on the Functioning of the European Union (TFEU)[2] are enforced. The previous enforcement regime, under Regulation 17,[3] which dated from 1962, was characterised by a centralised notification and authorisation system for Article 101(3) TFEU. Regulation 1/2003 abolished this system and replaced it with a system of decentralised *ex post* enforcement, in which the European Commission and the competition authorities of the EU Member States (national competition authorities or NCAs), forming together the European Competition Network (ECN), pursue infringements of Articles 101 and 102 TFEU.

This chapter provides an overview of the genesis of Regulation 1/2003, its objectives, and its main results, as apparent twenty years later.

Regulation 1/2003 was adopted by the Council of the European Union on 16 December 2002. It bears the number 1/2003 because it was the first regulation published in the Official Journal of the European Union in the year 2003, on 4 January 2003. According to its Article 45, it entered into force on the 20th day following that publication, but it only applied from 1 May 2004.[4] There will thus be twenty years of experience with the application of Regulation 1/2003 by the end of April 2024. On the other hand, much of the thinking behind Regulation 1/2003 goes back to more than twenty years ago. Indeed, as described below, the basic ideas underlying Regulation 1/2003 were already conceived inside the European Commission in 1997.

---

1 Council Regulation (EC) No 1/2003 of 16 December 2002 on the implementation of the rules on competition laid down in Articles 81 and 82 of the Treaty [2003] OJ L1/1, last amended by Council Regulation (EC) No 1419/2006 [2006] OJ L269/1. For a detailed analysis of Regulation 1/2003, in comparison with the regime preceding it, see my *Community Report* in D. Cahill and J. D. Cooke (eds), *The Modernisation of EU Competition Law Enforcement in the EU – FIDE 2004 National Reports* (Cambridge 2004), 661–736; my book *Principles of European Antitrust Enforcement* (Hart 2005); and K. Dekeyser, C. Gauer, J. Laitenberger, N. Wahl, W. Wils and L. Prete (eds), *Regulation 1/2003 and EU Antitrust Enforcement – A Systematic Guide* (Wolters Kluwer 2022).

2 Article 101 TFEU prohibits agreements between undertakings and decisions by associations of undertakings that may affect trade between EU Member States and restrict competition without redeeming virtue. Article 102 TFEU prohibits any abuse by one or more undertakings of a dominant position within the EU internal market or in a substantial part of it in so far as it may affect trade between EU Member States. These two prohibitions were previously contained in Articles 85 and 86 of the Treaty establishing the European Economic Community (EEC) and in Articles 81 and 82 of the Treaty establishing the European Community (EC). In this book, I will systematically refer to the current numbers and name.

3 Council Regulation No 17 [1962] OJ 13/204 (Special English Edition 1959-62, p 87).

4 The latter date is also the date on which the number of EU Member States increased from 15 to 25. This is not a coincidence; indeed the perspective of this enlargement was the main impetus for the European Commission to start working in 1997 on new rules for the implementation of Articles 101 and 102 TFEU.

B. Genesis

1. Modernisation Group

The origin of Regulation 1/2003 lies in January 1997, when a group of approximately a dozen officials of the European Commission started meeting, at the initiative and under the chairmanship of Gianfranco Rocca, then Deputy Director-General of the Commission's Directorate-General for Competition, in what was called the Modernisation Group (or rather *groupe de modernisation*, as everything happened in French).[5]

The starting point for the Modernisation Group's reflections was that the procedural rules for the application of Articles 101 and 102 TFEU had been laid down in 1962 in Regulation 17, which had never been reviewed since, whereas the EU had undergone substantial change, and would change further as a result of the planned accession of ten Central and Eastern European countries, which would significantly increase the workload of the Commission's Directorate-General for Competition.

When examining what type of procedural rules would be most appropriate in this new context, the Modernisation Group quickly came to the view that the centralised notification and authorisation system for Article 101(3) TFEU, as created by Regulation 17, should be abandoned and replaced by a directly applicable exception system. The choice between these two enforcement systems had been much discussed already at the time of the drafting of the Treaty provisions in the 1950s, and at the time of the adoption of Regulation 17 in the early 1960s. At that time, Germany favoured a notification and authorisation system, while France favoured a directly applicable exception system. The question was left open at the level of the Treaty. In its proposal for what became Regulation 17, the Commission opted for a centralised notification and authorisation system, and the Council eventually endorsed this choice in Regulation 17. The analysis made by the Modernisation Group in 1997 was that the Commission and Council had made the right choice in the conditions prevailing in 1962, but that, given the development of the EU and of competition policy in the EU since that time, a directly applicable exception system had now become preferable.[6]

Having obtained the agreement of Karel Van Miert, the Member of the European Commission then responsible for competition policy, the Modernisation Group subsequently went to work on the modalities of the change to a directly applicable exception

---

5 See further S. Norberg, 'Making Virtue out of Necessity and at Same Time Strengthening European Competition Law Enforcement – How the White Paper on Modernisation Reform came about', in M. Monti, Prinz N. von und zu Lichtenstein, B. Vesterdorf, J. Westbrook and L. Wildhaber (eds), *Economic Law and Justice in Times of Globalisation – Festschrift for Carl Baudenbacher* (Nomos 2007), 523.

6 See further G. Marenco, 'Does the Legal Exception System Require an Amendment of the Treaty?' in C.-D. Ehlermann and I. Atanasiu, *European Competition Law Annual 2000: The Modernisation of EC Antitrust Policy* (Hart 2001), 145, as well as, for a systematic analysis of why the notification system made sense in 1962 but no longer today, my publications 'Notification, Clearance and Exemption in EC Competition Law: An Economic Analysis' (1999) 24 *European Law Review* 139; 'The Modernisation of the Enforcement of Articles 81 and 82 EC: A Legal and Economic Analysis of the Commission's Proposal for a New Council Regulation Replacing Regulation No 17', in B. Hawk (ed), *Annual Proceedings of the Fordham Corporate Law Institute 2000* (Juris 2001), 313; my book *The Optimal Enforcement of EC Antitrust Law* (Kluwer 2002), Chapters 5 and 6, and my book *Principles of European Antitrust Enforcement* (Hart 2005), Section 1.1.3.

system, and examined, article by article, the whole of Regulation 17, so as to identify any other changes or improvements that could be made. After two years and around fifty half-day or day-long meetings, a draft White Paper setting out the proposed reforms was produced.

2. White Paper on Modernisation, legislative proposal and final compromise

The European Commission adopted and published the White Paper on Modernisation in 1999.[7] It advocated the ending of the notification and authorisation system, and its replacement by a system of *ex post* enforcement, allowing the Commission to refocus its action on combating the most serious competition infringements, and allowing an enhanced role for national competition authorities and national courts. It also proposed to strengthen the European Commission's investigatory powers.

The publication of the White Paper on Modernisation came as a complete surprise. Indeed, the work which the Modernisation Group had been doing over the two preceding years had been carefully kept secret, also inside the European Commission. The general view at the time, both inside and outside the European Commission, was that the Commission would never propose to replace Regulation 17, for fear of losing the substantial powers which it had been granted by the Council in 1962.[8] While occasionally the notification system was criticised by some authors, nobody had made a sustained argument for its abolition.[9]

Once the initial surprise had subsided, however, the reactions to the White Paper were mostly (very) positive,[10] though with one exception and one qualification.

The one exception was Germany, where in particular some highly respected professors, mostly of an older generation, and thus more likely to remember the discussions of the 1950s and early 1960s in which the German arguments in favour of a notification and authorisation system had ultimately convinced the Commission and the Council at the time of Regulation 17, were strongly opposed to the abolition of the notification system.[11] Moreover, the Bundeskartellamt (German Federal Competition Authority) had in 1998 (without any knowledge of the work being done at that time by the Modernisation Group inside the European Commission) proposed to decentralise the notification and

---

7 White Paper on modernisation of the rules implementing Articles 85 and 86 of the EC Treaty [1999] OJ C132/1.

8 See C.-D. Ehlermann, 'The Modernization of EC Antitrust Policy: A Legal and Cultural Revolution' (2000) 37 *Common Market Law Review* 537.

9 See for instance the at that time very influential paper by B. E. Hawk, 'System Failure: Vertical Restraints and EC Competition Law' (1995) 32 *Common Market Law Review* 973, which criticised the notification system at page 984, but did not include its abolition through a revision of Regulation 17 among the list of possible solutions at pages 986–988; see also the discussion of the notification system in the Commission's Green Paper on vertical restraints in EC competition policy, COM(96)721, and in the reactions to this Green Paper, summarised in the Communication from the Commission on the application of the Community competition rules to vertical restraints (Follow-up to the Green Paper on Vertical Restraints) [1998] OJ C365/3.

10 See for instance B. Hawk, 'EU "modernisation": a latter-day Reformation' (August/September 1999) *Global Competition Review* 12.

11 See for instance E.-J. Mestmäcker, 'The EC Commission's Modernization of Competition Policy: a Challenge to the Community's Constitutional Order' (2000) 1 *European Business Organization Law Review* 401.

authorisation system, thus sharing the work between the European Commission and the national competition authorities.[12]

The one qualification concerned the reaction of industry and the European Parliament, which expressed the fear that the decentralisation of the application of EU competition law would lead to a renationalisation of competition policy.

This last concern explains the main addition, as compared to the White Paper, which the European Commission included in the legislative proposal it submitted to the Council in 2000.[13] Article 3 of the proposed regulation excluded the application of national competition laws to all agreements or concerted practices within the meaning of Article 101 TFEU and all abuses of a dominant position within the meaning of Article 102 TFEU that affect trade between Member States, thus ensuring the sole applicability of EU law.

This last proposal in turn caused significant opposition from a number of Member States, and proved the most contentious point in the deliberations of the Council. The compromise which was ultimately found, and enacted in Article 3 of Regulation 1/2003, obliges national competition authorities and national courts, when applying national competition law to agreements or practices falling within the scope of application of Articles 101 or 102 TFEU, to apply also EU law.[14] It further provides that the application of national competition law may not lead to the prohibition of agreements or concerted practices affecting trade between Member States that are not prohibited under Article 101 TFEU, but it leaves Member States the freedom to apply on their territory national laws that are stricter than Article 102 TFEU in prohibiting unilateral conduct.[15]

Another contentious issue in the deliberations of the Council concerned the respective roles of the European Commission and the national competition authorities, and the functioning of the European Competition Network. Some national competition authorities, in particular the Bundeskartellamt, the national authority with the proudest tradition of competition law enforcement, feared that the Commission would play too dominant a role in the new system. This issue was resolved through the adoption of the Joint Statement of the Council and the Commission on the functioning of the network of competition authorities, entered into the Council Minutes at the time of the adoption of Regulation 1/2003.[16] The principles set out in this Joint Statement were later fleshed out in the Commission's Notice on cooperation within the network of competition authorities,[17] which was agreed with all national competition authorities.

---

12 See White Paper on modernisation, footnote 48.

13 Proposal for a Council Regulation implementing Articles 81 and 82 of the Treaty, COM(2000)582.

14 See also Judgment of 14 February 2012, *Toshiba*, C-17/10, EU:C:2012:72, paragraph 83.

15 See Communication from the Commission to the European Parliament and Council – Report on the functioning of Regulation 1/2003, COM(2009)206, Chapter 4; Commission Staff Working Paper accompanying the Report on the functioning of Regulation 1/2003, SEC(2009)574, section 4.4; and I. Kokkoris, *A Gap in the Enforcement of Article 82* (British Institute of International and Comparative Law 2009).

16 Council Document 15435/02 ADD 1 of 10 December 2002, available at http://register.consilium.europa.eu; see Judgment of 8 March 2007, *France Télécom v Commission*, T-339/04, EU:T:2007:80, paragraph 85, and Opinion of Advocate General Mazák of 16 December 2010, *Pfleiderer*, C-360/09, EU:C:2010:782, paragraph 26.

17 [2004] OJ C101/43.

C. Objectives

The White Paper on Modernisation, the explanatory memorandum of the legislative proposal, and the recitals of Regulation 1/2003 highlight two objectives: intensified enforcement by the European Commission, and decentralisation of enforcement to national authorities and national courts, while maintaining EU-wide consistency in the interpretation of Articles 101 and 102 TFEU.

1. Intensified enforcement by the European Commission

The first objective was to allow the European Commission to become more active in the pursuit of serious infringements of Articles 101 and 102 TFEU.[18]

At the time of the White Paper, the European Commission dealt every year with 150 to 200 notification cases through comfort letters.[19] It thus spent substantial resources on cases of little or no value for the effective enforcement of Articles 101 and 102 TFEU. The abolition of the notification system would allow the Commission to redirect these resources to curbing the more serious infringements of Articles 101 and 102 TFEU.[20] The White Paper predicted that thus 'the number of individual prohibition decisions can be expected to increase substantially'.[21]

This intensified enforcement by the European Commission was further helped by strengthening the Commission's powers of investigation,[22] and by encouraging the victims of antitrust infringement to approach the Commission as complainants, in particular by introducing a time limit of four months by the end of which the Commission would inform the complainant of the action it proposed to take on the complaint.[23]

2. Decentralisation of enforcement, while maintaining EU-wide consistency

The second objective was to decentralise the application of Articles 101 and 102 TFEU more to the Member States' competition authorities and to the national courts, making both the national competition authorities and the national courts play an enhanced role in the application of the EU antitrust rules.[24]

To this effect, Regulation 1/2003 not only abolished the European Commission's monopoly for applying Article 101(3) TFEU. It also obliged all Member States to designate national competition authorities empowered to apply Articles 101 and 102 TFEU,[25] and obliged both national competition authorities and national courts to also apply

---

18 White Paper on Modernisation, paragraphs 10, 13 and 42.

19 White Paper on Modernisation, paragraph 34.

20 Recital 3 of Regulation 1/2003.

21 White Paper on Modernisation, paragraph 87.

22 White Paper on Modernisation, paragraphs 109 to 116 and 124 to 126, and recitals 25, 26 and 29 and Articles 19 to 21 and 23(1) of Regulation 1/2003.

23 White Paper on Modernisation, paragraph 120, and Commission Notice on the handling of complaints by the Commission under Articles 81 and 82 of the EC Treaty [2004] OJ C101/65.

24 White Paper on Modernisation, paragraphs 46, 91 and 99, and recitals 6 and 7 of Regulation 1/2003.

25 Article 35(1) and Article 5 of Regulation 1/2003.

Articles 101 and 102 TFEU whenever they apply national competition law to agreements or practices within the scope of Articles 101 and 102 TFEU.[26]

At the same time, this decentralisation was not to lead to inconsistent application of EU antitrust law.[27]

To this effect, the European Commission was to continue adopting block exemptions, and draw up more notices and guidelines to provide guidance on the application of Articles 101 and 102 TFEU.[28] The European Competition Network (ECN) was created, bringing together the European Commission and the national competition authorities to make them apply Articles 101 and 102 TFEU in close cooperation.[29] Arrangements were also established for cooperation between the national courts and the European Commission.[30]

D. Results

1. National competition authorities and the European Competition Network

Twenty years after the adoption of Regulation 1/2003, there can be no doubt that, as far as the national competition authorities and the functioning of the European Competition Network are concerned, the new enforcement system has been a major success, beyond expectations.

From the start of the application of Regulation 1/2003 on 1 May 2004 until 31 December 2021, the national competition authorities have informed the European Commission and their fellow national competition authorities of 2,515 investigations under Articles 101 and 102 TFEU, and of envisaged final decisions ordering termination of infringements, imposing fines or accepting commitments in 1,336 cases.[31]

During the same period, the European Commission informed the Network of 429 investigations of its own, and 137 draft final decisions.

The national competition authorities have thus in quantitative terms become the primary public enforcers of Articles 101 and 102 TFEU, adopting 90% of all decisions. Given that under Regulation 17 the number of cases in which the national competition authorities applied Articles 101 and 102 TFEU was negligible, this means that the overall number of decisions ordering termination of infringements of Articles 101 or 102 TFEU, imposing fines or accepting commitments has increased very substantially.

---

26 Article 3 of Regulation 1/2003.

27 White Paper on Modernisation, paragraphs 42, 47 and 83, and recitals 17 and 21 of Regulation 1/2003.

28 White Paper on Modernisation, paragraphs 84 to 86.

29 Recital 15 and Articles 11 to 14 of Regulation 1/2003, and Commission Notice on cooperation within the Network of Competition Authorities [2004] OJ C101/43.

30 Recital 21 and Article 15 of Regulation 1/2003, and Commission Notice on the cooperation between the Commission and the courts of the EU Member States in the application of Articles 81 and 82 EC [2004] OJ C101/54.

31 I have taken these and the immediately following statistics from the European Commission's website https://competition-policy.ec.europa.eu/european-competition-network/statistics_en.

The list below shows per Member State, and in descending order, the number of envisaged final decisions submitted by the national competition authorities under Article 11(4) of Regulation 1/2003 in the period from 1 May 2004 to 31 December 2021, as well as the number of draft final decisions submitted by the European Commission in the same period:

Italy	178	
France	173	
Spain	140	
Commission	*137*	
Germany	128	
Romania	67	*(since EU accession on 1 January 2007)*
Denmark	66	
Greece	61	
Netherlands	61	
Hungary	54	
UK	49	*(until 31 December 2020)*
Austria	47	
Portugal	46	
Slovakia	33	
Slovenia	31	
Sweden	28	
Czechia	27	
Belgium	26	
Poland	25	
Finland	22	
Lithuania	20	
Cyprus	13	
Bulgaria	8	*(since EU accession on 1 January 2007)*
Latvia	8	
Luxembourg	8	
Ireland	5	
Croatia	4	*(since EU accession on 1 July 2013)*
Estonia	4	
Malta	4	

This list makes visible that the national competition authorities with the largest output each adopt as many or indeed more decisions than the European Commission. It also shows that generally the competition authorities of the larger Member States adopt the highest number of decisions, with the notable exceptions of Poland and the United Kingdom (which remained bound by Regulation 1/2003 until 31 December 2020, the end of the transition period of its withdrawal from the EU).[32]

---

[32] The UK government has recognised the low number of decisions as a problem: see Department for Business Innovation & Skills (BIS), *A Competition Regime for Growth: A Consultation on Options for Reform* (March 2011), paragraph 5.6.

The differences between Member States also show the potential for further increase, as national competition authorities increase their output over time.[33]

The functioning of the European Competition Network has also been a clear success. Work sharing between the different competition authorities has generally been unproblematic, and the cooperation and coordination mechanisms provided for in Regulation 1/2003 have generally worked well. The application of Regulation 1/2003 has also given rise to a significant degree of voluntary convergence of Member States' laws as to the procedures and sanctioning powers of national competition authorities, supported by the policy work in the European Competition Network.[34]

This process of convergence has been accelerated through Directive 2019/1, often referred to as the 'ECN + Directive'.[35] This Directive, adopted by the European Parliament and the Council at the end of 2018, sets out certain rules to ensure that national competition authorities have the necessary guarantees of independence, resources, and enforcement and fining powers to be able to effectively apply Articles 101 and 102 TFEU. It harmonises to a large extent the investigation, decision and fining powers of the national competition authorities, broadly along the lines of the European Commission's powers under Regulation 1/2003. It also contains further provisions on mutual assistance between the national competition authorities and on the functioning of the European Competition Network, adding to the provisions contained in Regulation 1/2003.[36] Member States were required to adapt their national laws to conform to this Directive by 4 February 2021.

---

33 Indeed, the European Competition Network, with its statistics, creates a basis of comparison that may lead Member States and national competition authorities that perform relatively less well to take measures so as to increase their output.

34 See Communication from the Commission to the European Parliament and Council – Report on the functioning of Regulation 1/2003, COM(2009)206, chapter 5; Commission Staff Working Paper accompanying the Report on the functioning of Regulation 1/2003, SEC(2009)574, chapter 5; '10th Anniversary of Regulation 1/2003: Convergence and Cooperation in the ECN', *ECN Brief 05/2011*, accessible at http://ec.europa.eu/competition/ecn/brief/05_2011/brief_05_2011.pdf, 5–6; ECN Working Group Cooperation Issues and Due Process, *Investigative Powers Report* and *Decision-Making Powers Report* (31 October 2012), accessible at https://competition-policy.ec.europa.eu/european-competition-network/documents_en; L. Idot, 'Regards sur le règlement n° 1/2003', in *Études à la mémoire de Fernand-Charles Jeantet* (Lexis Nexis 2010), 193; C. Lemaire and J. Gstalter, 'The Silent Revolution Beyond Regulation 1/2003', *Global Competition Policy*, October 2008 (2); B. Lasserre, 'Effective Enforcement of Competition Rules in Europe: The Leading Role of the European Competition Network', in Studienvereinigung Kartellrecht, *Kartellrecht in Theorie und Praxis: Festschrift für Cornelis Canenbley zum 70. Geburtstag* (Beck 2012), 307, and M. Snoep and J. Steenbergen, 'The Growing Powers of National Competition Authorities', in K. Dekeyser, C. Gauer, J. Laitenberger, N. Wahl, W. Wils and L. Prete (eds), Regulation 1/2003 and EU Antitrust Enforcement – A Systematic Guide (Wolters Kluwer 2022).

35 Directive (EU) 2019/1 of the European Parliament and of the Council of 11 December 2018 to empower the competition authorities of the Member States to be more effective enforcers and to ensure the proper functioning of the internal market [2019] OJ L11/3 ('ECN + Directive').
On this Directive and its antecedents, see further E. Arsenidou, J. Capiau, A. Sinclair and J. Stanciute, 'Cooperation Within the ECN and Strengthening of National Competition Authorities', in E. Rousseva (ed), *EU Antitrust procedure* (Oxford 2020), 689, and my paper 'The European Commission's "ECN+" Proposal for a Directive to empower the competition authorities of the Member States to be more effective enforcers', *Concurrences* no 4-2017, 60, also accessible at http://ssrn.com/author=456087.

36 Articles 24 to 28 and Articles 10(2), 11(1), last sentence, and 33 of Directive 2019/1.

2. National courts

Three different roles of national courts should be distinguished:[37]

First, in some Member States the national competition authority does not adopt decisions finding infringements of Articles 101 or 102 TFEU and imposing fines, but rather brings the case before a national court that acts as first-instance decision-maker.[38] When thus adopting decisions finding infringements of Articles 101 or 102 TFEU and/or imposing fines, these national courts act as national competition authorities,[39] and their decisions are included in the above statistics of national competition authorities' decisions.

Second, in all Member States an appeal or application for judicial review can be brought against the decisions of national competition authorities before a (higher) court that acts as review court. Obviously, the more decisions are adopted by national competition authorities, the more appeals or applications for judicial review can be brought before these review courts. It is probably in respect of this second role that Regulation 1/2003 has had its main impact on national courts.

Third, national courts deal with litigation between private parties in which Articles 101 and 102 TFEU may be applied. The impact of Regulation 1/2003 on the application of Articles 101 and 102 TFEU in litigation between private parties has been as expected:

As explained in the White Paper on Modernisation,[40] under Regulation 17 the notification system and exclusive competence of the European Commission to apply Article 101(3) TFEU constituted an obstacle to the application of Article 101 TFEU by national courts.

The first impact of the change to a directly applicable exception system is in the area of contractual litigation, where Article 101 TFEU can be used as a shield to avoid contractual liability. Regulation 1/2003 has brought to an end the phenomenon of agreements falling under Article 101(1) TFEU and fulfilling the conditions of Article 101(3) TFEU but not covered by a block exemption being unenforceable simply because they had not been notified to the European Commission. In all situations where in a contractual dispute before a national court the defendant invokes Article 101(2) TFEU, the claimant can now fully rely on Article 101(3) TFEU and the national court can itself decide on the matter.[41]

---

37 See Commission Notice on co-operation between the Commission and the courts of the EU Member States in the application of Articles 81 and 82 EC [2004] OJ C101/4, paragraph 2; Commission Staff Working Paper accompanying the Report on the functioning of Regulation 1/2003, SEC(2009)574, paragraph 269; and ECN Working Group Cooperation Issues and Due Process, *Decision-Making Powers Report* (31 October 2012), accessible at https://competition-policy.ec.europa.eu/european-competition-network/documents_en, section 2.3.

38 See ECN Working Group Cooperation Issues and Due Process, *Decision-Making Powers Report* (31 October 2012), accessible at https://competition-policy.ec.europa.eu/european-competition-network/documents_en, section 2.3.

39 See Article 35 of Regulation 1/2003, and my book *Principles of European Antitrust Enforcement* (Hart 2005), section 1.2.10.

40 White Paper on Modernisation, at paragraphs 99–100.

41 See further my paper 'The Modernisation of the Enforcement of Articles 81 and 82 EC: A Legal and Economic Analysis of the Commission's Proposal for a New Council Regulation Replacing Regulation No 17', in B. Hawk (ed), *Annual Proceedings of the Fordham Corporate Law Institute 2000* (Juris 2001), at 352–353 and my book *Principles of European Antitrust Enforcement* (Hart 2005), section 1.1.4.1.

As to the use of Article 101 TFEU as a sword, in actions for injunctive relief or for damages brought in national courts by victims of anti-competitive agreements, the abolition of the European Commission's exclusive competence to apply Article 101(3) TFEU also has a beneficial effect in that it is no longer possible, in particular in cases where injunctive relief is sought, for defendants to delay the national court procedure by notifying the agreement to the European Commission.

Apart from this change, which merely aligned the legal situation as to Article 101 TFEU to the situation already existing under Regulation 17 as to Article 102 TFEU, Regulation 1/2003 did not contain any measure to encourage the bringing of actions in national courts seeking injunctive relief or damages for infringements of Articles 101 or 102 TFEU.

Independently from Regulation 1/2003, the European Commission published in 2005 a Green Paper on Damages actions for breach of the EU antitrust rules,[42] in which it put up for discussion measures to encourage private actions for damages as an instrument for deterrence,[43] inspired by the US conception of private antitrust enforcement.[44] The reactions to this Green Paper were mostly negative, and this led to a change of orientation: The Commission published in 2008 a White Paper on Damages actions for breach of EU antitrust rules,[45] which focused no longer on deterrence and private enforcement, but rather on the right of victims to obtain compensation for damage suffered as a result of antitrust infringements.[46]

---

42 COM(2005)672 of 19 December 2005; see also D. Waelbroeck and D. Slater, 'The Commission's Green Paper on Private Enforcement: "Americanization" of EC Competition Law Enforcement?', in C.-D. Ehlermann and I. Atanasiu (eds), *European Competition Law Annual 2006: Enforcement of Prohibition of Cartels* (Hart Publishing 2007), 425.

43 See idem, page 3: 'public and private antitrust enforcement [. . .] serve the same aims: to deter anti-competitive practices [. . .]'; see also the comment by the then Director-General for Competition of the European Commission at the OECD Roundtable on private remedies in February 2006 (i.e. shortly after the publication of the 2005 Green Paper): 'compensation of victims should not be seen as an end in itself, but part of an overall strategy to enhance deterrence'; OECD, *Private Remedies*, DAF/COMP(2006)34 of 11 January 2008, at 271.

44 See generally my paper 'Should Private Antitrust Enforcement Be Encouraged in Europe?' (2003) 26 *World Competition* 473; my book *Principles of European Antitrust Enforcement* (Hart 2005), Chapter 4; W. Möschel, 'Should Private Enforcement of Competition Law Be Strengthened?', in D. Schmidtchen, M. Albert and S. Voigt, *The More Economic Approach to European Competition Law – Conferences on New Political Economy 24* (Mohr Siebeck 2007), 101, and (2013) 6 *Global Competition Litigation Review* 1; P. Nebbia, 'Damages actions for the infringement of EC competition law: compensation or deterrence?' (2008) *European Law Review* 23; K.S. Bernard, 'Private Antitrust Litigation in the European Union – Why Does the EC Want to Embrace What the US Federal Trade Commission is Trying to Avoid?' (2010) 3 *Global Competition Law Review* 69; and Opinion of Advocate General Jääskinen of 7 February 2013, *Donau Chemie*, C-536/11, EU:C:2013:67, paragraph 48.

45 COM(2008) 165 of 2 April 2008; see also F. W. Bulst, 'Of Arms and Armour – The European Commission's White Paper on Damages Actions for Breach of EC Antitrust Law' (2008) *Bucerius Law Journal* 81.

46 Indeed, the 2008 White Paper states, at page 3, that its 'primary objective [. . .] is to improve the legal conditions for victims to exercise their right under the Treaty to reparation of all damage suffered as a result of a breach of the EC antitrust rules. Full compensation is, therefore, the first and foremost guiding principle. [. . .] Another important guiding principle of the Commission's policy is to preserve strong public enforcement of Articles 81 and 82 by the Commission and the competition authorities of the Member States.' The European Commission has thus returned to the classic, time-honoured conception of the different roles of public enforcement and private actions for damages, not just in the area of antitrust but in the law more generally, as notably set out by John Locke in 1690 in his *Second Treatise on Civil Government*, Chapter II; see further my paper 'The Relationship between Public Antitrust Enforcement and Private Actions for Damages' (2009) 32 *World Competition* 3. Since its judgment of 20 September 2001, *Courage and Crehan*, C-453/99, EU:C:2001:465,

In line with the 2008 White Paper, and following the European Commission's 2013 legislative proposal,[47] the European Parliament and Council adopted Directive 2014/104 in November 2014.[48] This Directive sets out certain rules to ensure the effective exercise by victims of antitrust infringements of their right to full compensation from the antitrust infringers for the harm suffered.[49] It also contains some provisions to safeguard public enforcement, and in particular the use of leniency in public enforcement,[50] by protecting leniency and settlement submissions from disclosure and use in actions for damages and by limiting the joint and several liability of immunity recipients to their own direct and indirect customers and providers.[51] Member States were required to adapt their national laws to conform to this Directive by 27 December 2016.[52]

The principal intended and likely effect of Directive 2014/104 on the practice of private enforcement is an increase in the number of (purely compensatory) follow-on actions for damages. Significant change as to the frequency of stand-alone actions for damages was not intended by the legislator and is most unlikely to result from the Directive.[53]

To some extent the intended effect of Directive 2014/104 appears to have already materialised before the Directive became applicable on 27 December 2016. Indeed, it appears that already since 2005 there has been in several EU Member States a marked increase in the number of follow-on actions for damages.[54] In part this increase may be the

---

paragraph 27, the EU Court of Justice has, however, continued referring to the deterrent effect as an objective justifying private actions for damages; see Judgments of 6 October 2021, *Sumal*, C-882/19, EU:C:2021:800, paragraph 35, and of 11 November 2021, *Stichting Cartel Compensation and Equilib Netherlands*, C-819/19, EU:C:2021:904, paragraph 50.

47 European Commission, Proposal for a Directive of the European Parliament and of the Council on certain rules governing actions for damages under national law for infringements of the competition law provisions of the Member States and of the European Union, COM(2013)404 of 11 June 2013.

48 Directive 2014/104/EU of the European Parliament and of the Council of 26 November 2014 on certain rules governing actions for damages under national law for infringements of the competition law provisions of the Member States and of the European Union [2014] OJ L349/1. Among the many commentaries on this Directive, see in particular P. Van Nuffel, Institutional Report – Private enforcement of EU competition law, XXVII FIDE Congress (Budapest, 18–21 May 2016); as well as H. Schweitzer, 'Die neue Richtlinie für wettbewerbsrechtliche Schadenersatzklage' (2014) Neue Zeitschrift für Kartellrecht 335; P. Roth, 'Too much or too little? The EU initiatives to promote private redress', in Antitrust between EU law and National law / Antitrust fra diritto Nazionale e diritto dell'Unione Europea (Bruylant 2015) 51; F. Wagner-von Papp, 'Access to Evidence and Leniency Materials' (18 February 2016), accessible at http://ssrn.com/abstract=2733973; F. G. Wilman, The End of the Absence? The Growing Body of EU Legislation on Private Enforcement and the Main Remedies it Provides for' (2016) 53 *Common Market Law* Review 887; and my paper 'Private Enforcement of EU Antitrust Law and its Relationship with Public Enforcement: Past, Present and Future' (2017) 40 *World Competition* 3, also accessible at http://ssrn.com/author=456087.

49 Article 1(1) of Directive 2014/104/EU.

50 See generally my paper 'The Use of Leniency in EU Cartel Enforcement: An Assessment After Twenty Years' (2016) 39 *World Competition* 327, also accessible at http://ssrn.com/author=456087.

51 Recitals 26, 27 and 38 and Articles 1(2), 6(6), 7(1) and 11(4) and (5) of Directive 2014/104/EU.

52 Article 21 of Directive 2014/104/EU.

53 See P. Van Nuffel, Institutional Report – Private enforcement of EU competition law, XXVII FIDE Congress (Budapest, 18–21 May 2016), at 239, and P. Roth, 'Too much or too little? The EU initiatives to promote private redress', in Antitrust between EU law and National law / Antitrust fra diritto Nazionale e diritto dell'Unione Europea (Bruylant 2015) 51 at 52. The text of the Directive does not, however, distinguish between follow-on and stand-alone actions for damages and applies to both; see Opinion of Advocate General Pitruzzella of 8 September 2022, *Repsol Comercial de Productos Petrolíferos*, C-25/21, EU:C:2022:659, paragraph 44.

54 See B. Rodger, *Competition Law Comparative Private Enforcement and Collective Redress across the EU* (Wolters Kluwer, 2014).

result of increased awareness as a result of (the discussions surrounding) the European Commission's 2005 Green Paper, 2008 White Paper and 2013 legislative proposal.[55]

Indeed, already in the last years before Directive 2014/104 became applicable, in Germany, the Netherlands and the UK, practically every infringement decision of the European Commission or of the national competition authority appears to have triggered follow-on actions for damages.[56] The Directive has helped spread this development to other EU Member States.[57]

In particular the European Commission's decision in the *Trucks cartel* case[58] appears to have given rise to follow-on actions for damages in many Member States, also resulting in requests for preliminary rulings by the EU Court of Justice originating in several Member States.[59]

3. European Commission

The impact of Regulation 1/2003 on the activity of the European Commission has in many respects been as expected.

The European Commission has made good use of the increased investigatory and sanctioning powers which it obtained through Regulation 1/2003, such as the increased possibility to ask oral questions during inspections, the possibility to put seals,[60] the possibility to inspect private homes, the increased penalties for obstruction of investigations,[61] and the higher level of periodic penalty payments for non-compliance with decisions.[62]

The European Commission has also made use of the increased scope for prioritising its action.[63] It has published a list of general prioritisation criteria in its Annual Report on Competition Policy 2005.[64]

---

55 In part the increase may also be a consequence of legislative initiatives at the national level, some of which may have reflected competition between jurisdictions to attract legal business; see C.-D. Ehlermann, 'Foreword', in A. P. Komninos, EC Private Antitrust Enforcement – Decentralised Application of EC Competition Law by National Courts (Hart Publishing 2008), at x.

56 See P. C. Müller-Graf, General Report – Private enforcement of EU competition law, XXVII FIDE Congress (Budapest, 18–21 May 2016), at 94.

57 See European Commission, Report of 14 December 2020 on the implementation of Directive 2014/104/EU, SWD(2020)338 final, at 3–4.

58 Summary of Commission Decision of 19 July 2016 relating to a proceeding under Article 101 TFEU and Article 53 EEA (Case AT.39842 – Trucks) [2017] OJ C108/6.

59 See, among others, Judgments of 29 July 2019, *Tibor-Trans*, C-451/18, EU:C:2019:635 (reference from a Hungarian court), of 6 October 2021, *Sumal*, C-882/19, EU:C:2021:800 (reference from a Spanish court) and of 1 August 2022, *Daimler*, C-588/20, EU:C:2022:607 (reference from a German court).

60 See Commission Decisions of 30 January 2008 in Case COMP/39.326 *E.ON Energie* [2008] OJ C240/6 and of 24 May 2011 in Case COMP/39.796 *Suez Environnement breach of seal* [2011] OJ C251/4; Judgments of 15 December 2010, *E.ON Energie v Commission*, T-141/08, EU:T:2010:516, and of 22 November 2012, *E.ON Energie v Commission*, C-89/11 P, EU:C:2012:738; and A. Riley, 'Seal Breaking: Practical Compliance Lessons from Recent Cases' (2012) 3 *Journal of European Competition Law & Practice* 141.

61 See Commission Decision of 28 March 2012 in Case COMP/39.793 *EPH and Others* [2012] OJ C316/8, as well as the decisions mentioned in the footnote just above.

62 See Commission Decisions of 12 July 2006 and of 27 February 2008 in Case COMP/37.792 *Microsoft* [2008] OJ C138/10 and [2009] OJ C166/20, and Judgment 27 June 2012, *Microsoft v Commission*, T-167/08, EU:T:2012:323.

63 See Chapter IV of this book.

64 SEC(2006)761, June 2006, at 26–27. See also Commission Notice on the handling of complaints by the Commission under Articles 81 and 82 of the EC Treaty [2004] OJ C101/65.

As to the number of decisions adopted by the European Commission, the White Paper on Modernisation had predicted that, following the abolition of the notification system, 'the number of individual prohibition decisions can be expected to increase substantially'.[65]

A look at the figures shows that this prediction has been too optimistic.

a. *Comparative enforcement statistics*

The first column of Table 1 below shows, for the years 2005 to 2021 included (the 17 full years of application of Regulation 1/2003 for which figures were available at the time of writing), the number of prohibition decisions adopted by the European Commission.[66]

Strictly speaking prohibition decisions are decisions finding an infringement of Articles 101 or 102 TFEU, ordering its termination and/or imposing fines (Articles 7 and 23(2) of Regulation 1/2003). These are grouped into four categories: decisions concerning cartels adopted following the normal (non-settlement) procedure,[67] decisions concerning cartels adopted following the settlement procedure,[68] decisions concerning non-cartel infringements following the normal procedure (without cooperation), and decisions concerning non-cartel infringements in cases in which the companies investigated admitted the infringement and agreed to follow a streamlined procedure (with cooperation).[69] Even if these are not strictly speaking prohibition decisions, I have also added the number of decisions pursuant to Article 9 of Regulation 1/2003, through which the European Commission makes binding commitments offered by the companies under investigation in lieu of a prohibition decision (commitment decisions).[70]

---

65 White Paper on Modernisation, paragraph 87.

66 The statistics in this table 1 and the following tables 2 and 3 are of my own making. As Winston Churchill may or may not have said, I only believe in statistics that I doctored myself. The full list of the cases that I have counted, with their name, year and type, can be found in the annexes to my paper 'Regulation 1/2003: An Assessment After Twenty Years' (2023) 46 *World Competition* 3, also accessible at http://ssrn.com/aithor=456087.

67 Article 2(14) of the Directive 2014/104/EU defines 'cartel' as 'an agreement or concerted practice between two or more competitors aimed at coordinating their competitive behaviour on the market or influencing the relevant parameters of competition through practices such as, but not limited to, the fixing or coordination of purchase or selling prices or other trading conditions, including in relation to intellectual property rights, the allocation of production or sales quota, the sharing of markets and customers, including bid-rigging, restrictions of imports or exports or anti-competitive actions against other competitors'.

68 On the cartel settlement procedure, see Article 10a of Regulation 773/2004, as inserted by Commission Regulation (EC) No 622/2008 of 30 June 2008 amending Regulation (EC) No 773/2004, as regards the conduct of settlement procedures in cartel cases [2008] OJ L171/3; Commission Notice on the conduct of settlement procedures in view of the adoption of decisions pursuant to Article 7 and Article 23 of Council Regulation (EC) No 1/2003 in cartel cases [2008] OJ C167/1, amended by Communication from the Commission – Amendments to the Commission Notice on the conduct of settlement procedures [2015] OJ C256/2; and Chapter VI of this book.

69 On such cooperation in non-cartel antitrust proceedings, see European Commission, Fact Sheet – Cooperation – FAQ (17 December 2018), accessible at https://ec.europa.eu/competition/publications/data/factsheet_guess.pdf.

70 On commitment decisions, see my papers 'Settlements of EU Antitrust Investigations: Commitment Decisions under Article 9 of Regulation no 1/2009' (2006) 29 *World Competition* 345, 'The Use of Settlements in Public Antitrust Enforcement: Objectives and Principles' (2008) 31 *World Competition* 335, and 'Ten Years of Commitment Decisions under Article 9 of Regulation 1/2003: Too Much of a Good Thing?' *Concurrences* no 3-2015, all three also accessible at http://ssrn.com/author=456078.

The second column of Table 1 below similarly indicates, for the last 17 years of application of Regulation 17, that is 1988 to 2004,[71] the prohibition decisions adopted by the European Commission. No distinction is made according to whether the cartel settlement procedure was followed or whether cooperation took place, given that the cartel cooperation procedure was only introduced in 2008, and the practice of cooperation in non-cartel antitrust proceedings only started in 2016.[72] The right column also indicates the number of negative clearance and exemption decisions in notification cases (formal decisions, as opposed to comfort letters), in particular the decisions containing commitments offered by the notifying companies, which are comparable to commitment decisions under Article 9 of Regulation 1/2003.

To avoid double counting, re-adoptions of decisions annulled on procedural grounds by the EU Courts have not been included in the statistics. Also to avoid double counting, when a single investigation is closed through the adoption of more than one decision (for instance, because some parties to a cartel investigation opt for the settlement procedure, whereas a normal non-settlement decision is adopted for the other parties, or because for one half of the investigation a settlement or commitment outcome is reached early, whereas the other half of the investigation is closed through a later prohibition or commitment decision), such multiple decisions are only counted as one.[73]

Table 1: Number of prohibition decisions 2005–2021 compared to 1988–2004

Enforcement under Regulation 1/2003: Seventeen-year period 2005–2021	**Enforcement under Regulation 17: Seventeen-year period 1988–2004**
52 cartel non-settlement decisions 30 + ½ cartel settlement decisions	
= 82 + ½ cartel decisions	**61 cartel decisions**
26 + ½ non-cartel prohibition decisions without cooperation 12 + ½ non-cartel prohibition decisions with cooperation	
= 39 non-cartel prohibition decisions	**69 non-cartel prohibition decisions**
= 121 + ½ prohibition decisions	**= 130 prohibition decisions**
42 commitment decisions	118 negative clearance and exemption decisions of which **47 decisions with commitments**

71 Even if Regulation 1/2003 entered into application on 1 May 2004, it appears appropriate to consider the entire year 2004 as representative of the decisional output under Regulation 17 rather than under Regulation 1/2003. Indeed, the proceedings leading to the decisions adopted between 1 May and 31 December 2004 had been conducted mostly under Regulation 17.

72 See Summary of Commission Decision of 20 September 2016 in Case AT.39759 ARA Foreclosure [2016] OJ C432/6; see further C. Gauer and J. Lübking, 'Cooperation with the European Commission in antitrust cases: A new way paved by the ARA case', *Concurrences* no 1-2017, 81.

73 Thus, for instance, the cartel settlement decision in *Ethanol benchmarks* in 2021 is counted as a half decision, because it only closed the investigation with respect to one of the three suspected cartel parties, the proceedings still being ongoing in relation to the two other parties. Similarly, the three commitment decisions in the *Visa MIF* case in 2010, 2014 and 2021 are each counted as one third of a decision, because the three decisions concern parts of a single investigation.

It thus appears that, in the 17 full years of application of Regulation 1/2003, the European Commission adopted 121 and a half prohibition decisions, that is on average seven decisions per year, while in the last 17 years of application of Regulation 17, 130 prohibition decisions were adopted, that is on average seven and a half per year. Instead of a 'significant increase', there has thus in fact been a slight decrease in the number of prohibition decisions.

It may be fair to add to the 121 and a half prohibition decisions the 41 commitment decisions adopted in the 2005–2021 period, but then a fair comparison would also require taking into account the 47 negative clearance or exemption decisions with commitments in the 1988–2004 period. Adding the commitment decisions does thus not alter the finding of a slight decrease in enforcement output.

Table 2 below takes a closer look at the last five full years for which figures were available at the time of writing, 2017 to 2021, in comparison with an equal five-year period twenty years earlier, 1997 to 2001.[74]

Table 2: Number of prohibition decisions 2017–2021 compared to 1997–2001

Enforcement under Regulation 1/2003: Five-year period 2017–2021	Enforcement under Regulation 17: Five-year period 1997–2001
5 + ½ cartel non-settlement decisions 12 + ½ cartel settlement decisions	
= 18 cartel decisions	**18 cartel decisions**
9 + ½ non-cartel prohibition decisions without cooperation 11 + ½ non-cartel prohibition decisions with cooperation	
= 21 non-cartel prohibition decisions	**22 non-cartel prohibition decisions**
= 39 prohibition decisions	**= 40 prohibition decisions**
7 commitment decisions	35 negative clearance and exemption decisions of which **11 decisions with commitments**

Like for the entire 17-year periods in Table 1, Table 2 shows a slight decrease in the number of prohibition decisions compared with the European Commission's enforcement output under Regulation 17 twenty years earlier. Adding commitment decisions to the comparison again does not alter this conclusion.

We are thus presented with a real puzzle: Why is it that the abolition of the notification system, which was meant to free up resources and allow the European Commission to adopt a significantly higher number of prohibition decisions, has in fact resulted in a slightly lower number of prohibition decisions?

---

74 The full list of the cases that I have counted, with their name, year and type, can be found in the annexes to my paper 'Regulation 1/2003: An Assessment After Twenty Years' (2023) 46 *World Competition* 3, also accessible at http://ssrn.com/aithor=456087. The figure for the commitment decisions in the 2017–2021 period was rounded up from six plus a half and a third to seven decisions.

As mentioned above, under Regulation 17, the Commission dealt every year with 150 to 200 notification cases through comfort letters.[75] In addition, a number of notification cases were dealt with through formal negative clearance and exemption decisions without commitments. It appears from Table 2 just above that there were 24 such decisions in the five-year period 1997–2001, which is almost five per year.[76] The resource savings from no longer dealing with all these notifications must have been significant indeed.

In addition, many cases may in fact require fewer resources to deal with today than twenty years ago, because of the use of leniency and of settlement and cooperation procedures.[77] The European Commission already started operating a leniency programme for cartels in 1996, but the use of leniency in cartel enforcement became generalised only after a few years. In Table 2 above comparing the enforcement in the five-year period 2017–2021 under Regulation 1/2003 with the five-year period 1997–2001 under Regulation 17, the number of cartel decisions equals 18 for both periods. All the 18 cartel decisions in the 2017–2021 period benefited from the full use of leniency, whereas only some of those in the 1997–2001 period benefited from leniency.[78] Moreover, as indicated in Table 2 above, two thirds of the cartel decisions in the 2017–2021 period additionally benefited from the use of the cartel settlement procedure. Among the 21 non-cartel prohibition decisions in the 2017–2021 period (one fewer than during the 1997–2001 period), more than half similarly benefited from cooperation by the companies under investigation. Cases benefiting from leniency, settlement and/or cooperation require fewer resources to handle than fully contested cases.[79]

I do not have the answer to this puzzle, which undoubtedly merits further research. Below are some initial, in part speculative, thoughts about possible explanations.

b. *Ten possible explanations*

(1) *Resources*

A first possible explanation is that the European Commission's resources dedicated to the enforcement of Articles 101 and 102 TFEU would have gone down. This is not what happened, however. Resources have gone up rather than down.[80]

---

75 White Paper on Modernisation, paragraph 34.

76 The equivalent of such decisions under Regulation 1/2003 would be non-infringement decisions (finding of inapplicability) pursuant to Article 10 of Regulation 1/2003, but not a single such decision has been adopted since the entry into application of Regulation 1/2003; see R. Whish, 'Reflections on Regulation 1/2003, declarations of inapplicability and informal guidance', *Concurrences* no 2-2022, 2.

77 See Chapters 5 and 6 of this book.

78 See the lists of cases in the annex of my paper 'The Use of Leniency in EU Antitrust Enforcement: An Assessment after Twenty Years' (2016) 39 *World Competition* 327, also accessible at http://ssrn.com/author=456087.

79 See Chapters 5 and 6 of this book.

80 Within the European Commission, the staff dedicated to the enforcement of Articles 101 and 102 TFEU are in the Directorate-General for Competition (which also deals with merger and State aid control) and in the Competition Team of the Legal Service. Compared with twenty years ago, the number of lawyers in this Competition Team (which also deals with merger control) has roughly doubled. The number of staff in the Directorate-General for Competition dealing with the enforcement of Articles 101 and 102 TFEU appears to have followed a similar evolution.

(2) *Informal guidance*

A second possible explanation for the lack of increase in the number of prohibition decisions is that, instead of spending its newly freed resources on more enforcement, the European Commission would have continued spending those resources on providing informal guidance to businesses, continuing the old practice of comfort letters under another guise. While confirming that the European Commission could still provide informal guidance, recital 38 of Regulation 1/2003 limited this possibility to cases giving rise to genuine uncertainty because they present novel or unresolved questions for the application of Articles 101 and 102 TFEU. This strict approach was also followed in the initial Informal Guidance Notice published in 2004.[81] While the European Commission has provided informal guidance in a few cases,[82] though not under the Informal Guidance Notice, and has recently revised its Informal Guidance Notice, broadening the definition of 'novel (or unresolved)' issues,[83] this activity has remained very limited and can thus not explain the lack of increase in the number of prohibition decisions.[84]

(3) *Coordination work*

A third possible explanation for the lack of increase in the number of prohibition decisions is that the European Commission may spend a substantial amount of resources on its coordination tasks under Regulation 1/2003, monitoring the enforcement of Articles 101 and 102 TFEU by the national competition authorities and the national courts. In its Report on the functioning of Regulation 1/2003, the European Commission indicated that its Directorate-General for Competition had developed a practice of submitting (oral or written) observations to the national competition authorities in many cases.[85]

(4) *Inherently more complex cases*

A fourth possible explanation is that, as a result of increased prioritisation, the European Commission may deal to a larger extent with cases that are inherently more complex and thus consume more resources.[86]

---

81 Commission Notice on informal guidance relating to novel questions concerning Articles 81 and 82 of the EC Treaty that arise in individual cases (guidance letters) [2004] OJ C101/78.

82 In the context of the coronavirus outbreak, the European Commission has issued two comfort letters; see https://competition-policy.ec.europa.eu/antitrust/coronavirus_en. In the *Car Emissions* case, the European Commission also provided, in the margin of a cartel prohibition decision, the car producers concerned with guidance on aspects of their cooperation that raised no competition concerns; see Press release IP/21/3581 of 8 July 2021.

83 See Commission Notice on informal guidance relating to novel or unresolved questions concerning Articles 101 and 102 of the Treaty on the Functioning of the European Union that arise in individual cases (guidance letters) [2022] OJ C381/9, and Press release IP/22/5887 of 3 October 2022.

84 The European Commission has not adopted any formal non-infringement decisions (finding of inapplicability) pursuant to Article 10 of Regulation 1/2003 either; see R. Whish, 'Reflections on Regulation 1/2003, declarations of inapplicability and informal guidance', *Concurrences* no 2-2022, 2.

85 Communication from the Commission to the European Parliament and Council – Report on the functioning of Regulation 1/2003, COM(2009)206 of 29 April 2009, paragraph 28, and Commission Staff Working Paper accompanying the Report on the functioning of Regulation 1/2003, SEC(2009)574 of 29 April 2009, paragraph 257.

86 The activity of prioritisation also in itself consumes resources; see Chapter 4 of this book.

(5) *The so-called more economic approach*

A fifth possible explanation is that, due to the so-called more economic approach,[87] more resources are needed to produce economic evidence to show consumer harm, or to deal with claims of absence of consumer harm. The so-called more economic approach was initiated by the European Commission itself. The emblematic example is the 2009 *Intel* decision, in which the European Commission included a 150-page long 'as efficient competitor analysis' not required by the case law of the EU Courts.[88] To some extent, the so-called more economic approach has since been adopted by the EU Court of Justice, and hence become part of the binding interpretation in particular of Article 102 TFEU.[89] The so-called more economic approach does not, however, affect all types of antitrust cases. In particular, cartel cases have remained unaffected by this approach.

(6) *Increased intensity of judicial review*

A sixth possible explanation for the lack of increase in the number of prohibition decisions is an increase in the intensity of judicial review by the EU Courts,[90] requiring the European Commission to spend more care on handling its cases and to strengthen the reasoning of its decisions, as well as making the European Commission spend resources on readopting annulled decisions.[91]

(7) *Increased internal quality control*

A seventh possible explanation, closely related to the intensification of judicial review, is that the European Commission has increased the levels of internal quality control. Indeed, in 2003, the European Commission created the office of the Chief Economist inside the Directorate-General for Competition,[92] and introduced the practice of peer review panels in Article 102 TFEU cases and in some non-cartel Article 101 TFEU cases.[93] An important

---

87 See A. C. Witt, *The More Economic Approach to EU Antitrust Law* (Hart 2016); my paper 'The Judgment of the EU General Court in *Intel* and the So-called "More Economic Approach" to Abuse of Dominance' (2014) 37 *World Competition* 405, also accessible at http://ssrn.com/author=456078; and speech by Sven Giegold, Secretary of State in the German Federal Ministry for Economic Affairs, at the International Cartel Conference (IKK) Berlin (4 May 2022), accessible at https://www.d-kart.de/en/blog/2022/05/04/antitrust-pendulum-swinging-back/.

88 See Decision C(2009) 3726 final of 13 May 2009 in Case COMP/C-3/37.990 – Intel; Judgment of 12 June 2014, *Intel v European Commission*, T-286/09, EU:T:2014:547 and Judgment of 26 January 2022, *Intel v European Commission*, T-286/09 RENV, EU:T:2022:19; G. Monti, 'Rebates After the General Court's 2022 *Intel* Judgment' (2023) 60 *Common Market Law Review* 107 and my paper 'The Judgment of the EU General Court in *Intel* and the So-called "More Economic Approach" to Abuse of Dominance' (2014) 37 *World Competition* 405, also accessible at http://ssrn.com/author=456078.

89 See Judgments of 6 September 2017, *Intel v European Commission*, C-413/14 P, EU:C:.2017:632, and of 12 May 2022, *ENEL*, C-377/20, EU:C:2022:379, and A. Witt, 'The European Court of Justice and the More Economic Approach – Is The Tide Turning?' (2019) 64 *Antitrust Bulletin* 172.

90 See M. Jaeger, 'The Standard of Review in Competition Cases Involving Complex Economic Assessments: Towards the Marginalisation of the Marginal Review?' (2011) 2 *Journal of European Competition Law & Practice* 295; J. L. da Cruz Vilaça, 'The intensity of judicial review in complex economic matters – recent competition law judgments of the Court of Justice of the EU' (2018) 6 *Journal of Antitrust Enforcement* 173; and Interview with M van der Woude, 'The Reform of the General Court for a better and faster judicial review', *Concurrences* no 2-2020, 16.

91 See Chapter XVI of this book.

92 See https://competition-policy.ec.europa.eu/chief-competition-economist_en.

93 See speech by Commissioner Monti, 'EU competition policy after May 1994', at the 30th Annual Fordham Conference on International Law and Policy (New York, 24 October 2003), available at https://ec.europa.eu/commission/presscorner/detail/en/SPEECH_03_489.

quality control function is also performed by the European Commission's Legal Service.[94] While the Legal Service has always existed, its role appears to have expanded in practice, as reflected by the doubling in size of its Competition Team in the past twenty years.[95] Obviously, increased quality control entails increased use of resources.[96] Apart from being costly, systematic and extensive quality control also risks having a deresponsibilising effect on the primary case handlers, thus perversely lowering quality. It also risks increasing the duration of investigations, which, as explained below (tenth possible explanation), may in turn have a further negative effect on the number of decisions.

(8) *Detection of infringements and the treatment of complaints*

An eighth possible explanation for the lack of increase in the number of prohibition decisions might be a failure to detect more infringements. The White Paper on Modernisation had pointed out that, in order to detect the infringements that would be the object of the additional infringement decisions, the European Commission would have to make more use of sector inquiries and of complaints.[97] The lodging of complaints by victims of antitrust infringements was to be encouraged in particular by introducing a time limit of four months by the end of which the Commission would inform the complainant of the action it proposed to take on the complaint.[98]

The European Commission has indeed conducted more sector inquiries under Regulation 1/2003 than previously under Regulation 17. In particular the inquiries in the energy sector and in the pharmaceutical sector have also been followed by a series of prohibition or commitment decisions in those sectors.

As to the encouragement of complaints through the four-month time limit, a detailed study by Ben Van Rompuy has found that, during the twelve-year period 2009–2020, the median time period until the sending of a pre-rejection letter for those complaints that were formally rejected for lack of Union interest was more than one and a half years, far above the target of four months.[99]

Still in relation to complaints, it has been argued that the obligation for the European Commission to reject non-priority complaints through a formal decision, preceded by a pre-rejection letter, is a source of inefficiency that consumes substantial resources.[100]

---

94 See https://ec.europa.eu/dgs/legal_service/index_en.htm.

95 Similarly, while the function of the Hearing Officer was created in 1982, and their tasks were already expanded in 1990, 1994 and 2001, a further extension of the role of the Hearing Officer took place in 2011; see Decision 2011/695/EU of the President of the European Commission of 13 October 2011 on the function and terms of reference of the Hearing Officer in competition proceedings [2011] OJ L275/29; Chapter XI of this book; and Interview conducted by J. Jourdan, 'Wouter Wils: Looking back at his experience as Hearing Officer for competition proceedings at the European Commission', *Concurrences* no 2-2022, 14.

96 See also my papers 'The Combination of the Investigative and Prosecutorial Function and the Adjudicative Function in EC Antitrust Enforcement: A Legal and Economic Analysis' (2004) 27 *World Competition* 201, also accessible at http://ssrn.com/author=456087, and Chapter 9 of this book.

97 White Paper on Modernisation, paragraphs 115 and 118.

98 White Paper on Modernisation, paragraph 120, and Commission Notice on the handling of complaints by the Commission under Articles 81 and 82 of the EC Treaty [2004] OJ C101/65.

99 B. Van Rompuy, 'The European Commission's Handling of Non-priority Antitrust Complaints: An Empirical Assessment' (2022) 45 *World Competition* 265 at 289.

100 See in particular Directorate-General for Competition, Ex-post evaluation of key procedural aspects of Regulation (EC) No 1/2003 access to file and complaint – Final report (Publication Office of the European Union 2016) at 111.

While it is undoubtedly true that the formal rejection of non-priority complaints requires a non-insignificant amount of resources, this cannot, however, help explain the lack of increase in the number of prohibition decisions. Indeed, the obligation to reject non-priority complaints through a formal decision, preceded by a pre-rejection letter, already existed under Regulation 17,[101] and the number of formal decisions rejecting complaints has decreased rather than increased.[102]

(9) *Loss of expertise*

A ninth possible explanation for the lack of increase in the number of prohibition decisions is a loss of expertise due to increased staff turnover. Two types of expertise are relevant for the enforcement of Articles 101 and 102 TFEU: *primo* knowledge of the relevant markets, products, industry structures and business practices; and *secundo* practical mastery of the legal instruments and procedures, for instance how to conduct inspections effectively, how to formulate requests for information that elicit useful information without overburdening the file with superfluous information, or how to draft statements of objections.

As already mentioned, sector inquiries are one of the ways for the European Commission to obtain knowledge about markets and business practices. For the knowledge thus gained subsequently to be fully used, the same staff dealing with the sector inquiry should subsequently deal with the antitrust investigations in the same sector. Similarly, knowledge about markets can also be obtained through merger control. The effective transfer of knowledge gained through merger control does, however, require that the same staff who have dealt with merger cases in a certain sector subsequently deal with antitrust enforcement in that sector. Also for the second type of expertise (the practical mastery of legal instruments and procedures), staff retention is obviously a very important factor.

(10) *Duration of investigations*

Finally, a tenth possible explanation is related to the long duration of antitrust investigations.

It appears very difficult to assemble statistics on the duration of the European Commission's antitrust investigations, because the date on which the European Commission received the first information about the infringement (through a complaint, informant, leniency application, or otherwise) is in most cases not made public. Decisions typically mention the date on which the European Commission formally initiated proceedings, but this information is of little use, as the initiation of proceedings happens after a more or less extended period of preliminary investigation (or inaction).[103] It thus remains unknown

---

[101] See White Paper on Modernisation, paragraph 121.

[102] According to paragraph 121 of the White Paper on Modernisation, under Regulation 17, formal decisions rejecting complaints were more numerous than other formal decisions, and, according to the statistics in Annex 2 of the present chapter, there were on average fourteen and a half other formal decisions per year in the 1988–2004 period. There must thus have been at least fifteen formal decisions rejecting complaints per year under Regulation 17. According to the study by Ben Van Rompuy cited just above, at 279 and 280, there were eighty-six formal rejection decisions in the 2009–2020 period, that is around seven per year, and 164 pre-rejection letters, that is fourteen per year.

[103] See Article 2 of Commission Regulation (EC) No 773/2004 of 7 April 2004 relating to the conduct of proceedings by the Commission pursuant to Articles 81 and 82 of the EC Treaty [2004] OJ L123/18, and paragraphs 17 to 24 of Commission notice on best practices for the conduct of proceedings concerning Articles 101 and 102 TFEU [2011] OJ C308/6.

whether or not the European Commission's antitrust investigations are slower today than they were twenty years ago.

What appears more clearly is that complaints about the slowness of the European Commission's antitrust investigations have increased. This has, for instance, become a recurrent theme in the European Parliament's annual resolution on competition policy in response to the European Commission's annual report on competition policy.[104] Concern about the slowness of antitrust proceedings has also been one of the drivers behind the recent adoption of the Digital Markets Acts,[105] as well as behind the calls for more frequent use of interim measures pursuant to Article 8 of Regulation 1/2003, a power which the European Commission has used in 2019 for the first (and so far only) time since the entry into application of Regulation 1/2003.[106]

When antitrust investigations continue for many years, the opening of new investigations becomes more difficult, as resources remain tied up by the old investigations. The longer investigations last, the more likely that case handlers will leave before the end of the investigation, either for reasons unrelated to the duration of the investigation or precisely because they feel they have been dealing with the same case for too long. New case handlers then need time to familiarise themselves with the case, leading to a further slowing down of the investigation, and an increased difficulty of opening new investigations. When antitrust investigations proceed slowly, it also takes longer before new staff gain the expertise allowing them to deal faster and more effectively with subsequent other cases. A vicious circle of slowness and fewer investigations might thus develop.

4. Conclusion

Taking together the figures for the European Commission and the national competition authorities, however, there can be no doubt that Regulation 1/2003 has led to a spectacular increase in the enforcement of Articles 101 and 102 TFEU, and that Regulation 1/2003 has thus been a great success.

---

104 See for instance European Parliament resolution of 9 June 2021 on competition policy – annual report 2020, P9_TA(2021)0275, paragraph 33 ('regrets the slowness of antitrust investigations'), and European Parliament resolution of 18 June 2020 on competition policy – annual report 2019, P9_TA(2020)0158, paragraph 40 ('stresses the slowness of the antitrust investigations').

105 Regulation (EU) 2022/1925 of the European Parliament and of the Council of 14 September 2022 on contestable and fair markets in the digital sector (Digital Markets Act) [2022] OJ L265/1.

106 See Summary of Commission decision of 16 October 2019 in Case AT.40608 *Broadcom* [2021] OJ C81/23.

II. The Obligation for the Competition Authorities of the EU Member States to Apply EU Antitrust Law

Article 3 of Regulation 1/2003 obliges the competition authorities of the EU Member States (national competition authorities or NCAs) to apply Articles 101 and 102 TFEU (EU antitrust law) whenever they apply national competition law to conduct falling within the scope of EU antitrust law. Moreover, the application of national competition law cannot lead to the prohibition of agreements or concerted practices that affect trade between Member States but are not prohibited by Article 101 TFEU. National competition authorities can, however, use national competition law to prohibit unilateral conduct that is not prohibited by Article 102 TFEU. This chapter examines the content and rationale of these provisions of Article 3 of Regulation 1/2003, and the legal consequences in case of non-respect of these provisions, using as an example the Facebook Decision of 6 February 2019 of the Bundeskartellamt (German Federal Competition Authority).

A. Article 3 of Regulation 1/2003

Under Regulation 1/2003,[107] both the European Commission and the competition authorities of the EU Member States (national competition authorities or NCAs), forming together the European Competition Network (ECN), pursue infringements of Articles 101 and 102 TFEU.

In the words of the Joint Statement of the EU Council and the European Commission on the functioning of the network of competition authorities, entered in the Council Minutes at the time of the adoption of Regulation 1/2003,[108] the decentralisation of the enforcement of Articles 101 and 102 TFEU brought about by Regulation 1/2003 has 'strengthen[ed]

---

107 Council Regulation (EC) No 1/2003 of 16 December 2002 on the implementation of the rules on competition laid down in Articles 81 and 82 of the Treaty [2003] OJ L1/1, last amended by Council Regulation (EC) No 1419/2006 [2006] OJ L269/1. For a detailed analysis of Regulation 1/2003, in comparison with the regime preceding it, see my *Community Report* in D. Cahill and J. D. Cooke (eds), *The Modernisation of EU Competition Law Enforcement in the EU – FIDE 2004 National Reports* (Cambridge 2004), 661–736; my book *Principles of European Antitrust Enforcement* (Hart 2005); and K. Dekeyser, C. Gauer, J. Laitenberger, N. Wahl, W. Wils and L. Prete (eds), *Regulation 1/2003 and EU Antitrust Enforcement – A Systematic Guide* (Wolters Kluwer 2022).

108 Council Document 15435/02 ADD 1 of 10 December 2002, accessible at http://register.consilium.eu.int. According to its paragraphs 3 and 4, 'this Joint Statement is political in nature and does therefore not create any legal rights or obligations. It is limited to setting out common political understanding shared by all Member States and the Commission on the principles of the functioning of the Network. Details will be set out in a Commission notice which will be drafted and updated as necessary in close cooperation with Member States.' The said notice is Commission Notice on cooperation with the Network of Competition Authorities [2004] OJ C101/43. According to its paragraph 72, the principles set out in that notice have been agreed to by the NCAs. On the Joint Statement, see further Judgment in *France Télécom v Commission*, T-339/04, EU:T:2007:80, paragraph 85, and Opinion of Advocate General Mazák in *Pfleiderer*, C-360/09, EU:C:2010:782, paragraph 26.

the position of the NCAs [which have been made] fully competent to apply [Articles 101 and 102 TFEU], actively contributing to the development of [EU] competition policy, law and practice'.[109]

In accordance with settled case law of the EU Court of Justice, EU law and national law on competition apply in parallel. Competition rules at European and at national level view restrictions of competition from different angles and their areas of application do not coincide.[110]

Article 103(2)(e) TFEU enables the EU Council to regulate the relationship between national laws and Articles 101 and 102 TFEU. The Council has done so through Article 3 of Regulation 1/2003, which reads as follows:

Article 3

Relationship between [Articles 101 and 102 TFEU] and national competition laws

'*1. Where the competition authorities of the Member States or national courts apply national competition law to agreements, decisions by associations of undertakings or concerted practices within the meaning of [Article 101(1) TFEU] which may affect trade between Member States within the meaning of that provision, they shall also apply [Article 101 TFEU] to such agreements, decisions or concerted practices. Where the competition authorities of the Member States or national courts apply national competition law to any abuse prohibited by [Article 102 TFEU], they shall also apply [Article 102 TFEU].*

2. The application of national competition law may not lead to the prohibition of agreements, decisions by associations of undertakings or concerted practices which may affect trade between Member States but which do not restrict competition within the meaning of [Article 101(1) TFEU], or which fulfil the conditions of [Article 101(3) TFEU] or which are covered by a Regulation for the application of [Article 101(3) TFEU]. Member States shall not under this Regulation be precluded from adopting and applying on their territory stricter national laws which prohibit or sanction unilateral conduct engaged in by undertakings.

3. Without prejudice to general principles and other provisions of [EU] law, paragraphs 1 and 2 do not apply when the competition authorities and the courts of the Member States apply national merger control laws nor do they preclude the application of provisions of national law that predominantly pursue an objective different from that pursued by [Articles 101 and 102 TFEU].'

Article 3 of Regulation 1/2003 thus in essence contains two distinct rules, each with its own rationale and scope:

- **Article 3(1)** contains an obligation for national competition authorities and national courts also to apply Articles 101 or 102 TFEU when applying national competition law to conduct falling within the scope of Articles 101 or 102 TFEU.

---

109 Joint Statement, paragraph 6.

110 Judgment of 14 February 2012, *Toshiba Corporation and Others*, C-17/10, EU:C:2012:72, paragraph 81 and the case law cited, and Judgment of 3 April 2019, *Powszechny Zakład Ubezpieczeń na Życie*, C-617/17, EU:C:2019:283, paragraph 25.

According to recital 8 of Regulation 1/2003, the purpose of this rule is 'to ensure the effective enforcement of the [EU] competition rules and the proper functioning of the cooperation mechanisms contained in [Regulation 1/2003]'.
As far as national competition authorities (NCAs) are concerned, these cooperation mechanisms are those set out in Article 11 of Regulation 1/2003.[111] Article 11(1) provides that the European Commission and the NCAs must apply Articles 101 and 102 TFEU 'in close cooperation'. Article 11(3) provides that the NCAs, when acting under Article 101 or Article 102 TFEU, must inform the European Commission in writing before or without delay after commencing the first formal investigative measure. Article 11(4) provides that, no later than 30 days before the adoption of a decision requiring that an infringement be brought to an end or accepting commitments, the NCAs must inform the Commission of the envisaged decision. Finally, Article 11(6) provides that the European Commission can relieve the NCAs of their competence to apply Articles 101 and 102 TFEU in a given case by initiating itself proceedings.[112]

– The first sentence of **Article 3(2)** contains what has been called a 'convergence rule',[113] precluding the prohibition under national competition law of agreements, decisions of associations of undertakings and concerted practices that fall within the scope of Article 101(1) TFEU but are not prohibited by Article 101 TFEU.
According to recital 8 of Regulation 1/2003, the purpose of this rule is 'to create a level playing field for agreements, decisions of associations of undertakings and concerted practices within the [EU] internal market'.
This convergence rule only relates to Article 101 TFEU. As for Article 102 TFEU, the second sentence of Article 3(2) provides that EU Member States are not precluded from adopting and applying on their territory stricter national competition laws that prohibit unilateral conduct not prohibited by Article 102 TFEU.
According to recital 8, '[t]hese stricter national laws may include provisions which prohibit or impose sanctions on abusive behaviour toward economically dependent undertakings'. According to the European Commission's 2009 Report on the application of Regulation 1/2003, stricter national competition laws that prohibit unilateral conduct not prohibited by Article 102 TFEU 'exist in a number of Member States and include notably: national provisions which regulate the abuse of economic dependence, "superior bargaining power" or "significant influence"; legal provisions concerning resale below cost or

---

111 Details on the application of these cooperation mechanisms have been set out in the Commission Notice on cooperation with the Network of Competition Authorities [2004] OJ C101/43. According to its paragraph 72, the principles set out in that notice have been agreed to by the NCAs.

112 It follows from Article 3 and Article 11(6) of Regulation 1/2003 taken together that, once the European Commission initiates proceedings, the NCAs can no longer apply not only Articles 101 and 102 TFEU but also their national competition law, except for stricter national laws prohibiting unilateral conduct not prohibited by Article 102 TFEU, national merger control laws and provisions of national law that predominantly pursue an objective different from that pursued by Articles 101 and 102 TFEU; see Judgment of 14 February 2012, *Toshiba Corporation and Others*, C-17/10, EU:C:2012:72, paragraphs 75 and 76.

113 European Commission, *Report on the functioning of Regulation 1/2003*, COM(2009)206 of 29 April 2009, paragraph 21.

at a loss; national laws that foresee different standards for assessing dominance and stricter national provisions governing the conduct of dominant undertakings'.[114]

Article 3(3) provides that Article 3(1) and Article 3(2) do not apply when national competition authorities or national courts apply national merger control laws and that they do not preclude the application of provisions of national law 'that predominantly pursue an objective different from that pursued by [Articles 101 and 102 TFEU]'. According to recital 9 of Regulation 1/2003, Articles 101 and 102 TFEU 'have as their objective the protection of competition on the market'. Recital 9 further mentions as an example of provisions of national law that predominantly pursue an objective different from that pursued by Articles 101 and 102 TFEU 'national legislation that prohibits or imposes sanctions on acts of unfair trading practice, be they unilateral or contractual. Such legislation pursues a specific objective, irrespective of the actual or presumed effects of such acts on competition on the market. This is particularly the case of legislation which prohibits undertakings from imposing on their trading partners, obtaining or attempting to obtain from them terms and conditions that are unjustified, disproportionate or without consideration'.

The relationship between Articles 101 and 102 TFEU and national competition laws was one of the most contentious issues in the legislative history of Regulation 1/2003.[115]

Regulation 17, which governed the application of Articles 101 and 102 TFEU from 1962 until its replacement by Regulation 1/2003, did not regulate the relationship between EU competition law and national competition laws.[116] Under Regulation 17, the European Commission had exclusive competence to apply Article 101(3) TFEU through a notification and authorisation system.[117] Whereas Regulation 17 did not prevent the application of Article 102 TFEU by national competition authorities, in practice national competition authorities tended to apply only national competition law.

In its White Paper on Modernisation of 1999,[118] the European Commission advocated the ending of the notification and authorisation system, and its replacement by a system

---

114 European Commission, *Report on the functioning of Regulation 1/2003*, COM(2009)206 of 29 April 2009, paragraph 21; see also Commission Staff Working Paper accompanying the Report on the functioning of Regulation 1/2003, SEC(2009)574 of 29 April 2009, section 4.4. More Member States have introduced national laws on abuse of economic dependence since 2009, for instance Belgium in 2019. As to the economic justification for such laws, see I. Kokkoris, *A Gap in the Enforcement of Article 82* (British Institute of International and Comparative Law 2009). The European Commission's Decision 77/327/EEC of 19 April 1977 in Case IV/28.841 *ABG oil companies operating in the Netherlands* [1977] OJ L117/1, suggests that Article 102 TFEU could also be interpreted more broadly to cover abuse of economic dependence.

115 See E. Paulis and C. Gauer, 'La réforme des règles d'application des articles 81 et 82 du Traité' (2003) 11 *Journal des tribunaux Droit européen* 65, and Chapter I of this book.

116 Council Regulation No 17 [1962] OJ 13/204 (Special English Edition 1959-62, p 87).

117 For a detailed analysis as to why a notification and authorisation system made sense in 1962 but no longer made sense at the turn of the century, see my paper 'Notification, Clearance and Exemption in EC Competition Law: An Economic Analysis' (1999) 24 *European Law Review* 139, and my book *The Optimal Enforcement of EC Antitrust Law* (Kluwer 2002). For a detailed comparison between Regulation 17 and Regulation 1/2003, see my *Community Report* in D. Cahill and J. D. Cooke (eds), *The Modernisation of EU Competition Law Enforcement in the EU – FIDE 2004 National Reports* (Cambridge 2004), 661–736, also accessible at http://ssrn.com/author=456087, and my book *Principles of European Antitrust Enforcement* (Hart 2005).

118 White Paper on modernisation of the rules implementing Articles 85 and 86 of the EC Treaty [1999] OJ C132/1.

of *ex post* enforcement, allowing the Commission to refocus its action on combating the most serious competition infringements, and allowing an enhanced role for national competition authorities and national courts. In their reaction to the White Paper, industry and the European Parliament expressed the fear that the decentralisation of the application of EU competition law would lead to a renationalisation of competition policy.[119] This concern explains the main addition, as compared to the White Paper, which the European Commission included in the legislative proposal it submitted to the EU Council in 2000. Article 3 of the proposed regulation excluded the application of national competition laws to all agreements or concerted practices within the meaning of Article 101 TFEU and all abuses of a dominant position within the meaning of Article 102 TFEU that affect trade between Member States, thus ensuring the sole applicability of EU law.[120] This proposal in turn caused significant opposition from a number of Member States, whose national competition laws prohibited types of unilateral conduct not prohibited by Article 102 TFEU.[121] Article 3 of Regulation 1/2003 reflects the compromise that was ultimately found.[122]

B. The Facebook Decision of the Bundeskartellamt

On 6 February 2019, the Bundeskartellamt (German Federal Competition Authority) adopted a decision, in which it finds that Facebook abuses its dominant position in the private social network market in Germany by making the use of the Facebook social network conditional on Facebook being allowed to collect user- and device-related data from Facebook-owned services (such as WhatsApp and Instagram) and from websites visited or third-party mobile apps used and to combine those data with the facebook.com user account (the Facebook Decision).[123]

The Facebook Decision is based on Section 19(1) of the German Act against Restraints on Competition (Competition Act – GWB), the generic German competition law provision concerning abuse of dominance, which provides that '[t]he abuse of a dominant position by one or several undertakings is prohibited'.[124]

Based on the concept of demand-side substitutability, the Bundeskartellamt defines the relevant product market as the market for social networks for private use. The

---

119 See E. Paulis and C. Gauer, 'La réforme des règles d'application des articles 81 et 82 du Traité' (2003) 11 *Journal des tribunaux Droit européen* 65 at 67, and my paper 'Ten Years of Regulation 1/2003 – A Retrospective' (2013) 4 *Journal of European Competition Law & Practice* 293, also accessible at http://ssrn.com/author=456087, at footnotes 12 to 16.

120 Proposal for a Council Regulation implementing Articles 81 and 82 of the Treaty, COM(2000)582; see also Judgment of 14 February 2012, *Toshiba Corporation and Others*, C-17/10, EU:C:2012:72, paragraph 83.

121 See Chapter I of this book.

122 See E. Paulis and C. Gauer, 'La réforme des règles d'application des articles 81 et 82 du Traité' (2003) 11 *Journal des tribunaux Droit européen* 65 at 67, and my paper 'Ten Years of Regulation 1/2003 – A Retrospective' (2013) 4 *Journal of European Competition Law & Practice* 293, also accessible at http://ssrn.com/author=456087, at footnotes 12 to 16.

123 Facebook Decision (6 February 2019), B6-22/16, accessible at https://www.bundeskartellamt.de/SharedDocs/Entscheidung/DE/Entscheidungen/Missbrauchsaufsicht/2019/B6-22-16.html?nn=3591568; see also Press Release (7 February 2019), Frequently Asked Questions (7 February 2019) and Case Summary (15 February 2019) in English accessible at https://www.bundeskartellamt.de/SharedDocs/Meldung/EN/Meldungen%20News%20Karussell/2019/07_02_2019_Facebook.html.

124 English translation at https://www.bundeskartellamt.de/SharedDocs/Publikation/EN/Others/GWB.

geographical market is defined as Germany, based on the finding that the service is predominantly used to connect with people in the users' own country, special national user habits and the lack of opportunities for supply-side substitution.

The finding that Facebook is dominant in the German private social network market is based on an overall assessment of all factors of market power, including market shares, direct network effects and the difficulty of switching to another social network, indirect network effects through the advertising market, and access to competitively relevant data.

As to the abuse, the Bundeskartellamt finds that Facebook's terms of service, which allow it to collect user- and device-related data from sources outside the Facebook social network and to merge it with data collected via facebook.com, constitute exploitative business terms to the detriment of consumers. In addition, the Bundeskartellamt finds that Facebook's conduct impedes competitors in that it gives Facebook access to a large number of further data sources, thus giving Facebook a further competitive edge over its competitors and elevating barriers to market entry, thus in turn strengthening Facebook's market power vis-à-vis consumers.

In assessing whether Facebook's terms of service constitute exploitative business terms, the Bundeskartellamt relies on the *VBL Gegenwert* case law of the German Federal Court of Justice (Bundesgerichtshof), according to which, to determine whether business terms are exploitative and constitute an abuse pursuant to Section 19(1) GWB, account must be taken of any legal principle that aims to protect a contracting party in an unbalanced negotiation position.[125] The Bundeskartellamt follows this approach by applying the data protection principles contained in particular in the EU General Data Protection Regulation (GDPR).[126] It finds that the collection of data from sources outside the Facebook social network and the merging of these data with the data collected via facebook.com constitute unlawful data processing in breach of Articles 5(1)(a) and 6 GDPR. This data processing is not necessary to fulfil contractual obligations and the balancing of interests under Article 6(1)(f) GDPR does not result in the conclusion that Facebook's interests in data processing (also taking into account Facebook's dominant position[127]) outweigh the users' interests. Also, Facebook did not obtain its users' effective consent for the purposes of Articles 6(1)(a) and 7 GDPR, given Facebook's dominant position and the fact that the provision of the service of facebook.com is made subject to this condition.[128]

---

125 Judgment of 24 January 2017, KZR 47/14, *VBL Gegenwert II*.

126 Regulation (EU) 2016/679 of the European Parliament and of the Council of 27 April 2016 on the protection of natural persons with regard to the processing of personal data and on the free movement of such data, and repealing Directive 95/46/EC (General Data Protection Regulation) [2016] OJ L119/1.

127 In line with Opinion 06/2014 of the Article 29 Data Protection Working Party of 9 April 2014 on the notion of legitimate interests of the data controller under Article 7 of Directive 95/46/EC.

128 According to Article 7(4) GDPR, '[w]hen assessing whether consent is freely given, utmost account shall be taken of whether, inter alia, the performance of a contract, including the provision of a service, is conditional on consent to the processing of personal data that is not necessary for the performance of the contract'. See also Article 29 Data Protection Working Party Guidelines on consent under Regulation 2016/679 (revised 10 April 2018).

As to the applicability of Article 102 TFEU, paragraph 914 of the Facebook Decision acknowledges that, pursuant to Article 3(1), second sentence, of Regulation 1/2003, Article 102 TFEU must also be applied when national competition law is applied to abuses prohibited by Article 102 TFEU, and that according to Article 102(2)(a) TFEU an abuse can also consist in the direct or indirect imposition of unfair purchase or selling prices or other unfair trading conditions. However, according to the Facebook Decision, the *VBL Gegenwert* case law of the German courts, according to which, when assessing the existence of abuse under Section 19(1) GWB, account must be taken of fundamental rights and secondary legislation, has not yet found equivalent expression in the EU case law and decisional practice, and, for this reason, the Facebook Decision is based on Section 19(1) GWB and the corresponding case law. According to Article 3(2), second sentence, of Regulation 1/2003, Member States are not precluded from adopting and applying on their territory stricter national laws that prohibit or sanction unilateral conduct engaged in by undertakings.[129]

In the 'Frequently Asked Questions' accompanying the Press Release following the adoption of the Facebook Decision,[130] the question 'Is European competition law also applicable in this case?' is answered as follows:

'*In such proceedings the application of European abuse control provisions is always an issue. Such an abuse control proceeding against Facebook would generally also be possible under the relevant norm of Article 102 TFEU. So far, however, only the case-law of the highest German court has been established which can take into account constitutional or other legal principles (in this case data protection) in assessing abusive practices of a dominant company. However, due to the cross-border dimension of this case, the Bundeskartellamt closely liaised with the European Commission and other competition authorities in the course of the proceeding.*'

Speaking in Brussels on 17 April 2019, Andreas Mundt, the president of the Bundeskartellamt, expressed the view that the Facebook Decision could easily be replicated under EU competition law, German competition law being practically identical to EU competition law.[131]

---

129 In the German original: 'Nach Art. 3 Abs. 1 S. 2 VO 1/2003 ist im Fall, dass einzelstaatliches Wettbewerbsrecht auf nach Art. 102 AEUV verbotene Missbräuche angewendet wird, auch Art. 102 AEUV anzuwenden. Zwar kann nach dem Katalogtatbestand des Art. 102 Satz 2 lit. a AEUV ein Missbrauch auch in der unmittelbaren oder mittelbaren Erzwingung von unangemessenen Einkaufs- oder Verkaufspreisen oder sonstigen Geschäftsbedingungen bestehen. Die Prüfung hat jedoch gezeigt, dass das von der deutschen Rechtsprechung zur Generalklausel des § 19 Abs. 1 GWB entwickelte Schutzkonzept, das sich zur Feststellung der Missbräuchlichkeit maßgeblich auf grundrechtliche oder einfachgesetzliche Wertentscheidungen bezieht, in der europäischen Rechtsprechung und Anwendungspraxis bisher keine Entsprechung gefunden hat. Die beabsichtigte Untersagung wird daher auf § 19 Abs. 1 GWB i.V.m. der hierzu ergangenen innerstaatlichen Rechtsprechung gestützt. Den Mitgliedstaaten ist es nach Art. 3 Abs. 2 S. 2 VO 1/2003 nicht verwehrt, in ihrem Hoheitsgebiet strengere innerstaatliche Vorschriften zur Unterbindung oder Ahndung einseitiger Handlungen von Unternehmen zu erlassen oder anzuwenden.'

130 Frequently Asked Questions (7 February 2019) accessible at https://www.bundeskartellamt.de/SharedDocs/Meldung/EN/Meldungen%20News%20Karussell/2019/07_02_2019_Facebook.html.

131 Global Competition Law Centre (GCLC) 108th Lunch Talk (17 April 2019), reported by MLex, 'Facebook's antitrust order in Germany "easily" replicated in EU law, Mundt says' (17 April 2019). President Mundt referred on this point also to the statement by Professor von Danwitz at the 19th International Conference on Competition (IKK) in Berlin on 15 March 2019, mentioned in the footnote just below.

C. The question of the applicability of Article 102 TFEU

It could indeed be argued that conduct such as that at issue in the Facebook Decision also falls under Article 102 TFEU.[132]

Like Section 19(1) GWB, on which the Facebook Decision is based, Article 102 TFEU prohibits abuse of a dominant position. However, Article 102 TFEU additionally requires that the dominant position must be held in the whole or a substantial part of the EU internal market and that the abuse may affect trade between EU Member States.

As to the first of these conditions, the Bundeskartellamt finds that Facebook has a dominant position in the German market for social networks for private use. Germany being the largest EU Member State, there can be little doubt that this market constitutes a substantial part of the EU internal market.[133] While the Bundeskartellamt did not make any finding in this respect, it is also plausible that Facebook could be found to be dominant throughout the whole EU.

As to the potential effect of the abuse on trade between EU Member States, the Facebook Decision mentions that the facebook.com services are provided in Germany by Facebook Ireland Ltd., whereas most of the smaller competitors are based in Germany.[134] The exclusionary effect of Facebook's conduct vis-à-vis competing private social network providers, as found by the Bundeskartellamt, thus appears capable of influencing the pattern of trade between Member States.[135] Moreover, while this was not examined by the Bundeskartellamt, there might be smaller social network providers active in Member States other than Germany whose potential entrance into the German market Facebook's conduct, as found by the Bundeskartellamt, would be capable of affecting negatively.

The concept of dominance in Section 19(1) GWB and in Article 102 TFEU being in essence identical, there appears to be no reason why the finding of dominance made by the Bundeskartellamt under Section 19(1) GWB could not have equally been made under Article 102 TFEU.

As for the concept of abuse, it is true that there is no judgment of the EU Courts or decision of the European Commission concerning Article 102 TFEU that is identical to the *VBL Gegenwert* judgment of the German Federal Court of Justice concerning Section 19(1) GWB. However, according to Article 1(3) of Regulation 1/2003, '[t]he

---

132 See also T. von Danwitz, 'Privacy and competition law', Statement for the 19th IKK International Conference on Competition (Berlin, 15 March 2019), reported by MLex, 'Privacy-abusing tech companies could attract EU antitrust enforcement, judge warns' (15 March 2019).

133 Indeed, each Member State is likely to be considered to be a substantial part of the EU; see R. Whish and D. Bailey, *Competition Law* (9th edition, Oxford 2018) at 196.

134 Facebook Decision, paragraphs 3, 187, 197, 199, 207, 268 to 271 and 392.

135 Patterns of trade are also affected when the abuse causes an increase in trade; see Judgments of 13 July 1966, *Consten and Grundig v Commission*, C-56/64 and C-58/64, EU:C:1966:41, p 341; and of 23 November 2006, *Asnef-Equifax and Administración del Estado*, C-238/05, paragraph 38. See also European Commission, Guidelines on the effect on trade concept in Articles 81 and 82 of the Treaty [2004] OJ C101/81, paragraph 34.

abuse of a dominant position referred to in [Article 102 TFEU] shall be prohibited, no prior decision to that effect being required'.

The second sentence of Article 102 TFEU expressly provides that 'abuse may, in particular consist in (a) directly or indirectly imposing unfair purchase or selling prices or other unfair conditions'.

It would thus seem that Article 102 TFEU could also cover the imposition of unfair conditions in relation to access to personal data. This would appear all the more true in a market such as that for private social networks, where services like that of facebook.com are offered ostensibly for 'free' to users, while in economic reality the 'purchase price' of those services is the personal data that users must make available in order to use the services offered.[136]

As has also been pointed out by Professor von Danwitz,[137] according to the case law of the EU Court of Justice, the application of EU competition law always needs to take into account the legal context of a practice,[138] and non-compliance with other branches of the law can be a relevant factor.[139]

Article 7 TFEU provides that the EU is to 'ensure consistency between its policies and activities, taking all of its objectives into account'. According to Article 6(1) of the Treaty on European Union (TEU), the Charter of Fundamental Rights of the European Union has 'the same legal value as the Treaties'. Article 8 of the Charter provides that '[e]veryone has the right to the protection of personal data concerning him or her' and that such data 'must be processed fairly for specified purposes and on the basis of the consent of the person concerned or some other legitimate basis laid down by law'. The General Data Protection Regulation (GDPR) sets out in detail the rights of data subjects and the obligations of those who process and determine the processing of personal data.[140]

As has also been pointed out by Professor von Danwitz, the case law of the EU Court of Justice shows that the 'fairness' of trading conditions within the meaning of Article 102(a) TFEU can be assessed by using the principles of necessity, proportionality and transparency as relevant benchmarks.[141] These are also core principles of data protection law.[142]

---

136 See also Article 3(1) and recital 24 of Directive (EU) 2019/770 of the European Parliament and of the Council of 20 May 2019 on certain aspects concerning contracts for the supply of digital content and digital services [2019] OJ L136/1, which equates the provision of personal data by a consumer to obtain digital content or a digital service with the payment of a price.

137 T. von Danwitz, 'Privacy and competition law', Statement for the 19th IKK International Conference on Competition (Berlin, 15 March 2019), reported by MLex, 'Privacy-abusing tech companies could attract EU antitrust enforcement, judge warns' (15 March 2019).

138 Judgments of 26 September 2018, *Infineon Technologies v Commission*, C-99/17 P, EU:C:2018:773, paragraph 156 and the case law cited, and of 10 December 1991, *Merci Convenzionali Porto di Genova*, C-179/90, EU:C:1991:464, paragraphs 3, 4 and 17 to 20.

139 Judgment of 14 March 2013, *Allianz Hungária*, C-32/11, EU:C:2013:160, paragraphs 46 and 47. However, see also Judgment of 6 December 2012, *AstraZeneca v Commission*, C-457/10 P, EU:C:2012:770, paragraph 132.

140 Article 1(1) and recital 11 GDPR.

141 Judgments of 21 March 1974, *BRT and SABAM*, 127/73, EU:C:1974:25, of 16 July 2009, *Der Grüne Punkt – Duales System Deutschland v Commission*, C-385/07 P, EU:C:2009:456, paragraph 142, and of 6 December 2012, *AstraZeneca v Commission*, C-457/10 P, EU:C:2012:770, paragraph 93.

142 See Articles 5 and 6 GDPR; see also H. Kalimo and K. Majcher, 'The concept of fairness: linking EU competition and data protection law in the digital marketplace' (2017) *European Law Review* 210 at 213; G. Schneider, 'Testing Art. 102 TFEU in the Digital Marketplace: Insights from the *Bundeskartellamt*'s investigation against

It would thus appear possible also under Article 102 TFEU to use the principles of the General Data Protection Regulation (GDPR) as a benchmark for the assessment of the unfairness of trading conditions and hence the existence of an abuse.

Indeed, in its recent judgment on a preliminary question from the German court that is reviewing the Facebook Decision, the EU Court of Justice has confirmed that 'the compliance or non-compliance of [the conduct of a dominant undertaking] with the provisions of the GDPR may, depending on the circumstances, be a vital clue among the relevant circumstances of the case in order to establish whether that conduct entails resorting to methods governing normal competition and to assess the consequences of a certain practice in the market or for consumers'.[143]

Of course, this in no way means that any infringement of data protection law automatically constitutes an infringement of EU competition law. Indeed, the EU Court of Justice has stated in *Asnef-Equifax* that privacy issues are not **as such** competition law issues.[144] As has been pointed out by Professor von Danwitz, it is thus necessary to examine individually, according to the specific circumstances of the case at hand, whether conduct caught under the privacy rules may amount to an anticompetitive practice.[145]

In the Facebook Decision, the Bundeskartellamt conducts such an examination. In doing so, it finds not only that Facebook's terms of service constitute exploitative business terms to the detriment of consumers, but also that Facebook's conduct impedes competitors in that it gives Facebook access to a large number of further data sources, thus giving Facebook a further competitive edge over its competitors and reinforcing market entry barriers, which in turn strengthen Facebook's market power vis-à-vis consumers. The Facebook Decision thus goes well beyond a mere 'recycling' of a finding of infringement of data protection law.[146]

The applicability of Article 102 TFEU to conduct such as that found in the Facebook Decision could thus not be denied either on the ground that there would be an insufficient link between the conduct and the dominant position.[147] Indeed, the Facebook Decision shows a double link: *first*, Facebook's dominance is relevant for both the interest balancing and the effectiveness of the consent under data protection principles and thus for the assessment of the unfairness of the terms of use, and *second*, Facebook's conduct has an exclusionary effect vis-à-vis competitors, reinforcing Facebook's dominant position vis-à-vis consumers.

The conclusion of the above is that conduct such as that found in the Facebook Decision of the Bundeskartellamt arguably also falls under Article 102 TFEU. If this is indeed the

---

Facebook' (2018) 9 *Journal of European Competition Law & Practice* 213 at 223; and I. Graef, D. Clifford and P. Valcke, 'Fairness and enforcement: bridging competition, data protection, and consumer law' (2018) 8 *International Data Privacy Law* 200.

143 Judgment of 4 July 2023, *Meta Platforms and Others*, C-252/21, EU:C:2023:537, paragraph 47.

144 Judgment of 23 November 2006, *Asnef-Equifax and Administración des Estado*, C-238/05, EU:C:2006:734, paragraph 63.

145 See also Judgment of 4 July 2023, *Meta Platforms and Others*, C-252/21, EU:C:2023:537, paragraph 47.

146 Compare with Judgments of the EU General Court of 10 March 1992, *SIV v Commission*, T-68/89, EU:T:1992:38, paragraph 360 and of 23 October 2003, *Van den Bergh Foods v Commission*, T-65/98, EU:T:2003:281, paragraph 162.

147 On this requirement, see Judgment of the EU Court of Justice of 13 February 1979, *Hoffmann-La Roche v Commission*, 85/76, EU:C:1979:36, paragraph 91, and P. Vogelsang, 'Abuse of a Dominant Position in Article 86: The Problem of Causality and Some Applications' (1976) 13 *Common Market Law Review* 61.

case, it would follow that the Bundeskartellamt has infringed Article 3(1), second sentence, of Regulation 1/2003 by not also applying Article 102 TFEU in its Facebook Decision.

D. The distinct question of optimal case selection

Beyond the legal question of the applicability of Article 102 TFEU to the conduct at issue in the Facebook Decision of the Bundeskartellamt, a different question is whether, as a matter of policy, it is desirable or appropriate that the European Commission and/or the competition authorities of the EU Member States take up cases such as the Facebook case taken up by the Bundeskartellamt.

Following the adoption of the Facebook Decision by the Bundeskartellamt, a member of the European Parliament asked the European Commission whether it 'consider[s] it desirable to convert the decision of the German Federal Cartel Office into a European standard in order to further strengthen the position of consumers'.[148] Commissioner Vestager responded on behalf of the European Commission that the Commission 'took note of the decision of the German Federal Cartel Office. The German Federal Cartel Office's concerns are based on German competition law. The European legislator has made sure that the type of conduct in question is addressed by the General Data Protection Regulation (Regulation (EU) 2016/679)'.[149]

This appears to express the view that conduct such as that found by the Bundeskartellamt in the Facebook Decision should be addressed by the data protection supervisory authorities empowered by the EU General Data Protection Regulation rather than by the European Commission and the competition authorities of the EU Member States applying EU competition law.[150]

According to the case law of the EU Court of Justice, the European Commission has a broad discretion to select the cases that it deals with under Articles 101 and 102 TFEU.[151] Article 4(5) of the 'ECN+' Directive 2019/1 ensures that the competition authorities of the EU Member States have a similar discretion to set their enforcement priorities.[152]

---

148 Question for written answer P-001183/2019 by Ms Ruohanen-Lerner.

149 Answer given by Ms Vestager on behalf of the European Commission to Question P-001183/2019 (8 May 2019).

150 As to the European Commission's views, see also Judgment of 4 July 2023, *Meta Platforms and Others*, C-252/21, EU:C:2023:537, paragraph 51: 'As pointed out by the Commission, inter alia, access to personal data and the fact that it is possible to process such data have become a significant parameter of competition between undertakings in the digital economy. Therefore, excluding the rules on the protection of personal data from the legal framework to be taken into consideration by the competition authorities when examining an abuse of a dominant position would disregard the reality of this economic development and would be liable to undermine the effectiveness of competition law within the European Union.'

151 Judgments of 14 December 2000, *Masterfoods*, C-344/98, EU:C:2000:689, paragraph 46, of 4 March 1999, *Ufex and Others v Commission*, C-119/97 P, EU:C:1999:116, paragraphs 88 and 89, and of 17 May 2001, *IECC v Commission*, C-449/98 P, EU:C:2001:276, paragraphs 35 to 37; see further chapter IV of this book.

152 Directive (EU) 2019/1 of the European Parliament and of the Council of 11 December 2018 to empower the competition authorities of the Member States to be more effective enforcers and to ensure the proper functioning of the internal market [2019] OJ L11/3; see further my paper 'Competition authorities: Towards more independence and prioritisation? The European Commission's "ECN+" Proposal for a Directive to empower the competition authorities of the Member States to be more effective enforcers', *Concurrences* no 4-2017, 60, also accessible at http://ssrn.com/author=456087; L. Idot, 'Reform of Regulation 1/2003: Power to set priorities', *Concurrences* no 3-2015, 51; and Chapter III of this book.

In setting enforcement priorities, the fact that another authority is also capable of dealing with the issue, and may indeed be better placed to do so, is obviously a highly relevant consideration.[153]

Under the EU General Data Protection Regulation (GDPR), each EU Member State has an independent data protection supervisory authority responsible for monitoring the application of the GDPR, and empowered to investigate possible infringements, order their termination and impose fines up to 4% of the undertaking's annual turnover.[154]

Pursuant to Article 56 GDPR, the supervisory authority of the Member State of the main establishment of the company concerned is competent to act as lead supervisory authority for the cross-border data processing by that company. In the case of Facebook, this is the Irish Data Protection Commission.

If the Irish Data Protection Commission had taken up a case against Facebook instead of the Bundeskartellamt, it might have adopted a decision ordering the termination of Facebook's conduct throughout the European Union, whereas the Bundeskartellamt's decision only covers the German territory. This would obviously have been preferable. The fact remains, however, that the Irish Data Protection Commission had not taken up a case against Facebook in respect of the conduct at issue in the Facebook Decision.[155] Also, the Bundeskartellamt has indicated that it 'closely cooperated with data protection authorities in this case which explicitly supported the authority's proceeding'.[156] The EU Court of Justice has confirmed that the Bundeskartellamt thus appears to have fulfilled its obligations of sincere cooperation with the data protection supervisory authorities.[157]

E. Legal consequences of the non-respect of Article 3 of Regulation 1/2003

The question arises what the legal consequences are of the non-respect by a national competition authority of the obligations set out in Article 3 of Regulation 1/2003.

---

153 See, on the possibility for the European Commission to reject a complaint because the case can be dealt with by a national court, Judgment of 18 September 1992, *Automec v Commission*, T-24/90, EU:T:1992:97, paragraphs 88 to 96, and European Commission Notice on the handling of complaints by the Commission under Articles 81 and 82 of the EC Treaty [2004] C 101/65, paragraphs 17 and 44, and, on the possibility for the European Commission or a national competition authority to reject a complaint because another competition authority is dealing with the case, Article 13 of Regulation 1/2003 and Judgment of 21 January 2015, *EasyJet v Commission*, T-355/13, EU:T:2015:36.

154 Articles 51(1), 58 and 83 GDPR.

155 A Transatlantic Politico Investigation (N. Vinocur, 'One Country Blocks the World on Data Privacy – Millions of Americans rely on Europe's tough new privacy rules to safeguard their data, but the law's chief enforcer – Ireland – is in bed with the companies it regulates' (24 April 2019), accessible at https://www.politico.eu/interactive/ireland-blocks-the-world-on-data-privacy) argues that there might be a structural weakness in the GDPR lead supervisory authority system, given Member States' possible incentives to attract international companies through lax regulatory enforcement. In contrast, the system of parallel competence of the European Commission and the competition authorities of the EU Member States under Regulation 1/2003 does not suffer from a similar weakness; see further my book *Principles of European Antitrust Enforcement* (Hart 2005), sections 1.1.4.3.4 and 1.2.8.

156 Frequently Asked Question (7 February 2019), accessible at https://www.bundeskartellamt.de/SharedDocs/Meldung/EN/Meldungen%20News%20Karussell/2019/07_02_2019_Facebook.html, at 7.

157 Judgment of 4 July 2023, *Meta Platforms and Others*, C-252/21, EU:C:2023:537, paragraphs 53, 60 and 61.

It has been argued in the literature that 'decisions adopted in breach of the obligations contained in Article 3 are invalid and unenforceable'.[158]

Such a remedy may indeed be suitable to enforce respect for the rule in Article 3(2), first sentence, of Regulation 1/2003, which precludes the prohibition under national competition law of agreements, decisions of associations of undertakings and concerted practices that fall within the scope of Article 101(1) TFEU but are not prohibited by Article 101 TFEU. If a national competition authority breaches this rule, the undertakings whose agreement has been prohibited will have the ability and the incentive to challenge the decision of the national competition authority and to raise before the national review court the non-respect of Article 3(2), first sentence, of Regulation 1/2003. The national review court can then assess, possibly with assistance from the EU Court of Justice pursuant to Article 267 TFEU or from the European Commission pursuant to Article 15(1) of Regulation 1/2003, whether the agreement indeed falls within the scope of Article 101 TFEU and is not prohibited by it, and, in case of a positive conclusion, annul the decision of the national competition authority. Such an outcome would be fully in line with the purpose of Article 3(2), first sentence, of Regulation 1/2003.

Such a remedy would, however, appear neither workable nor desirable in a case like that of the Facebook Decision of the Bundeskartellamt, where, as advanced above, Article 3(1), second sentence, of Regulation 1/2003 has arguably not been respected by the national competition authority. In such a case, the undertaking whose behaviour has been found to violate national competition law will have no incentive to request the national review court to make a finding that its behaviour in addition also violates Article 102 TFEU. An annulment of the decision of the national competition authority on this ground by the national review court would also not appear satisfactory in the light of the purpose of Article 3(1), second sentence, of Regulation 1/2003. As explained above, the purpose of this provision is not to prevent national competition authorities from applying their national competition law to conduct prohibited by Article 102 TFEU but to ensure that the prohibition is also based on Article 102 TFEU.

Another possibility would be for the European Commission to bring proceedings pursuant to Article 258 TFEU against the Member State whose competition authority has not respected Article 3(1), second sentence, of Regulation 1/2003, with a view to obtaining a judgment by the EU Court of Justice that the Member State has failed in its obligations under EU law. While it is not common for the European Commission to bring such proceedings for a single failure by an independent authority of a Member State,[159] the legal possibility exists.[160] Such proceedings would not, however, directly affect the decision of the national competition authority, which would continue to be based only on national competition law. In the case of the Facebook Decision of the Bundeskartellamt, it is most unlikely that the European Commission would bring such proceedings, given that,

---

158 Faull & Nikpay, *The EU Law of Competition* (3rd edition, Oxford 2014), at 107.

159 On the independence of national competition authorities, see Article 4 of Directive (EU) 2019/1 of the European Parliament and of the Council of 11 December 2018 to empower the competition authorities of the Member States to be more effective enforcers and to ensure the proper functioning of the internal market [2019] OJ L11/3, and Chapter III of this book.

160 See Judgment of 4 October 2018, *European Commission v French Republic*, C-416/17, EU:C:2018:811.

as mentioned above, it appears to consider that conduct such as that apprehended by the Facebook Decision of the Bundeskartellamt should be dealt with by data protection supervisory authorities rather than by competition authorities.

In my view, the best remedy lies in the direct application of Article 3(1), second sentence, of Regulation 1/2003 by the national court reviewing the decision of the national competition authority. Indeed, the addressees of decisions of national competition authorities finding a violation of national competition law often appeal against such decisions before the competent national review courts. In the case of the Facebook Decision of the Bundeskartellamt, an appeal is indeed pending before the Düsseldorf Higher Regional Court (Oberlandesgericht Düsseldorf). As is clear from the text of Article 3 of Regulation 1/2003, the obligations contained in it apply not only to national competition authorities but also to national courts. In cases where national courts are reviewing a decision of a national competition authority that applies only national competition law to conduct that is also prohibited by Article 102 TFEU, those courts should thus, on their own motion, and possibly with assistance from the EU Court of Justice pursuant to Article 267 TFEU or from the European Commission pursuant to Article 15(1) of Regulation 1/2003, also apply Article 102 TFEU. In this way, the primary purpose of Article 3(1), second sentence, of Regulation 1/2003 is served, in that in the end not only national competition law but also Article 102 TFEU is applied.[161]

161 As mentioned above, the secondary purpose of Article 3(1), second sentence, of Regulation 1/2003, as apparent from recital 8 and the legislative history of Regulation 1/2003, is that the cooperation mechanisms set out in Regulation 1/2003 are applied. In the case of the Facebook Decision, this aspect does not appear to pose problems, as it appears that 'due to the cross-border dimension of this case, the Bundeskartellamt closely liaised with the European Commission and other competition authorities in the course of the proceeding' (Frequently Asked Question (7 February 2019), accessible at https://www.bundeskartellamt.de/SharedDocs/Meldung/EN/Meldungen%20News%20Karussell/2019/07_02_2019_Facebook.html, at 6). In any event, the use by the national review court of Article 267 TFEU and Article 15(1) of Regulation 1/2003 could further remedy any deficiencies in this respect.

III. Independence of Competition Authorities: The Example of the EU and its Member States

Directive 2019/1, often referred to as the 'ECN+ Directive', contains, among other things, provisions ensuring the independence of the competition authorities of the EU Member States (national competition authorities or NCAs), which are, together with the European Commission, responsible for the enforcement of the EU antitrust rules laid down in Articles 101 and 102 TFEU. In early 2019, the European Commission visibly showed its own independence by prohibiting Siemens' takeover of Alstom's rail transport business, a proposed merger publicly backed by the German and French governments. This chapter gives an overview of the independence guarantees in EU law and discusses more in general the notion of independence of competition authorities and its rationale.

A. The enforcement of EU competition law

EU competition law refers here to the prohibition of cartels and other restrictive agreements and the prohibition of abuse of a dominant position contained in Articles 101 and 102 TFEU, as well as merger control under the EU Merger Regulation.[162]

Under Regulation 1/2003,[163] both the European Commission and the competition authorities of the EU Member States (national competition authorities or NCAs), forming together the European Competition Network (ECN), pursue infringements of Articles 101 and 102 TFEU.

In the words of the Joint Statement of the EU Council and the European Commission on the functioning of the network of competition authorities, entered in the Council Minutes at the time of the adoption of Regulation 1/2003,[164] the decentralisation of the enforcement of Articles 101 and 102 TFEU brought about by Regulation 1/2003 has 'strengthen[ed] the position of the NCAs. These [have been made] fully competent to

---

162 Council Regulation (EC) No 139/2004 of 20 January 2004 on the control of concentrations between undertakings (the EC Merger Regulation) [2004] OJ L24/1 ('EU Merger Regulation').

163 Council Regulation (EC) No 1/2003 of 16 December 2002 on the implementation of the rules on competition laid down in Articles 81 and 82 of the Treaty [2003] OJ L1/1, last amended by Council Regulation (EC) No 1419/2006 [2006] OJ L269/1. For a detailed analysis of Regulation 1/2003, in comparison with the regime preceding it, see my *Community Report* in D. Cahill and J. D. Cooke (eds), *The Modernisation of EU Competition Law Enforcement in the EU – FIDE 2004 National Reports* (Cambridge 2004), 661–736; my book *Principles of European Antitrust Enforcement* (Hart 2005); and K. Dekeyser, C. Gauer, J. Laitenberger, N. Wahl, W. Wils and L. Prete (eds), *Regulation 1/2003 and EU Antitrust Enforcement – A Systematic Guide* (Wolters Kluwer 2022).

164 Council Document 15435/02 ADD 1 of 10 December 2002, accessible at http://register.consilium.eu.int. According to its paragraphs 3 and 4, 'this Joint Statement is political in nature and does therefore not create any legal rights or obligations. It is limited to setting out common political understanding shared by all Member States and the Commission on the principles of the functioning of the Network. Details will be set out in a Commission notice which will be drafted and updated as necessary in close cooperation with Member States'. The said notice is Commission Notice on cooperation with the Network of Competition Authorities [2004]

apply [Articles 101 and 102 TFEU], actively contributing to the development of competition policy, law and practice'.[165]

The powers that Regulation 1/2003 has granted to the NCAs are not, however, identical to the European Commission's powers. In particular, Article 5 of Regulation 1/2003 precludes the NCAs from adopting non-infringement decisions similar to the decisions which the Commission may adopt under Article 10 of Regulation 1/2003.[166]

The power of the European Commission to adopt non-infringement decisions under Article 10 of Regulation 1/2003, the rule laid down in Article 11(6) of Regulation 1/2003, according to which the initiation of proceedings by the European Commission relieves the NCAs of their competence to deal with the same case, and the rule laid down in Article 16(2) of Regulation 1/2003, according to which NCAs cannot take decisions which would run counter to an earlier decision by the European Commission concerning the same agreement or practice, differentiate the position of the European Commission from that of the NCAs.[167]

These differences all reflect the fact that, according to the case law of the EU Court of Justice, Article 105(1) TFEU, which constitutes the specific expression in the area of competition law of the general supervisory role conferred on the European Commission (under the control of the EU Court of Justice) by Article 17(1) TEU,[168] makes the European Commission responsible for defining and implementing the orientation of EU competition policy.[169]

From the start of the application of Regulation 1/2003 on 1 May 2004 until 31 December 2021, the national competition authorities have informed the European Commission and their fellow national competition authorities of 2,515 investigations under Articles 101 and 102 TFEU, and of envisaged final decisions ordering termination of infringements, imposing fines or accepting commitments in 1,336 cases.[170]

During the same period, the European Commission informed the Network of 429 investigations of its own, and 137 draft final decisions.

OJ C101/43. According to its paragraph 72, the principles set out in that notice have been agreed to by the NCAs. On the Joint Statement, see further Judgment in *France Télécom v Commission*, T-339/04, EU:T:2007:80, paragraph 85, and Opinion of Advocate General Mazák in *Pfleiderer*, C-360/09, EU:C:2010:782, paragraph 26.

165 Joint Statement, paragraph 6.

166 Judgments in *Tele2 Polska*, C-375/09, EU:C:2011:270, paragraphs 19 to 30, and in *Schenker*, C-681/11, EU:C:2013:404, paragraph 42.

167 Furthermore, pursuant to Article 105(3) TFEU, only the Commission can adopt block exemption regulations and, under Article 29 of Regulation 1/2003, the Commission has wider powers than the NCAs to withdraw the benefits of such block exemption regulations in an individual case; see further my book *Principles of European Antitrust Enforcement* (Hart 2005), section 1.2.1.

168 Judgments in *Automec v Commission*, T-24/90, EU:T:1992:97, paragraph 73, and in *Limburgse Vinyl Maatschappij and Others v Commission*, T-305/94, EU:T:1999:80, paragraph 46.

169 Judgment in *Masterfoods*, C-344/98, EU:C:2000:689, paragraph 46; see also paragraph 9 of the above-mentioned Joint Statement of the Council and the Commission: 'The Commission, as guardian of the Treaty, has the ultimate but not the sole responsibility for developing policy and safeguarding efficiency and consistency. Therefore the instruments of the Commission on the one hand and of the NCAs on the other hand are not identical. The additional powers the Commission has been granted to fulfil its responsibilities will be exercised with the utmost regard for the cooperative nature of the Network.'

170 I have taken these statistics from the European Commission's website https://competition-policy.ec.europa.eu/european-competition-network/statistics_en.

The national competition authorities have thus in quantitative terms become the primary public enforcers of Articles 101 and 102 TFEU, adopting 90% of all decisions.

Under the EU Merger Regulation, concentrations meeting certain thresholds of EU dimension must be notified to the European Commission prior to their implementation, and the European Commission has exclusive competence to authorise or prohibit such concentrations.

B. Provisions on independence applicable to the European Commission

Article 17(3) TEU provides that '[i]n carrying out its responsibilities, the Commission shall be completely independent. [. . .] the members of the Commission shall neither seek nor take instructions from any Government or other institution, body, office or entity. They shall refrain from any action incompatible with their duties or the performance of their tasks'.

Article 245 TFEU adds that 'Member States shall respect their independence and shall not seek to influence them in the performance of their tasks'.

Within the College of Commissioners, the Working Methods of the European Commission 2014–2019, laid down by then President of the Commission, Jean-Claude Juncker, provided that 'the Commissioner for Competition will liaise closely with the Vice-President for Jobs, Growth, Investment and Competitiveness only in defining the general lines of the Commission competition and State aid policies and the instruments of general scope related to them. She will act independently in all competition cases'.[171]

As to the European Commission's staff, Articles 11 and 12 of the EU Staff Regulations provide that an official 'shall carry out his duties and conduct himself solely with the interests of the Union in mind. He shall neither seek nor take instructions from any government, authority, organisation or person outside his institution. He shall carry out the duties assigned to him objectively, impartially and in keeping with his duty of loyalty to the Union' and 'shall refrain from any action or behaviour which might reflect adversely upon his position'.[172]

In early 2019, the European Commission visibly showed its independence by prohibiting under the EU Merger Regulation Siemens' takeover of Alstom's rail transport business, a proposed merger publicly backed by the German and French governments.[173]

---

171 Communication from the President to the Commission, The Working Methods of the European Commission 2014–2019, C(2014)9004 of 11 November 2014, accessible at **Register of Commission Documents – C(2014)9004 (europa.eu)**, at 15, footnote 6.

172 Regulation No 31 (EEC), 11 (EAEC), laying down the Staff Regulations of Officials and the Conditions of Employment of Other Servants of the European Economic Community and the European Atomic Energy Community [1962] OJ 45/1385, last amended by Regulation (EU) No 423/2014 of the European Parliament and the Council of 16 April 2014 [2014] OJ L129/12.

173 See European Commission Press release IP/19/881 of 6 February 2019, http://europa.eu/rapid/press-release_IP-19-881_en.htm; T. Patel and A. White, 'Siemens-Alstom's Expected EU Veto Unleashes Political Storm' (Bloomberg, 4 February 2019), https://www.bloomberg.com/news/articles/2019-02-04/european-champions-may-

C. The ECN+ Directive

At the end of 2018, the European Parliament and EU Council adopted Directive 2019/1, often referred to as the 'ECN+ Directive',[174] which sets out certain rules to ensure that national competition authorities have the necessary guarantees of independence, resources, and enforcement and fining powers to be able to effectively apply Articles 101 and 102 TFEU.[175]

In the 2015–2016 public consultation that preceded the European Commission's 2017 proposal for the Directive,[176] some respondents had referred to problems relating to the independence of some NCAs.[177] The Bundeskartellamt (German NCA), while confirming that it is itself sufficiently independent, indicated that it is 'aware of several cases where the president of the NCA of a larger EU Member State was dismissed ahead of the normal end of the term, reportedly because the respective Member State's government did not agree with decisions taken by the authority'.[178] The Italian business association Assonime referred to 'recent experience in some Member States (for instance, Poland and Greece)' and indicated that 'the credibility of the whole system of protection of competition [in the EU], including compliance with the principle of equal treatment of national and non-national undertakings, strongly depends on the independence of competition authorities from external influence when performing their task'.[179]

The Impact Assessment which accompanied the European Commission's 2017 proposal for the Directive mentioned in particular that 'a genuine risk of influence by other state

---

yet-rise-from-the-siemens-alstom-rubble; and A. Lamadrid, 'This is not a post on Siemens/Alstom – Congratulations to DG Comp (and brace for what's coming)' (Chillin'Competition, 6 February 2019), https://chillingcompetition.com/2019/02/06/this-is-not-a-post-on-siemens-alstom-congratulations-to-dg-comp-and-brace-for-whats-coming/. See also M. Vestager, 'Independence is non-negotiable' (Chatham House Competition Policy Conference, 18 June 2015), https://ec.europa.eu/commission/commissioners/2014-2019/vestager/announcements/independence-non-negotiable_en; as well as G. Gutierrez and T. Philippon, 'How EU Markets Became More Competitive than US Markets: A Study of Institutional Drift', NBER Working Paper 24700 (June 2018), http://www.nber.org/papers/w24700, at 2 (pointing out that the European Commission as competition authority is more independent than the US Department of Justice and the Federal Trade Commission), and J. Tepper and D. Hearn, *The Myth of Capitalism – Monopolies and the Death of Competition* (Wiley 2019) at 162 (claiming that 'the [US] Department of Justice now essentially works to serve the interests of companies').

174 Directive (EU) 2019/1 of the European Parliament and of the Council of 11 December 2018 to empower the competition authorities of the Member States to be more effective enforcers and to ensure the proper functioning of the internal market [2019] OJ L11/3.

175 Article 1(1) of Directive 2019/1.

176 For a detailed overview of the European Commission's 2017 proposal and all its antecedents, see my paper 'Competition authorities: Towards more independence and prioritisation? The European Commission's "ECN+" Proposal for a Directive to empower the competition authorities of the Member States to be more effective enforcers', *Concurrences* no 4-2017, 60, also accessible at http://ssrn.com/author=456087.

177 The consultation questionnaire, all the replies to the consultation (some in redacted, anonymised form) and a summary report of the replies are accessible at http://ec.europa.eu/competition/consultations/2015_effective_enforcers/index_en.html.

178 Reply of the Bundeskartellamt, at 9 and 15.

179 Reply of Assonime, at 1–2; see also reply of the American Chamber of Commerce to the European Union (AmChamEU), at 2 (referring to 'recent unfortunate developments in Poland and Greece'); as well as anonymous replies numbers 2, 14, 22, 30, 35 and 42 (concerning also three other Member States). Obviously, anonymous replies need to be interpreted with due caution.

bodies exists where state-owned companies or activities by state bodies are subject of an investigation by the NCA or where its enforcement action would interfere with other public interests'.[180] Without naming the Member States concerned, the Impact Assessment also described three cases where improper interference with the independent functioning of NCAs has taken place.[181]

Article 4 of the ECN+ Directive reads as follows:

Article 4

Independence

'1. *To guarantee the independence of national administrative competition authorities when applying Articles 101 and 102 TFEU, Member States shall ensure that such authorities perform their duties and exercise their powers impartially and in the interests of the effective and uniform application of those provisions, subject to proportionate accountability requirements and without prejudice to close cooperation between competition authorities in the European Competition Network.*

2. *In particular, Member States shall at a minimum ensure that the staff and persons who take decisions exercising the powers in Articles 10 to 13 and Article 16 of this Directive[[182]] in national administrative competition authorities:*
   (a) *are able to perform their duties and to exercise their powers for the application of Articles 101 and 102 TFEU independently from political and other external influence;*
   (b) *neither seek nor take any instructions from government or any other public or private entity when carrying out their duties and exercising their powers for the application of Articles 101 and 102 TFEU, without prejudice to the right of a government of a Member State, where applicable, to issue general policy rules that are not related to sector inquiries or specific enforcement proceedings; and*
   (c) *refrain from taking any action which is incompatible with the performance of their duties and/or with the exercise of their powers for the application of Articles 101 and 102 TFEU and are subject to procedures that ensure that, for a reasonable period after leaving office, they refrain from dealing with enforcement proceedings that could give rise to conflicts of interest.*

3. *The persons who take decisions exercising the powers in Articles 10 to 13 and Article 16 of this Directive in national administrative competition authorities shall not be dismissed from such authorities for reasons related to the proper performance of their duties or to the proper exercise of their powers for the*

180 Commission Staff Working Document, Impact Assessment accompanying the Proposal for a Directive of the European Parliament and of the Council to empower the competition authorities of the Member States to be more effective enforcers and to ensure the proper functioning of the internal market, SWD(2017)114 of 22 March 2017, Part 1/2, at 26.

181 Idem, at 26–27.

182 The powers referred to in Articles 10 to 13 and Article 16 of the Directive are the powers to find infringements of Articles 101 or 102 TFEU and to require that these be brought to an end, to order interim measures, to accept commitments, and to impose fines and periodic penalty payments.

application of Articles 101 and 102 TFEU, as referred to in Article 5(2) of this Directive.[183] *They may be dismissed only if they no longer fulfil the conditions required for the performance of their duties or if they have been found guilty of serious misconduct under national law. The conditions required for the performance of their duties, and what constitutes serious misconduct, shall be laid down in advance in national law, taking into account the need to ensure effective enforcement.*

4. *Member States shall ensure that the members of the decision-making body of national administrative competition authorities are selected, recruited or appointed according to clear and transparent procedures laid down in advance in national law.*
5. *National administrative competition authorities shall have the power to set their priorities for carrying out the tasks for the application of Articles 101 and 102 TFEU as referred to in Article 5(2) of this Directive. To the extent that national administrative competition authorities are obliged to consider formal complaints, those authorities shall have the power to reject such complaints on the grounds that they do not consider such complaints to be an enforcement priority. This is without prejudice to the power of national administrative competition authorities to reject complaints on other grounds defined by national law.'*

D. The notion of independence: A few selected definitions

The *Shorter Oxford English Dictionary* defines 'independence' as 'the condition or quality of being independent', and defines 'independent' as 'not subject to the authority or control of any person, country, etc.: free to act as one pleases, autonomous'.[184]

Independence understood as absence-of-any-control or freedom-to-act-as-one-pleases is not a desirable state of affairs, at least not from the perspective of the general interest. Independence should not be a licence for laziness, inefficiency, dereliction of duty, non-transparency, arbitrariness, self-dealing, corruption, abuse of powers, self-aggrandisement and the like. Competition authorities have been created and have been given powers and resources to fulfil a task in the general interest, and there should be adequate controls to ensure that they use their powers and resources for that purpose.

---

183 The powers referred to in Article 5(2) of the Directive are the powers of NCAs to conduct investigations with a view to applying Articles 101 and 102 TFEU; to adopt decisions requiring that an infringement of Article 101 or 102 TFEU be brought to an end, ordering interim measures, accepting commitments, imposing fines, periodic penalty payments or any other penalty provided for in their national law, and finding that there are no grounds for action on their part; to cooperate closely in the European Competition Network with a view to ensuring the effective and uniform application of Articles 101 and 102 TFEU; as well as, to the extent provided for under national law, to advise public institutions and bodies, where appropriate, on legislative, regulatory and administrative measures which may have an impact on competition in the internal market as well as promote public awareness of Articles 101 and 102 TFEU.

184 *Shorter Oxford English Dictionary* (Oxford University Press, Sixth edition 2007).

For this reason, it is generally accepted that independence should go hand in hand with accountability.[185] As independence means absence of controls, and accountability means controls, the crucial issue is to determine which types of controls are inappropriate and which are appropriate to ensure that competition authorities fulfil their task.

The ECN+ Directive clearly recognises this distinction. Indeed, according to Article 4(1) of the Directive, the independence of NCAs shall be 'subject to proportionate accountability requirements and without prejudice to close cooperation between competition authorities in the European Competition Network'. Recital 22 of the proposed Directive adds that 'the operational independence of national administrative competition authorities should not preclude either judicial review or parliamentary supervision in accordance with national law. Accountability requirements should also contribute to ensuring the credibility and the legitimacy of the actions of national administrative competition authorities. Proportionate accountability requirements include the publication by national administrative competition authorities of periodic reports on their activities to a governmental or parliamentary body. National administrative competition authorities might also be subject to control or monitoring of their financial expenditure, provided this does not affect their independence'.

In the context of interpreting the notion of 'complete independence' as applicable to national data protection supervisory authorities[186] – a notion that is arguably distinct from mere 'independence' – the EU Court of Justice has held that 'in relation to a public body, the term "independence" normally means a status which ensures that the body concerned can act completely freely, without taking instructions or being put under any pressure'.[187] This definition, or at least the first part of it ('completely freely'), raises the same problem as the *Shorter Oxford English Dictionary* definition discussed above, and does not appear to have been repeated by the Court in later judgments.[188]

In the context of interpreting the notion of 'court or tribunal' for the purposes of Article 267 TFEU, the Court of Justice has held that independence 'entails that the body is protected against external intervention or pressure liable to jeopardise the independent judgment of its members as regards the proceedings before them'.[189] The qualifier 'liable

---

185 See A. Ottow, *Market & Competition Authorities: Good Agency Principles* (Oxford University Press 2015, at 85 ('Clearly, accountability and independence are two sides of the same coin.')); S. Peers and M. Costa, 'Reassessing the Accountability of European Union Decentralized Agencies: Mind the Independence Gap' (2016) 22 *European Public Law* 645; M. Scholten, "Independent, hence unaccountable?' The Need for a Broader Debate on Accountability of the Executive' (2011) 4 *Review of European Administrative Law* 5; and International Competition Network, Competition Policy Implementation Working Group, Seminar on Competition Agency Effectiveness Summary Report (Brussels, January 2009), accessible at http://www.internationalcompetitionnetwork.org/uploads/library/doc376.pdf, at 25.

186 See Article 8(3) of the Charter of Fundamental Rights of the European Union, Article 16(2) TFEU, and Articles 52 and 53 of Regulation (EU) 2016/679 of the European Parliament and of the Council of 27 April 2016 on the protection of natural persons with regard to the processing of personal data and on the free movement of such data (General Data Protection Regulation) [2016] OJ L119/1, and Judgments in *Commission v Germany*, C-518/07, EU:C:2010:125, in *Commission v Austria*, C-614/10, EU:C:2012:631, and in *Commission v Hungary*, C-288/12, EU:C:2014:237.

187 Judgment in *Commission v Germany*, C-518/07, EU:C:2010:125, paragraph 18.

188 See for instance Judgment in *Commission v Hungary*, C-288/12, EU:C:2014:237, paragraph 51.

189 Judgment in *Wilson*, C-506/04, EU:C:2006:587, paragraph 51, and in *RTL Belgium*, C-517/09, EU:C:2010:821, paragraph 39.

to jeopardise the independent judgment of its members as regards the proceedings before them' is a useful one, as it reflects the need to distinguish between appropriate and inappropriate controls. Recital 17 of the ECN+ Directive similarly refers to the need for NCAs being protected 'against external intervention or political pressure that is liable to jeopardise their independent assessment of the matters before them'.

In the context of interpreting the EU law requirement of independence for airport coordinators,[190] the EFTA Court has held that it must be ensured that 'neither the authorities of the [Member State] concerned nor any other party can unduly influence the coordinator before, during and after the allocation process'.[191] The qualifier 'unduly' is again a useful one, as it reflects the need for appropriate accountability controls, as well as the need to respect procedural requirements, including the fundamental right to be heard. The latter need is also reflected in Article 3 of the ECN+ Directive, according to which 'proceedings concerning infringements of Articles 101 or 102 TFEU, including the exercise of the powers referred to in this Directive by national competition authorities, shall comply with general principles of Union law and the Charter of Fundamental Rights of the European Union' and must be 'subject to appropriate safeguards in respect of the undertakings' rights of defence, including the right to be heard and the right to an effective remedy before a tribunal'.[192]

According to a report of the International Competition Network (ICN), that competition authorities should be 'independent' means 'that their actions should be based on the facts and the law and not on political considerations'.[193]

Last but not least, Chris Fonteijn, former chairman of the board of the Netherlands Authority for Consumers and Markets (ACM), has defined independence as 'having the freedom to reach conclusions, in accordance with the task that lawmakers have bestowed upon us, without having to face inappropriate pressure (the notion of no pressure is unrealistic)'.[194]

E. The competition authorities' task

The above discussion of the notion of independence has made it clear that the crucial issue is to determine which types of controls, interference or influence are inappropriate

---

190 See Article 4 of Council Regulation (EEC) No 95/93 of 18 January 1993 on common rules for the allocation of slots at Community airports [1993] OJ L14/1, and Judgment of the EFTA Court of 10 December 2014 in Case E-18/14 *Wow air v Icelandic Competition Authority and Others*.

191 Judgment in Case E-18/14, paragraph 37.

192 The obligation for NCAs, when applying Articles 101 and 102 TFEU, to respect fundamental rights as laid down in the Charter of Fundamental Rights of the European Union and in general principles of Union law already existed before the ECN+ Directive; see my paper 'EU Antitrust Enforcement Powers and Procedural Rights and Guarantees: The Interplay between EU Law, National Law, the Charter of Fundamental Rights of the EU and the European Convention on Human Rights' (2011) 34 *World Competition* 189, also accessible at http://ssrn.com/author=456087.

193 International Competition Network, Competition Policy Implementation Working Group, Seminar on Competition Agency Effectiveness Summary Report (Brussels, January 2009), accessible at http://www.internationalcompetitionnetwork.org/uploads/library/doc376.pdf, at 25.

194 Chris Fonteijn, 'Regulators are independent, but 'noblesse oblige" (14 October 2011), accessible (in Dutch language original) at https://www.acm.nl/nl/publicaties/publicatie/11469/Chris-Fonteijn-Toezichthouder-is-onafhankelijk-maar-noblesse-oblige/, at 2.

and which are appropriate to ensure that competition authorities fulfil their task. The preliminary question to be answered is thus what the competition authorities' task is.

As already mentioned above, according to the case law of the EU Court of Justice, 'the [European] Commission, entrusted by [Article 105(1) TFEU] with the task of ensuring application of the principles laid down in [Articles 101 and 102 TFEU], is responsible for defining and implementing the orientation of [EU] competition policy. It is for the Commission to adopt, subject to review by the [EU Courts], individual decisions in accordance with the procedural rules in force and to adopt exemption regulations'.[195]

As to the NCAs, Article 35(1) of Regulation 1/2003 stipulates that the EU Member States are to 'designate the competition authority or authorities responsible for the application of [Articles 101 and 102 TFEU] in such a way that the provisions of this regulation are effectively complied with'. In *VEBIC*, the Court of Justice has clarified that '[t]he authorities so designated must, in accordance with the regulation, ensure that those Treaty Articles are applied effectively in the general interest', and that 'the objective of the regulation, which is to ensure that Articles 101 and 102 TFEU are applied effectively by those authorities'.[196]

In *Schenker*, the Court of Justice has, in addition to the requirements of **effective** enforcement **in the general interest** already set out in *VEBIC*, also subjected the enforcement of Articles 101 and 102 TFEU by the NCAs to a requirement of **uniform** application of those Treaty Articles.[197]

It thus appears from the *VEBIC* and *Schenker* judgments of the Court of Justice that the NCAs' task is **the effective and uniform application of Articles 101 and 102 TFEU in the general interest**.

The Court's language is reflected in the wording of the ECN+ Directive, in particular its Article 4(1) ('in the interests of the effective and uniform enforcement of those provisions') and recital 16 ('in the common interest of the effective enforcement of the Union competition rules').

F. Independence from economic operators and business interests

The decisions which competition authorities take in the application of Articles 101 and 102 TFEU (opening and closing investigations, making findings of infringement, imposing remedies and penalties, accepting commitments and settlements, rejecting complaints) are obviously of great import to the economic operators whom they affect (not only the economic operators targeted by the investigation, but also other economic operators such as competitors and customers).

While competition authorities must respect the undertakings' right to be heard,[198] their decisions should be based on their own, impartial judgment, with a view to the effective

195 Judgment in *Masterfoods*, C-344/98, EU:C:2000:689, paragraph 46.

196 Judgment in *VEBIC*, C-439/08, EU:C:2010:739, paragraphs 56 and 57.

197 Judgment in *Schenker*, C-681/11, EU:C:2013:404, paragraphs 36, 46 and 49.

198 See Article 3 of the ECN+ Directive.

and uniform application of Articles 101 and 102 TFEU in the general interest, without any bias in favour or against any particular economic operator or category of economic operators.

As the EU Court of Justice has held, 'a system of undistorted competition, as laid down in the Treaty, can be guaranteed only if equality of opportunity is secured between the various economic operators'.[199] For this reason, the Court of Justice has considered that it is justified for EU secondary law to entrust regulatory tasks in the telecommunications sector 'to a body independent of public or private undertakings offering competing goods and/or services in the telecommunications sector'.[200] The same reason justifies requiring that competition authorities, whose duties and powers affect all sectors of the economy, be independent of all public and private economic operators.

Article 4(1) and (2)(b) and (c) of the ECN+ Directive requires Member States to ensure that NCAs 'perform their duties and exercise their powers impartially and in the interests of the effective and uniform enforcement of [Articles 101 and 102 TFEU]', that the staff and persons exercising the decisional powers of the NCAs 'neither seek nor take any instructions from [. . .] any [. . .] public or private entity' and 'refrain from taking any action which is incompatible with the performance of their duties and/or with the exercise of their powers'. With regard to the latter requirement, recitals 18 and 19 of the Directive explain that this includes that they 'should refrain from any incompatible actions, whether gainful or not', 'not have any interest in any businesses or organisations which are subject to proceedings for the application of Articles 101 or 102 TFEU in which they take part, if this has the potential to compromise their impartiality in a specific case'. Recital 21 adds that '[e]very national administrative competition authority should publish a code of conduct that [. . .] covers rules on conflicts of interest'.

Independence from economic operators is necessary not only to prevent unequal treatment between different economic operators, but also to prevent regulatory capture by business interests.[201] Regulatory capture is the phenomenon where an authority entrusted with a regulatory task in the general interest ends up identifying with the businesses it regulates and defending the interests of those businesses rather than the public interest.[202] As John Kay has pointed out, 'the most common form of capture is honest and may be characterised as intellectual capture'.[203] This can in particular occur when the staff and members of the decision-making body of competition authorities identify

---

199 Judgment in *French Republic v Commission*, C-202/88, EU:C:1991:120, paragraph 51.

200 Idem, paragraph 52.

201 L.M. Schouten and A.J.C. de Moor-van Vugt, 'De onafhankelijkheid van de Autoriteit Consument en Markt' (2015) *SEW Tijdschrift voor Europees en economisch recht* 62 at 64.

202 Idem, at 64, and D. Carpenter and D. A. Moss (eds), *Preventing Regulatory Capture: Special Interest Influence and How to Limit It* (Cambridge University Press 2014), at 13. See in this respect J. Tepper and D. Hearn, *The Myth of Capitalism – Monopolies and the Death of Competition* (Wiley 2019) at 162, claiming that 'the [US] Department of Justice now essentially works to serve the interests of companies'.

203 J. Kay, 'Better a distant judge than a pliant regulator – Why overseers are so often captured by their industries', *Financial Times*, 2 November 2010; see also J. Kwak, 'Cultural Capture and the Financial Crisis', in D. Carpenter and D. A. Moss (eds), *Preventing Regulatory Capture: Special Interest Influence and How to Limit It* (Cambridge University Press 2014), 71.

professionally and maybe also socially with and end up feeling accountable to a competition expert community that is structurally biased towards the outlook and interests of big business.[204] As I have argued elsewhere,[205] the risk of such bias in the competition expert community is in particular visible in the area of abuse of dominance. The beneficiaries of full enforcement of Article 102 TFEU are, apart from the EU general interest, European consumers and the smaller companies that are the actual or potential competitors of dominant companies. These benefits are spread out over many beneficiaries, many of whom may never even become aware of it. They are thus unlikely to effectively defend their interests.[206] Indeed, as Dieter Wolf, former president of the Bundeskartellamt, has pointed out, competition has no lobby.[207] On the other hand, the loss to the dominant undertakings that are prevented from abusing their dominant position is highly concentrated. Dominant companies can thus be expected to lobby strongly against full enforcement. For antitrust practitioners, dominant companies are the largest and most lucrative clients. Antitrust practitioners thus have an interest in positioning themselves as proponents of views that chime with dominant company interests. Many antitrust academics are also practitioners, or may want to become practitioners at a later stage of their career. Large parts of the publication and conference markets are also run by and for practitioners. Many academics may thus face similar incentives as those faced by practitioners.[208]

---

204 On the concept of expert community or epistemic community, see F. van Waarden and M. Drahos, 'Courts and (epistemic) communities in the convergence of competition policies' (2002) 9 *Journal of European Public Policy* 913 at 928, and P. M. Haas, 'Introduction: Epistemic communities and international policy coordination' (1992) 46 *International Organization* 1 at 3, defining 'epistemic community' as 'a network of professionals with recognized expertise and competence in a particular domain and an authoritative claim to policy-relevant knowledge within that domain or issue-area'.

205 See my paper 'The Judgment of the EU General Court in *Intel* and the So-Called More Economic Approach to Abuse of Dominance' (2014) 37 *World Competition* 405, at 432–434, also accessible at http://ssrn.com/author=456087.

206 On diffused interests being less able to defend themselves than concentrated interests, see generally M. Olson, *The Logic of Collective Action: Public Goods and the Theory of Groups* (Harvard University Press 1965) and *The Rise and Decline of Nations* (Yale University Press 1982).

207 D. Wolf, in C.-D. Ehlermann and L. L. Laudati, *European Competition Law Annual 1997: The Objectives of Competition Policy* (Hart 1998), Panel Discussion on Competition Policy Objectives, at 24, adding: 'Institutional safeguards are needed to ensure that competition has at least one clear voice. [. . .] economists have learned to be advocates of the interests of their clients, just as lawyers have learned to do so. Thus, reliance on economic arguments does not protect the process. Independent institutions combined with judicial review by courts is the best way to guarantee objective results. Competition authorities must, of course, be staffed with lawyers and economists. However, as long as competition authorities are not independent, the risk is always present that specific interests will influence their decisions'.

208 See also L. Zingales, 'Preventing Economists' Capture', in D. Carpenter and D. A. Moss (eds), *Preventing Regulatory Capture: Special Interest Influence and How to Limit It* (Cambridge University Press 2014), 124–151, developing the argument and providing some empirical evidence consistent with the hypothesis that capture of (academic) economists by business interests exists, and is pervasive; J. Broulik, 'Economics in Antitrust Enforcement and the Private Benefit of Scholarly Commentators', TILEC Discussion Paper DP 2017-001 (January 2017), accessible at http://ssrn.com/abstract=2898753; J. Eisinger and J. Elliott, 'These Professors Make More Than a Thousand Bucks an Hour Peddling Mega-Mergers: The economists are leveraging their academic prestige with secret reports justifying concentration. Their predictions are often wrong and consumers pay the price.' (ProPublica, 16 November 2016), accessible at https://www.propublica.org/article/these-professors-make-more-than-thousand-bucks-hour-peddling-mega-mergers; and Campaign for Accountability, Google Transparency Project, 'Google Academics Inc.' (11 July 2017), accessible at http://googletransparencyproject.org/articles/google-academics-inc; see also MLex, 'Comment: Where does the Scott Morton scandal leave EU competition enforcement?' (19 July 2023).

G. Independence from government, other state bodies and politics

The need to prevent unequal treatment between economic operators, which, as explained above, justifies the independence of competition authorities from economic operators, also justifies their independence from national governments and from political interference.[209]

Indeed, as explained above, competition authorities should take their decisions (opening and closing investigations, making findings of infringement, imposing remedies and penalties, accepting commitments and settlements, rejecting complaints) impartially, with a view to the effective and uniform application of Articles 101 and 102 TFEU in the general interest, without any bias in favour or against any particular economic operator or category of economic operators. It should thus be avoided that certain economic operators end up being favoured by competition authorities because those operators benefit from political support.

As indicated in the Impact Assessment accompanying the European Commission's proposal for the ECN+ Directive, a specific risk exists when state-owned companies or economic activities by state bodies are the subject of an investigation by the NCA. More broadly, as has been pointed out in the public consultation, the credibility of the whole system of protection of competition in the EU, which requires compliance with the principle of equal treatment of national and non-national undertakings, strongly depends on the independence of NCAs from their national government and politics.

The need to avoid unequal treatment justifies keeping governments, other public bodies or elected politicians out of competition authorities' decisions **in individual cases**. On the other hand, it is normal for independent authorities to be accountable to their governments and/or parliaments **for their general activities**, in particular through annual reports.[210]

The ECN+ Directive also reflects this distinction: Article 4(2)(a) and (b) provide that Member States must ensure that the staff and persons exercising the decisional powers of the NCAs can perform their duties and exercise their powers for the application of Articles 101 and 102 TFEU 'independently from political and other external influence', and that they shall 'neither seek nor take instructions from government or any other public [. . .] entity'. Recital 17 clarifies that the required protection is against 'external intervention or political pressure liable to jeopardise their independent assessment of the matters before them', and that it is also 'for that purpose' that Article 4(3) lays down rules regarding the grounds for the dismissal of the persons exercising the decisional powers of the NCAs 'in order to remove any reasonable doubt as to their impartiality and their imperviousness to external factors'. On the other hand, Article 4(1) recognises

---

209 In the literature, some further justifications for the independence of competition authorities from their governments or from elected politicians have been advanced; for a critical overview of these justifications, see A. Walckiers, B. Crutzen and N. Sahuguet, 'An Economic Perspective on Independent Competition Enforcement', in M. Merola, N. Petit and J. Rivas, *10 Years of Regulation 1/2003: Challenges and Reform* (Bruylant 2015) 105–117.

210 See for instance, similarly, Article 6 of Council Regulation (EU) 2017/1939 of 12 October 2017 implementing enhanced cooperation on the establishment of the European Public Prosecutor's Office ('the EPPO') [2017] OJ L283/1, which provides that 'the EPPO shall be independent', but also that 'the EPPO shall be accountable to the European Parliament, to the Council and to the Commission for its general activities, and shall issue annual reports [. . .]'.

the appropriateness of 'proportionate accountability requirements'. Recital 22 affirms that 'the operational independence of national administrative competition authorities does not preclude [. . .] parliamentary supervision in accordance with national law'. That this rather broad statement should not be understood as also allowing parliamentary interference **in individual cases** is, however, clear from Article 4(1) and from the further explanation in recital 22 that 'proportionate accountability requirements include the publication by national administrative competition authorities of periodic reports on their activities to a governmental or parliamentary body. National administrative competition authorities might also be subject to control or monitoring of their financial expenditure, provided this does not affect their independence'. The distinction between interference in individual cases and accountability for the NCAs' general activities is also reflected in recital 23, according to which 'the power of national administrative competition authorities to prioritise their enforcement proceedings is without prejudice to the right of a government of a Member State to issue to national administrative competition authorities general policy rules or priority guidelines to national competition authorities that are not related to sector inquiries or specific proceedings for the enforcement of Articles 101 and 102 TFEU'.

H. The role of the European Commission and the European Competition Network

According to the Joint Statement of the EU Council and the European Commission on the functioning of the network of competition authorities, entered in the Council Minutes at the time of the adoption of Regulation 1/2003, 'all competition authorities within the [European Competition] Network are independent from one another'.[211]

As far as the relationship between, on the one hand, the NCAs and, on the other hand, the European Commission is concerned, this appears not entirely true. Indeed, as already mentioned above, according to Article 11(6) of Regulation 1/2003, the initiation of proceedings by the Commission relieves the NCAs of their competence to deal with the same case. Combined with the obligations, laid down in Article 11(3) and (4) of Regulation 1/2003, for NCAs to inform the Commission of the start of their investigation and to provide the Commission with a summary of their draft decisions finding an infringement or accepting commitments, this power undeniably reduces the NCAs' independence,[212] even if, according to the Joint Statement of the Council and the Commission,

---

211 Council Document 15435/02 ADD 1 of 10 December 2002, accessible at http://register.consilium.eu.int, paragraph 7.

212 See Judgment in *Syfait and Others*, C-53/03, EU:C:2005:333, paragraphs 34–36, in which the Court of Justice took into account Article 11(6) of Regulation 1/2003 as an element among others leading to the conclusion that the Greek Competition Council did not constitute a 'court or tribunal' for the purposes of Article 267 TFEU; see also A. Riley, 'EC Antitrust Modernisation: The Commission Does Very Nicely – Thank You!; Part Two: Between the Idea and the Reality: Decentralisation under Regulation No 1' (2003) *European Competition Law Review* 657; G. Monti, 'Independence, Interdependence and Legitimacy: The EU Commission, National Competition Authorities, and the European Competition Network' (EUI Working Paper LAW 2014/01), accessible at http://ssrn.com/abstract=2379320, and G. Monti, '*Alrosa* and Commitment Decisions in perspective', in B. E. Hawk, *Annual Proceedings of the Fordham Competition Law Institute International Antitrust Law & Policy 2014* (Juris 2015), 461 at 479 ('NCAs lost their independence . . . to the Commission').

the Commission is to exercise its powers vis-à-vis the NCAs 'with the utmost regard for the cooperative nature of the Network'.[213]

This lack of full independence of NCAs vis-à-vis the European Commission is however unproblematic. Indeed, as explained above, it reflects the fact that, according to the case law of the EU Court of Justice, Article 105(1) TFEU, which constitutes the specific expression in the area of competition law of the general supervisory role conferred on the Commission (under the control of the Court of Justice) by Article 17(1) TEU, makes the Commission responsible for defining and implementing the orientation of EU competition policy. The Commission's powers vis-à-vis the NCAs do not endanger the fulfilment by the NCAs of their task of applying Articles 101 and 102 TFEU effectively and uniformly in the general interest, but rather constitute a safeguard to ensure the fulfilment of this task.

The Commission's powers vis-à-vis the NCAs, and more generally the close cooperation within the European Competition Network, can also help ensure the NCAs' independence from their national government and politics, as NCAs may be able to call upon the Commission's authority when put under pressure in their Member State.[214]

Finally, the ECN also provides a professional network with which the staff and members of the decision-making bodies of the NCAs can identify, and which, because it includes only competition authorities, does not present the same risk of intellectual capture by big business interests discussed above in relation to the wider competition expert community.[215]

I. The role of judicial review

Recital 22 of the ECN+ Directive states that the independence of NCAs 'should not preclude [. . .] judicial review'.

Indeed, judicial review does not limit the NCAs' independence, as properly understood. On the contrary, it strengthens their independence.[216]

---

213 Joint Statement, paragraph 9.

214 See my book *Principles of European Antitrust Enforcement* (Hart 2005), section 1.2.8.

215 The absence of (direct or indirect) representation of business interests also distinguishes the ECN from some other international groupings of competition authorities that have institutionalised channels of business representation creating a risk of intellectual capture. For instance, the OECD Competition Committee includes participation by the Business and Industry Advisory Committee to the OECD (BIAC), in practice without any counterbalancing representation of consumer views and interests. The International Competition Network (ICN) involves so-called Non-Governmental Advisors ('NGAs'). While it has been claimed that 'the goals of NGAs are in principle aligned with those of the [competition authorities]' (P. Lugard, *The International Competition Network at Ten: Origins, Accomplishments and Aspirations* (Intersentia, 2011), at 15), the fact remains that the interests of big business in relation to antitrust enforcement are not aligned with the general interest and that the logic of collective action makes it all but inevitable that, among the different NGAs, those representing (directly or indirectly) the views and interests of big business will end up being most vocal. Indeed, it would appear that the desire of the big business community to exercise influence over international antitrust enforcement was part of the impetus to create the ICN in the first place; see M. E. Janow and J. F. Rill, 'The Origins of the ECN', in P. Lugard (ed), *The International Competition Network at Ten: Origins, Accomplishments and Aspirations* (Intersentia, 2011), 21 at 34.

216 Compare with W. E. Kovacic, 'Competition agencies, independence, and the political process', in J. Drexl, W. Kerber and R. Podszun (eds), *Competition Policy and the Economic Approach: Foundations and Limitations* (Edward Elgar 2011), 291 at 296–297; see also D. Wolf, in C.-D. Ehlermann and L.L. Laudati, *European*

For example, political pressure on an NCA to impose higher fines on the non-national members of a cartel than on the national members will be ineffective if the NCA's fining decision is subject to judicial review and the reviewing court can remedy unequal treatment.

As already mentioned, Article 3 of the Directive provides that 'proceedings concerning infringements of Articles 101 or 102 TFEU, including the exercise of the powers referred to in this Directive by national competition authorities, shall comply with general principles of Union law and the Charter of Fundamental Rights of the European Union' and must be 'subject to appropriate safeguards in respect of the undertakings' rights of defence, including the right to be heard and the right to an effective remedy before a tribunal'.

That judicial review strengthens independence is also true for the rejection of complaints. As explained further below, the possibility for complainants to seek judicial review protects an NCA against political pressure not to act on complaints against politically favoured companies.

J. De facto independence and the limits of legislating for independence

It is generally recognised that there is not necessarily a full correspondence between legal (formal, *de jure*) independence and *de facto* (actual, real) independence of competition authorities.[217] *De facto* independence depends on various factors, including the general political and administrative culture of the state in which the competition authority functions, the length of existence and the track record of the competition authority, and the personalities of its top management.[218]

The divergence between formal and *de facto* independence does not, however, justify abstaining from legislating for independence. Indeed, as the OECD Secretariat has pointed out, 'although legal independence does not automatically bring about *de facto* independence, it still matters. Aspects of legal independence provide [competition authorities] with those minimum safeguards which may not prevent all political pressures, but nonetheless make it less probable'.[219]

On the other hand, the fact that actual independence depends on numerous factors that significantly vary between EU Member States justifies limiting EU legislation to the most general and basic minimum requirements, such as those contained in Article 4 of the ECN+ Directive.[220]

Competition Law Annual 1997: The Objectives of Competition Policy (Hart 1998), Panel Discussion on Competition Policy Objectives, at 24: 'Independent institutions combined with judicial review by courts is the best way to guarantee objective results.'

217 OECD, Global Forum on Competition (1–2 December 2016), 'Independence of Competition Authorities – From Designs to Practices', Background Paper by the OECD Secretariat, DAF/COMP/GF(2016)5, at 18.

218 Idem, at 18–19.

219 Idem, at 18.

220 As David Currie, former chairman of the UK Competition and Markets Authority, has pointed out: '[A]lthough the debate about independence is often around particular statutes and mechanisms, the effectiveness of these is crucially influenced by the wider political culture in which they are embedded, and that culture itself is shaped by evolution and experience over time, sometimes decades. And this influence itself is complex: mechanisms

K. Prioritisation and independence

Article 4(5) of the ECN+ Directive provides that NCAs shall have the power to set their priorities for carrying out their tasks for the application of Articles 101 and 102 TFEU and that, to the extent that they are obliged to consider formal complaints, they shall have the power to reject such complaints on the grounds that they do not consider such complaints to be an enforcement priority.

This provision thus appears to do three things:

1) It obliges Member States to ensure that NCAs have the **power to set positive priorities**, i.e. the power to initiate investigations and proceedings on their own initiative (*ex officio*), without having received any formal notification or complaint. All NCAs, like the European Commission, already appear to have this power today.[221]
2) It obliges Member States to ensure that NCAs have the **power to set negative priorities**, in that, if according to national law the NCA is obliged to consider formal complaints, it must have the power to reject such complaints on the ground that it does not consider them to be an enforcement priority.
In this respect the Directive has led to significant changes in a number of EU Member States. Indeed, some NCAs, such as the French Autorité de la concurrence and the Spanish Comisión Nacional de los Mercados y la Competencia (CNMC), previously had no discretion to reject complaints under Articles 101 and 102 TFEU for lack of priority interest. The Autorité de la concurrence could be seized with a complaint by a company, the minister of economics, a local authority, a professional organisation, a trade union or a consumer association. Unless the facts are more than five years old or the complaint is manifestly lacking in supporting evidence, the Autorité de la concurrence was obliged to investigate the complaint and adopt a final decision.[222] This old French system, in which the NCA was obliged to investigate all complaints and adopt a final decision on them, has been outlawed by the ECN+ Directive.
3) It obliges Member States to ensure that NCAs set priorities **independently**, in the interest of the effective and uniform enforcement of Articles 101 and 102 TFEU. As is apparent from the last sentence of recital 23 of the Directive, this refers only to the setting of priorities in individual cases, 'without prejudice to the right of a government of a Member State to issue [to NCAs] general policy rules or

---

that in one culture may be benign and help to foster independence may in other cultures become a device for subverting independence'; D. Currie, 'Resources, Capacity and Independence of National Authorities', 21st Annual EU Competition Law and Policy Workshop – Stronger NCAs – Procedures, Powers and Prospects (European University Institute, 3–4 June 2016).

221 For a more detailed discussion of the different types of prioritisation and discretion, see my paper 'Discretion and Prioritisation in Public Antitrust Enforcement, in Particular EU Antitrust Enforcement' (2011) 34 *World Competition* 353, also accessible at http://ssrn.com/author=456087, and L. Idot, 'Reform of Regulation 1/2003: Power to set priorities', *Concurrences* no 3–2015, 51.

222 Article 5 of Regulation 1/2003 does not, however, allow national competition authorities to take decisions finding that Article 101 TFEU or Article 102 TFEU have not been infringed, only decisions that there are no grounds for action by the national competition authority; see Judgments in *Tele2 Polska*, C-375/09, EU:C:2011:270, paragraphs 19 to 30, and in *Schenker*, C-681/11, EU:C:2013:404, paragraph 42.

priority guidelines that are not related to sector inquiries or specific proceedings for the enforcement of Articles 101 and 102 TFEU'.

Of the three things which Article 4(5) of the Directive does, as set out just above, the third element – namely, that NCAs should be able to set priorities independently without government interference in individual cases – clearly constitutes a measure to strengthen NCAs' independence, and hence justifies that Article 4(5) forms part of Article 4 of the Directive, which deals with independence.

The first and second elements – namely, that NCAs should have the power to initiate cases on their own initiative and that they should not bc obliged to investigate and decide upon cases that they consider not to be an enforcement priority – do not directly relate to independence.

Indeed, courts, which are the purest case of independent state bodies,[223] do not normally have the power to initiate cases on their own initiative nor to refuse cases for lack of priority interest, and the wording of Article 4 of the Directive has been carefully limited so as to cover only national **administrative** competition authorities, not national **judicial** competition authorities.[224]

It cannot be argued either that the fact that the French Autorité de la concurrence previously had the power to reject complaints under Articles 101 and 102 TFEU on priority grounds would in any way have undermined or negatively affected its independence.

It could even be argued that having the power to reject complaints for lack of priority might weaken a competition authority's independence, in the absence of sufficient other independence guarantees. Imagine for instance that the head of a competition authority is nearing the end of his mandate and would like to be renewed in his office, that the decision to give him a second mandate is in the hands of a minister, and that the competition authority happens to have received a complaint against a state-owned company under the jurisdiction of the same minister, or a company which is based in the minister's constituency, or which has contributed financially to her election campaign, or in which the minister's spouse is the main shareholder. In such a situation, the impossibility for the competition authority to reject the complaint on priority grounds would clearly strengthen the authority's independence. Whether or not the possibility to reject complaints on priority grounds actually presents an independence risk depends, however, on the presence or absence of other independence guarantees. Judicial review of decisions rejecting complaints, even if limited as in the case of the European Commission,[225] strongly reduces

---

223 On judicial independence, see the Judgments of the EU Court of Justice in *Wilson*, C-506/04, EU:C:2006:587, paragraphs 49 to 53, in *Associação Sindical dos Juízes Portugueses*, C-64/16, EU:C:2018:117 and in *LM*, C-216/18 PPU, EU:C:2018:586, paragraphs 48 to 54 and 63 to 67; see also C. Baudenbacher, *Judicial Independence – Memoirs of a European Judge* (Springer 2019).

224 See Article 2(2) and (3) of the ECN+ Directive.

225 In the case of the European Commission (and several NCAs, for instance in The Netherlands), any person who submits a written, reasoned complaint and whose interests are likely to be materially affected by the conduct that is the subject matter of the complaint can obtain formal complainant status. If the authority decides to close its file because a (further) investigation does not fit in its priorities, it must address to the complainant a reasoned decision, which is subject to judicial review, but, as it is recognised that the authority has discretion

the risks of political interference.[226] In the case of Germany, where there is no formal status of 'complainant' before the Bundeskartellamt and informal complainants cannot challenge in court the non-opening of proceedings by the Decision Division concerned,[227] the above hypothetical could not even arise, as the president of the Bundeskartellamt is appointed for life and the heads of the Decision Divisions are permanent officials of the Bundeskartellamt. Indeed, the absence of complainant rights in the German system has not prevented the Bundeskartellamt from being one of the most independent, if not the most independent of all NCAs.

Article 10(2) of the ECN+ Directive, which provides that NCAs must inform the European Commission when, after having informed the Commission in accordance with Article 11(3) of Regulation 1/2003 about the opening of formal investigations, they decide that there are no grounds to continue enforcement proceedings and as a result close their enforcement proceedings, is also helpful in strengthening the NCAs' independence in this respect.

The fact that two of the three elements contained in Article 4(5) of the ECN+ Directive – namely, that NCAs should have the power to initiate cases on their own initiative and that they should not be obliged to investigate and decide upon cases that they consider not to be a priority – cannot be considered to strengthen independence does not, of course, mean that these elements are not justified on other grounds.[228]

---

to set its enforcement priorities, the judicial review is limited to whether the contested decision is based on materially incorrect facts or vitiated by an error of law, a manifest error of appraisal or misuse of powers; see further Chapters IV and XIV of this book.

226 See further my paper 'Competition authorities: Towards more independence and prioritisation? The European Commission's "ECN+" Proposal for a Directive to empower the competition authorities of the Member States to be more effective enforcers', *Concurrences* no 4-2017, 60, also accessible at http://ssrn.com/author=456087, at footnotes 145 to 186.

227 See K. Ost, *Münchener Kommentar Europäisches und Deutsches Wettbewerbsrecht (Kartellrecht)*, vol 2 (Beck 2008), at 738-739.

228 See on this my paper 'Competition authorities: Towards more independence and prioritisation? The European Commission's "ECN+" Proposal for a Directive to empower the competition authorities of the Member States to be more effective enforcers', *Concurrences* no 4-2017, 60, also accessible at http://ssrn.com/author=456087, at footnotes 159 to 186.

IV. Discretion and Prioritisation in Public Antitrust Enforcement

This chapter discusses discretion and prioritisation in public antitrust enforcement, in particular in the enforcement of EU antitrust law by the European Commission. First, it defines the notion of discretion and discusses the rationale of discretion. Second, it examines the enforcement of Articles 101 and 102 TFEU by the European Commission, showing that the Commission has a broad discretion concerning the question which suspected or alleged infringements to pursue, but no discretion as to the content of the antitrust prohibitions. With regard to fines, the Commission has a significant degree of discretion, although this discretion is potentially neutralised by the General Court's unlimited jurisdiction. The third section of this chapter sets out various reasons for allowing competition authorities discretion to set priorities as to which cases of suspected or alleged infringements of the antitrust prohibitions they investigate and pursue, as well as a number of risks related to prioritisation.

A. The notion of discretion

1. Definition

A competition authority (like any other administrative authority or agency) can be said to have discretion with regard to a certain matter (for instance whether to investigate and pursue a suspected or alleged antitrust infringement, whether a certain practice constitutes an infringement of the antitrust prohibitions, whether to impose a fine, or what the amount of the fine should be) whenever the law leaves the authority certain freedom to choose among different possible courses of action according to the authority's own judgment.[229]

For the authority to have discretion, it is thus required that neither the applicable legislative, constitutional or Treaty provisions nor the applicable case law have laid down rules that fully specify which course of action the authority must take, and that the courts which have the power to review the authority's decision have neither been given by the legislature nor themselves assumed the power to fully substitute their own judgment as to what course of action should be taken for that of the authority, or, if given such power, do not exercise it.

Discretion is a matter of degree. An authority will have a narrower or wider discretion regarding a certain decision, depending upon the extent to which the legislation empowering the authority to take the decision, other legislative or constitutional provisions and the courts' case law have circumscribed the range of possible choices (by excluding

---

229 See generally D. J. Galligan, *Discretionary Powers – A Legal Study of Official Discretion* (Oxford University Press 1986) and A.-L. Sibony, *Le juge et le raisonnement économique en droit de la concurrence* (LGDJ 2008), §§ 1176-1179.

certain courses of action, by spelling out the objectives to be pursued by the authority, or by prescribing or proscribing that certain elements be taken into account in the decision-making), and depending upon the extent to which the reviewing courts are able and willing to substitute their own judgment for that of the authority.

Discretion may be narrower or wider, but is unlikely ever to be unlimited. The rule of law requires that no discretion should be unconstrained so as to be potentially arbitrary.[230] The legislation empowering the authority to take the decision will always have some underlying rationale, even if unarticulated or vague, thus excluding as arbitrary those decisions that do not have any intelligible relationship to this rationale.

Every decision (for instance the decision whether or not to investigate a certain practice, the decision whether or not a certain practice constitutes an infringement of the antitrust prohibitions, the decision whether or not to impose a fine, or the decision on the amount of the fine) can be said to involve three primary elements: (a) finding facts, (b) settling the standards or criteria on which the decision should be based, and (c) applying the standards to the facts. Discretion in its central sense relates to (b), meaning that the authority has a certain freedom of choice as to the standards or criteria which govern the decision.[231]

An authority can have discretion either because the legislature and the courts have not laid down any rules or standards, explicitly or implicitly leaving the authority to create its own standards, or because the legislature and the courts have only laid down vague rules or standards that leave room for various interpretations and the courts give deference to the authority's interpretation.[232] Legislative or jurisprudential rules or standards are often at least to some extent vague or open-textured.[233] The vagueness of the applicable rules or standards is not, however, a sufficient condition for an authority to have discretion. The authority will only have discretion to the extent that the courts that have the power to review the authority's decisions give deference to the authority's interpretations of the vague rules or standards, thus not fully substituting their own interpretation for that of the authority.

It would appear incompatible with the rule of law for a decision-maker to have discretion as to the (primary) facts on which it proceeds.[234] Applying the relevant rules or standards to the (primary) facts may, however, require an assessment of those facts (in the light of the rule or standard). The authority can have a certain margin of appreciation in this

---

230 T. Bingham, *The Rule of Law* (Allen Lane 2010), at 54; Judgment of the European Court of Human Rights of 25 February 1992 in *Margareta and Roger Andersson v Sweden*, Series A No 226, paragraph 75, and Judgment in *Lafarge v Commission*, C-413/08 P, EU:C:2010:346, paragraph 94: '[T]he fact that a law confers a discretion is not in itself inconsistent with the requirement of foreseeability, provided that the scope of the discretion and the manner of its exercise are indicated with sufficient clarity, having regard to the legitimate aim in question, to give the individual protection against arbitrary interference'.

231 D. J. Galligan, *Discretionary Powers – A Legal Study of Official Discretion* (Oxford University Press 1986), at 9.

232 Idem, at 9.

233 See generally H. L. A. Hart, *The Concept of Law* (2nd edition, Oxford University Press 1994), Chapter VII; T. A. O. Endicott, *Vagueness in Law* (Oxford University Press 2000); and V.K. Bhatia, J. Engberg, M. Gotti and D. Heller (eds), *Vagueness in Normative Texts* (Peter Lang 2005).

234 T. Bingham, 'The Rule of Law' (2007) 66 *Cambridge Law Journal* 67 at 72.

assessment, to the extent that the reviewing courts do not fully substitute their own assessment for that of the authority but rather limit their review, for instance by censuring only manifest errors of assessment. Such a margin of appreciation, which does not involve a freedom of choice as to the standards or criteria which govern the decision, but only reflects the limits of judicial review, should not be confused with discretion.[235]

2. Why discretion?

The degree of discretion that an authority has, or ideally should have, regarding a certain type of decision depends on the answers that the legislature and the courts give, or should give, to two fundamental questions, namely (i) how precise or vague the applicable rules or standards are, or should be, and (ii), to the extent that the applicable rules or standards are vague, how much deference the reviewing courts give, or should give, to the authority's interpretation of these rules or standards.

At first blush one might consider that it would always be preferable for the legislature to avoid vagueness by enacting precise rules, thus ensuring foreseeability and limiting the risk of arbitrariness. However, precision is not always preferable over vagueness.[236] Because of the complexity of the world, and the inherent limitations of human foresight and language, it may be impossible for a lawmaker to formulate a precise rule that consistently achieves its purposes. Precise rules can thus in practice lead to arbitrary results.[237] The enactment of a vague standard may also be a useful way of imposing legal control without fully working out the rationale for the standard, by delegating power to a decision-maker (authority or court) that may be in a better position than the legislature to develop just and convenient standards, through case-by-case decision-making.[238]

Whether the legislature should require the courts to give deference, or whether the courts on their own motion should give deference, to the authority's interpretations of vague rules or standards depends on the type of decision and on the comparative institutional

---

235 This margin of appreciation is sometimes called 'technical discretion' (see for instance Opinion of Advocate General Léger in *Rica Foods v Commission*, C-40/03 P, EU:C:2005:93, paragraph 46), as opposed to 'policy discretion', but this usage does not appear very helpful; see A. Meij, 'Judicial Review in the EC Courts: *Tetra Laval* and Beyond', in O. Essens, A. Gerbrandy and S. Lavrijssen (eds), *National Courts and the Standard of Review in Competition Law and Economic Regulation* (Europa Law Publishing 2009), at 16 and 20; M. Schimmel and R. Widdershoven, 'Judicial Review after *Tetra* Laval – Some Observations From a European Administrative Law Point of View', in O. Essens, A. Gerbrandy and S. Lavrijssen (eds), as just above, at 65; M. Adam, *Beurteilungsspielraum und Legalausnahme im Europäischen Kartellrecht* (Stämpfli 2007), at 7–24; and D. Bailey, 'Scope of Judicial Review under Article 81 EC' (2004) 41 *Common Market Law Review* 1327 at 1337–1338.

236 See T. A. O. Endicott, 'The Value of Vagueness', in V.K. Bhatia, J. Engberg, M. Gotti and D. Heller (eds), *Vagueness in Normative Texts* (Peter Lang 2005), 27; H. L. A. Hart, *The Concept of Law* (2nd edition, Oxford University Press 1994), Chapter VII; V. Fon and F. Parisi, 'On the optimal specifity of legal rules' (2007) 3 *Journal of Institutional Economics* 147; and F. Parisi and V. Fon, *The Economics of Lawmaking* (Oxford University Press 2009), Part I, Chapter 2; see also Judgment of the European Court of Human Rights of 17 September 2009 in Case of *Scoppola v Italy* (no 2), Application no 10249/03, paragraphs 100–101.

237 Both precision and vagueness can thus lead to forms of arbitrariness, and legislatures should strive to strike the optimal balance between both concerns; see T. A. O. Endicott, 'The Value of Vagueness', in V. K. Bhatia, J. Engberg, M. Gotti and D. Heller (eds), *Vagueness in Normative Texts* (Peter Lang 2005), at 48.

238 Idem, at 42.

competence of the authority and the reviewing courts. The authority may have specialist expertise that (generalist) courts lack, and the authority's information-gathering powers, decision-making procedures and political accountability may be more suited for resolving certain issues than judicial proceedings. On the other hand, the rule of law generally requires that individual determinations of civil rights and obligations and of criminal or quasi-criminal liability are made by independent courts.[239]

B. Antitrust enforcement by the European Commission

1. Investigation, prosecution and settlement

a. *Discretion to set priorities: positive priorities*

According to the case law of the EU Court of Justice, 'the Commission, entrusted by [Article 105(1) TFEU] with the task of ensuring application of the principles laid down in [Articles 101 and 102 TFEU], is responsible for defining and implementing the orientation of [EU] competition policy. It is for the Commission to adopt, subject to review by the [EU Courts], individual decisions in accordance with the procedural rules in force'. In order to perform that task effectively, the Commission has a broad discretion to select the cases which it investigates and in which it continues the proceedings up to the stage of a final decision.[240]

The Commission can investigate cases and proceed to the finding of an infringement either acting on a complaint or on its own initiative.[241] It may also, on its own initiative, conduct an inquiry into a particular sector of the economy or into a particular kind of agreement across various sectors.[242] A company targeted by an investigation or by a final decision finding an infringement cannot escape by invoking the fact that the Commission has not investigated or prosecuted other infringements, provided the investigation was

---

239 See Article 6 of the European Convention on Human Rights; and my paper 'The Increased Level of EU Antitrust Fines, Judicial Review, and the European Convention on Human Rights' (2010) 33 *World Competition* 1, also accessible at http://ssrn.com/author=456087.

240 Judgments in *Masterfoods*, C-344/98, EU:C:2000:689, paragraph 46, in *Ufex and Others v Commission*, C-119/97 P, EU:C:1999:116, paragraphs 88 and 89, and in *IECC v Commission*, C-449/98 P, EU:C:2001:276, paragraphs 35 to 37; see also Judgment in *Limburgse Vinyl Maatschappij and Others v Commission (PVC II)*, T-305/94 etc., EC:T:1999:80, paragraphs 148 to 154 (discretion to take a new decision following annulment of a first decision on purely procedural grounds).

241 Article 7(1) of Council Regulation (EC) No 1/2003 of 16 December 2002 on the implementation of the rules on competition laid down in Articles 81 and 82 of the Treaty [2003] OJ L1/1, last amended by Council Regulation (EC) No 1419/2006 [2006] OJ L269/1. For a detailed analysis of Regulation 1/2003, in comparison with the regime preceding it, see my *Community Report* in D. Cahill and J. D. Cooke (eds), *The Modernisation of EU Competition Law Enforcement in the EU – FIDE 2004 National Reports* (Cambridge 2004), 661–736; my book *Principles of European Antitrust Enforcement* (Hart 2005); and K. Dekeyser, C. Gauer, J. Laitenberger, N. Wahl, W. Wils and L. Prete (eds), *Regulation 1/2003 and EU Antitrust Enforcement – A Systematic Guide* (Wolters Kluwer 2022).

242 Article 17 of Regulation 1/2003. The opening of a sector inquiry requires a finding that 'the trend of trade between Member States, the rigidity of prices or other circumstances suggest that competition may be restricted or distorted within the common market'. The information obtained through a sector inquiry can subsequently be used to start individual infringement proceedings. The Commission has no powers to impose remedies as part of a sector inquiry comparable to the remedies that can be imposed for instance by the UK Competition and Markets Authority as part of a market investigation.

properly conducted and the infringement properly established.[243] The Commission decision would only be vitiated by misuse of powers if it is evident, on the basis of objective, relevant and consistent evidence, that it was taken with the exclusive or main purpose of achieving an end other than the enforcement of Articles 101 and 102 TFEU.[244]

The Commission can at any time open an investigation and adopt a decision under Articles 101 or 102 TFEU, even where an agreement or practice has already been the subject of a decision by a national court and the decision contemplated by the Commission conflicts with that national court's decision.[245] When the Commission initiates proceedings for the adoption of a decision, the national competition authorities are relieved of their competence to apply Articles 101 and 102 TFEU to the same case.[246]

b. *Discretion to set priorities: negative priorities*

Companies whose agreements or practices may be contested under Articles 101 or 102 TFEU cannot notify their agreements or practices to the Commission, nor through any means force the Commission to take a position on the legality of their agreements or practices.[247] An immunity or leniency applicant in a cartel case cannot force the Commission to investigate the cartel or to adopt a final decision finding the infringement.[248]

A complainant cannot compel the Commission to carry out an investigation or to take a decision as to the existence or non-existence of an alleged infringement.[249] In order to

---

243 Judgments in *British Airways v Commission*, T-219/99, EU:T:2003:343, paragraphs 66 to 70, and in *Deutsche Telekom v Commission*, T-271/03, EU:T:2008:101, paragraph 243.

244 See Judgment in *Deutsche Telekom v Commission*, T-271/03, EU:T:2008:101, paragraph 270.

245 Judgment in *Masterfoods*, C-344/98, EU:C:2000:689, paragraph 48. This appears to preclude the award of punitive damages for violations of Articles 101 or 102 TFEU by national courts, as such an award would prevent the Commission from later imposing fines for the same infringement without breaching the principle of *ne bis in idem*; see my paper 'The Relationship between Public Antitrust Enforcement and Private Actions for Damages' (2009) 32 *World Competition* 3 at 22, also available at http://ssrn.com/author=456087.

246 Article 11(6) of Regulation 1/2003. However, where a decision has already been taken by a national competition authority, the Commission's power to deal with the same case risks being limited by the principle of *ne bis in idem*; see Article 50 CFREU; Judgment in *Nordzucker*, C-151/20, EU:C:2022:203; my paper 'The Principle of "Ne Bis in Idem" in EC Antitrust Enforcement: A Legal and Economic Analysis' (2003)26 *World Competition* 131, also accessible at http://ssrn.com/author=456087 and S. Frisch, '*Ne bis in idem* under an optimal antitrust enforcement framework' (2023) 24 *ERA Forum*.

247 The notification system previously existing under Regulation 17 was abolished by Regulation 1/2003 because of its negative impact on the Commission's enforcement priorities; see my book *Principles of European Antitrust Enforcement* (Hart 2005), section 1.1.4.2. The Commission has the power under Article 10 of Regulation 1/2003 to adopt non-infringement decisions, but only acting on its own initiative in the EU public interest. According to its Notice on informal guidance relating to novel questions [2004] OJ C101/6, the Commission may also issue guidance letters on novel questions, but the Commission retains full discretion to refuse to deal with a request for guidance, in particular to ensure that the provision of informal guidance does not interfere with its enforcement priorities. No non-infringement decisions or guidance letters have been adopted yet; see Commission Report on the functioning of Regulation 1/2003, COM(2009)206 of 29 April 2009, and accompanying Commission Staff Working Paper SEC(2009)574.

248 An immunity or leniency applicant only has a right to an acknowledgement of receipt of its application, and, if the requirements set out in the Leniency Notice are fulfilled, a conditional (provisional) immunity decision; see Commission Notice on Immunity from fines and reduction of fines in cartel cases [2006] OJ C298/17, paragraphs 17, 18 and 28,

249 Judgments in *Automec v Commission*, T-24/90, EU:T:1992:97, paragraphs 75 and 76, and in *IECC v Commission*, C-449/98 P, EU:C:2001:275, paragraphs 35 to 37. The Commission can, however, be required to give a decision if the subject matter of the complaint falls within its exclusive competence, as in the case of the withdrawal

perform effectively its task of defining and implementing the orientation of EU competition policy, the Commission is entitled to give differing degrees of priority to the complaints brought before it, and hence to decline to continue with the examination of a complaint for lack of sufficient EU interest.[250]

The discretion which the Commission has for that purpose is not unlimited, however.[251] First, the Commission must consider attentively all the matters of fact and of law which the complainants bring to its attention, and, if it declines to continue with the examination of a complaint, it must state sufficiently precise and detailed reasons to enable the EU General Court to carry out an effective review of the Commission's use of its discretion to define priorities.[252] The Court's review is, however, limited to whether or not the contested decision is based on materially incorrect facts or vitiated by an error of law, a manifest error of appraisal or a misuse of powers.[253]

Second, 'when deciding the order of priority for dealing with the complaints brought before it, the Commission may not regard as excluded in principle from its purview certain situations which come under the task entrusted to it by the Treaty', but must in each case make an individual assessment of the EU interest in (further) investigating the complaint.[254]

c. *Guidance on enforcement priorities*

Where the Commission, through accumulated experience with the exercise of its discretion to set priorities, finds that certain criteria are usually pertinent in deciding on

---

in an individual case of the benefit of an exemption regulation; see *Automec v Commission*, as just above, paragraph 75, and Articles 29(1) and (2) of Regulation 1/2003.

250 Judgments in *Ufex and Others v Commission*, C-119/97 P, EU:C:1999:116, paragraph 88, and *Automec v Commission*, T-24/90, EU:T:1992:97, paragraphs 77 and 85. As has been pointed out by Advocate General Ruiz-Jarabo Colomer in his Opinion in *IECC v Commission*, C-449/98 P, EU:C:2001:7, paragraph 57, the 'lack of EU interest' (or 'lack of Community interest' in the pre-Lisbon Treaty terminology) 'is no more than an abbreviated formula, a short-cut to describe, succinctly, the discretion – neither unfettered nor arbitrary, since it is subject to judicial review – which the Treaties confer on the Commission for its examination of a complaint alleging the existence of anti-competitive practices. The substance of that concept varies considerably, to the same extent as the widely differing circumstances which surround cases involving infringements of the competition rules.'

251 Judgment in *Ufex and Others v Commission*, C-119/97 P, EU:C:1999:116, paragraph 89.

252 Idem, paragraphs 86, 90 and 91. Complainants only have the right to a reasoned and reviewable decision rejecting their complaint if they can show a legitimate interest (Article 7(2) of Regulation 1/2003; as to what constitutes a legitimate interest, see Commission Notice on the handling of complaints [2004] OJ C101/5, paragraphs 33–40, and Judgment in *Österreichische Postsparkasse and Bank für Arbeit und Wirtschaft v Commission*, T-231/01 and T-214/01, EU:T:2006:151, paragraph 114) and if they provide the information required by Form C (Article 5 and Annex of Commission Regulation (EC) No 773/2004 of 7 April 2004 relating to the conduct of proceedings by the Commission pursuant to Articles 81 and 82 of the EC Treaty [2004] OJ L123/28). Complainants cannot request interim measures, which the Commission can only take on its own initiative; see Article 8(1) of Regulation 1/2003, and A. Nordsjo, 'Regulation 1/2003: Power of the Commission to Adopt Interim Measures' (2006) *European Competition Law Review* 299.

253 Judgment in *Automec v Commission*, T-24/90, EU:T:1992:97, paragraph 80. A similar review to that undertaken by the General Court can also be undertaken by the European Ombudsman; see Decision of the European Ombudsman of 25 September 2009 closing his enquiry into complaint 1142/2008/(BEH)KM against the European Commission.

254 Judgment in *Ufex and Others v Commission*, C-119/97 P, EU:C:1999:116, paragraphs 92 and 93; see also Judgment in *Treuhand v Commission*, T-99/04, EU:T:2008:256, paragraph 163, and, more generally, D. J. Galligan, *Discretionary Powers – A Legal Study of Official Discretion* (Oxford University Press 1986), at 281–284.

priorities, or develops a certain decision method, it is desirable for reasons of transparency that it makes these criteria or this method public.

The Commission published a list of general prioritisation criteria in its Annual Report on Competition Policy 2005.[255] In 2009, the Commission also published guidance on its enforcement priorities in applying Article 102 TFEU to abusive exclusionary conduct by dominant undertakings, setting out a general framework of analysis which it employs in determining which cases it should pursue.[256]

Because the Commission cannot regard as excluded in principle from its purview certain situations which come under its task of enforcing Articles 101 and 102 TFEU,[257] such guidance must not be treated as rules to be applied automatically but must allow consideration of the merits of each case.[258]

d. *Discretion how to conduct investigations*

According to the case law of the EU Courts, the Commission has 'freedom of action in the conduct of its investigations in competition cases' so as to ensure their effectiveness.[259] Regulation 1/2003 gives the Commission a number of investigative powers, such as the power to request information and the power to inspect business premises. These powers are subject to a number of limitations, conditions or guarantees for the rights of the defence.[260] Provided that it respects these limitations, the Commission has a broad discretion to decide which investigative measures to take, according to its own judgment of what is most effective for its investigation. The EU Courts have confirmed for instance that 'the Commission is under no obligation to put the same questions, during its investigation, to all the undertakings which it suspects of participating in an infringement',[261]

---

255 SEC(2006)761, June 2006, at 26–27. See also Commission Notice on the handling of complaints by the Commission under Articles 81 and 82 of the EC Treaty [2004] OJ C101/65.

256 Commission Communication – Guidance on the Commission's enforcement priorities in applying Article 82 of the EC Treaty to abusive exclusionary conduct by dominant undertakings [2009] OJ C45/7; see G. Monti, 'Article 82 EC: What Future for the Effects-Based Approach?' (2010) 1 *Journal of European Competition Law & Practice* 2, my paper 'The Judgment of the EU General Court in *Intel* and the So-Called More Economic Approach to Abuse of Dominance' (2014) 37 *World Competition* 405, G. Monti, 'Rebates After the General Court's 20222 *Intel* Judgment (2023) 60 *Common Market Law Review* 107, and H. Schweitzer, 'Art. 102 AEUV: Irrwege und Auswege' (2023) *Wirtschaft und Wettbewerb* 61. In 2023, the Commission amended the Guidance and announced its future replacement by Guidelines; see European Commission Press release, 'Antitrust: Commission announces Guidelines on exclusionary abuses and amends Guidance on enforcement priorities' (IP/23/1911, 27 March 2023).

257 Judgment in *Ufex and Others v Commission*, C-119/97 P, EU:C:1999:116, paragraphs 92 and 93.

258 See D. J. Galligan, *Discretionary Powers – A Legal Study of Official Discretion* (Oxford University Press 1986), at 281: '[C]onsideration of the merits of each case means that the authority must direct itself to the case, and then decide whether the standards should apply, whether they should be modified, or whether, in the circumstances, an exception should be made to them'; see also F.W. Bulst, 'Mehr Licht – Zur Anwendung des Art. 82 EG auf Behinderungsmissbräuche' (2009) 73 *Rabel Journal of Comparative and International Private Law* 703 at 716–718.

259 Judgment in *Corus UK v Commission*, T-48/00, EU:T:2004:219, paragraph 212.

260 See my paper 'EU Antitrust Enforcement Powers and Procedural Rights and Guarantees: The Interplay between EU Law, National Law, the Charter of Fundamental Rights of the EU and the European Convention on Human Rights' (2011) 34 *World Competition* 187, also available at http://ssrn.com/author=456087, and Chapter X of this book.

261 Judgment in *Corus UK v Commission*, T-48/00, EU:T:2004:219, paragraph 212. However, the General Court has also stressed that, under the general principle of equal treatment, the Commission must ensure that it does not distort the conditions of competition between undertakings in a (potential) race to be the first to cooperate under

that 'the Commission has a reasonable margin of discretion to decide how expedient it may be to hear persons whose evidence may be relevant to the inquiry',[262] and that 'the guarantee of the rights of the defence [. . .] does not require the Commission [. . .] to carry out further investigations or to hear witnesses put forward by the party concerned, where it considers that the preliminary investigation of the case has been sufficient'.[263]

e. *Discretion to limit the investigation or the finding of infringement to only part of a case*

The Commission's discretion in choosing which cases to pursue also includes discretion to pursue only part of a case.[264] For instance, it can decide to limit its investigation of a cartel to a certain time period because also investigating earlier periods would consume too many resources. Or in a case concerning an excessively long non-compete clause incorporated in an agreement for the transfer of an undertaking, it could decide to limit itself to making a finding that beyond four years the non-compete clause is in any event excessive, even if a more thorough investigation would reveal that the clause already became anti-competitive at some earlier point.[265] Furthermore, where a practice infringes Articles 101 or 102 TFEU on several grounds, the Commission could limit itself to pursuing only one of these grounds. For instance, in the *Virgin / British Airways* case, the rebate scheme operated by British Airways infringed Article 102 TFEU both because it was exclusionary and because it was discriminatory.[266] In its discretion, the Commission could have decided to pursue the case on only one of these two grounds. Similarly, the Commission has discretion whether or not to proceed against all members of a cartel.[267] Finally, the fact that the Commission may initially have investigated more widely does not prevent it from later including in the statement of objections or the final decision only more limited findings.[268]

---

the Commission's Leniency Notice, by contacting one of them, or giving them unequal access when they contact the European Commission; see Judgments in *Krupp Thyssen and Others v Commission*, T-45/98 and T-47/98, EU:T:2001:288, paragraphs 237–248, and in *BASF v Commission*, T-15/02, EU:T:2006:74, paragraph 504.

262 Judgment in *HFB and Others v Commission*, T-9/99, EU:T:2002:70, paragraph 383.

263 Judgment in *Thyssen Stahl v Commission*, T-141/94, EU:T:1994:48, paragraph 110; see also Judgments in *GEA Group v Commission*, T-45/10, EU:T:2015:507, paragraph 311, and in *Silver Plastics and Johannes Reifenhäuser v Commission*, T-582/15, EU:T:2019:497, paragraph 202.

264 See Judgment in *LG Display and LG Display Taiwan, Commission*, T-128/11, EU:T:2014:88, paragraphs 223 to 228, and in *Amazon.com and Others v Commission*, C-815/21 P, EU:C:2023:308, paragraph 36.

265 Compare with Judgment in *Remia v Commission*, C-42/84, EU:C:1985:327.

266 Commission Decision of 14 July 1999 relating to a proceeding under Article 82 of the EC Treaty (IV/D-2/34.780 – Virgin/British Airways) [2000] OJ L30/1, confirmed by Judgments in *British Airways v Commission*, T-219/99, EU:T:2003:343 and in *British Airways v Commission*, C-95/04 P, EU:C:2007:166.

267 See Judgment of 8 July 2004, *JFE and Others v Commission*, T-67/00, T-68/00, T-71/00 and T-78/00, EU:T:2004:221, paragraph 414: '[T]he Commission was not under any obligation to set out, in the contested decision, the reasons for which the Latin American producers were not among its addressees. The obligation to state the reasons on which a measure is based cannot embody an obligation for the institution from which it emanates to give reasons for the fact that it did not adopt other measures of a similar kind addressed to third parties'; see also Judgment of 1 February 2018, *Schenker*, C-263/16, EU:C:2018:58, paragraphs 48 to 50.

268 See Judgment in *Prym v Commission*, C-534/07 P, EU:C:2009:505, paragraph 33, confirming that the Commission has no obligation to state reasons in a statement of objections or final decision as to why it does not propose to act on the basis of certain matters which it had initially investigated or intended to investigate; see also Commission Decision of 20 June 2001 in Case COMP/E-2/36.041/ PO – Michelin [2002] OJ L143/1, paragraph 359 (Commission concentrated its enquiries on a limited time period).

f. *Discretion to settle*

Finally, the Commission's discretion in choosing which cases to pursue also includes discretion to settle or to refuse to settle a case.[269] Article 9 of Regulation 1/2003 provides that, where the Commission intends to adopt a decision requiring that an infringement be brought to an end and the undertakings concerned offer commitments to meet the concerns expressed to them by the Commission in its preliminary assessment, the Commission may by decision make those commitments binding on the undertakings. Such a commitment decision closes the case, without making a finding of infringement. The EU Courts have confirmed that 'the Commission is never obliged under Article 9(1) of Regulation No 1/2003 to decide to make commitments binding instead of proceeding under Article 7 of that regulation [taking a decision finding the infringement and ordering its termination]'.[270] Similarly, the Commission Notice on the conduct of settlement procedures in cartel cases clearly states that 'the Commission retains a broad margin of discretion to determine which cases may be suitable [. . .] to settle'.[271]

2. Content of the antitrust prohibitions

a. *Article 102 TFEU*

By virtue of the Treaty itself, the prohibition of abuse of a dominant position laid down in Article 102 TFEU (and earlier in Articles 82 EC and 86 EEC) is (and has always been) directly applicable, without any need for a prior decision.[272] It is applied by the companies active in the European market, whose conduct it is meant to guide, and can be applied, in case of breach, by the European Commission as well as by national competition authorities and national courts.[273]

---

[269] On the policy question of how the discretion to settle or not to settle should be exercised from the perspective of optimal antitrust enforcement, see Chapter VI of this book.

[270] Judgment of 11 July 2007, *Alrosa v Commission*, T-170/06, EU:T:2007:220, paragraph 130 (continuing: 'It is therefore not required to give reasons for which commitments are not in its view suitable to be made binding, so as to bring the proceedings to an end.'); this judgment was annulled on appeal before the Court of Justice by Judgment of 29 June 2010, *Commission v Alrosa*, C-441/07 P, EU:C:2010:377, but this point was not contested on appeal. See also Judgment of 17 December 2015, *Orange Polska*, T-486/11, EU:T:2015:1002, paragraphs 218 to 224, Judgment of 30 June 2016, *CB v Commission*, T-491/07 RENV, EU:T:2016:379, paragraph 470, and Judgment of 10 November 2021, *Google and Alphabet v Commission (Google Shopping)*, T-612/17, EU:T:2021:763, paragraph 638.

[271] Commission Notice on the conduct of settlement procedures in view of the adoption of Decisions pursuant to Article 7 and Article 23 of Council Regulation (EC) No 1/2003 in cartel cases [2008] OJ C167/1, paragraph 5. Paragraph 6 of the Notice, however, adds: 'While parties to the proceedings do not have a right to settle, should the Commission consider that a case may, in principle, be suitable for settlement, it will explore the interest in settlement of all parties to the same proceedings'; see also recital 4 of Commission Regulation (EC) No 622/2008 of 30 June 2008 amending Regulation (EC) No 773/2004, as regards the conduct of settlement procedures in cartel cases [2008] OJ L171/3, and Judgments of 20 May 2015, *Timab Industries and CFPR v Commission*, T-456/10, EU:T:2015:296, paragraph 64, of 29 February 2016, *Schenker v Commission*, T-265/12, EU:T:2016:111, paragraphs 395 to 422, and of 15 December 2016, *Philips and Philips France v Commission*, T-762/14, EU:T:2016:738, paragraph 255.

[272] See Judgments in *Giuseppe Sacchi*, C-155/73, EU:C:1974:40, at 431, and in *Ahmed Saeed Flugreisen*, C-66/86, EU:C:1989:140, paragraph 32.

[273] On the substantive rules of criminal law (in the broad sense; see Chapters IX and X of this book) being applied primarily by the members of society whose conduct they are set up to guide, and only secondarily by officials operating a system of penalties, see H.L.A. Hart, H.L.A. Hart, *The Concept of Law* (2nd edition, Oxford University Press 1994), at 38–39.

Because the prohibition of abuse of a dominant position laid down in Article 102 TFEU is to a significant extent vague or open-textured, it requires interpretation so as to specify its precise legal content to be applied in specific cases. By virtue of Article 19 of the Treaty on European Union (TEU), it is the EU Court of Justice which is ultimately responsible for interpreting EU law.[274]

The EU judicature has, indeed, in its case law, progressively clarified the interpretation of the prohibition of abuse of a dominant position laid down in Article 102 TFEU. For instance, in *Hoffmann-La Roche* the Court of Justice clarified in general that 'the concept of abuse is an objective concept relating to the behaviour of an undertaking in a dominant position which is such as to influence the structure of a market where, as a result of the very presence of the undertaking in question, the degree of competition is weakened and which, through the recourse to methods different from those which condition normal competition in products or services on the basis of the transactions of commercial operators, has the effect of hindering the maintenance of the degree of competition still existing in the market or the growth of that competition'.[275] Building upon this general interpretation, the Court of Justice laid down in *Akzo* the following 'criterion of legality of conduct of a dominant undertaking in relation to prices': 'Prices below average variable costs (that is to say, those which vary depending on the quantities produced) by means of which a dominant undertaking seeks to eliminate a competitor must be regarded as abusive. [. . .] Moreover, prices below average total costs, that is to say, fixed costs plus variable costs, must be regarded as abusive if they are determined as part of a plan for eliminating a competitor'.[276] In *France Télécom*, the Court further clarified that 'it does not follow from the case law of the Court that proof of the possibility of recoupment of losses suffered by the application, by an undertaking in a dominant position, of prices lower than a certain level of costs constitutes a necessary precondition to establishing that such a pricing policy is abusive'; the possibility of recoupment may, however, be 'a relevant factor in assessing whether or not the practice concerned is abusive, in that it may, for example where prices lower than average variable cost are applied, assist in excluding economic justifications other than the elimination of a competitor, or, where prices below average total costs but above average variable costs are applied, assist in establishing that a plan to eliminate a competitor exists'.[277]

The interpretations of Article 102 TFEU given by the Court of Justice are binding on the European Commission, as they are on national competition authorities and national courts. As Advocate General Kokott has pointed out, 'the Commission would [always] have to act within the framework prescribed for it by [Article 102 TFEU] as interpreted by the Court of Justice'.[278] Or, in the words of Judge Meij of the General Court, writing extrajudicially, 'an abuse of a dominant position is what the Court says it is'.[279]

---

274 See also A.-L. Sibony, A.-L. Sibony, *Le juge et le raisonnement économique en droit de la concurrence* (LGDJ 2008), §§ 620 and 621.

275 Judgment in *Hoffmann-La Roche v Commission*, 85/76, EU:C:1979:36, paragraph 91.

276 Judgment in *Akzo v Commission*, C-62/86, EU:C:1991:286, heading above paragraph 63 and paragraphs 71 and 72.

277 Judgment in *France Télécom v Commission*, C-202/07 P, EU:C:2009:214, paragraphs 110 and 111.

278 Opinions of Advocate General Kokott in *British Airways v Commission*, C-95/04 P, EU:C:2006:133, paragraph 28, and in *Solvay v Commission*, C-109/10 P, EU:C:2011:256, paragraph 21.

279 A. Meij, 'Judicial Review in the EC Courts: *Tetra Laval* and Beyond', in O. Essens, A. Gerbrandy and S. Lavrijssen (eds), *National Courts and the Standard of Review in Competition Law and Economic Regulation* (Europa Law Publishing 2009), at 16.

The Commission can thus not be said to have any discretion as to the interpretation of Article 102 TFEU. Many of the judgments in which the EU judicature has clarified the interpretation of Article 102 TFEU, such as the *Hoffmann-La Roche*, *Akzo* and *France Télécom* judgments, concerned appeals against Commission decisions, and the Commission may thus have been more or less successful in convincing the Courts to adopt the interpretation which it advocated.[280] However, the Courts do not defer to the Commission's views as to the correct interpretation of Article 102 TFEU but make their own judgment.[281]

b. *Article 101 TFEU*

Prior to the entry into application of Regulation 1/2003 on 1 May 2004, it could be argued that the Commission had a discretion to interpret the third paragraph of Article 101 TFEU (then Article 81 EC or earlier Article 85 EEC), which the Treaty itself had not made directly applicable, and for the application of which Regulation 17, the predecessor of Regulation 1/2003,[282] had given exclusive competence to the Commission.[283] Regulation 1/2003 has however made the whole of Article 101 TFEU directly applicable.[284] Today the situation for Article 101 TFEU is thus the same as for Article 102 TFEU.[285] As is the case with Article 102 TFEU, the Court of Justice is ultimately responsible for the interpretation of Article 101 TFEU, the Court's interpretations are binding upon the Commission, and the Court of Justice and General Court do not defer to the Commission's views as to the correct interpretation of Article 102 TFEU but make their own judgment.[286] The Commission can thus not be said to have any discretion as to the interpretation of Article 101 TFEU.[287]

The above conclusion that the Commission has no discretion as to the interpretation of Articles 101 and 102 TFEU is not called into question by the *Masterfoods* judgment and its partial codification in Article 16 of Regulation 1/2003.

In *Masterfoods* the Court of Justice held that the Commission 'is responsible for defining and implementing the orientation of Community competition policy', and is entitled to

---

280 See also B. Allan, 'Rule-Making in the Context of Article 102 TFEU' (2014) *Competition Law Journal* 7 at 14–15: '[T]he rule-making process may be viewed as, primarily, a dialogue in which the Commission proposes and the Court ultimately disposes.'

281 Similarly, in cases upon preliminary reference from a national court, the Commission, which makes systematic use of its right under Article 23 of the Statute of the Court of Justice (Protocol No 3 TEU) to submit observations to the Court of Justice, may be more or less successful in convincing the Court to adopt the interpretation of Article 102 TFEU which it advocates, but the Court makes its own judgment.

282 Council Regulation No 17 [1962] OJ 13/204 (Special English Edition 1959-62, p 87).

283 See O. Odudu, 'Article 81(3), Discretion and Direct Effect' (2002) *European Competition Law Review* 17; D. Bailey, 'Scope of Judicial Review under Article 81 EC' (2004) 41 *Common Market Law Review* 1327; G. Marenco, 'Does a Legal Exception System Require an Amendment of the Treaty?', in C.-D. Ehlermann and I. Atanasiu (eds), *European Competition Law Annual 2000: The Modernisation of EC Antitrust Policy* (Hart Publishing 2001) 145, at 164–167; and my book *Principles of European Antitrust Enforcement* (Hart 2005), at 6–7.

284 Articles 1 and 6 of Regulation 1/2003.

285 See also Opinion of Advocate General Léger in *Rica Foods v Commission*, C-40/03 P, EU:C:2005:93, paragraph 50, referring to the Commission's discretion under Article 101(3) TFEU (then Article 81(3) EC) 'before the entry into force of Regulation (EC) No 1/2003'.

286 See Judgment in *Treuhand v Commission*, T-99/04, EU:T:2008:256, paragraph 163.

287 As to the Commission's role in adopting exemption regulations and interpretative communications, see further below.

adopt at any time decisions under Articles 101 and 102 TFEU, even where an agreement or practice has already been the subject of a conflicting decision by a national court. It further held that a national court ruling on an agreement or practice that is already the subject of a Commission decision cannot take a decision running counter to that of the Commission; if the national court has doubts as to the validity of the Commission decision, it may, or must, in accordance with Article 267 TFEU, refer a question to the Court of Justice for a preliminary ruling.[288] The latter points have since been codified in Article 16 of Regulation 1/2003.

The discretion that this case law grants the Commission is the discretion to choose which cases of suspected infringement of Articles 101 and 102 TFEU to pursue,[289] not a discretion as to the content of the antitrust prohibitions laid down in those provisions. The deference to Commission decisions which *Masterfoods* and its codification in Article 16 of Regulation 1/2003 require from national courts does not relate to the Commission's interpretation of Articles 101 or 102 TFEU but only to the operative part of the Commission's decisions, and merely serves to protect the Court of Justice's exclusive competence to review the legality of Commission decisions.[290]

Neither is the conclusion that the Commission has no discretion as to the interpretation of Articles 101 and 102 TFEU called into question by the case law concerning the EU Courts' (allegedly) limited review of complex economic assessments made by the Commission in applying Articles 101 or 102 TFEU to the facts of a specific case.[291] As I have argued elsewhere, it is unclear whether or to what extent this review is really limited.[292] In any event, the limited review, to the extent that it really exists, only gives the Commission a margin of appreciation, not discretion, as it does not grant the Commission any freedom of choice as to the standards or criteria which govern its decision.[293]

c. *Exemption regulations*

Regulation 1/2003 has maintained the possibility for the Commission to adopt, on the basis of empowerments in Council regulations, so-called block exemption regulations,

---

288 Judgment in *Masterfoods*, C-344/98, EU:C:2000:689, paragraphs 46 to 54.

289 As well as the discretion for which categories of agreements that fulfil the requirements of Article 101(3) TFEU to adopt exemption regulations; see further below.

290 See E. Gippini-Fournier, Community Report for the FIDE XXIII Congress 2008, in H. F. Koeck and M. M. Karollus (eds), *The Modernisation of European Competition Law: Initial Experiences with Regulation 1/2003* (Nomos 2008), at 470–474; F. Castillo de la Torre, 'Decisiones de la Comisión en materia de política de competencia ante los tribunales nacionales: la sentencia Masterfoods' (2001) 213 *Gaceta jurídica de la Unión Europea y de la competencia* 29; A. P. Komninos, 'Effect of Commission Decisions in Private Litigation: Setting the Story Straight' (2007) 44 *Common Market Law Review* 1387; and Judgment of the UK House of Lords of 19 July 2006 in *Inntrepreneur Pub Company (CPC) and Others v Crehan* [2006] UKHL 38.

291 See my paper 'The Increased Level of EU Antitrust Fines, Judicial Review and the ECHR' (2010) 33 *World Competition* 5 at 26–28.

292 As footnote just above; see also J. Bornkamm, 'Richtliche Kontrolle von Entscheidungen im deutschen und europäischen Kartellverwaltungsverfahren' (2010) *Zeitschrift für Wettbewerbsrecht* 34 at 43; J. Nothdurft, 'Die Entscheidung des EuGH im Fall Tetra Laval' (2006) *Zeitschrift für Wettbewerbsrecht* 306; and P. Craig, *EU Administrative Law* (Oxford 2006) at 470; and Chapter IX of this book.

293 See F. Castillo de la Torre, 'Evidence, Proof and Judicial Review in Cartel Cases' (2009) 32 *World Competition* 505 at 565–566.

by which it declares Article 101(1) TFEU inapplicable to categories of agreements, decisions and practices that fulfil the requirements of Article 101(3) TFEU.[294]

When adopting exemption regulations, the Commission is bound by Article 101 TFEU, as interpreted by the Court of Justice. The Commission has thus no discretion to exempt categories of agreements that do not fulfil the requirements of Article 101(3) TFEU.[295] The Commission does, however, have a discretion whether or not to adopt exemption regulations for any category of agreements that fulfil the requirements of Article 101(3) TFEU.[296]

d. *Guidelines, notices and other interpretative communications*

The Commission has published a number of guidelines, notices and other communications, such as the Guidelines on vertical restraints and the Guidelines on horizontal co-operation agreements,[297] the Guidelines on the effect on trade concept,[298] which concern the interpretation of Articles 101 and 102 TFEU and of exemption regulations.[299]

The Commission has wide discretion whether or not, or on which subjects to, publish interpretative communications. As to the content of these communications, the Commission is, however, bound by Articles 101 and 102 TFEU, as well as by the exemption regulations, as interpreted by the Court of Justice.[300] On questions of interpretation on which the Court has not yet spoken, the Commission may provide its own interpretation, provided that these additions are coherent with the case law of the Court of Justice, and that the communication does not create any confusion as to what is the Court's case

---

294 See recital 10 and Articles 29 and 40 of Regulation 1/2003, and my book *Principles of European Antitrust Enforcement* (Hart 2005), section 1.2.1; see also Article 105(3) TFEU.

295 The fact that Article 29 of Regulation 1/2003 allows the Commission and national competition authorities to withdraw the benefit of an exemption regulation in individual cases where an agreement falling under the exemption regulation is found to have effects incompatible with Article 101(3) TFEU does not suggest otherwise, as it merely reflects the difference between the abstract assessment made at the stage of the adoption of the exemption regulation and the assessment on the basis of a specific agreement; see J. Bornkamm, 'Die Freistellung vom Kartellverbot nach dem Systemwechsel', in M. Monti, N. Prinz von und zu Lichtenstein, B. Vesterdorf, J. Westbrook and L. Wildhaber (eds), *Economic Law and Justice in Times of Globalisation – Festschrift for Carl Baudenbacher* (Nomos 2007) 299 at 308; my book *The Optimal Enforcement of EC Antitrust Law* (Kluwer 2002), section 6.2.3.2; and my book *Principles of European Antitrust Enforcement* (Hart 2005), section 1.2.1.

296 This discretion is of the same nature as the discretion which individual cases to pursue; see above and Judgment in *Masterfoods*, C-344/98, EU:C:2000:689, paragraph 46: '[T]he Commission, entrusted by [Article 105(1) TFEU] with the task of ensuring application of the principles laid down in [Articles 101 and 102 TFEU], is responsible for defining and implementing the orientation of [EU] competition policy. It is for the Commission to adopt, subject to review by the [EU Courts], individual decisions in accordance with the procedural rules in force and to adopt exemption regulations.'

297 Guidelines on Vertical Restraints [2022] OJ C248/1; Guidelines on the applicability of Article 101 TFEU to horizontal co-operation agreements [2023] OJ C259/1.

298 Commission Notice – Guidelines on the effect on trade concept contained in Articles 81 and 82 of the Treaty [2014] OJ C291/1.

299 Such interpretative communications are of a different nature than communications from the Commission on its enforcement priorities. Whether a communication interprets the law or sets out the Commission's enforcement priorities depends not just on its title but on its content. A single communication may be in part interpretative of the law and in part setting out the Commission's enforcement priorities.

300 Once adopted, an exemption regulation is a binding act of EU law, to be interpreted by the Court of Justice like any other part of EU law; see Article 288 TFEU and Article 19 TEU.

law and what is the Commission's additional interpretation, and does not suggest that the Commission's interpretation is binding.[301] While the Commission's interpretation is without prejudice to the case law of the EU Courts, 'it is not unreasonable to suppose that the Courts are at least influenced by well-reasoned and informed statements that emanate from the Commission'.[302] If the Commission later comes to the view that the interpretation given in one of its communications is not correct, it must communicate its amended views as quickly as possible.[303]

3. Fines

a. *The Commission's discretion*

Article 23(2) of Regulation 1/2003 provides that the Commission 'may by decision impose fines' on undertakings that 'either intentionally or negligently' have infringed Articles 101 or 102 TFEU. For each undertaking, 'the fine shall not exceed 10% of its total turnover in the preceding business year [. . .]. In fixing the amount of the fine, regard shall be had both to the gravity and to the duration of the infringement'.

These provisions leave the Commission a significant degree of discretion. First, the Commission is never obliged to impose fines, even if the conditions allowing it to do so are fulfilled.[304] Second, as to the amount of the fine, according to the case law of the EU Courts, the Commission has 'a particularly wide discretion as regards the choice of factors to be taken into account for the purposes of determining the amount of the fines',[305] as well as a discretion to raise the general level of fines so as to reinforce their deterrent effect.[306] The Commission is however 'bound to comply with general principles of law, in particular the principles of equal treatment and proportionality, as developed by the case-law of the Court of Justice and the [General Court]'.[307]

The EU Courts have commended the Commission 'for having adopted guidelines to direct the exercise of its discretion concerning the fixing of fines, and for thus better

---

301 See Judgment in *France v Commission*, C-57/95, EU:C:1997:164; B. M. P. Smulders, 'Institutional Aspects of European Commission Guidance in the Area of Antitrust Law', *Competition Policy International*, vol 5, no 1, Spring 2009, 25; Commission Guidelines on the application of Article 81(3) of the Treaty [2004] OJ C101/97, paragraph 7; and Judgment in *Visa v Commission*, T-461/07, EU:T:2011:181, paragraph 172.

302 R. Whish and D. Bailey, 'Regulation 330/2010: The Commission's New Block Exemption for Vertical Agreements' (2010) 47 *Common Market Law Review* 1757 at 1760.

303 Opinion of Advocate General Geelhoed in *VW-Audi Forhandlerforenigingen v Skandinavisk Motor*, C-125/05, EU:C:2006:262, paragraph 38.

304 While the Commission must reason its decision to impose a fine, as well as the level at which the fine is set, EU law does not require any reasoning for not imposing a fine; see my book *The Optimal Enforcement of EC Antitrust Law* (Kluwer 2002), section 2.4.1.3 (footnote 88).

305 Judgments in *Showa Denko v Commission*, C-289/04 P, EU:C:2006:431, paragraph 36, and in Case *Danone v Commission*, C-3/06 P, EU:C:2007:88, paragraph 37.

306 Judgments in *Musique Diffusion Française and Others v Commission*, 100/80 to 103/80, EU:C:1983:158, paragraphs 106–109, and in *Aristrain v Commission*, C-196/99 P, EU:C:2003:529, paragraph 81.

307 Judgments in *Evonik Degussa v Commission*, T-279/02, EU:T:2006:103, paragraph 77, and in *Evonik Degussa v Commission*, C-266/06 P, EU:C:2008:295; see further Opinion of Advocate General Tizzano in *Dansk Rørindustri v Commission*, C-189/02 P, EU:C:2004:415, paragraphs 107 to 109, and Judgment in *Ahlström Osakeyhtiö and others v Commission*, C-89/85, C-104/85, C-114/85, C-116/85, C-117/85 and C-125/85 to C-129/85, EU:C:1993:120, paragraphs 196–197, and my paper 'Optimal Antitrust Fines: Theory and Practice' (2006) 29 *World Competition* 183 at 205–206.

ensuring equal treatment of the undertakings concerned'.[308] The Commission has adopted Guidelines on the method of setting fines, in which it sets out its general method for setting fines,[309] a Leniency Notice, in which it offers immunity from fines and reduction of fines to undertakings that voluntarily provide evidence of secret cartels,[310] and a Notice on settlement procedures in cartel cases, offering in appropriate cases a further reduction of fines to undertakings that admit their liability and waive certain procedural rights.[311]

The Court of Justice has held that, 'in adopting [guidelines] and announcing by publishing them that they will henceforth apply to the cases to which they relate, [the Commission] imposes a limit on the exercise of its discretion and cannot depart from those rules under the pain of being found, where appropriate, to be in breach of the general principles of law, such as equal treatment or the protection of legitimate expectations'.[312] While the Guidelines 'may not be regarded as rules of law which [the Commission] is always bound to observe, they nevertheless form rules of practice from which [the Commission] may not depart in an individual case without giving reasons that are compatible with the principle of equal treatment'.[313]

However, 'the self-limitation on the Commission's discretion arising from the adoption of the Guidelines is not incompatible with the Commission's maintaining a substantial margin of discretion. The Guidelines display flexibility in a number of ways, enabling the Commission to exercise its discretion in accordance with the provisions of [Regulation 1/2003], as interpreted by the Court of Justice'.[314]

b. *The General Court's unlimited jurisdiction*

The Commission's discretion with regard to the amount of fines is, however, without prejudice to the exercise by the General Court of its unlimited jurisdiction.[315] Under Article 261 TFEU and Article 31 of Regulation 1/2003, the General Court has 'unlimited

---

308 Judgments in *Metsä-Serla Sales v Commission*, C-298/98 P, EU:C:2000:634, paragraph 57, and in *Danone v Commission*, T-38/02, EU:T:2005:367, paragraph 523; see further my paper 'The European Commission's 2006 Guidelines on Antitrust Fines: A Legal and Economic Analysis' (2007) 30 *World Competition* 197 at 202.

309 Guidelines on the method of setting fines imposed pursuant to Article 23(2)(a) of Regulation No 1/2003 [2006] OJ C210/2; see 'The European Commission's 2006 Guidelines on Antitrust Fines: A Legal and Economic Analysis', as footnote just above.

310 Commission Notice on Immunity from fines and reduction of fines in cartel cases [2006] C298/11; see Chapter V of this book.

311 Commission Notice on the conduct of settlement procedures in view of the adoption of Decisions pursuant to Article 7 and Article 23 of Council Regulation (EC) No 1/2003 in cartel cases [2008] OJ C167/1; see Chapter VI of this book.

312 Judgment in *Dansk Rørindustri and Others v European Commission*, C-189/02 P, C-202/02 P, C-205/02 P to C-208/02 P and C-213/02 P, EU:C:2005:408, paragraph 211. The guidelines thus 'ensure legal certainty for the undertakings concerned'; Judgments in *Evonik Degussa v Commission*, C-266/06 P, EU:C:2008:295, paragraphs 53 and 60, and in *Lafarge v Commission*, C-413/08 P, EU:C:2010:346, paragraph 93.

313 Judgment in *Archer Daniels Midland v Commission*, C-397/03 P, EU:C:2006:328, paragraph 91.

314 Judgments in *Wieland-Werke v Commission*, T-116/04, EU:T:2009:140, paragraph 31, and in *Dansk Rørindustri and Others v European Commission*, C-189/02 P, C-202/02 P, C-205/02 P to C-208/02 P and C-213/02 P, EU:C:2005:408, paragraph 267. While this is clearly the case for the Commission's Guidelines on the method of setting fines, it is much less so for the Leniency Notice and the Notice on settlement procedures in cartel cases, which display much less flexibility.

315 Judgment in *Wieland-Werke v Commission*, T-116/04, EU:T:2009:140, paragraph 33.

jurisdiction' with regard to the fines, allowing it to 'assess [. . .] the appropriateness of the amount of the fine'.[316] On this basis, the General Court has 'unlimited jurisdiction not only to appraise the facts but also to cancel or amend the fine as it sees fit'.[317] It is 'empowered, in addition to carrying out a mere review of the lawfulness of the penalty, to substitute their own appraisal for the Commission's and, consequently, to cancel, reduce or increase the fine or penalty payment imposed'.[318]

Depending on how actively the General Court exercises its powers, this unlimited jurisdiction more or less neutralises the Commission's discretion. There has been some debate in the past as to whether the General Court exercises its full jurisdiction sufficiently.[319] As I have argued elsewhere,[320] the General Court cannot be criticised for not using more often its unlimited jurisdiction to depart from the methodology used by the Commission in setting the initial fine, where either the parties before the Court have not requested such departure, or the Court, when making its own assessment as to the appropriate fine, ends up agreeing with the Commission's methodology.

C. Prioritisation

1. Arguments in favour of prioritisation

At first blush, one may consider that competition authorities should investigate and pursue all cases of alleged or suspected infringements of the antitrust prohibitions that are brought to their attention, thus giving equal consideration to all victims of all antitrust infringements.[321] There are, however, a number of reasons which may justify not dealing with all cases.

a. *Over-inclusiveness of the antitrust prohibitions*

A first possible reason for allowing competition authorities to set priorities as to which cases they pursue is to enable selective non-enforcement of antitrust prohibitions that are considered too broad.

---

316 Judgment in *SCA Holding v Commission*, C-297/98 P, EU:C:2000:633, paragraph 55.

317 Judgment in *Aristrain v Commission*, T-156/94, EU:T:1999:53, paragraph 116, quoting the Report of the French Delegation on the ECSC Treaty on the notion of 'full jurisdiction' as first introduced in that Treaty and later in Article 172 of the EEC Treaty (later Article 229 EC and now Article 261 TFEU).

318 Judgment of 8 December 2011, *Chalkor v Commission*, C-386/10 P, EU:C:2011:815, paragraph 63; see also Judgment of 21 January 2016, *Galp Energía España and Others v Commission*, C-603/13 P, EU:C:2016:38, paragraphs 75 and 76.

319 See in particular B. Vesterdorf, 'The Court of Justice and Unlimited Jurisdiction: What Does it Mean in Practice?', *Global Competition Policy*, June 2009; F. Castillo de la Torre, 'Evidence, Proof and Judicial Review in Cartel Cases' (2009) 32 *World Competition* 505 at 578, and 'The 2006 Guidelines on Fines: Reflections on the Commission's Practice' (2010) 33 *World Competition* 359 at 364 (footnote 30); E. Barbier de La Serre and C. Winckler, 'Legal Issues Regarding Fines Imposed in EU Competition Proceedings' (2010) 1 *Journal of European Competition Law & Practice* 327 at 345–347; D. Bailey, 'Scope of Judicial Review under Article 81 EC' (2004) 41 *Common Market Law Review* 1327 at 1333; and my paper 'The Increased Level of EU Antitrust Fines, Judicial Review, and the European Convention on Human Rights' (2010) 33 *World Competition* 1 at 25–26.

320 See my paper 'The Increased Level of EU Antitrust Fines, Judicial Review, and the European Convention on Human Rights'(2010) 33 *World Competition* 1 at 25–26; see also Chapter IX of this book.

321 See N. Petit, 'How much discretion do, and should, competition authorities enjoy in the course of their enforcement activities? A multi-jurisdictional assessment', *Concurrences* no 1-2010, 44 at 48.

It is inherent in the nature of rules that they may be over-inclusive, covering some cases which do not fit under the rationale justifying the rule.[322] The only way to avoid over-inclusiveness would be to have very narrow prohibitions, which would then inevitably be under-inclusive.

If competition authorities have discretion as to which cases they pursue, they could use this discretion to avoid enforcing the antitrust prohibitions in cases that could technically be brought under the antitrust prohibitions but that would not fit under the rationale of the prohibitions, and where enforcement would thus not be considered desirable.[323]

This use of discretion appears unproblematic where it concerns unforeseeable anomalous cases, for which one can confidently assume that the legislature has not considered them, and that, if they had been considered, the legislature would not have wanted them to be covered.[324]

Far more problematic would be the systematic non-enforcement of the antitrust prohibitions to entire categories of infringements. In the absence of a legislative authorisation to do so, this could be criticised as a usurpation by the competition authority of powers belonging to the legislature or as a failure of the competition authority to carry out its functions.[325]

As mentioned above, the EU Court of Justice has held that the European Commission, when setting its enforcement priorities, 'may not regard as excluded in principle from its purview certain situations which come under the task entrusted to it by the Treaty'.[326] The Commission cannot, for instance, decide to pursue under Article 102 TFEU only exclusionary abuses and not exploitative abuses.

b. *Enforcement costs exceeding enforcement benefits*

A second possible justification for not pursuing all cases of alleged or suspected infringement of the antitrust prohibitions is that the cost of investigating and pursuing a case may exceed the benefits of doing so. Relevant costs here are not only the resources spent by the competition authority and the courts but also the costs borne by the companies defending themselves or responding to information requests.

---

322 See generally F. Schauer, *Playing by the Rules: A Philosophical Examination of Rule-Based Decision-Making in Law and in Life* (Clarendon 1991) and F. Schauer and R. Zeckhauser, 'Regulation by generalization' (2007) 1 *Regulation & Governance* 68; see also Opinion of Advocate General Kokott in *T-Mobile Netherlands*, C-8/08, EU:C:2009:110, paragraph 47.

323 See O. Odudu, 'Developing private enforcement in the EU: Lessons from the Roberts Court' (2008) 53 *Antitrust Bulletin* 873 at 885–886, and more generally W. M. Landes and R. A. Posner, 'The Private Enforcement of Law' (1975) 4 *Journal of Legal Studies* 1 at 38–41.

324 See J. Vorenberg, 'Decent Restraint of Prosecutorial Power' (1981) 94 *Harvard Law Review* 1521 at 1551, and G. E. Lynch, 'Our Administrative System of Criminal Justice' (1998) 66 *Fordham Law Review* 2117 at 2138.

325 See S. Schauer, *Playing by the Rules: A Philosophical Examination of Rule-Based Decision-Making in Law and in Life* (Clarendon 1991), at 158–162, and M. E. Stucke, 'Better Competition Advocacy' (2008) 82 *St John's Law Review* 951 at 954, and compare with W. E. Kovacic, 'The Modern Evolution of U.S. Competition Policy Enforcement Norms' (2003) 71 *Antitrust Law Journal* 377 at 414.

326 Judgments in *Ufex and Others v Commission*, C-119/97 P, EU:C:1999:116.

Should a competition authority for instance spend a million euros to investigate price fixing in a market worth ten thousand euros?[327] Not if the investigation yields no benefits beyond the market concerned, either in terms of deterrence of others or in terms of clarification of the law. Very often the main benefit of enforcement action in a given case lies, however, precisely in the deterrent and precedent effect beyond the case concerned,[328] and the size of those benefits is usually difficult to assess.[329]

c. *Limited enforcement resources*

A third possible reason for a competition authority not to investigate and pursue all cases of alleged or suspected infringements is that the authority's limited resources may not allow it to do so.

As the English High Court held in *Cityhook*: 'The allocation of limited resources in pursuit of statutory objectives necessarily involves the establishment of priorities for administrative action.'[330]

Whether or not the resources of a competition authority allow it to deal with all the complaints it receives is, of course, a factual question. Some competition authorities may have larger budgets than others. And a competition authority may receive more or fewer complaints depending on many factors, including the general awareness of the antitrust prohibitions and of the possibility of bringing complaints, the cost and effectiveness of private litigation, the formal and evidentiary requirements imposed on complainants, and the reputation of and trust in the competition authority.

That it is not inconceivable that competition authorities deal with all complaints is shown by the example of the French Autorité de la concurrence, which, until the French transposition of Directive 2019/1,[331] was obliged to deal with all complaints brought before it, without a particularly large budget, and that time topped the list of European competition authorities in terms of the number of decisions taken under Articles 101 and 102 TFEU.[332]

---

327 D. W. Carlton, 'How should Economic Evidence be Presented and Evaluated?', paper presented at the 14th Annual EU Competition Law and Policy Workshop (EUI, Florence, 19–20 June 2009), forthcoming in C.-D. Ehlermann and M. Marquis (eds), *European Competition Law Annual 2009: Evaluation of Evidence and its Judicial Review in Competition Cases* (Hart 2010), at 2.

328 See UK Office of Fair Trading, 'The Deterrent Effect of Competition Enforcement by the OFT: a report prepared for the OFT by Deloitte' (2007).

329 See M. A. Bergman, 'Quis Custodiet Ipsos Custodes? Or Measuring and Evaluating the Effectiveness of Competition Enforcement' (2008) 156 *De Economist* 387.

330 Judgment of 20 January 2009, *Cityhook v OFT* [2009] EWHC 57 (Admin), paragraph 89; see also Judgment in *Automec v Commission*, T-24/90, EU:T:1992:97, paragraph 77.

331 Directive (EU) 2019/1 of the European Parliament and of the Council of 11 December 2018 to empower the competition authorities of the Member States to be more effective enforcers and to ensure the proper functioning of the internal market [2019] OJ L11/3; see further my paper 'Competition authorities: Towards more independence and prioritisation? The European Commission's "ECN+" Proposal for a Directive to empower the competition authorities of the Member States to be more effective enforcers', *Concurrences* no 4-2017, 60, also accessible at http://ssrn.com/author=456087, and L. Idot, 'Reform of Regulation 1/2003: Power to set priorities', *Concurrences* no 3-2015, 51.

332 See B. Lasserre, 'La nouvelle Autorité de la concurrence – Interview', *Concurrences* no 1-2009, and 'An interview with Bruno Lasserre', *Global Competition Review*, August/September 2010 (vol 13, no 8).

The obligation to deal with all complaints may have the beneficial effect of forcing competition authorities to work harder and be more productive.[333]

d. *Unrepresentativeness of complaints and leniency applications*

Even if it is possible for a competition authority to pursue all the complaints it receives, it may still be undesirable to do so if the complaints received only concern certain types of infringements and the resources spent on pursuing these complaints mean that insufficient resources remain to pursue *ex officio* other types of infringements of similar or even greater importance.

Complaints are for instance more likely to be brought by competitors affected by exclusionary practices than by victims of exploitative practices, such as secret price cartels, who may not even be aware of the infringement.

Similarly, obliging a competition authority to deal with all cartel cases in which it receives leniency applications may lead to an excessive focus on those types of cartels that are more prone to leniency applications.[334]

e. *Deterrence through infrequently imposed high penalties*

A fifth possible justification for not pursuing all cases of suspected antitrust infringements is that it may be possible to achieve the same level of deterrence at a lower cost by pursuing fewer infringements but punishing these more harshly.

Under the standard economic model of deterrence, deterrence requires that, from the perspective of the company contemplating whether or not to commit a violation, the expected fine or other penalty exceeds the expected gain from the violation. Given that the expected penalty equals the nominal amount of the penalty discounted by the probability that a penalty is effectively imposed, deterrence can be achieved through different combinations of the level of penalties and of the probability of detection and punishment. Since the detection and prosecution of antitrust violations have a significant administrative cost, elementary economic reasoning would call for a strategy of very high penalties that are only rarely imposed.[335]

As I have argued in more detail elsewhere,[336] there are, however, two (sets of) reasons why this strategy may not be optimal, or could at least not be carried too far. The first possible reason relates to the psychological phenomenon of availability bias.[337] If com-

---

333 See N. Garoupa, 'Some reflections on the economics of prosecutors: Mandatory vs. selective prosecution' (2009) 29 *International Review of Law and Economics* 25.

334 See H. W. Friederiszick and F. P. Maier-Rigaud, 'Triggering inspections ex officio: Moving beyond a passive EU cartel policy' (2008) 4 *Journal of Competition Law and Economics* 89. It is also important for competition authorities to continue detecting cartels otherwise than through leniency because leniency can only work if potential leniency applicants believe that the authority risks detecting the cartel or at least believe that at least one other cartel participant may believe so; see further my paper 'Leniency in Antitrust Enforcement: Theory and Practice' (2007) 30 *World Competition* 25 at 47–48, and Chapters V and XVIII of this book.

335 See G. S. Becker, 'Crime and Punishment: An Economic Approach' (1968) 76 *Journal of Political Economy* 169.

336 See my paper 'Optimal Antitrust Fines: Theory and Practice' (2006) 29 *World Competition* 183 at 195–199.

337 See R. B. Korobkin and T. S. Ulen, 'Law and Behavioral Science: Removing the Rationality Assumption from Law and Economics' (2000) 88 *California Law Review* 1051, at 1085–1090 and A. Tversky and D. Kahneman, 'Availability: A Heuristic for Judging Frequency and Probability', in D. Kahneman, P. Slovic and A. Tversky (eds), *Judgment under Uncertainty: Heuristics and Biases* (Cambridge UP 1982), 163.

panies or individual decision-makers are biased in their estimates of the probability of detection and punishment and of the amount of the penalty in that they rely disproportionately on those incidents that can easily be brought to mind, because they are recent, happened close to them, or were well publicised, a strategy of very high penalties that are rarely imposed may make sense in that the very high amounts of the penalties imposed may give them more publicity and thus make them more memorable. On the other hand, a sufficient frequency of punishment would seem more efficient, assuming that if a company (or the individual decision-maker within the company) knows of a company which has been punished for a comparable antitrust violation, this information is likely to be available and thus to cause an overestimate of the probability of being fined.[338]

The second set of reasons why a strategy of very high fines combined with a low probability of detection and punishment may not be optimal, or could at least not be carried too far, is that very high fines may be problematic in several respects, in particular because they risk exceeding the ceiling of companies' ability to pay, because high fines, even if they do not exceed the ability to pay, may have substantial social and economic costs, and because they may be unacceptable from the perspective of proportional justice.[339]

f. *Other enforcers are better placed*

A sixth possible reason for a competition authority not to pursue every case of alleged or suspected infringement that comes to its attention is that another enforcer may be better placed to deal with the case.

This reason is particularly relevant for the European Commission. Article 35 of Regulation 1/2003 obliges all EU Member States to designate and empower national competition authorities responsible for the application of Articles 101 and 102 TFEU. National competition authorities are often closer to the markets concerned and may be able to act more quickly and at lower cost, inter alia for language reasons.[340]

In its Notice on cooperation within the Network of Competition Authorities,[341] the Commission has explained that it considers itself particularly well placed to deal with a case if the practices concerned have effects in more than three Member States or if the EU interest requires the adoption of a Commission decision to develop the law when a new competition issue arises.[342]

It may also be justified for a competition authority not to deal with certain cases because they can be dealt with better through private litigation.[343]

---

338 R.B. Korobkin and T.S. Ulen, 'Law and Behavioral Science: Removing the Rationality Assumption from Law and Economics' (2000) 88 *California Law Review* 1051, at 1089.

339 See further my paper 'Optimal Antitrust Fines: Theory and Practice' (2006) 29 *World Competition* 183, at 196–199.

340 See further my book *Principles of European Antitrust Enforcement* (Hart 2005), section 1.1.4.3.4.

341 [2004] OJ C101/3.

342 Paragraphs 14 and 15; see further my book *Principles of European Antitrust Enforcement* (Hart 2005), section 1.2.5.

343 See Judgments in *Automec v Commission*, T-24/90, EU:T:1992:97, paragraphs 87 to 96; in *BEMIM v Commission*, T-114/92, EU:T:1995:11, paragraphs 86–93; and in *CEAHR v Commission*, T-427/08, EU:T:2010:517, paragraph 174–176; on private litigation, see chapter XVII of this book.

2. Prioritisation risks

While there are thus a number of reasons for allowing competition authorities to set priorities as to which cases of alleged or suspected infringements of the antitrust prohibitions they deal with, there are also some risks related to prioritisation.[344]

a. *Arbitrariness or discrimination risk*

The first risk is that competition authorities abuse their discretion and select cases on the basis of criteria unrelated to either optimal antitrust enforcement or efficient resource allocation. As far as refusals to pursue complaints are concerned, this risk can be controlled by requiring the competition authority to give reasons for its decisions not to pursue a complaint, and to allow limited judicial review of these rejection decisions. As mentioned above, this is the case for the European Commission.[345]

b. *Short-sightedness risks*

As the individuals taking decisions in competition authorities are, like everyone else, subject to the psychological phenomenon of availability bias,[346] and as competition authorities and the individuals working in them are also likely to be judged by others primarily on the basis of the most readily visible output, there is a risk of excessive focus on whatever is immediate and apparently big.[347]

There is in particular a risk of only dealing with big cases in big markets, while seemingly smaller cases in smaller markets may actually be equally or more important, because they occur more frequently and intervention in some small cases could have considerable deterrence and precedent effects for many other cases.[348]

c. *Predictability risk*

Where a competition authority announces in advance that it will focus its enforcement activity on particular sectors of the economy or types of practices, such announcements

---

344 See also the above-mentioned risk of competition authorities working less hard when not obliged to deal with all the cases brought to their attention.

345 The review should be limited, so as not to annihilate the discretion and transfer the power to set priorities from the competition authority to the reviewing court. As a matter of comparative institutional competence, competition authorities are manifestly better placed than courts to make judgments of optimal enforcement and efficient resource allocation.

346 R. B. Korobkin and T. S. Ulen, 'Law and Behavioral Science: Removing the Rationality Assumption from Law and Economics' (2000) 88 *California Law Review* 1051, at 1085–1090 and A. Tversky and D. Kahneman, 'Availability: A Heuristic for Judging Frequency and Probability', in D. Kahneman, P. Slovic and A. Tversky (eds), *Judgment under Uncertainty: Heuristics and Biases* (Cambridge UP 1982), 163.

347 As to the risk of excessive use of settlements, which bring an immediate result in the specific case, as compared to the later and less visible deterrent and precedent benefits of fully litigating a case, see Chapter VI of this book and my papers 'The Use of Settlements in Public Antitrust Enforcement: Objectives and Principles' (2008) 31 *World Competition* 335 at 341–348, and 'Settlements of EU Antitrust Investigations: Commitment Decisions under Article 9 of Regulation No. 1/2003' (2006) 29 *World Competition* 345 at 348–352, and S. Baker and C. Mezzetti, 'Prosecutorial Resources, Plea Bargaining, and the Decision to Go to Trial' (2001) 17 *Journal of Law, Economics & Organization* 149 at 166.

348 See also M. A. Bergman, 'Quis Custodiet Ipsos Custodes? Or Measuring and Evaluating the Effectiveness of Competition Enforcement' (2008) 156 *De Economist* 387, at 404.

risk not only allowing the infringers in the sectors concerned better to prepare themselves by concealing the evidence of infringements, but also being taken by businesses in other sectors as a signal that they can do what they want without fear of attracting the attention of the competition authority.

Similarly, where a perception arises that competition authorities are only interested in dealing with big cases involving large companies in big markets, this risks having a negative deterrent effect on smaller companies and on companies active in smaller markets.[349]

d. *Prioritisation process risks*

The process of prioritisation itself may consume substantial resources. Where a competition authority employs people specifically to work on prioritisation, these people could alternatively be employed as case handlers, allowing more cases to be pursued. Similarly, where case teams have to spend a significant part of their time verifying and justifying the priority status of their cases, they can deal with fewer cases. Finally, where prioritisation decisions are not taken by the case-handling divisions but by others within the competition authority, there may also be a risk of negative motivational effects on the case handlers.

All these risks can, of course, be mitigated in a well-managed competition authority.

349 See UK National Audit Office, 'The Office of Fair Trading: Progress Report on Maintaining Competition in Markets', HC 127 Session 2008–2009, 5 March 2009, at 6.

V. The Use of Leniency in EU Cartel Enforcement: An Assessment after more than Twenty Years

Since 1996, the European Commission has been operating a leniency programme, under which companies cooperating with its cartel investigations can obtain immunity from fines or a reduction of fines. Leniency plays a prominent role in EU cartel enforcement today. This chapter assesses the positive effects and the possible negative effects of leniency, in the light of more than twenty years of experience.

A. Introduction

1. Overview of the applicable provisions

According to the definition provided by the EU legislator, a 'leniency programme' is 'a programme [. . .] on the basis of which a participant in a secret cartel, independently of the other undertakings involved in the cartel, cooperates with an investigation of the competition authority, by voluntarily providing presentations regarding that participant's knowledge of, and role in, the cartel in return for which that participant receives [. . .] immunity from, or a reduction in, fines for its involvement in the cartel'.[350]

The European Commission adopted its first Leniency Notice in 1996.[351] This initial

---

350 Article 2(15) of Directive 2014/104/EU of the European Parliament and of the Council of 26 November 2014 on certain rules governing actions for damages under national law for infringements of the competition law provisions of the Member States and of the European Union [2014] OJ L349/1. Article 2(14) of the same Directive defines 'cartel' as 'an agreement or concerted practice between two or more competitors aimed at coordinating their competitive behaviour on the market or influencing the relevant parameters of competition through practices such as, but not limited to, the fixing or coordination of purchase or selling prices or other trading conditions, including in relation to intellectual property rights, the allocation of production or sales quota, the sharing of markets and customers, including bid-rigging, restrictions of imports or exports or anti-competitive actions against other competitors'.

351 Commission Notice on the non-imposition or reduction of fines in cartel cases [1996] OJ C207/4. For a detailed analysis of this 1996 Leniency Notice, see my paper 'The Commission Notice on the Non-Imposition or Reduction of Fines in Cartel Cases: A Legal and Economic Analysis' (1997) 22 *European Law Review* 125. The 1996 Leniency Notice was clearly inspired by the US Department of Justice's Corporate Leniency Policy of 1993. This was even more visible in the earlier draft notice, which was published by the European Commission as part of the consultation procedure preceding the adoption of the 1996 Leniency Notice; [1995] OJ C341/13. The contemporary practice of leniency in antitrust enforcement is generally considered to have been started by the US Department of Justice in 1978, when it adopted its first Corporate Leniency Policy. The basic idea of granting immunity or a reduced penalty in exchange for cooperation to help convict co-conspirators is, however, probably as old as criminal prosecution; see N. K. Katyal, 'Conspiracy Theory' (2003) 112 *Yale Law Journal* 1307, at 1330–1331, referring to practices in English law going back to the early 12th century, as well as in early American law. The European Commission had already in a number of cases before 1996 reduced fines or even abstained from imposing fines in recognition of cooperation received. Examples of reduced fines include Decision of 19 December 1984, *Wood Pulp* [1985] OJ L85/1, paragraph 148; Decision of 24 April 1986, *Polypropylene* [1986] OJ L230/1, paragraph 109; and Decision of 13 July 1994, *Cartonboard* [1994]

Leniency Notice was replaced by a new one in 2002.[352] The main changes were that immunity became automatic, and that fine reductions became more strictly aligned to the timing of the cooperation.[353] In 2006 the European Commission again amended its Leniency Notice, mainly to clarify the threshold for immunity in terms of information to be provided and to clarify the duty of cooperation of all leniency applicants.[354]

The 2006 Leniency Notice, as currently applicable, provides as follows:

- The European Commission will grant **immunity** from any fine that would otherwise have been imposed to an undertaking disclosing its participation in a cartel if that undertaking is the **first to submit information and evidence** which, in the Commission's view, will enable it to carry out a targeted inspection in connection with the cartel, and if, at the time of the application for immunity, the Commission did not yet have sufficient evidence to adopt a decision to carry out an inspection and had not yet carried out such an inspection.[355]
- The immunity applicant must provide the Commission with a **leniency corporate statement**,[356] which may be written or oral and which must include, in so far as it is known to the applicant at the time of the submission, a detailed description of the cartel arrangement, as well as other evidence relating to the alleged cartel in possession of the applicant or available to it at the time of the submission, including in particular any evidence contemporaneous to the infringement.[357]

OJ L243/1, paragraphs 169–171. In its Decision of 1 April 1992, *French-West African Shipowners' Committees* [1992] OJ L134/1, paragraph 74, sub (e), the European Commission decided that 'there are grounds for exempting from fines the four shipping companies which although members of the committees contributed in drawing the attention of the Commission to the practices dealt with in this decision'. For more details on the history of leniency, see my paper 'Leniency in Antitrust Enforcement: Theory and Practice' (2007) 30 *World Competition* 25, also accessible at http://ssrn.com/author=456087, and A. O'Brien, 'Leadership of Leniency', in C. Beaton-Wells and C. Tran (eds), *Anti-Cartel Enforcement in a Contemporary Age Leniency Religion* (Hart 2015), 17.

352 Commission Notice on immunity from fines and reduction of fines in cartel cases [2002] OJ C45/3.

353 See F. Arbault and F. Peiró, 'The Commission's new notice on immunity and reduction of fines in cartel cases: building on success', *EC Competition Policy Newsletter*, June 2002, 15–22, accessible at http://ec.europa.eu/comm/competition/publications/cpn/cpn2002_2.pdf.

354 Commission Notice on immunity from fines and reduction of fines in cartel cases [2006] OJ C298/17.

355 Idem, points 8(a) and 10. On what information is needed to carry out a targeted inspection, see Judgment in *EGL and Others v Commission*, T-251/12, EU:T:2016:114, paragraphs 148–169. Contrary to the US Department of Justice's Corporate Leniency Policy, immunity under the European Commission's Leniency Notice does not mean absence of prosecution. The Commission will normally still adopt a decision finding an infringement of Article 101 TFEU. The fact that the undertaking cooperated with the Commission during its administrative procedure will be indicated in the decision, so as to explain the non-imposition of a fine; see 2006 Leniency Notice, point 38.

356 The term 'leniency corporate statement' is defined in Article 4a of Commission Regulation (EC) No 773/2004 of 7 April 2004 relating to the conduct of proceedings by the Commission pursuant to Articles 81 and 82 of the EC Treaty [2004] OJ L123/18, as amended by Commission Regulation (EU) 2015/1348 of 3 August 2015 [2015] OJ L208/3, as a 'voluntary presentation of [the undertaking's] knowledge of a secret cartel and [its] role therein, which may also be in the form of voluntary presentations of the knowledge of former or current employees or representatives of the undertaking', 'drawn up specifically for submission to the Commission with a view to obtaining immunity from or reduction of fines under the Commission's leniency programme'.

357 2006 Leniency Notice, point 9.

- If no undertaking has been granted immunity on the above ground, the Commission will alternatively grant immunity to the undertaking that is the first to submit information and evidence that will enable the Commission to find an infringement of Article 101 TFEU in connection with the cartel, provided that the Commission did not yet have, at the time of the submission, enough evidence to make such a finding. The undertaking must provide the Commission with contemporaneous, incriminating evidence of the alleged cartel as well as a leniency corporate statement.[358]
- A number of **additional conditions** must be met in any case to qualify for immunity: the undertaking must cooperate genuinely, fully, on a continuous basis and expeditiously from the time it submits its application throughout the Commission's administrative procedure; and the undertaking must have ended its involvement in the cartel immediately following its application, except for what would, in the Commission's view, be reasonably necessary to preserve the integrity of the inspections.[359] Moreover, an undertaking that took steps to coerce other undertakings to join the cartel or to remain in it is not eligible for immunity.[360]
- Undertakings disclosing their participation in a cartel that do not meet the conditions for immunity may still be eligible for a **reduction** from any **fine** that would otherwise have been imposed, if they provide the European Commission with evidence that represents **significant added value** compared to the evidence already in the European Commission's possession, and provided that they fulfil the same conditions of genuine, full cooperation and termination of the infringement as applicable to immunity applicants.[361]
- The first undertaking to provide such significant added value will receive a reduction of 30 to 50% of the fine that would otherwise have been imposed, the second undertaking a reduction of 20 to 30%, and subsequent undertakings a reduction of up to 20%.[362]
- The degree of added value depends on the extent to which the evidence provided strengthens, by its very nature and/or its level of detail, the European Commission's

358 2006 Leniency Notice, points 8(b) and 11.

359 2006 Leniency Notice, points 12 and 22. If the undertaking does not meet these conditions, it cannot qualify for a fine reduction either.

360 2006 Leniency Notice, point 13. Such an undertaking may, however, still qualify for a fine reduction if it fulfils all the relevant requirements and conditions.

361 2006 Leniency Notice, points 23 and 24. In the United States, second and subsequent applicants cannot qualify for reduced sanctions under the leniency programme, but they can enter into plea agreements with the Department of Justice, which reward them for their cooperation; see my paper 'Leniency in Antitrust Enforcement: Theory and Practice' (2007) 30 *World Competition* 25, also accessible at http://ssrn.com/author=456087, at footnotes 15 to 25; A. O'Brien, 'Leadership of Leniency', in C. Beaton-Wells and C. Tran (eds), *Anti-Cartel Enforcement in a Contemporary Age Leniency Religion* (Hart 2015), 17, at 28; and OECD Policy Roundtable, *Leniency for Subsequent Applicants* (2012), available at http://www.oecd.org/competition/Leniencyforsubsequentapplicants2012.pdf. Plea bargaining in the United States is simultaneously an investigatory tool and a way to dispose of cases, and hence corresponds to the combination of (the reduction-of-fine part of) leniency and settlements in the European Commission's cartel enforcement. On settlements, see Chapter V of this book.

362 2006 Leniency Notice, point 26.

> ability to prove the infringement. The degree of corroboration from other sources required for the evidence submitted to be relied upon against other undertakings involved in the cartel will have an impact on the value of that evidence, so that compelling evidence will be attributed a greater value than uncorroborated or simply corroborating statements.[363]

Guidance as to the normal amount of the fine, and thus the size of the reduction in absolute terms available under the Leniency Notice, can be found in the European Commission's Fining Guidelines. Indeed, the desire to offer potential leniency applicants a somewhat higher degree of predictability as to the amount of the fines normally imposed was among the reasons why the Commission adopted in 1998 its first Fining Guidelines,[364] and why it replaced these in 2006 with the currently applicable Fining Guidelines.[365]

In 2008, the European Commission introduced a cartel settlement procedure, under which, in cases deemed suitable by the Commission, undertakings can obtain an additional fine reduction of 10% if they make a formal settlement submission, containing a recognition of the infringement and of the undertaking's liability for it, acceptance of a range of likely fines, and a waiver of some procedural rights.[366]

The European Commission's Leniency Notice, Fining Guidelines and cartel settlement procedure only apply to the European Commission's own cartel enforcement.

Following the example of the European Commission, most EU Member States' competition authorities have also introduced a leniency programme, starting with the British and German competition authorities in 2000. The leniency programmes of the European Commission and of the various national competition authorities are autonomous and independent of each other.[367] They are, however, broadly similar. The European Competition Network (ECN) adopted a first ECN Model Leniency Programme in 2006 and a second,

---

363 2006 Leniency Notice, point 25.

364 Guidelines on the method of setting fines imposed pursuant to Article 15(2) of Regulation No 17 and Article 65(5) of the ECSC Treaty [1998] OJ C9/3. For a detailed analysis of these guidelines, see my paper 'The Commission's New Method for Calculating Fines in Antitrust Cases' (1998) 23 *European Law Review* 125 and Chapter 4 of my book *The Optimal Enforcement of EC Antitrust Law – Essays in Law and Economics* (Kluwer 2002).

365 Guidelines on the method of setting fines imposed pursuant to Article 23(2)(a) of Regulation No 1/2003 [2006] OJ C210/2. For a detailed analysis, see my paper 'The European Commission's 2006 Guidelines on Antitrust Fines: A Legal and Economic Analysis' (2007) 30 *World Competition* 197, also accessible at http://ssrn.com/author=456087. On the complex relationship between the foreseeability of fines and their deterrent and other enforcement effects, see my paper 'The European Commission's 2006 Guidelines on Antitrust Fines: A Legal and Economic Analysis', as just above, at 204–206.

366 See Article 10a of Commission Regulation (EC) No 773/2004 of 7 April 2004 relating to the conduct of proceedings by the Commission pursuant to Articles 81 and 82 of the EC Treaty [2004] OJ L123/18, as amended by Commission Regulation (EC) No 622/2008 of 30 June 2008 amending Regulation (EC) No 773/2004, as regards the conduct of settlement procedures in cartel cases [2008] OJ L171/3 (further amended in 2015 by Commission Regulation (EU) 2015/1348 [2015] OJ L208/3), and Commission Notice on the conduct of settlement procedures in view of the adoption of Decisions pursuant to Article 7 and Article 23 of Council Regulation (EC) No 1/2003 in cartel cases [2008] OJ C167/1 (amended in 2015 by a Communication from the Commission [2015] OJ C256/2). For an analysis of the cartel settlement procedure, see Chapter VI of this book.

367 See Judgment in *DHL Express*, C-428/14, EU:C:2016:27, and Opinion of Advocate General Wathelet in the same case, EU:C:2015:587.

revised one in 2012. This soft harmonisation was later replaced by Directive (EU) 2019/1, which obliged each EU Member State to have a leniency programme and harmonised the content of these leniency programmes along the lines of the European Commission's Leniency Notice.[368]

In addition to the harmonisation of the leniency programmes of the national competition authorities, Directive 2019/1 also provides for a system of summary applications before national competition authorities by applicants that have applied to the European Commission for leniency, provided that the leniency application to the European Commission covers more than three Member States.[369]

2. Some statistics

Table 3 below contains, for the thirty-five-year period 1986–2020, divided into periods of five years, the total number of decisions in which the European Commission imposed fines for cartel infringements,[370] and the number of these decisions in which immunity was granted under the European Commission's leniency programme to the first undertaking cooperating.[371]

368 Directive (EU) 2019/1 of the European Parliament and of the Council of 11 December 2018 to empower the competition authorities of the Member States to be more effective enforcers and to ensure the proper functioning of the internal market [2019] OJ L11/3, Chapter VI.

369 Article 22 of Directive 2019/1.

370 The statistics are of my own making, based on the information about individual decisions available on the European Commission's website, http://ec.europa.eu/competition/cartels/cases/cases.html. The full list of the cases I have counted for the 1986–2015 period can be found in the annex to my paper 'The Use of Leniency in EU Cartel Enforcement: An Assessment After Twenty Years' (2016) 39 *World Competition* 327, also accessible at http://ssrn.com/author=456087. For the period 2016–2020, see the annex to my paper 'Regulation 1/2003: An Assessment After Twenty Years' (2023) 46 *World Competition* 3, also accessible at http://ssrn.com/author=456087. I have counted decisions as initially adopted by the European Commission, ignoring possible later annulments by the EU Courts (as well as possible re-adoptions of decisions by the Commission following such annulments). In a number of cases (as identified by a single case number, reflecting a single investigation and set of administrative proceedings conducted by the Commission), the decision contains the finding of several infringements, for instance eight infringements in the 2001 decision in Case 37.512 *Vitamins*, or seven infringements in the 2013 decision in Case 39.861 *Yen Interest Rate Derivatives*. I have counted each of those cases as a single case, and I have done the same for cases where, following a single investigation, the Commission split the case into two decisions (1990 decisions in Case 33.133 *Soda-ash* and 2014 decisions in Case 39.924 *Swiss Franc Interest Rate Derivatives*). Where, for the same cartel, two decisions, covering different undertakings party to that cartel, were taken in different years, I have included only the decision covering more than half of the undertakings concerned (for instance the 2013 decision in Case 39.861 *Yen Interest Rate Derivatives*, the 2014 decisions in Case 39.792 *Steel Abrasives* and Case 39.965 *Mushrooms*, and the 2016 decision in Case 39.914 *Euro Interest Rate Derivatives*).

371 Including cases in which a 'very substantial reduction' or a 'substantial reduction' of the fine was granted under the 1996 Leniency Notice. Indeed, the 1996 Leniency Notice did not guarantee complete immunity to the first undertaking cooperating. In practice, however, the Commission invariably granted a 100% reduction as 'very substantial fine reduction'. Also included is the one case (2001 decision in Case 36.490 *Graphite Electrodes*) in which the Commission granted a 'substantial reduction' under the 1996 Leniency Notice, at the maximum rate of 75%, because immunity would also have been granted in that case if the 2002 Leniency Notice or the 2006 Leniency Notice had been applicable.

Table 3: European Commission cartel decisions with fines

Period	Total number of European Commission cartel decisions with fines	Number of decisions in which immunity was granted under the European Commission's leniency programme to the first undertaking cooperating
1986–1990	9	0
1991–1995	8	0
1996–2000	10	1
2001–2005	33	20
2006–2010	31	25
2011–2015	23	21
2016–2020	17	17

For the 1986–1990 and 1991–1995 periods, no decisions are listed in the right-hand column of Table 3 because the European Commission's leniency programme only started with the 1996 Leniency Notice. In the 1996–2000 period, there was only one decision in which immunity was granted, reflecting the time lag between applications for immunity and final decisions at the end of the European Commission's administrative proceedings.

As a percentage of the total number of cartel decisions with fines, the above figures correspond to an increase in the number of decisions involving immunity under the European Commission's leniency programme from 10% (1 out of 10) in the 1996–2000 period, over 61% (20 out of 33) in the 2001–2005 period, 81% (25 out of 31) in the 2006–2010 period, and 91% (21 out of 23) in the 2011–2015 period, to 100% (17 out of 17) in the 2016–2020 period.

In most of the cases in which an undertaking received immunity from fines under the European Commission's leniency programme, a 30 to 50% reduction of the fine was also granted to a second undertaking under the leniency programme. In many cases, a 20 to 30% reduction was also granted to a third undertaking, and in a number of cases, reductions of up to 20% to further undertakings. Also, in many of the cases in which no undertaking received immunity from fines, reductions of the fine on account of leniency were granted to one or more undertakings.[372]

A statistical study of 52 European Commission cartel decisions adopted between 1 May 2004 and 1 May 2014 found that in 94% of these cases, at least one undertaking had applied for leniency, that, of the 333 undertakings involved in all 52 cases, 56% had applied for leniency and 46% were granted leniency, including 11% immunity, and that on average the fines of the 186 undertakings that applied for leniency were reduced by

372 For instance, in the most recent case in the 1986–2020 period in which no immunity was granted, four of the five undertakings fined received reductions of respectively 50%, 25% and 10% on account of leniency; see Summary of Commission Decision of 10 December 2014 in Case AT.39780 *Envelopes* [2015] OJ C74/5 at 7.

37.8%. For the whole sample of 333 undertakings, the average fine reduction on account of leniency thus amounted to 21.1%.[373]

Leniency thus clearly plays a prominent role in EU cartel enforcement today.

B. Positive effects of leniency

1. Improved collection of intelligence and evidence

In order to be able to punish cartels, competition authorities need intelligence of the existence of the cartel, and evidence sufficient for the penalties to be upheld in court.

Competition authorities can try to obtain the necessary intelligence and evidence from three possible sources. First, they could themselves monitor markets, observing publicly available information and data, and possibly use economic analysis of these data to try to detect and prove antitrust infringement. For cartels, this first method has not been very important in practice. Economic evidence is generally insufficient in court to establish collusion, and, at least in jurisdictions with a history of successful cartel enforcement,[374] screening for cartels appears difficult.[375]

Secondly, competition authorities could obtain information from third parties. Customers or competitors harmed by antitrust violations may bring complaints to the authorities,[376] and third parties may otherwise volunteer to provide information. As Donald Baker has put it: 'The desire for revenge is more picturesque, but it is still very much present. In my experience, disgruntled current employees, fired employees, former trade association officials, and even ex-spouses and ex-lovers may be anxious to finger the individuals who they think have done them in.'[377]

The third, and usually best, source of information is the companies and individuals that have committed the antitrust violations themselves. For secret cartels, the undertakings that have committed the violations and their staff may be the only ones holding the information that competition authorities need to detect and punish the violations.

The European Commission could try to obtain the information necessary to detect and punish cartels from the companies concerned by using its investigatory powers, in particular requests for information and inspections.[378] The use of these instruments is, however,

---

373 S. Broos, A. Gautier, J. Marcos Ramos and N. Petit, 'Analyse statistique des affaires d'ententes dans l'UE (2004-2014)' (2016) 67 *Revue économique* 79 at 85.

374 In jurisdictions where cartels have until recently not been prohibited or at least not successfully prosecuted, traces of their existence are likely to be much easier to detect.

375 See OECD Policy Roundtable, *Ex officio cartel investigations and the use of screens to detect cartels* (2013), available at http://www.oecd.org/daf/competition/exofficio-cartel-investigation-2013.pdf.

376 See European Commission's Notice on the handling of complaints by the Commission under articles 81 and 82 of the EC Treaty [2004] OJ C101/5.

377 D. I. Baker, 'The Use of Criminal Law Remedies to Deter and Punish Cartels and Bid-Rigging' (2001) 69 *George Washington Law Review* 693 at 708.

378 Article 18 and Articles 20 and 21 of Regulation 1/2003. For a detailed legal and economic analysis of the European Commission's investigatory powers and their limitations, see my paper 'Self-incrimination in EC Antitrust Enforcement: A Legal and Economic Analysis' (2003) 26 *World Competition* 567, also accessible at http://ssrn.com/author=456087.

legally only possible if the European Commission already has a relatively precise indicia of the suspected cartel infringement.[379] In the absence of full cooperation by the companies concerned, the use of these investigatory powers is also difficult and consumes much time and administrative resources.[380] In jurisdictions with a history of successful cartel enforcement, cartelists will also have learnt their lessons and take great care to minimise written traces of their conspiracies.

The leniency programme significantly reduces the difficulty, time and administrative cost of collecting intelligence and evidence of cartel infringements, as the European Commission receives the assistance of the leniency applicants, through their leniency applications and their continuing cooperation during the administrative procedure.

This allows the European Commission to detect and punish more cartels, while keeping the resources spent on cartel enforcement constant. It may also allow cartel investigations to be completed faster, and to be more extensive and more thorough, in that more and stronger evidence can be obtained, thus also enabling the imposition of higher fines.[381]

The statistics in Table 3 above confirm that the introduction of the leniency programme has indeed allowed the European Commission to significantly increase the number of cartels detected and punished. Indeed, the comparison between the figures for the 1996–2000 period and the figures for the 2001–2005 period shows that the number of cartel decisions tripled following the introduction of the leniency programme.

There can be no doubt that this tripling of the number of cartel decisions has significantly increased deterrence.[382] Indeed, increasing the probability of detection and punishment is a very effective method to increase deterrence.[383]

2. Increased difficulty of creating and maintaining cartels

Setting up and maintaining a successful cartel requires effort. The cartel members have to select and coordinate their behaviour on mutually consistent, collusive strategies,

---

379 See Judgments in *HeidelbergCement v Commission*, C-247/14 P, EU:C:2016:149 and in *Nexans v Commission*, T-135/09, EU:T:2012:596.

380 Their use is also limited by the privilege against self-incrimination, which prohibits the use of compulsion to elicit answers to questions that may involve admission of an infringement; see 'Self-incrimination in EC Antitrust Enforcement: A Legal and Economic Analysis' (2003) 26 *World Competition* 567, and 'EU Antitrust Enforcement Powers and Procedural Rights and Guarantees: The Interplay between EU Law, National Law, the Charter of Fundamental Rights of the EU and the European Convention on Human Rights' (2011) 34 *World Competition* 189, both also accessible at http://ssrn.com/author=456087.

381 See further my paper 'Leniency in Antitrust Enforcement: Theory and Practice' (2007) 30 *World Competition* 25, also accessible at http://ssrn.com/author=456087, at footnotes 84 to 94.

382 Apart from the deterrent effect, the imposition of fines on cartel participants also has a moral effect, in that it sends a message to the spontaneously law-abiding, reinforcing their moral commitment to the antitrust prohibitions; see my paper 'Optimal Antitrust Fines: Theory and Practice' (2006) 29 *World Competition* 183, also accessible at http://ssrn.com/author=456087, at footnotes 12 to 37.

383 See A. von Hirsch, A. E. Bottoms, E. Burney and P.-O. Wikström, *Criminal Deterrence and Sentence Severity: An Analysis of Recent Research* (Hart 1999), at 47; C. Parker and V. Lehmann Nielsen, 'Deterrence and the Impact of Calculative Thinking on Business Compliance with Regulation' (2009), accessible at http://ssrn.com/abstract=1527326, at 33; and my 'Optimal Antitrust Fines: Theory and Practice' (2006) 29 *World Competition* 183, at footnotes 62 to 80, and 'Recidivism in EU Antitrust Enforcement: A Legal and Economic Analysis' (2012) 35 *World Competition* 5, both also accessible at http://ssrn.com/author=456087, at footnote 93.

allowing the cartel participants as a group to increase profits, and providing for a fair distribution of profits between them. They also need to develop mechanisms to discourage cheating, involving monitoring, rewards and punishments. In a dynamic economy, successful cartels may have to develop an organisational structure that allows them to solve these problems continuously.[384]

A well-designed leniency programme makes these tasks more difficult. The possibility for a deviator to apply for leniency increases the payoff of cheating, thus making collusion more difficult to sustain.[385] It increases uncertainty, making it more difficult for cartel participants to reach agreement, diminishing trust among them, and increasing the need for costly monitoring.[386]

This effect of raising the cost of setting up and maintaining cartels[387] is not unique to leniency. The same logic underlies the legal rule that cartels or other agreements restrictive of competition are legally unenforceable,[388] and the practice of imposing higher penalties for cartel members that play active roles in setting up and running the cartel.[389]

This effect of leniency may lead to cartels breaking down earlier than they would otherwise or even not being formed in the first place.[390]

It is impossible to know how many (or how few) cartels have not come into existence as a result of this effect of the European Commission's leniency programme.

As to how many cartels have broken down earlier than they would have in the absence of the European Commission's leniency programme, one could count the number of European Commission decisions in cases in which the cartel was detected exclusively

---

384 M. C. Levenstein and V. Y. Suslow, 'What Determines Cartel Success?' (2006) 44 *Journal of Economic Literature* 43, at 44–45; see also J.E. Harrington, 'How Do Cartels Operate?' (2006) 2 *Foundations and Trends in Microeconomics* 1, and R. C. Marshall and L. M. Marx, *The Economics of Collusion – Cartels and Bidding Rings* (MIT Press 2012).

385 J. E. Harrington, 'Optimal Corporate Leniency Programs' (2008) 56 *The Journal of Industrial Economics* 215, at 217, has called this the 'Deviator Amnesty Effect' of leniency.

386 N. K. Katyal, 'Conspiracy Theory' (2003) 112 *Yale Law Journal* 1307, at 1342–1350, and G. Spagnolo, 'Divide et Impera: Optimal Leniency Programmes', CEPR Discussion Paper No 4840 (December 2004), available at http://www.cepr.org/pubs/dps/DP4840.asp, at 6.

387 N. K. Katyal, 'Conspiracy Theory' (2003) 112 *Yale Law Journal* 1307, at 1363, calls this 'cost deterrence'.

388 See Article 101(2) TFEU.

389 See paragraph 28, third indent, of the 2006 Fining Guidelines. This makes the setting up and functioning of cartels more difficult, because, faced with the prospect of higher fines, there will be fewer volunteers to play active roles. Those who nevertheless accept to do so are likely to want compensation in the form of a larger part of the gain, which is likely to be difficult to agree on, and to weaken the sense of solidarity and mutual trust within the group; see N. K. Katyal, 'Conspiracy Theory' (2003) 112 *Yale Law Journal* 1307, at 1341–1346 and 1363–1367, and my paper 'Optimal Antitrust Fines: Theory and Practice' (2006) 29 *World Competition* 183, also accessible at http://ssrn.com/author=456087, at footnotes 88 to 90.

390 The two are, of course, linked, as the earlier breakdown means that a prospective cartel is less profitable and thus less likely to be entered into in the first place; see my paper 'The Commission Notice on the Non-Imposition or Reduction of Fines in Cartel Cases: A Legal and Economic Analysis' (1997) 22 *European Law Review* 125, at 130, 133 and 140, and J.E. Harrington, 'Optimal Corporate Leniency Programs' (2008) 56 *The Journal of Industrial Economics* 215, at 220–221. See further my paper 'Leniency in Antitrust Enforcement: Theory and Practice' (2007) 30 *World Competition* 25, also accessible at http://ssrn.com/author=456087, at footnotes 102 to 106.

through leniency and the cartel was still ongoing at the time of the first leniency application.[391]

Table 4 below shows that, on a conservative count,[392] there have been 41 such cases. This is a significant number.[393]

Table 4: Cartels that were ongoing when first detected through leniency

Period	Number of European Commission cartel decisions concerning cartels detected exclusively through leniency where the cartel was clearly ongoing at the time of the first leniency application
1996–2000	1
2001–2005	7
2006–2010	15
2011–2015	11
2016–2020	7
Total 1996–2020	**41**

C. Risks of negative effects

1. Lowering of the penalty level

It would seem obvious at first sight that leniency leads to a lowering of the average fine level. Several commentators have indeed made this observation and expressed concern about it.[394]

---

391 Not all cartels for which immunity from fines was granted under the leniency programme, as counted in Table 3 above, were detected **exclusively** through leniency, as in some cases the European Commission had already obtained some information about the cartel before it received the first leniency application. Those cases are not counted in Table 4. As to whether the cartel was still ongoing at the time of the first leniency application, in four cases the public version of the decision does not allow the drawing of a clear conclusion. These unclear cases have not been included in Table 4, which thus reflects a conservative counting. More generally, the fact that the Commission decision sets as the end date of the infringement a date before the date of the immunity application does not exclude that the cartel may still have been ongoing at the latter date. Indeed, the Commission tends to take a cautious approach setting the end date at the last date for which it has firm evidence of ongoing cartel activity. Also in this respect, Table 4 thus reflects a conservative counting.

392 See footnote immediately above.

393 The total number of cases exclusively detected through leniency being 75, the 41 cases in which it is clear that the cartel was still ongoing at the time of the first leniency application thus represent 55% of the total. The detection and punishment of cartels that are no longer ongoing, of course, also contribute to deterrence.

394 See my paper 'The Commission Notice on the Non-Imposition or Reduction of Fines in Cartel Cases: A Legal and Economic Analysis' (1997) 22 *European Law Review* 125 at 130; M. Motta and M. Polo, 'Leniency programs and cartel prosecution' (2003) 21 *International Journal of Industrial Organization* 347, who, through a mathematical model, 'showed that, by reducing the expected fines, leniency programs may induce a pro-collusive reaction' (idem, at 375); and, C. Marvão and G. Spagnolo, 'Pros and cons of leniency, damages and screens' (2015) 1 *Competition Law & Policy Debate* 47.

In reality, this issue turns out to be a red herring. The introduction of a leniency programme only leads to a lowering of the fine level if it is not accompanied by a compensating increase in the level of the fines that would be imposed in the absence of cooperation under the leniency programme.[395]

Most or indeed all legislators and competition authorities have understood this, and have raised the general fine level around the same time as they introduced a leniency programme.[396]

This is also true for the European Commission: The introduction of the leniency programme in 1996 and its subsequent development (as well as the addition of the cartel settlement procedure in 2008) were accompanied by a sustained increase in the level of the fines, marked in particular by the adoption of the 1998 and 2006 Fining Guidelines.

Before the 1998 Fining Guidelines, fines were typically calculated as a percentage of the turnover in the product concerned by the cartel, and the percentage tended to be in the order of 2 to 4%, and certainly never exceeded 8%.[397] Under the 2006 Fining Guidelines, fines are again calculated as a percentage of the turnover in the product concerned by the cartel, but the percentages are now in the order of 15 to 25%.[398] The level of the fines imposed in the absence of cooperation under the leniency programme has thus more than doubled.[399]

This means that, even if the application of the leniency programme were on average to lead to fine reductions of 50%, the level of the fines ultimately imposed would still be higher than it was before the introduction of the leniency programme. In reality, the average fine reduction on account of leniency is well below 50%. As mentioned above, a study shows an average fine reduction on account of leniency of only 21%.[400]

There is thus no ground for concern that the European Commission's leniency programme would have weakened deterrence by lowering the overall fine level.[401]

---

395 See my paper 'Leniency in Antitrust Enforcement: Theory and Practice' (2007) 30 *World Competition* 25, also accessible at http://ssrn.com/author=456087, at footnotes 124 to 127.

396 In France, for instance, a leniency programme was introduced in 2001 by the same Act of Parliament, which also increased the maximum fine; see D. Voillemot, *Gérer la clémence* (Bruylant, 2005), at 59.

397 See M. Reynolds, 'EC Competition Policy on Fines' (1992) *European Business Law* Review 263 at 263, and my book *The Optimal Enforcement of EC Antitrust law* (Kluwer Law International, 2002) at 32 and at 70.

398 See E. Barbier de La Serre and E. Lagathu, 'The Law on Fines Imposed in EU Competition Proceedings: Faster, Higher, Harsher' (2013) 4 *Journal of European Competition Law & Practice* 325 at 329, and 'The Law on Fines Imposed in EU Competition Proceedings: On the Road to Consistency' (2014) 5 *Journal of European Competition Law & Practice* 400 at 404.

399 For cartels that last more than one year, the increase is in fact much higher than a doubling, because before the 1998 Guidelines, only a percentage of the turnover during one year was taken into account, whereas under the 2006 Guidelines, this is multiplied by the number of years of participation in the cartel.

400 S. Broos, A. Gautier, J. Marcos Ramos and N. Petit, 'Analyse statistique des affaires d'ententes dans l'UE (2004-2014)' (2016) 67 *Revue économique* 79 at 85. For cases in which the settlement procedure is followed, a further reduction of 10% has to be added.

401 One could argue that these general penalty increases could have been introduced anyway, irrespective of the introduction of a leniency policy, so that the fact remains that the leniency policy has the effect of lowering the penalty level. However, the existence of a leniency policy, which allows antitrust offenders to reduce their exposure to penalties by cooperating with the authorities and which results in more and better evidence of the antitrust violations being discovered, may precisely allow the higher penalty levels, because the antitrust offenders' failure to take advantage of the possibility to cooperate increases their culpability, and hence the

2. Facilitation of the creation and maintenance of cartels

As I have pointed out in previous publications,[402] successful cartels tend to be sophisticated organisations capable of learning. It is thus safe to assume that cartel participants will try to adapt their organisation to leniency policies, not only so as to minimise the destabilising effect, but also, where possible, to exploit leniency policies to facilitate the creation and maintenance of cartels. This raises the question whether there could be features of leniency programmes that risk being exploited to perverse effect.

The limitation of immunity to the single first cooperating cartel participant is clearly important in avoiding perverse effects. If this condition did not exist, one could imagine all the members of a cartel collectively denouncing it to the antitrust enforcement authorities and claiming leniency, only after having fully implemented the cartel agreement up to its time of natural death.[403]

In situations where the same companies participate in a number of cartels in different markets, or repeatedly form cartels over time, one could imagine a system in which cartel participants take turns to apply for leniency, every time one of the cartels is (about to be) detected by the competition authority. In jurisdictions where cartels are punished not only by fines on companies but also by imprisonment of individuals, such a system is most unlikely to be attractive,[404] but in jurisdictions without such individual penalties, it might conceivably work.

More than twenty years after the introduction of the European Commission's leniency programme, can any evidence of such a possible perverse effect be found?

The issue has been thoroughly examined by Robert Marshall and Leslie Marx.[405] The strongest example they found of a possible instance of cartel participants taking turns to apply for immunity concerns the European Commission's following three decisions:

- The 2003 decision in *Organic Peroxides*, in which Akzo was granted immunity on the ground of a leniency application made in April 2000 for a cartel lasting from 1971 until the end of 1999[406]

---

acceptability of higher penalties, and because the stronger evidence equally makes higher penalties acceptable; see my 'Leniency in Antitrust Enforcement: Theory and Practice' (2007) 30 *World Competition* 25, also accessible at http://ssrn.com/author=456087, after footnote 127.

402 See my paper 'Leniency in Antitrust Enforcement: Theory and Practice' (2007) 30 *World Competition* 25, also accessible at http://ssrn.com/author=456087, at footnotes 133 to 140, and my book *Efficiency and Justice in European Antitrust Enforcement* (Hart 2008), paragraphs 422 to 425.

403 Cartels tend to die natural deaths, be it sometimes only after a long life, because of the entry or expansion of non-cartel members; see M. C. Levenstein and V. Y. Suslow, 'What Determines Cartel Success?' (2006) 44 *Journal of Economic Literature* 43.

404 See also C. Aubert, P. Rey and W. E. Kovacic, 'The Impact of Leniency and Whistleblowing Programs on Cartels' (2006) 24 *International Journal of Industrial Organization* 1241 at 1250.

405 R. C. Marshall and L. M. Marx, 'Participation in Multiple Cartels Through Time and the Potentially Strategic Use of leniency', paper presented at the Swedish Competition Authority's 2015 Pros and Cons seminar on leniency, available at http://www.konkurrensverket.se/en/research/seminars/the-pros-and-cons/leniency-and-criminalization-2015/. See also C. Harding, C. Beaton-Wells and J. Edwards, 'Leniency and Criminal Sanctions in Anti-Cartel Enforcement: Happily Married or Uneasy Bedfellows?', in C. Beaton-Wells and C. Tran (eds), *Anti-Cartel Enforcement in a Contemporary Age Leniency Religion* (Hart 2015), 233 at 254–257.

406 Commission Decision of 10 December 2003 in Case COMP/37.857 *Organic Peroxides*, Summary publication in [2005] OJ L110/44.

- The 2006 decision in *Hydrogen Peroxide and Perborate*, in which Degussa was granted immunity on the ground of a leniency application made in December 2002 for a cartel lasting from 1994 until the end of 1999[407]
- The 2009 decision in *Calcium Carbide*, in which Akzo was granted immunity on the ground of a leniency application made before 8 December 2006 for a cartel lasting from 2004 until 16 January 2007, the day on which the European Commission conducted surprise inspections on the business premises of the other cartel participants.[408]

I do not find this a convincing example of possible 'taking turns' to apply for leniency, for two reasons. First, while Akzo and Degussa participated in all three cartels, several other large companies were also involved in one or more of these cartels, notably Atochem/Atofina (second largest in the *Organic Peroxides* and *Hydrogen Peroxide and Perborate* cartels) and Solvay (largest in the *Hydrogen Peroxide and Perborate* cartel). It is difficult to see how Akzo and Degussa could between the two of them have controlled the strategic use of leniency. Secondly, one would expect that the taking of turns to apply for leniency would happen when the cartel either has died a natural death or has just been detected or is about to be detected by a competition authority, whereas in the case of the *Calcium Carbide* cartel, the cartel was still ongoing and undetected when Akzo applied for leniency. A more convincing explanation for Akzo's leniency applications is the one provided by Akzo itself – namely, that, after having expanded through a series of acquisitions and having been caught in several cartels through its relatively autonomous divisions, Akzo introduced in 2000 an Internal Amnesty Programme, in order to be able to detect cartels engaged in by its divisions and report them under the European Commission's leniency programme.[409]

Another potential perverse scenario to be considered is the use of leniency as a mechanism to punish deviations from the cartel agreement. Again, the limitation of immunity to the single first cooperating cartel participant very much reduces the risk of such perverse effect, as it makes it impossible for all the other cartel members together to denounce the cartel to the antitrust enforcement authority, obtain immunity themselves, and have the deviator penalised by the authority. One may nevertheless wonder whether it would be possible to set up a system in which one cartel member would play a central role in organising and administering the cartel, and would be the only one to have all the evidence of the cartel, and could use this position to deter the other cartel members from deviating from the cartel agreement under the threat of a leniency application. It would, however, seem very unlikely that the other cartel members would be willing to enter into such an agreement, as they would have to trust the ringleader to act exclusively in the common interest, and would risk being the co-victim of deviations by one of the other non-ringleaders. This would only be different if the ringleader could coerce

---

407 Commission Decision of 3 May 2006 in Case COMP/38.620 *Hydrogen Peroxide and Perborate*, Summary publication in [2006] OJ L353/54.

408 Commission Decision of 22 July 2009 in Case COMP/39.396 *Calcium Carbide*, Summary publication in [2009] OJ C301/18. That Akzo's leniency application was made before 8 December 2006 can be deduced from the fact that immunity was granted under the 2002 Leniency Notice, which was replaced on 8 December 2006 by the 2006 Leniency Notice.

409 Story as told by Jan Eijsbouts, Akzo's General Counsel, at http://www.goodgovernance.nu/verhalen/jan-eijsbouts-deel-1/.

the other cartel members into the agreement. The European Commission's leniency programme, however, excludes coercers from immunity.[410]

3. Negative moral effects and the problem of recidivism

Corporate managers are not necessarily just maximisers of profits for themselves and their principals. They may feel a moral responsibility to live within the law whether or not they are likely to be caught, and this normative commitment could trump their interest calculus. The public punishment of those who violate the antitrust prohibitions has thus not only a deterrent effect, in that it helps create a credible threat of punishment for those who would be willing to commit violations on the basis of a profit calculation, but also moral effects, in that it sends a message to the spontaneously law-abiding, reinforcing their moral commitment to the rules.[411]

For people to have such moral commitment to the law, however, it is important that the law and its enforcement are perceived to be fair.[412] Leniency, in particular in its strongest form of immunity, may raise two (closely related) concerns in this respect.[413]

First, there may be concerns about the retributive injustice of an antitrust offender escaping punishment. The main response to this concern is to design and apply leniency programmes in such a way as to ensure that no more leniency is granted than strictly necessary to obtain the positive enforcement effects, and to stress the condition for any beneficiary of leniency, and in particular of immunity, to provide genuine and full cooperation to the enforcement authorities. This appears to be reflected in the case law of the EU Court of Justice, which has emphasised that for companies to benefit from leniency under the European Commission's Leniency Notice, their conduct must reveal 'a genuine spirit of cooperation'.[414] Requiring restitution to injured parties as a condition for leniency may also help to assuage justice concerns.[415]

---

410 2006 Leniency Notice, point 13. In some jurisdictions, including the US, leniency programmes go further in that they also exclude non-coercing sole ringleader; see further my paper 'Leniency in Antitrust Enforcement: Theory and Practice' (2007) 30 *World Competition* 25, also accessible at http://ssrn.com/author=456087, at footnote 140.

411 See C. D. Stone, 'Sentencing the corporation' (1991) 71 *Boston University Law Review* 383 at 389; J. Adenaes, 'The Moral or Educative Influence of Criminal Law' (1971) 27 *Journal of Social Issues* 17, and 'General prevention revisited: research and policy implications' (1975) 66 *Journal of Criminal Law & Criminology* 338, at 341–343; K. G. Dau-Schmidt, 'An Economic Analysis of the Criminal Law as a Preference-Shaping Policy' (1990) *Duke Law Journal* 1, C. R. Sunstein, 'On the Expressive Function of the Law' (1996) 144 *University of Pennsylvania Law Review* 2021, D. M. Kahan, 'Social Influence, Social Meaning, and Deterrence' (1997) 83 *Virginia Law Review* 349, N.K. Katyal, 'Deterrence's Difficulty' (1997) 95 *Michigan Law Review* 2385, G. E. Lynch, 'The Role of Criminal Law in Policing Corporate Misconduct' (1997) 60 *Law and Contemporary Problems* 23, D.M. Kahan, 'Social Meaning and the Economic Analysis of Crime' (1998) 27 *Journal of Legal Studies* 609, and K. G. Dau-Schmidt, 'Preference shaping by the law', in P. Newman (ed), *The New Palgrave Dictionary of Economics and the Law* (Macmillan 1998) 84.

412 See T. R. Tyler, *Why People Obey the Law* (Yale UP 1990), as well as the literature listed in the footnote just above.

413 See also OECD, *Fighting Hard-Core Cartels – Harm, Effective Sanctions and Leniency Programmes* (2000), available at http://www.oecd.org/dataoecd/41/44/1841891.pdf, at 26.

414 Judgments in *Dansk Rørindustri and Others v European Commission*, C-189/02 P, C-202/02 P, C-205/02 P to C-208/02 P and C-213/02 P, EU:C:2005:408, paragraphs 388–403, in *Commission v SGL Carbon*, C-301/04 P, EU:C:2006:432, paragraph 68, and in *Schenker*, C-681/11, EU:C:2013:404, paragraphs 36, 46 and 49.

415 See further my papers 'Leniency in Antitrust Enforcement: Theory and Practice' (2007) 30 *World Competition* 25, at footnote 146, and 'The Relationship between Public Antitrust Enforcement and Private Actions for Damages' (2009) 32 *World Competition* 3, both also accessible at http://ssrn.com/author=456087, at footnotes 101 to 106;

A second (closely related) concern focuses on the unequal treatment between the beneficiary of immunity or leniency and the other cartel participants, who receive full punishment for the same antitrust violation.[416] Again, the main response is to ensure that leniency is only granted to the extent that the company or individual has genuinely and effectively cooperated with the competition authority, thus objectively distinguishing its situation from the other cartel participants that have not done so, or not to the same extent, or at the same early point in time. Equally important is to ensure that leniency policies are applied in a transparent and consistent way, thus providing an equal chance for all cartel participants to benefit from them. In this respect, the EU General Court has stressed that, under the general principle of equal treatment, the European Commission must ensure that it does not distort the conditions of competition between undertakings in a (potential) race to be the first to cooperate, by contacting one of them, or giving them unequal access when they contact the European Commission.[417]

Both concerns, as to the guilty remaining unpunished and as to co-conspirators being treated unequally, would appear to be particularly acute in the case of immunity being granted to the ringleader of a cartel, in particular if that ringleader has coerced other cartel members into committing the infringement. As already mentioned above, under the European Commission's leniency programme, coercers are excluded from immunity.[418]

Both concerns, as to the guilty remaining unpunished and as to co-conspirators being treated unequally, would also appear to be particularly acute in the case of immunity being granted to a **recidivist**, in particular if the other cartelists being fined are not recidivists.[419]

One could consider excluding recidivists from leniency, or at least from the benefit of immunity from fines: Until 2011, the leniency programme of the Greek competition authority excluded recidivists from immunity from fines.[420]

However, the exclusion of recidivists from leniency comes at a substantial cost. As explained above, leniency generally has very significant benefits in terms of improved

---

J. Rivas and G. Eclair-Heath, 'Striking the balance between public and private enforcement: The case for consensual compensation as a mitigating circumstance in setting fines for violations of EU competition law' (2014) *Concurrences*, art no 62573; and C. Prieto, 'Incitations aux réparations spontanées dans le cadre du public enforcement' (2016) *Concurrences* no 2-2016.

416 See also D. Voillemot, *Gérer la clémence* (Bruylant, 2005), at 99–100.

417 Judgments in *Krupp Thyssen Stainless and Acciai Speciali Terni v Commission*, T-45/98 and T-47/98, EU:T:2001:288, paragraphs 237–248, and in *BASF v Commission*, T-15/02, EU:T:2006:74, paragraph 504. The European Commission would thus not be allowed to adopt the US Department of Justice's practice of 'affirmative amnesty', under which the latter authority approaches a company – which may at the time not even know that it or its competitors are under investigation – to cooperate and seek leniency; see S. D. Hammond, 'Measuring the Value of Second-In Cooperation in Corporate Plea Negotiations', address to the 54th Annual American Bar Association Section of Antitrust Law Spring Meeting (Washington, DC, 29 March 2006), at 11.

418 2006 Leniency Notice, point 13.

419 See my paper 'Recidivism in EU Antitrust Enforcement: A Legal and Economic Analysis' (2012) 35 *World Competition* 5, also accessible at http://ssrn.com/author=456087, at footnotes 77 to 82.

420 Decision No 299/V/2006 of the Plenary of the Hellenic Competition Commission, point A.4(e) ('the undertaking must not have participated in the past in a prohibited collusive practice for which a decision by a National Competition Authority or the European Commission has been issued'). In 2011, however, the Greek competition authority changed its leniency programme, and recidivists can now also obtain immunity from fines; see Decision 526/VI/2011 of 30 August 2011.

collection of evidence and intelligence of cartel infringements and in terms of increased difficulty of creating and maintaining cartels. The more cartelists are excluded from seeking immunity or leniency, the less these benefits can accrue. In the extreme case where the same group of undertakings, which were all found to have participated in a cartel, subsequently starts a new cartel, the exclusion of recidivists from leniency would shelter this new cartel from the positive enforcement effects of leniency, and would thus render this new cartel easier to create and maintain and more difficult to detect and punish. Paradoxically, excluding recidivists from leniency thus encourages recidivism.

On balance, excluding recidivists from leniency or from immunity from fines would thus not appear to be a good idea.

Table 5 below shows, for the cartel decisions adopted by the European Commission in the period 2006–2015, the total number of undertakings that were held liable for cartel infringements, and the number among these that were found to be recidivists, as well as the number of immunity recipients, and the number among these that were recidivists.[421]

Table 5: Recidivists and immunity recipients

Period	2006–2010	2011–2015	Total 2006–2015
Total number of detected cartel participants	228	125	353
of which recidivists	27 = 12%	1 = 1%	28 = 8%
Number of immunity recipients	25	21	46
of which recidivists	8 = 32%	1 = 5%	9 = 20%

Table 5 shows that recidivists are statistically better represented among immunity recipients (20%) than among the total population of detected cartel participants (8%). On the other hand, it should be noted that only 9 out of 28 recidivists were granted immunity. Most recidivists were thus fined, and more heavily than other cartelists, because of the treatment of recidivism as an aggravating circumstance.[422] Moreover, where several participants in the same cartel are recidivists, only one of them can possibly receive immunity.

---

421 The full list of the cases I have counted can be found in the annex to my paper 'The Use of Leniency in EU Cartel Enforcement: An Assessment After Twenty Years' (2016) 39 *World Competition* 327, also accessible at http://ssrn.com/author=456087.

422 The European Commission's 2006 Fining Guidelines threaten an increase of up to 100% in case of one prior infringement, 200% in case of two prior infringements, 300% in case of three prior infringements, 400% in case of four prior infringements, and so on *ad infinitum*. However, the Commission has not made full use of the possibilities offered by its 2006 Fining Guidelines, increasing in practice fines by 50% in case of one prior infringement, 60% in case of two prior infringements, 90% in case of three prior infringements, and 100% in case of four prior infringements; see E. Barbier de La Serre and C. Winckler, 'Legal Issues Regarding Fines Imposed in EU Competition Proceedings' (2010) 1 *Journal of Competition Law & Practice* 327 at 336–337 and 'A Survey of Legal Issues Regarding Fines Imposed in EU Competition Proceedings (2010)' (2011) 2 *Journal of Competition Law & Practice* 356 at 360–361 and Chapter 8 of this book.

That recidivists are statistically better represented among the immunity recipients than among the total population of detected cartel participants is not necessarily abnormal or worrying. One would want and expect an undertaking that has been found to have participated in an antitrust infringement to take measures so as to avoid continued or new violations, including by establishing effective compliance programmes.[423] The first-best outcome of these measures would, of course, be that no new infringements are committed. However, if this is not achieved, the second-best outcome is that, thanks to the compliance programme, the new infringements are quickly detected and reported to the competition authorities.[424] The higher percentage of recidivists among immunity recipients may reflect this second-best outcome.

What is also apparent from Table 5 above, when comparing the figures for the 2006–2010 period with those of the 2011–2015 period, is that the number of (detected) recidivists has spectacularly declined.[425]

4. The impact of fines on the market structure

As Advocate General Geelhoed has pointed out, 'in the event of a collective infringement like a cartel as opposed to an infringement by a single offender, the [European] Commission must also consider the subsequent effects of the fines and take into account the size of a given company. [. . .] The example [. . .] is a cartel consisting of one big player and several small players. The big player cooperated with the Commission and receives immunity under the Leniency Notice. In such cases very high fines could have put the smaller players out of business, in which case the Commission's intervention would have resulted in a monopoly'.[426]

Table 6 provides some statistics for all the decisions adopted in the 2006–2015 period in which immunity was granted.[427] It appears that in 46% of the cases, the immunity recipient was the cartel participant with the highest turnover in the market affected by the cartel, whereas on average there were 7 participants per cartel, and the undertaking with the highest turnover should thus have been the immunity recipient in only 15% of the cases if there had been no correlation between being the undertaking with the largest turnover and being the immunity recipient.

---

423 On compliance programmes, see Chapter VII of this book; B. Fisse, 'Reconditioning Corporate Leniency: The Possibility of Making Compliance Programmes a Condition for Immunity', in C. Beaton-Wells and C. Tran (eds), *Anti-Cartel Enforcement in a Contemporary Age Leniency Religion* (Hart 2015), 179; and H. Bergman and D. D. Sokol, 'The Air Cargo Cartel: Lessons for Compliance', in C. Beaton-Wells and C. Tran (eds), as just above, 301; see also above the example of Akzo.

424 Compare with Judgment in *Shell v Commission*, T-38/07, EU:T:2011:355, paragraph 96, last sentence, and see above for the example of Akzo.

425 See already my paper 'Recidivism in EU Antitrust Enforcement: A Legal and Economic Analysis' (2012) 35 *World Competition* 5, also accessible at http://ssrn.com/author=456087, at footnotes 86 to 89, and OECD Policy Roundtable, *Serial offenders: Why some industries seem prone to endemic collusion* (2015), DAF/COMP/GF(2015)4, available at http://www.oecd.org/officialdocuments/publicdisplaydocumentpdf/?cote=DAF/COMP/GF(2015)4&docLanguage=En, at 35–37.

426 Opinion in *Showa Denko v Commission*, C-289/04 P, EU:C:2006:52, paragraph 61 and footnote 16; see also my paper 'Optimal Antitrust Fines: Theory and Practice' (2006) 29 *World Competition* 183, also accessible at http://ssrn.com/author=456087, at footnotes 94 to 96.

427 The full list of the cases I have counted can be found in the annex to my paper 'The Use of Leniency in EU Cartel Enforcement: An Assessment After Twenty Years' (2016) 39 *World Competition* 327, also accessible at http://ssrn.com/author=456087.

Table 6: Immunity recipients with the highest turnover in the affected market

Period	2006–2015
Number of immunity recipients	46
Number of immunity recipients with the highest turnover in the market affected by the cartel	21 = 46%
Total number of undertakings involved	316
Average number of undertakings per cartel	7

Given that under the European Commission's 2006 Fining Guidelines the fines are calculated as a percentage of each undertaking's turnover in the goods or services affected by the cartel, the above result should not come as a surprise: The undertakings with the largest affected turnover can expect the highest fine, and hence have the most to gain from applying for leniency.

Should we thus be concerned about the scenario identified by Advocate General Geelhoed, in which the imposition of fines would result in the market becoming monopolistic?

On the reassuring side, it should be pointed out that whereas in 46% of the cases, the immunity recipient has the largest turnover affected by the cartel, in many of these cases, the other cartel participants are also large companies that cannot easily be fined out of business.

Moreover, and most importantly, the European Commission has a policy of capping fines so as to avoid undertakings going out of business because of a fine. Indeed, in addition to the 10% of total turnover cap laid down in Article 23(2) of Regulation 1/2003, the European Commission reduces fines on the grounds of inability to pay.[428]

On the other hand, in the absence of perfect capital markets, high fines can have a negative effect on the competitiveness of smaller companies, even below the level of inability to pay, and may thus negatively affect market structure.[429]

5. Exclusive reliance on leniency

As explained above, the main benefit of a well-designed leniency programme is that it significantly reduces the difficulty, time and administrative cost of collecting intelligence and evidence of cartel infringements.

It is important to note, however, that leniency is not a substitute but a complement to other methods of collecting intelligence and evidence of cartel infringements. Indeed, leniency will work well if the cartel participants concerned perceive a risk that the competition authorities

---

428 See paragraph 35 of the 2006 Fining Guidelines; Commission Document SEC(2010)737, 'Inability to pay under paragraph 35 of the 2006 Fining Guidelines and payment conditions pre-and post-decision finding an infringement and imposing fines' (June 2010), available at the Register of Commission documents, http://ec.europa.eu/transparency/regdoc/registre.cfm?CL=en; and paragraph 87 of the European Commission's Notice on best practices for the conduct of proceedings concerning Articles 101 and 102 TFEU [2011] OJ C308/6.

429 See my paper 'Optimal Antitrust Fines: Theory and Practice' (2006) 29 *World Competition* 183, also accessible at http://ssrn.com/author=456087, at footnotes 67 to 71. In addition, negative effects on the market structure could also result from follow-on actions for damages, which may be difficult to anticipate in the assessment of inability to pay; see Chapter XVIII of this book.

will detect and establish the cartel infringement without recourse to leniency. The risk could be a specific one, where the competition authority is already collecting or receiving information of the cartel infringement by other means (or is believed to be doing so, or to be doing so in the near future), or a more general one, where a competition authority, as a result of many other recent cases of successful detection and prosecution, is believed to be good at it. If leniency policies are well designed in that immunity is only granted to the first co-conspirator to come forward, and reductions in penalties are linked to the timing of the cooperation as compared to the other co-conspirators, cartel participants may decide to cooperate out of fear that a co-conspirator may do so before them.[430] Such a 'race to cooperate' may amplify the positive effects of leniency, but again such a race is most likely to start if there is a risk that the competition authorities will detect and establish the antitrust violation without recourse to leniency, or at least a belief by at least one of the conspirators that at least one of the other co-conspirators may believe that there is such a risk.[431]

A leniency policy will thus work well if the antitrust enforcement authority concerned has first built up a sufficient level of credibility as to its capacity to detect and punish cartel infringements on its own. As the statistics in Table 1 of Chapter I above show, the European Commission had already a good track record in detecting and punishing cartels by the time it introduced its leniency programme in 1996. Without this track record, the leniency programme could not have achieved the same rapid success.

For authorities that have managed to build up sufficient credibility, and subsequently operate a successful leniency programme, there may be a risk in relying too much on this success. If for a prolonged period they do not detect and prosecute any case anymore other than through leniency, they may lose their capacity to do so, or at least cartelists may start doubting their continued capacity to do so. If this were to happen, the success of their leniency programmes would risk coming to an end.[432]

Table 7 below shows the number of European Commission decisions concerning cartels that were not detected through leniency (so-called *ex officio* cartel investigations).[433] As can be seen from the comparison of these statistics with those in Table 3 above, in some of the cases where the cartel was not detected through leniency there was still a grant of immunity to the first cartel participant to cooperate, because at the time of this first leniency application, the European Commission, while having already some information obtained from another source, did not yet have sufficient information to establish the cartel infringement up to the requisite legal standard.

---

430 See also M. Bigoni, S. O. Fridolfsson, C. Le Coq and G. Spagnolo, 'Trust, Leniency and Deterrence' (2014), available at http://ssrn.com/abstract=2469778.

431 See my paper 'Leniency in Antitrust Enforcement: Theory and Practice' (2007) 30 *World Competition* 25, also accessible at http://ssrn.com/author=456087, at footnotes 91 to 94; and OECD Policy Roundtable, *Ex officio cartel investigations and the use of screens to detect cartels* (2013), available at http://www.oecd.org/daf/competition/exofficio-cartel-investigation-2013.pdf.

432 See my paper 'Leniency in Antitrust Enforcement: Theory and Practice' (2007) 30 *World Competition* 25, also accessible at http://ssrn.com/author=456087, at footnotes 131 and 132.

433 The full list of the cases I have counted for the period 1986–2015 period can be found in the annex to my paper 'The Use of Leniency in EU Cartel Enforcement: An Assessment After Twenty Years' (2016) 39 *World Competition* 327, also accessible at http://ssrn.com/author=456087. For the period 2016–2020, see the annex to my paper 'Regulation 1/2003: An Assessment After Twenty Years' (2023) 46 *World Competition* 3, also accessible at http://ssrn.com/author=456087.

Table 7: Decisions following ***ex officio*** *cartel investigations*

Period	Number of decisions following *ex officio* cartel investigations
1986–1990	9
1991–1995	8
1996–2000	9
2001–2005	15
2006–2010	9
2011–2015	4
2016–2020	0

Whereas in the 2001–2005 and 2006–2010 periods, there were still many decisions concerning cartels that had not been detected through leniency, there were only four such decisions in the 2011–2015 period, the most recent of these being the December 2014 decision concerning the *Envelopes* cartel, which was detected thanks to information received from an informant.[434] In the 2016–2020 period, there were none.[435]

While some *ex officio* investigations have started with information obtained from other authorities or gleaned from the specialised press, informants have always been the main source of information allowing the detection of cartels other than through leniency.[436]

It is thus important that the European Commission keeps signalling that it welcomes information from informants, including, of course, anonymous informants, and follows up leads provided by informants so as to continue detecting cartels without leniency, and thus to ensure the continued success of its leniency programme.

---

434 Decision of 10 December 2014 in Case AT.39780 *Envelopes*, Summary publication in [2015] OJ C74/5.

435 In 2022, the European Commission adopted a decision following an *ex* officio cartel investigation that had been started by the German Federal Competition Authority (Bundeskartellamt), which transferred the case to the European Commission; see Decision of 12 July 2022 in Case AT.405220 *Metal packaging*, Summary publication in [2023] OJ C57/5.

436 See also M. E. Stucke, 'Leniency, Whistle-Blowing and the Individual: Should We Create Another Race to the Competition Agency?', in C. Beaton-Wells and C. Tran (eds), *Anti-Cartel Enforcement in a Contemporary Age Leniency Religion* (Hart 2015), 209.
Whereas it has often been suggested (not always disinterestedly) that econometric tools could be used to detect cartels, the experience with such tools has not been good, with some limited exceptions in public procurement markets; see OECD Competition Policy Roundtable Background Note, *Data Screening Tools for Competition Investigations* (2022), https://www.oecd.org/daf/competition/data-screening-tools-in-competition-investigations-2022.pdf. In the United States, the Department of Justice Antitrust Division has in the past employed several methods for cartel screening and found that those methods did not produce solid leads for cartel investigations; see OECD Policy Roundtable, *Ex officio cartel investigations and the use of screens to detect cartels* (2013), http://www.oecd.org/daf/competition/exofficio-cartel-investigation-2013.pdf, at 38, footnote 129. Similarly, the European Commission's attempt to use economic data analysis in the *Cement* cartel investigation has delivered no results, while consuming a huge amount of resources; see information on the opening and closure of proceedings in Case 39520 *Cement and related products* on the European Commission's website http://ec.europa.eu/competition/antitrust/cases/index.html; Opinion of Advocate General Wahl in *HeidelbergCement v Commission*, C-247/14 P, EU:C:2015:694; and Judgment in *HeidelbergCement v Commission*, C-247/14 P, EU:C:2016:149.

VI. The Use of Settlements in Public Antitrust Enforcement: Objectives and Principles

This chapter discusses two general questions concerning the use of settlements in public antitrust enforcement, namely, under which conditions the use of settlements contributes to optimal antitrust enforcement and under which conditions self-incrimination and waivers of procedural rights by settlement candidates are compatible with fundamental rights of defence. The discussion of these general questions will be illustrated with the specific example of two settlement procedures for the enforcement by the European Commission of the antitrust prohibitions contained in Articles 101 and 102 TFEU – namely, the commitment procedure under Article 9 of Regulation 1/2003 and the settlement procedure in cartel cases.

A. Introduction

1. Settlements as opposed to the fully adversarial disposal of cases

The notion of **settlement** can be best understood in contrast with the normal, **fully adversarial disposal** of cases.[437]

As to antitrust enforcement by the European Commission, the procedural rules governing the normal, fully adversarial disposal of cases are laid down in the EU Treaties, Council Regulation 1,[438] Council Regulation 1/2003,[439] Commission Regulation 773/2004,[440] various Commission notices or guidelines, and the case law of the EU Courts. Cases of infringement of Articles 101 or 102 TFEU are closed by a Commission decision, based on Articles 7 and 23 of Regulation 1/2003, finding the infringement, imposing remedies to bring the infringement to an end, and/or imposing fines. Before adopting such a decision, the Commission notifies to the defendant companies a full statement of the objections raised. Following receipt of

---

437 The fully adversarial disposal can be said to be 'normal' at least in the sense that it applies by default and by right, being substituted by settlement only with the consent of both the competition authority and the defendant.

438 Council Regulation No 1 determining the languages to be used by the European Economic Community [1958] OJ 17/385 (Special English Edition 1952-58, p 59), last amended by Council Regulation (EU) No 517/2013 [2013] OJ L158/1.

439 Council Regulation (EC) No 1/2003 of 16 December 2002 on the implementation of the rules on competition laid down in Articles 81 and 82 of the Treaty [2003] OJ L1/1, last amended by Council Regulation No 1419/2006 [2006] OJ L269/1.

440 Commission Regulation (EC) No 773/2004 of 7 April 2004 relating to the conduct of proceedings by the Commission pursuant to Articles 81 and 82 of the EC Treaty [2004] OJ L123/18, last amended by Commission Regulation (EU) 2015/1348.

the statement of objections, the defendants receive access to the Commission's file, and can respond to the objections both in writing and orally, during a hearing presided over by an independent Hearing Officer. The Commission decision must be fully reasoned. The statement of objections and decision must be addressed to each company in an official language of the EU Member State in which the company is based, and the companies can also use these languages in their written response and at the hearing. The Commission decision can be appealed to the EU General Court on factual and legal grounds.[441] The Court can entirely or partially annul the decision and cancel, reduce or increase the fine.[442] A further appeal, limited to points of law, lies to the EU Court of Justice. If the Courts annul the Commission decision on merely procedural grounds, the Commission may, correcting the procedural defect, readopt the decision, which can then again be subjected to judicial review.[443]

In many cases the defendant companies fully contest the Commission's analysis throughout the whole procedure, but this is far from always the case. Some defendants contest the Commission's objections during the administrative procedure, but abstain from challenging the Commission's decision before the Courts. Some already do not contest the statement of objections in their response to it. Defendants may also waive their right to access to the file, or to an oral hearing, or waive their language rights. Some already take or announce remedial action.

Where the defendant in public antitrust enforcement proceedings abstains from using all possibilities of contesting the competition authority's analysis, decision or action, or waives some of its procedural rights, it may do so, at least in part, in the hope of receiving some benefits, such as a faster end to the procedure, less adverse publicity, milder penalties, less burdensome remedies, or a narrower finding of infringement, or even no finding at all if the case is dropped by the competition authority.

Competition authorities or legislators may encourage such non-contestation or voluntary remedial action by granting such benefits, or promising to grant them, as part of a **settlement policy**. This may involve the creation of specific **settlement procedures**, distinct from the normal, fully adversarial procedures, and designed to be used in cases where the defendant does not contest or recognises the infringement and/or offers or accepts remedies and/or penalties. The notion of **settlement** thus refers to the disposal by a competition authority of a case of suspected antitrust infringement through a specific procedure, or in application of a policy, under which some benefit is granted to the defendant in recognition of the defendant's admission or non-contestation of the infringement and/or offer or acceptance of remedies and/or penalties.

---

441 Articles 229 and 230 EC and Article 31 of Regulation 1/2003.

442 Increases have been rare, but the General Court notably used this power in its judgment in *BASF v Commission*, T-101/05, EU:T:2007:380.

443 See Chapter XVI of this book.

As to the enforcement of Articles 101 and 102 TFEU by the European Commission, two main settlement procedures currently exist:

- The commitments procedure laid down in Article 9 of Regulation 1/2003
- The settlement procedure in cartel cases under Article 10a of Commission Regulation 773/2004 and the Commission Notice on the conduct of settlement procedures in cartel cases.[444]

These two settlement procedures are summarily described in the two sections below.

2. Commitment decisions (Article 9 of Regulation 1/2003)

The commitments procedure was introduced in 2004 through Article 9 of Regulation 1/2003.[445] This Article provides that '[w]here the Commission intends to adopt a decision requiring that an infringement be brought to an end and the undertakings concerned offer commitments to meet the concerns expressed to them by the Commission in its preliminary assessment, the Commission may by decision make those commitments binding on the undertakings'.[446] Commitment decisions 'are not appropriate in cases where the Commission intends to impose a fine'.[447] A commitment decision 'shall conclude that there are no longer grounds for action by the Commission', 'without concluding whether or not there has been or still is an infringement'.[448] 'Commitment decisions are without prejudice to the powers of competition authorities and courts of the Member States to make such a finding [i.e. a finding that there has been or still is an infringement] and decide upon the case.'[449] As to the Commission, it may only reopen the proceedings 'where there has been a material change in any of the facts on which the decision was based', 'where the undertakings concerned act contrary to their commitments' or 'where the decision was based on incomplete, incorrect or misleading information provided by the parties'.[450] Finally, the Commission may compel compliance with a commitment made binding by a commitment decision through periodic penalty payments (of equal severity to those it can use to compel compliance with a normal decision finding an

---

444 In non-cartel cases in which a prohibition decision is taken, the European Commission has also rewarded cooperation, but without setting out a specific procedure; see Summary of Commission Decision of 20 September 2016 in Case AT.39759 ARA Foreclosure [2016] OJ C432/6; C. Gauer and J. Lübking, 'Cooperation with the European Commission in antitrust cases: A new way paved by the ARA case', *Concurrences* no 1-2017, 81; and European Commission, Fact Sheet – Cooperation – FAQ (17 December 2018), accessible at https://ec.europa.eu/competition/publications/data/factsheet_guess.pdf.

445 For a detailed analysis of this procedure, see my paper 'Settlements of EU Antitrust Investigations: Commitment Decisions under Article 9 of Regulation No. 1/2003' (2006) 29 *World Competition* 345, also accessible at http://ssrn.com/author=456087, and L. Kjolbye, E. Leduc and J. Lübking, 'Article 9 Commitments' in K. Dekeyser, C. Gauer, J. Laitenberger, N. Wahl, W. Wils and L. Prete (eds), *Regulation 1/2003 and EU Antitrust Enforcement – A Systematic Guide* (Wolters Kluwer 2022), 273.

446 Article 9(1), first sentence, of Regulation 1/2003; see Judgment in *Google and Alphabet v Commission (Google Shopping)*, T-612/17, EU:T:2021:763, paragraphs 635 to 638 and 692 to 694.

447 Fourth sentence of recital 13 of Regulation 1/2003.

448 Article 9(1), second sentence, and second sentence of recital 13 of Regulation 1/2003; see also Judgment in *Gasorba and Others v Commission*, C-547/16, EU:C:2017:891, paragraph 28.

449 Third sentence of recital 13. Similarly, in the third sentence of recital 21: 'Commitment decisions adopted by the Commission do not affect the power of the courts and the competition authorities of the Member States to apply Articles 81 and 82 of the Treaty'; however, see also Judgment in *Gasorba and Others v Commission*, C-547/16, EU:C:2017:891, paragraph 29.

450 Article 9(2).

infringement and ordering its termination), and it can impose fines in case of failure to comply with a commitment made binding (of equal severity as those it can impose for an infringement of Articles 101 or 102 TFEU which it has found).[451]

A decision under Article 9, making commitments binding, is thus a substitute for a decision under Article 7 of Regulation 1/2003 finding an infringement and imposing remedies for its termination. Article 9 can only be used instead of Article 7 if the undertakings concerned offer commitments that meet the Commission's concerns, and if the Commission chooses to dispose of the case in this way. As has been confirmed by the EU Courts, 'the Commission is never obliged under Article 9(1) of Regulation No 1/2003 to decide to make commitments binding instead of proceeding under Article 7 of that regulation'.[452]

A decision under Article 9 is not a substitute for a decision under Article 23 of Regulation 1/2003, imposing fines for an infringement of Articles 101 or 102 TFEU, and cannot be combined with it either because the imposition of fines requires the finding of an infringement, and hence a decision under Article 7 of Regulation 1/2003. Commitment decisions are therefore 'not appropriate in cases where the Commission intends to impose a fine',[453] and are thus not to be used in cartel cases, where the imposition of fines is at the heart of the Commission's enforcement activity.

In application of the general rules contained in Article 263 TFEU, commitment decisions can be appealed before the EU Courts by the undertakings whose commitments have been made binding. As the undertakings have themselves offered the commitments, one can, however, expect that such appeals will be much less frequent than appeals by the addressees of decisions under Article 7 of Regulation 1/2003, finding an infringement and imposing remedies for its termination. Indeed, at the time of writing, no commitment decision has been the object of such an appeal.[454]

Commitment decisions under Article 9 of Regulation 1/2003 are broadly comparable to consent orders or consent decrees, as used in antitrust enforcement by the Federal Trade Commission and the Department of Justice in the United States.[455] Indeed, the introduction of the commitment procedure in Regulation 1/2003 was inspired by the American example.[456]

---

451 Articles 24(1)(b) and 23(2)(c) of Regulation 1/2003.

452 Judgment in *Alrosa v Commission*, T-170/06, EU:T:2007:220, paragraph 130 (continuing: 'It is therefore not required to give reasons for which commitments are not in its view suitable to be made binding, so as to bring the proceedings to an end.'); this judgment was annulled on appeal before the Court of Justice by Judgment in *Commission v Alrosa*, C-441/07 P, EU:C:2010:377, but this point was not contested on appeal. See also Judgments in *Orange Polska*, T-486/11, EU:T:2015:1002, paragraphs 218 to 224, in *CB v Commission*, T-491/07 RENV, EU:T:2016:379, paragraph 470, and in *Google and Alphabet v Commission (Google Shopping)*, T-612/17, EU:T:2021:763, paragraph 638.

453 Fourth sentence of recital 13 of Regulation 1/2003.

454 Appeals have, however, been brought by third parties, successfully in one case: see Judgment in *Groupe Canal + v Commission*, C-132/19 P, EU:C:2020:1007.

455 See D.P. Ducrore, 'Settlement of Competition Conduct Violations at the United States Antitrust Agencies and at the European Commission – Some Observations', in B. E. Hawk (ed), *2005 Annual Proceedings of the Fordham Corporate Law Institute – International Antitrust Law and Policy* (Juris Publishing 2006), 227.

456 See my book *The Optimal Enforcement of EC Antitrust Law* (Kluwer 2002), section 6.5.2.2.

3. The settlement procedure in cartel cases

The European Commission introduced in 2008 a settlement procedure for cartel cases, laid down in a new Article 10a of Commission Regulation 773/2004 and a Commission Notice on the conduct of settlement procedures in cartel cases.[457]

The settlement procedure is a specific procedure, which can only be used in cartel cases.[458] It is based on Articles 7 and 23 of Regulation 1/2003, like the normal, fully adversarial procedure. The result of a settlement procedure is thus, like that of a fully adversarial procedure, a decision, based on Articles 7 and 23, finding an infringement and imposing fines. But the new Article 10a of Commission Regulation 773/2004 and Notice on the conduct of settlement procedures in cartel cases provide for a different procedure leading to such a decision. Where the Commission, after having collected the intelligence and evidence of a cartel using the normal investigatory instruments (primarily inspections and applications for leniency), considers the case suitable for settlement discussions, it invites all parties to declare whether they envisage engaging in settlement discussions.[459] If all or some of the parties express such interest, and the Commission still considers the case suitable for settlement discussions, it will conduct settlement discussions with each settlement candidate.[460] During these discussions, the Commission will inform the settlement candidates of the essential elements of the case as the Commission sees it, such as the facts alleged, the classification of those facts, the gravity and duration of the alleged cartel, the attribution of liability, an estimation of the range of likely fines (in the light of the Commission's Guidelines on fines[461] and Leniency Notice[462]), and the evidence used, thus enabling the parties to assert their views.[463] The settlement discussions allow the parties to exercise their rights of the defence, thus ensuring the accuracy of the finding of the infringement and of the setting of the fine, but the Commission 'does not negotiate the question of the existence of an infringement [. . .] and the appropriate sanction'.[464] If the settlement discussions are successful, each party must make a formal settlement submission, containing a recognition of the infringement and the party's liability for it, acceptance of the range of likely fines, a waiver of further access to the file and of an oral hearing after the statement of objections,

---

457 Commission Regulation (EC) No 622/2008 of 30 June 2008 amending Regulation (EC) No 773/2004, as regards the conduct of settlement procedures in cartel cases [2008] OJ L171/3 and Commission Notice on the conduct of settlement procedures in view of the adoption of Decisions pursuant to Article 7 and Article 23 of Council Regulation (EC) No 1/2003 in cartel cases [2008] OJ C167/1 ('Settlement Notice').

458 The notion of cartels is the same here as in the European Commission's Leniency Notice; see Chapter V of this book.

459 Settlement Notice, points 5 and 6 and 8 to 13.

460 Where proceedings are initiated against several legal entities controlled by the same undertaking, they must appoint joint representatives for the purpose of conducting the settlement discussions, without prejudice as to their individual responsibility.

461 Guidelines on the method of setting fines imposed pursuant to Article 23(2)(a) of Regulation No 1/2003 [2006] OJ C210/2; see my paper 'the European Commission's 2006 Guidelines on Fines: A Legal and Economic Analysis' (2007) 30 *World Competition* 197, and chapter 4 of my book *Efficiency and Justice in European Antitrust Enforcement* (Hart 2008).

462 Commission Notice on immunity from fines and reduction of fines in cartel cases [2006] OJ C298/17; see Chapter V of this book.

463 Settlement Notice, points 14 to 18. Upon request by a party, the Commission services will also grant it access to non-confidential versions of any specified accessible document listed in the case file at that point in time, in so far as this is justified for the purpose of enabling the party to ascertain its position regarding a time period or any other aspect of the cartel.

464 Settlement Notice, point 2; see also Judgment in *Daimler*, C-588/20, EU:C:2022:607, paragraph 53.

and acceptance of receiving the decision in an agreed language.[465] The Commission will then normally issue a streamlined statement of objections, reflecting the settlement submissions, to which the parties will respond with a simple confirmation, followed by a streamlined final decision, reflecting again the settlement submissions.[466] By way of settlement reward, the normally applicable amount of the fine will be reduced by 10%.[467] The Notice explicitly confirms that the decision is subject to the normal judicial review by the EU Courts.[468] One can, however, expect that appeals will be much less frequent than against decisions adopted following the normal, fully adversarial procedure, as already noted in the context of Article 9 commitment decisions.[469]

It is important to note that the settlement procedure in cartel cases is separate from leniency. Under its Leniency Notice,[470] the European Commission grants immunity from fines as well as reduction of fines in recognition of the voluntary provision of intelligence and evidence that enables the Commission to detect and punish the cartel, whereas under the settlement procedure a (further) reduction of the fine is granted in recognition of the acceptance of the finding of the infringement and of the fine, and waivers of some procedural rights. Also, in the timing of the procedures, there is a clear separation between leniency and settlement, as the settlement procedure is only started after the Commission has collected the intelligence and evidence of the cartel infringement. This separation between leniency and settlement is different from the procedures used by the United States Department of Justice in its cartel enforcement.[471] Under its Leniency Policy, the Department of Justice grants immunity, not only from punishment but also from prosecution, to the first corporation or individual to provide intelligence and evidence of the cartel. Other defendants cooperating with the Department of Justice are granted reduced penalties through plea or plea/cooperation agreements that cover the provision of intelligence and evidence, as well as the acceptance of the infringement and the penalties, and the waiver of a number of procedural rights, including the right to appeal. Plea bargaining in the United States is thus simultaneously an investigatory tool and a way to dispose of cases. Plea bargaining in the United States therefore corresponds to the combination of (the reduction-of-fine part of) leniency and settlements in the European Commission's cartel enforcement.[472]

---

465 Settlement Notice, points 17 and 20 to 22.

466 Settlement Notice, points 23 to 29. If the Commission were to decide to depart from the settlement submissions, it has to send a new statement of objections, following the normal, fully adversarial procedure, and the settlement submissions would be deemed to be withdrawn and could not be used in evidence.

467 Settlement Notice, point 32.

468 Settlement Notice, last point.

469 Indeed, there have been only a few such appeals: see Order in *Société Générale v Commission*, T-98/14, EU:T:2016:131, and Judgments in *Printeos v Commission*, T-95/15, EU:T:2016:722 and in *Printeos v Commission*, T-466/17, EU:T:2019:671, and currently pending cases T-587/22 *Crown Holdings v Commission* and T-589/22 *Silgan Holdings v Commission*.

470 See Chapter V of this book.

471 See OECD, *Plea Bargaining / Settlement of Cartel Cases*, DAF/COMP(2007)38 (22 January 2008), at 149–202, and 'Leniency in Antitrust Enforcement: Theory and Practice' (2007) 30 *World Competition* 25, also accessible at http://ssrn.com/author=456087, at 26–29, and my book *Efficiency and Justice in European Antitrust Enforcement* (Hart 2008), paragraphs 347–361. See also Judgment in *Schenker v Commission*, T-265/12, EU:T:2016:111, paragraph 421.

472 The primary explanation for the difference is historical. The plea bargaining used by the United States Department of Justice in its cartel enforcement is the same plea bargaining that has been used for a long time in American criminal law enforcement in general. The European Commission adopted its first Leniency Notice in 1996, and modified it in 2002 and 2006, to improve its effectiveness in collecting intelligence and evidence of cartels. The idea of a settlement procedure in cartel cases only arose more recently, precisely as a result of the success of the

B. Settlements and optimal antitrust enforcement

1. Enforcement benefits of fully adversarial proceedings

As I have discussed in more detail elsewhere,[473] the enforcement of antitrust prohibitions such as Articles 101 and 102 TFEU entails three broad tasks: clarifying and developing the content of the prohibitions, preventing violations of the prohibitions, and dealing with the consequences when violations have nevertheless happened.

The normal, fully adversarial disposal of a case by the European Commission, through a decision, based on Articles 7 and 23 of Regulation 1/2003, finding the infringement, imposing remedies to bring the infringement to an end, and/or imposing fines, can thus in six ways contribute to the enforcement of Articles 101 and 102 TFEU:[474]

(1) The finding of the infringement can contribute to clarifying the content of the prohibitions laid down in Articles 101 or 102 TFEU, thus allowing better respect for these prohibitions in the future.

(2) The termination order helps to bring the infringement to an end.

(3) Especially if accompanied by a fine, the finding of the infringement acts as a public censure, which – apart from contributing to the deterrence and punishment effects mentioned under (4) and (5) below – tends to confirm those who already respect the prohibitions of Articles 101 and 102 TFEU in their law-abiding attitude.

(4) The imposition of fines, if sufficiently high, will contribute to deterring both the undertakings concerned and others from committing future infringements.

(5) To the extent that the fines equal the gain obtained through the infringement, their imposition leads to disgorgement of the illicit gains; to the extent that the fines exceed this gain, they may be valued as punishment.

(6) The finding of the infringement may facilitate follow-on private actions for damages, leading to compensation for the victims of the infringement.

Leniency Notice, in its 2002 and 2006 versions, which has led to a large increase in the number of cartels detected; see my paper 'The Commission Notice on the Non-Imposition or Reduction of Fines in Cartel Cases' (1997) 22 *European Law Review* 125; chapter 5 ('The Collection of Intelligence and Evidence from Antitrust Violators') of my book *Principles of European Antitrust Enforcement* (Hart 2005); and 'Leniency in Antitrust Enforcement: Theory and Practice' (2007) 30 *World Competition* 25, also accessible at http://ssrn.com/author=456087, and chapter 5 of my book *Efficiency and Justice in European Antitrust Enforcement* (Hart 2008). Separating leniency and settlement, i.e. giving separate discounts for the provision of intelligence and evidence, on the one hand, and for the guilty plea, on the other hand, also has the advantage of providing more transparency as to the penalty reductions granted in exchange for the intelligence and evidence provided, thus facilitating control of proportionality and equal treatment (see my paper 'Leniency in Antitrust Enforcement: Theory and Practice' (2007) 30 *World Competition* 25, also accessible at http://ssrn.com/author=456087, at 49–51 and 53–54, my book *Efficiency and Justice in European Antitrust Enforcement* (Hart 2008), paragraphs 426–430 and 437–439), as well as the avoidance of too high settlement discounts that could undermine optimal case selection or have a coercive effect. See also below as to the risk of underenforcement when cases are settled at a too early stage of the investigation.

473 See my book *Efficiency and Justice in European Antitrust Enforcement* (Hart 2008), paragraphs 167–182; 'Optimal Antitrust Fines: Theory and Practice' (2006) 29 *World Competition* 183 at 185–190; my book *The Optimal Enforcement of EC Antitrust Law* (Kluwer 2002), section 2.1.3; and my book *Principles of European Antitrust Enforcement* (Hart 2005), section 4.2.

474 See my book *Efficiency and Justice in European Antitrust Enforcement* (Hart 2008), paragraph 93, and my paper 'Settlements of EU Antitrust Investigations: Commitment Decisions under Article 9 of Regulation No. 1/2003' (2006) 29 *World Competition* 345, also accessible at http://ssrn.com/author=456087, at 349.

Whereas the fully adversarial disposal of a case can thus contribute much to the enforcement of Articles 101 and 102 TFEU, these results are only obtained at the end of relatively long and costly procedures. This can be illustrated by two examples (among others):

In the *Irish Ice Cream* case, the Commission adopted in March 1998, after an administrative procedure that had taken several years, a decision finding that the practice of Unilever's Irish subsidiary to provide its distributors with freezer cabinets for free but under the condition that they only be used to store Unilever's ice cream products, constituted, in the circumstances of the Irish market at the time, an infringement of Articles 101 and 102 TFEU, and ordering Unilever to put an end to this practice. Unilever brought an application for annulment of the decision before the General Court and obtained from its president an order staying the execution of the Commission's decision while the case was pending. The order to terminate the infringement thus only became effective after the General Court rejected the application for annulment in October 2003.[475]

In the *PVC Cartel* case, the Commission adopted in December 1988, following an investigation started in 1983, a decision finding that since 1980 fourteen producers of PVC had operated a price-fixing cartel in violation of Article 101 TFEU, and imposing fines on them. Most of the PVC producers brought actions for annulment of the decision. After a first judgment by the General Court declaring the Commission's decision non-existent, and an appeal against that judgment by the Commission, the Court of Justice in 1994 annulled the Commission's decision, because the Commission had failed to authenticate its decision in the way provided for in its own Rules of Procedure.[476] Following this judgment, the Commission readopted its decision, now duly authenticated, reimposing the same fines. The PVC producers again brought an application for annulment to the General Court, and a further appeal to the Court of Justice, which finally confirmed the Commission's decision in October 2002, almost fourteen years after the initial Commission decision.[477]

2. Enforcement gains and losses from settlements

The use of settlements can deliver two potential enforcement gains: speed and lower costs. A settlement may enable the competition authority to obtain **earlier results**. Timeliness is particularly valuable for remedies that bring to an end ongoing infringements. It is, however, also of value for finding infringements and imposing penalties, since a shorter time distance between the infringement and the punishment tends to increase the punishment's deterrent effects.[478] The second potential enforcement gain results from **cost savings**. If a shorter, more streamlined procedure can be followed, and if there are

---

475 Unilever subsequently brought an appeal against the judgment of the General Court, which was rejected by the Court of Justice by Order of 28 September 2006 (*Unilever v Commission*, C-552/03 P, EU:C:2006:607), but Unilever did not seek a further suspension of the execution of the termination order while its appeal before the Court of Justice was pending.

476 Judgment in *Commission v BASF and Others*, C-137/92 P, EU:C:1994:247.

477 Judgment in *Limburgse Vinyl Maatschappij and Others v Commission*, C-238/99 P etc., EU:C:2002:582.

478 On the difficulties for deterrence resulting from the passage of time between the infringement and the punishment, see my book *The Optimal Enforcement of EC Antitrust Law* (Kluwer 2002), section 8.4.2.3, and my book *Efficiency and Justice in European Antitrust Enforcement* (Hart 2008), sections 3.2.1 (footnote 41) and 6.3.1.1 (footnote 103).

no or fewer appeals, less administrative resources will have to be spent per case, which means, if the competition authority's budget is fixed, that more antitrust infringements can be detected and dealt with.

These enforcement gains can, however, only be obtained if the defendants are willing to settle, and they will only be prepared to do so if they derive some benefit from it, which makes settling more attractive to them than fully contesting the case. Two categories of possible benefits could be distinguished, depending on whether or not they correspond to enforcement losses. Like the competition authority, the defendant may benefit from saving some of the costs of fully contesting the case (cost of lawyers, management time, etc.). Depending on the circumstances, the defendant may also have an interest in an earlier outcome of the case. To the extent that defendants can be made to accept settlements solely for these reasons, settlements appear unambiguously desirable from the perspective of optimal enforcement. However, in many instances such benefits may not be enough to induce defendants to settle. Other benefits will have to be offered, such as lesser or no findings of infringement, lower penalties or less burdensome remedies. Such **settlement rewards**, however, directly correspond to enforcement losses. If such settlement rewards are granted to the defendants to induce them to settle, settlements will only be desirable from the perspective of optimal enforcement if the corresponding enforcement losses are outweighed by the enforcement gains resulting from the speedier outcome of the case and the administrative cost savings.

The **balance between the potential enforcement gains and losses** obviously depends upon the type of settlement procedure and the type of settlement reward granted.

As to commitment decisions under Article 9 of Regulation 1/2003, the settlement reward consists in the absence of a finding of infringement, as well as the absence of a fine, whereas the potential enforcement gains are the earlier termination of the infringement and the administrative cost savings. Optimally, commitment decisions should thus be used (only) in those cases where the benefit in terms of an earlier termination of the infringement and the saving of the cost of longer proceedings outweigh the loss of the other contributions to the enforcement of Articles 81 and 82 EC which infringement decisions could make, in terms of clarification of the law, public censure, deterrence, disgorgement of illicit gains and punishment, and facilitation of follow-on actions for compensation.

In the above-mentioned example of the *Irish Ice Cream* case, the main interest of the case probably consisted in the clarification of the law, because of the novel character of the infringement.[479] This required a fully adversarial disposal of the case, as an authoritative clarification of the law can only be obtained by bringing the case before the courts. In the case of serious and clear-cut infringements such as cartels, the main enforcement objectives should be deterrence and public censure through the finding of the infringement and the imposition of penalties. Commitment decisions would thus be inappropriate, as is indeed indicated in recital 13 of the preamble of Regulation 1/2003. In some other cases, where the infringement is neither novel nor very serious, the benefits of earlier

---

479 No fine was imposed in this case, precisely reflecting the novel character of the infringement.

termination and administrative cost savings may outweigh other considerations, and the use of commitment decisions would thus be desirable.[480]

As to the settlement procedure in cartel cases, the settlement reward consists of a reduction of the fine by 10%. This obviously entails an enforcement loss. If the settlement procedure were to become generally used, the average expected fine would be reduced by 10%. In order to ensure that the use of the settlement procedure on the whole increases deterrence, the increase in the number of cartels detected and fined, resulting from the use of the resources saved thanks to the settlement procedure, would thus have to exceed 11%.[481]

More generally, the following points could be made as to how to ensure that the enforcement gains from settlements exceed the enforcement losses:

First, defendants should not be given a right to settle. The use of settlements should be at the competition authority's discretion, in the light of each specific case, so that it can be restricted to those cases where the enforcement gains exceed the enforcement losses. This is indeed the situation for commitment decisions under Article 9 of Regulation 1/2003, the EU Courts having confirmed that 'the Commission is never obliged under Article 9(1) of Regulation No 1/2003 to decide to make commitments binding instead of proceeding under Article 7 of that regulation'.[482] Similarly, the Commission Notice on the conduct of settlement procedures in cartel cases clearly states that 'the Commission retains a broad margin of discretion to determine which cases may be suitable [. . .] to settle'.[483]

Second, it is important that the competition authority builds and maintains a credible reputation for being able to handle cases successfully under the normal, fully adversarial procedures. Indeed, the stronger the authority's reputation for obtaining forceful remedies and penalties through the fully adversarial route, the more defendants will be willing to

---

480 See also E. Gippini-Fournier, Community Report for the FIDE XXIII Congress 2008, in H. F. Koeck and M. M. Karollus (eds), *The Modernisation of European Competition Law: Initial Experiences with Regulation 1/2003* (Nomos 2008), text accompanying footnotes 126 to 127, and P. Lowe and F. Maier-Rigaud, 'Quo Vadis Antitrust Remedies', in B. E. Hawk (ed), *2007 Annual Proceedings of the Fordham Corporate Law Institute – International Antitrust Law and Policy* (Juris Publishing 2008), 597, at 607–609.

481 Similarly, if a competition authority were to grant settlement rebates of 33%, an increase of more than 50% in the number of cartels detected and penalised would be required for the net enforcement effect to be positive, the general formula being that a systematically applied settlement rebate of n % requires a compensatory increase in the number of cartels detected and penalised of at least (n * 100) / (100 – n) % in order to avoid a net reduction of the expected fine (i.e. the nominal fine discounted by the probability of detection and punishment), and hence a weakening of deterrence.

482 Judgment in *Alrosa v Commission*, T-170/06, EU:T:2007:220, paragraph 130 (continuing: 'It is therefore not required to give reasons for which commitments are not in its view suitable to be made binding, so as to bring the proceedings to an end.'); this judgment was annulled on appeal before the Court of Justice by Judgment in *Commission v Alrosa*, C-441/07 P, EU:C:2010:377, but this point was not contested on appeal. See also Judgments in *Orange Polska*, T-486/11, EU:T:2015:1002, paragraphs 218 to 224, in *CB v Commission*, T-491/07 RENV, EU:T:2016:379, paragraph 470, and in *Google and Alphabet v Commission (Google Shopping)*, T-612/17, EU:T:2021:763, paragraph 638.

483 Settlement Notice, paragraph 5; see also recital 4 of Commission Regulation (EC) No 622/2008 of 30 June 2008 amending Regulation (EC) No 773/2004, as regards the conduct of settlement procedures in cartel cases [2008] OJ L171/3, and Judgments in *Timab Industries and CFPR v Commission*, T-456/10, EU:T:2015:296, paragraph 64, in *Schenker v Commission*, T-265/12, EU:T:2016:111, paragraphs 395 to 422, and in *Philips and Philips France v Commission*, T-762/14, EU:T:2016:738, paragraph 255.

settle without the need for large settlement rewards. Only if the Commission demonstrates that it can win contested cases, such as the *Microsoft* case,[484] can it expect to obtain good settlements in other cases under Article 9 of Regulation 1/2003. Similarly, the introduction of the settlement procedure for cartel cases, with only a modest settlement reward, was only feasible thanks to the many fully contested cartel decisions that were upheld by the Courts in the previous years.

Third, the competition authority should avoid settling a case at a too early stage of the investigation, when it has not yet established all the relevant facts.[485] Indeed, if the competition authority settles a case before it has discovered the full extent and seriousness of the infringement, it is likely to grant (unknowingly) a too large (*de facto*) settlement reward. This is particularly important in settlement procedures such as the Commission's settlement procedure for cartel cases, where it would no doubt be impossible, because of the principle of *ne bis in idem*,[486] to reopen the case at a later point in time, if it appears that the infringement was more serious than thought at the time of settlement, and thus requiring higher fines. As to commitment decisions under Article 9 of Regulation 1/2003, there may be less risk of inadequate settlement due to incomplete investigation, because Article 9(2) allows for the case to be reopened notably where the decision was based on incomplete, incorrect or misleading information provided by the parties, and because a commitment decision under Article 9 does not prevent the competition authorities and courts of the Member States finding an infringement of Articles 101 and 102 TFEU, even if the commitment decision is complied with.[487] Also helpful in this respect is Article 27(4) of Regulation 1/2003, which provides that, where the Commission intends to adopt a commitment decision, it must first publish a summary of the case and the main content of the commitments, thus allowing third parties to provide additional relevant information as to the adequacy of the commitments offered.[488]

Finally, it may be useful periodically to evaluate settlement policies and procedures, so as verify *ex post* whether they indeed generate the net enforcement gains that justify their use.[489]

---

484 Judgment in *Microsoft v Commission*, T-201/04, EU:T:2007:289.

485 See also OECD, *Plea Bargaining / Settlement of Cartel Cases*, DAF/COMP(2007)38 (22 January 2008), at 10 and 34.

486 See my paper 'The Principle of *Ne Bis in Idem* in EC Antitrust Enforcement: A Legal and Economic Analysis' (2003) 26 *World Competition* 131, and chapter 3 and section 2.5.2 of my book *Principles of European Antitrust Enforcement* (Hart 2005).

487 This possibility of further action at Member State level creates an incentive for the companies concerned to offer sufficiently effective commitments to the Commission; 'Settlements of EU Antitrust Investigations: Commitment Decisions under Article 9 of Regulation No. 1/2003' (2006) 29 *World Competition* 345, also accessible at http://ssrn.com/author=456087, at 361–363, and my book *Efficiency and Justice in European Antitrust Enforcement* (Hart 2008), paragraphs 141 to 150.

488 See 'Settlements of EU Antitrust Investigations: Commitment Decisions under Article 9 of Regulation No. 1/2003' (2006) 29 *World Competition* 345, also accessible at http://ssrn.com/author=456087, at 355–356, and my book *Efficiency and Justice in European Antitrust Enforcement* (Hart 2008), paragraphs 117 and 118.
The publication and possibility for third-party comments, and the ensuing possibility for third-party complainants to bring an action before the EU Courts, constitute the functional equivalent of the publication for public comments and the public interest determination by the district court under the Tunney Act, 15 USC § 16, for consent judgments in civil proceedings brought by the United States Department of Justice.

489 See generally W. E. Kovacic, 'Using Evaluation to Improve the Performance of Competition Policy Authorities – Background note', in OECD, *Evaluation of the Actions and Resources of Competition Authorities*, DAF/COMP(2005)30 (16 December 2005), 19-58.

3. Case selection and prioritisation

The above analysis of the potential enforcement gains and losses resulting from the use of settlements focused on the question whether a given case, which has been investigated by the competition authority, should be disposed of through the fully adversarial route or by way of settlement. The possibility of disposing of cases by way of settlement may, however, also have an impact on the initial decision of the competition authority whether or not to start investigating a case.[490]

Competition authorities inevitably have only limited resources compared to the many cases of possible antitrust infringements that could be investigated. It would obviously be desirable for competition authorities to spend their limited resources on those investigations that are likely to lead to the finding, remedying and punishing of the most serious antitrust infringements. In a system where cases can only be disposed of through fully adversarial proceedings, there is a strong incentive for the competition authority, starting from the initial case selection, to spend its resources according to the likelihood of finding a serious infringement that can be remedied or punished. Indeed, at the end of the fully adversarial proceedings, it will become apparent whether or not such an infringement can be established. If it turns out that there is no infringement, or only a minor one, the authority will not be able to show any result, or only a minor result, for all the resources spent.[491]

The possibility of disposing of cases through a settlement procedure may alter these incentives for optimal case selection and prioritisation. If the settlement procedure allows for large settlement rewards, and is flexible, in that the size of the award can be negotiated on a case-by-case basis, there is a risk of a negative effect on case selection and prioritisation incentives. Indeed, it may be feasible for a competition authority to settle a case which, if disposed of through fully adversarial proceedings, is likely to result in no finding of an infringement, or only a minor one. Indeed, the defendant may accept to settle such a case, provided that a sufficiently large settlement reward is granted, reflecting the low probability of the authority obtaining a substantial result through fully adversarial proceedings. This possibility of settling weak cases, and thus still show a result, could reduce the incentives for optimal case selection and prioritisation.

If, however, the settlement procedure only allows for small settlement rewards, and is inflexible, in that the rewards cannot be significantly varied through case-by-case negotiation, incentives for optimal case selection and prioritisation may actually be strengthened. Indeed, as the rewards are only small, and cannot be adapted to reflect the weakness of a case, only strong cases will be settled. And given that settlements allow resources to be saved, the authority will be induced to select those cases that can be settled, thus strong cases.

---

490 See also R. Wright and M. Miller, 'The Screening/Bargaining Tradeoff' (2002) 55 *Stanford Law Review* 29 and O. Gazal-Ayal, 'Partial Ban on Plea Bargains' (2006) 27 *Cardozo Law Review* 2295.

491 On the incentives for competition authorities to show results, see my paper 'The Combination of the Investigative and Prosecutorial Function and the Adjudicative Function in EC Antitrust Enforcement: A Legal and Economic Analysis' (2004) 27 *World Competition* 201 at 214–217, and my book *Principles of European Antitrust Enforcement* (Hart 2005), paragraphs 594–603.

As described above, the European Commission's settlement procedure for cartel cases only allows for a fixed settlement reward of 10%. It is also clearly stated that the Commission 'does not negotiate the question of the existence of an infringement [. . .] and the appropriate sanction',[492] which means that there will be no other settlement reward than the fine reduction. Under such a system, only strong cases will be settled, and the incentives for optimal case selection and prioritisation between cases are strengthened rather than weakened.

The commitments procedure under Article 9 of Regulation 1/2003 is much more flexible, and hence produces some risk as to the weakening of incentives for optimal case selection and prioritisation. To avoid such negative effects, it is thus important that the Commission maintains strict and effective internal procedures and controls ensuring that weak cases are not opened, or, if already opened, swiftly closed, without recourse to formal commitments.

C. Settlements and fundamental rights of defence

As defined above, settlement procedures or policies are based on the granting of some benefit to the defendant in recognition of the defendant's admission or non-contestation of the infringement and/or offer or acceptance of penalties and/or remedies. Apart from admitting the infringement and consenting to the penalties or remedies, the defendant will usually also waive various procedural rights.

For instance, under the European Commission's settlement procedure for cartel cases, companies that choose to settle must not only admit to the infringement and their liability, and accept the (reduced) fine, but are also required to waive their right to separate representation from other companies within the same undertaking (corporate group), their right to further access to the file and to a formal oral hearing after the statement of objections, and their right to receive the decision in an official language of the Member State in which they are based. The settling companies are not asked to waive their right to have the Commission decision reviewed by the EU Courts.[493] However, their recognition of the infringement and of their liability, and acceptance of the fine is likely to affect their chances of successful judicial review.[494]

The self-incrimination and waiver of procedural rights by settlement candidates, and the encouragement thereof by the grant of settlement rewards, may raise concerns with regard to the privilege against self-incrimination and other fundamental rights of defence.[495]

---

492 Settlement Notice, point 2; see also Judgment in *Daimler*, C-588/20, EU:C:2022:607, paragraph 53.

493 See Settlement Notice, last point.

494 See D. Waelbroeck, 'Le développement en droit européen de la concurrence des solutions négociées (engagements, clémence, non-contestation des faits et transactions): que va-t-il rester aux juges?', *GCLC Working Paper 01/08* (2008), at 23–24, and K. Lenaerts, 'Some Thoughts on Evidence and Procedure in European Community Competition Law' (2007) 30 *Fordham International Law Journal* 1463 at 1490–1491. There certainly remains scope for judicial review based on grounds of procedural irregularities during the settlement procedure or on grounds of unequal treatment between different settlement candidates.

495 On the privilege against self-incrimination, see Judgment in *Orkem v Commission*, 374/87, EU:C:1989:387, paragraphs 35–40; Judgment and Opinion of Advocate General Geelhoed in *Commission v SGL Carbon*, C-301/04 P, EU:C:2006:432 and EU:C:2006:53; Judgment in *Qualcomm and Qualcomm Europe v Commission*,

The general answer of the law appears to be that self-incrimination and waivers of procedural rights are unproblematic provided that they are **voluntary**, which requires both **adequate knowledge** and **absence of improper compulsion.**[496]

Indeed, under those conditions the values underlying both the privilege against self-incrimination and other fundamental rights of defence are not endangered. All rights of the defence could generally be said to serve two purposes. First, they serve to avoid miscarriages of justice, or more generally, to ensure accuracy in the outcome of law enforcement procedures.[497] Second, they serve to uphold the defendant's dignity during the enforcement process.[498] Where the outcome of the enforcement procedure is based on the defendant's voluntary acceptance, both accuracy and dignity would appear to be safeguarded.[499]

One of the obvious conditions to be satisfied for a settlement to be voluntary is that the defendant has not been the victim of any misrepresentation by the competition authority, regarding the expected or possible outcome of a fully adversarial disposal of the case,

---

T-371/17, EU:T:2019:232, paragraphs 177 to 194; Opinion of Advocate General Wahl in *HeidelbergCement v Commission*, C-247/14 P, EU:C:2015:694, paragraphs 149 to 164; recital 23 of Regulation 1/2003; and my paper 'Self-Incrimination in EC Antitrust Enforcement: A Legal and Economic Analysis' (2003) 26 *World Competition* 567, also accessible at http://ssrn.com/author=456087.

496 See inter alia Judgment of the European Court of Human Rights, *Saunders v United Kingdom* (17 December 1996, Reports 1996-VI, p 2064), Concurring Opinion of Judge Walsh: 'Persons are always free to incriminate themselves if in doing so they are exercising their own free will'; Admissibility Decision of the European Court of Human Rights, *Borghi v Italy* (20 June 2002, Application 54767/00): '[T]he prospect of obtaining an advantage cannot be taken to affect a defendant's freedom to waive all grounds of appeal on the facts or on points of law [. . .] the applicant's decision must be considered to have been free and voluntary'; Judgment of the EU Court of Justice in *ThyssenKrupp v Commission*, C-65/02 P and C-73/02 P, EU:C:2005:454, paragraphs 52–53: '[A] dmission of an infringement is a matter entirely within the will of the undertaking concerned. The latter is not in any way coerced to admit the existence of the agreement. It must therefore be considered that the fact that the Commission took account of the degree of cooperation with it shown by the undertaking concerned, including admission of the infringement, for the purpose of imposing a lower fine does not constitute any breach of its rights of the defence'; and US Supreme Court, *United States v Ruiz*, 536 US 622 (2002): 'When a defendant pleads guilty he or she, of course, forgoes not only a fair trial, but also other accompanying constitutional guarantees [. . .] Given the seriousness of the matter, the Constitution insists, among other things, that the defendant enter a guilty plea that is "voluntary" and that the defendant must make related waivers "knowing[ly], intelligent[ly] [and] with sufficient awareness of the relevant circumstances and likely consequences." *Brady v United States*, 397 US 742, 748 (1970).' Among the extensive literature on the subject, see in particular the enlightening analysis in C. G. Brunk, 'The Problem of Voluntariness and Coercion in the Negotiated Plea' (1979) 13 *Law and Society Review* 527.

497 That only the guilty should be punished, and that sanctions should be proportionate to the infringement, not only reflects the most basic requirements of justice, but is also essential for the effectiveness of deterrence. Indeed, it is through the differential in expected sanctions between non-infringement and infringement, and between lesser and more serious infringements, that potential infringers are deterred from entering into infringements, or infringers are deterred from prolonging, extending or otherwise aggravating their infringements.

498 Concerns about the defendant's dignity would appear more relevant in the case of natural persons than in the case of corporate defendants; see generally M. Emberland, *The Human Rights of Companies* (Oxford University Press 2006). Procedural fairness not only constitutes a value in itself but also contributes to the objective of ensuring compliance with the substantive law, to the extent that perceptions of fairness lead to greater voluntary compliance; see T. R. Tyler, *Why People Obey the Law* (Yale University Press 1990).

499 Obviously, the defendant's agreement can only guarantee that the finding of infringement is not too broad, and the remedies or penalties not disproportionately heavy, but does not exclude that the finding may be too narrow and the remedies or penalties disproportionately weak. As to how to avoid the latter type of inaccuracy in the settlement context, see the discussion on settlements and optimal antitrust enforcement above.

as well as regarding the conditions and consequences of a settlement. Clear rules or guidelines on the normally applicable sanctions and on the available settlement rewards are certainly useful in this respect. To avoid settlements being coerced through bluffing, access to the authority's file should be possible.[500]

Second, the defendant must receive enough time, and have adequate access to counsel so as to be able to make an intelligent settlement decision in its own interests, as well as the means to defend itself through fully adversarial proceedings. While concerns as to access to adequate counsel have often been raised in the context of plea bargaining in general criminal law,[501] this condition would not appear to pose problems in the context of antitrust enforcement, certainly not in the case of the European Commission, whose antitrust enforcement proceedings are usually directed against large companies that have access to the best legal advice money can buy.[502]

Third, a settlement could obviously not be said to be voluntary if it were coerced through physical threats, or any other threats or promises of a nature not properly related to the antitrust enforcement proceedings.

Fourth, improper compulsion would also exist if a defendant's refusal to settle would result in an increase in the penalty above the normal penalty, i.e. above the penalty that would have been imposed if the competition authority had not offered the defendant a possibility to settle.[503]

On the other hand, a settlement does not become involuntary merely because a penalty reduction below the normal penalty level is offered. Indeed, if the penalty imposed in case the defendant refuses to settle is the normal penalty, i.e. the penalty that would also have been imposed if the authority had not granted the possibility to settle, the offer of a lower penalty in case of settlement merely enlarges the options available to the defendant, thus increasing rather than reducing the defendant's freedom of choice.[504] If large reductions were offered, the voluntariness of settlements could, however, still be questioned, for two reasons. First, if the settlement reward were so large that a 'flagrant disproportion' would exist been the two alternatives facing the defendant, it might be argued that the pressure to settle would be compelling.[505] Second, as argued above, large settlement rewards may allow competition authorities to obtain settlements in weak cases

---

500 *See* E. J. Ostrow, 'The Case for Preplea Disclosure' (1981) 90 *Yale Law Journal* 1581.

501 See inter alia S. J. Schulhofer, 'Plea Bargaining as Disaster' (1992) 101 *Yale Law Journal* 1979.

502 See also OECD, *Plea Bargaining / Settlement of Cartel Cases*, DAF/COMP(2007)38 (22 January 2008), at 11–12 and 33. As to the limited (and never used) possibility for the European Commission to bring antitrust enforcement proceedings against natural persons, see my book *Efficiency and Justice in European Antitrust Enforcement* (Hart 2008), paragraphs 502–504.

503 Similarly, improper compulsion would exist if a defendant's refusal to settle would result in a wider or more serious finding of infringement, or the imposition of more burdensome remedies than would have been the case if the competition authority had not offered the defendant a possibility to settle.

504 See Admissibility Decision of the European Court of Human Rights, *Borghi v Italy* (20 June 2002, Application no 54767/00).

505 See European Court of Human Rights, *Deweer v Belgium* (27 February 1980; Application no 6903/75). This case concerned an infringement of (then in force) Belgian price regulations by Mr Deweer, a butcher. Mr Deweer was offered the choice by the public prosecutor between either directly paying a modest fine (in the order of €250) without any further prosecution, or facing a criminal prosecution, which could have taken several months, during which his butcher shop would have been provisionally closed, depriving him of his income.

(or including weak parts of cases), which, in the absence of the settlement option, would never have been opened, or would have been discontinued by the competition authority. In such cases, the voluntary nature of settlements could be contested on the ground that the competition authority has placed the defendant into an unfavourable choice situation, compared to the situation in which the defendant would have been if no possibility of settlement had existed.[506]

In the European Commission's settlement procedure for cartel cases, the fine reduction is 10%. Such a small reduction, applied to the normal fine as resulting from the Commission's Guidelines on fines and Leniency Notice, appears entirely unproblematic.[507]

The situation of Mr Deweer would, however, appear to be substantially different from that of a large company assisted by sophisticated counsel in an antitrust procedure. On the impossibility of simply transposing the case law of the European Court of Human Rights concerning natural persons in the context of 'classical' criminal procedures to the different situation of companies in antitrust proceedings such as those conducted by the European Commission, see Chapter X of this book.

506 See C. G. Brunk, 'The Problem of Voluntariness and Coercion in the Negotiated Plea' (1979) 13 *Law and Society Review* 527.

507 See also A. Ashworth and M. Redmayne, *The Criminal Process*, 3rd edition (Oxford University Press 2005), at 292 (arguing that the sentence discount for guilty pleas should be 'no more than a 10 per cent reduction').

VII. Antitrust Compliance Programmes and Optimal Antitrust Enforcement

A. Introduction

Should companies that have antitrust compliance programmes[508] be granted a reduction in the amount of fines or even immunity from fines when they are found to have committed antitrust infringements? Should the absence of a compliance programme constitute an aggravating factor leading to higher fines for antitrust infringements? Should the adoption of a compliance programme be imposed as part of infringement decisions or settlements?

These are the questions which this chapter examines, on the basis of an analysis of the nature of antitrust infringements, the rationale of company liability for antitrust infringements, and the possible positive and possible negative effects of compliance programmes.

In November 2011, the European Commission published a brochure, in which it reaffirmed its policy not to grant a reduction in the amount of fines because of the existence of a compliance programme:

'*The Commission welcomes and supports all compliance efforts by companies [. . .]. For the purpose of setting the level of fines, the specific situation of a company is duly taken into account. But the mere existence of a compliance programme will not be considered as an attenuating circumstance. Nor will the setting-up of a compliance programme be considered as a valid argument justifying a reduction of the fine in the wake of investigation of an infringement.*'[509]

---

508 An antitrust compliance programme is a set of measures adopted within a company or corporate group to inform, educate and instruct its personnel about the antitrust prohibitions (Articles 101 and 102 TFEU and similar prohibitions) and the company's or group's policy regarding respect for these prohibitions, and to control or monitor respect for these prohibitions or this policy. Antitrust compliance programmes are thus a type of organisational control system aimed at standardising staff behaviour, specifically within the domain of antitrust compliance; see G. R. Weaver, L. K. Treviño and P. L. Cochran, 'Corporate Ethics Programs as Control Systems: Influences of Executive Commitment and Environmental Factors' (1999) 42 *Academy of Management Journal* 41 at 42, as well as C. Angelucci and M. A. Han, 'Monitoring Managers Through Corporate Compliance Programs', Amsterdam Center for Law & Economics Working Paper no 2010-14, accessible at http://ssrn.com/abstract=1729135, and Chapter 2 of M. A. Han, *Vertical Relations in Cartel Theory* (PhD thesis, University of Amsterdam, ACLE Dissertation Series No 4, September 2011), accessible at http://www.carteltheory.com.

509 European Commission, *Compliance matters – What companies can do better to respect EU competition rules* (November 2011), accessible at http://ec.europa.eu/competition/antitrust/compliance/, at 19–20; see also speeches by Joaquín Almunia, Vice President of the European Commission responsible for Competition Policy, 'Cartels: the priority in competition enforcement' (SPEECH/11/268; Berlin, 14 April 2011) and 'Compliance and Competition policy' (SPEECH/10/586; Brussels, 25 October 2012).

The European Commission has never granted a reduction of a fine because of the existence of a compliance programme at the time of the infringement. In seven decisions, adopted between 1982 and 1992, however, the Commission granted a fine reduction because the companies concerned had set up a compliance programme after the start of the Commission's investigations.[510] The Commission has never since granted any reductions because of compliance programmes.[511]

The EU Courts have consistently upheld this policy, pointing out that the implementation of a competition compliance programme 'does not alter the reality of the infringement and does not oblige the Commission to grant a reduction in the amount of the fine'.[512]

This policy has been criticised by some authors calling for 'a substantial fine reduction for firms with effective compliance programs'.[513]

A few authors have gone further, arguing that, 'if a company has made a reasonable effort to comply with the antitrust law, and an employee nevertheless engages in price-fixing, then it makes no sense to fine the corporation'.[514] Their idea would thus be that

---

510 Commission Decisions of 7 December 1982, *National Panasonic* [1982] L 354/28; of 14 December 1984, *John Deere* [1985] OJ L35/58; of 16 December 1985, *Sperry New Holland* [1985] OJ L376/21; of 18 December 1987, *Fisher-Price/Quaker Oats – Toyco* [1988] OJ L49/19; of 22 December 1987, *Eurofix-Bauco/Hilti* [1988] OJ L65/19; of 18 July 1988, *British Sugar* [1988] OJ L284/41; of 5 June 1991, *Viho/Toshiba* [1991] OJ L287/39; and of 15 July 1992, *Viho/Parker Pen* [1992] OJ L233/27; all these decisions concerned vertical agreements or abuse of a dominant position, which were the main types of cases the Commission prosecuted in those years. When *British Sugar* was later found to have committed another infringement, the Commission took the violation of the compliance programme, together with the fact of the recidivism, into account as an aggravating factor leading to a higher second fine; Commission Decision of 14 October 1998, *British Sugar* [1999] OJ L76/1; on recidivism, see Chapter VIII of this book.

511 In a decision in 2001, the Commission took into account the introduction of a compliance programme as one of a number of elements indicating that the infringement had been terminated and that there was thus no need for the Commission to order its termination; Commission Decision of 5 December 2001, *Interbrew and Alken*-Maes [2003] OJ L200/1, paragraph 291. More importantly, since 1996, the Commission grants fine reductions and even immunity from fines to companies that put an end or have put an end to their participation in a secret cartel and cooperate with the Commission in providing intelligence and evidence of the cartel under the conditions set out in the Commission's Leniency Notice; see Chapter V of this book.

512 Judgments in *UPM-Kymmene v European Commission*, T-53/06, EU:T:2012:101, paragraphs 123–124; in *Dansk Rørindustri and Others v European Commission*, C-189/02 P, C-202/02 P, C-205/02 P to C-208/02 P and C-213/02 P, EU:C:2005:408, paragraph 373; in *BASF and UCB v Commission*, T-101/05 and T-111/05, EU:T:2007:380, paragraph 52; and in *Schindler Holding and Others v Commission*, T-138/07, EU:T:2011:362, paragraph 88.

513 F. Brunet, 'The role of antitrust compliance programs in competition law enforcement', New Frontiers of Antitrust Conference (Paris, 10 February 2012), *Concurrences* no 2-2012, 16 at 22.

514 D. H. Ginsburg and J. D. Wright, 'Antitrust Sanctions', *Competition Policy International*, vol 6, no 2 (Autumn 2010), at 18. Judge Ginsburg and Professor Wright make this statement as part of a broader argument against continuously increasing the level of corporate fines and in favour of adding more individual penalties, with which I largely agree, and which indeed corresponds to arguments made in several publications of mine ('Does the Effective Enforcement of Articles 81 and 82 EC Require Not Only Fines on Undertakings But Also Individual Penalties, In Particular Imprisonment?', in C.-D. Ehlermann and I. Atanasiu (eds), *European Competition Law Annual 2001: Effective Private Enforcement of EC Antitrust Law* (Hart 2002); my book *The Optimal Enforcement of EC Antitrust Law* (Kluwer 2002), chapters 8 and 9; 'Is Criminalization of EU Competition Law the Answer?' (2005) 28 *World Competition* 117; 'Optimal Antitrust Fines: Theory and Practice' (2006) 29 *World Competition* 183; *Efficiency and Justice in European Antitrust Enforcement* (Hart 2008); 'Recidivism in EU Antitrust Enforcement: A Legal and Economic Analysis' (2012) 35 *World Competition* 5). There is an important difference though between, on the one hand, adding individual penalties to corporate penalties (instead of further increasing corporate penalties), and, on the other hand, granting corporations immunity from fines and relying exclusively on individual penalties.

a company with a compliance programme should not merely receive reduced fines for antitrust infringements, but immunity from such fines.[515]

While most of the literature focuses on granting fine reductions to companies that had a compliance programme in place when committing an antitrust infringement, some authors have suggested a number of other measures which competition authorities could also take to promote investment in compliance programmes, including considering the absence of genuine antitrust compliance efforts as an aggravating factor in assessing the level of any penalty and imposing a requirement on companies to adopt a credible compliance programme as part of infringement decisions or settlements.[516]

The purpose of this chapter is to examine, from the perspective of optimal antitrust enforcement (taking into account considerations of cost and effectiveness as well as considerations of principle),[517] whether reductions in the amount of fines or immunity from fines should be granted to companies that have compliance programmes, whether the absence of a compliance programme should lead to higher fines, and whether the adoption of a compliance programme should be imposed as part of infringement decisions or settlements.

In order to do so, the following sections first examine the nature of antitrust infringements, the rationale of company liability for antitrust infringements, and the possible positive and possible negative effects of compliance programmes.

B. The nature of antitrust infringements

Antitrust infringements have the following four characteristics:

1. Antitrust infringements involve directors or employees that have been given authority to act on behalf of the company

Antitrust infringements involve directors or employees that have been given by their company authority to act on its behalf.[518] Indeed, for an individual working in a company to be able to fix prices or share markets with other companies, or to make the company practise exclusionary rebates or predatory prices, the individual must have been given by the company the power to set or negotiate prices or to conclude or negotiate contracts.

---

515 See also K. Hofstetter and M. Ludescher, 'Fines against Parent Companies in EU Antitrust Law: Setting Incentives for "Best Practice Compliance"' (2010) 33 *World Competition* 55.

516 A. Riley and M. Bloom, 'Antitrust Compliance Programmes – Can Companies and Antitrust Agencies Do More?' (2011) *Journal of Competition Law* 21 at 39–40.

517 See generally my books *The Optimal Enforcement of EC Antitrust Law* (Kluwer Law International, 2002) and *Efficiency and Justice in European Antitrust Enforcement* (Hart 2008), and my papers 'Optimal Antitrust Fines: Theory and Practice' (2006) 29 *World Competition* 183, 'Leniency in Antitrust Enforcement: Theory and Practice' (2007) 30 *World Competition* 25, and Chapters VI and VIII of this book.

518 See Judgments in *Musique Diffusion française* v *Commission*, 100/80 – 103/80, EU:C:1983:97, and in *Scania and Others* v *Commission*, T-799/17, EU:T:2022:48, paragraph 339.

The empirical evidence from the population of antitrust infringements that have been detected and prosecuted by antitrust authorities is that most infringements involve senior management.[519]

The 'rogue employee' explanation, a classic defence in cartel cases, does clearly not fit the many cases where the highest levels of the company are involved. In the remaining cases, where no involvement of senior management can be established, the 'rogue employee' must be someone to whom the company has given authority to set or negotiate prices or to conclude or negotiate contracts.

2. Antitrust infringements are financially beneficial to the company

Unless they are detected and punished sufficiently heavily to take away the illegal gain, antitrust infringements are beneficial to the company, in that they increase profits or reduce losses, or, in some cases of marginal companies, prevent the company from having to lay off staff or even going out of business. In the absence of detection and punishment, the company has thus a financial interest, and in some extreme cases even an existential interest, in antitrust infringements being committed on its behalf.

In the area of antitrust, there is thus no natural alignment of interests between companies and authorities, in that companies would naturally want to reduce the number of illegal acts engaged in by their staff.[520] This is an important difference from some other types of employee wrongdoing, such as embezzlement, that victimise the company or at least benefit no one else than the individual wrongdoer.[521]

---

519 See M. Berzins and F. Sofo, 'The inability of compliance strategies to prevent collusive conduct' (2008) 8 *Corporate Governance* 669 at 675 (finding that senior management were involved in 80% of 69 publicly available cases from Australia, Canada, Denmark, the European Commission, Ireland, Japan, Korea, The Netherlands, New Zealand, the UK and the USA between 2000 and 2006); A. Stephan, 'Hear no Evil, See no Evil: Why Antitrust Compliance Programmes may be Ineffective at Preventing Cartels', University of East Anglia CCP Working paper 09-09 (July 2009) at 8–10 (listing the positions of individuals involved in 40 international cartels and named in decisions of the European Commission or press releases of the US Department of Justice between 1998 and 2008); J. C. Gallo, K. Dau-Schmidt, J. L. Craycraft and C. J. Parker, 'Department of Justice Antitrust Enforcement, 1955–1997: An Empirical Study' (2000) 17 *Review of Industrial Organization* 75 at 104–107 (69% of all individual criminal defendants in cases brought by the US Department of Justice Antitrust Division between 1955 and 1997 were corporate officers); 'Antitrust Compliance Programs: The Government Perspective', Address by W. J. Kolasky, Deputy Assistant Attorney General, before the Corporate Compliance 2002 Conference (San Francisco, July 12, 2002), at 5; and J. M. Connor, *Global Price Fixing: Our Customers are the Enemy* (Kluwer 2001) at 11–12.

520 See M. H. Baer, 'Governing Corporate Compliance' (2009) 50 *Boston College Law Review* 1 at 35 and footnote 213, and compare with *How your business can achieve compliance with competition law* (OFT1341, June 2011), at 1.1, and T. R. Tyler, 'The psychology of self-regulation: normative motivations for compliance', in C. Parker and V. Lehmann Nielsen, *Explaining Compliance: Business Responses to Regulation* (Edward Elgar, 2011) 78 at 81.

521 See M. H. Baer, 'Governing Corporate Compliance' (2009) 50 *Boston College Law Review* 1, at 48–49; A. Stephan, 'Hear no Evil, See no Evil: Why Antitrust Compliance Programmes may be Ineffective at Preventing Cartels', University of East Anglia CCP Working paper 09-09 (July 2009), at 11; and M. E. Stucke, 'Am I a Price Fixer? A Behavioural Economic Analysis of Cartels', in C. Beaton-Wells and A. Ezrachi, *Criminalising Cartels: Critical Studies of an International Regulatory Movement* (Hart 2011) 263 at 267 and 274.

3. Employees are primarily motivated by what they perceive to be their company's interest and/or by the incentives the company has set for them

All available studies of the motivations of employees engaging in antitrust infringements show that these employees are primarily motivated by what they perceive to be their company's interest, or what they think is expected from them, and/or by the incentives the company has set for them.[522] While it cannot be excluded in theory that employees may be primarily motivated by considerations disconnected from what they perceive to be their company's interest or the expectations towards them and from the incentives their company has set for them, for instance by the desire to help out a personal friend in a competing company,[523] there is no evidence that this happens with any frequency.

4. The importance of performance targets and incentives

The same studies referred to just above show that a particularly important factor driving employees to commit antitrust infringements is the pressure they feel from overly ambitious profit targets or performance goals or overly strong incentives set for them by the company.[524]

C. The rationale of company liability for antitrust infringements

There are essentially three reasons that justify company liability for antitrust infringements. These reasons reflect the nature of antitrust infringements described just above.

---

522 See J. Sonnenfeld and P. R. Lawrence, 'Why do companies succumb to price fixing?' (July-August 1978) *Harvard Business Review* 145; J. Sonnenfeld, 'Executive Apologies for Price Fixing: Role Biased Perceptions of Causality' (1981) 24 *Academy of Management Journal* 192; W. E. Baker and R.R. Faulkner, 'The Social Organization of Conspiracy: Illegal Networks in the Heavy Electrical Equipment Industry' (1993) 58 *American Sociological Review* 837; J. M. Conley and W. M. O'Barr, 'Crime and Custom in Corporate Society: A Cultural Perspective on Corporate Misconduct' (1997) 60 *Law and Contemporary Problems* 5; C. Parker, P. Ainsworth and N. Stepanenko, *ACCC Enforcement and Compliance Project: The Impact of ACCC Enforcement Activity in Cartel Cases* (Australian National University, Centre for Competition and Consumer policy, May 2004); Interview of B. Allison by M. O'Kane, 'Does prison work for cartelists? – The view from behind the bars' (2011) 56 *Antitrust Bulletin* 483 at 498; 'Antitrust Compliance Programs: The Government Perspective', Address by W. J. Kolasky, Deputy Assistant Attorney General, before the Corporate Compliance 2002 Conference (San Francisco, July 12, 2002), at 14; see also C. Parker, 'Criminal Cartel Sanctions and Compliance: The Gap between Rhetoric and Reality', in C. Beaton-Wells and A. Ezrachi, *Criminalising Cartels: Critical Studies of an International Regulatory Movement* (Hart 2011) 239; and M. E. Stucke, 'Am I a Price Fixer? A Behavioural Economic Analysis of Cartels', in C. Beaton-Wells and A. Ezrachi, *Criminalising Cartels: Critical Studies of an International Regulatory Movement* (Hart 2011) 263.

523 See my book *The Optimal Enforcement of EC Antitrust Law* (Kluwer 2002), at 193.

524 See the literature referred to in the last but one footnote above; see also D. D. Sokol, 'Cartels, Corporate Compliance, and What Practitioners Really Think About Enforcement' (2012) 78 *Antitrust Law Journal* 201 at 224; M. H. Baer, 'Governing Corporate Compliance' (2009) 50 *Boston College Law Review* 1, at 60–61 and 66; D. A. DeMott, 'Organizational Incentives to Care About the Law' (1997) 60 *Law and Contemporary Problems* 39 at 45; S. H. Elsen, 'Commentary' (1997) 60 *Law and Contemporary Problems* 87; A. R. Beckenstein and H. L. Gabel, 'The Economics of Antitrust Compliance' (1985) 52 *Southern Economic Journal* 673 at 676–677; and A. Riley and M. Bloom, 'Antitrust Compliance Programmes – Can Companies and Antitrust Agencies Do More?' (2011) *Journal of Competition Law* 21, at 34.

1. Companies are generally best placed to prevent antitrust infringements, and to do so in the most cost-effective way

The first reason justifying company liability for antitrust infringements is that companies are generally best placed to influence the main factors that determine the likelihood of antitrust infringements being committed by their employees, and to do so in the most cost-effective way.[525] Indeed, companies select the employees they hire, and determine what authority they give them to set or negotiate prices or to conclude or negotiate contracts. They also define the profit targets or performance goals and the incentive structure under which their employees act. Through their internal culture, they also influence the likelihood of infringements being committed.[526]

Companies are also best placed to determine, for their specific situation, which is the most cost-effective way to prevent antitrust infringements. As Stephen Calkins has pointed out:

> 'A company has a wide array of ways to increase its compliance with various laws. It can emphasize the quality of its people, by hiring honest employees, encouraging them to lead healthy lives, and taking care of them in times of need. It can create good incentives, by tying compensation to long-term results, by refraining from exerting undue pressure, and by paying supra-competitive wages employees will not want to risk losing. It can teach and remind. It can monitor and audit. And it can threaten with whatever draconian consequences are in its powers [. . .]. Some companies will be better at one approach, some at another, most at some mix; but it would be surprising were the same approach right for all. Accordingly, it would seem self-evident that government should set out penalties for violating the law and leave it to firms to determine how best to respond to those penalties'.[527]

2. Avoiding perverse incentives

If companies were not liable for the antitrust infringements engaged in by their employees, serious incentive problems would result.[528] Because companies benefit from the antitrust infringements engaged in by their employees, companies would have an incentive to encourage violations. Companies would have an incentive to recruit those employees most likely to engage in antitrust infringements, and to give them the authority necessary to do so. Companies would have an incentive to set for their employees overly ambitious profit targets or performance goals and overly strong incentive structures that pressurise their employees into committing antitrust infringements. Companies would also have an incentive to develop internal cultures conducive to antitrust infringements.

---

525 See my book *The Optimal Enforcement of EC Antitrust Law* (Kluwer 2002), at 197.

526 See J. M. Conley and W. M. O'Barr, 'Crime and Custom in Corporate Society: A Cultural Perspective on Corporate Misconduct' (1997) 60 *Law and Contemporary Problems* 5.

527 S. Calkins, 'Corporate Compliance and the Antitrust Agencies' Bi-Modal Penalties' (1997) 60 *Law and Contemporary Problems* 127 at 147.

528 See my book *The Optimal Enforcement of EC Antitrust Law* (Kluwer 2002), at 198.

3. Avoiding unfairness

Because companies, through the selection of, and authority given to, their employees, through the performance targets and incentive structures they set, and through their internal culture, influence the likelihood of antitrust infringements being committed, and because companies benefit from antitrust infringements, it would be unfair if companies were not liable for the antitrust infringements engaged in by their employees.

4. Parent company liability

It should be noted that all three of the above reasons for holding companies liable for antitrust infringements committed by their employees equally justify holding parent companies liable for antitrust infringements engaged in by (employees of) subsidiaries under their control.[529]

Indeed, parent companies are generally well placed to influence the likelihood of their subsidiaries committing antitrust infringements, in particular through the setting of financial targets.[530] Given that parent companies, as shareholders, benefit from their subsidiaries' antitrust infringements, not holding parent companies liable would create a perverse incentive for parent companies to encourage their subsidiaries to engage in antitrust infringements, in particular by setting excessive financial targets or incentives that create pressure to commit infringements. Finally, as the EU General Court has held, 'since any gains resulting from illegal activities accrue to shareholders, it is only fair that those who have the power of supervision should assume liability for the illegal business activities of their subsidiaries'.[531]

D. The value of antitrust compliance programmes

What is the value of antitrust compliance programmes for society or from the perspective of optimal antitrust enforcement?

1. The value of compliance programmes depends on their effects and cost

From the point of view of society, antitrust compliance programmes only have value to the extent that they have positive effects for the enforcement of the antitrust prohibitions, that these positive effects outweigh possible negative enforcement effects as well as the cost of the resources spent on the compliance programmes, and that the net positive enforcement benefits cannot be obtained at lower cost in some other way.

---

529 See also my paper 'The Undertaking as Subject of EC Competition Law and the Imputation of Infringements to Natural or Legal Persons' (2000) 25 *European Law Review* 99; and Chapter 7 of my book *The Optimal Enforcement of EC Antitrust Law* (Kluwer 2002).

530 See also I. Simonsson, *Legitimacy in EU Cartel Control* (Hart 2010) at 172.

531 Judgment in *Dow Chemical v Commission*, T-77/08, EU:T:2012:47, paragraph 101.

2. Possible positive and possible negative effects of compliance programmes

Antitrust compliance programmes have positive enforcement effects in three situations:

i) when they (directly or indirectly, through their impact on company culture or norms) prevent the occurrence of antitrust infringements that would have taken place in the absence of the compliance programme;

ii) when they lead to an ongoing antitrust infringement being terminated earlier than would have happened in the absence of the compliance programme;

iii) when they lead to an infringement being reported to the competition authorities, thus allowing the authorities to prosecute and punish the infringement and victims to obtain redress, and this would not have happened in the absence of the compliance programme or would only have happened at a later point in time or at a higher cost to the authorities or the victims.

On the other hand, antitrust compliance programmes can have two types of negative enforcement effects:[532]

i) A first type of negative effect can arise when employees inclined to engage in antitrust infringements learn from compliance training how to engage more effectively in antitrust infringements or how to avoid detection and punishment. For instance, a divisional manager who is afraid of not reaching his performance targets, and who is not yet engaged in cartel activity but knows that his counterparts in the competitor firms would be open to do so, may, after having sat a day in an antitrust compliance training, come to the insight that the probability of detection is low, that any detection will be only ten years later, by which time he will have retired, and will anyway only lead to fines for the company, and this may prompt him to start engaging in cartel activity.[533] The risk of perverse learning effects is particularly high with dawn raid training, especially through mock raids, as this may teach cartelists or prospective cartelists how to avoid detection.[534]

ii) Negative enforcement effects also arise where a compliance programme leads to the detection of an infringement but where, instead of reporting the

532 See M. P. Schinkel, 'Nalevingsprogramma's' (2011) *Markt & Mededinging* 231, as well as C. Angelucci and M.A. Han, 'Monitoring Managers Through Corporate Compliance Programs', Amsterdam Center for Law & Economics Working Paper no 2010-14, accessible at http://ssrn.com/abstract=1729135, and Chapter 2 of M.A. Han, *Vertical Relations in Cartel Theory* (PhD thesis, University of Amsterdam, ACLE Dissertation Series No 4, September 2011), accessible at http://www.carteltheory.com.

533 Obviously, the threat of personal penalties for the manager, in particular imprisonment, would substantially alter this risk calculation.

534 See, on the one hand, F. Brunet, 'The role of antitrust compliance programs in competition law enforcement', New Frontiers of Antitrust Conference (Paris, 10 February 2012), *Concurrences* no 2-2012, 16, at 16 (listing dawn raid training as a normal element that antitrust compliance programmes can entail) and, on the other hand, A. Riley and M. Bloom, 'Antitrust Compliance Programmes – Can Companies and Antitrust Agencies Do More?' (2011) *Journal of Competition Law* 21, at 36–37 and A. Riley, Seal Breaking – Practical Compliance Lessons from Recent Cases' (2012) 3 *Journal of European Competition Law & Practice* 141 at 147 (arguing convincingly that mock raids should not be part of compliance programmes since they dilute the main message of the importance of real compliance).

infringement to the antitrust authorities, the company decides to conceal or destroy the evidence of the infringement.[535]

3. Empirical evidence

Do we have any empirical evidence indicating that generally the positive enforcement effects of antitrust compliance programmes outweigh the negative enforcement effects?

The answer is no: there is no such empirical evidence, and it may be impossible to obtain it.

There have been no attempts in the literature to estimate empirically the general effects, positive or negative, of antitrust compliance programmes.

There have been some empirical studies in the United States on the effectiveness of compliance programmes in preventing violations in other areas of the law, such as health and safety regulation. These studies have not shown positive results.[536]

The only evidence available in the antitrust area is evidence derived from cases that have been dealt with by competition authorities.

Obviously, those instances in which antitrust infringements have not happened thanks to compliance programmes will not show up in the cases dealt with by competition authorities. So, we have no idea how often antitrust infringements are prevented by antitrust compliance programmes.

On the other hand, there are many examples of cases in which antitrust infringements were committed in (flagrant) disregard of compliance programmes.[537] A particularly striking example of a case detected by the US Department of Justice was recounted as follows by William Kolasky:

> 'A good example is the extent to which one executive of a corporation we recently prosecuted went to frustrate the efforts of the company's general counsel to enforce the company's antitrust compliance program. This general counsel had instituted

---

535 Companies might even decide to reward the employees involved in the detected infringement; see M. P. Schinkel, 'Nalevingsprogramma's' (2011) *Markt & Mededinging* 231, at 233, and M. Han, M. A. Han, *Vertical Relations in Cartel Theory* (PhD thesis, University of Amsterdam, ACLE Dissertation Series no 4, September 2011), accessible at http://www.carteltheory.com.

536 See M. McKenndall, B. DeMarr and C. Jones-Rikkers, 'Ethical Compliance Programs and Corporate Illegality: Testing the Assumptions of the Corporate Sentencing Guidelines' (2002) 37 *Journal of Business Ethics* 367; K. D. Krawiec, 'Cosmetic Compliance and the Failure of Negotiated Governance' (2003) 81 *Washington University Law Quarterly* 487 at 510–515; and M. H. Baer, 'Governing Corporate Compliance' (2009) 50 *Boston College Law Review* 1, at 29–30 and 63.

537 See M. Berzins and F. Sofo, 'The inability of compliance strategies to prevent collusive conduct' (2008) 8 *Corporate Governance* 669, at 675–678; C. Parker, P. Ainsworth and N. Stepanenko, *ACCC Enforcement and Compliance Project: The Impact of ACCC Enforcement Activity in Cartel Cases* (Australian National University, Centre for Competition and Consumer policy, May 2004), at 34, 35 and 60; and 'Antitrust Compliance Programs: The Government Perspective', Address by W. J. Kolasky, Deputy Assistant Attorney General, before the Corporate Compliance 2002 Conference (San Francisco, July 12, 2002); see also the case of Intel, whose antitrust compliance programme was once heralded in the Harvard Business Review to have prevented antitrust infringements, but later turned out not to have: D. B. Yoffie and M. Kwak, 'Playing by the Rules: How Intel Avoids Antitrust Litigation' (2001) 79 *Harvard Business Review* 119 and C. Roquilly, 'Intel, dix ans après: Le mythe de la compliance revisité?' *Concurrences* no 2-2010, 50.

> a comprehensive antitrust compliance program, and had made sure that the senior executives were well schooled on the antitrust laws. He had laid out specific rules to follow and adopted stiff penalties for failure to follow those rules. When a top executive at his firm arranged a meeting with his chief foreign competitor to discuss exchanging technological information, the executive, as required by the policy, notified the general counsel's office of the meeting. The general counsel (perhaps suspecting the worst) insisted on accompanying the executive to the meeting and remaining at his side throughout the meeting – never letting him out of his sight even when the executive went to the bathroom. He was certain that this way there could be no chance conversation between the company executive and his competitor, and the general counsel would be a witness to everything said. Surely no antitrust problems could arise in such a setting. And the general counsel must have taken some comfort when he, the executive, and the executive from the competitor firm greeted one another at the start of the meeting and the two executives introduced themselves to each other, exchanged business cards, and engaged in small talk about their careers and families that indicated that the two had never met each other before. Imagine how that general counsel must have felt when he learned, during the course of our investigation, that the introduction between the two executives had been completely staged for his benefit – to keep him in the dark. In fact, the two executives had been meeting, dining, socializing, playing golf, and participating together and with others in a massive worldwide price-fixing conspiracy for years. Furthermore, other employees at the company knew of this relationship and were instructed to keep the general counsel in the dark by referring to the competitor executive by a code name when he called the office and the general counsel was around.'[538]

As to the positive effect that compliance programmes may have in detecting infringements and reporting them to the authorities, this appears to have happened in some cases.[539]

As to how often antitrust compliance programmes may have had perverse learning effects or may have led to the suppression of evidence of detected infringements, we have again no empirical evidence, and we are unlikely ever to obtain it, irrespective of how often or how rarely these negative effects may in reality occur.

4. A tale of four companies

The fundamental difficulty of relying on empirical evidence to judge the value of antitrust compliance programmes should, of course, not prevent us from making judgments on the basis of reasonable argument, informed by the limited empirical knowledge we have and by what we can learn from research into corporate law-breaking and compliance more generally.[540]

---

538 'Antitrust Compliance Programs: The Government Perspective', Address by W. J. Kolasky, Deputy Assistant Attorney General, before the Corporate Compliance 2002 Conference (San Francisco, July 12, 2002), at 5–6.

539 See Study by Europe Economics for the French Conseil de la concurrence, *État des lieux et perspectives des programmes de conformité* (September 2008), at 3.20.

540 See in particular C. Parker and V. Lehmann Nielsen (eds), *Explaining Compliance: Business Responses to Regulation* (Edward Elgar, 2011); K. D. Krawiec, 'Organizational Misconduct: Beyond the Principal-Agent Model' (2005) 32 *Florida State University Law* Review 57.

I will do so by telling a tale of four companies, describing types of situations that can realistically arise, and which any public policy with regard to antitrust compliance programmes should thus take into account:[541]

- Company A has been run for several decades by its current chief executive, a strong and inspiring personality, who has moulded the company in his own image and who exerts close control over all the company's business. Strongly principled, the chief executive of company A could not even imagine ever engaging in any illegal activity. Indeed, he would rather see his company go bankrupt than betray his moral principles. The culture of the company reflects this attitude, which is shared by all staff. Company A has never committed any antitrust infringement. It does not have an antitrust compliance programme.
- Company B has been on the receiving end of several decisions imposing fines for cartel infringements. The chief executive, who was not involved in or aware of these cartels, and who is profoundly shocked by the discovery of illegal behaviour engaged in by some of his managers, decides at some point to make a clean break. The managers who were responsible for the illegal activities are replaced, and compliance counsel is recruited and given a large budget to set up a state-of-the-art compliance programme. The new chief compliance officer, assisted by reputable outside counsel, sets up a state-of-the-art compliance programme. The staff of company B perceives that the chief executive sincerely wants to put an end to any illegal activity, even if this may affect the company's profitability, and the new ethical culture spreads throughout the company. Since then, company B is not involved in any antitrust infringement anymore.
- Company C, like company B, has been on the receiving end of several decisions imposing fines for cartel infringements. The chief executive of company C was not involved in or aware of these cartels. Indeed, he would never know about such things, being a practitioner of management through delegation, who conceives his role as setting very ambitious and closely monitored financial targets for the different divisions of the company, with highly powered incentives for the divisional managers, and letting the divisional managers swim or sink. However, the fines and the attendant negative publicity are a serious problem. The chief executive thus decides that something should be done. Exactly as in company B, compliance counsel is recruited and given a large budget to set up a state-of-the-art compliance programme. The new chief compliance officer, assisted by reputable outside counsel, sets up a state-of-the-art compliance programme. However, the chief executive of company C keeps setting the same very ambitious financial targets and highly powered incentives for his divisional managers. The divisional managers perceive that, even if the chief executive clearly dislikes fines and negative publicity, fulfilling the financial targets is what really counts for the chief executive and for their own survival. The divisional managers continue engaging in cartel activities, but they now pay very careful attention to hiding

541 I am not making any claims as to which of these four types of companies is more common in the real world. I do not know this, and have strong doubts as to whether it is possible to know this. My only claim is that all four types are realistic, and that all four should thus be taken into account when designing policy in relation to antitrust compliance programmes.

their activities from the companies' compliance counsel and the chief executive, while projecting an image of dutiful compliance.

- Company D has a chief executive with substantial experience in cartel matters. Indeed, one of the factors explaining his rise to the top of the company is that, in the different divisions which he headed over the years, he always succeeded in obtaining excellent results through effective cartel arrangements that were never detected. Still today, the chief executive of company D personally manages a number of cartels in which his company is involved. In order to follow the general business trend, and to avoid attracting negative attention from the competition authorities, compliance counsel is recruited and given a large budget to set up a state-of-the-art compliance programme, exactly as in companies B and C. The chief executive of company D, who has over the years acquired substantial experience in avoiding detection, and actually rather enjoys this type of game,[542] weaves an elaborate net of deception around his company's compliance counsel, like the top executive in the example recounted by William Kolasky,[543] and continues successfully managing the various cartels in which company D is engaged.

5. Are formal compliance programmes a necessary or a sufficient condition for real compliance?

The above tale of four companies helps us answer the question whether having a compliance programme is a necessary or sufficient condition for real compliance (that is, absence of antitrust infringements).

The example of company A illustrates that real compliance with the antitrust prohibitions can also happen without any formal compliance programme, at least in smaller or relatively centralised companies.

On the other hand, the situation of company B, which has a history of cartel activity but honestly wants to make a clean break with this past, illustrates the potential usefulness of antitrust compliance programmes: at least for a large company or corporate group, with decentralised decision-making on prices and contracts, an antitrust compliance programme may be a necessary component in a change from a past of antitrust infringements to a new culture and practice of real compliance.

The comparison between company B and company C illustrates, however, that setting up a compliance programme is not a sufficient condition to bring about real change and achieve real compliance. The reason for this is that real compliance (absence of antitrust infringements) depends on a complex interaction between several factors, including formal compliance programmes, but also other incentives that the

---

542 Compare with C. Harding, 'An emotional issue: Why do cartelists do what they do and risk going to jail?' (29 July 2008) *Competition Law Insight* 9 at 10, and 'The Anti-Cartel Enforcement industry: Criminological Perspectives on Cartel Criminalisation', in C. Beaton-Wells and A. Ezrachi, *Criminalising Cartels: Critical Studies of an International Regulatory Movement* (Hart 2011) 359 at 368–369.

543 'Antitrust Compliance Programs: The Government Perspective', Address by W. J. Kolasky, Deputy Assistant Attorney General, before the Corporate Compliance 2002 Conference (San Francisco, July 12, 2002).

company sets for its staff, exemplary behaviour by the company's leading individuals, and wider corporate culture.[544] The compliance programme set up by company C is exactly the same as the one set up by company B, but it has no impact, because of the pressure created by the excessive performance targets and incentives and because the divisional managers correctly perceive that the chief executive's commitment to antitrust compliance is not genuine, or at least entirely subordinate to the company's financial objectives.

6. Is it possible for authorities to identify a set of characteristics of formal compliance programmes that ensure real compliance?

The comparison between company B and companies C and D illustrates that ostensibly identical antitrust compliance programmes can be part of a culture and practice of real compliance, an irrelevant sideshow, or part of a calculated attempt to project a misleading image of compliance.[545] Merely by observing the characteristics of the compliance programmes, it would not be possible to distinguish between the situations of company B and of companies C and D. Indeed, even the compliance counsel of companies C and D may have exactly the same impression as to whether their compliance programmes are working as company B's compliance counsel.

This problem cannot be solved by making a better, more complete checklist of what characteristics compliance programmes should have to be credited, because the multiple and complexly interacting factors of structure, culture and agency that determine real compliance cannot be reduced to a set of characteristics that can be reliably measured or observed by outsiders, at least not at reasonable cost. Indeed, this is a key finding of compliance research. In the words of Christine Parker and Sharon Gilad:

> '[I]t is certainly possible that regulation (whether official and governmental or private and voluntary) can directly influence the adoption of formal compliance systems, [. . .]. However it does not make sociological sense to suppose that regulation can directly engineer how these systems are implemented and understood in practice, nor how they interact with the motivations and commitments of various actors throughout the organization';
>
> 'The influence of regulator-mandated formal compliance systems on culture and agency – how they are implemented and understood in practice, and how they interact with pre-existing motivations and commitments – cannot be engineered or predicted in detail';

---

544 See C. Parker and S. Gilad, 'Internal corporate compliance management systems: structure, culture and agency', in C. Parker and V. Lehmann Nielsen, *Explaining Compliance: Business Responses to Regulation* (Edward Elgar, 2011) 170.

545 See further K. D. Krawiec, 'Cosmetic Compliance and the Failure of Negotiated Governance' (2003) 81 *Washington University Law Quarterly* 487; and M. H. Baer, 'Governing Corporate Compliance' (2009) 50 *Boston College Law Review* 1; and more generally C. E. Parker, R. E. Rosen and V. Lehmann Nielsen, 'The Two Faces of Lawyers: Professional Ethics and Business Compliance With Regulation' (2009) 22 *Georgetown Journal of Legal Ethics* 201.

> 'To merely measure implementation of a formal compliance management system is to grasp at an epiphenomenon.'[546]

Even if it were possible, at least to some extent, to identify characteristics of compliance programmes that ensure real compliance, competition authorities would be particularly badly placed to develop such insight. Indeed, competition authorities never see the full picture: they never see the cases where compliance programmes have successfully prevented infringements, only the cases where this has not happened. They can thus not compare the two situations so as to learn better to distinguish between successful compliance programmes and symbolic or cosmetic compliance, otherwise than on the basis of the finding that an infringement has been committed.[547]

E. Discussion of the different questions

1. Should companies that have antitrust compliance programmes be granted immunity from fines?

a. *The answer is negative*

On the basis of our analysis above, the answer to the question whether companies that have an antitrust compliance programme matching some best practices determined by the legislator, the competition authorities or the courts should be granted immunity from fines is clearly negative. As explained above, it is not possible to identify a list of characteristics of formal compliance programmes that ensure real compliance and that can be applied at reasonable cost. It is thus not possible for authorities and courts to distinguish reliably and at reasonable cost between situations where antitrust compliance programmes are part of a culture and practice of real compliance and situations of symbolic or cosmetic compliance.[548]

Granting immunity from fines to companies that have a compliance programme would create perverse incentives for companies: Given that antitrust infringements can bring great financial benefit to companies,[549] that a company can easily encourage antitrust

546 C. Parker and S. Gilad, 'Internal corporate compliance management systems: structure, culture and agency', in C. Parker and V. Lehmann Nielsen, *Explaining Compliance: Business Responses to Regulation* (Edward Elgar, 2011) 170, at 178, 189 and 189–190.

547 See also M. H. Baer, 'Governing Corporate Compliance' (2009) 50 *Boston College Law Review* 1, at 50, and G. R. Weaver, L. K. Treviño and P. L. Cochran, 'Corporate Ethics Programs as Control Systems: Influences of Executive Commitment and Environmental Factors' (1999) 42 *Academy of Management Journal* 41, at 46.

548 See also J. Harrington, 'Comment on Antitrust Sanctions', *Competition Policy International*, vol 6, no 2 (Autumn 2010) at 48–49; K. D. Krawiec, 'Cosmetic Compliance and the Failure of Negotiated Governance' (2003) 81 *Washington University Law Quarterly* 487; K. D. Krawiec, 'Organizational Misconduct: Beyond the Principal-Agent Model' (2005) 32 *Florida State University Law* Review 57; W. S. Laufer, 'Integrity, Diligence, and the Limits of Good Corporate Citizenship' (1996) 34 *American Business Law Journal* 157; and M. H. Baer, 'Governing Corporate Compliance' (2009) 50 *Boston College Law Review* 1.

549 See OECD, 'Report on the Nature and Impact of Hard Core Cartels and Sanctions under National Competition Laws', DAFFE/COMP(2002)7 (9 April 2002), at 9 (median overcharge in 14 price-fixing cases between 15 and 20%); L. M. Froeb, R. A. Koyak and G. J. Werden, 'What is the effect of bid-rigging on prices?' (1993) 42 *Economics Letters* 419 (finding that a fairly typical bid-rigging scheme had raised prices by over 20% for over 4 years); my books *The Optimal Enforcement of EC Antitrust Law* (Kluwer 2002), at 191–201; and *Efficiency and Justice in European Antitrust Enforcement* (Hart 2008), at 178–179.

infringements, notwithstanding any antitrust compliance programme, in particular by setting excessive financial targets and incentives, and that the cost of setting up a compliance programme is low compared to the potential benefits from antitrust infringements, companies would have a clear incentive to set up a compliance programme so as to obtain immunity from fines, while maximising antitrust infringements through excessive performance targets and incentives.[550]

Granting immunity from fines to companies that have a compliance programme thus encourages companies to behave like company C in the above tale of four companies. It also immunises from fines companies like company D, or the company in the example reported by William Kolasky,[551] in which the top management deliberately engages in cartel activity while concealing this activity from the company's own legal or compliance counsel.

Having an antitrust compliance programme then becomes a cheap insurance policy against antitrust liability.[552] This is problematic not only from a narrow deterrence perspective but also from a broader normative perspective.[553] By granting immunity from fines to companies that have an antitrust compliance programme (but that have nevertheless committed antitrust infringements – otherwise, the issue of immunity from fines does not arise), the law would send the message that antitrust infringements are some sort of natural accidents, part of the normal course of business, and that companies have no responsibility for avoiding such infringements.

Granting immunity from fines to companies that have an antitrust compliance programme would also be unfair, as companies would keep the financial benefit of the antitrust infringements while escaping liability.

Finally, granting immunity from fines to companies that detect infringements through a compliance programme but that do not report the infringement to the competition

---

550 See also J. Harrington, 'Comment on Antitrust Sanctions', *Competition Policy International*, vol 6, no 2 (Autumn 2010), at 49.

551 'Antitrust Compliance Programs: The Government Perspective', Address by W. J. Kolasky, Deputy Assistant Attorney General, before the Corporate Compliance 2002 Conference (San Francisco, July 12, 2002).

552 See also W. S. Laufer, 'Integrity, Diligence, and the Limits of Good Corporate Citizenship' (1996) 34 *American Business Law Journal* 157, at 3.

553 Law and law enforcement have both deterrent and norm-generating effects, which are both important; see generally my book *Efficiency and Justice in European Antitrust Enforcement* (Hart 2008), at 52 and 185; K. G. Dau-Schmidt, 'An Economic Analysis of the Criminal Law as a Preference-Shaping Policy' (1990) *Duke Law Journal* 1; C. R. Sunstein, 'On the Expressive Function of the Law' (1996) 144 *University of Pennsylvania Law Review* 2021; D. M. Kahan, 'Social Influence, Social Meaning, and Deterrence' (1997) 83 *Virginia Law Review* 349; N. K. Katyal, 'Deterrence's Difficulty' (1997) 95 *Michigan Law Review* 2385; G. E. Lynch, 'The Role of Criminal Law in Policing Corporate Misconduct' (1997) 60 *Law and Contemporary Problems* 23; R. A. Kagan, N. Gunnigham, and D. Thornton, 'Fear, duty, and regulatory compliance: lessons from three research projects', in C. Parker and V. Lehmann Nielsen, *Explaining Compliance: Business Responses to Regulation* (Edward Elgar, 2011) 37; R. Paternoster and S. Simpson, 'Sanction Threats and Appeals to Morality: Testing a Rational Choice Model of Corporate Crime' (1996) 30 *Law & Society Review* 549; C. Parker, 'Criminal Cartel Sanctions and Compliance: The Gap between Rhetoric and Reality', in C. Beaton-Wells and A. Ezrachi, *Criminalising Cartels: Critical Studies of an International Regulatory Movement* (Hart 2011) 239; and S. S. Simpson and M. Rorie, 'Motivating compliance: economic and material motives for compliance', in C. Parker and V. Lehmann Nielsen, *Explaining Compliance: Business Responses to Regulation* (Edward Elgar, 2011) 59.

authorities would undermine the important incentives, created by the competition authorities' leniency programmes, to report infringements to the competition authorities as quickly and as fully as possible.

b. *Punishing individuals instead of the company is not the solution*

These problems cannot be resolved by punishing, instead of the company, the individuals within the company who have engaged in the antitrust infringement. As I have argued elsewhere,[554] it would be good from the perspective of optimal antitrust enforcement to **add** to company liability for antitrust infringements also penalties for individuals, for several reasons, the most important of which being that in order to effectively deter antitrust infringements, corporate fines would often need to be so high as to be impracticable or to cause significant negative effects.[555] Having a realistic threat of individual punishment would also be helpful for those companies – like company B in the above tale of four companies – that sincerely want to avoid their staff engaging in antitrust infringements, as it would allow compliance counsel, as part of compliance training, to attract attention to this risk. It is, however, a bad idea to have **only** individual liability for antitrust infringements.

Indeed, under a regime of individual liability only, companies, parent companies and other shareholders would still have the perverse incentive to encourage antitrust infringements through excessive profit targets and performance incentives. Moreover, the unfairness of companies profiting from antitrust infringements while escaping liability would actually be exacerbated if individuals within the company who were pressurised by excessive performance targets and incentives into engaging in antitrust infringements were punished.[556]

2. Should companies that had a compliance programme at the time of the infringement be granted a reduction in the amount of the fine?

a. *The answer is again negative*

Granting a fine reduction to companies that had a compliance programme at the time of their infringement has the same negative effects as granting immunity from fines to such companies, only to a lesser extent, depending on the size of the reduction of the fine.

Indeed, the more the fine is reduced on account of the compliance programme, the more the incentive for companies to avoid infringements by all possible means so as to

---

554 See my publications 'Does the Effective Enforcement of Articles 81 and 82 EC Require Not Only Fines on Undertakings But Also Individual Penalties, In Particular Imprisonment?', in C.-D. Ehlermann and I. Atanasiu (eds), *European Competition Law Annual 2001: Effective Private Enforcement of EC Antitrust Law* (Hart 2002); *The Optimal Enforcement of EC Antitrust Law* (Kluwer 2002), chapters 8 and 9; 'Is Criminalization of EU Competition Law the Answer?' (2005) 28 *World Competition* 117; and *Efficiency and Justice in European Antitrust Enforcement* (Hart 2008), chapter 6.

555 See also J. Harrington, 'Comment on Antitrust Sanctions', *Competition Policy International*, vol 6, no 2 (Autumn 2010), at 43–44.

556 For further reasons why individual penalties should be a complement to corporate penalties, not a substitute, see my book *The Optimal Enforcement of EC Antitrust Law* (Kluwer 2002), at 217–218.

avoid being fined is replaced by an incentive to set up a compliance programme so as to obtain the fine reduction, while maximising antitrust infringements through excessive performance targets and incentives.

The higher the fine reduction, the more compliance programmes become a cheap insurance policy against full antitrust liability.

The negative normative effects of fine reductions are also the same as the negative normative effects of immunity, only to a lesser degree, depending on the size of the reduction. Indeed, the higher the reduction of the fine given to companies that have a compliance programme but nevertheless committed infringements, the stronger the message that antitrust infringements are part of normal business and that companies have no full responsibility for avoiding such infringements.

Fine reductions also create the same unfairness as immunity from fines, only to a lesser degree, depending on the size of the reduction. Indeed, the higher the reduction, the more companies can keep the financial benefit of the antitrust infringements while escaping liability.

Finally, granting a fine reduction to companies that detect infringements through a compliance programme but that do not report the infringement to the competition authorities would undermine the important incentives, created by the competition authorities' leniency programmes, to report infringements to the competition authorities as quickly and as fully as possible.

b. *Subsidies for compliance programmes should not be conditional upon an antitrust infringement being committed*

It is often argued that granting a fine reduction to companies with compliance programmes is a way to encourage the adoption of compliance programmes. Indeed, granting a fine reduction to companies that had an antitrust compliance programme at the time of the infringement comes down to the state giving a subsidy (equal to the amount of the reduction of the fine) to companies that have set up antitrust compliance programmes, but only to those companies that have also committed an antitrust infringement. Whatever view one may have as to the question whether the state should give financial aid to companies to set up compliance programmes,[557] it cannot possibly make sense to condition such aid upon the company committing an antitrust infringement.

3. Response to some concerns

Having thus come to the conclusion that it is a bad idea to grant fine reductions or immunity from fines to companies that had an antitrust compliance programme when committing an antitrust infringement, it may be useful to respond to some of the concerns that may have led others to argue in favour of such reductions or immunity.

---

557 In my view, the answer to this question is negative, for reasons of principle. Indeed, by defining antitrust infringements as infringements committed by companies (or groups of companies forming a single undertaking), the legislator has made a legislative choice that companies are responsible for avoiding antitrust infringements. By subsidising the adoption of compliance programmes, the government would go against this legislative choice, and undermine its normative message.

a. *Current antitrust enforcement policy is not working*

Some of the discussion about whether antitrust authorities and courts should credit compliance programmes in their fining decisions appears to have sprung from a concern that current antitrust enforcement policy, based on imposing fines on companies in the EU, and corporate fines combined with imprisonment in the US, may not be working.[558] These doubts as to the effectiveness of current policies are based on the observation that, notwithstanding the imposition of high fines in the past years, many antitrust infringements, in particular cartels, are still detected.[559]

One should be very cautious with inferring from the number of infringements currently detected any conclusions as to the effectiveness of current policies. When an enforcement policy is strengthened at some point in time, by increasing the level of the fines, improving leniency programmes, and/or increasing detection and prosecution capacity, the normal effect in a first period is that more cartels are detected than before, because a category of cartels that could survive under the previous weaker enforcement policy can no longer survive under the new stronger enforcement policy. The effect of the new stronger enforcement policy on the formation of new cartels can only show up many years later in the enforcement statistics. If, as has been the case in the EU in the last years of the twentieth century and the first decade of the twenty-first century, there is a continuous or repeated strengthening of the enforcement policy through improved leniency policies, increased fines and increased detection and prosecution capacity, the first-period effect of increased detection of cartels may continue to predominate in the enforcement statistics for some time.

I have personally no doubts that large financial penalties on companies have an influence on the behaviour of companies and managers,[560] in that it changes incentives and affects prevailing norms,[561] and that there is less cartel activity in Europe today than there would have been in the absence of the enforcement actions of the European Commission and the competition authorities of the EU Member States.

At the same time, I am also convinced that the US enforcement policy of not only imposing financial penalties on companies but also imprisoning individuals has a stronger deterrent and normative effect.[562]

---

558 See OECD, *Roundtable on Promoting Compliance with Competition Law – Issues Paper by the Secretariat*, DAF/COMP(2011)4 (1 June 2011).

559 Idem, at 2. John Connor has in particular attracted attention with his claim that recidivism would be increasing rapidly; see J. M. Connor, 'Recidivism Revealed: Private International Cartels 1990–2009' (Autumn 2010) *Competition Policy International* 101 at 116. However, this claim has since been shown to be significantly overstated; see G. J. Werden, S. D. Hammond and B. A. Barnett, 'Recidivism Eliminated: Cartel Enforcement in the United States Since 1999' (October 2011) *CPI Antitrust Chronicle* 1, and my paper 'Recidivism in EU Antitrust Enforcement: A Legal and Economic Analysis' (2012) 35 *World Competition* 5.

560 See also J. Harrington, 'Comment on Antitrust Sanctions', *Competition Policy International*, vol 6, no 2 (Autumn 2010), at 47.

561 Law enforcement has both deterrent and norm-generating effects; R. A. Kagan, N. Gunnigham, and D. Thornton, 'Fear, duty, and regulatory compliance: lessons from three research projects', in C. Parker and V. Lehmann Nielsen, *Explaining Compliance: Business Responses to Regulation* (Edward Elgar, 2011) 37.

562 See my publications 'Does the Effective Enforcement of Articles 81 and 82 EC Require Not Only Fines on Undertakings But Also Individual Penalties, In Particular Imprisonment?', in C.-D. Ehlermann and I. Atanasiu (eds), *European Competition Law Annual 2001: Effective Private Enforcement of EC Antitrust Law* (Hart 2002);

Finally, completely eliminating antitrust infringements is an unattainable objective.[563] Indeed, even if the competition authorities managed at some point in time to detect so many violations and to impose such high fines that all companies will be deterred from committing new violations, this situation will not last, as over time the memory of those successful prosecutions will fade, and violations will thus again be committed.[564]

In any event, whatever one may think about the effectiveness of current enforcement policies, changing these policies by granting reductions in the amount of fines imposed on companies that had a compliance programme at the time of the infringement could only make matters worse. Indeed, as explained above, such a change would, in proportion to the size of the reduction, replace the incentive for companies to avoid infringements by all possible means so as to avoid being fined by an incentive to set up a compliance programme so as to obtain the fine reduction, while maximising antitrust infringements through excessive performance targets and incentives. It would also send the normative message that antitrust infringements are part of normal business and that companies have no full responsibility for avoiding such infringements, and allow companies unfairly to keep the benefit of antitrust infringements while escaping liability.

b. *It makes no sense to punish a company that has 'done everything it could'*

It is sometimes argued that lower fines or even no fines should be imposed on companies with compliance programmes because it makes no sense to punish companies that have 'done everything they could'.

The problem with this argument is that it is based either on a much too narrow conception of what it is that companies can do to encourage or prevent antitrust infringements, or on unrealistic assumptions as to what competition authorities and courts can investigate and assess at reasonable cost, or a combination of both. As explained above, and illustrated by the above tale of four companies, whether or not antitrust infringements are engaged in by a company's employees depends on much more than the presence or absence of a compliance programme. In particular performance targets and incentives are crucial. For a company to do everything it could do to avoid antitrust infringements, it would,

---

The Optimal Enforcement of EC Antitrust Law (Kluwer 2002), chapters 8 and 9; 'Is Criminalization of EU Competition Law the Answer?' (2005) 28 *World Competition* 117; and *Efficiency and Justice in European Antitrust Enforcement* (Hart 2008), chapter 6.

563 See my publications 'Optimal Antitrust Fines: Theory and Practice' (2006) 29 *World Competition* 183, at 188 and 194, and *Efficiency and Justice in European Antitrust Enforcement* (Hart 2008), at 53–54 and 60.

564 See also W. Eucken 'The Competitive Order and Its Implementation' (Autumn 2006) 2 *Competition Policy International* 219 (English translation of 'Die Wettbewerbsordnung und ihre Verwirklichung' (1949) 2 *Ordo – Jahrbuch für die Ordnung von Wirtschaft und Gesellschaft* 1), at 222 ('There is an omnipresent, strong and irrepressible urge to eliminate competition and to acquire a monopolistic position.'); S. Wilks and I. Bartle, 'The Unanticipated Consequences of Creating Independent Competition Agencies' (January 2002) 25 *Western European Politics* 148 at 152 ('Since abuse of market power is endemic in every market economy and is indeed a major component in the competitive strategies of most large companies, the elimination of anti-competitive practices (rather like the elimination of racial intolerance) is an impossible goal. Yet, as with racial equality, it is essential for governments to confirm support for free competition.'); and D. D. Sokol, 'Antitrust in 2025: Cartels, Agency Effectiveness, and a Return to Back to the Future' (December 2010) 2 *CPI Antitrust Journal*, accessible at http://ssrn.com/abstract=1733246, at 2 ('In many cases the same industries are recidivists because, as a new generation retires, the next generation relearns how to coordinate with competitors. This illustrates the social norm within society and within the industry.').

like the chief executive of company A, have to adopt wholeheartedly the attitude that it would rather go bankrupt than violate the antitrust prohibitions, and the company's performance targets and incentives would have to reflect this. Also important is the company's internal culture, which makes it more or less likely that unethical behaviour, including cartel activity, takes place. Finally, companies control whom they recruit and how much authority to negotiate and set prices or to negotiate and conclude contracts they give to which of their employees. All these elements should be considered before concluding that a company has 'done everything it could'. It is not possible for competition authorities or courts reliably to investigate and assess all these elements at reasonable cost.

Given the many and complex ways in which companies can influence the likelihood of antitrust infringements being committed by their employees, the impossibility of reliably capturing all these ways in a list of characteristics of supposedly 'effective' compliance programmes that can be applied by competition authorities or courts at reasonable cost, and the fact that companies financially benefit from antitrust infringements irrespective of how exactly they were committed, company liability for all antitrust infringements engaged in by their employees is both efficient and fair.

It has been argued that 'it seems strange to penalise a company whose top management deliberately and systematically planned its cartel activities in the same fashion as a company whose vigorously-communicated compliance policy was ignored by several employees in one department of one wholly-owned subsidiary'.[565]

Again, this ignores the various ways in which companies can encourage antitrust infringements. In the above tale of four companies, company C has a vigorously communicated compliance policy that is ignored by divisional managers because of the excessive performance targets and incentives the company sets for them. It is far from obvious that company C should be punished less than company D, where the chief executive personally manages the antitrust infringements. In both cases, fines on the company are fully justified. Otherwise companies would be incentivised to behave like company C, and would be able unfairly to benefit from antitrust infringements while escaping full liability.

c. *Current policy neglects the need to create proper incentives for companies to monitor, investigate and report employee wrongdoing*

Some authors have, in support of their arguments in favour of fine reductions or even immunity from fines for companies with compliance programmes,[566] referred to the academic work by Jennifer Arlen and Reinier Kraakman on the potentially adverse effects of strict vicarious liability of companies for the wrongdoing of their employees.[567]

---

565 I. Forrester, 'Due process in EC competition cases: A distinguished institution with flawed procedures' (2009) 34 *European Law Review* 817 at 826.

566 See in particular K. Hofstetter and M. Ludescher, 'Fines against Parent Companies in EU Antitrust Law: Setting Incentives for "Best Practice Compliance"' (2010) 33 *World Competition* 55, at 67–68.

567 J. Arlen, 'The Potentially Perverse Effects of Corporate Criminal Liability' (1994) 23 *Journal of Legal Studies* 833, and J. Arlen and R. Kraakman, 'Controlling Corporate Misconduct: An Analysis of Corporate Liability Regimes' (1997) 72 *New York University Law Review* 687; see also S. Oded, 'Inducing Corporate Compliance: A Compound Corporate Liability Regime' (2011) 31 *International Review of Law & Economics* 272.

What Jennifer Arlen and Reinier Kraakman have pointed out is that strict vicarious liability of companies for the wrongdoing of their employees, in addition to its positive incentive effect in that companies are incentivised to use all means at their disposal to prevent such wrongdoing, may also have a perverse incentive effect, in that companies may hesitate to monitor too closely their employees' behaviour and to detect wrongdoing for fear that this will lead to detection by the government and punishment for the company. This potential perverse effect can be reduced by mitigation rules under which the company is punished less if it effectively monitors its employees' behaviour and reports wrongdoing to the government.

I entirely agree with this point. However, I do not think that it can support an argument for modifying the current enforcement policy of the European Commission by adding fine reductions or immunity from fines for companies with compliance programmes, for two reasons:

First, Jennifer Arlen and Reinier Kraakman's argument is about liability of companies for 'the wrongdoing of their employees'.[568] The starting assumption is that employees 'commit crimes to benefit themselves'.[569] This would appear an adequate assumption for certain types of wrongdoing by employees, such as embezzlement or harassment, which are committed by employees solely for their own benefit, without any benefit for the company, so that there is a natural alignment of the interests of the government and the company to prevent such wrongdoing. However, it is not an adequate assumption in the case of antitrust infringements.[570] As explained above, the characteristics of antitrust infringements are that they are financially beneficial to the company, that employees engaging in them are primarily motivated by what they perceive to be their company's interest and/or by the incentives the company has set for them, and that in particular performance targets and incentives play a crucial role.

Second, the enforcement policy of the European Commission already contains a leniency programme under which companies that are the first to detect cartel activity engaged in by their employees and report it to the authority can obtain immunity from fines, and other companies involved in the same cartel can obtain fine reductions if they are the first to provide additional information that has significant additional value for the authority.[571]

Such a leniency programme is a much better way to incentivise companies to detect and report cartel behaviour engaged in by their employees than granting fine reductions or immunity to all companies that have a compliance programme. Indeed, under the leniency programme, companies are only given immunity from fines or reductions in the amount of fines if they report the infringement to the authority and assist the

---

568 J. Arlen and R. Kraakman, 'Controlling Corporate Misconduct: An Analysis of Corporate Liability Regimes' (1997) 72 *New York University Law Review* 687, at 687.

569 J. Arlen, 'The Potentially Perverse Effects of Corporate Criminal Liability' (1994) 23 *Journal of Legal Studies* 833, at 834.

570 See also J. Harrington, 'Comment on Antitrust Sanctions', *Competition Policy International*, vol 6, no 2 (Autumn 2010), at 48.

571 See European Commission, Notice on immunity from fines and reduction of fines in cartel cases [2006] OJ C298/17; and my paper 'Leniency in Antitrust Enforcement: Theory and Practice' (2007) 30 *World Competition* 25.

authority in prosecuting it. This is essential. Indeed, as explained above, the detection of infringements through a compliance programme actually has negative effects from the perspective of optimal enforcement if it leads to the company concealing or destroying the evidence of the infringement, whereas it has only positive enforcement effects if it leads to the infringement being reported to the authority, thus allowing the authority to prosecute.

The requirement under the leniency programme that the company must be the first to report the infringement to the authority so as to obtain immunity is also very important, because it leads to infringements coming to an end more quickly (given the requirement for immunity applicants to put an end to their participation in the infringement) and being punished more quickly. Similarly, the requirement to be the first to provide information that has significant added value in order to benefit from fine reductions is important in order to incentivise companies to assist the authorities as quickly and as fully as possible.[572]

d. *Current antitrust enforcement policy is not in line with enforcement policies in other areas of the law*

It is sometimes argued that the absence of immunity from fines or reductions in the amount of the fine for companies that had an antitrust compliance programme at the time of the infringement is not in line with enforcement policies in other areas of the law where such immunity from fines or such fine reductions are granted or are said to be granted in some jurisdictions. I am not convinced by this argument, for two reasons:

First, antitrust enforcement policy should be informed by, and adapted to, the nature of antitrust infringements. As explained above, the characteristics of antitrust infringements are that they are financially beneficial to the company, that employees engaging in them are primarily motivated by what they perceive to be their company's interest and/or by the incentives the company has set for them, and that in particular performance targets and incentives play a crucial role. This distinguishes antitrust enforcement from some other types of wrongdoing by employees, such as embezzlement or harassment, which are committed by employees solely for their own benefit, without any benefit for the company, so that there is a natural alignment of the interests of the government and the company to prevent such wrongdoing.

Cartels have the further distinguishing characteristic that they are conspiracies between several wrongdoers (several companies or employees in several companies).[573] This specific characteristic explains the use by competition authorities of leniency programmes. As explained above, these leniency programmes provide better incentives for detecting and reporting infringements than could be provided by granting immunity from fines or reductions of the fine to companies with compliance programmes, and granting immunity from fines or reductions of the fine to all companies that have compliance programmes would undermine the superior incentives created by these leniency programmes.

Second, to the extent that in some jurisdictions immunity from fines or reduced fines for companies with compliance programmes are granted for types of wrongdoing that are

572 See further my paper 'Leniency in Antitrust Enforcement: Theory and Practice' (2007) 30 *World Competition* 25.
573 See N. K. Katyal, 'Conspiracy Theory' (2003) 112 *Yale Law Journal* 1307.

comparable to antitrust infringements, the above analysis indicates that such policies are misguided. These policies may not have been sufficiently thought through, and/or may result from lobbying by the beneficiaries of such policies. Indeed, large companies, which can afford compliance programmes, no doubt benefit from such enforcement policies, as such policies limit their liability, and deflect prosecution to smaller companies and to individuals.[574] The compliance industry also obviously benefits from such enforcement policies.[575]

4. Should companies that did not have a compliance programme at the time of the infringement be fined more heavily?

Some authors have suggested, as an alternative to giving a reduced fine to companies with a compliance programme, to consider the absence of genuine compliance efforts as an aggravating factor in assessing the level of any fine.[576]

Increasing fines for companies without antitrust compliance programmes does indeed not have the same disadvantages as reducing fines for companies with antitrust compliance programmes: Unless the baseline level of the fine is lowered correspondingly (in which case the incentive and fairness effects would be the same as those of granting a reduction to companies with a compliance programme), increasing fines for companies without antitrust compliance programmes does not weaken the incentives for real compliance and does not allow companies unfairly to benefit from infringements while escaping liability. In any event, it does not undermine the normative message that companies are responsible for avoiding antitrust infringements.

On the other hand, increasing fines because of the absence of a compliance programme comes down to adding to the existing obligation for companies not to commit antitrust infringements a second, implied obligation to have a compliance programme. It is difficult to see what would be the justification for adding such an obligation, given that compliance programmes are not a necessary condition for real compliance.

5. Should companies that set up compliance programmes after the detection of an infringement be granted a reduction in the amount of the fine?

As mentioned above, between 1982 and 1992 the European Commission granted fine reductions to companies that had set up a compliance programme after the start of the Commission's investigations.

---

574 See W.S. Laufer, 'Integrity, Diligence, and the Limits of Good Corporate Citizenship' (1996) 34 *American Business Law Journal* 157, at 6, K.D. Krawiec, 'Cosmetic Compliance and the Failure of Negotiated Governance' (2003) 81 *Washington University Law Quarterly* 487, at 533-537, and L.B. Edelman and S.A. Talesh, 'To comply or not to comply – that isn't the question: how organizations construct the meaning of compliance', in C. Parker and V. Lehmann Nielsen, *Explaining Compliance: Business Responses to Regulation* (Edward Elgar, 2011) 103.

575 See K.D. Krawiec, 'Cosmetic Compliance and the Failure of Negotiated Governance' (2003) 81 *Washington University Law Quarterly* 487, at 528-532.

576 A. Riley and M. Bloom, 'Antitrust Compliance Programmes – Can Companies and Antitrust Agencies Do More?' (2011) *Journal of Competition Law* 21, at 38.

Compared to granting fine reductions to companies that had an antitrust compliance programme when they committed the infringement, granting fine reductions to companies that commit to adopt or upgrade a compliance programme so as to reduce the risk of recidivism is indeed a better (or less bad) idea. Whereas the former sends the normative message that antitrust infringements are part of normal business and that companies have no full responsibility for avoiding such infringements, the latter sends the normative message that companies are responsible for avoiding antitrust infringements, and, when found to have committed an infringement, should take measures to avoid repeating infringements.

I see two risks or drawbacks to granting fine reductions to companies that commit to adopting or upgrading a compliance programme.

The first risk is that by lowering the fine, and by making this fine reduction conditional upon the company not having a compliance programme at the time of the infringement, the incentive to avoid infringements in the first place and the incentive to adopt a compliance programme before a first infringement is committed are weakened. However, this risk may be remote, at least if the reduction remains low.

The second risk is that companies would adopt or upgrade a compliance programme so as to benefit from the reduced fine, but continue to engage in antitrust infringements, either by maintaining or introducing excessive performance targets or incentives that pressurise staff into committing infringements, like company C in the above tale of four companies, or by deceiving the company's compliance counsel, like company D. For the reasons explained above, competition authorities or courts are unlikely to be able to distinguish between, on the one hand, companies that genuinely want to make a clean break with their past of antitrust infringements, like company B in the above tale of four companies, and that may thus merit a reduced fine, and, on the other hand, companies that cynically exploit the possibility of obtaining a reduced fine.

Because of this second risk, it may make sense to make the fine reduction conditional upon the company not contesting the first infringement, as this may be a (no doubt imperfect) indicator that the company is genuinely committed to changing its behaviour.

Another way to reduce the second risk would be to specifically increase the fine for any second or later infringement committed notwithstanding the compliance programme for which a fine reduction was granted.[577]

6. Should the adoption of a compliance programme be imposed as part of infringement decisions or settlements?

Some authors have suggested that antitrust authorities could impose the adoption of a compliance programme as part of an infringement decision or a settlement.[578]

---

577 This is what the European Commission did in the *British Sugar* case; see Commission Decision of 14 October 1998, *British Sugar* [1999] OJ L76/1. To counter the second risk, this increase would have to come on top of the normal increase for recidivism; see generally my paper 'Recidivism in EU Antitrust Enforcement: A Legal and Economic Analysis' (2012) 35 *World Competition* 5.

578 A. Riley and M. Bloom, 'Antitrust Compliance Programmes – Can Companies and Antitrust Agencies Do More?' (2011) *Journal of Competition Law* 21, at 38.

Adopting this suggestion would not weaken incentives for real compliance, nor undermine the normative message that companies are responsible for avoiding antitrust infringements, nor allow companies unfairly to benefit from infringements while escaping liability.

However, one may object that, as explained above, compliance programmes can have negative enforcement effects of two types: employees may learn how to engage more effectively in antitrust infringements and to avoid detection, and companies may decide to conceal or destroy the evidence of infringements they detect through the compliance programme. The risk of such negative effects is no doubt higher when the compliance programme has not been introduced as part of a company's own voluntary decision to improve its respect for the antitrust prohibitions, but has been imposed on the company by a competition authority or court.

On the other hand, it may be possible to reduce to some extent the risk of perverse learning effects by prohibiting the elements of compliance programmes that are most likely to have such perverse effects, in particular dawn raid training through mock raids. As to the risk that companies may conceal or destroy evidence of infringements detected through the compliance programme, this risk would appear to be neutralised by leniency programmes such as those operated by the European Commission.

7. What else could or should be done?

What else could or should competition authorities, courts or legislators do to encourage genuine compliance efforts by companies, without creating perverse incentives or undermining the normative message of the antitrust prohibitions?

First, antitrust authorities should prosecute and punish many infringements, not just deal with a low number of high-profile cases. As has been pointed out by Christine Parker, 'empirical deterrence research persistently finds that the factors that make the most difference to compliance behaviour are the perceived likelihood of detection and enforcement, rather than the objective severity and subjective fearsomeness of the sanctions imposed'.[579] To generate normative commitment to the law, it is equally important to detect and punish as many infringements as possible, as many companies and individuals may be willing to comply with the law on condition that those who do not are caught and punished.[580]

Second, as already mentioned above, adding individual penalties to fines for companies would help companies that sincerely want to avoid their staff engaging in antitrust

---

579 C. Parker, 'Criminal Cartel Sanctions and Compliance: The Gap between Rhetoric and Reality', in C. Beaton-Wells and A. Ezrachi, *Criminalising Cartels: Critical Studies of an International Regulatory Movement* (Hart 2011) 239 at 250; see also, for a discussion of the reasons why a strategy of infrequently imposed very high penalties is not optimal, my paper 'Optimal Antitrust Fines: Theory and Practice' (2006) 29 *World Competition* 183 at 196–199, and, for a discussion of the risks of excessive prioritisation, my paper 'Discretion and Prioritisation in Public Antitrust Enforcement, in Particular EU Antitrust Enforcement' (2011) 34 *World Competition* 353 at 381–382, and Chapter IV of this book.

580 See R. A. Kagan, N. Gunnigham, and D. Thornton, 'Fear, duty, and regulatory compliance: lessons from three research projects', in C. Parker and V. Lehmann Nielsen, *Explaining Compliance: Business Responses to Regulation* (Edward Elgar, 2011) 37, at 46.

infringements, as it would allow compliance counsel, as part of compliance training, to attract attention to this risk.[581]

Third, antitrust authorities should ensure that the content of the antitrust prohibitions is sufficiently clear and is clearly communicated to the business community, so that companies that want to respect the law can figure out at reasonable cost what they can and cannot do.[582]

---

581 See my publications 'Does the Effective Enforcement of Articles 81 and 82 EC Require Not Only Fines on Undertakings But Also Individual Penalties, In Particular Imprisonment?', in C.-D. Ehlermann and I. Atanasiu (eds), *European Competition Law Annual 2001: Effective Private Enforcement of EC Antitrust Law* (Hart 2002); *The Optimal Enforcement of EC Antitrust Law* (Kluwer 2002), chapters 8 and 9; 'Is Criminalization of EU Competition Law the Answer?' (2005) 28 *World Competition* 117; and *Efficiency and Justice in European Antitrust Enforcement* (Hart 2008), chapter 6.

582 See also A. Riley and M. Bloom, 'Antitrust Compliance Programmes – Can Companies and Antitrust Agencies Do More?' (2011) *Journal of Competition Law* 21, at 39; D. Bailey, 'Restrictions of Competition by Object under Article 101 TFEU' (2012) 49 *Common Market Law Review* 559 at 566; and B. J. Rodger, 'A Study of Compliance Post-OFT Infringement Action' (2009) *European Competition Journal* 65 at 95.

VIII. Recidivism in EU Antitrust Enforcement: A Legal and Economic Analysis

Recidivism has attracted much attention and controversy in the context of EU antitrust enforcement. The treatment of recidivism by the European Commission and the EU Courts has often been criticised, and the observed incidence of recidivism has led to some questioning of the overall effectiveness of EU antitrust enforcement. This chapter first clarifies the concept of recidivism and then analyses the treatment of recidivism as an aggravating circumstance in setting the amount of fines, the interplay between recidivism and leniency, and the difficulty of drawing conclusions as to the overall effectiveness of EU antitrust enforcement from the observed incidence of recidivism.

A. Introduction

Recidivism has attracted much attention and controversy in the context of EU antitrust enforcement:

- In the conclusions of their study, published in 2005, of appeals against decisions of the European Commission in cartel cases, Christopher Harding and Alun Gibbs identified an 'awesome level of recidivism on the part of major companies who appear as usual suspects in the world of business cartels. In short this suggests a confirmed culture of business delinquency'.[583]
- In 2006, the European Commission revised its Guidelines for setting fines in antitrust cases.[584] One of three main changes was that repeat offenders would be fined more than in the past: the European Commission now takes into account not only its own previous decisions, but also those by the competition authorities of the EU Member States applying EU antitrust law; the increase of the fine on account of recidivism may be up to 100%; and each prior infringement will justify an increase of the fine.[585]

---

583 C. Harding and A. Gibbs, 'Why go to court in Europe? An analysis of cartel appeals 1995–2004' (2005) 30 *European Law Review* 349 at 369.

584 Guidelines on the method for setting fines imposed pursuant to Article 23(2)(a) of Regulation 1/2003 [2006] OJ C210/2; see H. de Broca, 'The Commission Revises its Guidelines for Setting Fines in Antitrust Cases' (Autumn 2006) *Competition Policy Newsletter* 1; my paper 'The European Commission's 2006 Guidelines on Antitrust Fines: A Legal and Economic Analysis' (2006) 29 *World Competition* 197; chapter 5 of my book *Efficiency and Justice in European Antitrust Enforcement* (Hart 2008); F. Castillo de la Torre, 'The 2006 Guidelines on Fines: Reflections on the Commission's Practice' (2010) 33 *World Competition* 359; and E. Barbier de La Serre and E. Lagathu, 'The Law on Fines Imposed in EU Competition Proceedings: A Post-Pandemic Boost of the Case Law' (2022) 13 *Journal of Competition Law & Practice* 448.

585 Idem, and European Commission press release IP/06/857 of 28 June 2006: 'Multiple offenders will therefore be fined more heavily, in line with Commissioner Kroes's repeated wish'; see also C. Baudenbacher, 'The Legacy of Neelie Kroes' (2010) 1 *Journal of European Competition Law & Practice* 169.

- Already before the 2006 Fining Guidelines, the European Commission had, in a significant number of cases, increased fines on account of recidivism, usually by 50% (irrespective of the number of previous offences).[586] These decisions have generally been confirmed by the EU Courts.[587]
- The European Commission's decisional practice and the EU Courts' case law have, however, been criticised by industry and legal practitioners as disproportionate and lacking limiting principles.[588]
- Noteworthy is also that some national competition authorities in EU Member States that have adopted fining guidelines more recently have chosen not to follow the example of the European Commission's 2006 Fining Guidelines, opting instead for a lower maximum increase of fines on account of recidivism and stricter conditions as to what instances of recidivism are taken into account.[589]
- On the other hand, it has been observed that the European Commission has not made full use of the possibilities offered by its 2006 Fining Guidelines, increasing in practice fines by 50% in case of one prior infringement, 60% in case of two prior infringements, 90% in case of three prior infringements, and 100% in case of four prior infringements, far below the 100%, 200%, 300% and 400% limits set out in the 2006 Fining Guidelines.[590]
- John Connor has claimed to have identified, on the basis of his own statistics on the incidence of recidivism, compared with the decisions taken by the European Commission in application of the 2006 Fining Guidelines, a 'large number of defendants convicted under the new guidelines that received no recidivism penalty when they clearly qualified for such. [. . .] One wonders whether such a severe undercounting is wilful or simply the result of poor record-keeping by the Commission'.[591]
- More generally, John Connor has claimed, on the basis of his (worldwide) statistics for international cartels during the last two decades, that 'recidivism appears to

586 See my book *Efficiency and Justice in European Antitrust Enforcement* (Hart 2008), paragraph 295.

587 See in particular Judgments in *Danone v Commission*, C-3/06 P, EU:C:2007:88, and in *Lafarge v Commission*, C-413/08 P, EU:C:2010:346.

588 See, among others, K. Nordlander, 'The Commission's Policy on Recidivism: legal certainty for repeat offenders?' (2005) 2 *Competition Law Review* 55–68; J. Lever, Opinion 'Whether, and if so how, the EC Commission's 2006 Guidelines on setting fines for infringements of Articles 81 and 82 of the EC Treaty are fairly subject to serious criticism', BDI – Federation of German Industries (12 November 2007); and A. Winckler, 'La récidive en droit européen de la concurrence: Un droit d'exception?', *Concurrences* no 4-2010, 21; compare with L. Truchot, 'Le régime de la récidive en matière de pratiques anticoncurrentielles: Garanties et dissuasion', *Concurrences* no 4-2010, 17.

589 See for example the French Competition Authority's Notice of 30 July 2021 on the Method Relating to the Setting of Financial Penalties, paragraphs 43 and 44 (increase of fines by 15 to 50%, and maximum period of 15 years between the first finding of infringement and the start of the second infringement), identical on this point to the French Competition Authority's previous Notice of 16 May 2011.

590 E. Barbier de La Serre and C. Winckler, 'Legal Issues Regarding Fines Imposed in EU Competition Proceedings' (2010) 1 *Journal of Competition Law & Practice* 327 at 336–337 and 'A Survey of Legal Issues Regarding Fines Imposed in EU Competition Proceedings (2010)' (2011) 2 *Journal of Competition Law & Practice* 356 at 360–361, and C. Veljanovski, 'Deterrence, Recidivism and European Cartel Fines' (14 July 2011), electronic copy available at http://ssrn.com/abstract=1758639, at 14; see also Judgment in *Arkema France v Commission*, T-343/08, EU:T:2011:218, paragraphs 19 and 102–103.

591 J. M. Connor, 'Has the Commission become more severe in punishing cartels? Effects of the 2006 Guidelines' (2011) *European Competition Law Review* 27 at 30.

be increasing rapidly, both in number and relative to all corporate cartelists. [. . .] This observation seems to justify a continuation of policies that impose brutally higher fines and other effective sanctions on cartel recidivists'.[592]

- Finally, the question has been raised whether it is just to allow recidivists to benefit from immunity from fines under the European Commission's Leniency Notice.[593] Under the 2006 Leniency Programme of the Greek competition authority, recidivists could not receive immunity from fines. In 2011, however, the Greek competition authority changed its leniency programme, and recidivists can now also obtain immunity from fines.[594]

B. The concept of recidivism

In its 2006 Fining Guidelines, the European Commission defines recidivism (or repeated infringement) as the situation 'where an undertaking continues or repeats the same or a similar infringement after the Commission or a national competition authority has made a finding that the undertaking infringed [Articles 101 or 102 TFEU]'.[595]

According to the EU General Court, 'recidivism, as understood in a number of national legal systems, implies that a person has committed fresh infringements after having been penalised for similar infringements'.[596]

---

592 J. M. Connor, 'Recidivism Revealed: Private International Cartels 1990–2009' (Autumn 2010) *Competition Policy International* 101, at 101 and 116; see also OECD, Roundtable on promoting compliance with competition law – Issues paper by the Secretariat, DAF/COMP(2011)4 of 1 June 2011, at 2.

593 L. Truchot, 'Le régime de la récidive en matière de pratiques anticoncurrentielles: Garanties et dissuasion', *Concurrences* no 4-2010, 17, at 20.

594 Decision No 299/V/2006 of the Plenary of the Hellenic Competition Commission, point A.4(e) ('the undertaking must not have participated in the past in a prohibited collusive practice for which a decision by a National Competition Authority or the European Commission has been issued'). The new leniency programme was adopted by Decision No 526/VI/2011 of 30 August 2011.

595 Guidelines on the method for setting fines imposed pursuant to Article 23(2)(a) of Regulation 1/2003 [2006] OJ C210/2. In fact, the 2006 Fining Guidelines do not use the word 'recidivism'. Similarly, in its previous 1998 Guidelines (Guidelines on the method of setting fines imposed pursuant to Article 15(2) of Regulation No 17 and Article 65(5) of the ECSC Treaty [1998] OJ C9/3), the Commission mentioned as aggravating circumstance 'repeated infringement of the same type by the same undertaking(s)'. The use by the Commission of the term 'repeated infringement' rather than 'recidivism' may have reflected a desire to distinguish EU antitrust enforcement from (hard-core) criminal law; see further L. Idot, 'Récidive ou réitération?', *Concurrences* no 4-2010, 26 at 29, and (on the criminal-law nature of EU antitrust enforcement) my paper 'The Increased Level of EU Antitrust Fines, Judicial Review and the ECHR' (2010) 33 *World Competition* 5 at 12–14.

596 Judgment in *Thyssen Stahl v Commission*, T-141/94, EU:T:1999:48, paragraph 617, and in *ICI v Commission*, T-66/01, EU:T:2010:255, paragraph 378; in other judgments, the Court has added that 'the concept of repeated infringement does not necessarily imply that a fine has been imposed in the past, but merely that a finding of infringement has been made in the past' (Judgment in *Danone v Commission*, T-38/02, EU:T:2005:367, paragraph 363, confirmed upon appeal in Judgment in *Danone v Commission*, C-3/06 P, EU:C:2007:88, paragraph 41). The EU Courts have also clarified that the Commission can take account of recidivism even if the prior decision is still subject to review by the courts; in case of later annulment of the prior decision, the Commission would, however, be required to amend its second decision (Judgment in *Lafarge v Commission*, C-413/08 P, EU:C:2010:346, paragraphs 81–90). As to the notion of 'similar' infringements, it appears from the case law that an infringement of Article 101 TFEU and an infringement of Article 102 TFEU cannot be considered similar (Judgments in *BASF and UCB v Commission*, T-101/05 and T-111/05, EU:T:2007:380, paragraph 64, and in *ICI v Commission*, T-66/01, EU:T:2010:255, paragraphs 378–381; see also L. Truchot, 'Le régime de la récidive en matière de pratiques anticoncurrentielles: Garanties et dissuasion', *Concurrences* no 4-2010, 17, at 19).

These two definitions have in common that the same person or undertaking is found to have started or continued an infringement after having been the addressee of a decision finding a similar infringement or imposing a fine for a similar infringement. Recidivism thus only exists if the second infringement starts or continues after the date on which the European Commission or a national competition authority adopted the decision finding the first infringement (second infringement after a first decision).

Under these definitions, there is thus no recidivism in a situation where two or more infringements take place partially or entirely during the same time period, but none of these infringements continues after the date on which the first decision finding one of these infringements is adopted (contemporaneous infringements).[597]

In his work on recidivism,[598] John Connor identifies a company or undertaking as recidivist 'if it is convicted a second time for cartel conduct'.[599] Under this definition, an undertaking which participated in four different cartels that all ended before the date on which the first decision finding any of these infringements was adopted is a multiple recidivist, whereas under the concept of recidivism as used by the European Commission and the EU Courts (as well as by the competition authorities and courts in other jurisdictions) such an undertaking is not a recidivist.

John Connor's use of an alternative definition of recidivism fully explains his surprising finding of 'severe undercounting' of recidivism by the European Commission.[600] One can legitimately debate the question whether optimal deterrence would require that fines be increased not only in case of a second infringement after a first decision but also in case of contemporaneous infringements.[601] It is, however, clearly erroneous to criticise

---

597 Judgments in *Thyssen Stahl v Commission*, T-141/94, EU:T:1999:48, paragraph 618, and in *BPB v European Commission*, T-53/03, EU:T:2008:254, paragraphs 391–396. The notion of recidivism is also distinct from the notion of '[continuing or] repeated infringements' in Article 25(2) of Regulation 1/2003, which concerns the situation where an infringement that has been interrupted and restarted is only later for the first time found by the Commission; see Judgment in *IMI v Commission*, T-18/05, EU:T:2010:202, paragraphs 96–97.

598 J. M. Connor, 'Recidivism Revealed: Private International Cartels 1990–2009' (Autumn 2010) *Competition Policy International* 101, and 'Has the Commission become more severe in punishing cartels? Effects of the 2006 Guidelines' (2011) *European Competition Law Review* 27.

599 J. M. Connor, 'Recidivism Revealed: Private International Cartels 1990–2009' (Autumn 2010) *Competition Policy International* 101, at 103.

600 J. M. Connor, 'Has the Commission become more severe in punishing cartels? Effects of the 2006 Guidelines' (2011) *European Competition Law Review* 27 at 30. For instance, in *Sodium Chlorate*, one of the examples cited by John Connor, the Commission found in its decision of 11 June 2008 that Akzo Nobel had ended its participation in the infringement on 9 February 2000, which is well before the six earlier antitrust decisions against Akzo Nobel, namely, *Sodium Gluconate* on 2 October 2001, *Choline Chloride* on 9 December 2004, *Organic Peroxides* on 10 December 2003, *Rubber Chemicals* on 21 December 2005, *MCAA* on 19 January 2005, and *Hydrogen Peroxide* on 3 May 2006. Another example cited by John Connor is the decision of 10 January 2008 in *Candle Wax*, in which the Commission found that Exxon Mobil and Repsol had ended their participation in the cartel on, respectively, 20 November 2003 and 4 August 2004. These dates precede the two earlier Commission decisions fining Exxon Mobil on 13 September 2006 for involvement in the *Dutch Bitumen* cartel, and Repsol on 21 December 2005 for participation in the *Rubber Chemicals* cartel and on 3 October 2007 for participation in the *Spanish Bitumen* cartel. A last example cited by John Connor is the *Power Transformer* case, in which the Commission found in its decision of 7 October 2009 that inter alia Toshiba, Hitachi and Siemens had participated in a cartel from 9 June 1999 to 15 May 2003. Again, these dates precede the Commission's decision of 24 January 2007 against the same undertakings in *Switchgear*. As regards Hitachi, the end date of involvement in the *Power Transformer* cartel also precedes the Commission decision of 20 November 2007 in *Professional videotape*.

601 This question is addressed further below.

the Commission for having under-applied its Guidelines in that it has not identified as recidivism situations that would only qualify as recidivism under a definition of recidivism different from that used in those Guidelines and in the case law of the EU Courts.[602]

C. Recidivism as an aggravating circumstance in setting the amount of fines

1. The role of fines

To understand the justification for treating recidivism as an aggravating circumstance in setting the amount of antitrust fines, it may be useful first to recall the general purpose of antitrust fines.

According to Article 103(2)(a) TFEU, the purpose of EU antitrust fines is 'to ensure compliance with the prohibitions laid down in [Articles 101 and 102 TFEU]'.

As I have argued in more detail elsewhere,[603] the imposition of fines on undertakings that are found to have breached the antitrust prohibitions can in three ways contribute to ensuring compliance with those prohibitions:

- First, the imposition of fines may have a deterrent effect, in that it creates a credible threat of prosecution and punishment that weighs sufficiently in the balance of expected costs and benefits to deter calculating undertakings from committing antitrust violations.
- Secondly, in the case of collective violations such as cartels, the differentiation of penalties according to the role played by the different conspirators can have the effect of raising the cost of setting up and running cartels. Setting up and maintaining a successful cartel requires effort. The cartel members have to select and coordinate their behaviour according to mutually consistent, collusive strategies, allowing the cartel participants as a group to increase profits, and providing for a fair distribution of profits between them. They also need to develop mechanisms to discourage cheating, involving monitoring, rewards and punishments. In a dynamic economy, successful cartels may have to develop an organisational structure that allows them to solve these problems continuously.[604] A well-designed fining policy can make these tasks more difficult, by imposing higher penalties for cartel members that play active roles in setting up and running the cartel, and lower penalties for cartel members that remain exclusively passive, and by offering deviators the possibility of applying for leniency.[605]

---

602 See also G. J. Werden, S. D. Hammond and B. A. Barnett, 'Recidivism Eliminated: Cartel Enforcement in the United States Since 1999' (October 2011) *CPI Antitrust Chronicle* 1.

603 See my paper 'Optimal Antitrust Fines: Theory and Practice' (2006) 29 *World Competition* 183, and chapter 3 of my book *Efficiency and Justice in European Antitrust Enforcement* (Hart 2008).

604 M. C. Levenstein and V. Y. Suslow, 'What Determines Cartel Success?' (2006) 44 *Journal of Economic Literature* 43–95, at 44–45; see also J.E. Harrington, 'How Do Cartels Operate?' (2006) 2 *Foundations and Trends in Microeconomics* 1.

605 See my paper 'Optimal Antitrust Fines: Theory and Practice' (2006) 29 *World Competition* 183, at 201–204; my paper 'Leniency in Antitrust Enforcement: Theory and Practice' (2007) 30 *World Competition* 25; and chapter 5 of my book *Efficiency and Justice in European Antitrust Enforcement* (Hart 2008); see also Chapter V of this book.

– Thirdly, the public punishment of those who violate the antitrust prohibitions may also have a moral effect, by sending a message to the spontaneously law-abiding, reinforcing their moral commitment to the antitrust prohibitions.[606] Indeed, corporate managers are not necessarily just maximisers of profits for themselves and their principals. They may feel a moral responsibility to live within the law whether or not they are likely to be caught, and this normative commitment could trump their interest calculus.[607] Psychological research suggests that normative commitment is generally an important factor explaining compliance with the law.[608]

2. Four reasons for imposing higher fines on recidivists

The Court of Justice has held that, in setting the amount of the fine, '[t]he analysis must [. . .] take into consideration [. . .] any repeated infringement',[609] and that the circumstance of recidivism is 'not only a relevant factor but also a particularly important factor and a very significant indication of the gravity of the infringement for the purpose of assessing the amount of the fine in the context of effective deterrence'.[610]

As to the justification for imposing higher fines in case of recidivism, the General Court has held that 'it must be recalled to mind that, for the purpose of determining the amount of the fine, the Commission must ensure that its action has the necessary deterrent effect [. . .]. Recidivism is a circumstance which justifies a significant increase in the basic amount of the fine. Recidivism constitutes proof that the sanction previously imposed was not sufficiently deterrent'.[611]

It would indeed appear that the fact that an undertaking continues or repeats an infringement not very long after it has been fined for a similar infringement shows that the first fine has not been sufficiently deterrent.

One may, however, wonder whether the solution to this problem should be to raise the second fine specifically for the repeat offender, or rather to increase the fine level generally

---

606 See J. Adenaes, 'The Moral or Educative Influence of Criminal Law' (1971) 27 *Journal of Social Issues* 17, and 'General prevention revisited: research and policy implications' (1975) 66 *Journal of Criminal Law & Criminology* 338, at 341–343; K. G. Dau-Schmidt, 'An Economic Analysis of the Criminal Law as a Preference-Shaping Policy' (1990) *Duke Law Journal* 1, C. R. Sunstein, 'On the Expressive Function of the Law' (1996) 144 *University of Pennsylvania Law Review* 2021, D. M. Kahan, 'Social Influence, Social Meaning, and Deterrence' (1997) 83 *Virginia Law Review* 349, N. K. Katyal, 'Deterrence's Difficulty' (1997) 95 *Michigan Law Review* 2385, G. E. Lynch, 'The Role of Criminal Law in Policing Corporate Misconduct' (1997) 60 *Law and Contemporary Problems* 23, D. M. Kahan, 'Social Meaning and the Economic Analysis of Crime' (1998) 27 *Journal of Legal Studies* 609, and K. G. Dau-Schmidt, 'Preference shaping by the law', in P. Newman (ed), *The New Palgrave Dictionary of Economics and the Law* (Macmillan 1998) 84.

607 C. D. Stone, 'Sentencing the corporation' (1991) 71 *Boston University Law Review* 383 at 389.

608 See T. R. Tyler, *Why People Obey the Law* (Yale University Press 1990).

609 Judgments in *Aalborg Portland and Others v Commission*, C-204/00 P etc., EU:C:2004:6, paragraph 91, and in *Danone v Commission*, C-3/06 P, EU:C:2007:88, paragraph 26.

610 Judgment in *Danone v Commission*, C-3/06 P, EU:C:2007:88, paragraph 47.

611 Judgment in *Michelin v European Commission*, T-203/01, EU:T:2003:250, paragraph 293; see also Judgments in *Danone v Commission*, T-38/02, EU:T:2005:367, paragraph 348, and in *Shell v Commission*, T-38/07, EU:T:2011:355, paragraph 98.

for all offenders.[612] If the first fine was insufficient to deter the specific undertaking, could one not assume a general problem of insufficient deterrence for all undertakings?[613] Indeed, according to settled case law of the Court of Justice, the Commission can at any time raise the level of fines so as to reinforce their deterrent effect, when it finds that practices that have long been established as being unlawful are still relatively frequent.[614]

I can, however, see at least four reasons why a finding of recidivism may justify an increased fine specifically for the recidivist rather than (or in addition to) a general increase in the level of fines:[615]

a. *Higher than average propensity to commit infringements*

As has been pointed out by the EU Courts, the fact of the repeated infringement may reveal 'a characteristic specific to the perpetrator of the infringement, namely its propensity to commit such infringements'.[616] Indeed, some undertakings may have a higher propensity to commit antitrust violations than others, because they, or rather the individuals taking the decisions inside them, have a weaker moral commitment to respect the law, or are more willing to take legal risks, or differ in some other relevant aspect from the average undertaking.[617] To deter such undertakings from committing infringements (not only repeated ones, but also first infringements), higher fines would be required for them than for other undertakings. At the time of a first infringement, however,

---

612 Another difficulty with this justification for increasing fines specifically for recidivists is that, according to the case law of the EU Courts, the concept of recidivism 'does not necessarily imply that a fine has been imposed in the past, but merely that a finding of infringement has been made in the past' (Judgment in *Danone v Commission*, T-38/02, EU:T:2005:367, paragraph 363, confirmed upon appeal in Judgment in *Danone v Commission*, C-3/06 P, EU:C:2007:88, paragraph 41).

613 One could even argue that the problem of insufficient deterrence could be greater for the other undertakings, as their subjective estimate of the probability that they will be caught and punished may be lower than that of the undertaking that has already been fined; see the discussion on subjective estimates and availability bias in my paper 'Optimal Antitrust Fines: Theory and Practice' (2006) 29 *World Competition* 183, 193–195, and D. A. Dana, 'Rethinking the Puzzle of Escalating Penalties for Repeat Offenders' (2001) 110 *Yale Law Journal* 733 at 743–753 and 759–772.

614 Judgment in *Musique Diffusion Française and Others v Commission*, 100/80 to 103/80, EU:C:1983:158, paragraphs 108–109, and Judgment in *Dansk Rørindustri and Others v European Commission*, C-189/02 P, C-202/02 P, C-205/02 P to C-208/02 P and C-213/02 P, EU:C:2005:408, paragraph 169.

615 See already my paper 'The European Commission's 2006 Guidelines on Antitrust Fines: A Legal and Economic Analysis' (2007) 30 *World Competition* 197 at 215–216, and my book *Efficiency and Justice in European Antitrust Enforcement* (Hart 2008), at 96–97. A fifth possible reason is that higher fines for repeat offenders may be needed to compensate for decreasing social sanctions, in that the reputational, commercial or social damage from being fined for an antitrust violation may be lower the second or subsequent time than the first time; see D. A. Dana, 'Rethinking the Puzzle of Escalating Penalties for Repeat Offenders' (2001) 110 *Yale Law Journal* 733, 772–776; compare also with T. J. Miceli and C. Bucci, 'A Simple Theory of Increasing Penalties for Repeat Offenders' (2005) Review of Law and Economics, vol 1, no 1, Article 5. On the other hand, social sanctions might actually increase if the first infringement is perceived as being accidental, whereas the repetition of infringements is perceived as a sign of a deeper problem with the company's culture.

616 Judgment in *Danone v Commission*, T-38/02, EU:T:2005:367, paragraph 349, confirmed upon appeal in Judgment in *Danone v Commission*, C-3/06 P, EU:C:2007:88, paragraph 39.

617 On the role of an undertaking's culture, with a case study of Archer Daniels Midland, see J. M. Conley and W. M. O'Barr, 'Crime and Custom in Corporate Society: A Cultural Perspective on Corporate Misconduct' (1997) 60 *Law and Contemporary Problems* 5; see also J. Sonnenfeld and P. R. Lawrence, 'Why do companies succumb to price fixing?' (July-August 1978) *Harvard Business Review* 145; and my book *The Optimal Enforcement of EC Antitrust Law* (Kluwer 2002), at 193–194.

it may not be possible for a competition authority or a court to observe these specific characteristics with an acceptable degree of accuracy or at a reasonable cost, allowing a differentiation in fines between the undertakings with these specific characteristics and the other ones.[618] It may not be possible either, in particular for reasons of proportional justice, to set the level of fines for all undertakings at the higher level that would be required to deter the undertakings with a higher propensity to commit infringements.[619] The best that can then be done in practice is to wait until the undertakings with a higher propensity to commit infringements have committed repeated infringements, and then to raise the fines specifically for them.[620]

b. *Need to express increased moral condemnation*

Higher fines for recidivists may be required for moral reasons. Indeed, the visible fact of repeat offending risks weakening the moral commitment to the law of the spontaneously law-abiding, and the imposition of higher fines counters this effect, by expressing increased moral condemnation.[621]

c. *Lower probability of detection*

Higher fines for repeat offenders may be needed to compensate for a lower probability of detection, on the assumption that undertakings learn from a first investigation and prosecution by a competition authority how they can better hide their infringements or better organise their defence.[622]

d. *Discovery of the profitability of infringements*

In a situation where the fines imposed (discounted for the probability of detection and punishment) are in reality below the illicit gains from the antitrust violations, but where

---

618 Even if it were possible to observe these characteristics before a first infringement has been found, reliance on these characteristics before a first infringement has been found may also be contrary to the fundamental legal principle of respect for the presumption of innocence.

619 On the principle of proportionality as a constraint on the pursuit of optimal deterrence, as well as other limits to high fines, see my paper 'Optimal Antitrust Fines: Theory and Practice' (2006) 29 *World Competition* 183, at 196–199, and my book *Efficiency and Justice in European Antitrust Enforcement* (Hart 2008), at 61–65.

620 See also R. A. Posner, *Economic Analysis of Law* (3rd ed; Little, Brown & Company, 1986), at 214; A.M. Polinsky and D.L. Rubinfeld, 'A model of optimal fines for repeat offenders' (1991) 46 *Journal of Public Economics* 291–306; D. A. Dana, 'Rethinking the Puzzle of Escalating Penalties for Repeat Offenders' (2001) 110 *Yale Law Journal* 733, at 755; and S. Shavell, *Foundations of Economic Analysis of Law* (Harvard UP 2004), at 529–530.

621 See D. A. Dana, 'Rethinking the Puzzle of Escalating Penalties for Repeat Offenders' (2001) 110 *Yale Law Journal* 733, at 776–783.

622 See my book *The Optimal Enforcement of EC Antitrust Law* (Kluwer 2002), at 36–37, and A. M. Polinsky and D. L. Rubinfeld, 'A model of optimal fines for repeat offenders' (1991) 46 *Journal of Public Economics* 291–306, at 303; see also, as to the importance of learning by cartels, M. C. Levenstein and V. Y. Suslow, 'What Determines Cartel Success?' (2006) 44 *Journal of Economic Literature* 43, and J. E. Harrington, 'How Do Cartels Operate?' (2006) 2 *Foundations and Trends in Microeconomics* 1, and, as to the role of the cartel defendant bar, C. Harding and A. Gibbs, 'Why go to court in Europe? An analysis of cartel appeals 1995–2004' (2005) 30 *European Law Review* 349, at 368–369; however, see also above as to the countervailing considerations relating to possible increased attention by the investigating authorities and relating to availability bias. See also N. K. Katyal, 'Conspiracy Theory' (2003) *Yale Law Journal* 1307 at 1381–1382, arguing for increased penalties in cases where the same group of cartelists commit repeated infringements together, with the argument that this circumstance suggests a tightly knit conspiracy in which defection is more difficult.

the amounts of the fines are not sufficiently foreseeable for undertakings fully to understand this,[623] it may take a first imposition of a fine for an undertaking fully to understand that violations are profitable. Higher fines for repeat offenders may then be required to reinforce deterrence for these undertakings.

3. Should contemporaneous infringements be treated in the same way as recidivism?

As mentioned above, the notion of recidivism as defined by the EU Courts and applied by the European Commission requires that an undertaking starts or continues an infringement after the date on which it was the addressee of a decision finding a similar infringement (second infringement after a first decision). Recidivism does thus not cover the situation where an undertaking commits two or more (separate) infringements partially or entirely during the same time period, but none of these infringements is continued after the date on which the first decision finding one of these infringements is adopted (contemporaneous infringements).

Would it be justified to treat contemporaneous infringements as an aggravating circumstance for the setting of the amount of the fines, similar to recidivism? As discussed above, John Connor uses a wider notion of recidivism, including contemporaneous infringements.

Considering the four reasons for increasing fines for recidivists identified above, it appears that there is much less justification to increase fines in case of contemporaneous infringements than in case of recidivism. The first reason for increasing fines for recidivists (higher than average propensity to commit infringements) also applies in case of contemporaneous infringements, but to a lesser extent, as repeated infringements after having been warned by a decision are more revealing of a high propensity to commit infringements than multiple infringements without such a warning. The second reason (need to express increased moral condemnation) also only applies to a lesser extent in case of contemporaneous infringements, as it is morally more reprehensible to reoffend after a first finding of infringement than without such a prior warning.[624] The third and fourth reasons (lower probability of detection, and discovery of the profitability of infringements) do not apply in case of contemporaneous infringements.

On balance, it would thus not appear justified to take account of contemporaneous infringements as an aggravating factor in setting the amount of fines in the same way as recidivism.

If an undertaking is found to have committed two or more (separate) contemporaneous infringements, each of these infringements should in principle be punished with the

---

623 On the relationship between the foreseeability of fines and their deterrent and other enforcement effects, see my paper 'The European Commission's 2006 Guidelines on Antitrust Fines: A Legal and Economic Analysis' (2007) 30 *World Competition* 197 at 204–206, and my book *Efficiency and Justice in European Antitrust Enforcement* (Hart 2008), at 85–86.

624 See generally A. von Hirsch, 'Desert and Previous Convictions in Sentencing' (1980–1981) 65 *Minnesota Law Review* 591, and A. von Hirsch and A. Ashworth, *Proportionate Sentencing: Exploring the Principles* (Oxford UP 2005) at 148–155.

same fine as if that infringement was the only infringement.[625] However, where several fines are imposed simultaneously or around the same time, there is an increased risk of inability to pay, and inability to pay may justify a fine reduction.[626]

4. Should there be a limitation period for recidivism?

Given that the European Commission's 2006 Fining Guidelines do not contain a maximum period of time between the starting date of the new infringement, or the date of the new decision, and the date at which the earlier infringement was penalised or found, concerns have been expressed that this would allow a system of 'everlasting' or 'perpetual' recidivism.[627]

The Court of Justice has held that the absence of such a maximum period does not infringe the principle of legal certainty. However, EU law does not authorise the European Commission to take account of recidivism without any limitation in time. Indeed, the principle of proportionality requires that the Commission takes into account the time elapsed between the infringements in assessing, in each individual case, whether or not these infringements demonstrate a tendency to infringe the antitrust prohibitions and hence justify a fine increase on account of recidivism.[628]

As mentioned above, some national competition authorities that have adopted fining guidelines more recently have chosen not to follow the example of the case-by-case approach of the European Commission, opting instead for a definite limitation period, for example, 15 years between the first finding of infringement and the start of the second infringement in France.[629]

Considering the four reasons for increasing fines for recidivists identified above, it would indeed appear in general that the longer the time period between (the finding of) the first infringement and the second infringement, the weaker the justification for a fine increase on account of recidivism.

For a same time period of, for instance, 15 years, there may, however, be significant differences from case to case. Particularly relevant in this respect is whether over this time

---

625 See also Judgment in *Arkema v Commission*, T-217/06, EU:T:2011:251, paragraphs 228–231, rejecting the argument that lower fines should be imposed in case of contemporaneous infringements.

626 See Judgment in *Arkema v Commission*, T-217/06, EU:T:2011:251, paragraphs 330–331; Commission Document SEC(2010)737, Inability to pay under paragraph 35 of the 2006 Fining Guidelines and payment conditions pre-and post-decision finding an infringement and imposing fines (June 2010), available at http://ec.europa.eu/transparency/regdoc/rep/2/2010/EN/2-2010-737-EN-2-0.Pdf; and Commission notice on best practices for the conduct of proceedings concerning Articles 101 and 102 TFEU [2011] OJ C308/6, paragraphs 87–89; see also my paper 'Optimal Antitrust Fines: Theory and Practice' (2006) 29 *World Competition* 183, at 196–198; my book *Efficiency and Justice in European Antitrust Enforcement* (Hart 2008), at 62–64; and M. C. Levenstein and V. Y. Suslow, 'Constant Vigilance: Maintaining Cartel Deterrence During the Great Recession' (Autumn 2010) 6 *Competition Policy International* 145.

627 See argumentation of Danone, as summarised in Judgment in *Danone v Commission*, C-3/06 P, EU:C:2007:88, paragraph 33, and K. Nordlander, 'The Commission's Policy on Recidivism: legal certainty for repeat offenders?' (2005) 2 *Competition Law Review* 55 at 66–68.

628 Judgments in *Danone v Commission*, C-3/06 P, EU:C:2007:88, paragraphs 37–39; in *Lafarge v Commission*, C-413/08 P, EU:C:2010:346, paragraphs 66–75; and in *Commission and Others v Versalis and Others*, C-93/13 P, EU:C:2015:150, paragraph 97.

629 French Competition Authority's Notice of 30 July 2021 on the Method Relating to the Setting of Financial Penalties, paragraph 44.

period the relevant individuals within the undertaking (both those directly committing the infringements and those encouraging or failing to prevent the infringements) are still at least in part the same or have been replaced by a different generation.[630]

In many undertakings, the relevant individuals may be an entirely different group from those in charge 15 years earlier. In such a case, the four reasons for increasing fines for recidivists identified above (higher than average propensity to commit infringements, need to express increased moral condemnation, lower probability of detection, and discovery of the profitability of infringements) appear much less or not at all applicable.

In other cases, however, there may be significant continuity: for example, in the *Belgian Beer* case, where the European Commission in its decision in 2001 increased the fine imposed on Danone on account of participation in two earlier cartels in the glass sector, which the Commission had found in 1984 and 1974, it appeared that 'during the period in which the three infringements were committed by BSN/Danone the same person occupied the post of chairman and chief executive. In addition, at least two of Danone's directors who were responsible for food operations during the [Belgian beer] cartel were employed in the company's plate glass division at the time of the earlier infringement(s)'.[631] In such a case, a fine increase on account of recidivism appears entirely justified, even if more than 15 years have elapsed since the prior findings of infringement.[632]

5. By how much should fines be increased on account of recidivism?

There are clearly different views, between competition authorities and over time, on the question by how much antitrust fines should be increased on account of recidivism. As mentioned above, the European Commission's 2006 Fining Guidelines threaten an increase of up to 100% in case of one prior infringement, 200% in case of two prior infringements, 300% in case of three prior infringements, 400% in case of four prior infringements, and so on *ad infinitum*. However, the Commission has not made full use of the possibilities offered by its 2006 Fining Guidelines, increasing in practice fines by 50% in case of one prior infringement, 60% in case of two prior infringements, 90% in case of three prior infringements, and 100% in case of four prior infringements.

---

630 Compare with J. Lever, Opinion 'Whether, and if so how, the EC Commission's 2006 Guidelines on setting fines for infringements of Articles 81 and 82 of the EC Treaty are fairly subject to serious criticism', BDI – Federation of German Industries (12 November 2007), at 11.

631 Commission Decision of 5 December 2001 relating to a proceeding under Article 81 of the EC Treaty (Case IV/37.614/F3 PO/ Interbrew and Alken-Maes) [2003] OJ L200/1, paragraph 314. As to the time period between the infringements (rather than the findings of infringement), this was in the case of Danone less than ten years; see Judgment in *Danone v Commission*, T-38/02, EU:T:2005:367, paragraphs 354–355. See also Judgment in *Saint-Gobain Glass France and Others v Commission*, T-56/09 and T-73/09, EU:T:2014:160, paragraphs 330 to 334.

632 This would also appear to be a case where individual (criminal) penalties for the directors concerned would be appropriate; see generally my paper 'Is Criminalization of EU Competition Law the Answer?' (2005) 28 *World Competition* 117; Chapters 8 and 9 of my book *The Optimal Enforcement of EC Antitrust Law* (Kluwer 2002); Chapter 6 of my book *Efficiency and Justice in European Antitrust Enforcement* (Hart 2008); S. Calkins, 'Coming to Praise Criminal Antitrust Enforcement', in C.-D. Ehlermann and I. Atanasiu, *European Competition Law Annual 2006: Enforcement of Prohibition of Cartels* (Hart 2007), 343; D.H. Ginsburg and J. D. Wright, 'Antitrust Sanctions' (Autumn 2010) 6 *Competition Policy International* 3; and A. Stephan, 'Disqualification Orders for Directors Involved in Cartels' (2011) 2 *Journal of European Competition Law & Practice*.

The Commission has thus stayed relatively close to its practice preceding the 2006 Fining Guidelines, when it usually increased fines by 50% on account of recidivism, irrespective of the number of prior infringements. The French Competition Authority, in its notice on fines, foresees an increase of 15 to 50% on account of recidivism.[633] The General Court has upheld a European Commission decision applying a 90% increase on account of three prior infringements.[634] However, in a judgment in which the General Court found that the Commission in a decision imposing a fine for violation of Article 102 TFEU had mistakenly made a finding of recidivism on the basis of a prior infringement of Article 101 TFEU, the General Court reduced the fine by only 5%.[635]

Considering again the four reasons for increasing fines for recidivists identified above (higher than average propensity to commit infringements, need to express increased moral condemnation, lower probability of detection, and discovery of the profitability of infringements), I would personally not think these reasons could ever justify trebling or quadrupling fines. On the other hand, an increase of only 5% would appear inappropriately low. The traditional Commission practice, often confirmed by the EU Courts, of increasing fines by 50% on account of recidivism would appear reasonable. As to multiple recidivism, the difference between no prior infringements and one or more prior infringements would appear much more relevant in the light of those four reasons than the difference between one prior infringement and two prior infringements. The Commission's practice of increasing fines by 50% in case of one prior infringement and 60% in case of two prior infringements thus again appears reasonable. The relevance of the difference between two prior infringements and three prior infringements would appear to be less than that of the difference between one prior infringement and two prior infringements. The more prior infringements there are, the less difference one additional prior infringement would appear to make.[636]

D. Recidivism and leniency

Under its Leniency Notice, the European Commission grants immunity from fines as well as reduction of fines in recognition of the voluntary provision of intelligence and evidence that enables the Commission to detect and punish cartels.[637]

Recidivists can benefit from the Leniency Notice under the same conditions as other cartelists.

---

633 French Competition Authority's Notice of 30 July 2021 on the Method Relating to the Setting of Financial Penalties, paragraph 45.

634 Judgment in *Arkema France v Commission*, T-343/08, EU:T:2011:218, paragraphs 19 and 102–104.

635 Judgment in *ICI v Commission*, T-66/01, EU:T:2010:255, paragraph 381. The Commission's decision did not specify by how much the fine had been increased on account of recidivism, but the Commission explained at the hearing before the Court that this factor had not played a large role in the setting of the amount of the fine. In its Judgment in *Saint-Gobain Glass France and Others v Commission*, T-56/09 and T-73/09, EU:T:2014:160, paragraphs 485 and 486, the General Court, having discarded one of the two previous decisions taken into account by the Commission for the purposes of recidivism, diminished the fine increase on account of recidivism from 60% to 30%.

636 Attention should also be paid to the sequence of the previous infringements: a further increase for multiple recidivism may be justified in a case where the previous infringements occur sequentially, but not where the multiple previous infringements were contemporaneous between themselves.

637 See Chapter V of this book.

Statistically, it appears that recidivists more than proportionately benefit from immunity from fines under the Leniency Notice: During the 5-year period 2006–2010, the European Commission adopted decisions finding 38 cartels.[638] The sum of the number of undertakings found to have participated in these cartels was 255, and the number of findings of recidivism 31. Slightly less than one out of eight (12%) of the undertakings found to have participated in cartels were thus recidivists. For 28 of the 38 cartels, the Commission granted immunity from fines to an undertaking in application of the Leniency Notice. Among the 28 immunity recipients, 7 were recidivists. One out of four (25%) of the immunity recipients were thus recidivists.

The question has been asked whether it is just that recidivists can receive immunity from fines.[639]

This fairness concern should be taken seriously, also because it may impact the effectiveness of antitrust enforcement.

As already mentioned above, corporate managers are not necessarily just maximisers of profits for themselves and their principals. They may feel a moral responsibility to live within the law whether or not they are likely to be caught, and this normative commitment could trump their interest calculus. The public punishment of those who violate the antitrust prohibitions has thus not only a deterrent effect, in that it helps create a credible threat of punishment for those who would be willing to commit violations on the basis of a profit calculation, but also moral effects, in that it sends a message to the spontaneously law-abiding, reinforcing their moral commitment to the rules.

For people to have such moral commitment to the law, however, it is important that the law and its enforcement are perceived to be fair.[640] Leniency, in particular in its strongest form of immunity, may raise two (closely related) concerns in this respect.[641]

First, there may be concerns about the retributive injustice of an antitrust offender escaping punishment. The main response to this concern is to design and apply leniency programmes in such a way as to ensure that no more leniency is granted than strictly

---

638 See list of decisions available at the European Commission's competition website http://ec.europa.eu/competition/index_en.html. These 38 cartels were found in 31 decisions, as in some cases (*Elevators & Escalators*, *Fasteners* and *Heat Stabilisers*) several distinct cartels were found in the same decision. I have not counted re-adoptions of decisions previously annulled by the EU Courts on procedural grounds.

639 See L. Truchot, 'Le régime de la récidive en matière de pratiques anticoncurrentielles: Garanties et dissuasion', *Concurrences* no 4-2010, 17, at 20.

640 See T. R. Tyler, *Why People Obey the Law* (Yale University Press 1990), as well as J. Adenaes, 'The Moral or Educative Influence of Criminal Law' (1971) 27 *Journal of Social Issues* 17, and 'General prevention revisited: research and policy implications' (1975) 66 *Journal of Criminal Law & Criminology* 338, at 341–343; K. G. Dau-Schmidt, 'An Economic Analysis of the Criminal Law as a Preference-Shaping Policy' (1990) *Duke Law Journal* 1, C. R. Sunstein, 'On the Expressive Function of the Law' (1996) 144 *University of Pennsylvania Law Review* 2021, D. M. Kahan, 'Social Influence, Social Meaning, and Deterrence' (1997) 83 *Virginia Law Review* 349, N. K. Katyal, 'Deterrence's Difficulty' (1997) 95 *Michigan Law Review* 2385, G. E. Lynch, 'The Role of Criminal Law in Policing Corporate Misconduct' (1997) 60 *Law and Contemporary Problems* 23, D. M. Kahan, 'Social Meaning and the Economic Analysis of Crime' (1998) 27 *Journal of Legal Studies* 609, and K. G. Dau-Schmidt, 'Preference shaping by the law', in P. Newman (ed), *The New Palgrave Dictionary of Economics and the Law* (Macmillan 1998) 84.

641 See OECD, *Fighting Hard-Core Cartels – Harm, Effective Sanctions and Leniency Programmes* (2000), available at http://www.oecd.org/dataoecd/41/44/1841891.pdf, at 26.

necessary to obtain the positive enforcement effects,[642] and to stress the condition for any beneficiary of leniency, and in particular of immunity, to provide genuine and full cooperation to the enforcement authorities. This appears to be reflected, for instance, in the case law of the Court of Justice, which has emphasised that for companies to benefit from leniency under the European Commission's Leniency Notice, their conduct must reveal 'a genuine spirit of cooperation'.[643] Requiring restitution to injured parties as a condition for leniency may also help to assuage justice concerns.[644]

A second (closely related) concern focuses on the unequal treatment between the beneficiary of immunity or leniency and the other cartel participants, who receive full punishment for the same antitrust violation.[645] Again, the main response is to ensure that leniency is only granted to the extent that the company or individual has genuinely and effectively cooperated with the competition authority, thus objectively distinguishing its situation from the other cartel participants that have not done so, or not to the same extent, or at the same early point in time. Equally important is to ensure that leniency policies are applied in a transparent and consistent way, thus providing an equal chance for all cartel participants to benefit from them.[646] In this respect, the General Court has stressed that, under the general principle of equal treatment, the European Commission must ensure that it does not distort the conditions of competition between undertakings in a (potential) race to be the first to cooperate, by contacting one of them, or giving them unequal access when they contact the European Commission.[647]

---

642 Limiting leniency to what is strictly necessary to obtain its enforcement benefits is also indicated to counter the penalty-reducing effect of leniency; my paper 'Leniency in Antitrust Enforcement: Theory and Practice' (2007) 30 *World Competition* 25, at 45–47, and my book *Efficiency and Justice in European Antitrust Enforcement* (Hart 2008), at 134–136.

643 Judgments in *Dansk Rørindustri and Others v European Commission*, C-189/02 P, C-202/02 P, C-205/02 P to C-208/02 P and C-213/02 P, EU:C:2005:408, paragraphs 388–403, and in *Commission v SGL Carbon*, C-301/04 P, EU:C:2006:432, paragraph 68.

644 See my paper 'Leniency in Antitrust Enforcement: Theory and Practice' (2007) 30 *World Competition* 25, at 44–45; my book *Efficiency and Justice in European Antitrust Enforcement* (Hart 2008), at 133–134; my paper 'The Relationship between Public Antitrust Enforcement and Private Actions for Damages' (2009) 32 *World Competition* 3 at 19–21, and C. J. S. Hodges, 'European Competition Enforcement Policy: Integrating Restitution and Behaviour Control' (2011) 34 *World Competition* 383.

645 See also D. Voillemot, *Gérer la clémence* (Bruylant 2005), at 99–100.

646 One could try to argue that a company that is willing to cooperate but detains less evidence that it can offer in exchange for leniency is disadvantaged as compared to another willing applicant with more evidence at its hands. This argument should, however, be rejected (and has indeed been rejected by the General Court in its Judgment in *SAS v Commission*, T-241/01, EU:T:2005:296, paragraphs 211–221), because distinguishing according to the usefulness of the cooperation appears objectively justified. Moreover, granting leniency in proportion to the evidence provided creates a desirable incentive for all cartel participants to create and keep evidence; see C. Aubert, P. Rey and W. E. Kovacic, 'The Impact of Leniency and Whistleblowing Programs on Cartels' (2006) 24 *International Journal of Industrial Organization* 1241 at 1260–1264, and my book *Efficiency and Justice in European Antitrust Enforcement* (Hart 2008), at 130.

647 Judgments in *Krupp Thyssen Stainless and Acciai Speciali Terni v Commission*, T-45/98 and T-47/98, EU:T:2001:288, paragraphs 237–248, and in *BASF v Commission*, T-15/02, EU:T:2006:74, paragraph 504. The European Commission would thus not be allowed to adopt the US Department of Justice's practice of 'affirmative amnesty', under which the latter approaches a company – which may at the time not even know that it or its competitors are under investigation – to cooperate and seek leniency; see S. D. Hammond, 'Measuring the Value of Second-In Cooperation in Corporate Plea Negotiations', address to the 54th Annual American Bar Association Section of Antitrust Law Spring Meeting (Washington, DC, 29 March 2006), available at http://www.usdoj.gov/atr/public/speeches/215514.pdf, at 11.

Both concerns, as to the guilty remaining unpunished and as to co-conspirators being treated unequally, would appear to be particularly acute in the case of immunity being granted to a recidivist, in particular if the other cartelists being fined are not recidivists.

One could consider excluding recidivists from leniency, or at least from the benefit of immunity from fines: As mentioned above, until 2011, the leniency programme of the Greek competition authority excluded recidivists from immunity from fines.

However, the exclusion of recidivists from leniency comes at a substantial cost. Leniency generally has very significant benefits in terms of improved collection of evidence and intelligence of cartel infringements and in terms of increased difficulty of creating and maintaining cartels.[648] The more cartelists are excluded from seeking immunity or leniency, the less these benefits can accrue. In the extreme case where the same group of undertakings, which were all found to have participated in a cartel, subsequently start a new cartel, the exclusion of recidivists from leniency would shelter this new cartel from the positive enforcement effects of leniency, and would thus render this new cartel easier to create and maintain and more difficult to detect and punish. Paradoxically, excluding recidivists from leniency thus encourages recidivism.

On balance, excluding recidivists from leniency or from immunity from fines would thus not appear to be a good idea.

Looking again at the statistics for cartels found by the European Commission in the 5-year period 2006–2010, it should be noted that only 7 out of 31 recidivists were granted immunity. Most recidivists were thus fined, and more heavily than other cartelists, because of the treatment of recidivism as an aggravating circumstance. Where several participants in the same cartel are recidivists, only one of them can possibly receive immunity.

That recidivists are statistically better represented among the immunity recipients (25%) than among the population of detected cartel participants (12%) is not necessarily abnormal or worrying. One would want and expect an undertaking that has been found to have participated in an antitrust infringement to take measures so as to avoid continued or new violations, including by establishing effective compliance programmes.[649] The first-best outcome of these measures would, of course, be that no new infringements are

---

648 For a detailed analysis, see my paper 'Leniency in Antitrust Enforcement: Theory and Practice' (2007) 30 *World Competition* 25, at 38–43, and my book *Efficiency and Justice in European Antitrust Enforcement* (Hart 2008), at 127–132.

649 On compliance programmes, see Chapter VII of this book. What measures should be taken to avoid continued or new infringements depends, of course, on what caused the earlier infringements. For instance, to the extent that infringements are caused by financial targets that can only be fulfilled through violations, these targets should be changed; see generally J. Sonnenfeld, 'Executive Apologies for Price Fixing: Role Biased Perceptions of Causality' (1981) 24 *Academy of Management Journal* 192; J. Sonnenfeld and P. R. Lawrence, 'Why do companies succumb to price fixing?' (July–August 1978) *Harvard Business Review* 145; A. Stephan, 'Hear no Evil, See no Evil: Why Antitrust Compliance Programmes may be Ineffective at Preventing Cartels', University of East Anglia Centre for Competition Policy Working Paper 09-09 (July 2009), available at http://www.uea.ac.uk/polopoly_fs/1.122147!ccp09-9wp.pdf; Chapter 3 ('Short-term Managerial Contracts and Cartels') in M. A. Han, *Vertical Relations in Cartel Theory*, as just above; and M. E. Stucke, 'Am I a Price Fixer? A Behavioural Economics Analysis of Cartels', in C. Beaton-Wells and A. Ezrachi (eds), *Criminalising Cartels: Critical Studies of an International Regulatory Movement* (Hart 2011), 263.

committed. However, if this is not achieved, the second-best outcome is that, thanks to the compliance programme, the new infringements are quickly detected and reported to the competition authorities.[650] The higher percentage of recidivists among immunity recipients may reflect this second-best outcome.

E. What conclusions can be drawn from the observed incidence of recidivism?

As already mentioned above, John Connor has claimed, on the basis of his (worldwide) statistics for international cartels during the 1990–2009 period, that 'recidivism appears to be increasing rapidly, both in number and relative to all corporate cartelists. [. . .] This observation seems to justify a continuation of policies that impose brutally higher fines and other effective sanctions on cartel recidivists'.[651]

As discussed above, John Connor's concept of recidivism covers not only the situation where an undertaking continues or starts a new infringement after having been found to have committed a first infringement, but also the situation where an undertaking simultaneously commits several infringements.[652]

In any event, as John Connor indicates elsewhere in his paper, his statistics in fact only show that the annual discovery rate of recidivists (according to his conception of recidivism) compared to all cartelists 'increased after 1990 and was quite high during 1995–2004. [. . .] The relative frequency of cartels discovered with recidivists as members did fall slightly after 2004 compared with the previous ten years'.[653]

Looking at the cartel decisions adopted by the European Commission, there does indeed not appear to be a continuing trend of increased recidivism:

As mentioned above, Christopher Harding and Alun Gibbs already reported in 2005, in their analysis of EU cartel appeals during the period 1995–2004, an 'awesome level of recidivism'. As also mentioned above,[654] the statistics of decisions adopted by the European Commission during the 5-year period 2006–2010 show that 12% (31 out of 255) of the undertakings found to have participated in cartels were found to be recidivists.

To the extent there is a trend within this 5-year period, it is a declining one: 24% in 2006 (11 out of 45), 11% in 2007 (7 out of 64), 13.5% in 2008 (5 out of 37), 13% in 2009 (5 out of 38), and 4% in 2010 (3 out of 71).

---

650 Compare with Judgment in *Shell v Commission*, T-38/07, EU:T:2011:355, paragraph 96, last sentence.

651 J. M. Connor, 'Recidivism Revealed: Private International Cartels 1990–2009' (Autumn 2010) *Competition Policy International* 101, at 101 and 116; see also OECD, Roundtable on promoting compliance with competition law – Issues paper by the Secretariat, DAF/COMP(2011)4 of 1 June 2011, at 2.

652 See also G. J. Werden, S. D. Hammond and B. A. Barnett, 'Recidivism Eliminated: Cartel Enforcement in the United States Since 1999' (October 2011) *CPI Antitrust Chronicle* 1.

653 J. M. Connor, 'Recidivism Revealed: Private International Cartels 1990–2009' (Autumn 2010) *Competition Policy International* 101, at 110 and 116.

654 C. Harding and A. Gibbs, 'Why go to court in Europe? An analysis of cartel appeals 1995–2004' (2005) 30 *European Law Review* 349 at 369.

The argument that the observed incidence of recidivism would justify further increases in the level of fines also requires qualification:

It is not untypical for the European Commission to find, for example, in 2011, that an undertaking participated in a cartel from 2001 to 2006, after having been fined in 1999 for a similar infringement. Such a finding of recidivism no doubt justifies, for the four reasons identified above, an increase in the fine imposed on the specific recidivist. It is, however, more difficult to draw any conclusions as to the overall fine level. If many similar findings of recidivism were made, one could conclude that the overall fine level in 1999 was not sufficiently deterrent. However, unless the overall fine level had remained stable or had decreased between 1999 and 2011, it does not appear possible to draw any immediate conclusions as to the need for a further increase of the fine level in 2011.

Indeed, the overall level of the fines imposed by the European Commission has significantly increased during this period,[655] thus making it difficult to draw any conclusions from the observed incidence of recidivism as to the need for a further increase in the overall fine level.

More generally, whereas in the past, when fines were significantly lower, a strong case could be made that EU antitrust fines were insufficiently deterrent,[656] more recent econometric work by Marie-Laure Allain, Marcel Boyer, Rachidi Kotchoni and Jean-Pierre Ponssard suggests that most fines imposed by the European Commission in more recent years are sufficiently high to deter.[657]

Furthermore, if the current enforcement level is insufficient to deter, it is not obvious that the best solution would be to increase the level of fines further. An increase in the number of infringements detected and punished may have a stronger marginal deterrence effect than a further increase in the level of fines.[658] Adding other types of penalties, in particular penalties for individuals, may also be more effective than further increasing fines on companies.[659]

---

655 See C. Veljanovski, 'Deterrence, Recidivism and European Cartel Fines' (14 July 2011), electronic copy available at http://ssrn.com/abstract=1758639, at 6; J. M. Connor, 'The predictability of global cartel fines', *Concurrences* no 2-2010, *New Frontiers of Antitrust Conference* (15 February 2010), 59 at 63 ; and my paper 'The Increased Level of EU Antitrust Fines, Judicial Review and the ECHR' (2010) 33 *World Competition* 5 at 10–12.

656 See my paper 'EC Competition Fines: To Deter or Not to Deter', in A. Barav and D. A. Wyatt (eds), *Yearbook of European Law 1995* (Oxford UP 1996), 17; and Chapter 2 of my book *The Optimal Enforcement of EC Antitrust Law* (Kluwer 2002).

657 M.-L. Allain, M. Boyer, R. Kotchoni and J.-P. Ponssard, 'The Determination of Optimal Fines in Cartel Cases: The Myth of Underdeterrence' (March 2011), accessible at http://ssrn.com/abstract=1787651.

658 See A. von Hirsch, A. E. Bottoms, E. Burney and P.-O. Wikström, *Criminal Deterrence and Sentence Severity: An Analysis of Recent Research* (Hart 1999), at 47; C. Parker and V. Lehmann Nielsen, 'Deterrence and the Impact of Calculative Thinking on Business Compliance with Regulation' (2009), accessible at http://ssrn.com/abstract=1527326, at 33; and my paper 'Optimal Antitrust Fines: Theory and Practice' (2006) 29 *World Competition* 183, at 195–199, and my book *Efficiency and Justice in European Antitrust Enforcement* (Hart 2008), at 61–65.

659 See my paper 'Is Criminalization of EU Competition Law the Answer?' (2005) 28 *World Competition* 117; Chapters 8 and 9 of my book *The Optimal Enforcement of EC Antitrust Law* (Kluwer 2002); Chapter 6 of my book *Efficiency and Justice in European Antitrust Enforcement* (Hart 2008); S. Calkins, 'Coming to Praise Criminal Antitrust Enforcement', in C.-D. Ehlermann and I. Atanasiu, *European Competition Law Annual 2006: Enforcement of Prohibition of Cartels* (Hart 2007), 343; D.H. Ginsburg and J. D. Wright,

Finally, one should also keep in mind that it will never be possible to achieve complete deterrence.[660] Indeed, even if the competition authorities managed at some point in time to detect so many violations and to impose such high fines that all companies will be deterred from committing new violations, this situation will not last, as over time the memory of those successful prosecutions will fade, and violations will thus again be committed.[661]

'Antitrust Sanctions' (Autumn 2010) 6 *Competition Policy International* 3; B. Fisse, 'Cartel Offences and Non-Monetary Punishment: The Punitive Injunction as a Sanction against Corporations', in C. Beaton-Wells and A. Ezrachi (eds), *Criminalising Cartels: Critical Studies of an International Regulatory Movement* (Hart 2011), 313; and A. Stephan, 'Disqualification Orders for Directors Involved in Cartels' (2011) 2 *Journal of European Competition Law & Practice*.

660 See my paper 'Optimal Antitrust Fines: Theory and Practice' (2006) 29 *World Competition* 183, at 188 and 194, and my book *Efficiency and Justice in European Antitrust Enforcement* (Hart 2008), at 53–54 and 60.

661 See also W. Eucken 'The Competitive Order and Its Implementation' (Autumn 2006) 2 *Competition Policy International* 219 (English translation of 'Die Wettbewerbsordnung und ihre Verwirklichung' (1949) 2 *Ordo – Jahrbuch für die Ordnung von Wirtschaft und Gesellschaft* 1), at 222 ('There is an omnipresent, strong and irrepressible urge to eliminate competition and to acquire a monopolistic position.'); S. Wilks and I. Bartle, 'The Unanticipated Consequences of Creating Independent Competition Agencies' (January 2002) 25 *Western European Politics* 148 at 152 ('Since abuse of market power is endemic in every market economy and is indeed a major component in the competitive strategies of most large companies, the elimination of anti-competitive practices (rather like the elimination of racial intolerance) is an impossible goal. Yet, as with racial equality, it is essential for governments to confirm support for free competition.'); and D. D. Sokol, 'Antitrust in 2025: Cartels, Agency Effectiveness, and a Return to Back to the Future' (December 2010) 2 *CPI Antitrust Journal*, electronic copy available at http://ssrn.com/abstract=1733246, at 2 ('In many cases the same industries are recidivists because, as a new generation retires, the next generation relearns how to coordinate with competitors. This illustrates the social norm within society and within the industry.').

IX. The Compatibility with Fundamental Rights of the EU Antitrust Enforcement System in which the European Commission Acts Both as Investigator and as First-Instance Decision Maker

Following the *Jussila* and *Menarini* judgments, it is now entirely clear that Article 6 ECHR, as interpreted by the European Court of Human Rights, provides no grounds for abandoning the system in which the European Commission both investigates suspected infringements of the EU antitrust prohibitions and takes decisions finding such infringements and imposing fines. Article 6(1) ECHR requires, however, that the EU General Court, when reviewing European Commission decisions, exercise full jurisdiction. What is decisive is whether the General Court in fact exercises full jurisdiction, not any general statements that the Courts may make as to its powers. It is nevertheless also important that the General Court is seen to exercise full jurisdiction. For this reason, potentially misleading general statements should be avoided. A number of internal checks and balances and procedural guarantees apply to the European Commission's administrative procedure, and regularly show their usefulness. This, however, in no way reduces the need for a full review by the General Court, when requested by the undertakings concerned. Indeed, the internal checks and balances and procedural guarantees derive their full effectiveness precisely from the possibility of a subsequent full review by the General Court.

A. Introduction

Under the system initially set up by Regulation 17,[662] and maintained under Regulation 1/2003,[663] the European Commission both investigates suspected infringements of the antitrust prohibitions contained in Articles 101 and 102 TFEU and takes decisions finding such infringements, ordering their termination, and imposing fines.

The question has been debated for many years whether this system is compatible with fundamental rights, in particular with Article 6(1) of the European Convention on Human Rights (ECHR), which provides that 'in the determination of his civil rights and obligations or of any criminal charge against him, everyone is entitled to a fair and public

662 Council Regulation No 17 [1962] OJ 13/204 (Special English Edition 1959-62, p 87). The system does not flow directly from the Treaties; see my paper 'The Combination of the Investigative and Prosecutorial Function and the Adjudicative Function in EC Antitrust Enforcement: A Legal and Economic Analysis' (2004) 27 *World Competition* 201 at 210–211, and my book *Principles of European Antitrust Enforcement* (Hart 2005) at 160–161.

663 Council Regulation (EC) No 1/2003 of 16 December 2002 on the implementation of the rules on competition laid down in Articles 81 and 82 of the Treaty [2003] OJ L1/1.

hearing within a reasonable time by *an independent and impartial tribunal*' (emphasis added).

Already in the late 1970s/early 1980s, the argument that the system would be incompatible with Article 6 ECHR was summarily raised and rejected in two cases before the Court of Justice.[664]

The question became prominent in the mid-1990s, when the EU was considering acceding to the ECHR.[665] Two studies, both based on a detailed examination of the case law of the European Court of Human Rights, appeared in the literature around this time.[666]

Both studies reached the same conclusions:

- EU antitrust proceedings, at least when involving a fine, concern 'criminal charges' within the wider, autonomous meaning of that concept in Article 6 ECHR, even if such proceedings are not classified as criminal under EU law;[667]
- notwithstanding the obvious fact that the European Commission is not an 'independent and impartial tribunal' because it acts both as investigator and as first-instance decision-maker, it does not automatically follow that the EU antitrust enforcement system is incompatible with Article 6 ECHR, because the case law of the European Court of Human Rights accepts that decisions are taken in the first instance by an administrative body provided that such decisions are subject to subsequent control by a judicial body that has 'full jurisdiction' and does provide the guarantees of Article 6 ECHR;[668]

---

664 Judgment in *Van Landewyck and Others v Commission*, 209 to 215 and 218/78, EU:C:1980:248, paragraphs 79–81 and at 3160–3161; Judgment in *Musique Diffusion Française and Others v Commission*, 100/80 to 103/80, EU:C:1983:158, paragraphs 6–11, and Opinion of Advocate General Sir Gordon Slynn in *Musique Diffusion Française and Others v Commission*, 100/80 to 103/80, EU:C:1983:29; see further my paper 'La compatibilité des procédures communautaires en matière de concurrence avec la Convention européenne des droits de l'homme' (1996) *Cahiers de droit européen* 329, at 339–340.

665 See Request by the Council of the European Union for an Opinion pursuant to Article 228(6) of the Treaty establishing the European Community [1994] OJ C174/8. The plans for accession were put on hold following Opinion 2/94 of the Court of Justice of 28 March 1996, EU:C:1996:140, which held that accession required a change of the Treaties.

666 D. Waelbroeck and D. Fosselard, 'Should the Decision-Making Power in EC Antitrust Procedures be left to an Independent Judge? – The Impact of the European Convention of Human Rights on EC Antitrust Procedures', in A. Barav and D. A. Wyatt (eds) *1994 Yearbook of European Law* (Clarendon 1995), and my paper 'La compatibilité des procédures communautaires en matière de concurrence avec la Convention européenne des droits de l'homme' (1996) *Cahiers de droit européen* 329.

667 D. Waelbroeck and D. Fosselard, 'Should the Decision-Making Power in EC Antitrust Procedures be left to an Independent Judge? – The Impact of the European Convention of Human Rights on EC Antitrust Procedures', in A. Barav and D. A. Wyatt (eds) *1994 Yearbook of European Law* (Clarendon 1995), at 122–125, and my paper 'La compatibilité des procédures communautaires en matière de concurrence avec la Convention européenne des droits de l'homme' (1996) *Cahiers de droit européen* 329, at 331–337; Judgment of 8 June 1976 in Case of *Engel and Others v The Netherlands* (Application no 5100/71); Article 15(4) of Regulation 17 and Article 23(5) of Regulation 1/2003.

668 D. Waelbroeck and D. Fosselard, 'Should the Decision-Making Power in EC Antitrust Procedures be left to an Independent Judge? – The Impact of the European Convention of Human Rights on EC Antitrust Procedures', in A. Barav and D. A. Wyatt (eds) *1994 Yearbook of European Law* (Clarendon 1995), at 126–127, and my paper 'La compatibilité des procédures communautaires en matière de concurrence avec la Convention européenne des droits de l'homme' (1996) *Cahiers de droit européen* 329, at 337–339; Judgment of 23 June 1981 in Case of *Le Compte, Van Leuven and De Meyere v Belgium* (Application no 6878/75), paragraph 51; Judgment of 10 February 1983 in Case of *Albert and Le Compte v Belgium* (Application no 7299/75), paragraph 29; Judgment of 21 February 1984

– the decisive issue is thus whether the General Court (then Court of First Instance) exercises sufficient jurisdiction when reviewing European Commission antitrust decisions.

On the decisive question whether the General Court exercises sufficient jurisdiction when reviewing European Commission antitrust decisions, the two studies gave somewhat different, but not necessarily incompatible, answers. One study emphasised that Articles 263 and 261 TFEU and Article 31 of Regulation 1/2003 (then Articles 173 and 172 EC and Article 17 of Regulation 17) grant the General Court sufficient jurisdiction,[669] whereas the other study expressed doubt as to whether the General Court exercised sufficient review in practice, because of its case law according to which, where complex economic facts are involved, judicial review of the legal characterisation of facts is limited to the possibility of the European Commission having committed a manifest error of assessment.[670]

Since the second half of the 2000s, the question of the compatibility with Article 6 ECHR of the EU antitrust enforcement system and the question whether the General Court exercises sufficient review have received renewed interest. This renewed interest appears to result from two developments: First, the Lisbon Treaty, which was signed on 13 December 2007 and entered into force on 1 December 2009, created in Article 6(2) TEU the legal basis and obligation for the EU to accede to the ECHR,[671] and elevated through Article 6(1) TEU to Treaty status the Charter of Fundamental Rights of the EU, which guarantees at least the same fundamental rights protection as the ECHR.[672] Article 47 of the Charter now implements in EU law the protection afforded by Article 6(1) ECHR.[673] Secondly, around the same time the European Commission changed its fining policy and, while still staying within the unaltered maximum as laid down in Article 15(2) of

---

in Case of *Öztürk v Germany* (Application no 8544/79), paragraph 56; Judgment of 24 February 1994 in Case of *Bendenoun v France* (Application no 12547/86), paragraph 46; and Report of the European Commission on Human Rights of 30 May 1991 in Case of *Stenuit v France* (Application no 11598/85), paragraph 72.

669 My paper 'La compatibilité des procédures communautaires en matière de concurrence avec la Convention européenne des droits de l'homme' (1996) *Cahiers de droit européen* 329, at 338.

670 D. Waelbroeck and D. Fosselard, 'Should the Decision-Making Power in EC Antitrust Procedures be left to an Independent Judge? – The Impact of the European Convention of Human Rights on EC Antitrust Procedures', in A. Barav and D. A. Wyatt (eds) *1994 Yearbook of European Law* (Clarendon 1995), at 132–133; see also my later paper 'The Increased Level of EU Antitrust Fines, Judicial Review and the ECHR' (2010) 33 *World Competition* 5 at 26–28.

671 Negotiations between the EU and the Council of Europe (the international organisation in charge of the ECHR) for an accession agreement were started in 2010, and a draft agreement was reached in April 2013. However, in its Opinion 2/13 of 18 December 2014, EU:C:2014:2454, the Court of Justice held that the draft agreement was not compatible with Article 6(2) TEU and with Protocol No 8 EU, which require that the accession agreement preserve the specific characteristics of the Union and Union law. New negotiations for an accession of the EU to the ECHR were started in 2020, and a draft revised accession agreement was reached in April 2023; see https://www.echr.coe.int/documents/d/echr/UE_Report_CDDH_ENG.

672 See further my paper 'EU Antitrust Enforcement Powers and Procedural Rights and Guarantees: The Interplay between EU Law, National Law, the Charter of Fundamental Rights of the EU and the European Convention on Human Rights' (2011) 34 *World Competition* 189, and Chapter 10 of this book.

673 Judgment in *Chalkor v Commission*, C-386/10 P, EU:C:2011:815, paragraph 51. According to Article 52(3) of the Charter, in so far as the Charter contains rights that correspond to rights guaranteed by the ECHR, the meaning and scope of those rights shall be the same as those laid down in the ECHR, but EU law may provide more extensive protection.

Regulation 17 and Article 23(2) of Regulation 1/2003, started imposing higher fines than it had previously done.[674]

A number of judgments of the European Court of Human Rights have also further clarified and confirmed the interpretation of Article 6 ECHR. The most important are the judgments of 23 November 2006 in *Jussila v Finland* and of 27 September 2011 in *Menarini v Italy.*[675]

B. The case law of the European Court of Human Rights

1. The Jussila judgment

The judgment in *Jussila v Finland* is relevant not because of its facts, which concerned the refusal of an oral hearing by the Finnish administrative court dealing with an appeal against a decision of the Finnish tax administration imposing tax surcharges on the applicant, but because of the broader (re)statement that the European Court of Human Rights, sitting as a Grand Chamber, made, also concerning competition law and the imposition of criminal penalties in the first instance by an administrative body. The relevant passage of the judgment reads as follows:

> '[T]he autonomous interpretation adopted by the Convention institutions of the notion of a "criminal charge" by applying the *Engel* criteria have underpinned a gradual broadening of the criminal head to cases not strictly belonging to the traditional categories of the criminal law, for example administrative penalties [. . .], prison disciplinary proceedings [. . .], customs law [. . .], competition law (*Société Stenuit v. France,* judgment of 27 February 1992, Series A no. 232-A) and penalties imposed by a court with jurisdiction in financial matters [. . .]. Tax surcharges differ from the hard core of criminal law; consequently, the criminal-head guarantees will not necessarily apply with their full stringency (see *Bendenoun* and *Janosevic,* § 46 and § 81 respectively, where it was found compatible with Article 6 § 1 for criminal penalties to be imposed, in the first instance, by an administrative or non-judicial body, and, *a contrario, Findlay v. the United Kingdom,* . . .)'.[676]

---

674 See C. Baudenbacher, 'The legacy of Neelie Kroes' (2010) *Journal of European Competition Law and Practice* 169 at 169, and my paper 'The Increased Level of EU Antitrust Fines, Judicial Review and the ECHR' (2010) 33 *World Competition* 5, at 10–12. As explained in more detail in the latter paper, at 17–18 and 28, this increase in the level of antitrust fines is not relevant for the assessment of the compatibility of the EU antitrust enforcement system with Article 6 ECHR, because the case law of the European Court of Human Rights looks at the maximum potential penalty for which the relevant law provides, and that maximum, laid down in Article 15(2) of Regulation 17 and Article 23(2) of Regulation 1/2003, has not changed. However, the level of the fines actually imposed may affect more general views on the appropriate intensity of the review of fining decisions by the General Court. It certainly also affects the incentives for defence lawyers and academics to write and speak on the issue and to raise it in court.

675 Judgment of 23 November 2006 in Case of *Jussila v Finland* (Application no 73053/01), and Judgment of 27 September 2011 in Case of *Menarini Diagnostics v Italy* (Application no 43509/08); see further also Judgment of 21 July 2011 in Case of *Sigma Radio Television Ltd. v Cyprus* (Application no 32181/05).

676 Judgment of 23 November 2006 in Case of *Jussila v Finland* (Application no 73053/01), paragraph 43.

The European Court of Human Rights thus confirmed that fines imposed on companies for violations of competition law fall under the broader, autonomous concept of 'criminal charge', but that they do not fall under the 'hard core of criminal law'; that the criminal-head guarantees of Article 6 ECHR do not necessarily apply with their full stringency outside the hard core of criminal law; and in particular that outside the hard core of criminal law, it is compatible with Article 6 ECHR for criminal penalties to be imposed, in the first instance, by an administrative or non-judicial body that combines investigative and decision-making powers, provided that there is a possibility of appeal before a judicial body that has full jurisdiction, including the power to quash in all respects, on questions of fact and of law, the challenged decision.[677]

It is important to note that, on the point of the compatibility with Article 6 ECHR of a first-instance decision by an administrative body that combines investigative and decision-making powers, the *Jussila* judgment refers to the *Bendenoun* and *Janosevic* judgments, and, *a contrario*, to the *Findlay* judgment. In *Bendenoun v France* and in *Janosevic v Sweden*, the European Court of Human Rights stated that the imposition of criminal penalties in the first instance by an administrative body is acceptable 'even if the [penalties] are large ones', or 'very substantial', or 'even if [these penalties] come to large amounts'.[678] This contradicts the argument made by some authors that an administrative first-instance decision would only be acceptable for 'minor infringements'.[679] The judgment in *Findlay v United Kingdom*, which concerned an individual sentenced to two years' imprisonment by a court martial on multiple charges of assault and threatening to kill, is also telling, in that it required a first-instance tribunal because the case concerned 'serious charges classified as "criminal" under both domestic and Convention law',[680] a criterion manifestly not fulfilled in the case of the imposition by the European Commission on companies of antitrust fines classified as 'not of a criminal law nature' by Article 23(5) of Regulation 1/2003.

2. The Menarini judgment

The judgment in *A. Menarini Diagnostics S.R.L. v Italy* directly concerns antitrust enforcement. The applicant, a company that had been fined for a violation of Italian competition law (which, apart from the condition of effect on trade between Member States, is identical to Articles 101 and 102 TFEU) by the *Autorità Garante della Concorrenza e del Mercato* (AGCM), the Italian competition authority (which, like

---

677 See, for a more detailed analysis of the *Jussila v Finland* judgment, read together with the earlier judgments to which it refers, my paper 'The Increased Level of EU Antitrust Fines, Judicial Review and the ECHR' (2010) 33 *World Competition* 5.

678 Judgment of 24 February 1994 in Case of *Bendenoun v France* (Application no 12547/86), paragraphs 46 and 47, and Judgment of 23 July 2002 in Case of *Janosevic v Sweden* (Application no 34619/97), paragraph 81.

679 See in particular A. Andreangeli, O. Brouwer, D. de Feydeau, I. Forrester, D. Geradin, A. Komninos, K. Hofstetter, Y. Katsoulakos, C. Lemaire, M. O'Regan, L. Ortiz Blanco, D. Slater, S. Thomas, D. Ulph, D. Waelbroeck and U. Zinsmeister, Chapter 3 'Enforcement by the Commission – The Decisional and Enforcement Structure in Antitrust Cases and the Commission's Fining System', in M. Merola and D. Waelbroeck (eds), *Towards an optimal enforcement of competition rules in Europe – Time for a revision of Regulation 1/2003?* (College of Europe Global Competition Law Centre; Bruylant 2010) 197 at 217–218.

680 Judgment of 25 February 1997 in Case of *Findlay v The United Kingdom* (Application no 22107/93), paragraph 79; see also Judgment of 26 October 1984 in Case of *De Cubber v Belgium* (Application no 9186/80), paragraph 32, to which the *Findlay* judgment refers.

the European Commission, combines investigative and first-instance decision-making powers), complained that the Italian administrative courts that had heard its appeal against the decision of the AGCM had not exercised full jurisdiction.

The European Court of Human Rights confirmed that the proceedings fell under the criminal head of Article 6 ECHR, and that Article 6 ECHR does not oppose a first-instance decision by an administrative body, provided that there is a possibility of appeal before a judicial body with full jurisdiction. This judicial body must have the power to quash in all respects, on questions of fact and law, the decision of the body below. It must in particular have jurisdiction to examine all questions of fact and law relevant to the dispute before it.[681]

In this specific case, the European Court of Human Rights found that the Italian administrative courts had exercised such full jurisdiction.[682] As explained by Judge Sajó in his concurring opinion, the Court's finding was that the Italian administrative courts had **in fact** exercised full jurisdiction, notwithstanding general statements as to their jurisdiction being limited. In his dissenting opinion, Judge Pinto de Albuquerque focused on these general statements, which reflected the principle of discretionary power of the administration, and pointed out that these were not in line with the concept of full jurisdiction, which should be without limits.[683]

3. Conclusion from the Jussila and Menarini judgments

Following the *Jussila* and *Menarini* judgments, it is now entirely clear that Article 6 ECHR, as interpreted by the European Court of Human Rights, provides no grounds for abandoning the system, as set up by Regulation 17 and maintained under Regulation 1/2003, in which the European Commission both investigates suspected infringements of the antitrust prohibitions contained in Articles 101 and 102 TFEU and takes decisions finding such infringements, ordering their termination, and imposing fines.[684]

The only question still open to debate is whether the General Court, when reviewing European Commission decisions, exercises sufficient jurisdiction to meet the 'full jurisdiction' standard laid down in the case law of the European Court of Human Rights. Either the General Court does exercise 'full jurisdiction', and there is no problem, or it does not, in which case the solution is for the Court to modify its practice.

---

681 *Menarini v Italy*, paragraphs 38–44 and 58–59.

682 *Menarini v Italy*, paragraphs 60–67.

683 *Menarini v Italy*, Dissenting Opinion of Judge Pinto de Albuquerque, paragraph 9.

684 This, of course, does not exclude a possible wider discussion as to whether or not this system is, among the various systems that are legally possible, the best system in terms of administrative cost, effectiveness, or other policy considerations; see J. Almunia, 'Due Process and competition enforcement', SPEECH/10/449 (IBA 14th Annual Competition Conference, Florence, 17 September 2010); J. Steenbergen, 'Decision-making in Competition Cases: The Investigator, the Prosecutor and the Judge', in L. Gormley (ed), *Current and Future Perspectives on EC Competition Law – A Tribute to Professor M. R. Mok* (Kluwer Law International 1997), 101; C. Baudenbacher, 'Switzerland as a Spearhead of Competition Law in Europe?' (2011) *European Law* Reporter 114 at 118; Charlemagne, 'A democratic nightmare', *The Economist*, October 26, 2013, p 35; and my paper 'The Combination of the Investigative and Prosecutorial Function and the Adjudicative Function in EC Antitrust Enforcement: A Legal and Economic Analysis' (2004) 27 *World Competition* 20.

A distinction should be made between the review that the General Court exercises as to the finding of the antitrust infringement, and the review exercised by that court over the fine.[685]

C. Review as to the finding of the antitrust infringement

As to the finding of the antitrust infringement, the General Court does not have unlimited jurisdiction under Article 261 TFEU but can only exercise a review of legality under Article 263 TFEU.[686]

In the light of the case law of the European Court of Human Rights, it is clear that a review of legality as to the finding of the antitrust infringement can meet the 'full jurisdiction' standard, provided that the reviewing court has the power to quash in all respects, on questions of fact and law, the administrative decision and has in particular jurisdiction to examine all questions of fact and law relevant to the dispute before it.[687]

Open to debate is the question whether the old case law, initially developed by the Court of Justice in cases not involving fines but later also applied by the EU Courts to cases involving fines, according to which the 'review of complex economic appraisals made by the Commission is necessarily limited to checking whether the relevant rules on procedure and on the stating of reasons have been complied with, whether the facts have been accurately stated and whether there has been any manifest error of assessment or a misuse of powers',[688] is compatible with the requirement of 'full jurisdiction'.[689]

It should be clarified at the outset that, contrary to the now-defunct ECSC Treaty, which contained in its Article 33 a limitation of the jurisdiction of the Court of Justice to manifest errors in relation to economic assessments, the current Treaties do not contain any wording that would mandate a limited review of economic assessments. Furthermore,

---

685 See also my paper 'The Increased Level of EU Antitrust Fines, Judicial Review and the ECHR' (2010) 33 *World Competition* 5, at 22–28.

686 At first sight, it might appear that Article 31 of Regulation 1/2003, which does not contain an express reference to Article 261 TFEU, goes further in that it refers to unlimited jurisdiction to review 'decisions whereby the Commission has fixed a fine', whereas Article 261 TFEU talks about unlimited jurisdiction 'with regard to the penalties'. The wider language in Article 31 of Regulation 1/2003 could be understood as covering not only the fine itself, but also the finding of an infringement of Articles 101 or 102 TFEU contained in the same Commission decision. Apart from the fact that the finding of an infringement is probably to be considered legally as a distinct 'decision' from the imposition of the fine, given the separate legal bases in Articles 7 and 23(2) of Regulation 1/2003, such a wider interpretation is contradicted by the preparatory works of Regulation 1/2003. Indeed, the text of Article 31 remained unaltered as from the Commission's initial proposal, and the explanatory memorandum of this proposal (Commission Proposal for a Regulation implementing Articles 81 and 82 of the Treaty, COM(2000)582 of 27 September 2000, at 29) explained that this Article 'is identical to Article 17 of the existing Regulation No 17'. Article 17 of Regulation 17 expressly referred to 'unlimited jurisdiction within the meaning of Article 172 of the Treaty [now Article 261 TFEU]'.

687 *Menarini v Italy*, paragraph 59.

688 Judgments in *Consten and Grundig v Commission*, C-56/64 and C-58/64, EU:C:1965:60, at 347, in *Remia and Others v Commission*, C-42/84, EU:C:1985:327, paragraph 34; in *Aalborg Portland and Others v Commission*, C-204/00 P etc., EU:C:2004:6, paragraph 279; in *Microsoft v Commission*, T-201/04, EU:T:2007:289, paragraph 87; in *Telefónica v Commission*, T-336/07, EU:T:2012:172, paragraph 69; and in *E.ON Ruhrgas v Commission*, T-360/09, EU:T:2012:332, paragraph 69.

689 See also Editorial Comments, 'Towards a more judicial approach? EU antitrust fines under the scrutiny of fundamental rights' (2011) 48 *Common Market Law Review* 1405 at 1410–1411.

under the ECSC Treaty, it was unclear whether the limitation of the jurisdiction of the Court of Justice in relation to economic assessments also applied to cases where the Commission imposed fines, as Article 36 ECSC gave the Court unlimited jurisdiction in appeals against pecuniary sanctions.

The case law of the European Court of Human Rights recognises that, in assessing the sufficiency of judicial review, regard should be had to whether the subject matter of the decision concerns a specialised issue requiring professional knowledge or experience and whether the decision under review involves the exercise of administrative discretion, and that respect must be given to decisions taken by administrative authorities on grounds of expediency.[690]

There are many areas of EU law other than competition law where the European Commission takes decisions involving the exercise of administrative discretion or decisions of a technical nature, justifying a limited review by the EU Courts. Also in the broad area of competition law, there are a number of instances where limited review appears justified. For instance, when deciding whether State aid is compatible with the internal market in the application of Article 107 TFEU, the Commission has a wide discretion, the exercise of which involves complex economic and social assessments, and this discretion justifies limited review by the EU Courts.[691] Or in the area of merger control, it seems right to consider that the EU Merger Regulation confers on the Commission a certain discretion, especially with respect to assessments of an economic nature, and that, consequently, the review by the EU Courts must take account of that margin of discretion.[692] Also, in the context of the application of Articles 101 and 102 TFEU, there are a number of situations where the European Commission takes decisions involving administrative discretion, and review by the EU Courts should be limited correspondingly.[693] For instance, in the case of rejection of complaints, review by the EU Courts is rightly limited to correcting manifest errors of appraisal.[694] Similarly, with regard to decisions whether or not to accept commitments under Article 9 of Regulation 1/2003, review by the EU Courts is rightly limited to correcting manifest errors of appraisal.[695]

The case of decisions imposing fines is, however, fundamentally different. In the light of the principle of *nullum crimen sine lege*, enshrined in Article 7 ECHR and Article 49(1) of the Charter, the existence or non-existence of the infringement found in a fining decision cannot be a matter of policy or of administrative discretion, but is exclusively a matter of fact and of law. As Judge Pinto de Albuquerque argued

---

690 Judgment of 21 July 2011 in Case of *Sigma Radio Television Ltd. v Cyprus* (Application no 32181/05), paragraphs 154 and 160–161.

691 Judgments in *Spain v Commission*, C-169/95, EU:C:1997:10, paragraph 34, and in *Andersen v Commission*, T-92/11, EU:T:2017:14, paragraph 58.

692 Judgments in *Commission v Tetra Laval*, C-12/03 P, EU:C:2005:87, paragraph 38, and in *Commission v CK Telecoms UK Investments*, C-376/20 P, EU:C:2023:561, paragraphs 82 to 84.

693 See Chapter IV of this book.

694 Judgments in *Automec v Commission*, T-24/90, EU:T:1992:97 and in *Diamanthandel A. Spira v Commission*, T-108/07 and T-354/08, EU:T:2013:367, paragraph 185.

695 Judgments in *Commission v Alrosa*, C-441/07 P, EU:C:2010:377, paragraphs 59–67, and in *Polskie Górnictwo Naftowe i Gazownictwo v Commission*, T-616/18, EU:T:2022:43, paragraph 93.

in *Menarini*, in this context administrative discretion appears incompatible with the rule of law.[696]

The editorial comments in the October 2011 issue of *Common Market Law Review* put the issue as follows:

> 'Judicial review "by an independent and impartial tribunal" (Art. 6(1) ECHR) is only meaningful if it purges all traces of partiality from the decision under review, including a prosecutorial bias of the body that made the decision. Notwithstanding the internal checks and balances introduced during the last ten years, the Commission as a whole publicly displays more than ever a healthy appetite for hunting and bringing down antitrust perpetrators. It is hard to believe that any matter relevant to the finding of an infringement is completely immune to the influence of such a prosecutorial disposition. If this is true, judicial self-restraint out of respect for the Commission's superior expertise in complex economic or technical matters creates the danger that, by approving the Commission's decision, the General Court is associating itself with a procedure that cannot be said to be wholly impartial. However, it seems that this danger can be avoided at comparably low cost: generally, the "margin of appreciation" doctrine has not prevented the General Court from looking into any economic or technical detail of a case that appeared remotely promising as a basis for a successful ground of appeal. Therefore, much would be won if the Court stopped paying lip-service to the old "complex appraisals" formula [. . .].'

In *Otis and Others*,[697] the Court of Justice, sitting in Grand Chamber, dealt with the argument that the review of legality carried out by the EU Courts under Article 263 TFEU in the sphere of competition law would be insufficient because of, in particular, the margin of discretion that those Courts allow the Commission in economic matters.[698] The Court of Justice concluded that the review provided for by the Treaties meets the requirements of the principle of effective judicial protection in Article 47 of the Charter.[699]

In coming to this conclusion, the Court of Justice reaffirmed that 'in areas giving rise to complex economic assessments, the Commission has a margin of discretion with regard to economic matters', only to add that 'that does not mean that the EU Courts must refrain from reviewing the Commission's interpretation of information of an economic nature. Those courts must, among other things, not only establish whether the evidence relied on is factually accurate, reliable and consistent but also to ascertain whether that evidence contains all the information which must be taken into account in order to assess a complex situation and whether it is capable of substantiating the conclusions drawn'.[700]

The Court of Justice did not use the 'manifest error' language, and a 'manifest error' test would indeed appear incompatible with the language used in *Otis and Others*.

---

696 *Menarini v Italy*, Dissenting Opinion of Judge Pinto de Albuquerque, paragraph 9.
697 Judgment in *Europese Gemeenschap v Otis and Others*, C-199/11, EU:C:2012:684.
698 Idem, paragraphs 58 to 63.
699 Idem, paragraph 63.
700 Idem, paragraph 59.

In *Posten Norge*, the EFTA Court explicitly held that, in the case of decisions imposing fines, 'the submission that the Court may intervene only if it considers a complex economic assessment to be manifestly wrong must be rejected'.[701]

The EFTA Court did, however, still see a limitation of its review in relation to complex economic assessments in decisions taken by the EFTA Surveillance Authority (ESA):

> 'Also as far as past events involving complex economic features are concerned, a situation may arise in which the Court, while still considering ESA's reasoning to be capable of substantiating the conclusions drawn from the economic evidence, may come to a different assessment of a complex economic situation. However, the fact that the Court is restricted to a review of legality precludes it from annulling the contested decision if there can be no legal objection to the assessment of ESA, even if it is not the one which the Court would consider to be preferable (compare *Commission v Alrosa*, cited above, paragraphs 65–67; and the Opinion of Advocate General Kokott in that case, points 81–84)'.[702]

In the context of decisions imposing fines, this position is problematic. In the light of the principle of *nullum crimen sine lege*, enshrined in Article 7 ECHR and Article 49(1) of the Charter, the existence of the infringement cannot depend on something that is beyond legal assessment. The *Alrosa* case did not concern a decision imposing a fine but a decision refusing commitments pursuant to Article 9 of Regulation 1/2003. In that context, the Court of Justice endorsed the 'manifest error' test.[703] As argued above, while it appears quite right for the EU Courts to leave the European Commission a (broad) margin of discretion when deciding whether or not to accept commitments pursuant to Article 9 of Regulation 1/2003, the case of decisions imposing fines for infringements of Articles 101 and 102 TFEU is fundamentally different.

In the context of decisions imposing fines, there should be no limitations to the review by the General Court under Article 263 TFEU other than the following two, which are unproblematic under Articles 6 and 7 ECHR.[704] First, the review to be exercised by the General Court does not amount to a review of the Court's own motion. With the exception of pleas involving matters of public policy which the Court is required to raise of its own motion, such as the failure to state reasons for a contested decision, it is for the applicant to raise pleas against that decision and to adduce evidence in support of those pleas.[705] Second, where the General Court comes to the conclusion that the finding of the infringement

---

701 Judgment of 18 April 2012 in Case E-15/10 *Posten Norge v EFTA Surveillance Authority*, paragraphs 100–102.

702 Idem, paragraph 98.

703 Judgment in *Commission v Alrosa*, C-441/07 P, EU:C:2010:377, paragraphs 63 and 64; and Opinion of Advocate General Kokott in *Commission v Alrosa*, C-441/07 P, EU:C:2009:555, paragraph 81.

704 See my paper 'The Increased Level of EU Antitrust Fines, Judicial Review and the ECHR' (2010) 33 *World Competition* 5, at 19–20.

705 See Judgment in *Chalkor v Commission*, C-386/10 P, EU:C:2011:815, paragraphs 64–66. As the Court points out in paragraph 65: 'That requirement, which is procedural in nature, does not conflict with the rule that, in regard to infringements of the competition rules, it is for the Commission to prove the infringements found by it and to adduce evidence capable of demonstrating to the requisite legal standard the existence of the circumstances constituting an infringement. What the applicant is required to do in the context of a legal challenge is to identify the impugned elements of the contested decision, to formulate grounds of challenge in that regard and to adduce evidence – direct or circumstantial – to demonstrate that its objections are well founded.'

in the Commission's decision is incorrect in law or in fact, it cannot replace it with a correct finding, but must annul the Commission's decision, either entirely or partially, if the incorrectness concerns part of the decision and the remaining part can still stand.[706]

I do not have the impression that the General Court, even in those cases, such as the *Microsoft* case, where it stated that its review was limited to manifest errors, in fact abstained from exercising a full review in respect of all the pleas raised by the applicant against the Commission's decision.[707] As already mentioned, it is clear from the case law of the European Court of Human Rights that what is decisive for compliance with Article 6 ECHR is whether the judicial body reviewing the administrative first-instance decision **in fact** exercises full jurisdiction, not any general statements that the judicial body may make as to the extent of its own powers.[708]

That being said, while it is essential that the General Court in fact exercises full jurisdiction, it is also important that that Court is seen to exercise such jurisdiction. It would therefore be preferable for the Court to no longer use the language of 'manifest error', 'discretion', 'margin of appreciation', 'complex economic assessments' and the like when reviewing decisions imposing fines, so as to avoid any confusion.[709]

D. Review as to the fine

The imposition of a fine by the European Commission involves a number of findings. First, the Commission must make a finding that the infringement has been committed intentionally or negligently.[710] Second, given that the antitrust prohibitions are addressed to undertakings but decisions imposing fines need to be addressed to legal persons, the Commission must make findings as to the imputability of the infringement to the legal persons on which the fines are imposed.[711] Third, the Commission must make findings as to the duration and the gravity of the infringement.[712] With regard to the gravity of the infringement, the case law of the Court of Justice requires the Commission to take into account objective factors such as the content of the anti-competitive conduct, the number of incidents and their intensity, the extent of the market affected and the damage to the economic public order, as well as the relative importance and market share of the undertakings responsible and also any repeated infringements.[713] In the interest of transparency, the Commission has adopted Guidelines in which it indicates the basis on

---

706 Article 264 TFEU, and Judgment in *Commission v Verhuizingen Coppens*, C-441/11 P, EU:C:2012:778, and Opinion of Advocate General Kokott in *Commission v Verhuizingen Coppens*, C-441/11 P, EU:C:2012:317.

707 In cases where the General Court in fact fails to exercise a full review, this can be redressed upon appeal by the Court of Justice; see for example Judgment in *CB v Commission*, C-67/13 P, EU:C:2014:2204, paragraphs 89 and 90.

708 See discussion of *Menarini v Italy* above; see also Judgment of 21 July 2011 in Case of *Sigma Radio Television Ltd. v Cyprus* (Application no 32181/05), paragraph 155.

709 See also Editorial Comments, 'Towards a more judicial approach? EU antitrust fines under the scrutiny of fundamental rights' (2011) 48 *Common Market Law Review* 1405.

710 Article 23(2) of Regulation 1/2003.

711 See Judgments in *Akzo Nobel and Others v European Commission*, C-97/08 P, EU:C:2009:536, and in *Alliance One v Commission*, C-628/10 P and C-14/11 P, EU:C:2012:479, and Opinions of Advocate General Kokott in *Akzo Nobel and Others v European Commission*, C-97/08 P, EU:C:2009:262, and in *Alliance One v Commission*, C-628/10 P and C-14/11 P, EU:C:2012:11.

712 Article 23(3) of Regulation 1/2003.

713 Judgment in *Aalborg Portland and Others v Commission*, C-204/00 P etc., EU:C:2004:6, paragraph 91.

which it will take account of one or the other aspect of the infringement and what this will imply as regards the amount of the fine.[714] The Commission has also published a Leniency Notice in which it promises, under certain conditions, immunity from fines or reductions in the amount of the fine to undertakings that help the Commission to discover and prove secret cartel infringements.[715] In a decision imposing fines, the Commission thus must make a number of findings as to whether or to what extent the factors set out in its Guidelines and the conditions and factors set out in its Leniency Notice are fulfilled. Finally, the Commission must make a finding as to the undertaking's total turnover in the preceding business year, because the fine shall not exceed 10% of that amount.[716]

With regard to all these findings, the General Court exercises a review of legality under Article 263 TFEU, similar to the review of legality of the finding of the infringement. An important difference, however, is that with regard to the amount of the fine, Regulation 1/2003, the case law of the EU Courts and the Guidelines and Leniency Notice still leave the European Commission a significant margin of discretion.

For instance, the case law provides that recidivism is a factor to be taken into account in determining the gravity of the infringement and that the circumstance of recidivism is 'not only a relevant factor but also a particularly important factor and a very significant indication of the gravity of the infringement for the purpose of assessing the amount of the fine in the context of effective deterrence',[717] but gives no more precise indications. According to the Guidelines, the basic amount of the fine will be increased by 'up to 100%' for each earlier infringement.[718] In practice, it appears that the Commission typically increases the basic amount by 50% in case of one earlier infringement, 60% in case of two earlier infringements, and 90% in case of three earlier infringements,[719] but it could equally have chosen higher or lower percentages.

The European Commission's margin of discretion in determining the amount of the fine it imposes is, however, counterbalanced by the General Court's unlimited jurisdiction with regard to the fines under Article 261 TFEU and Article 31 of Regulation 1/2003. That jurisdiction empowers the General Court, in addition to carrying out a review of

---

714 Judgment in *Chalkor v Commission*, C-386/10 P, EU:C:2011:815, paragraph 59; Commission Guidelines on the method of setting fines pursuant to Article 23(2)(a) of Regulation No. 1/2003 [2006] OJ C210/2; see further my paper 'The European Commission's 2006 Guidelines on Antitrust Fines: A Legal and Economic Analysis' (2007) 30 *World Competition* 197. According to the case law of the Court of Justice, the Commission may not depart from its Guidelines in an individual case without giving reasons that are compatible with the principle of equal treatment; Judgment in *Archer Daniels Midland v Commission*, C-397/03 P, EU:C:2006:328, paragraph 91.

715 Commission Notice on immunity from fines and reduction of fines in cartel cases ('Leniency Notice') [2006] OJ C298/17; see further my paper 'Leniency in Antitrust Enforcement: Theory and Practice' (2007) 30 *World Competition* 25, and Chapter V of this book. The Commission has itself indicated in its Leniency Notice that this notice creates legitimate expectations, which means that the Commission is bound by this notice.

716 Article 23(2) of Regulation 1/2003.

717 Judgment in *Danone v Commission*, C-3/06 P, EU:C:2007:88, paragraph 47.

718 Commission Guidelines on the method of setting fines pursuant to Article 23(2)(a) of Regulation No 1/2003 [2006] OJ C210/2, point 28, first indent.

719 E. Barbier de La Serre and C. Winckler, 'Legal Issues Regarding Fines Imposed in EU Competition Proceedings' (2010) 1 *Journal of Competition Law & Practice* 327 at 336–337 and 'A Survey of Legal Issues Regarding Fines Imposed in EU Competition Proceedings (2010)' (2011) 2 *Journal of Competition Law & Practice* 356 at 360–361.

the lawfulness of the penalty, to substitute its own appraisal for the Commission's and, consequently, to cancel, reduce or increase the fine as it sees fit.[720]

The only limitation to the review exercised by the General Court under Article 261 TFEU and Article 31 of Regulation 1/2003 is that it does not amount to a review of the Court's own motion. With the exception of matters of public policy, which the Courts are required to raise of their own motion, it is for the applicant to raise pleas against the contested decision and to adduce evidence in support of those pleas.[721]

There can be no doubt that the combination of the review of legality and this unlimited jurisdiction meets the 'full jurisdiction' standard laid down in the case law of the European Court of Human Rights.[722] Indeed, even Judge Pinto de Albuquerque, in his dissenting opinion in *Menarini*, refers to the unlimited jurisdiction pursuant to Article 31 of Regulation 1/2003 as an example of 'full jurisdiction'.[723]

In a number of cases, applicants have complained on appeal before the Court of Justice that the General Court had failed to exercise its jurisdiction by holding that the Commission has a considerable margin of discretion as to the amount of the fine it imposes and that only the manifest exceeding of the bounds of that margin could be challenged. This has allowed the Court of Justice in the *Chalkor* and *Schindler* cases to clarify that the General Court cannot use the Commission's margin of discretion, be it in the application of its Fining Guidelines or in the application of its Leniency Notice,[724] as a basis for dispensing with the conduct of an in-depth review of the law and of the facts.[725]

Indeed, while Regulation 1/2003 and the case law leave the European Commission a broad margin of discretion in the determination of the amount of the fines it imposes, and while the existence of that margin would be relevant for the extent of the General Court's powers if that court could only exercise a review of legality under Article 263 TFEU, that margin cannot limit the General Court's unlimited jurisdiction under Article 261 TFEU and Article 31 of Regulation 1/2003.[726]

In both *Chalkor* and *Schindler*, the Court of Justice did, however, find that, irrespective of the introductory statements that the General Court had made as to the extent of its

---

720 Judgment in *Chalkor v Commission*, C-386/10 P, EU:C:2011:815, paragraph 63, and in *Galp Energía España and Others v Commission*, C-603/13 P, EU:C:2016:38, paragraphs 75 to 90.

721 Judgment in *Chalkor v Commission*, C-386/10 P, EU:C:2011:815, paragraphs 64–66. As the Court points out in paragraph 65: 'That requirement, which is procedural in nature, does not conflict with the rule that, in regard to infringements of the competition rules, it is for the Commission to prove the infringements found by it and to adduce evidence capable of demonstrating to the requisite legal standard the existence of the circumstances constituting an infringement. What the applicant is required to do in the context of a legal challenge is to identify the impugned elements of the contested decision, to formulate grounds of challenge in that regard and to adduce evidence – direct or circumstantial – to demonstrate that its objections are well founded.'

722 See Opinion of Advocate General Sharpston in *KME v Commission*, C-272/09 P, EU:C:2011:63, paragraph 70.

723 Dissenting Opinion of Judge Pinto de Albuquerque in *Menarini v Italy*, paragraph 8.

724 Judgment in *Chalkor v Commission*, C-386/10 P, EU:C:2011:815, paragraph 59.

725 Judgments in *Chalkor v Commission*, C-386/10 P, EU:C:2011:815, paragraph 62, and in *Schindler v Commission*, C-501/11 P, EU:C:2013:522, paragraph 155.

726 See Opinion of Advocate General Kokott in *Schindler v Commission*, C-501/11 P, EU:C:2013:248, paragraph 190, and my paper 'The Increased Level of EU Antitrust Fines, Judicial Review and the ECHR' (2010) 33 *World Competition* 5, at 23–24.

powers, the General Court had, in fact, in response to all the pleas that had been raised by the applicant, carried out an in-depth review in which it itself assessed the evidence without referring to the Commission's margin of discretion, stating detailed grounds for its own decision.[727] The Court of Justice thus did not find a violation of the principle of effective judicial protection in Article 47 of the Charter of Fundamental Rights of the EU, which implements in EU law the protection afforded by Article 6(1) ECHR.[728]

Indeed, as already mentioned above, it is clear from the case law of the European Court of Human Rights that what is decisive for compliance with Article 6(1) ECHR is whether the judicial body reviewing the administrative first-instance decision **in fact** exercises full jurisdiction, not any general statements that the judicial body may make as to its own powers.[729]

That being said, as also mentioned above, while it is essential that the General Court in fact exercises full jurisdiction, it is also important that that court is seen to exercise such jurisdiction. Potentially misleading general statements should thus be avoided.[730]

E. Internal checks and balances and procedural guarantees

The fact that ECHR and EU law allow the European Commission to act both as investigator and as first-instance decision-maker does, of course, not mean that the Commission is free to indulge in prosecutorial bias.

First, the possibility of appeal before the General Court, with its full jurisdiction, obviously has a disciplining effect on the European Commission. The Commission has organised itself internally in a way that interiorises this discipline to maximum effect through the role of its Legal Service.[731] The Legal Service reports to the president of the Commission, and is thus independent from both the Directorate-General for Competition

---

727 Judgment in *Chalkor v Commission*, C-386/10 P, EU:C:2011:815, paragraphs 69–82, and in *Schindler v Commission*, C-501/11 P, EU:C:2013:522, paragraphs 156–158; see also Judgment in *Telefónica and Telefónica de España v Commission*, C-295/12 P, EU:C:2014:2062, paragraph 59, and in *Nexans France and Nexans v Commission*, C-606/18 P, EU:C:2020:571, paragraph 571; and compare with Judgment in *Infineon Technologies v Commission*, C-99/17 P, EU:C:2018:773, paragraph 206.

728 Judgment in *Chalkor v Commission*, C-386/10 P, EU:C:2011:815, paragraphs 51–52 and 67.

729 See discussion of *Menarini v Italy* above; see also Judgment of 21 July 2011 in Case of *Sigma Radio Television Ltd. v Cyprus* (Application no 32181/05), paragraph 155.

730 See, for example, the Judgment in *Kone v Commission*, C-510/11 P, EU:C:2013:696, paragraph 27, in which the Court of Justice stated that 'when it falls to the European Union judicature to review the legality of Commission decisions imposing fines for infringements of the EU competition rules, it cannot encroach upon the discretion available to the Commission in the administrative proceedings by substituting its own assessment of complex economic circumstances for that of the Commission, but, where relevant, must demonstrate that the way in which the Commission reached its conclusions was not justified in law (see, to that effect, Case C-441/07 P *Commission v Alrosa*, EU:C:2010:377, paragraph 67)'. The reference to *Alrosa* is problematic, because in *Alrosa*, which did not concern a decision imposing fines but a decision refusing commitments pursuant to Article 9 of Regulation 1/2003, the Court endorsed the 'manifest error' test. As argued above, while it appears quite right for the EU Courts to leave the European Commission a (broad) margin of discretion when deciding whether or not to accept commitments pursuant to Article 9 of Regulation 1/2003, the case of decisions imposing fines for infringements of Articles 101 and 102 TFEU is fundamentally different.

731 See http://ec.europa.eu/dgs/legal_service/index_en.htm.

and the Commissioner for Competition. It must be consulted on all draft decisions, and its opinion is provided to the College of Commissioners together with any draft decision. Given that the same Legal Service is also charged with defending the Commission's final decision when challenged before the Courts, it has a strong incentive to counteract any prosecutorial bias.

Secondly, the European Commission is bound to observe a number of procedural safeguards, laid down in the case law of the EU Courts and now enshrined in Article 41 of the Charter, and in part also codified in Regulation 1/2003, including the duty to examine carefully and impartially all the relevant aspects of the individual case, the right of the undertakings or persons concerned to be heard, the right of access to the file, and the right to an adequately reasoned decision.[732] The Commission has, in its Regulation 773/2004 (and the earlier implementing regulations under Regulation 17) and in its 2011 Notice on Best Practices,[733] added further procedural guarantees, notably the right to an oral hearing,[734] the practice of early review of key submissions in cases based on formal complaints,[735] and the practice of state of play meetings.[736] The respect of the procedural rights of the parties in the administrative procedure is ultimately guaranteed by the EU Courts, but the European Commission has also created in its internal organisation the function of the Hearing Officer, to whom the parties can turn during the administrative procedure for an independent review of any issues regarding the effective exercise of their procedural rights.[737] Apart from their procedural role, the Hearing Officer can also provide observations to the Commissioner for Competition on the substance of the case, thus possibly adding a third, independent assessment to the assessments by the Directorate-General for Competition and the Legal Service.[738]

These internal checks and balances and procedural guarantees regularly show their usefulness, as becomes apparent when looking at the outcomes of the European Commission's administrative proceedings during a two-year period.[739]

---

732 See generally H. P. Nehl, *Principles of Administrative Procedure in EC Law* (Hart 1999); N. Kahn, *Kerse & Kahn on EU Antitrust Procedure* (6th edition; Sweet & Maxwell 2012); L. Ortiz Blanco (ed) *EU Competition Procedure* (3rd edition; Oxford University Press 2013); and my paper 'EU Antitrust Enforcement Powers and Procedural Rights and Guarantees: The Interplay between EU Law, National Law, the Charter of Fundamental Rights of the EU and the European Convention on Human Rights' (2011) 34 *World Competition* 189.

733 Commission Regulation (EC) No 773/2004 of 7 April 2004 relating to the conduct of proceedings by the Commission pursuant to Articles 81 and 82 of the EC Treaty [2004] OJ L123/18, and Commission Notice on Best Practices for the conduct of proceedings concerning Articles 101 and 102 TFEU [2011] OJ C308/6.

734 Article 12 of Regulation 773/2004; see further Chapter XII of this book.

735 Commission Notice on Best Practices for the conduct of proceedings concerning Articles 101 and 102 TFEU [2011] OJ C308/6, paragraphs 71–74.

736 Idem, paragraphs 60–66.

737 Decision 2011/695/EU of the President of the European Commission of 13 October 2011 on the function and terms of reference of the hearing officer in certain competition proceedings [2011] OJ L275/29; see further Chapter XI of this book.

738 Articles 3(5) and 14(2) of Decision 2011/695/EU.

739 See also J. Almunia, 'Due Process and competition enforcement', SPEECH/10/449 (IBA 14th Annual Competition Conference, Florence, 17 September 2010), at 4: 'Between 2007 and 2009, 17 out of 21 cartel cases were amended after the parties exercised their rights of defence. Many of these changes were substantial and one case was dropped altogether. In the same period, 6 out of 7 abuses of dominance cases were amended, and one case was dropped.'

In the two-year period from the end of October 2011 to the end of October 2013,[740] the European Commission adopted decisions finding infringements and imposing fines in six cartel cases. In three of these cases,[741] the settlement procedure was followed,[742] which means that all the addressees of those decisions have acknowledged the infringement and accepted the amount of the fine.[743] In each of the three other cases,[744] as a result of the parties' written and oral replies to the statement of objections, the final decision was addressed to fewer legal entities than had been addressees of the statement of objections, and for one or more of the addressees of the decision, the duration of the infringement as found in the final decision is shorter than the duration that had preliminarily been found in the statement of objections. A seventh case of an alleged cartel involving fourteen undertakings was closed, following a negative opinion of the Legal Service on the draft statement of objections prepared by the Directorate-General for Competition. Nine other cases of suspected cartels, including two cases in which inspections had been carried out and two cases in which immunity had been granted,[745] were closed at an even earlier stage.

During the same period, the European Commission also adopted decisions in two cartel cases amending its earlier decision or readopting its earlier decision so as to reduce the time period of the finding of infringement and/or reduce the amount of the fines, following judgments by the EU Courts.[746] In another cartel case where the Commission had sent a statement of objections with a view to re-imposing a fine that had been partially annulled by the EU Courts, the proceedings were closed shortly before the oral hearing, following the written replies to the statement of objections and observations made by the Hearing Officer.

As to infringements of Article 101 or 102 TFEU other than cartels, the European Commission adopted during the same two-year period two decisions finding infringements and imposing fines,[747] whereas in eight cases the undertakings concerned offered commitments meeting the concerns expressed in the Commission's preliminary assessment and the proceedings were closed through a decision making those commitments

---

740 The beginning of this period corresponds to the introduction of the most recent changes in the procedural rules and practices, contained in the Notice on Best Practices and in Decision 2011/695/EU. The end of this period corresponds to the time of writing of my paper 'The Compatibility with Fundamental Rights of the EU Antitrust Enforcement System in Which the European Commission Acts Both as Investigator and as First-Instance Decision Maker' (2014) 37 *World Competition* 5, all also accessible at http://ssrn.com/author=456087, on which this chapter is based.

741 Cases AT.39600 *Refrigeration Compressors*, AT.39611 *Water Management Products* and AT.39748 *Automotive Wire Harnesses*.

742 Article 10a of Regulation 773/2004, and Commission Notice on the conduct of settlement procedures in view of the adoption of Decisions pursuant to Article 7 and Article 23 of Council Regulation (EC) No 1/2003 in cartel cases ('Settlement Notice') [2008] OJ C167/1.

743 Paragraph 18 of the Settlement Notice, and Article 15(2) of Decision 2011/695/EU provide that the parties may at any time during the settlement procedure call upon the Hearing Officer to ensure the effective exercise of their procedural rights. In none of the three cases did any of the parties call upon the Hearing Officer.

744 Cases AT.39462 *Freight Forwarding*, AT.39452 *Mountings for windows and window doors* and AT.39437 *TV and Computer Monitor Tubes*.

745 Article 20(4) of Regulation 1/2003 and Leniency Notice.

746 Cases AT.38695 *Sodium Chlorate* and AT.39966 *Gas Insulated Switchgear re-adoption*.

747 Cases AT.39839 *Telefónica and Portugal Telecom* and AT.39226 *Lundbeck*.

binding pursuant to Article 9 of Regulation 1/2003.[748] A few dozen other cases were closed, most often but not always before the initiation of formal proceedings,[749] requiring in half a dozen cases decisions rejecting formal complaints.[750]

Finally, during the same period, the European Commission adopted one decision imposing a fine for failure to comply with a commitment made binding by a decision pursuant to Article 9 of Regulation 1/2003.[751] The undertaking concerned did not contest the failure to comply. The Commission also adopted a decision imposing a fine for refusal to submit to an inspection ordered by decision.[752] Following the written reply to the statement of objections and the oral hearing, the final decision retains only two of the three incidents that had been used in the statement of objections. In another case in which the Commission had sent a statement of objections with a view to imposing a fine for supplying incorrect or misleading information in response to a request for information,[753] the proceedings were closed following the written reply to the statement of objections, the oral hearing, and observations made by the Hearing Officer.

While the above overview of the outcomes of the European Commission's administrative proceedings during a two-year period shows that the internal checks and balances and procedural guarantees are useful, it should be clear that these guarantees in no way reduce the need for a full review by the General Court, when requested by the undertakings concerned. Indeed, the internal checks and balances and procedural guarantees derive their full effectiveness precisely from the possibility of a subsequent full review by the General Court.

F. Summary and conclusions

Following the *Jussila* and *Menarini* judgments, it is now entirely clear that Article 6 ECHR, as interpreted by the European Court of Human Rights, provides no grounds for abandoning the system, as set up by Regulation 17 and maintained under Regulation 1/2003, in which the European Commission both investigates suspected infringements of the antitrust prohibitions contained in Articles 101 and 102 TFEU and takes decisions finding such infringements, ordering their termination, and imposing fines.

Article 6(1) ECHR and Article 47 of the Charter, which implements in EU law the protection afforded by Article 6(1) ECHR, require, however, that the General Court, when reviewing European Commission decisions, exercise full jurisdiction. What is decisive is whether the General Court in fact exercises full jurisdiction, not any general statements that the Courts may make as to its powers. It is nevertheless also important

---

748 Cases AT.39592 *Standard & Poor's*, AT.39692 *IBM Maintenance Services*, AT.37984 *Skyteam*, AT.39736 *Siemens/Areva*, AT.39847 *E-books*, AT.39230 *Reel/Alcan*, AT.39654 *Reuters Instrument Codes* and AT.39727 *CEZ*. Article 15(1) of Decision 2011/695/EU provides that the parties may at any time during the commitments procedure call upon the Hearing Officer to ensure the effective exercise of their procedural rights. In none of the eight cases did any of the parties call upon the Hearing Officer.

749 Article 11(6) of Regulation 1/2003 and Article 2 of Regulation 773/2004.

750 Article 7 of Regulation 773/2004.

751 Case AT.39530 *Microsoft (Tying)*.

752 Case AT.39793 *EPH and Others*.

753 Article 23(1)(a) of Regulation 1/2003.

that the General Court is seen to exercise full jurisdiction. For this reason, potentially misleading general statements should be avoided.

The fact that ECHR and EU law allow the European Commission to act both as investigator and as first-instance decision-maker does, of course, not mean that the Commission is free to indulge in prosecutorial bias. A number of internal checks and balances and procedural guarantees apply to the Commission's administrative procedure, and regularly show their usefulness. This, however, in no way reduces the need for a full review by the General Court, when requested by the undertakings concerned. Indeed, the internal checks and balances and procedural guarantees derive their full effectiveness precisely from the possibility of a subsequent full review by the General Court.

X. Fundamental Procedural Rights and Effective Enforcement of Articles 101 and 102 TFEU in the European Competition Network

This chapter deals with the fundamental procedural rights of companies that are targeted in the enforcement of Articles 101 and 102 TFEU by the European Commission or the competition authorities of the EU Member States, forming together the European Competition Network. The chapter first provides a (non-exhaustive) list of such rights as applicable to the enforcement of Articles 101 and 102 TFEU by the European Commission, and explains the source of these fundamental rights in the EU legal order. It then examines the relationship between fundamental procedural rights and effective enforcement of Articles 101 and 102 TFEU. It argues that procedural rights often contribute to effective enforcement, but not always. The interplay between fundamental rights of legal persons and competition enforcement remains a balancing exercise, and this balancing exercise is not the same as in traditional criminal law. Finally, this chapter examines the question whether or to what extent EU Member States can, for the enforcement of Articles 101 and 102 TFEU by their national competition authorities, provide for a lower or a higher level of procedural rights than the level of fundamental procedural rights applicable to the enforcement of Articles 101 and 102 TFEU by the European Commission.

A. Fundamental procedural rights applicable to the enforcement of Articles 101 and 102 TFEU by the European Commission

1. The European Commission's enforcement powers

To enable the European Commission to enforce Articles 101 and 102 TFEU, Regulation 1/2003 grants the European Commission a number of investigative and decisional powers. The European Commission's investigative powers are set out in Chapter V of Regulation 1/2003, the two main instruments being requests for information (Article 18) and inspections of business premises (Article 20). The European Commission's decisional powers are set out in Chapters III and VI of Regulation 1/2003, the two main instruments being decisions finding infringements and ordering their termination (Article 7) and imposing fines (Article 23(1)(a)).[754]

---

[754] For a detailed overview, see K. Dekeyser, C. Gauer, J. Laitenberger, N. Wahl, W. Wils and L. Prete (eds), *Regulation 1/2003 and EU Antitrust Enforcement – A Systematic Guide* (Wolters Kluwer 2022).

2. Enforcement only targets companies, not natural persons

In practice, the enforcement of Articles 101 and 102 TFEU by the European Commission targets only companies or other legal persons, not natural persons.[755]

The substantive antitrust prohibitions contained in Articles 101 and 102 TFEU are addressed to undertakings and associations of undertakings. The concept of undertaking in that context must be understood as designating an economic unit, even if in law that economic unit consists of several persons, natural or legal.[756] However, decisions by the European Commission (or by national competition authorities) ordering termination of infringements or imposing fines can only be addressed to persons, not least because such decisions must be enforced.[757] The same is true of investigative measures such as decisions requesting information or inspection decisions. The European Commission thus conducts the whole of its enforcement proceedings vis-à-vis the person or persons to whom the conduct of the undertaking can be imputed, typically a parent company and one or more of its subsidiaries. Each of these companies concerned by the proceedings is individually entitled to all the applicable procedural rights and safeguards.[758]

If the undertaking suspected of an infringement of Articles 101 or 102 TFEU were found to consist of an unincorporated business (a single trader, with or without employees, who has not incorporated her business, or a professional exercising her profession alone and unincorporated, or several natural persons operating a single business without any employment relationship between them and without any form of legal person), the European Commission would necessarily have to conduct its enforcement proceedings vis-à-vis the natural person or persons operating the business. However, this situation almost never occurs: in practice, proceedings are always conducted against companies or other legal persons.[759]

---

755 See further my paper 'Is Criminalization of EU Competition Law the Answer?' (2005) 28 *World Competition* 117, also accessible at http://ssrn.com/author=456087.

756 Judgments in *Akzo Nobel NV and Others v Commission*, C-97/08 P, EU:C:2009:536, paragraphs 54 and 55 and in *Schindler Holding Ltd and Others v Commission*, C-501/11 P, EU:C:2013:522, paragraph 102.

757 See Opinion of Advocate General Kokott in *Akzo Nobel NV and Others v Commission*, C-97/08 P, EU:C:2009:262, paragraph 37, and Article 299 TFEU.

758 See Judgments in *Akzo Nobel NV and Others v Commission*, C-97/08 P, EU:C:2009:536, paragraph 57, in *Akzo Nobel NV and Others v Commission*, T-47/10, EU:T:2015:506, paragraph 126 (confirmed on appeal in *Akzo Nobel NV and Others v Commission*, C-516/15 P, EU:C:2017:314) and in *LG Electronics Inc and Koninklijke Philips NV*, C-588/15 P and C-622/15 P, EU:C:2017:679, paragraphs 45–46.

759 In the *Pre-Insulated Pipes* case, one of the undertakings fined for participation in the cartel was controlled and managed by a natural person, Dr W. H., but the European Commission appears to have made an effort to avoid imposing the fine on him, identifying instead a collection of companies which it held jointly and severally liable for the fine; see recitals 157–160 and Article 3(d) of the Decision of 21 October 1998, *Pre-Insulated Pipe Cartel* [1999] OJ L24/1, and paragraph 105 of the Judgment in *HFB and Others v Commission*, T-9/99, EU:T:2002:70, in which the Court found that the European Commission had 'intentionally' not established Dr H.'s liability.
See also Judgment in *Aristrain v Commission*, C-196/99 P, EU:C:2003:529, paragraphs 91 and 101.

3. A (non-exhaustive) list of fundamental procedural rights

The companies targeted by the European Commission's enforcement of Articles 101 and 102 TFEU benefit from a number of fundamental procedural rights, including:

- protection against arbitrary or disproportionate intervention by public authorities in the sphere of private activities (protection of privacy / right to the inviolability of the home),[760]
- the right not to be compelled to admit their participation in an infringement (privilege against self-incrimination),[761]
- legal professional privilege,[762]
- the presumption of innocence,[763]
- the right to be heard, and its corollary, the right of access to the file,[764]
- the right to careful and impartial examination,[765]
- the right to an adequate statement of reasons,[766]
- the right to effective judicial protection,[767]

---

760 See Article 7 of the Charter of Fundamental Rights of the European Union (CFREU), and Judgments in *Hoechst v Commission*, 46/87 and 227/88, EU:C:1989:337, paragraph 19, in *Deutsche Bahn v Commission*, C-583/13 P, EU:C:2015:404, paragraphs 19 to 36, in *Nexans France and Nexans v Commission*, T-135/09, EU:T:2012:596, and in *České dráhy v Commission*, T-325/16, EU:T:2018:368.

761 See Judgment in *Orkem v Commission*, 374/87, EU:C:1989:387, paragraphs 35–40; Judgment and Opinion of Advocate General Geelhoed in *Commission v SGL Carbon*, C-301/04 P, EU:C:2006:432 and EU:C:2006:53; Judgment in *Qualcomm and Qualcomm Europe v Commission*, T-371/17, EU:T:2019:232, paragraphs 177 to 194; Opinion of Advocate General Wahl in *HeidelbergCement v Commission*, C-247/14 P, EU:C:2015:694, paragraphs 149 to 164; recital 23 of Regulation 1/2003; and my paper 'Self-Incrimination in EC Antitrust Enforcement: A Legal and Economic Analysis' (2003) 26 *World Competition* 567, also accessible at http://ssrn.com/author=456087. See also, on the compatibility of leniency and settlement procedures with the privilege against self-incrimination, Judgments in *Schindler v Commission*, T-138/07, EU:T:2011:362, paragraphs 148 to 158, and in *Timab Industries and CFPR v Commission*, C-411/15 P, EU:C:2017:11, paragraphs 84 to 87, and Chapter VI of this book.

762 See Judgment in *AM & S Europe v Commission*, 155/79, EU:C:1982:157; Judgment in *Akzo Nobel Chemicals and Akcros Chemicals v Commission*, T-125/03 and T-253/03, EU:T:2007:287; Judgment and Opinion of Advocate General Kokott in *Akzo Nobel Chemicals and Akcros Chemicals v Commission*, C-550/07 P, EU:C:2010:512 and EU:C:2010:229; and Chapter XIII of this book.

763 See Article 48(1) CFREU; Judgment in *Hüls v Commission*, C-199/92 P, EU:C:1999:358, paragraph 150; and Judgments in *Pometon v Commission*, C-440/19 P, EU:C:2021:214, paragraphs 57 to 86, and in *HSBC v Commission*, C-883/19 P, EU:C:2023:11, paragraphs 79 to 96 and 218 to 246.

764 See Article 41(2)(a) and (b) CFREU; Judgment in *Aalborg Portland and Others v Commission*, C-204/00 P etc., EU:C:2004:6, paragraphs 66 to 77; and Article 27(1) and (2) of Regulation 1/2003; and W. Wils and H. Abbott, 'Access to the File in Competition Proceedings Before the European Commission' (2019) 42 *World Competition* 255, updated version accessible at http://ssrn.com/author=456087.

765 See Article 41(1) CFREU; Judgments in *Technische Universität München*, C-269/90, EU:C:1991:438, paragraph 14, in *Teva v Commission*, T-679/14, EU:T:2018:919, paragraph 54, and in *Qualcomm and Qualcomm Europe v Commission*, T-371/17, EU:T:2019:232, paragraph 101.

766 See Article 41(2)(c) CFREU and Article 296 TFEU; Judgments in *Icap and Others v Commission*, C-39/18 P, EU:C:2019:584, in *Pometon v Commission*, T-433/16, EU:T:2019:201, paragraphs 348 to 394, in *HeidelbergCement v Commission*, C-247/14 P, EU:C:2016:149, in *Nexans and Nexans France v Commission*, C-37/13 P, EU:C:2014:2030, paragraphs 29 to 40, and in *Qualcomm and Qualcomm Europe v Commission*, T-371/17, EU:T:2019:232, paragraphs 35 to 55.

767 See Article 47 CFREU; Article 31 of Regulation 1/2003; Judgment in *Galp Energía España and Others v Commission*, C-603/13 P, EU:C:2016:38, paragraphs 71 to 77; Judgments in *Groupement des Cartes Bancaires v Commission*, C-67/13 P, EU:C:2014:2204, paragraphs 89 to 91, and in *Intel v Commission*, C-413/14 P, EU:C:2017:632, paragraphs 141 to 147; Judgment in *Deutsche Bahn v Commission*, C-583/13 P, EU:C:2015:404, paragraphs 41 to 48; and Judgment 9 March 2023, *Intermarché Casino Achats v Commission*, C-693/20 P, EU:C:2023:172, paragraphs 32 to 68.

- the right to a decision within a reasonable time,[768] and
- the principle of *ne bis in idem*.[769]

4. The source of fundamental procedural rights in the EU legal order

The fundamental rights applicable to the enforcement of Articles 101 and 102 TFEU by the European Commission are nowadays primarily enshrined in the Charter of Fundamental Rights of the EU (the Charter or CFREU), but can also be found in general principles of EU law.[770]

According to Article 6(1) of the Treaty on European Union (TEU), as amended by the Lisbon Treaty in 2009, 'the Union recognises the rights, freedoms and principles set out in the Charter of Fundamental Rights of the European Union of 7 December 2000, as adapted at Strasbourg, on 12 December 2007, which shall have the same legal value as the Treaties'.[771]

According to its Preamble, the purpose of the Charter is 'to strengthen the protection of fundamental rights [. . .] by making those rights more visible in a Charter'. The Charter 'reaffirms [. . .] the rights as they result, in particular, from the constitutional traditions and international obligations common to the Member States, the European Convention for the Protection of Human Rights and Fundamental Freedoms, [. . .] and the case-law of the Court of Justice of the European Union and of the European Court of Human Rights'.[772]

---

768 See Articles 41(1) and 47, second paragraph, CFREU; Judgment in *Nederlandse Federatieve Vereniging voor de Groothandel op Electrotechnisch Gebied v Commission*, C-105/04 P, EU:C:2006:592, paragraphs 35 to 62; Opinion of Advocate General Kokott in *Solvay v Commission*, C-109/10 P, EU:C:2011:256, paragraphs 229 to 277 and 305 to 357; Judgment in *Groupe Gascogne v Commission*, C-58/12 P, EU:C:2013:770, paragraphs 72 to 96; Judgment in *Bolloré v Commission*, C-414/12 P, EU:C:2014:301, paragraphs 104 to 109; View of Advocate General Kokott in Opinion procedure 2/13, EU:C:2014:2475, paragraphs 153 to 155; Judgment in *The Goldman Sachs Group v Commission*, T-419/14, EU:T:2018:445, paragraphs 245 to 251; Judgment in *Italmobiliare v Commission*, T-523/15, EU:T:2019:499, paragraphs 153 to 160; and Final Report of the Hearing Officer of 1 July 2019 in Case AT.37956 *Reinforcing bars*.

769 See Article 50 CFREU; Judgment in *Limburgse Vinyl Maatschappij and Others v Commission*, C-238/99 P etc., EU:C:2002:582, paragraphs 59 to 68; View of Advocate General Kokott in Opinion procedure 2/13, EU:C:2014:2475, paragraph 152; Judgment in *Powszechny Zakład Ubezpieczeń na Życie*, C-617/17, EU:C:2019:283; Judgment in *bpost*, C-117/20, EU:C:2022:202; Judgment in *Nordzucker*, C-151/20, EU:C:2022:203; my paper 'The Principle of "Ne Bis in Idem" in EC Antitrust Enforcement: A Legal and Economic Analysis' (2003)26 *World Competition* 131, also accessible at http://ssrn.com/author=456087 and S. Frisch, '*Ne bis in idem* under an optimal antitrust enforcement framework' (2023) 24 *ERA Forum*.

770 For a more detailed analysis, see my paper 'EU Antitrust Enforcement Powers and Procedural Rights and Guarantees: The Interplay between EU Law, National Law, the Charter of Fundamental Rights of the EU and the European Convention on Human Rights' (2011) 34 *World Competition* 189, also accessible at http://ssrn.com/author=456087.

771 The final text of the Charter has been published in: [2007] OJ C303/1.
See also recital 37 of Regulation 1/2003, which states that 'this Regulation respects the fundamental rights and observes the principles recognised in particular by the Charter of Fundamental Rights of the European Union. Accordingly, this Regulation should be interpreted and applied with respect to those rights and principles'.

772 See also Article 52 CFREU; the Explanations to the Charter [2007] OJ C303/17; and Declaration No 1 concerning the Charter of Fundamental Rights of the European Union, annexed to the Final Act of the Intergovernmental Conference which adopted the Treaty of Lisbon [2007] OJ C306/249.

According to Article 6(3) TEU, 'fundamental rights, as guaranteed by the European Convention for the Protection of Human Rights and Fundamental Freedoms and as they result from the constitutional traditions common to the Member States, [. . .] constitute general principles of the Union's law'.

Before the entry into force of the Lisbon Treaty, general principles of EU law (or 'general principles of Community law' as they were called at the time) were the main source of fundamental procedural rights.[773] Given that, since the entry into force of the Lisbon Treaty, the Charter of Fundamental Rights of the EU has the same legal value as the Treaties, and given that the Charter contains the rights guaranteed by the Convention, and also draws upon the common constitutional traditions of the Member States, general principles of EU law are now a subsidiary and complementary source of fundamental procedural rights, which mainly serves to fill any gaps in the Charter.[774]

Whilst, as Article 6(3) TEU confirms, fundamental rights recognised by the European Convention on Human Rights (ECHR) constitute general principles of EU law and whilst Article 52(3) CFREU provides that the rights in the Charter which correspond to rights guaranteed by the ECHR are to have the same meaning and scope as those laid down by the ECHR, the ECHR does not constitute, for as long as the European Union has not acceded to it,[775] a legal instrument that has been formally incorporated into EU law.[776]

5. The role of the EU Courts

The primary responsibility for respecting fundamental procedural rights in its enforcement of Articles 101 and 102 TFEU lies, of course, with the European Commission itself. The respect by the European Commission of the fundamental procedural rights applicable to its enforcement of Articles 101 and 102 TFEU is, however, ultimately ensured by the EU Courts (General Court and Court of Justice). While there is already a well-developed

---

773 See my paper 'Powers of Investigation and Procedural Rights and Guarantees in EU Antitrust Enforcement: The Interplay between European and National Legislation and Case-law' (2006) 29 *World Competition* 3, also accessible at http://ssrn.com/author=456087, and G. Delledonne and F. Fabbrini, 'The founding myth of European human rights law: revisiting the role of national courts in the rise of EU human rights jurisprudence' (2019) *European Law Review* 178.

774 The main gap in the Charter is not relevant for the enforcement of Articles 101 and 102 TFEU by the European Commission but is relevant for the enforcement of Articles 101 and 102 TFEU by the competition authorities of the EU Member States. Because of its specific wording, Article 41 CFREU only applies to the institutions, bodies, offices and agencies of the European Union, not to the Member States. However, the content of Article 41 CFREU reflects general principles of EU law that as such also apply to the enforcement of Articles 101 and 102 TFEU by the competition authorities of the EU Member States; see Judgment in *YS and Others*, C-141/12 and C-372/12, EU:C:2014:2081, paragraphs 67 and 68.

775 Article 6(2) TEU, as inserted by the Lisbon Treaty in 2009, provides that the EU shall accede to the ECHR. Negotiations between the EU and the Council of Europe for an accession agreement were started in 2010, and a draft agreement was reached in 2013. However, in Opinion 2/13 of 18 December 2014, EU:C:2014:2454, the EU Court of Justice held that the draft agreement is not compatible with Article 6(2) TEU and with Protocol No 8 EU, which require that the accession agreement preserve the specific characteristics of the Union and Union law. New negotiations for an accession of the EU to the ECHR were started in 2020, and a draft revised accession agreement was reached in April 2023; see https://www.echr.coe.int/documents/d/echr/UE_Report_CDDH_ENG.

776 Judgment in *Garlsson Real Estate and Others v Consob*, C-537/16, EU:C:2018:193, paragraph 24. As pointed out in paragraph 25 of the same judgment, according to the explanations relating to Article 52 of the Charter, Article 52(3) thereof is intended to ensure the necessary consistency between the Charter and the ECHR, 'without thereby adversely affecting the autonomy of Union law and [. . .] that of the Court of Justice of the European Union'.

case law going back several decades, novel issues of interpretation and application of those fundamental procedural rights keep coming up.

For example, in its judgment of 10 July 2019 in Case C-39/18 P *Commission v Icap and Others*,[777] the Court of Justice confirmed an earlier judgment of the General Court,[778] annulling a decision of the European Commission imposing a fine for an infringement of Article 101 TFEU for non-respect of the obligation to state reasons, enshrined in Article 296 TFEU and Article 41(2)(c) CFREU. The Court of Justice thus clarified that the right to an adequate statement of reasons requires that, when the European Commission, for the determination of the amount of a fine, uses a method of calculation (other than a simple lump sum) that deviates from the method set out in its Fining Guidelines,[779] the European Commission must indicate in its decision all the factors taken into account and explain the relevance and weighting of these factors (without being obliged to provide figures relating to the method of calculation or to explain in detail the internal calculations it has carried out).

In addition, in paragraph 34 of its judgment, the Court of Justice appears to have endorsed the view expressed by Advocate General Tanchev in his Opinion of 2 May 2019 that the right to be heard, enshrined in Article 41(2)(a) of the Charter, further requires that the company concerned is also heard during the administrative procedure on this method of calculation, allowing the company to express its views on all the factors to be taken into account and their relevance and weighting before the European Commission adopts its decision.[780] The Court of Justice thus appears to have departed from its previous case law, according to which the European Commission only needed to hear the companies concerned on the main factual and legal criteria on which it intended to base the calculation of the fine, without the need to specify the way in which it intended to use those elements.[781]

6. The role of the Hearing Officer

Inside the European Commission, the primary responsibility for respecting the procedural rights of all parties involved in competition proceedings lies with the Directorate-General for Competition (DG Competition).[782] The European Commission has, however, also created in its internal organisation the function of the Hearing Officer, to whom the parties can turn during the administrative procedure for an independent review of any issues regarding the effective exercise of their procedural rights.[783]

For example, in Case AT.40054 *Ethanol benchmarks*, which concerns an alleged infringement of Article 101 TFEU, the European Commission engaged in settlement discussions with all three of the groups of companies under investigation.[784] Whilst one

---

777 EU:C:2019:584.

778 Judgment in *Icap and Others v Commission*, T-180/15, EU:T:2017:795.

779 Guidelines on the method of fines pursuant to Article 23(2)(a) of Regulation No 1/2003 [2006] OJ C210/2.

780 Opinion of Advocate General Tanchev in *Commission v Icap and Others*, C-39/18 P, EU:C:2019:359.

781 See Judgment of 6 July 2017 in *Toshiba v Commission*, C-180/16 P, EU:C:2017:520, paragraphs 21 and 33, and the case law referred to therein. However, see also Judgment of the General Court of 7 November 2019 in *Campine and Campine Recycling v Commission*, T-240/17, EU:T:2019:778, paragraphs 350 to 360.

782 See recital 8 and Article 3(7) of Decision 2011/695/EU of the President of the European Commission of 13 October 2011 on the function and terms of reference of the hearing officer in certain competition proceedings [2011] OJ L275/29.

783 See further Chapter 11 of this book.

784 On the European Commission's cartel settlement procedure, see Chapter 6 of this book.

of the groups of companies (Lantmännen) made a formal settlement submission, the two other groups of companies abandoned the settlement procedure. When the European Commission subsequently sent under the normal non-settlement procedure a statement of objections to the two non-settling groups of companies, DG Competition initially granted the two non-settling groups of companies access to Lantmännen's settlement submission under the conditions set out in Article 15(1b) of Regulation 773/2004 and paragraph 35 of the Settlement Notice, but refused access to previous correspondence in the file concerning Lantmännen's settlement discussions, including in particular a number of so-called non-papers submitted by Lantmännen during the settlement discussions. One of the two non-settling groups of companies raised the issue with the Hearing Officer, claiming that its right of access to the file, enshrined in Article 41(2)(b) CFREU, extended to the settlement correspondence between Lantmännen and the European Commission preceding Lantmännen's settlement submission. The Hearing Officer accepted the request of that non-settling group of companies and ordered that access be given to the said settlement correspondence under the conditions set out in paragraph 35 of the Settlement Notice. Lantmännen brought an application for annulment of the Hearing Officer's decision before the General Court,[785] accompanied by an application for interim measures to stay the implementation of the Hearing Officer's decision. After the president of the General Court and the vice-president of the Court of Justice rejected the application for interim measures,[786] Lantmännen withdrew its application for annulment.[787]

B. Striking the right balance between fundamental rights and effective enforcement

1. Procedural rights often contribute to effective enforcement...

Procedural rights and effective law enforcement are not inherently antithetical. Rather to the contrary, procedural rights can contribute to effective enforcement in two ways:

- by enhancing the accuracy of the outcome of enforcement proceedings, and hence their deterrent effect; and
- by enhancing the perceived fairness of the law, and hence voluntary compliance with the law.

---

785 Case T-79/19 *Lantmännen and Lantmännen Agroetanol v Commission*. Among other arguments, Lantmännen claimed on the basis of the wording 'confidential vis-à-vis third parties' in Article 10a(2) of Regulation 773/2004 and in paragraph 7 of the Settlement Notice that settlement discussions between the European Commission and a party to the proceedings are confidential vis-à-vis other (settling or non-settling) parties to the same proceedings. However, it is clear from an overall reading of both Regulation 1/2003 and Regulation 773/2004 that the term 'third parties' in Article 10a(2) of Regulation 773/2004 means the same as elsewhere in Regulation 1/2003 and Regulation 773/2004, namely parties other than those that are the subject of given proceedings. This is corroborated by a combined reading of point 6 of the Settlement Notice and the first sentence of point 7 of that notice, where 'third parties' are opposed to 'parties to the proceedings', the latter including both settling and non-settling parties.

786 Order of the President of the General Court of 2 April 2019 in *Lantmännen and Lantmännen Agroetanol v Commission*, T-79/19 R, EU:T:2019:212, and Order of the Vice-President of the Court of Justice of 10 September 2019 in *Lantmännen and Lantmännen Agroetanol v Commission*, C-318/19 P(R), EU:C:2019:698.

787 See Order of the President of the Eighth Chamber of the General Court of 18 November 2019 in *Lantmännen and Lantmännen Agroetanol v Commission*, T-79/19, EU:T:2019:806.

In particular, the right to be heard before the competition authority adopts a decision finding an infringement, ordering its termination and/or imposing a fine and the right to effective judicial review of such decisions are useful for effective enforcement in that they safeguard against inaccurate decisions being taken or being upheld.

That only the guilty should be punished, and that sanctions should be proportionate to the infringement, not only reflects basic requirements of justice, but is also essential for the effectiveness of deterrence. Indeed, it is through the differential in expected sanctions between non-infringement and infringement, and between lesser and more serious infringements, that potential infringers are deterred from entering into infringements, or infringers are deterred from prolonging, extending or otherwise aggravating their infringements.

Secondly, procedural fairness not only constitutes a value in itself, but also contributes to the objective of ensuring compliance with the substantive law, to the extent that perceptions of fairness lead to greater voluntary compliance.[788]

Concerning in particular the right to effective judicial review, Commissioner Vestager has expressed as follows these twin benefits of procedural rights for effective enforcement:

> *'At every stage in a competition investigation, we're aware that our reasoning and our choices have to satisfy the courts. So for us, the rule of law is a constant presence, in the work that we do.*
>
> *And that is a good thing – because it helps us reach better decisions. It reminds us to make our assumptions explicit. It helps us to make sure that we've considered every angle, looked at every arguments that could prove – or disprove – our case.*
>
> *And it also helps to build trust and acceptance for the work that we do. Of course, we can't expect companies to welcome being fined. But it is important that our society – business, consumers, politicians – are confident that we're taking those decisions for the right reasons.'*[789]

2. ...but not always: the example of legal professional privilege

Whereas procedural rights can contribute to effective enforcement, this is not always or not necessarily the case. Legal professional privilege provides a good example.[790]

Legal professional privilege is the expression commonly used to describe what the EU Court of Justice has called the 'principle of confidentiality of written communications

---

788 See T. R. Tyler, *Why People Obey the Law* (Yale University Press 1990).

789 Speech 'Competition and the rule of law' (European Association of Judges, Copenhagen, 10 May 2019).

790 See further Chapter XIII of this book and E. Gippini-Fournier, 'Legal Professional Privilege in Competition Proceedings Before the European Commission: Beyond the Cursory Glance', in B. E. Hawk (ed) *2004 Annual Proceedings of the Fordham Corporate Law Institute – International Antitrust Law and Policy* (Juris Publishing 2005), 587.

between lawyer and client'.[791] As has been pointed out repeatedly,[792] the expression 'legal professional privilege' is a misnomer, because it is a right of the client, not a privilege of the legal profession.[793]

It follows from legal professional privilege, as recognised by the EU Court of Justice since its 1982 judgment in *AM & S Europe* v *Commission*, that the European Commission cannot use its powers of investigation to compel the disclosure of communications between lawyers and clients, provided that, on the one hand, such communications are made for the purpose and in the interests of the client's rights of defence and, on the other hand, the lawyers are independent lawyers, who are not bound to the client by a relationship of employment, and who are entitled to practise their profession in one of the EU (or EEA) Member States.[794]

In EU law, the protection of legal professional privilege thus circumscribed is a fundamental right, which constitutes a general principle of EU law and which can also be derived from Article 7 of the Charter of Fundamental Rights of the European Union (respect for communications) in conjunction with Article 47(1), second sentence of Article 47(2) and Article 48(2) of that Charter (right to be advised, defended and represented, respect for the rights of the defence).[795]

It is sometimes argued, in particular by the in-house lawyer and business lobbies that would want legal professional privilege to be extended to cover also in-house lawyers, that legal professional privilege would also be beneficial for effective enforcement in that it would lead to increased compliance with the antitrust prohibitions.[796]

---

791 Judgment in *AM & S Europe v Commission*, 155/79, EU:C:1982:157. In its more recent judgment in *Akzo Nobel Chemicals and Akcros Chemicals v Commission*, C-550/07 P, EU:C:2010:512, the Court of Justice also used the expression 'legal professional privilege'.

792 See Lord Wilberforce in *Waugh v British Railways Board* [1980] AC 251, at 531; Opinion of Advocate General Warner in *AM & S Europe v Commission*, 155/79, EU:C:1981:19 [1982] ECR 1619 at 1622 and 1633; and Opinion of Advocate General Sir Gordon Slynn in *AM & S Europe v Commission*, 155/79, EU:C:1982:17 [1982] ECR 1642 at 1650.

793 As has been pointed out by the EU Court of Justice, 'the principle of confidentiality does not prevent a lawyer's client from disclosing the written communications between them if it considers that it is in his interest to do so'; see Judgments in *AM & S Europe v Commission*, 155/79, EU:C:1982:157, paragraph 28, and in *Akzo Nobel Chemicals and Akcros Chemicals v Commission*, T-125/03 and T-253/03, EU:T:2007:287, paragraph 90. See also Order in *Hilti v Commission*, T-30/89, EU:T:1990:27, paragraph 12.

794 Judgment in *AM & S Europe v Commission*, 155/79, EU:C:1982:157, paragraphs 18 to 27, confirmed by Judgment in *Akzo Nobel Chemicals and Akcros Chemicals v Commission*, C-550/07 P, EU:C:2010:512. In subsequent judgments, the EU General Court has recognised that internal documents of a company summarising advice received in the exercise of the company's rights of defence from external lawyers are also protected; see Order in *Hilti v Commission*, T-30/89, EU:T:1990:27, paragraph 18. Similarly, internal preparatory documents, even if they were not exchanged with a lawyer or were not created for the purpose of being sent physically to a lawyer, are protected if drawn up exclusively for the purpose of seeking legal advice from an external lawyer in the exercise of the rights of defence; see Judgment in *Akzo Nobel Chemicals and Akcros Chemicals v Commission*, T-125/03 and T-253/03, EU:T:2007:287, paragraph 123. On the other hand, the mere fact that a document has been discussed with an external lawyer is not sufficient to give it protection; see Judgment in *Akzo Nobel Chemicals and Akcros Chemicals v Commission*, T-125/03 and T-253/03, EU:T:2007:287, paragraph 123.

795 See Opinion of Advocate General Kokott in *Akzo Nobel Chemicals and Akcros Chemicals v Commission*, C-550/07 P, EU:C:2010:229, paragraph 47.

796 See for instance the written contribution by BIAC for the discussion at the OECD on the treatment of legally privileged information in competition proceedings, DAF/COMP/WP3/WD(2018)50 of 19 November 2018.

This argument is neither convincing in theory, nor supported by empirical evidence.[797]

In theory, the argument would only work if legal professional privilege were limited to advice about future conduct (not past conduct) and conditional upon the legal advice being followed. Indeed, only if these cumulative conditions are met could the seeking of legal advice lead to more compliance. The fundamental right of legal professional privilege, as recognised by the EU Court of Justice, is not, however, subject to these conditions. Nor would it be if that right were to be extended to in-house lawyers.

Nor does the limited available evidence support the argument that legal professional privilege would lead to more compliance. For example, it turned out that AM & S Europe continued infringing Article 85 EEC (now Article 101 TFEU) for five years after it received the legal advice at stake in the *AM & S Europe* v *Commission* case.[798]

3. Reconciling fundamental rights and effective competition enforcement

To the extent that fundamental procedural rights and effective enforcement of Articles 101 and 102 TFEU may be in tension, the question arises as to how such tension should be resolved.

The answer to this question comes in two parts.

a. *A balancing exercise*

The first part of the answer is that a balancing exercise is required.

In the words of Advocate General Geelhoed:

> *'[T]he interplay between the fundamental rights of legal persons and competition enforcement remains a balancing exercise: at stake are the protection of fundamental rights versus effective enforcement of [EU] competition law. As the Court of Justice held in Eco Swiss [C-126/97, EU:C:1999:269], [Article 101 TFEU] is a fundamental provision which is essential for the accomplishment of the tasks entrusted to the [European Union] and, in particular for the functioning of the internal market. [Article 101 TFEU] forms part of public policy. . . . It is self-evident that the effective enforcement with reasonable means of the basic tenets*

---

797 See E. Gippini-Fournier, 'Legal Professional Privilege in Competition Proceedings Before the European Commission: Beyond the Cursory Glance', in B. E. Hawk (ed) *2004 Annual Proceedings of the Fordham Corporate Law Institute – International Antitrust Law and Policy* (Juris Publishing 2005), 587, at 596–606; L. Kaplow and S. Shavell, 'Legal Advice About Information to Present in Litigation: Its Effects and Social Desirability' (1989) 102 *Harvard Law Review* 565; L. Kaplow and S. Shavell, 'Legal Advice About Acts Already Committed' (1990) 10 *International Review of Law and Economics* 149; S. Shavell, 'Legal Advice', in P. Newman (ed), *New Palgrave Dictionary of Economics and the Law*, vol 2 (1998), 516–520; I. Baum, 'Attorney Corporate Client Privilege: Who Represents the Corporation?' (2007) *Review of Law & Economics*, vol 3, no 1, art 5; and C. E. Parker, R. E. Rosen and V. Lehmann Nielsen, 'The Two Faces of Lawyers: Professional Ethics and Business Compliance With Regulation' (2009) 22 *Georgetown Journal of Legal Ethics* 201.

798 See European Commission Decision of 6 August 1984 in Case IV/30.350 *Zinc Producer Group* [1984] OJ L220/27.

> *of the [EU] legal order should remain possible, just as it is evident that the rights of the defence should be respected too.*'[799]

In the hierarchy of norms of the EU legal order, fundamental rights, as recognised in particular by the Charter, on the one hand, and Articles 101 and 102 TFEU, on the other hand, are at the same level. Both are fundamental provisions. Whereas the enforcement of Articles 101 and 102 TFEU must respect fundamental rights, fundamental rights must also be interpreted and applied in a way that allows for effective enforcement of Articles 101 and 102 TFEU.

The latter requirement can also be found in Opinion 2/13 of the Court of Justice on the accession of the EU to the ECHR:

> '*The autonomy enjoyed by EU law in relation to the laws of the Member States and in relation to international law requires that the interpretation of [the] fundamental rights [recognised by the Charter of Fundamental Rights of the EU] be ensured within the framework of the structure and objectives of the EU. [. . .]*
>
> *The pursuit of the EU's objectives, [. . .], is entrusted to a series of fundamental provisions, such as those providing for [. . .] competition policy. Those provisions, which are part of the framework of a system that is specific to the EU, are structured in such a way as to contribute [. . .] to the implementation of the process of integration that is the raison d'être of the EU itself. [. . .]*
>
> *Fundamental rights, as recognised in particular by the Charter, must [. . .] be interpreted and applied within the EU in accordance with the [EU] constitutional framework [. . .]*'.[800]

For example, in the interpretation of the privilege against self-incrimination in the context of the enforcement of Articles 101 and 102 TFEU by the European Commission, the EU Courts have taken into account the need to preserve the effectiveness of this enforcement:

> '*Thus, an undertaking in receipt of a decision requesting information pursuant to Article 18(3) of Regulation No 1/2003 cannot be recognised as having an absolute right of silence. To acknowledge the existence of such a right would be to go beyond what is necessary in order to preserve the rights of defence of undertakings, and would constitute an unjustified hindrance to the Commission's performance of its duty to ensure that the rules on competition within the internal market are observed. A right of silence can be acknowledged only to the extent that the undertaking concerned would be compelled to provide answers which*

---

799 Opinion of Advocate General Geelhoed in *Commission v SGL Carbon*, C-301/04 P, EU:C:2006:53, paragraph 67. See also recital 14 of Directive (EU) 2019/1 of the European Parliament and of the Council of 11 December 2018 to empower the competition authorities of the Member States to be more effective enforcers and to ensure the proper functioning of the internal market [2019] OJ L11/3, according to which 'the design of [procedural] safeguards should strike a balance between the respect of fundamental rights of undertakings and the duty to ensure that Articles 101 and 102 TFEU are effectively enforced'.

800 Opinion 2/13 of the Court of Justice of 18 December 2014, EU:C:2014:2454, paragraphs 170, 172 and 177.

> *might involve an admission on its part of the existence of an infringement which it is incumbent upon the Commission to prove.*'[801]

Also, in the interpretation of the fundamental right to protection against arbitrary or disproportionate intervention by public authorities in the sphere of private activities, in the context of inspections ordered by the European Commission pursuant to Article 20(4) of Regulation 1/2003, the EU Courts have taken into account the need to preserve the effectiveness of investigations into suspected infringements of Articles 101 and 102 TFEU:

> '*If however, in order to establish that the inspection is justified, the Commission is required to show, in a properly substantiated manner, in the decision ordering the inspection that it is in possession of information and evidence providing reasonable grounds for suspending the infringement of which the undertaking subject to the inspection is suspected [. . .], at the preliminary investigation stage, it cannot be required to indicate, besides the putative infringements that it intends to investigate, the evidence, that is to say, the indicia leading it to consider that Article 102 TFEU has possibly been infringed. Such an obligation would upset the balance struck by the case law between preserving the effectiveness of the investigation and upholding the rights of defence of the undertaking concerned [. . .].*'[802]

Similarly, in relation to its case law according to which, where a parent company holds all the voting rights associated with its subsidiary's shares, the Commission is entitled to rely on a presumption that the parent company actually exercises decisive influence over its subsidiary's market conduct, the Court of Justice has held that:

> '*the presumption that decisive influence is exercised over a subsidiary by its parent company is intended, in particular, to strike a balance between, on the one hand, the importance of the objective of combating conduct contrary to the competition rules, in particular to Article 101 TFEU, and of preventing a repetition of such conduct and, on the other hand, the requirements flowing from certain general principles of European Union law such as the principle of the presumption of innocence, the principle that penalties should be applied solely to the offender and the principle of legal certainty as well as the rights of the defence, including the principle of equality of arms*'.[803]

Of course, in cases where the effective enforcement of Articles 101 and 102 TFEU is not seriously at stake, there is no need to adapt the interpretation and application of fundamental rights. For this reason, in *Icap* the General Court was undoubtedly right to reject the Commission's argument that, in a 'hybrid' cartel settlement procedure, the objectives of rapidity and efficiency of the settlement procedure could justify the violation of the presumption of innocence of a non-settling party consisting in the fact that the Commission had already in the earlier decision regarding the settling parties taken

---

801 Judgment in *Qualcomm and Qualcomm Europe v Commission*, T-371/17, EU:T:2019:232, paragraph 181, citing earlier case law, going back to Judgment in *Limburgse Vinyl Maatschappij and Others v Commission*, T-305/94 etc., EU:T:1999:80, paragraph 448, confirmed by Judgment in *Limburgse Vinyl Maatschappij and Others v Commission*, C-238/99 P etc., EU:C:2002:582, paragraph 272.

802 Judgment in *České dráhy v Commission*, T-325/16, EU:T:2018:368, paragraph 45, citing earlier case law, in particular Judgment in *Orange v Commission*, T-402/13, EU:T:2014:991, paragraph 81.

803 Judgment in *The Goldman Sachs Group v Commission*, C-595/18 P, EU:T:2021:73, paragraph 38.

a view on the non-settling party's participation in the infringement, before having heard the non-settling party in the normal procedure.[804] As the General Court pointed out, the Commission could easily have avoided the violation of the presumption of innocence by adopting the decision regarding the settlement parties and the decision regarding the non-settling party on the same day, as the Commission had done in another case.[805] As is apparent from the subsequent judgment in *Pometon*, depending on the facts of the case, a violation of the presumption of innocence can also be avoided by more careful drafting of the earlier decision regarding the settling parties.[806]

b. *Not the same balancing exercise as in traditional criminal law*

Whilst the first part of the answer to the question how to resolve any tension between fundamental procedural rights and effective enforcement of Articles 101 and 102 TFEU is that a balancing exercise is required, the second part of the answer is that this balancing exercise is not the same as in traditional criminal law. The balance must rather be struck with due regard to the particular nature of competition law enforcement.

In the words of Advocate General Ruiz-Jarabo Colomer:

> *'In general, [. . .], the body of safeguards developed in the field of criminal law, which has as its protagonists the penalising State, on the one hand, and the individual charged with an offence on the other, is not transferred* en bloc *to the field of competition law. Those safeguards are designed specifically to compensate for that imbalance of power. In the case of free competition, those parameters are altered, since it is sought to protect the community of individuals which constitutes society and is composed of groups of consumers against powerful corporations with significant resources. To accord such offenders the same procedural safeguards as those accorded to the most needy individuals, apart from being a mockery, would entail, essentially, a lower degree of protection, in this case economic protection, for the individual as the main victim of anti-competitive conduct. I therefore consider it important that the procedural rules be adapted to the specific field of competition.'*[807]

The need to have due regard to the particular nature of competition law enforcement is also fully recognised by the European Court of Human Rights.[808]

Lawyers advocating for more fundamental procedural rights protection in the enforcement of Articles 101 and 102 TFEU by the European Commission regularly argue along the following lines. *Primo*, EU antitrust enforcement is 'criminal' within the meaning

---

804 Judgment in *Icap and Others v Commission*, T-180/15, EU:T:2017:795, paragraphs 256 to 269, in particular paragraphs 264 to 268.

805 Idem, paragraph 268.

806 Judgment in *Pometon v Commission*, T-433/16, EU:T:2019:201, paragraphs 52 to 103, confirmed on appeal in *Pometon v Commission*, C-440/19 P, EU:C:2021:214, paragraphs 57 to 86.

807 Opinion of Advocate General Ruiz-Jarabo Colomer in *Volkswagen v Commission*, C-338/00 P, EU:C:2002:591, paragraph 66.

808 See, for example, Judgment of the European Court of Human Rights of 14 February 2019 in Case of *SA-Capital Oy v Finland*, Application no 5556/10, paragraphs 67 to 78.

of the ECHR. *Secundo*, a given judgment of the European Court of Human Rights appears to require in some criminal case a procedural right or guarantee that does not appear to be available in EU antitrust proceedings. *Ergo*, EU antitrust proceedings are incompatible with the ECHR.

Such reasoning is liable to lead to erroneous conclusions to the extent that it disregards the case law of the European Court of Human Rights, which distinguishes, as to the level of protection required by the ECHR, according to the circumstances of the particular case:

> '*While the right to a fair trial under Article 6 [ECHR] is an unqualified right, what constitutes a fair trial cannot be the subject of a single unvarying rule but must depend on the circumstances of the particular case.*'[809]

Particularly relevant in the context of the enforcement of Articles 101 and 102 TFEU by the European Commission are the distinction between the hard core of criminal law and other areas of the law that are only 'criminal' within the Convention's wider meaning of that term, and the distinction between natural persons and companies.

Since its seminal judgment in *Jussila v Finland*,[810] the European Court of Human Rights distinguishes, within the broad range of procedures or penalties that are 'criminal' within the meaning of Article 6 ECHR, between the 'hard core of criminal law', and 'cases not strictly belonging to the traditional categories of the criminal law', which 'differ from the hard core of criminal law'. Antitrust enforcement such as that undertaken by the European Commission, which only involves the imposition on companies of fines, belongs to the second category, outside the hard core of criminal law. The criminal-head guarantees laid down in Article 6 ECHR do 'not necessarily apply with their full stringency' to cases belonging to the second category, outside the hard core of criminal law.[811]

This need for such a differentiated approach was recalled by the European Court of Human Rights in its 2019 judgment in *SA-Capital Oy v Finland*:

> '*A differentiated approach [. . .] can be seen to reflect the Court's [. . .] general focus on regarding, as its primary concern, the fairness of the proceedings as a whole, with a view to ensuring the rights of defence while also remaining mindful of the interests of the public and the victims in the proper enforcement of the laws in question. [. . .]*
>
> *Thus, in the light of the Court's established case-law, it is not a requirement under Article 6 of the Convention that proceedings such as those concerning sanctions*

809 Judgments of the European Court of Human Rights (Grand Chamber) of 29 June 2007 in Case of *O'Halloran and Francis v United Kingdom*, Applications nos 15809/02 and 25624/02, paragraph 53, and of 13 September 2016 in Case of *Ibrahim and Others v United Kingdom*, Applications nos 50541/08 and others, paragraph 250.

810 Judgment of the European Court of Human Rights (Grand Chamber) of 23 November 2006 in Case of *Jussila v Finland*, Application no 73053/01.

811 Idem, paragraph 43. Competition enforcement proceedings that can only lead to the finding of an infringement of the competition rules, without any possibility of fines being imposed, may not even be 'criminal' within the wider meaning of Article 6 ECHR and hence fall entirely outside Article 6 ECHR; see Judgment of 23 October 2018 in Case of *Produkcija Plus storitveno podjete D. A.o. v Slovenia*, Application no 47072/15, paragraphs 40 to 43.

for breaches of competition law be conducted according to the classical model of a criminal trial. [. . .]

In this context, the Court is further called upon to assess those issues with due regard to the particular nature of competition proceedings. [. . .]

[…], the Court acknowledges that cases concerning restrictions of competition typically involve complex and often wide-ranging economic matters and related factual issues, which means that the relevant elements of evidence will also be multifaceted. The Court is also aware of the strong public interest involved in the effective enforcement of competition law. Moreover, it is mindful of the fact that as a rule, the financial penalties applicable in this field are not imposed on natural persons but on corporate entities, quantified on the basis of the harmful effect of the anti-competitive conduct and taking into account the business turnover of the entities found to be in breach of competition rules.'[812]

As already mentioned, the distinction between natural persons and companies also appears to be relevant for the level of protection offered by the ECHR.[813]

For instance, while the European Court of Human Rights has held that the protection of the home provided for in Article 8 ECHR may in certain circumstances be extended to cover business premises, it has also held that public authorities' entitlement to interfere with this right, in accordance with Article 8(2) ECHR, 'might well be more far-reaching where professional or business activities or premises were involved than would otherwise be the case'.[814]

As explained further below, the distinction between natural persons and companies also appears to be particularly relevant for the privilege against self-incrimination.[815]

C. The enforcement of Articles 101 and 102 TFEU by EU Member State competition authorities

The above discussion has focussed on the enforcement of Articles 101 and 102 TFEU by the European Commission. Articles 101 and 102 TFEU are however also enforced by the competition authorities of the EU Member States (national competition authorities or NCAs). In fact, the national competition authorities have in quantitative terms become the primary public enforcers of Articles 101 and 102 TFEU, adopting 90% of all decisions.[816]

---

812 Judgment of the European Court of Human Rights of 14 February 2019 in Case of *SA-Capital Oy v Finland*, Application no 5556/10, paragraphs 71, 72, 77 and 78.

813 See M. Emberland, *The Human Rights of Companies: Exploring the Structure of ECHR Protection* (Oxford 2006) and P. J. Oliver, *The Fundamental Rights of Companies: EU, US and International Law Compared* (Hart 2020 forthcoming); see also A. Winkler, *We the Corporations – How American Businesses Won Their Civil Rights* (Liveright 2018).

814 Judgments of the European Court of Human Rights of 16 April 2002 in *Colas Est and Others v France*, Application no 37971/97, paragraph 41, and of 16 December 1991 in *Niemitz v Germany*, Series A no 251-B, paragraph 19.

815 See also my papers 'Self-Incrimination in EC Antitrust Enforcement: A Legal and Economic Analysis' (2003) 26 *World Competition* 567 and 'EU Antitrust Enforcement Powers and Procedural Rights and Guarantees: The Interplay between EU Law, National Law, the Charter of Fundamental Rights of the EU and the European Convention on Human Rights' (2011) 34 *World Competition* 189, both also accessible at http://ssrn.com/author=456087.

816 See the statistics in Chapter I of this book.

This raises the question whether the same level of protection of fundamental procedural rights should apply to the enforcement of Articles 101 and 102 TFEU by the national competition authorities as that which applies to the enforcement of Articles 101 and 102 TFEU by the European Commission.

The remainder of this chapter deals with this question. The enforcement by national competition authorities of their national competition laws is not dealt with in this chapter. It should, however, be kept in mind that Article 3(1) of Regulation 1/2003 contains an obligation for national competition authorities and national courts also to apply Articles 101 or 102 TFEU when applying national competition law to conduct falling within the scope of Articles 101 or 102 TFEU.[817]

1. Can EU Member States reduce fundamental rights protection below the EU level?

Can EU Member States apply a lower standard of protection of fundamental procedural rights to the enforcement of Articles 101 and 102 TFEU by their national competition authorities than the standard applicable to the enforcement of Articles 101 and 102 TFEU by the European Commission?

The answer to this question is clear and simple: no.

Article 3(1) of the so-called ECN+ Directive (Directive 2019/1)[818] states:

> 'Proceedings concerning infringements of Articles 101 or 102 TFEU, including the exercise of the powers referred to in this Directive by national competition authorities, shall comply with general principles of Union law and the Charter of Fundamental Rights of the European Union.'

This provision merely repeats what already follows from the case law of the EU Court of Justice and from Article 51(1) of the Charter.

Indeed, according to the case law, the requirements flowing from the protection of fundamental rights in the EU legal order are also binding on the Member States when they implement EU rules.[819]

Article 51(1) of the Charter similarly provides that the provisions of the Charter also apply to the Member States when they are implementing EU law.[820]

---

817 See Chapter II of this book.

818 Directive (EU) 2019/1 of the European Parliament and of the Council of 11 December 2018 to empower the competition authorities of the Member States to be more effective enforcers and to ensure the proper functioning of the internal market [2019] OJ L11/3.

819 Judgments in *Karlsson and Others*, C-292/97, EU:C:2000:202, paragraph 37, and in *Eturas and Others*, C-74/14, EU:C:2016:42, paragraph 38.

820 As already mentioned above, because of its specific wording, Article 41 of the Charter only applies to the institutions, bodies, offices and agencies of the European Union, not to the Member States. However, the content of Article 41 CFREU reflects general principles of EU law that as such also apply to the enforcement of Articles 101 and 102 TFEU by the competition authorities of the EU Member States; see Judgment in *YS and Others*, C-141/12 and C-372/12, EU:C:2014:2081, paragraphs 67 and 68.

a. *The example of legal professional privilege*

As mentioned above,[821] in EU law, the protection of legal professional privilege has the status of a general legal principle in the nature of a fundamental right, deriving inter alia from the Charter of Fundamental Rights of the EU.

In most EU Member States, national law provides for legal professional privilege under the same or very similar conditions as under EU law.

It would be contrary to EU law for competition authorities or courts of the EU Member States in cases of enforcement of Articles 101 or 102 TFEU to grant legal professional privilege under more restrictive conditions than those laid down in the case law of the EU Courts.

According to a comparative study by the OECD from 2019, in Germany, the right to claim legal privilege arises only after a specific investigation has started.[822]

This is more restrictive than under EU law. Indeed, according to the case law of the EU Court of Justice, legal professional privilege covers correspondence between lawyers and clients 'made for the purposes and in the interests of the client's rights of defence', covering not only 'all written communications exchanged after the initiation of the administrative procedure under [Regulation 1/2003] which may lead to a decision on the application of [Articles 101 and 102 TFEU] or to a decision imposing a pecuniary sanction on the undertaking' but also 'earlier written communications which have a relationship to the subject-matter of that procedure'.[823] In *AM & S Europe v Commission*, the EU Court of Justice accepted on this ground the protection of communications that dated from several years before the initiation of proceedings but that were 'drawn up during the period preceding, and immediately following, the accession of the United Kingdom to the [European Economic] Community, and that [were] principally concerned with how far it might be possible to avoid conflict between the applicant and the Community authorities on the applicant's position, in particular with regard to the Community provisions on competition'.[824]

When enforcing Articles 101 or 102 TFEU, the German competition authority, Bundeskartellamt and the German courts supervising the Bundeskartellamt, must in this respect apply the broader EU law standard and not the narrower German law standard of legal professional privilege. Companies can directly invoke EU law to ensure their rights in this respect.[825]

---

821 See also Chapter XIII of this book.

822 'Treatment of Legally Privileged Information in Competition Proceedings', Background Paper by the OECD Secretariat, DAF/COMP/WP3(2018)5 of 31 January 2019, paragraph 28. The law in Austria appears to be similar; see OECD, 'Summary of discussion of the roundtable on the treatment of legally privileged information in competition proceedings 26 November 2018', DAF/COMP/WP3/M(2018)2/ANN1/FINAL of 2 October 2019, at 6.

823 Judgment in *AM & S Europe v Commission*, 155/79, EU:C:1982:157, paragraph 23.

824 Judgment in *AM & S Europe v Commission*, 155/79, EU:C:1982:157, paragraph 34.

825 See also OECD, 'Summary of discussion of the roundtable on the treatment of legally privileged information in competition proceedings 26 November 2018', DAF/COMP/WP3/M(2018)2/ANN1/FINAL of 2 October 2019, at 6.

2. Can EU Member States grant procedural rights above the EU level?

Can EU Member States in the enforcement of Articles 101 and 102 TFEU by their national competition authorities grant companies more extensive procedural rights than those available in the enforcement of Articles 101 and 102 TFEU by the European Commission?

The answer to this question is more complex: generally yes, but not if such further procedural rights undermine the effective and uniform application of Articles 101 and 102 TFEU.

Article 35(1) of Regulation 1/2003 stipulates that the Member States are to 'designate the competition authority or authorities responsible for the application of [Articles 101 and 102 TFEU] in such a way that the provisions of this regulation are effectively complied with'.

In *VEBIC*, the EU Court of Justice clarified that '[t]he authorities so designated must, in accordance with the regulation, ensure that those Treaty Articles are applied effectively in the general interest', and that the laws of the Member States governing the powers and functioning of the national competition authorities 'must not jeopardise the attainment of the objective of the regulation, which is to ensure that Articles 101 and 102 TFEU are applied effectively by those authorities'.[826]

On this basis, the Court of Justice ruled to be contrary to EU law a system such as that which existed at the time in Belgium and which precluded the Belgian competition authority from appearing as a defendant or respondent before the Brussels Appeal Court when its decisions applying Articles 101 or 102 TFEU were appealed by the companies concerned.[827]

In *Schenker*, the Court of Justice has, in addition to the requirements of **effective** enforcement in the general interest already set out in *VEBIC*, also subjected the enforcement of Articles 101 and 102 TFEU by the NCAs to a requirement of **uniform** application of those Treaty Articles.[828]

On the basis of this requirement of not only effective but also uniform application of Articles 101 and 102 TFEU, the Court of Justice held for instance in *Schenker* that, when national law establishes conditions relating to intention or negligence for the imposition of fines by their national competition authorities, those conditions should be at least as stringent as the conditions laid down in Article 23 of Regulation 1/2003 for the imposition of fines by the European Commission, and that immunity from fines under national leniency programmes can be accorded only in strictly exceptional situations,

---

826 Judgment in *VEBIC*, C-439/08, EU:C:2010:739, paragraphs 56 and 57.

827 Judgment in *VEBIC*, C-439/08, EU:C:2010:739; see further Article 30 of the Directive 2019/1.

828 Judgment in *Schenker*, C-681/11, EU:C:2013:404, paragraphs 36, 46 and 49. See also Judgment in *AKKA/LAA*, C-177/16, EU:C:2017:689, paragraph 64, as well as recitals 10, 14, 16, 17, 40, 46 and 76 and Articles 4(1), 5(2) and 13(4) of Directive 2019/1.

such as where an undertaking's co-operation has been decisive in detecting and actually suppressing the cartel.[829]

This requirement of effective and uniform application of Articles 101 and 102 TFEU appears to go further than the general principle of effectiveness as applicable in all areas of EU law where Member States are entrusted with a role in the enforcement of EU law.[830]

This stricter requirement of effectiveness and uniformity would indeed appear justified in the case of Articles 101 and 102 TFEU, which, as discussed above, constitute fundamental provisions of the EU constitutional framework.[831]

a. *The example of legal professional privilege for in-house lawyers*

In EU law, a necessary condition for communications between lawyers and clients to be protected by legal professional privilege is that the lawyers are independent lawyers, who are not bound to the client by a relationship of employment.[832]

Following a lengthy debate among practitioners and scholars, the EU Court of Justice, following the Opinion of Advocate General Kokott,[833] confirmed in *Akzo Nobel Chemicals and Akcros Chemicals* v *Commission* the exclusion of in-house lawyers from legal professional privilege, even if those in-house lawyers are enrolled with a Bar or Law Society and subject to the corresponding professional ethical obligations.[834]

As the Court of Justice and Advocate General Kokott explained, this exclusion of all in-house lawyers, even if enrolled with a Bar or Law Society and subject to the corresponding professional ethical obligations, is not discriminatory. Indeed, in-house lawyers are in a fundamentally different position from external lawyers, because of the economic dependence and personal identification of a lawyer in an employment relationship with his undertaking.[835]

---

829 Judgment in *Schenker*, C-681/11, EU:C:2013:404, paragraphs 36, 46 and 49; see also Article 13 and recital 42 and Article 17 of Directive 2019/1.

830 See Judgments in *Commission v Greece*, 68/88, EU:C:1989:339, paragraphs 23–25, in *Edis*, C-231/96, EU:C:1998:401, paragraphs 34 and 36–37, and in *Commission v Ireland*, C-354/99, EU:C:2001:550, paragraph 46.

831 See also Judgment in *Melloni*, C-399/11, EU:C:2013:107, paragraphs 59 and 60, in which the EU Court of Justice held, in the context of the execution of a European arrest warrant, that, by virtue of the principle of primacy of EU law, which is an essential feature of the EU legal order, rules of national law, even of a constitutional order, cannot be allowed to undermine the effectiveness of EU law, and the application of national standards of protection of fundamental rights cannot compromise the primacy, unity and effectiveness of EU law.

832 Judgment in *AM & S Europe v Commission*, 155/79, EU:C:1982:157, paragraphs 21 to 26.

833 Opinion of Advocate General Kokott in *Akzo Nobel Chemicals and Akcros Chemicals v Commission*, C-550/07 P, EU:C:2010:229.

834 Judgment in *Akzo Nobel Chemicals and Akcros Chemicals v Commission*, C-550/07 P, EU:C:2010:512.
In-house lawyers, including those that are enrolled with a Bar or Law Society, are similarly excluded from representing parties (other than the EU or EEA Member States and the EU or EEA institutions) before the EU Courts; see Judgment in *Prezes Urzędu Komunikacji Elektronicznej and Republic of Poland v Commission*, C-422/11 P and C-423/11 P, EU:C:2012:553.

835 Judgment in *Akzo Nobel Chemicals and Akcros Chemicals v Commission*, C-550/07 P, EU:C:2010:512, paragraphs 56 to 58 and Opinion of Advocate General Kokott in *Akzo Nobel Chemicals and Akcros Chemicals v Commission*, C-550/07 P, EU:C:2010:229, paragraphs 58 to 71 and 83.

As further explained by Advocate General Kokott:

'There is a structural danger that an enrolled in-house lawyer – even if, as is usually the case, he is himself of good character and has the best intentions – will encounter a conflict of interests between his professional obligations and the aims and wishes of his company.

The susceptibility of an enrolled in-house lawyer to conflicts of interest also makes it difficult for him to raise an effective opposition to any abuses of legal professional privilege. Such abuse may, for example, consist in handing over evidence and information to an undertaking's legal department, under cover of a request for legal advice, for the sole or primary purpose, ultimately, of preventing the competition authorities of gaining access to that evidence and information. At worst, the functional departments of an undertaking may be tempted to misuse the company's internal legal department as a place for storing illegal documents such as cartel agreements and records of meetings between the parties to those cartels and of the modus operandi of a cartel.'[836]

Several attempts have been made to argue that the exclusion of in-house lawyers would somehow be contrary to the European Convention on Human Rights. These arguments were cogently rejected by Advocate General Kokott.[837] The European Court of Human Rights has not expressed any support for extending legal professional privilege to communications inside a company involving legal advice provided by an in-house lawyer employed by that company.[838]

As I have argued elsewhere,[839] both the fundamental rights arguments and the instrumental arguments for extending legal professional privilege to in-house lawyers are very weak.

Indeed, it is difficult to see how the possibility to consult in confidence an independent lawyer would be insufficient to guarantee fundamental rights, thereby creating a need to extend legal professional privilege to in-house counsel.[840] There is a wide choice of

---

836 Opinion of Advocate General Kokott in *Akzo Nobel Chemicals and Akcros Chemicals v Commission*, C-550/07 P, EU:C:2010:229, paragraphs 149 and 150.

837 Opinion of Advocate General Kokott in *Akzo Nobel Chemicals and Akcros Chemicals v Commission*, C-550/07 P, EU:C:2010:229, in particular paragraphs 47, 141, 148 and 152.

838 Idem, paragraph 141; see further the judgments of the European Court of Human Rights of 6 December 2012 in *Michaud v France* (Application no 12323/11), of 2 April 2015 in *Vinci Construction and GMT génie civil et services v France* (Applications nos 63629/10 and 60567/10), and of 26 July 2002 in *Meftah and Others v France* (Applications nos 32911/96, 35267/97 and 34595/97), paragraphs 45 to 47.

839 See my papers 'Powers of investigation and Procedural Rights and Guarantees in EU Antitrust Enforcement: The Interplay between European and National Legislation and Case-law' (2006) 29 *World Competition* 3, text accompanied by footnotes 75 to 81, and 'EU Antitrust Enforcement Powers and Procedural Rights and Guarantees: The Interplay between EU Law, National Law, the Charter of Fundamental Rights of the EU and the European Convention on Human Rights' (2011) 34 *World Competition* 189, text accompanied by footnotes 100 and 101, and Chapter XIII of this book.

840 See also Judgment in *Akzo Nobel Chemicals and Akcros Chemicals v Commission*, C-550/07 P, EU:C:2010:512, paragraphs 95 and 96: '[E]ven assuming that the consultation of in-house lawyers employed by the undertaking or group were to be covered by the right to obtain legal advice and representation, that would not exclude the application, were in-house lawyers are involved, of certain restrictions and rules relating to the exercise of the profession without that being regarded as adversely affecting the rights of the defence. Thus, in-house lawyers are not always able to represent their employer before all the national courts, although such

independent lawyers companies can turn to, and those companies that can afford to have in-house counsel can also afford to pay an independent lawyer.[841]

As mentioned above, instrumental arguments, to the effect that extending legal professional privilege to in-house lawyers would lead to better compliance with Articles 101 and 102 TFEU, are not convincing either.

Instrumental arguments were also brought up in the legislative process leading to the adoption of Regulation No 1/2003. Indeed, the Economic and Monetary Committee of the European Parliament initially adopted an amendment providing for the extension of legal professional privilege to in-house counsel,[842] but this amendment, which was strongly opposed by the European Commission, was subsequently rejected in plenary session of the Parliament by 404 votes against and 69 votes in favour.[843] The EU Council also declined to include any such extension in Regulation No 1/2003. The European Parliament, EU Council and European Commission thus rejected the arguments that extension of legal professional privilege to in-house counsel would be beneficial for the enforcement of Articles 101 and 102 TFEU.

Finally, the American model cannot be invoked as an argument for extending legal professional privilege to in-house lawyers under EU law. Indeed, no direct comparison can be drawn with the enforcement system in the USA.

In the EU system, extending legal professional privilege to in-house lawyers would be detrimental to the effectiveness of inspections and thus the possibility of detecting and collecting evidence of cartels and other infringements of Articles 101 and 102 TFEU. Inspections are a crucial instrument in EU antitrust enforcement.[844] European Commission decisions heavily rely on documentary evidence, which must be collected on the spot and cannot be complemented by summoning witnesses.

Extending legal professional privilege to in-house lawyers would be detrimental to the effectiveness of inspections in two ways. First, it would reduce the universe of the documents that can be found during an inspection that may contain useful evidence of the

---

rules restrict the possibilities open to potential clients in their choice of the most appropriate legal counsel. It follows from those considerations that any individual who seeks advice from a lawyer must accept the restrictions and conditions applicable to the exercise of that profession. The rules on legal professional privilege form part of those restrictions and conditions'; see also Judgment of the European Court of Human Rights of 26 July 2002 in *Meftah and Others v France* (Applications nos 32911/96, 35267/97 and 34595/97), paragraphs 45 to 47.

841 In fact, extension of legal professional privilege to in-house lawyers might lead to less protection of fundamental rights, in that it could lead large undertakings to use only in-house counsel, thus reducing the availability of independent lawyers on the open market, to the detriment of smaller companies that cannot afford in-house counsel.
See also, on legal aid for companies, Judgment in *DEB v Bundesrepublik Deutschland*, C-279/09, EU:C:2010:811.

842 Amendment No 10 contained in the Evans Report, EP Session document of 21 June 2001, PE 296.005.

843 Plenary of 6 September 2001, PE 308.749, page 35; see also Opinion of Advocate General Kokott in *Akzo Nobel Chemicals and Akcros Chemicals v Commission*, C-550/07 P, EU:C:2010:229, paragraph 106.

844 The success of leniency does not reduce the need for effective inspections; rather to the contrary, effective investigation powers and effective sanctions are preconditions for operating a successful leniency programme; see further my papers 'Leniency in Antitrust Enforcement: Theory and Practice' (2007) 30 *World Competition* 25, and Chapters V and XVIII of this book.

suspected infringement. More so than legal opinions of in-house lawyers,[845] the descriptions of facts contained in, and documents attached to, the communications to in-house lawyers from other members of staff regularly contain useful evidence. Secondly, extending legal professional privilege to in-house lawyers would significantly complicate and slow down inspections, as difficult and time-consuming discussions would take place between the inspectors and the company's lawyers to determine which communications with in-house lawyers are privileged. Speed in inspections is often of great importance in practice.

If legal professional privilege were extended to in-house lawyers, it would be difficult to define its precise scope in a way that does not invite abuse. In the US, where in-house lawyers are not, as a matter of principle, excluded from attorney-client privilege protection, the law appears to be rather uncertain. The problem is that unqualified application of the privilege to communications between all corporate employees and in-house counsel risks leading to zones of silence, through which the corporation could potentially channel all potentially incriminating documents and information. Lower court judgments and academic writing have proposed numerous competing tests to determine the acceptable scope of protection, mostly by limiting who is to be considered as the 'client' to whom communications are confidential (only the board, not other staff, etc.). In *Upjohn*,[846] the US Supreme Court opted for a case-by-case approach under which each case has to be judged in the light of the rationale of legal privilege protection. This approach arguably leaves a lot of legal uncertainty.

One can easily imagine this borderline problem being much more serious in the case of the European Union, in the absence of a common practice or understanding concerning the role and nature of in-house lawyers in the EU Member States. In the US at least, in-house counsel is a well-established function, present in all (large) corporations.

The US investigation system does not in any event rely to the same extent as that of the EU on on-the-spot inspections to collect documentary evidence. The US enforcement agencies work with discovery orders and witnesses. Disputes on the scope of legal professional privilege do not impinge directly on the powers of the US Department of Justice to gather the necessary evidence. This is partly explained by the extensive investigatory powers at the US Department of Justice's disposal, in particular the power to perform secret recordings by informants of telephone calls and meetings. Furthermore, the basic features of the US system, including criminal sanctions on individuals, grand jury and plea bargaining, give the US Department of Justice very significant leverage to obtain admissions from direct witnesses.[847]

---

845 As to the legal opinions of in-house lawyers, the European Commission stated in paragraph 37 of its *XXXIInd Report on Competition Policy 2002* (2003) that it 'will in future not consider, pursuant to its guidelines on the method of setting fines, as an aggravating circumstance to be taken into account in determining the amount of a pecuniary penalty to be imposed on a company, the fact that in-house legal advisers had warned the management of the illegality of the conduct forming the subject-matter of the Commission's decision. Such a communication may, however, be used as evidence of the existence of an infringement'. On the European Commission's method of setting fines, see further my paper 'The European Commission's 2006 Guidelines on Antitrust Fines: A Legal and Economic Analysis' (2007) 30 *World Competition* 197, also accessible at http://ssrn.com/author=456087.

846 *Upjohn Co. v United States*, 449 US 383 (1981).

847 For a critical assessment of the US system from a defence perspective, see L. W. Jacobs, 'Criminal Enforcement of Antitrust Laws – Problems with the US Model', in B. E. Hawk (ed) *2006 Annual Proceedings of the Fordham Corporate Law Institute – International Antitrust Law and Policy* (Juris Publishing 2007), 25.

Whilst the large majority of EU Member States exclude in-house lawyers from legal professional privilege, a few EU Member States also grant, under varying conditions, legal professional privilege protection to exchanges with in-house lawyers.[848]

In Portugal for instance, the Tribunal do Comércio de Lisboa (Lisbon Commercial Court) held in 2007 that in-house lawyers who are enrolled with the Ordem dos Advogados (Portuguese Bar Association) are also covered by legal professional privilege, even if the Autoridade da Concorrência (Portuguese Competition Authority) is investigating a suspected infringement of Articles 101 or 102 TFEU.[849]

However, the Tribunal do Comércio de Lisboa did not examine the question whether such extension of legal professional privilege beyond the EU law standard would undermine the effective and uniform application of Articles 101 and 102 TFEU.

As explained above, one of the reasons why under EU law legal professional privilege has not been extended to in-house lawyers, even if those in-house lawyers are enrolled with a Bar or Law Society and subject to the corresponding professional ethical obligations, is that such an extension would undermine the effectiveness of the enforcement of Articles 101 and 102 TFEU by the European Commission.

There is no sound basis for assuming that the extension of legal professional privilege to in-house lawyers would not similarly affect the effectiveness of the enforcement of Articles 101 and 102 TFEU by the competition authorities of the Member States.[850]

It follows that those Member States that currently recognise legal professional privilege for in-house lawyers in the context of the enforcement of Articles 101 and 102 TFEU by their national competition authorities appear in breach of EU law.

I am not necessarily arguing that the competition authorities or courts of all those Member States can directly invoke EU law to deny legal professional privilege to exchanges with in-house lawyers. In particular in Member States where (contrary to the Portuguese example) legal professional privilege for in-house lawyers has an explicit legislative basis, such direct invocation of EU law risks offending against the principle of legal certainty, which is a general principle of EU law.[851] In any event, the Member States concerned are under an obligation to enact the necessary legislation to exclude all in-house lawyers from legal professional privilege in cases of enforcement of Articles 101 or 102 TFEU

---

848 See 'Treatment of Legally Privileged Information in Competition Proceedings', Background Paper by the OECD Secretariat, DAF/COMP/WP3(2018)5 of 31 January 2019, paragraph 19 and footnote 3.

849 Tribunal do Comércio de Lisboa, Judgment of 6 December 2007 in *Unilever Jéronimo Martins v Autoridade da Concorrência*.

850 In none of the Member States concerned do the competition authorities, when enforcing Articles 101 and 102 TFEU, have criminal enforcement powers similar to those of the US Department of Justice that might counterbalance the weakening of enforcement powers resulting from the extension of legal professional privilege to in-house lawyers. Moreover, Article 13(1) of Directive 2019/1 obliges EU Member States to provide for the effective imposition of fines for violations of Articles 101 and 102 TFEU in **non-criminal** proceedings.

851 See Judgments in *X*, C-60/02, EU:C:2004:10, paragraph 61, in *Berlusconi*, C-387/02 etc., EU:C:2005:270, paragraph 74, and in *M.A.S.*, C-42/17, EU:C:2017:936.

by their national competition authorities.[852] The European Commission could bring proceedings pursuant to Article 258 TFEU against those Member States that fail to do so.

b. *The example of the right to remain silent for legal persons*

Under EU law, companies or other legal persons investigated by the European Commission for possible infringement of Articles 101 or 102 TFEU are under an obligation to cooperate actively with the investigation. They cannot claim a general right to remain silent, the privilege against self-incrimination being limited to the right not to be compelled to provide the Commission with answers that might involve admission on the company's part of the existence of an infringement.[853]

As already mentioned above, in refusing, in the context of the enforcement of Articles 101 and 102 TFEU by the European Commission, to extend the privilege against self-incrimination to a general right to remain silent, the EU Courts have taken into account the need to preserve the effectiveness of this enforcement:

> '*Thus, an undertaking in receipt of a decision requesting information pursuant to Article 18(3) of Regulation No 1/2003 cannot be recognised as having an absolute right of silence. To acknowledge the existence of such a right would be to go beyond what is necessary in order to preserve the rights of defence of undertakings, and would constitute an unjustified hindrance to the Commission's performance of its duty to ensure that the rules on competition within the internal market are observed. A right of silence can be acknowledged only to the extent that the undertaking concerned would be compelled to provide answers which might involve an admission on its part of the existence of an infringement which it is incumbent upon the Commission to prove.*'[854]

Whilst EU law does not grant a right to remain silent for companies and other **legal persons**, it recognises the right to remain silent for **natural persons** who are suspects or accused persons in criminal proceedings, in line with the case law of the European Court of Human Rights.[855]

---

852 In Belgium, the extension of legal professional privilege to in-house counsel results from Article 5 of the Law of 1 March 2000, and could thus be reversed by repealing or amending this provision; see Judgment of the Brussels Court of Appeals of 5 March 2013 in Case 2011/MR/3.
It would not appear that in any of those Member States that extend legal professional privilege to in-house counsel, this extension is in the nature of a constitutional or fundamental right. In any event, according to the case law of the EU Court of Justice, by virtue of the principle of primacy of EU law, which is an essential feature of the EU legal order, rules of national law, even of a constitutional order, cannot be allowed to undermine the effectiveness of EU law, and the application of national standards of protection of fundamental rights cannot compromise the primacy, unity and effectiveness of EU law; see Judgment in *Melloni*, C-399/11, EU:C:2013:107, paragraphs 59 and 60.

853 See Judgment in *Orkem v Commission*, 374/87, EU:C:1989:387, paragraphs 35–40; Judgment and Opinion of Advocate General Geelhoed in *Commission v SGL Carbon*, C-301/04 P, EU:C:2006:432 and EU:C:2006:53; Judgment in *Qualcomm and Qualcomm Europe v Commission*, T-371/17, EU:T:2019:232, paragraphs 177 to 194; Opinion of Advocate General Wahl in *HeidelbergCement v Commission*, C-247/14 P, EU:C:2015:694, paragraphs 149 to 164; recital 23 of Regulation 1/2003; and my paper 'Self-Incrimination in EC Antitrust Enforcement: A Legal and Economic Analysis' (2003) 26 *World Competition* 567, also accessible at http://ssrn.com/author=456087.

854 Judgment in *Qualcomm and Qualcomm Europe v Commission*, T-371/17, EU:T:2019:232, paragraph 181, citing earlier case law, going back to Judgment in *Limburgse Vinyl Maatschappij and Others v Commission*, T-305/94 etc., EU:T:1999:80, paragraph 448, confirmed by Judgment in *Limburgse Vinyl Maatschappij and Others v Commission*, C-238/99 P etc., EU:C:2002:582, paragraph 272.

855 See Articles 2 and 7(1) of Directive (EU) 2016/343 of the European Parliament and of the Council of 9 March 2016 on the strengthening of certain aspects of the presumption of innocence and the right to be present at the trial in criminal proceedings [2016] OJ L65/1, and Judgment of 2 February 2021, *DB v Consob*, C-481/19, EU:C:2021:84.

All the judgments in which the European Court of Human Rights has recognised a right to remain silent under Article 6 ECHR concern natural persons.[856] The German Constitutional Court has held that the privilege against self-incrimination contained in the German Constitution does not extend to legal persons, because it is grounded in the protection of individual human dignity.[857] Similarly, under the US Constitution, legal persons cannot invoke the privilege against self-incrimination.[858]

Distinguishing between natural and legal persons, and granting only the former a right to remain silent, indeed makes eminent sense.[859]

The right to remain silent protects suspects from being subjected to improper physical or psychological pressure, thus avoiding miscarriages of justice (as statements made under pressure risk being unreliable) and safeguarding human dignity and autonomy.[860]

The importance of the right to remain silent for natural persons in the context of traditional criminal law cannot be overstated, and can easily be illustrated with examples, such as that of the Birmingham Six.[861] In 1974, within hours of the explosion of bombs planted by the IRA in two crowded Birmingham pubs, five Irishmen were arrested. A sixth was arrested the next day. They were kept in police custody for three days and two nights, and subjected to violence and intimidation, resulting in four confessions. In the subsequent trial, the six men were found guilty of murder and sentenced to multiple life sentences. It later turned out that they had actually nothing to do with the bombings, and they finally were released in 1991, after 16 years in prison.

More generally, confession evidence has been implicated in numerous wrongful convictions, and psychological research has shown that false confessions are worryingly simple to extract.[862]

None of these serious concerns applies, however, to the situation of a company or other legal person being compelled to respond in writing, through its external lawyers or with

---

856 See inter alia *Funke v France* (judgment of 25 February 1993, Series A no 256-A), *John Murray v United Kingdom* (judgment of 8 February 1996, *Reports* 1996-I, p 49), *Saunders v United Kingdom* (judgment of 17 December 1996, *Reports* 1996-VI, p 2064), *J.B. v Switzerland* (judgment of 3 May 2001, Application no 31827/96), *Weh v Austria* (judgment of 8 April 2004, Application no 38544/97), *O'Halloran and Francis v United Kingdom* (judgment of 29 June 2007, Applications nos 15809/02 and 25624/02). See also Opinion of Advocate General Geelhoed in *Commission v SGL Carbon*, C-301/04 P, EU:C:2006:53, paragraphs 62 to 67, and Opinion of Advocate General Pikamäe of 27 October 2020, *DB v Consob*, C-481/19, EU:C:2020:861, paragraphs 97 to 99.

857 BVerfG, 26 February 1997, 1 BvR 2172/96.

858 *Braswell v United States*, 487 US 99 (1988).

859 See also J. Dine, 'Criminal Law and the Privilege Against Self-Incrimination', in S. Peers and A. Ward, *The European Union Charter of Fundamental Rights* (Hart 2004), 269–286.

860 See European Court of Human Rights, *Saunders v United Kingdom*, 17 December 1996, *Reports of Judgments and Decisions* 1996-VI, p 2064.

861 See C. Mullin, *Error of Judgment: The Truth About the Birmingham Bombings* (Chatto & Windus 1986), and C. Mullin, 'Diary', *London Review of Books*, 21 February 2019.

862 See J. T. Perillo and S. M. Kassin, 'Inside Interrogation: The Lie, The Bluff, and False Confessions' (2011) 35 *Law and Human Behaviour* 327; 'False confessions – Silence is golden – People have a strange and worrying tendency to admit things they have not, in fact, done', *The Economist*, 13 August 2011; and S. M. Kassin, 'False Confessions: Causes, Consequences, and Implications for Reform' (2014) 1 *Policy Insights from the Behavioral and Brain Sciences* 112.

their help,[863] to a written request for information from the European Commission or a national competition authority investigating a possible infringement of Articles 101 and 102 TFEU.

From a fundamental rights perspective, there is no justification whatsoever for treating the situation of legal persons responding in writing to written requests for information in competition investigations as similar to the questioning of natural persons in the context of traditional criminal law. Equating the two would be – to use the words of Advocate General Ruiz-Jarabo Colomer quoted above[864] – a mockery.

As already mentioned, according to the German Constitutional Court, the privilege against self-incrimination contained in the German Constitution does not extend to legal persons, because it is grounded in the protection of individual human dignity. Until before the transposition of Directive 2019/1 into German law,[865] secondary (non-constitutional) German law had however extended the right to remain silent to legal persons in proceedings by the Bundeskartellamt that can lead to the imposition of a fine (*Bußgeldverfahren*).

As mentioned above, one of the reasons why the EU Courts have refused, in the context of the enforcement of Articles 101 and 102 TFEU by the European Commission, to extend the privilege against self-incrimination to a general right to remain silent, is that such extension would hinder the effective enforcement of Articles 101 and 102 TFEU by the European Commission. There is no reason to assume that this would be any different for the Bundeskartellamt.[866] In this respect, German law thus appeared in breach of the EU law requirement of effective and uniform application of Articles 101 and 102 TFEU, and the German legislator was under an obligation to amend its law.

That German law had to be changed in this respect followed also from Directive 2019/1, Article 8 of which provides as follows:

> '*Member States shall ensure that national administrative competition authorities may require undertakings and associations of undertakings to provide all necessary information for the application of Articles 101 and 102 TFEU [. . .]. Such requests for information shall be proportionate and not compel the addressees of the requests to admit an infringement of Articles 101 and 102 TFEU. [...]*'

---

863 See Article 18(4) of Regulation 1/2003.

864 Opinion of Advocate General Ruiz-Jarabo Colomer in *Volkswagen v Commission*, C-338/00 P, EU:C:2002:591, paragraph 66.

865 Directive (EU) 2019/1 of the European Parliament and of the Council of 11 December 2018 to empower the competition authorities of the Member States to be effective enforcers and to ensure the proper functioning of the internal market [2019] OJ L11/3. According to its Article 34(1), Member States must bring into force the laws, regulations and administrative provisions necessary to comply with this Directive by 4 February 2021.

866 See also K. Ost, 'The Right to an Independent and Impartial Tribunal and the Right not to Incriminate Oneself – With Special Regard to the Situation in Germany', in C. Baudenbacher (ed), *Current Developments in European and International Competition Law – 14th St Gallen International Competition Law Forum ICF 2007* (Helbing Lichtenhahn 2008) 201, and Bundeskartellamt, 'Kartellbußgeldverfahren zwischen deutschem Systemdenken und europäischer Konvergenz', Hintergrundpapier, Arbeitskreis Kartellrecht, 4.10.2012.

That this provision is meant to harmonise the privilege against self-incrimination for legal persons along the lines of the case law of the EU Courts is clear from the accompanying recital 35, which reads as follows:

> '*While the right to require information is crucial for the detection of infringements, such requests [. . .] should not compel an undertaking [. . .] to admit that it has committed an infringement, which is incumbent on the NCAs to prove. This should be without prejudice to the obligations of undertakings [. . .] to answer factual questions and to provide documents. [...]*'

As part of its transposition of the Directive 2019/1, Germany has indeed changed its national law in this respect.[867]

[867] See Gesetz zur Änderung des Gesetzes gegen Wettbewerbsbeschränkungen für ein fokussiertes, proaktives und digitales Wettbewerbsrecht 4.0 und anderer Bestimmungen (GWB-Digitalisierungsgesetz), 18 January 2021.

XI. The Role of the Hearing Officer in Antitrust Proceedings before the European Commission

This chapter deals with the role of the Hearing Officer in proceedings conducted by the European Commission for the enforcement of Articles 101 and 102 TFEU. After a brief discussion of the history and status of the Hearing Officer, this chapter examines the various powers and tasks of the Hearing Officer (other than the organisation and conduct of the oral hearing, which is discussed in the next chapter of this book).

A. Introduction

Council Regulation 1/2003,[868] the main implementing regulation of Articles 101 and 102 TFEU, does not mention the Hearing Officer. Indeed, the Hearing Officer is a creature not of the Council but of the Commission itself in its internal organisation.

Antitrust proceedings conducted by the European Commission are further regulated by Commission Regulation 773/2004.[869] This implementing regulation provides for a (formal) oral hearing as a step in (certain of) the Commission's proceedings, and stipulates that such oral hearings shall be conducted by a Hearing Officer.[870]

B. History

As the Commission recalled in its Eighteenth Report on Competition Policy, '[a]t the suggestion of the business and industrial community, endorsed by the European Parliament, the Commission created the post of Hearing Officer on 1 September 1982'.[871]

In its Eleventh Report on Competition Policy, the Commission had announced for the first time that it envisaged 'appointing hearing officers, duly authorized to chair hearings, vested with genuine autonomy and the right of access to the responsible Member of the Commission. This would provide an even better guarantee that the Commission, when stating its view on an individual case as a decision-making authority, would be

---

868 Council Regulation (EC) No 1/2003 of 16 December 2002 on the implementation of the rules on competition laid down in Articles 81 and 82 of the Treaty [2003] OJ L1/1, last amended by Council Regulation (EC) No 1419/2006 [2006] OJ L269/1.

869 Commission Regulation (EC) No 773/2004 of 7 April 2004 relating to the conduct of proceedings by the Commission pursuant to Articles 81 and 82 of the EC Treaty [2004] OJ L123/18, last amended by Commission Regulation (EU) 2015/1348 of 3 August 2015 [2015] OJ L208/3.
See also Commission notice on best practices for the conduct of proceedings concerning Articles 101 and 102 TFEU [2011] OJ C308/6 ('Notice on Best Practices').

870 Article 14 of Regulation 773/2004.

871 Commission, Eighteenth Report on Competition Policy 1988 (1989), paragraph 44.

fully informed of all the features of the case whether favourable or unfavourable to the undertakings'.[872]

At the same time, the Commission stressed that its antitrust procedures are administrative, that the oral hearing should not be turned into a trial, and that the Hearing Officer could not have powers similar to those of administrative law judges at the Federal Trade Commission in the United States, as this would not seem compatible with the EU Treaties.[873]

According to Marc van der Woude, the creation of the Hearing Officer was thus a means to soften the contradiction between the administrative and inquisitorial nature of the Commission's antitrust procedures and the need to guarantee rights of a contradictory nature, as resulting from the case law of the Court of Justice on fair proceedings and rights of the defence.[874]

In 1994, the Commission extended the role of the Hearing Officer to cover not only the oral hearing but the whole of the administrative procedure and granted them decisional powers to resolve certain procedural disputes between the Directorate-General for Competition and the parties.[875]

Following this extension, the role of the 'Hearing Officer', as they are still called today, would arguably be better described by the title 'Procedural Officer', as the similar function introduced by the UK Competition and Markets Authority in 2014 is called.

The powers and functions of the Hearing Officer are currently defined by Decision 2011/695 of the President of the European Commission on the function and terms of reference of the Hearing Officer in certain competition proceedings (hereafter: 'Decision 2011/695' or 'the Terms of Reference').[876]

C. Status

The European Commission is a collegiate body composed of a number of commissioners equal to the number of EU Member States.[877] One of these commissioners has special responsibility for competition ('the Competition Commissioner'). The Directorate-General for Competition ('DG Competition') is the department of the Commission

---

[872] Commission, Eleventh Report on Competition Policy 1981 (1982), paragraph 26.

[873] Commission, Eleventh Report on Competition Policy 1981 (1982), paragraph 27.

[874] M. van der Woude, 'Hearing Officers and EU Antitrust Procedures: The Art of Making Subjective Procedures More Objective' (1996) 33 Common Market Law Review 531–546 at 532.

[875] For a full overview of the successive extensions of the role of the Hearing Officer until before Decision 2011/695/EU, see M. Albers and J. Jourdan, 'The Role of the Hearing Officers in EU Competition Proceedings: A Historical and Practical Perspective' (2011) 2 *Journal of European Competition Law & Policy* 185–200.

[876] Decision 2011/695/EU of the President of the European Commission of 13 October 2011 on the function and terms of reference of the Hearing Officer in competition proceedings [2011] OJ L275/29.

[877] According to Article 17(3) of the Treaty on European Union (TEU), 'in carrying out its responsibilities, the Commission shall be completely independent', and 'the members of the Commission shall neither seek nor take instructions from any Government'; see further Chapter III of this book.

services that conducts competition investigations, under the authority of the Competition Commissioner.

The Hearing Officer is a member of the Commission's staff, appointed by the Commission in accordance with the normal staff regulations.[878] In a departure from the normal rules, Decision 2011/695 provides that 'the appointment shall be published in the *Official Journal of the European Union*. Any interruption, termination or transfer of the Hearing Officer shall be the subject of a reasoned decision of the Commission. That decision shall be published in the *Official Journal of the European Union*'.[879] One of the recitals of Decision 2011/695 adds that the Hearing Officer should be 'an independent person experienced in competition matters who has the integrity necessary to contribute to the objectivity, transparency and efficiency of [competition] proceedings'.[880]

Decision 2011/695 stipulates that, in order to ensure independence from DG Competition, the Hearing Officer is attached, for administrative purposes, to the Competition Commissioner,[881] and that, 'in exercising his or her functions, the Hearing Officer shall act independently'.[882]

D. General mission

Article 1(2) of the Terms of Reference sets out the general mission of the Hearing Officer as follows:

'The Hearing Officer shall safeguard the effective exercise of procedural rights throughout competition [antitrust and merger] proceedings before the Commission.'

These procedural rights include all rights set out in the applicable regulations, all rights recognised by the Charter of Fundamental Rights of the EU (and hence also all rights guaranteed by the European Convention on Human Rights), as well as all rights recognised in the case law of the Court of Justice.[883]

---

878 Article 2(1), first sentence, and recital 6 of Decision 2011/695; recital 6 recalls that 'in accordance with those rules, consideration may also be given to candidates who are not officials of the Commission'.

879 Second, third and fourth sentence of Article 2(1) of Decision 2011/695; for examples of such publications, see Communication from the Commission – Termination of appointment of Hearing Officer [2010] OJ C78/1, and Appointment of the Hearing Officer [2010] OJ C278/16, as well as Press release IP/10/1114.

880 Recital 3 of Decision 2011/695.

881 Article 2(2) and recital 5 of Decision 2011/695; recital 7 adds that the Commission should provide for supporting staff.

882 Article 3(1) of Decision 2011/695. The attachment to the Competition Commissioner is thus only for administrative purposes. In exercising their functions, the Hearing Officer shall act independently, and shall thus neither seek nor take instructions from the Competition Commissioner.

883 Recital 2 of Decision 2011/695 and recital 37 of Regulation 1/2003; the reference to the Court of Justice must be understood as referring to the Court of Justice of the European Union, the EU institution which also includes the General Court; see Articles 13(1) and 19(1) TEU.
For an analysis of the different sources of procedural rights in EU competition enforcement (including the relationship between the Charter of Fundamental Rights of the EU and the European Convention on Human Rights), see my paper 'EU Antitrust Enforcement powers and Procedural Rights and Guarantees: The Interplay between EU Law, National Law, the Charter of Fundamental Rights of the EU and the European Convention on Human Rights', accessible at http://ssrn.com/author=456087. See also Judgment in *Tele2 Sverige*, C-203/15, EU:C:2016:970, paragraphs 127 to 129, and Chapter 10 of this book.

It is also clear from the Terms of Reference that in principle the procedural rights of all parties involved in competition proceedings are covered, thus also the rights of complainants and third persons.[884]

The Hearing Officer's mission is limited to competition proceedings before the European Commission. The Hearing Officer is thus not competent to deal with complaints in relation to the effective exercise of procedural rights in competition proceedings before the competition authorities of the Member States, even if these complaints concern the cooperation between the Commission and a national competition authority.[885]

Whereas the focus of the Hearing Officer's mission is on safeguarding the effective exercise of procedural rights, Article 3(2) of the Terms of Reference adds as follows:

'In exercising his or her functions, the Hearing Officer shall take account of the need for effective application of the competition rules in accordance with Union legislation in force and the principles laid down by the Court of Justice.'[886]

As the Terms of Reference recall, the primary obligation to respect the procedural rights of all parties involved in competition proceedings lies with DG Competition, which is responsible for the conduct of these proceedings. The Hearing Officer provides a safeguard, in that parties may refer to the Hearing Officer for independent review any issues regarding the effective exercise of their procedural rights that have not been resolved in prior contacts with DG Competition.[887]

Whereas Article 1(2) of the Terms of Reference sets out the general mission of the Hearing Officer, this provision is largely programmatic, the precise powers and functions of the Hearing Officer being set out in the various detailed provisions of the Terms of Reference.[888]

These powers and functions can be grouped into four categories, which are discussed in detail in the following sections: First, the Hearing Officer plays a direct role in the

---

884 Recital 3 of Decision 2011/695.

885 See for instance Order in *Henkel and Henkel France v Commission*, T-64/12, EU:T:2013:116, concerning the refusal by the Commission to transmit certain documents to the French Competition Authority for use in proceedings before the latter.

886 See also Judgment in *SKW Stahl-Metallurgie v Commission*, T-384/09, EU:T:2014:27, paragraph 61 (referring to the requirements of a proper progress of the administrative proceedings, which must lead, within a reasonable time after the opening of proceedings, to a decision by the Commission), and Opinion of Advocate General Geelhoed in *Commission v SGL Carbon*, C-301/04 P, EU:C:2006:53, paragraph 67 ('it must be said that the interplay between the fundamental rights of legal persons and competition enforcement remains a balancing exercise: at stake are the protection of fundamental rights versus effective enforcement of [EU] competition law. As the Court of Justice held in *Eco Swiss* [Article 101 TFEU] is a fundamental provision which is essential for the accomplishment of the tasks entrusted to the [Union] and, in particular, for the functioning of the internal market. [Article 101 TFEU] forms part of public policy. [. . .] It is self-evident that the effective enforcement with reasonable means of the basic tenets of the [EU] public order should remain possible, just as it is evident that the rights of the defence should be respected too').

887 Recital 8 and Article 3(7) of Decision 2011/695.

888 See Article 1(1) of Decision 2011/695. Article 1(2) can, however, be relevant for the interpretation of the other more detailed provisions of the Terms of Reference; see Judgment in *Evonik Degussa v Commission*, C-162/15 P, EU:C:2017:205, paragraph 40: 'Article 1(2) of Decision 2011/695, as clarified by recital 9 of that decision, provides that the terms of reference of the hearing officer must be framed in such a way as to safeguard the effective exercise of procedural rights throughout proceedings before the Commission pursuant to Articles 101 TFEU and 102 TFEU, in particular the right to be heard.'

conduct of competition proceedings, in that they organise and conduct the oral hearing, and decide on applications to be heard by interested third persons. Secondly, parties involved in competition proceedings may refer issues relating to the effective exercise of their procedural rights to the Hearing Officer for independent review. Depending on the procedural right and the situation concerned, the Hearing Officer has decisional powers, may make a recommendation, or may report on the matter to the Competition Commissioner and to the College of Members of the Commission. Thirdly, on their own initiative, the Hearing Officer may, and to a certain extent must, verify the respect for procedural rights, and report on the matter to the Competition Commissioner and to the College of Members of the Commission. Finally, the Hearing Officer may provide advice to the Competition Commissioner on any matter arising out of any antitrust proceeding, including thus not only procedural but also substantive matters.

E. Direct role in the conduct of competition proceedings

Commission competition proceedings are in principle conducted by DG Competition. By way of exception, two parts of the proceedings are conducted directly by the Hearing Officer: the oral hearing, and decisions on applications to be heard by interested third persons.

1. Oral hearing

At the request of parties to whom the Commission has addressed a statement of objections, an oral hearing will be held, so that such parties can further develop their written submissions. The Hearing Officer organises and conducts this oral hearing.[889]

This is the oldest task of the Hearing Officer, going back to the creation of the function in the early 1980s.

For a detailed discussion of the oral hearing, the reader is referred to Chapter XII of this book.

2. Decisions on applications to be heard by interested third persons

In antitrust proceedings, the Commission must, before taking an adverse decision, give the undertakings or associations of undertakings that are the subject of the proceedings the opportunity of being heard.[890] Complainants must also be given the opportunity to be heard.[891] Other natural or legal persons also have a right to be heard, provided that they show a sufficient interest.[892]

---

889 Articles 6(1) and 10 of Decision 2011/695.

890 Article 27 of Regulation 1/2003 and Articles 10 and 11 of Regulation 773/2004.

891 See Articles 7(2) and 27(1) of Regulation 1/2003 and Articles 5, 6 and 7 of Regulation 773/2004, and Commission Notice on the handling of complaints [2004] OJ C101/5.

892 Article 27(3) of Regulation 1/2003 and Article 13 of Regulation 773/2004. Recital 32 of Regulation 1/2003 clarifies what is meant by 'a sufficient interest' – namely, that the third party's interests may be affected by a decision – and recital 11 of Regulation 773/2004 indicates that consumer associations that apply to be heard should generally be regarded as having a sufficient interest, where the proceedings concern products or services used by the end consumer or products or services that constitute a direct input into such products or services.

Article 5 of the Terms of Reference empowers the Hearing Officer to decide whether third persons are to be heard, after consulting the Director from DG Competition responsible for the case.[893]

Applications to be heard by interested third persons must be submitted in writing, and explain the applicant's interest in the outcome of the procedure.[894] In antitrust proceedings, applications to be heard can be submitted from the date of the initiation of proceedings and until the Commission consults the Advisory Committee on the basis of a draft decision.[895]

Where the Hearing Officer considers that an applicant has not shown a sufficient interest to be heard, they must inform the applicant in writing of the reasons thereof, and set a time limit for a further written submission. If the applicant responds within the time limit and the written submission does not lead to a different assessment, the Hearing Officer will take a reasoned decision.[896]

If the application to be heard is granted by the Hearing Officer, DG Competition will then inform the interested third person in writing of the nature and subject matter of the procedure,[897] and set a time limit within which it may make known its views in writing.[898]

The Hearing Officer must inform the parties to the proceedings as from the initiation of proceedings of the identities of interested third persons to be heard, unless such disclosure would significantly harm a person or undertaking.[899] In particular, according to the case law of the Court of Justice and the General Court, keeping the identity of third parties confidential is justified where there is a risk that an undertaking holding a dominant position in the market might adopt retaliatory measures against competitors, suppliers or customers that have collaborated in the investigation carried out by the Commission.[900]

---

893 Article 5(2) of Decision 2011/695 adds that, in assessing whether a third person shows a sufficient interest, the Hearing Officer shall take into account whether and to what extent the applicant is sufficiently affected by the conduct that is the subject of the competition proceedings. The second sentence of recital 12 of Decision 2011/695 adds that consumer associations that apply to be heard should generally be regarded as having a sufficient interest, where the proceedings concern products or services used by end consumers or products or services that constitute a direct input into such products or services.

894 Article 5(1) of Decision 2011/695.

895 See Article 11(6) of Regulation 1/2003, Article 2 of Regulation 773/2004 and paragraphs 17 to 23 of the Notice on Best Practices; Judgment in *Österreichische Postsparkasse and Bank für Arbeit und Wirtschaft v Commission*, T-213/01 and T-214/01, EU:T:2006:151, paragraphs 148 to 151; and, by analogy, W. Wils and H. Abbott, 'Access to the File in Competition Proceedings Before the European Commission' (2019) 42 *World Competition* 255, updated version accessible at http://ssrn.com/author=456087, text accompanied by footnotes 178 to 181.

896 Article 5(3) of Decision 2011/695.

897 The General Court has held that the Commission may, without being obliged to do so, provide this information by transmitting to the interested third person a non-confidential version of the statement of objections; see Judgment in *Österreichische Postsparkasse and Bank für Arbeit und Wirtschaft v Commission*, T-213/01 and T-214/01, EU:T:2006:151, paragraph 107.

898 Article 13(1) of Regulation 733/2004. In these written comments, the interested third person may also request to develop its arguments at the oral hearing, if there is an oral hearing.

899 Article 5(4) of Decision 2011/695; see Article 11(6) of Regulation 1/2003, Article 2 of Regulation 773/2004 and paragraphs 17 to 23 of the Notice on Best Practices.

900 Judgments in *BPB Industries and British Gypsum v Commission*, C-310/93 P, EU:C:1995:101, paragraphs 26 and 27, and in *General Electric v Commission*, T-210/01, EU:T:2005:456, paragraph 650.

F. Independent review of issues concerning the effective exercise of procedural rights

As the Terms of Reference recall, the primary obligation to respect the procedural rights of all parties involved in competition proceedings lies with DG Competition, which is responsible for the conduct of these proceedings. The Hearing Officer provides a safeguard, in that parties may refer to the Hearing Officer for independent review any issues regarding the effective exercise of their procedural rights that have not been resolved in prior contacts with DG Competition.[901] Depending on the procedural right and the situation concerned, the Hearing Officer has decisional powers, may make a recommendation, or may report on the matter to the Competition Commissioner and to the College of Members of the Commission.

1. Decisional powers

The Terms of Reference have granted the Hearing Officer decisional powers in relation to five matters: extension of the time limit for replying to a decision requesting information in antitrust proceedings; right to be informed of one's procedural status in antitrust investigations; extension of the time limit for replying to a statement of objections or for making known one's views; access to the file or access to documents or information; and disclosure of business secrets or other confidential information.

a. *Extension of the time limit for replying to a decision requesting information in antitrust proceedings*

The Commission can, pursuant to Article 18(3) of Regulation 1/2003, by decision require undertakings and associations of undertakings to provide all necessary information (that is, either to hand over existing documents or to provide answers to questions) specified in the decision within a time limit fixed in the decision.[902]

---

901 Recital 8 and Article 3(7) of Decision 2011/695. In order to refer a matter to the Hearing Officer, it is not sufficient to put the Hearing Officer in copy of the prior request addressed to DG Competition. A separate request to the Hearing Officer following the rejection by DG Competition of the prior request is required; see Judgment in *Toshiba Samsung Storage Technology v Commission*, T-8/16, EU:T:2019:522, paragraphs 111 and 114 to 117. The request must also be clear and specific; see Judgment in *United Parcel Service v Commission*, T-834/17, EU:T:2022:84, paragraph 167. Not referring the matter to the Hearing Officer after the issue has not been resolved with DG Competition may negatively affect the possibility of later seeking in court the annulment of the Commission's final decision on the ground of violation of one's rights of the defence; see Judgments in *Mannesmannröhren-Werke v Commission*, T-44/00, EU:T:2004:218, paragraph 53, in *Campine and Campine Recycling v Commission*, T-240/17, EU:T:2019:778, paragraph 98, in *HeidelbergCement and Schwenk Zement v Commission*, T-380/17, EU:T:2020:471, paragraph 663, and in *United Parcel Service v Commission*, T-834/17, EU:T:2022:84, paragraphs 171 and 181; see also Opinion of Advocate General Mazák in *Knauf v Commission*, C-407/08 P, EU:C:2010:70, paragraph 38.

902 Article 18(1) and (3) of Regulation 1/2003 specifies that the Commission can only make requests for information 'in order to carry out the duties assigned to it by this Regulation' and that the decision 'shall stipulate the legal basis and purpose of the request'; see Judgments in *HeidelbergCement v Commission*, C-247/14 P, EU:C:2016:149, *Schwenk Zement v Commission*, C-248/14 P, EU:C:2016:150, *Buzzi Unichem v Commission*, C-267/14 P, EU:C:2016:151, and *Italmobiliare v Commission*, C-268/14 P, EU:C:2016:152, in *Slovak Telekom v Commission*, T-458/09 and T-171/10, EU:T:2012:145, and in *Schwenk Zement v Commission*, T-306/11, EU:T:2014:123, *Cemex v Commission*, T-292/11, EU:T:2014:125, *Cementos Portland Valderrivas v Commission*, T-296/11, EU:T:2014:121, *Buzzi Unichem v Commission*, T-297/11, EU:T:2014:122, *HeidelbergCement v Commission*, T-302/11, EU:T:2014:128, and *Italmobiliare v Commission*, T-305/11, EU:T:2014:126.

Article 18(3) of Regulation 1/2003 only requires the Commission to fix a time limit and not to provide reasons for its choice thereof.[903] The request for information, and the time limit included in it, must, however, comply with the principle of proportionality and the obligation imposed on an undertaking to supply information should not be a burden on that undertaking that is disproportionate to the needs of the inquiry.[904]

The Commission may, under Article 23(1)(b) of Regulation 1/2003, impose a fine of up to 1% of their total turnover in the preceding business year on undertakings or associations of undertakings that, intentionally or negligently, supply incorrect, incomplete or misleading information or do not supply information within the required time limit.[905]

The General Court has held that, because of this threat of a fine, the examination of the appropriateness of the time limit fixed in a decision requesting information is particularly important. That time limit must enable the addressee of the decision not only to provide its reply in practical terms, but also to satisfy itself that the information is complete, correct and not misleading.[906]

Paragraph 38 of the Notice on Best Practices provides that, in general, the time limit will be at least two weeks from the receipt of the request. When the scope of the request is limited, for example if it only covers a short clarification of information previously provided or information readily available to the addressee of the request, the time limit will normally be shorter (one week or less).

The General Court has held that, in the absence of a specific need of the inquiry which warranted the fixing of a particularly short time limit, the imposition of a two-week time limit for a German cement manufacturer to provide information on all contacts, including informal ones, between two of its employees and other manufacturers of cement and related products or their representatives in Germany, over periods of three and seven years, was disproportionate.[907] On the other hand, a time limit of 12 weeks for the provision of a particularly large amount of information, to be provided in a particularly demanding format, was not disproportionate, given the means available to the undertaking concerned because of its economic size.[908]

Paragraph 39 of the Notice on Best Practices provides that, if the addressee of a decision requesting information considers that the time limit imposed for its reply is too short, it can make a reasoned request for extension to DG Competition, sufficiently in advance

---

903 Judgment in *Schwenk Zement v Commission*, T-306/11, EU:T:2014:123, paragraph 41.

904 Judgment in *Schwenk Zement v Commission*, T-306/11, EU:T:2014:123, paragraph 71.

905 Article 24(1)(d) of Regulation 1/2003 further allows the Commission to impose periodic penalty payments of up to 5% of the average daily turnover in the preceding business year per day in order to compel undertakings or associations of undertakings to supply complete and correct information which it has requested by decision.

906 Judgment in *Schwenk Zement v Commission*, T-306/11, EU:T:2014:123, paragraphs 72 and 73. By virtue of a general duty of care, any undertaking or association of undertakings is required to ensure the proper maintenance of records in its books or files of information enabling details of its activities to be retrieved, in order, in particular, to make the necessary evidence available in the event of legal or administrative proceedings; Judgments in *Heineken Nederland and Heineken v Commission*, T-240/07, EU:T:2011:284, paragraph 301, and in *Schwenk Zement v Commission*, T-306/11, EU:T:2014:123, paragraph 83.

907 Judgment in *Schwenk Zement v Commission*, T-306/11, EU:T:2014:123, paragraphs 80 to 92.

908 Judgment in *Cemex v Commission*, T-292/11, EU:T:2014:125, paragraphs 132 to 135.

of the expiry of the time limit. If DG Competition considers the request to be justified, additional time will be granted. DG Competition may also agree with the addressee of the request that certain parts of the requested information that are of particular importance or easily available for the addressee will be supplied within a shorter time limit, whereas additional time will be granted for supplying the remaining information.

Article 4(2)(c), read in conjunction with Article 3(7), of the Terms of Reference, provides that, if the addressee is unsuccessful in resolving its concerns about the time limit with DG Competition, it may refer the matter to the Hearing Officer, in due time before the expiry of the original time limit set. The Hearing Officer shall decide on whether an extension of the time limit should be granted, taking account of the length and complexity of the request for information and the requirements of the investigation.[909]

The General Court has held that, if the addressee of a decision requesting information fails to request an extension of the time limit, the time limit is deemed to be sufficient.[910]

The possibility to request from the Hearing Officer an extension of the time limit for replying to a request for information does not exist for simple requests for information, pursuant to Article 18(2) of Regulation 1/2003. This makes sense, because the addressees of such simple requests for information cannot be fined for not supplying information within the required time limit, only for supplying incorrect or misleading information.[911] Addressees of simple requests for information that consider that the time limit for their reply is too short, and that cannot obtain an extension from DG Competition, can thus not be sanctioned for not replying within the time limit.[912]

b. *Right to be informed of one's procedural status*

According to the case law, undertakings or associations of undertakings that are subject to an investigative measure under Chapter V of Regulation 1/2003 (inspection or request for information) have the right to be informed of their procedural status – namely, whether they are subject to an investigation and, if so, the subject matter and purpose of that investigation.[913]

---

909 The possibility to request first from DG Competition and subsequently from the Hearing Officer an extension of the time limit fixed in a Commission decision requesting information pursuant to Article 18(3) of Regulation 1/2003 does not alter the time limit for bringing an application for annulment against that Commission decision before the General Court. As Article 18(3) of Regulation 1/2003 requires to be indicated in any decision based on that provision, the addressee of a Commission decision requesting information pursuant to Article 18(3) of Regulation 1/2003 can have that decision reviewed by the General Court; see also Judgment in *Schwenk Zement v Commission*, T-306/11, EU:T:2014:123, paragraph 75. According to Article 263 TFEU and Articles 58 and 60 of the Rules of procedure of the General Court ([2015] OJ L105/1), the application for annulment of the Commission decision must be brought within two months and ten days of the notification of the decision to the addressee.

910 Judgments in *Finnboard v Commission*, T-338/94, EU:T:1998:99, paragraph 54 and in *Cementos Portland Valderrivas v Commission*, T-296/11, EU:T:2014:121, paragraph 95.

911 Article 23(1)(a) of Regulation 1/2003.

912 The absence of a reply within the time limit may, of course, prompt the Commission to request the information by decision pursuant to Article 18(3) of Regulation 1/2003, in which case Article 4(2)(c) of the Terms of Reference becomes applicable.

913 Judgment in *AC-Treuhand v Commission*, T-99/04, EU:T:2008:256, paragraphs 44 to 60. It is, however, only upon receipt of the statement of objections that the parties concerned are informed of all the objections made and the evidence used against them and are able to rely in full on their rights of defence. If such rights were

Article 4(2)(d), read in conjunction with Article 3(7), of the Terms of Reference, provides that, where an undertaking or association of undertakings subject to an investigative measure considers, after having raised the matter first with DG Competition, that it has not been properly informed of its procedural status, it may refer the matter to the Hearing Officer. If the Hearing Officer finds that the undertaking or association of undertakings has not been properly informed, they will take a decision that DG Competition will inform the undertaking or association of undertakings of its procedural status.

c. *Extension of the time limit for replying to a statement of objections or for making known one's views*

Before taking a decision finding an infringement and ordering its termination, ordering interim measures, imposing fines, or fixing the definitive amount of periodic penalty payments, the Commission must inform the intended addressees of the decision of the objections raised against them through a written statement of objections, and set a time limit within which these parties may express their views in writing.[914] According to Regulation 773/2004, in setting this time limit, which may not be shorter than four weeks, the Commission must have regard both to the time required for preparation of the submission and to the urgency of the case.[915] In its Notice on Best Practices, the Commission has indicated that DG Competition will grant a longer period, normally a period of two months, depending on the circumstances of the case.[916] The time limit will start to run from the date when access to the main documents of the file has been granted.[917]

Article 9(1) of the Terms of Reference provides that, if an addressee of a statement of objections considers that the time limit imposed for its reply to the statement of objections is too short, it may seek an extension of that time limit by means of a reasoned request addressed to the director responsible. Such a request must be made in due time before the expiry of the original time limit. If such a request is not granted or the addressee of the statement of objections making the request disagrees with the length of the extension granted, it may refer the matter to the Hearing Officer for review before the expiry of the original time limit. After hearing the director responsible, the Hearing Officer shall decide on whether an extension of the time limit is necessary to allow the addressee of a statement of objections to exercise its right to be heard effectively, while also having regard to the need to avoid undue delay in proceedings.[918]

---

in effect extended to the period before the statement of objections, the effectiveness of the Commission's investigation would be undermined; see Judgments in *Elf Aquitaine v Commission*, C-521/09 P, EU:C:2011:620, paragraphs 113 to 122, and in *AC-Treuhand v Commission*, T-27/10, EU:T:2014:59, paragraphs 165 to 196; see also Final Report of the Hearing Officer of 22 June 2015 in Case AT.39563 *Retail Food Packaging* [2015] OJ C402/6.

914 Article 27 of Regulation 1/2003 and Article 10 of Regulation 773/2004.

915 Article 17(1) and (2) of Regulation 773/2004; for proceedings initiated with a view to adopting interim measures pursuant to Article 8 of Regulation 1/2003, the time limit may be shortened to one week.

916 Paragraph 100 of the Notice on Best Practices.

917 Paragraph 102 of the Notice on Best Practices; see Judgment in *Mannesmannröhren-Werke v Commission*, T-44/00, EU:T:2004:218, paragraph 65.

918 Article 9(1) of the Terms of Reference adds that the Hearing Officer shall take into account, among other elements, the size and complexity of the file, whether the addressee of the statement of objections making the request has had prior access to information, and any other objective obstacles that may be faced by the addressee.

A decision refusing an extension is an intermediate procedural measure, which does not affect the applicant's legal situation until the Commission has adopted a final decision finding an infringement, or otherwise adversely affecting the applicant. The applicant can thus not bring a separate action before the General Court against the decision refusing the extension, but can later raise the matter in an action against such final decision.[919]

Apart from the addressees of a statement of objection, also complainants and interested third persons have a right to provide written comments within a time limit set by the Commission.[920]

Article 9(2) of the Terms of Reference provides that, if a complainant or an interested third person considers that the time limit to make its views known is too short, it may seek an extension of that time limit by means of a reasoned request addressed to the director responsible in due time before the expiry of the original time limit. If such a request is not granted or the complainant or interested third person disagrees with this decision, it may refer the matter to the Hearing Officer for review. After hearing the director responsible, the Hearing Officer shall decide on whether an extension of the time limit should be granted.

d. *Access to the file or access to documents or information*

The addressees of a statement of objections have a right of access to the Commission's investigation file, so as to allow them to effectively express their views on the preliminary conclusions reached by the Commission in the statement of objections.[921] The right of access covers in principle the entire investigation file, but with exceptions for internal documents and correspondence with the competition authorities of the Member States (unless these add relevant evidence to the file[922]), and for business secrets or other confidential information of other undertakings or persons.[923] The right of other undertakings or persons to the protection of their business secrets or other confidential information

---

It is apparent from recital 17 of Decision 2011/695 that Article 9(1) also applies to time limits for the reply to supplementary statements of objections and letters of fact; see further Notice on Best Practices, paragraphs 109 to 112. In its Judgment in *Infineon Technologies v Commission*, T-758/14, EU:T:2016:737, paragraphs 60 to 69, the General Court held that the period that the Commission must grant an undertaking to provide its observations on a letter of facts should take account of the relative complexity and the volume of the evidence submitted, that, in the circumstances of that case, a period of five working days was 'an extremely short period', but that the Commission had not infringed the undertaking's rights of defence, inter alia because the undertaking did not seek from the Hearing Officer an extension of the period set.

919 See Order in *Intel v Commission*, T-457/08 R, EU:T:2009:18.

920 Articles 6(1) and 7(1) and Article 13(1) of Regulation 773/2004.

921 For a detailed discussion of access to the file, see W. Wils and H. Abbott, 'Access to the File in Competition Proceedings Before the European Commission' (2019) 42 *World Competition* 255, updated version accessible at http://ssrn.com/author=456087.

922 See Judgment in *Infineon Technologies v Commission*, T-758/14, EU:T:2016:737, paragraphs 77 to 89 for an example of an internal forensic IT report constituting inculpatory evidence. Evidence which the Commission receives, in the context of its investigation, from a competition authority of a Member State pursuant to Article 12 of Regulation 1/2003 forms in principle part of the accessible file; see Final Report of the Hearing Officer in Case AT.39610 *Power Cables* [2014] OJ C319/5.

923 An example of such other confidential information is the identity of third parties where there is a risk of retaliation; see Judgments in *BPB Industries and British Gypsum v Commission*, C-310/93 P, EU:C:1995:101, paragraphs 26 and 27, and in *General Electric v Commission*, T-210/01, EU:T:2005:456, paragraph 650, and Judgment in *Stanley Adams v Commission*, 145/83, EU:C:1985:323.

must, however, be balanced against and reconciled with the right of access to the file,[924] through the use of non-confidential versions of documents or the provision of access in a restricted manner, for instance through a data room procedure.[925]

Article 7(1) and (3), read in conjunction with Article 3(7), of the Terms of Reference provide that, where a party which has exercised its right of access to the file has reason to believe that the Commission has in its possession documents which have not been disclosed to it and those documents are necessary for the proper exercise of the right to be heard, it may, after having raised the matter with DG Competition, make a reasoned request for access to these documents to the Hearing Officer. The Hearing Officer shall take a reasoned decision, granting or rejecting the request for additional access.

Where information which may constitute a business secret or other confidential information of another undertaking or person is at stake, and this other undertaking or person objects to the disclosure, a decision granting access pursuant to Article 7(3) of the Terms of Reference may necessitate a prior decision pursuant to Article 8(2) of the Terms of Reference allowing disclosure, or a decision pursuant to Article 8(4) of the Terms of Reference allowing access in a restricted manner, for instance through a data room procedure.

A decision refusing access or granting access only in a restricted manner is an intermediate procedural measure, which does not affect the applicant's legal situation until the Commission has adopted a final decision finding an infringement, or otherwise adversely affecting the applicant. The applicant can thus not bring a separate action before the General Court against the decision refusing access, but can later raise the matter in an action against such final decision.[926]

Article 7(1) of the Terms of Reference only covers access to documents which the Commission has in its possession. It does not empower the Hearing Officer to order the Commission to obtain or seek to obtain documents which are not in its possession in order to complete an allegedly incomplete file.[927]

Article 7(2) and (3) of the Terms of Reference further empower the Hearing Officer to decide upon requests by complainants pursuant to Article 8(1) of Regulation 773/2004 for access to the documents on which the Commission bases its intention to reject the

---

924 Judgment in *Cimenteries CBR and Others v Commission*, T-25/95 etc., EU:T:2000:77, paragraph 147; Judgment in *General Electric v Commission*, T-210/01, EU:T:2005:456, paragraph 653; Judgment in *Varec v Belgian State*, C-450/06, EU:C:2008:91, paragraphs 46 to 54; and recital 14 of Regulation 773/2004.

925 On the data room procedure, see paragraph 97 of the Notice on Best Practices, and DG Competition Best Practices on the disclosure of information in data rooms in proceedings under Articles 101 and 102 TFEU and under the EU Merger Regulation (2 June 2015), accessible at http://ec.europa.eu/competition/antitrust/legislation/legislation.html.

926 Order in *Commerzbank v Commission*, T-219/01, EU:T:2003:201.

927 See Final report of the Hearing Officer in Case COMP/C-3/37.990 *Intel* [2009] OJ C227/7 at 9. See further, as to whether the Commission can be obliged to obtain certain documents at the request of an undertaking which is the subject of an investigation, Judgments in *Intel v Commission*, T-286/09, EU:T:2014:547, paragraphs 349 to 436, and in *Infineon Technologies v Commission*, T-758/14, EU:T:2016:737, paragraphs 73, 74 and 110, and Chapter IV of this book.

complaint, requests by complainants to receive an adequate non-confidential version of the statement of objections, and requests by interested third persons to be informed of the nature and subject matter of the procedure.

Article 7 of the Terms of Reference does not cover requests for public access to Commission documents under Regulation 1049/2001.[928] The Hearing Officer does not have any role in the application of Regulation 1049/2001.[929]

e. *Disclosure of business secrets and other confidential information*

Article 8(1) and (2) of the Terms of Reference provides that, where the Commission intends to disclose information which may constitute a business secret or other confidential information of any undertaking or person, the latter shall be informed in writing of this intention and the reasons thereof by the Directorate-General for Competition. A time limit shall be fixed within which the undertaking or person concerned may submit any written comments. Where the undertaking or person concerned objects to the disclosure of the information, it may refer the matter to the Hearing Officer. If the Hearing Officer finds that the information may be disclosed because it does not constitute a business secret or other confidential information or because there is an overriding interest in its disclosure, that finding shall be stated in a reasoned decision which shall be notified to the undertaking or person concerned. The decision shall specify the date after which the information will be disclosed. This date shall not be less than one week from the date of notification.

Article 8(4) of the Terms of Reference adds that, where appropriate in order to balance the effective exercise of a party's rights of defence with legitimate interests of confidentiality, the Hearing Officer may decide that parts of the file that are indispensable for the exercise of the party's rights of defence will be made accessible to the party requesting access in a restricted manner, the details of which shall be determined by the Hearing Officer. Recital 16 of the Terms of Reference further explains that such access in a restricted manner may involve, for example, a limitation of the number or category of persons having access, and a limitation of the use of the information being accessed.[930] The so-called data room procedure is a type of such restricted access.[931]

The undertaking or person the disclosure of whose alleged business secrets or other confidential information the Hearing Officer's decision allows can immediately bring

---

928 Regulation (EC) No 1049/2001 of the European Parliament and of the Council of 30 May 2001 regarding public access to European Parliament, Council and Commission documents [2001] OJ L145/43; on the application of this regulation in the antitrust context, see Judgments in *EnBW Energie Baden-Württemberg v Commission*, C-365/12 P, EU:C:2014:112, and in *Deutsche Telekom v Commission*, T-210/15, EU:T:2017:224.

929 The rules for the application by the Commission of Regulation 1049/2001 are laid down in the annex to the Commission Decision of 5 December 2001 amending its rules of procedure [2001] OJ L345/94.

930 The general rule being that information obtained in the course of antitrust proceedings may only be used for the purposes of judicial or administrative proceedings for the application of Articles 101 and 102 TFEU; see Article 16a of Regulation 773/2004, as amended by Regulation 2015/1348.

931 See paragraphs 97 and 98 of the Notice on Best Practices, and DG Competition Best Practices on the disclosure of information in data rooms in proceedings under Articles 101 and 102 TFEU and under the EU Merger Regulation (2 June 2015), accessible at http://ec.europa.eu/competition/antitrust/legislation/legislation.html.

before the General Court an action for annulment against the Hearing Officer's decision, as well as a request for suspension or other interim measures.[932]

Article 8(1) of the Terms of Reference only covers disclosure of information to addressees of a statement of objections, complainants and interested third persons having a right to be heard in the context of antitrust (or merger) proceedings before the Commission.[933] It does not cover disclosure of information in the application of Regulation 1049/2001, nor disclosure after the closing of the Commission's proceedings.

Article 8(3) of the Terms of Reference, however, provides that Article 8(1) and (2) shall apply *mutatis mutandis* to the disclosure of information by publication in the *Official Journal of the European Union.*

Article 30 of Regulation 1/2003 requires the Commission to publish its final antitrust decisions. Pursuant to the second paragraph of this provision, the published decision must state the names of the parties and the main content of the decision and must have regard to the legitimate interests of the undertakings in the protection of their business secrets.

The Commission's current practice is to comply with those obligations by publishing a summary of antitrust decisions in the Official Journal, containing the main content of the decision. In addition, a full-length version of the decision is published on DG Competition's website subject to legitimate requests for confidentiality.[934]

While Article 8(3) of the Terms of Reference only mentions publication in the Official Journal, a practice has developed according to which undertakings that do not accept DG Competition's assessment as to the confidentiality of information in the full-length version of the decision to be published on DG Competition's website can also turn to the Hearing Officer, who then decides on behalf of the Commission whether the information can be published.[935]

The Hearing Officer's competence covers any objection based on a ground, arising from rules or principles of EU law, relied on by the interested person in order to claim

---

932 Judgment in *AKZO v Commission*, 53/85, EU:C:1986:256; see also Order in *Commission v Pilkington Group*, C-278/13 P(R), EU:C:2013:558, paragraphs 56 to 58, and Order in *Lantmännen v Commission*, T-79/19 R, EU:T:2019:212.

933 Judgment in *Bank Austria Creditanstalt v Commission*, T-198/03, EU:T:2006:136, paragraph 29.

934 See DG Competition Guidance on the preparation of public versions of Commission Decisions adopted under Articles 7 to 10, 23 and 24 of Regulation 1/2003 (4 June 2015), accessible at http://ec.europa.eu/competition/antitrust/information_en.html.
The General Court has confirmed that the Commission is entitled to publish, with due regard to its obligation to protect business secrets and other confidential information, versions of its decisions that are fuller than the minimum required by Article 30 of Regulation 1/2003, and that the Commission is entitled to adjust its approach as to the publication of its decisions to the needs of its competition policy; Judgment in *Pilkington Group v Commission*, T-462/12, EU:T:2015:508, paragraph 77.

935 See also Judgments in *Pergan v Commission*, T-474/04, EU:T:2007:306, paragraph 62, and in *Evonik Degussa v Commission*, C-162/15 P, EU:C:2017:205.
This extension in practice of the Hearing Officer's competence does not, however, cover other publications on DG Competition's website than the publication of the full-length version of the decisions listed in Article 30 of Regulation 1/2003. For instance, publication on DG Competition's website of decisions rejecting complaints pursuant to Article 7(2) of Regulation 773/2004 falls outside the scope of the Hearing Officer's competence.

protection of the confidentiality of the contested information,[936] as well as whether there is an overriding interest in its disclosure.

Undertakings the publication of whose business secrets or other confidential information the Hearing Officer's decision allows can immediately bring before the General Court an action for annulment against the Hearing Officer's decision, as well as a request for suspension or other interim measures.[937]

2. Recommendation powers

The Terms of Reference have granted the Hearing Officer the power to make recommendations in relation to two matters: legal professional privilege, and the privilege against self-incrimination.

a. *Legal professional privilege*

The Commission's powers of investigation are limited by legal professional privilege. According to the case law of the Court of Justice, the protection of the confidentiality of certain communications between lawyer and client is an essential corollary to the rights of the defence and serves the important requirement that everyone should be able without restraint to consult a lawyer to obtain independent legal advice.[938] The communications protected are, however, limited to those between a client and an independent lawyer (not in-house counsel) entitled to practise in one of the EU or EEA Member States.[939] The protected communications are those made 'for the purpose and in the interests of the client's rights of defence', that is to say which come into existence after the initiation of proceedings or which, although made earlier, 'have a relationship to the subject-matter of that procedure'.[940] Internal documents of an undertaking summarising advice received from independent lawyers are also protected.[941] Similarly, internal preparatory documents are protected if drawn up exclusively for the purpose of seeking legal advice from an external lawyer in exercise of the rights of defence.[942]

Where during an inspection an undertaking claims that a document is protected by legal professional privilege, it must substantiate its claim and, unless this would not be possible without revealing the protected information, allow the Commission officials to have a cursory look at the general layout, heading, title or other superficial features of the document so as to enable them to confirm the accuracy of

936 Judgments in *Evonik Degussa v Commission*, C-162/15 P, EU:C:2017:205, paragraphs 40 to 56, and in *AGC Glass Europe and Others v Commission*, C-517/15 P, EU:C:2017:598, paragraphs 51 to 59.

937 See Judgments in *Evonik Degussa v Commission*, C-162/15 P, EU:C:2017:205, in *AGC Glass Europe and Others v Commission*, C-517/15 P, EU:C:2017:598, and in *Pilkington Group v Commission*, T-462/12, EU:T:2015:508 and Orders in *Commission v Pilkington Group*, C-278/13 P(R), EU:C:2013:558, in *AGC Glass Europe and Others v Commission*, C-517/15 P-R, EU:C:2016:21, and in *Nexans France and Nexans v Commission*, T-423/17 R, EU:T:2017:835.

938 Judgment in *AM&S v Commission*, 155/79, EU:C:1982:157, paragraphs 18 and 23. See further Chapter XIII of this book.

939 Judgments in *AM&S v Commission*, 155/79, EU:C:1982:157, and in *Akzo Nobel v Commission*, C-550/07 P, EU:C:2010:512.

940 Judgment in *AM&S v Commission*, 155/79, EU:C:1982:157, paragraph 23.

941 Order in *Hilti v Commission*, T-30/89, EU:T:1990:27.

942 Judgment in *Akzo Nobel v Commission*, T-125/03, EU:T:2007:287, paragraph 123.

the claim. In case of disagreement as to whether the document is privileged, the Commission officials may place a copy of the document in a sealed envelope and take it with them.[943]

Article 4(2)(a), read in conjunction with Article 3(7), of the Terms of Reference, provides that, where an undertaking or association of undertakings has withheld from the Commission a document, claiming that it is covered by legal professional privilege within the meaning of the case law of the Court of Justice, the undertaking or association of undertakings may, after having raised the matter with DG Competition, ask the Hearing Officer to examine the claim. The Hearing Officer may only review the matter if the undertaking or association of undertakings making the claim consents to the Hearing Officer viewing the information claimed to be covered by legal professional privilege as well as related documents that the Hearing Officer considers necessary for their review. Without revealing the potentially privileged content of the information, the Hearing Officer shall communicate to the director responsible and the undertaking or association of undertakings concerned their preliminary view, and may take appropriate steps to promote a mutually acceptable resolution. Where no resolution is reached, the Hearing Officer may formulate a reasoned recommendation to the Competition Commissioner, without revealing the potentially privileged content of the document. The party making the claim shall receive a copy of this recommendation.

The Hearing Officer's recommendation has no binding force.[944] If, after the intervention of the Hearing Officer, the undertaking maintains its claim, and the Commission still wants to read and use the document, then the Commission must do what it would also have to do if the intervention of the Hearing Officer had not been asked, namely, take a decision ordering production of the document or opening the sealed envelope, allowing the undertaking to bring the matter immediately before the General Court through an application for annulment of that decision and an accompanying request for interim relief.[945]

This possibility to ask the intervention of the Hearing Officer is, according to the text of Article 4(2)(a) of the Terms of Reference, only available if two cumulative conditions are fulfilled: first, the document for which legal professional privilege is claimed has been requested by the Commission in the exercise of its powers to request information pursuant to Article 18 of Regulation 1/2003 or in the exercise of its powers of inspection pursuant to Articles 20 and 21 of Regulation 1/2003; secondly, the document must have been withheld from the Commission (including having been put in a sealed envelope).

The intervention of the Hearing Officer can thus not be asked in a situation where the undertaking has not initially withheld the document from the Commission but only later claims that, because of legal professional privilege, the document should be removed from the Commission's investigation file.

---

943 Judgment in *Akzo Nobel v Commission*, T-125/03, EU:T:2007:287, paragraphs 80 to 83.

944 Article 288 TFEU.

945 Judgments in *AM&S v Commission*, 155/79, EU:C:1982:157, paragraph 32, and in *Akzo Nobel v Commission*, T-125/03, EU:T:2007:287, paragraphs 79 and 85.

The condition that the document must have been withheld from the Commission makes sense in that in those circumstances DG Competition and the Commission's Legal Service cannot see the document and thus cannot determine in full knowledge of the facts whether it is covered by legal professional privilege, making it useful for the Commission to receive the view of the Hearing Officer who has seen the document.

b. *Privilege against self-incrimination*

The Commission's powers of investigation in antitrust proceedings are further limited by the privilege against self-incrimination. According to the case law of the Court of Justice, whilst the Commission is entitled to compel an undertaking to provide all necessary information concerning such facts as may be known to it and to disclose to it, if necessary, such documents relating thereto as are in its possession, even if the latter may be used to establish, against it or another undertaking, the existence of anti-competitive conduct, the Commission may not compel an undertaking to provide it with answers which might involve an admission on its part of the existence of an infringement which it is incumbent upon the Commission to prove.[946] The privilege against self-incrimination thus only extends to directly incriminating questions (involving an admission of infringement), not to purely factual questions, nor to the disclosure of documents.[947]

The privilege against self-incrimination can only be violated in case of compulsion, i.e. only in case of a request for information by decision pursuant to Article 18(3) of Regulation 1/2003, not in case of a simple request pursuant to Article 18(2) of Regulation 1/2003.[948] It is, however, the Commission's policy to avoid directly incriminating questions also in simple requests for information.

Article 4(2)(b), read in conjunction with Article 3(7), of the Terms of Reference, provides that, where the addressee of a simple request for information pursuant to Article 18(2) of Regulation 1/2003 refuses to reply to a question in such a request invoking the privilege against self-incrimination, as determined by the case law of the Court of Justice, it may refer the matter, in due time following the receipt of the request, and after having first raised the issue with DG Competition, to the Hearing Officer. In appropriate

---

946 Judgment in *Orkem v Commission*, 374/87, EU:C:1989:387, paragraphs 34 and 35.

947 The question of the extent of the privilege was reconsidered by the Court of Justice in the *SGL Carbon* case (Judgment in *Commission v SGL Carbon*, C-301/04 P, EU:C:2006:432), in particular in the light of the case law of the European Court of Human Rights (ECtHR). In his Opinion in *SGL Carbon* (C-301/04 P, EU:C:2006:53), Advocate General Geelhoed pointed out that in the United States companies cannot invoke the privilege against self-incrimination (Fifth Amendment of the United States Constitution), which applies to natural persons only, that the case law of the ECtHR regarding the right to be silent concerns natural persons in the context of 'classical' criminal procedures, that the ECtHR generally makes a distinction between the level of protection conferred on natural persons, on the one hand, and legal persons on the other, and that, in the case law of the ECtHR, the right to be silent is not absolute, and does not extend to the use in criminal proceedings of material which may be obtained from the accused through the use of compulsory powers but which has an existence independent of the will of the suspect, such as documents. Following this Opinion, the Court of Justice reiterated its *Orkem* case law; see also my papers 'Self-incrimination in EC Antitrust Enforcement: A Legal and Economic Analysis' (2003) 26 *World Competition* 567, 'EU Antitrust Enforcement Powers and Procedural Rights and Guarantees: The Interplay between EU Law, National Law, the Charter of Fundamental Rights of the EU and the European Convention on Human Rights' (2011) 34 *World Competition* 189 at 204–206, and Chapter X of this book.

948 Judgment in *Dalmine v Commission*, C-407/04 P, EU:C:2007:53, paragraphs 31 to 35.

cases, and having regard to the need to avoid undue delay in proceedings, the Hearing Officer may make a reasoned recommendation as to whether the privilege against self-incrimination applies and inform the director responsible of the conclusions drawn, to be taken into account in case of any decision taken subsequently pursuant to Article 18(3) of Regulation 1/2003. The addressee of the request shall receive a copy of the reasoned recommendation.

3. Reporting powers

Beyond the specific decisional powers or recommendation powers described above, the Hearing Officer has general reporting powers, which may be triggered by parties referring to the Hearing Officer for independent review any other issues regarding the effective exercise of their procedural rights that have not been resolved in prior contacts with DG Competition. The Terms of Reference specifically mention that the possibility to call upon the Hearing Officer is also available during commitment and settlement procedures.[949]

a. *Commitment and settlement procedures*

Article 15(1), read in conjunction with Article 3(7), of the Terms of Reference provides that parties to the proceedings which offer commitments to meet the concerns expressed to them by the Commission in its preliminary assessment pursuant to Article 9 of Regulation 1/2003 may, after having raised the issue with DG Competition, call upon the Hearing Officer at any stage in the commitment procedure, in order to ensure the effective exercise of their procedural rights.

Similarly, Article 15(2), read in conjunction with Article 3(7), of the Terms of Reference provides that parties to proceedings in cartel cases which engage in settlement discussions pursuant to Article 10a of Regulation 773/2004 may, after having raised the issue with DG Competition, call upon the Hearing Officer at any stage during the settlement procedure in order to ensure the effective exercise of their procedural rights.

b. *Other issues regarding the effective exercise of procedural rights in antitrust proceedings*

It is apparent from Article 1(2) and recital 8, read in conjunction with Article 3(7), of the Terms of Reference that parties may also in any antitrust proceeding call upon the Hearing Officer for any other issue regarding the effective exercise of their procedural rights that has not been resolved in prior contacts with DG Competition.

In the absence of specific decisional powers or recommendation powers, the Hearing Officer may, if they considers the complaint founded, and the issue is not immediately resolved following informal discussion with DG Competition, present observations on the matter to the Competition Commissioner in their interim report pursuant to Article 14(1) of the Terms of Reference and/or in the form of separate observations pursuant to Article 3(5) of the Terms of Reference, and to the Competition Commissioner and the

---

949 On commitment and settlement procedures generally, see Chapter VI of this book.

College of Members of the Commission in their final report pursuant to Articles 16 and 17 of the Terms of Reference.[950]

Whilst the interim report and any observations pursuant to Article 3(5) of the Terms of Reference are only for internal use by the Commission and are not communicated to any of the parties to the proceedings,[951] the final report is also (in draft version) communicated to the competition authorities of the Member States represented in the Advisory Committee, and (in its final version) communicated, together with the final decision of the Commission, to the addressees of the decision, and published in the *Official Journal of the European Union*.

The General Court has held that the Hearing Officer, in their capacity as an objective and independent officer, is not required to communicate in their final report all objections of a procedural nature put forward by the parties during the administrative procedure, but only the objections relevant to the assessment of the lawfulness of the conduct of the administrative procedure.[952]

G. Verification of the respect for procedural rights on the Hearing Officer's own initiative

Apart from reviewing issues referred to them by parties, the Hearing Officer may, and to a certain extent must, verify on their own initiative the respect for procedural rights, and report on the matter to the Competition Commissioner and to the College of Members of the Commission.

1. General reporting powers

Pursuant to Article 14 of the Terms of Reference, the Hearing Officer must, after the oral hearing, submit to the Competition Commissioner an interim report on the oral hearing and on the respect for the effective exercise of procedural rights up to that point in the proceedings.[953]

Pursuant to Articles 16 and 17 of the Terms of Reference, the Hearing Officer must, towards the end of the proceedings, on the basis of the draft decision to be submitted to the Advisory Committee,[954] submit to the Competition Commissioner and to the College of Members of the Commission a final report on the respect for the effective exercise of

---

950 It is apparent from the text of Article 14 of the Terms of Reference that the Hearing Officer is only required to submit an interim report if an oral hearing has taken place, and from the text of Article 16 of the Terms of Reference that the Hearing Officer is only required to submit a final report in those cases in which the Advisory Committee is consulted; see Article 14(1) of Regulation 1/2003.

951 See Judgments in *FMC Foret v Commission*, T-191/06, EU:T:2011:277, paragraph 143, and in *Infineon Technologies v Commission*, T-758/14, EU:T:2016:737, paragraph 112.

952 Judgment in *Tokai Carbon and Others v Commission*, T-236/01 etc., EU:T:2004:118, paragraph 53.

953 It is apparent from the text of Article 14 of the Terms of Reference that the Hearing Officer is only required to submit an interim report if an oral hearing has taken place.
The interim report is only for internal use by the Commission and is not communicated to any of the parties to the proceedings; see Judgments in *FMC Foret v Commission*, T-191/06, EU:T:2011:277, paragraph 143, and in *Infineon Technologies v Commission*, T-758/14, EU:T:2016:737, paragraph 112.

954 It is apparent from the text of Article 16 of the Terms of Reference that the Hearing Officer is only required to submit a final report in those cases in which the Advisory Committee is consulted; see Article 14(1) of Regulation 1/2003.

procedural rights throughout the proceedings.[955] This final report is also communicated to the competition authorities of the Member States represented in the Advisory Committee, and communicated, together with the final decision of the Commission, to the addressees of the decision, and published in the *Official Journal of the European Union.*

In these interim and final reports,[956] the Hearing Officer may report on the procedural issues that parties have referred to the Hearing Officer, and is required to report those objections relevant for the assessment of the lawfulness of the conduct of the administrative procedure.

The Hearing Officer may also report on procedural issues that have not been referred to them by any party. The Hearing Officer may be aware of such issues through their direct role in organising and conducting the oral hearing, or through information received or obtained from DG Competition throughout the proceedings. Indeed, according to Article 3(4) of the Terms of Reference the Hearing Officer must be kept informed about the development of the procedure by DG Competition, and according to Article 3(3) of the Terms of Reference the Hearing Officer shall have access to any files relating to competition proceedings.

As a general rule, the Hearing Officer would not appear to be required to report on any issue that parties could have referred to their but have not.[957] Indeed, final reports of the Hearing Officer often conclude that the effective exercise of procedural rights has been respected precisely on the ground that no issues have been raised with the Hearing Officer.[958]

2. Specific reporting obligation as to whether the draft decision deals only with objections in respect of which the parties have been afforded the opportunity of making known their views

The second sentence of Article 16(1) of the Terms of Reference provides that the final report of the Hearing Officer must consider whether the draft decision deals only with objections in respect of which the parties have been afforded the opportunity of making known their views.

In line with Article 41(2)(a) of the Charter of Fundamental Rights of the European Union and the case law of the Court of Justice, Article 27(1) of Regulation 1/2003 states that the Commission shall base its decisions only on objections on which the parties concerned have been able to comment.

---

955 Article 17(2) of the Terms of Reference provides that the final report may be modified by the Hearing Officer in the light of any amendments to the draft decision prior to its adoption by the Commission. In *Ferriere Nord v Commission*, T-90/10, EU:T:2014:1035, paragraphs 150 to 161, the General Court held that the fact that the final report was submitted to the College of Members of the Commission in French, German and English, but not in Italian, the authentic language of the Commission's decision, was not a ground for annulment of that decision, in the absence of any indication that the College of Members of the Commission had not been able to take note of the content of the final report and to adopt its decision in full knowledge of its content.

956 The Hearing Officer may also at any time present observations to the Competition Commission pursuant to Article 3(5) of the Terms of Reference.

957 See Judgment in *Mannesmannröhren-Werke v Commission*, T-44/00, EU:T:2004:218, paragraph 53; however, see also Opinion of Advocate General Mazák in *Knauf v Commission*, C-407/08 P, EU:C:2010:70, paragraph 38.

958 See, for example, Final Report of the Hearing Officer in Case COMP/39.692 *IBM Maintenance Services* [2012] OJ C18/5, and Final Report of the Hearing Officer in Case AT.39939 *Samsung – Enforcement of UMTS standard essential patents* [2014] OJ C350/6.

If, after the statement of objections has been issued, the Commission wants to add new objections or to materially alter the objections (otherwise than in favour of the parties), or wants to rely on new evidence to support its objections, this should be brought to the attention of the parties through a supplementary statement of objections or a letter of facts, and the parties should be given the opportunity to present their observations.[959]

Given that the parties are not shown the draft decision before its adoption by the Commission, and that they thus cannot themselves verify at this stage whether the draft decision deals only with objections in respect of which they have been afforded the opportunity of making known their views, and raise any issues concerning this with the Hearing Officer, it makes sense that the Hearing Officer on their own initiative makes this verification and reports on it in the final report.

H. Advice to the Competition Commissioner on any matter arising out of any antitrust proceeding

Pursuant to Article 3(5) of the Terms of Reference, the Hearing Officer may at any point in time present to the Competition Commissioner observations on any matter arising out of any Commission antitrust (or merger) proceeding. This potentially includes not only observations on procedural matters, but also observations on matters of substance, and not only observations concerning one specific case, but also observations concerning more general issues of policy or practice arising out of specific proceedings.

Specifically for cases where an oral hearing has been held, and the Hearing Officer may thus have become particularly knowledgeable about the case, Article 14(2) of the Terms of Reference provides that the Hearing Officer may, in addition to the interim report on procedural issues, make observations to the Competition Commissioner on the further progress of the proceedings. In so doing, the Hearing Officer shall seek to ensure in particular that, in the preparation of draft Commission decisions, due account is taken of all the relevant facts, including the factual elements relevant to the gravity and duration of any infringement. Such observations may relate to, inter alia, the need for further information, the withdrawal of certain objections, the formulation of further objections or suggestions for further investigative measures.[960]

Such observations are only for internal use by the Commission and are not communicated to any of the parties to the proceedings.[961]

---

959 Notice on Best Practices, paragraphs 109 to 112; Judgments in *AEG v Commission*, 107/82, EU:C:1983:293, paragraphs 24 to 29, in *Atlantic Container Line and Others v Commission*, T-191/98 etc., EU:T:2003:245, paragraphs 115, 170 to 173, and 287, in *France Télécom v Commission*, T-340/03, EU:T:2007:22, paragraphs 15 to 53, in *Telefónica v Commission*, T-336/07, EU:T:2012:172, paragraphs 75 to 109, in *Panasonic and MT Picture Display v Commission*, T-82/13, EU:T:2015:612, paragraphs 48 to 62, confirmed by Order in *Panasonic v Commission*, C-608/15 P, EU:C:2016:538, in *Generics (UK) v Commission*, T-469/13, EU:T:2016:454, paragraphs 376 to 386, and in *Infineon Technologies v Commission*, T-758/14, EU:T:2016:737, paragraphs 94 to 100.

960 See also Interview conducted by J. Jourdan, 'Wouter Wils: Looking back at his experience as Hearing Officer for competition proceedings at the European Commission', *Concurrences* no 2-2022, 14.

961 See also Judgments in *FMC Foret v Commission*, T-191/06, EU:T:2011:277, paragraph 143, and in *Infineon Technologies v Commission*, T-758/14, EU:T:2016:737, paragraph 112.

XII. The Oral Hearing in Antitrust Proceedings before the European Commission

This chapter deals with the (formal) oral hearing in proceedings conducted by the European Commission for the enforcement of Articles 101 and 102 TFEU. It analyses the legal basis and the nature and purpose of the oral hearing, examines who can request an oral hearing, and who can attend and speak at the oral hearing, compares the oral hearing with state of play meetings, and provides some general observations as to what factors may make addressees of a statement of objections decide in favour or against requesting an oral hearing.

A. Legal basis

Article 41(2)(a) of the Charter of Fundamental Rights of the European Union affirms 'the right of every person to be heard, before any individual measure which would affect him or her adversely is taken'.[962]

According to the Explanations to the Charter,[963] this provision restates case law of the Court of Justice of the EU on general principles of EU law. According to this case law:

'Observance of the right to be heard is, in all proceedings initiated against a person which are liable to culminate in a measure adversely affecting that person, a fundamental principle of [EU] law which must be guaranteed even in the absence of any rules governing the proceedings in question [. . .]. That principle requires that the addressees of decisions which significantly affect their interests should be placed in a position in which they may effectively make known their views.'[964]

If the right to be heard is thus recognised as a fundamental right in EU law, it would not appear, however, that there is a fundamental right to be heard **orally**, as long as the addressees of decisions can effectively make known their views in writing.[965]

---

962 [2007] OJ C303/1; see generally my paper 'EU Antitrust Enforcement Powers and Procedural Rights and Guarantees: The Interplay between EU Law, National Law, the Charter of Fundamental Rights of the EU and the European Convention on Human Rights' (2011) 34 *World Competition* 189, also accessible at http://ssrn.com/author=456087, and I. Rabinovici, 'The Right to Be Heard in the Charter of Fundamental Rights of the European Union' (2012) 18 *Public Law* 149.

963 [2007] OJ C303/17.

964 Judgment in *Commission v Lisrestal and Others*, C-32/95 P, EU:C:1996:402, paragraph 21.

965 See Judgments of the European Court of Human Rights of 23 November 2006 in *Jussila v Finland* (Application no 73053/01), paragraphs 40 to 49; of 19 April 2007 in *Vilho Eskelinen & Ors v Finland* (Application no 63235/00), paragraphs 72 to 75; and of 23 October 2018 in *Produkcija Plus storitveno podjetje d.o.o. v Slovenia* (Application no 47072/15), paragraph 54; and Decision of the European Court of Human Rights of 13 March 2012 in *Bouygues Telecom v France* (Application no 2324/08), paragraphs 69 to 71; as well as Orders in *Troszczynski v Parliament*, C-462/18 P, EU:C:2019:239, paragraphs 52 to 55, in *Gollnisch v Parliament*, C-330/18 P, EU:C:2019:240, paragraphs 60 and 61, and Judgment in *Syrian Lebanese Commercial Bank v Council*, T-174/12

Article 27 of Regulation 1/2003[966] provides for the hearing of parties, complainants and others, but again no right to an **oral** hearing is granted. Such a right only results from Regulation 773/2004.[967] Article 12(1) of Regulation 773/2004 provides as follows:

'The Commission shall give the parties to whom it has addressed a statement of objections the opportunity to develop their arguments at an oral hearing, if they so request in their written submissions.'[968]

B. The nature and purpose of the oral hearing

1. The purpose of the oral hearing

Recital 19 of Decision 2011/695/EU of the President of the European Commission of 13 October 2011 on the function and terms of reference of the Hearing Officer in competition proceedings summarises as follows the purpose of the oral hearing:

'The oral hearing allows the parties to whom the Commission has addressed a statement of objections to further exercise their right to be heard by developing their arguments orally before the Commission, which should be represented by the Directorate-General for Competition as well as other services that contribute to the further preparation of a decision taken by the Commission. It should provide an additional opportunity to ensure that all relevant facts – whether favourable or unfavourable to the parties concerned, including the factual elements relating to the gravity and duration of the alleged infringement – are clarified as much as possible. The oral hearing should also allow the parties to present their arguments as to the matters that may be of importance for the possible imposition of fines.'[969]

---

and T-80/13, EU:T:2014:52, paragraph 147; and Opinion of Advocate General Wahl in *SKW Stahl-Metallurgie v Commission*, C-154/14 P, EU:C:2015:543, paragraphs 49 and 58; Judgment in *Lucchini v Commission*, T-185/18, EU:T:2019:298, paragraph 49; Judgment in *HeidelbergCement and Schwenk Zement v Commission*, T-380/17, EU:T:2020:471, paragraph 634, and Judgment in *Wieland-Werke v Commission*, T-251/19, EU:T:2022:296, paragraph 694.
In its Judgment in *Limburgse Vinyl Maatschappij and Others v Commission*, T-305/94 etc., EU:T:1999:80, paragraph 248, the General Court wrote: 'The right of the undertakings and associations of undertakings concerned to put their case on the matters to which the Commission has taken objection, at both the written and oral stages of the administrative procedure, is an essential part of the rights of the defence (*Hoechst*, paragraph 52)', but this appears to reflect the secondary legislation providing for a right to an oral hearing rather than a fundamental right to an oral hearing; the Judgment in *Hoechst v Commission*, 46/87 and 227/88, EU:C:1989:337, to which the General Court refers, does not mention the oral hearing.

966 Council Regulation (EC) No 1/2003 of 16 December 2002 on the implementation of the rules on competition laid down in Articles 81 and 82 of the Treaty [2003] OJ L1/1, last amended by Council Regulation (EC) No 1419/2006 [2006] OJ L269/1.

967 Commission Regulation (EC) No 773/2004 of 7 April 2004 relating to the conduct of proceedings by the Commission pursuant to Articles 81 and 82 of the EC Treaty [2004] OJ L123/18, last amended by Commission Regulation (EU) 2015/1348.

968 Article 12(2) of Regulation 773/2004 adds an exception for settlement proceedings in cartel cases.

969 Decision 2011/695/EU of the President of the European Commission of 13 October 2011 on the function and terms of reference of the Hearing Officer in competition proceedings [2001] OJ L275/29.

2. Administrative proceedings

The antitrust proceedings conducted by the European Commission are administrative proceedings, in which the Commission, which is an administrative, non-judicial body, acts both as investigator and as first-instance decision-maker.[970] The addressees of Commission decisions can subsequently appeal against the Commission decision before the EU Courts, thus ensuring the compatibility of the enforcement system with the fundamental right of access to an independent court.[971]

The oral hearing in the Commission proceedings is thus not a court hearing or a trial.[972]

3. Primarily written proceedings

The antitrust proceedings conducted by the European Commission are primarily written proceedings. Before adopting a decision, the Commission must address its objections in writing to the parties concerned, who may submit in writing their comments on these objections within a set time limit.[973] In these written comments, the parties may request the opportunity 'to develop their arguments' at an oral hearing.[974]

The fact that the proceedings are primarily written does not, however, exclude the bringing of new arguments at the stage of the oral hearing. According to the Commission's Notice on best practices for the conduct of antitrust proceedings (hereafter also: 'Notice on Best Practices'):

'*The oral hearing allows the parties to develop orally the arguments they have submitted in writing and to supplement, where appropriate, the written evidence, or to inform the Commission of other matters that may be relevant.*'[975]

4. Hearing primarily of the addressees of the statement of objections

The oral hearing is always 'the oral hearing of the parties to whom a statement of objections has been addressed'.[976] Only they can request an oral hearing, and the main purpose of the oral hearing is to allow them to develop orally their arguments.[977]

---

970 See further my papers 'The Combination of the Investigative and Prosecutorial Function and the Adjudicative Function in EC Antitrust Enforcement: A Legal and Economic Analysis' (2004) 27 *World Competition* 201, 'The Increased Level of EU Antitrust Fines, Judicial Review and the ECHR' (2010) 33 *World Competition* 5, both also accessible at http://ssrn.com/author=456087, and Chapter IX of this book.

971 Idem; Judgments in *Chalkor v Commission*, C-386/10 P, EU:C:2011:815, in *Schindler v Commission*, C-501/11 P, EU:C:2013:522, and in *Emesa-Trefilería and Industrias Galycas v Commission*, T-406/10, EU:T:2015:499; View of Advocate General Kokott, Opinion procedure 2/13 (Accession of the EU to the ECHR), EU:C:2014:2475, paragraphs 146 to 150; Judgment of the European Court of Human Rights of 27 September 2011 in *Menarini Diagnostics v Italy* (Application no 43509/08), and Decision of the European Court of Human Rights of 13 March 2012 in *Bouygues Telecom v France* (Application no 2324/08).

972 See, inter alia, Judgments in *FMC Foret v Commission*, T-191/06, EU:T:2011:277, paragraphs 134 to 141, and in *Coats Holdings v Commission*, T-439/07, EU:T:2012:320, paragraphs 171 to 177 (rejecting the argument that cross-examination of witnesses should be possible at the oral hearing).

973 Article 10 of Regulation 773/2004.

974 Article 12(1) of Regulation 773/2004.

975 Commission notice on best practices for the conduct of proceedings concerning Articles 101 and 102 TFEU [2011] OJ C308/6 ('Notice on Best Practices'), paragraph 107; see also Judgment in *General Electric v Commission*, T-210/01, EU:T:2005:456, paragraph 704.

976 Article 13(2) of Regulation 773/2004.

977 Article 12(1) of Regulation 773/2004 and Article 6(1) of Decision 2011/695.

Third persons may, where appropriate, be allowed to attend the oral hearing and to express their views, but this is only secondary to the main purpose of the oral hearing, which is to allow the addressees of the statement of objections to develop their arguments.[978]

5. Not an investigative hearing

The oral hearing is not an investigative hearing, where the parties could be compelled to appear (or failure to appear could result in changes in the Commission's burden of proof) and where they would be obliged to answer questions. Whereas other participants at the hearing (including Commission services, authorities of the Member States, complainants) may be allowed to ask questions during the oral hearing, as a general rule there is no obligation to answer.

The Commission has other instruments at its disposal to conduct its investigation, notably requests for information and inspections.[979]

C. Who can request an oral hearing, and when or how?

1. Only addressees of a statement of objections

Before taking a decision provided for in Articles 7 (finding and termination of infringement), 8 (interim measures), 23 (fines) or 24(2) (fixation of the definitive amount of periodic penalty payments) of Regulation 1/2003, the Commission must inform the intended addressees of the decision of the objections raised against them through a written statement of objections, and set a time limit within which these parties may express their views in writing.[980] The addressees of a statement of objections can, in their written reply, request an oral hearing.[981]

There is however an exception for cartel settlement proceedings: Article 10a of Regulation 773/2004, and the Commission Notice on the conduct of settlement procedures in cartel cases[982] provide for a special procedure for settlements in cartel cases.[983] If both the Commission and the parties concerned agree to opt for this procedure, the parties are heard through bilateral settlement discussions. If these settlement discussions lead to a common understanding regarding the scope of the objections and the estimation of the range of likely fines, the parties that want to settle must then make a formal settlement submission acknowledging their liability for the infringement and accepting

---

978 See also Judgment in *Diamanthandel A. Spira v Commission*, T-108/07 and T-354/08, EU:T:2013:367, paragraph 59.

979 Articles 18, 20 and 21 of Regulation 1/2003.

980 Article 27 of Regulation 1/2003 and Article 10 of Regulation 773/2004. According to paragraphs 85 and 90 of the Notice on Best Practices, when the Commission intends to impose fines, it will also include in the statement of objections further information as to any subsequent calculation of the fine, allowing the addressees of the statement of objections to give their views on the matters that may be of importance for the possible imposition of fines in their written reply and at the oral hearing.

981 Article 12(1) of Regulation 773/2004.

982 Commission Notice on the conduct of settlement procedures in view of the adoption of Decisions pursuant to Article 7 and Article 23 of Council regulation (EC) No 1/2003 in cartel cases [2008] OJ C167/1, amended [2015] OJ C256/2 ('Settlement Notice').

983 See Chapter VI of this book.

the fine, and waiving their right to an oral hearing, unless the subsequent statement of objections does not reflect the contents of their settlement submission.[984]

In commitment proceedings under Article 9 of Regulation 1/2003,[985] there is no possibility for the parties concerned to request an oral hearing, unless the preliminary assessment takes the form of a statement of objections.[986]

Complainants or other third persons cannot request an oral hearing. They may, where appropriate, be allowed to participate in the oral hearing of the addressees of the statement of objections, but this presupposes that those addressees have requested an oral hearing.

The Commission cannot organise an oral hearing if no addressee of the statement of objections has requested one.[987]

2. Request in the written reply to the statement of objections

According to Article 12(1) of Regulation 773/2004, the addressees of a statement of objections must make any request for an oral hearing in their written submissions in reply to the statement of objections.

This written reply, and hence any request for an oral hearing, must be made within the time limit set by the Commission when notifying the statement of objections.[988] In setting this time limit, which may not be shorter than four weeks, the Commission must have regard both to the time required for preparation of the submission and to the urgency of the case.[989] An addressee of a statement of objections may seek an extension of this time limit through a reasoned request first to the Commission's Directorate-General for Competition, and, if unsuccessful, subsequently to the Hearing Officer.[990]

Once this time limit has passed, any request for an oral hearing is inadmissible.[991]

---

984 Article 12(2) of Regulation 773/2004 and paragraph 20(d) of the Settlement Notice. Outside the cartel settlement procedure, waiving the right to an oral hearing does not constitute cooperation entitling a party to a fine reduction; see Judgment in *CD-Contact Data v Commission*, T-18/03, EU:T:2009:132, paragraph 125.

985 See my papers 'Settlements of EU Antitrust investigations: Commitment Decisions under Article 9 of Regulation No. 1/2003' (2006) 29 *World Competition* 345, and 'Ten years of commitment decisions under Article 9 of Regulation 1/2003: Too much of a good thing?' (New frontiers of antitrust Concurrences Journal 6th International Conference, Paris, 15 June 2015), both also accessible at http://ssrn.com/author=456087, and Chapter VI of this book.

986 See paragraph 123 of Notice on Best Practices.

987 See also Final Report of the Hearing Officer in Case AT.40099 *Google Android* [2019] OJ C402/12, paragraph 19. The Commission could however hold other types of meetings with complainants or other third parties.

988 Article 10(2) of Regulation 773/2004, and paragraph 106 of the Notice on Best Practices.

989 Article 17(1) and (2) of Regulation 773/2004; for proceedings initiated with a view to adopting interim measures pursuant to Article 8 of Regulation 1/2003, the time limit may be shortened to one week.
In paragraph 100 of the Notice on Best Practices, the Commission has indicated that a longer period, normally two months, will be granted, depending on the circumstances of the case.

990 Paragraph 101 of the Notice on Best Practices, and Article 9(1) of Decision 2011/695; see also Order in *Intel v Commission*, T-457/08 R, EU:T:2009:18.

991 Judgments in *Ferriere v Commission*, T-667/19, EU:T:2022:692, paragraph 94 and in *Intel v Commission*, T-286/09, EU:T:2014:547, paragraph 326 ('The obligation for the addressee of a statement of objections to request an oral hearing within the time-limit set by the Commission, failing which it is barred from the right to an oral hearing, is justified by reasons of procedural economy.'). Decision 2011/695/EU does not contain any empowerment for the Hearing Officer to grant an oral hearing requested after the expiry of the time limit for the written

3. Second oral hearing

Where, after the issuing of the statement of objections, because it discovers new evidence or changes its assessment, the Commission wants to raise additional objections or substantially to alter the content of the objections, it must send a supplementary statement of objections. Such a supplementary statement of objections triggers a new possibility for the addressees to request an oral hearing in their written reply to the supplementary statement of objections.[992]

Where the Commission merely intends to rely on new evidence to corroborate the same objections already set out in the statement of objections, without substantially altering the content of the objections, no new statement of objections is needed. The Commission will then bring the new evidence and its intention to rely on it to the attention of the parties concerned through a letter of facts, allowing the parties concerned to submit written comments, but without a possibility to request again an oral hearing.[993]

The fact that an addressee of a statement of objections may not have been able, for reasons outside the responsibility of the Commission, to develop certain arguments at the oral hearing does not create a right to a second oral hearing.[994]

D. Who attends or can attend the oral hearing?

1. Oral hearings are not public

Oral hearings are not public.[995] According to the Commission Notice on Best Practices, 'the fact that the hearing is not public guarantees that all attendees can express themselves freely'.[996]

Only persons invited or admitted by the Hearing Officer can attend the oral hearing.[997] Article 11(4) of Decision 2011/695 provides that the Hearing Officer 'may set a time limit for all persons invited to the oral hearing to provide a list of participants who will

---

reply to the statement of objections; *contra* Final Report of the Hearing Officer in Case COMP/C-3/37.990 – Intel [2009] OJ C227/7, section II.2.(b) (interpreting the then applicable Commission Decision 2001/462/EC, ECSC of 23 May 2001 on the terms of reference of Hearing Officers in certain competition proceedings).

992 See paragraphs 110 and 112 of the Notice on Best Practices, and Judgments in *Geigy v Commission*, 52/69, EU:C:1972:73, paragraph 14, in *Intel v Commission*, T-286/09, EU:T:2014:547, paragraph 325, and in *Google and Alphabet v Commission*, T-604/18, EU:T:2022:541, paragraphs 962 to 1005.

993 See paragraphs 111 and 112 of the Notice on Best Practices, and Judgments in *France Télécom v Commission*, T-340/03, EU:T:2007:22, paragraphs 15 to 53, in *Intel v Commission*, T-286/09, EU:T:2014:547, paragraph 327, in *HeidelbergCement and Schwenk Zement v Commission*, T-380/17, EU:T:2020:471, paragraphs 629 to 639, and in *Wieland-Werke v Commission*, T-251/19, EU:T:2022:296, paragraphs 683 to 703. See also Judgment in *GEA Group v Commission*, T-640/16 RENV, EU:T:2023:18, paragraphs 208 to 224.

994 Judgment in *SKW Stahl-Metallurgie v Commission*, T-384/09, EU:T:2014:27, paragraph 61 (referring to the requirements of a proper progress of the administrative proceedings, which must lead, within a reasonable time after the opening of proceedings, to a decision by the Commission).

995 Article 14(6) of Regulation 773/2004. The absence of a public hearing in the administrative procedure before the European Commission is not contrary to Article 6 ECHR, because a public hearing is available on appeal before the General Court; see Decision of the European Court of Human Rights of 13 March 2012 in *Bouygues Telecom v France* (Application no 2324/08), paragraphs 69 to 71.

996 Paragraph 107 of the Notice on Best Practices; see also recital 20 of Decision 2011/695 and Final Report of the Hearing Officer in Case COMP/C-3/37.792 – Microsoft [2008] OJ C138/4 at 8.

997 Article 14 of Regulation 773/2004 and Chapter 6 of Decision 2011/695.

attend the hearing on their behalf. The Hearing Officer shall make this list available to all persons invited to the oral hearing in due time before the date of the hearing'.

2. Addressees of the statement of objections

As explained above, it is the request by an addressee of a statement of objections to be allowed to develop its defence arguments at an oral hearing that triggers the organisation of an oral hearing.

a. *Hearing in the presence of other addressees of the statement of objections*

Statements of objections in antitrust proceedings often have more than one addressee, because the alleged infringement involves several undertakings or because the undertaking concerned consists of several legal persons, for instance a parent company and a subsidiary.[998]

Article 12(1) of Regulation 773/2004 gives each addressee of the statement of objections an individual right to develop its arguments at an oral hearing, if it requests so in its written submissions.

The case law of the EU Courts leaves the Commission a choice whether to hear each addressee that has requested to be heard orally in a separate oral hearing or to hear all those addressees in a single oral hearing,[999] subject to two limitations:

First, the rights of the defence must be observed. This means that the Commission cannot use in its final decision information gathered at the hearing of one addressee of the statement of objections against another addressee not present at that hearing without having allowed the latter addressee to examine that information and give its view thereon. It also means that, if at the hearing of one addressee of the statement of objections evidence exculpating another addressee is disclosed, the Commission must, if it wants to maintain its objections against the latter addressee in the final decision, allow the latter addressee to examine that information and give its view.[1000]

---

998 The antitrust prohibitions contained in Articles 101 and 102 TFEU are addressed to undertakings. According to the case law of the Court of Justice, the concept of an undertaking must be understood as designating any entity engaged in an economic activity, even if that economic unit consists of several legal persons. In order to be applied and enforced, decisions taken pursuant to Articles 101 or 102 TFEU must, however, be addressed to entities possessing legal personality. As a result, those legal persons have the right to be heard, including the right to receive a statement of objections, to reply in writing and to develop their arguments at an oral hearing; see Judgments in *Akzo Nobel v Commission*, T-47/10, EU:T:2015:506, paragraph 126, confirmed by Judgment in *Akzo Nobel v Commission*, C-516/15 P, EU:C:2017:314, in *Akzo Nobel v Commission*, C-97/08 P, EU:C:2009:536, paragraphs 54–57, in *Compagnie maritime belge v Commission*, C-395/96 P etc., EU:C:2000:132, paragraph 143, and in *ThyssenKrupp v Commission*, C-65/02 P etc., EU:C:2005:454, paragraphs 86 and 94.

999 Judgments in *Cimenteries CBR and Others v Commission*, T-25/95 etc., EU:T:2000:77, paragraph 697, and in *Ferriere v Commission*, T-667/19, EU:T:2022:692, paragraph 84, and Opinion of Advocate General Darmon in *Ahlström Osakeyhtiö and Others v Commission*, C-89/85 etc., EU:C:1988:258, paragraph 155.

1000 Judgment in *Cimenteries CBR and Others v Commission*, T-25/95 etc., EU:T:2000:77, paragraph 682, and Opinion of Advocate General Darmon in *Ahlström Osakeyhtiö and Others v Commission*, C-89/85 etc., EU:C:1988:258, paragraph 156, and Judgment in *SKW Stahl-Metallurgie v Commission*, T-384/09, EU:T:2014:27, paragraphs 38 to 58. The principles here are the same as those applicable to the written replies of the different addressees of the statement of objections; see Judgment in *Mitsubishi Electric v Commission*, T-133/07, EU:T:2011:345, paragraphs 41 to 47.

Secondly, the different addressees' legitimate interests in the protection of their business secrets and other confidential information must be respected.[1001] This means that, to the extent that it is necessary for an addressee of the statement of objections, in order effectively to develop its defence arguments, to refer to business secrets or other confidential information, that addressee must be allowed to be heard in the absence of the other parties.[1002]

According to Article 13 of Decision 2011/695, all addressees of the statement of objections that have requested to be heard orally are normally heard in a single oral hearing, with occasionally a (short) closed session within the hearing to allow an addressee to refer to business secrets or other confidential information in the absence of the other parties. Addressees that want such a closed session must make a reasoned request to the Hearing Officer, who is empowered to accept or reject such requests.[1003]

Addressees of the statement of objections that have not in their written reply to the statement of objections requested to be heard orally have no right to attend the oral hearing of those addressees that have requested an oral hearing. The Commission may, however, invite such parties (like any other third person) to attend the oral hearing.[1004]

b. *Who can appear on behalf of an addressee of the statement of objections?*

The question which natural persons are allowed to appear at the oral hearing on behalf of an addressee of the statement of objections is governed by Article 14(4) and (5) of Regulation 773/2004,[1005] which reads as follows:

> '4. *Persons invited to attend shall either appear in person or be represented by legal representatives or by representatives authorised by their constitution as appropriate. Undertakings and associations of undertakings may also be represented by a duly authorised agent appointed from among their permanent staff.*

1001 See Article 339 TFEU and Article 28(2) of Regulation 1/2003, and Judgment in *Bank Austria Creditanstalt v Commission*, T-198/03, EU:T:2006:136, paragraph 71.

1002 See Article 14(6) of Regulation 773/2004 and Article 13 of Decision 2011/695.

1003 Article 13 of Decision 2011/695; see also Judgment in *SKW Stahl-Metallurgie v Commission*, T-384/09, EU:T:2014:27, paragraphs 38 to 58, and Judgment in *SKW Stahl-Metallurgie v Commission*, C-154/14 P, EU:C:2016:445, paragraphs 61 to 68. If the request is granted but it turns out during the closed session that the closed session was not justified, the Hearing Officer may ask the party concerned to repeat its presentation in the presence of the other parties and/or to submit a written version of its presentation to be distributed to the other parties; see Final Report of the Hearing Officer in Case COMP/39.462 *Freight Forwarding* [2012] OJ C375/4, paragraph 8.

1004 Article 13(3) of Regulation 773/2004; In the *Animal feed phosphates* cartel case, the cartel settlement procedure was followed for most addressees of the final decision, but not for two companies (belonging to the same undertaking). Given that waiving the right to an oral hearing is one of the conditions of the cartel settlement procedure, the settling parties had not requested an oral hearing, but the Hearing Officer invited them to attend the oral hearing of the two non-settling parties; see Final Report of the Hearing Officer in Case COMP/38.866 *Animal feed phosphates* [2011] OJ C111/13 at 14. The *Animal feed phosphates* case has, however, remained an exception in this respect. In all the other (more recent) similar cases, the settling parties were not invited to attend the oral hearing of the non-settling parties.

1005 These provisions apply not only to addressees of the statement of objections but also to complainants, interested third parties and other third persons admitted to the oral hearing.

5. *Persons heard by the Commission may be assisted by their lawyers or other qualified persons admitted by the Hearing Officer.*'

Two points should be noted in particular:

First, a party is thus not allowed to be represented at the oral hearing only by its lawyer. As the Court of Justice has pointed out, the requirement 'that undertakings may be represented only by a duly authorised agent appointed from among their permanent staff or by legal representatives or representatives authorised by their constitution, is justified by the fact that as a general rule those persons are the best informed as to the facts and technical or economic aspects of their undertakings' actions which may be of decisive importance in applying the rules on competition'.[1006]

Secondly, a party is not entitled to bring along to the oral hearing, as part of its own delegation, representatives of other undertakings or organisations (customers, suppliers, consumer organisations, business associations, etc.). Apart from members of their permanent staff and legal representatives or representatives authorised by their constitution, companies can only bring to the oral hearing their lawyers, as well as other qualified persons (such as economic advisors or public affairs consultants) admitted by the Hearing Officer.

Article 10(3) of Regulation 773/2004 provides, however, that a party may, in its written reply to the statement of objections, propose that the Commission hear other persons who may corroborate the facts set out in its written reply. If such a proposal is made in the written reply to the statement of objections, and the Commission accepts this proposal, these other persons may also be heard at the oral hearing, like other third persons which the Commission may invite.[1007] The General Court has confirmed that 'the Commission has a reasonable discretion to decide how expedient it may be to hear persons whose evidence may be relevant to the inquiry. The guarantee of the rights of the defence does not require the Commission to hear witnesses put forward by the party concerned, where it considers that the investigation of the case has been sufficient'.[1008]

3. Commission

a. *Hearing Officer*

The oral hearing is chaired by the Hearing Officer.[1009] The Hearing Officer is a member of the Commission's staff, who is not part of the Commission's Directorate-General for

---

1006 Judgment in *Badische Anilin- & Soda-Fabrik v Commission*, 49/69, EU:C:1972:71, paragraph 11.

1007 See Article 13(3) of Regulation 773/2004.

1008 Judgments in *FSL Holdings and Others v Commission*, T-655/11, EU:T:2015:383, paragraph 406; in *HFB and Others v Commission*, T-9/99, EU:T:2002:70, paragraph 383; in *Thyssen Stahl v Commission*, T-141/94, EU:T:1999:48, paragraph 110; and in *Silver Plastics and Johannes Reifenhäuser v Commission*, T-582/15, EU:T:2019:497, paragraphs 201–214.

1009 For the historical origin of this role of the Hearing Officer, see I. S. Forrester, 'Due process in EC competition cases: A distinguished institution with flawed procedures' (2009) 34 *European Law Review* 817 at 834 and M. Albers and J. Jourdan, 'The Role of the Hearing Officers in EU Competition Proceedings: A Historical and Practical Perspective' (2011) 2 *Journal of European Competition Law & Practice* 185 at 186; for a description of the status of the Hearing Officer and of his other current functions, see Chapter X of this book.

Competition, and who has been entrusted by the president of the Commission with a number of powers and functions in order to safeguard the effective exercise of procedural rights in antitrust and merger proceedings before the Commission.[1010] One of the tasks of the Hearing Officer is to organise and conduct the oral hearings. Article 3(1) of Decision 2011/695/EU of the President of the Commission on the function and terms of reference of the Hearing Officer in competition proceedings states generally that 'in exercising his or her functions, the Hearing Officer shall act independently', and Article 14(1) of Regulation 773/2004 and Article 6(2) of Decision 2011/695 provide more specifically that 'the oral hearing shall be conducted by the Hearing Officer in full independence'.

b. *Commission services*

The European Commission is a collegiate body composed of a number of commissioners equal to the number of EU Member States.[1011] One of these commissioners has special responsibility for competition ('the Competition Commissioner'). Neither the Competition Commissioner nor the other commissioners normally take part in the oral hearing.[1012]

Recital 19 of Decision 2011/695 states that at the oral hearing the Commission 'should be represented by the Directorate-General for Competition as well as other services that contribute to the further preparation of a decision to be taken by the Commission'.

The Directorate-General for Competition ('DG Competition') is the department of the Commission services that conducts competition investigations, under the authority of the Competition Commissioner. According to the Commission Notice on Best Practices,[1013] 'in view of the importance of the oral hearing, it is the practice of the Directorate-General for Competition to ensure the continuous presence of senior management (Director or Deputy Director-General), together with the case team of Commission officials responsible for the investigation'.

Members of DG Competition's Chief Economist's team may also attend the oral hearing, as well as members of the Cabinet (that is, the private office) of the Competition Commissioner.

As to the presence of other Commission services at the hearing, there will normally be a member of the Commission's Legal Service, which is a central service under the authority of the president of the Commission, often also a representative of the Directorate-General for Internal Market, Industry, Entrepreneurship and SMEs, and possibly, depending on the case, representatives of other departments, for instance the

---

1010 See Decision 2011/695/EU of the President of the European Commission of 13 October 2011 on the function and terms of reference of the Hearing Officer in competition proceedings [2011] OJ L275/29, and Chapter XI of this book.

1011 According to Article 17(3) of the Treaty on European Union (TEU), 'in carrying out its responsibilities, the Commission shall be completely independent', and 'the members of the Commission shall neither seek nor take instructions from any Government'.

1012 According to constant case law, the fact that the commissioners do not themselves attend the oral hearing is unproblematic: see Judgments in *Buchler v Commission*, 44/69, EU:C:1970:72, paragraphs 19 to 23, in *Boehringer Mannheim v Commission*, 45/69, EU:C:1970:73, in *Bolloré v Commission*, T-372/10, EU:T:2012:325, paragraphs 56 to 61, in *Emesa-Trefilería and Industrias Galycas v Commission*, T-406/10, EU:T:2015:499, paragraph 120, and in *Servier v Commission*, T-691/14, EU:T:2018:922, paragraph 136.

1013 Paragraph 108 of the Commission notice on best practices for the conduct of proceedings concerning Articles 101 and 102 TFEU [2011] OJ C308/6.

Directorate-General for Energy if the case concerns the energy sector, or the Directorate-General for Communications Networks, Content and Technology if the case concerns the sectors it deals with.

4. Other (competition) authorities

Article 14(3) of Regulation 773/2004 provides as follows:

'The Commission shall invite the competition authorities of the Member States to take part in the oral hearing. It may likewise invite officials and civil servants of other authorities of the Member States.'[1014]

The competition authorities of the Member States form the Advisory Committee, which the Commission must consult before adopting its final decision.[1015]

In cases concerning Article 53 or Article 54 of the Agreement on the European Economic Area (EEA), the EFTA Surveillance Authority and the EEA EFTA States may also be represented at the oral hearing.[1016]

The last sentence of Article 6(2) of Decision 2011/695 further provides:

'The Hearing Officer may also invite representatives from competition authorities from third countries to attend the oral hearing as observers in accordance with agreements concluded between the Union and third countries.'

Within the framework of the 1991 Cooperation Agreement between the EU and the USA, the Commission has agreed administrative arrangements with the US competition authorities (Department of Justice and Federal Trade Commission), which provide for the possibility of the US competition authorities attending, as observers, in appropriate cases of mutual concern, oral hearings before the Commission. Attendance is only possible with the express consent of the persons concerned by the enforcement proceedings.[1017] A similar administrative agreement with the Competition Bureau of Canada, within the framework of the 1999 Cooperation Agreement between the EU and Canada, was agreed on 27 March 2017.

1014 The invitation of the competition authorities of the Member States constitutes an essential procedural requirement; see Judgment in *Feralpi v Commission*, C-88/15 P, EU:C:2017:709, paragraphs 53 and 54. There is, however, no obligation for the competition authorities of the Member States to attend the oral hearing; see Judgments in *Servier v Commission*, T-691/14, EU:T:2018:922, paragraph 163, and in *Ferriere v Commission*, T-667/19, EU:T:2022:692, paragraphs 171 to 194.
For an example of other authorities being invited, see the *Telefónica* case, in which representatives of the Spanish Telecommunications Market Commission participated in the oral hearing; see Judgment in *Spain v Commission*, T-398/07, EU:T:2012:173, paragraph 48.

1015 Article 14 of Regulation 1/2003.

1016 Article 5 of Protocol 23 to the EEA Agreement, as replaced by Decision No 130/2004 of the EEA Joint Committee of 24 September 2004 [2005] OJ L64/57.

1017 Report from the Commission to the Council and the European Parliament on the application of the Agreement between the European Communities and the Government of the United States of America regarding the application of their competition laws 1 January 1999 to 31 December 1999, COM(2000)618 of 4 October 2000, at 4–5. Attendance is also conditioned upon confirmation of satisfactory assurances or arrangements regarding confidentiality and use of information. In the *Intel* case, not only a representative of the Federal Trade Commission but also the attorney general of the State of New York was admitted at the hearing, with the agreement of Intel, and following undertakings as to confidentiality and use of information; see Final Report of the Hearing Officer in Case COMP/C-3/37.990 *Intel* [2009] OJ C227/7 at 10.

5. Complainants

Article 7 of Regulation 1/2003 provides for a status of complainant in relation to the finding and termination of infringements of Articles 101 and 102 TFEU.[1018] Complaints by EU Member States are always admissible.[1019] Natural or legal persons can become complainants provided that they can show a legitimate interest and that their complaint contains the information required by Form C, as set out in the Annex to Regulation 773/2004.[1020]

The last sentence of Article 27(1) of Regulation 1/2003 provides that 'complainants shall be associated closely with the proceedings'. Article 6 of Regulation 773/2004 provides in more detail as follows:

> '*1. Where the Commission issues a statement of objections relating to a matter in respect of which it has received a complaint, it shall provide the complainant with a copy of the non-confidential version of the statement of objections, except in [cartel] cases where the settlement procedure applies, where it shall inform the complainant in writing of the nature and the subject matter of the procedure. The Commission shall also set a time limit within which the complainant may make known its views in writing.*
>
> *2. The Commission may, where appropriate, afford complainants the opportunity of expressing their views at the oral hearing of the parties to which a statement of objections has been issued, if complainants so request in their written comments.*'

Article 6(2) of Decision 2011/695 empowers the Hearing Officer to decide on the admission of complainants to the oral hearing:[1021]

'*The Hearing Officer may, where appropriate and after consulting the Director responsible, decide to afford complainants [. . .] the opportunity to express their views at the oral hearing of the parties to which a statement of objections has been issued, provided they so request in their written comments.*'

Recital 13 of Decision 2011/695 adds:

'*The Hearing Officer should decide whether to admit complainants [. . .] to the oral hearing, taking into account the contribution they can make to the clarification of the relevant facts of the case.*'

1018 The status of complainant is not provided for in relation to the imposition of fines pursuant to Article 23 of Regulation 1/2003.

1019 Article 7(2) of Regulation 1/2003.

1020 Article 7(2) of Regulation 1/2003 and Article 5 of Regulation 773/2004; see also Commission Notice on the handling of complaints by the Commission under Articles 81 and 82 of the EC Treaty [2004] OJ C101/5, and Judgment in *Österreichische Postsparkasse and Bank für Arbeit und Wirtschaft v Commission*, T-213/01 and T-214/01, EU:T:2006:151, and Chapter XIV of this book.

1021 Different from the case of interested third persons, the Hearing Officer has not been granted the power to decide whether persons that want to be admitted as complainants can show a legitimate interest; see Judgment in *Österreichische Postsparkasse and Bank für Arbeit und Wirtschaft v Commission*, T-213/01 and T-214/01, EU:T:2006:151, paragraph 132, and Decision 2011/695.

Several points should be noted:

First, complainants cannot request an oral hearing. They can only request to be allowed to express their views at the oral hearing of the addressees of the statement of objections, which presupposes that at least one of these addressees has requested an oral hearing.

Second, complainants can only request to be allowed to express their views at the oral hearing if they have first made written comments, and have in these written comments requested the opportunity to participate in the oral hearing.[1022]

Third, even if they have made the request in their written comments, complainants have no right to participate at the oral hearing. The Hearing Officer has a discretionary power to decide whether or not it is appropriate to admit a complainant to the oral hearing. The provision in Article 27(1) of Regulation 1/2003 according to which 'complainants shall be associated closely with the proceedings' is clearly relevant for this decision. As indicated in recital 13 of Decision 2011/695 quoted just above, a further consideration that the Hearing Officer should take into account in making this decision is the contribution that the complainant can make to the clarification of the relevant facts of the case. Normally a good indicator for this is the contribution that the complainant has already made to the Commission's investigation through the complaint, responses to requests for information and written comments on the statement of objections.

6. Interested third persons

Article 13(1) and (2) of Regulation 773/2004 provide as follows:

'1. *If natural or legal persons other than [complainants and addressees of the statement of objections] apply to be heard and show a sufficient interest, the Commission shall inform them in writing of the nature and subject matter of the procedure and shall set a time-limit within which they may make known their views in writing.*

2. *The Commission may, where appropriate, invite persons referred to in paragraph 1 to develop their arguments at the oral hearing of the parties to whom a statement of objections has been addressed, if the persons referred to in paragraph 1 so request in their written comments.'*

Article 5 of Decision 2011/695 empowers the Hearing Officer to decide on applications of interested third persons to be heard in writing:

'1. *Applications to be heard from persons other than [complainants and addressees of the statement of objections] [. . .] shall be submitted in writing and explain the applicant's interest in the outcome of the procedure.*

2. *The Hearing Officer shall decide as to whether third persons are to be heard after consulting the Director responsible. In assessing whether a third person shows a sufficient interest, the Hearing Officer shall take into account whether*

1022 The written observations must be made within the time limit set by the Commission. The complainant can make a reasoned request for an extension of the time limit, first to the director responsible and in second instance to the Hearing Officer; see Article 6(1) of Regulation 773/2004 and Article 9(2) of Decision 2011/695.

and to what extent the applicant is sufficiently affected by the conduct which is the subject of the competition proceedings [. . .].'[1023]

Article 6(2) of Decision 2011/695 also empowers the Hearing Officer to decide on the admission of interested third persons to the oral hearing:

'The Hearing Officer may, where appropriate and after consulting the Director responsible, decide to afford [. . .] interested third persons [. . .] the opportunity to express their views at the oral hearing of the parties to which a statement of objections has been issued, provided they so request in their written comments.'

Recital 13 of Decision 2011/695 adds:

'The Hearing Officer should decide whether to admit [. . .] interested third persons to the oral hearing, taking into account the contribution they can make to the clarification of the relevant facts of the case.'

As in the case of complainants, several points should be noted:

First, interested third persons cannot request an oral hearing. They can only request to be allowed to express their views at the oral hearing of the addressees of the statement of objections, which presupposes that at least one of these addressees has requested an oral hearing.

Second, interested third persons can only request to be allowed to express their views at the oral hearing if they have first requested and been allowed to be heard in writing, and have in their written comments requested the opportunity to participate in the oral hearing.[1024]

Third, even if they have made the request in their written comments, interested third persons have no right to participate at the oral hearing. The Hearing Officer has a discretionary power to decide whether or not it is appropriate to admit an interested third person to the oral hearing.[1025] As indicated in recital 13 of Decision 2011/695 quoted just above, an important consideration which the Hearing Officer must take into account

---

1023 The second sentence of recital 12 of Decision 2011/695 provides that consumer associations that apply to be heard should generally be regarded as having a sufficient interest, where the proceedings concern products or services used by end consumers or products or services that constitute a direct input into such products or services; see also Judgment in *Association belge des consommateurs test-achats v Commission*, T-224/10, EU:T:2011:588, paragraphs 40 to 44.
The third and fourth paragraphs of Article 5 of Decision 2011/695 add that, if the Hearing Officer considers that the applicant has not shown a sufficient interest, the applicant is entitled to a two-stage reasoned rejection decision, and that the Hearing Officer shall inform the parties to competition proceedings as from the formal initiation of proceedings of the identity of interested parties to be heard, unless such disclosure would significantly harm a person or undertaking.

1024 The written observations must be made within the time limit set by the Commission. The interested third person can make a reasoned request for an extension of the time limit, first to the Director responsible and in second instance to the Hearing Officer; see Article 13(1) of Regulation 773/2004 and Article 9(2) of Decision 2011/695.

1025 See Judgments in *VBVB and VBBB v Commission*, 43/82 and 63/82, EU:C:1984:9, paragraph 18, in *Compagnie générale maritime and Others v Commission*, T-86/95, EU:T:2002:50, paragraph 468, and in *Ferriere v Commission*, T-667/19, EU:T:2022:692, paragraph 133, and Final Report of the Hearing Officer in Case AT.40608 *Broadcom – Interim Measures Procedure* [2021] OJ C81/13, paragraphs 59 and 60.

in making this decision is the contribution that the interested third person can make to the clarification of the relevant facts of the case. Normally a good indicator for this is the contribution that the interested third person has already made to the Commission's investigation through written comments and responses to requests for information.

7. Other third persons

Article 13(3) of Regulation 773/2004 provides as follows:

'The Commission may also invite any other person to express its views in writing and to attend the oral hearing of the parties to whom a statement of objections has been addressed. The Commission may also invite such persons to express their views at that oral hearing.'

The difference with complainants and interested third persons is that these other third persons are invited by the Commission and do not need to show either a legitimate interest or a sufficient interest. Another difference is that they may be invited to attend the oral hearing without being allowed to express their views, whereas complainants and interested third persons can only be admitted to the oral hearing in order to express their views.[1026] In practice such other third persons are only rarely invited.[1027]

E. Who speaks at the oral hearing? – Presentations and questions

1. Presentations

The oral hearing essentially consists of a succession of presentations, interspersed with question-and-answer sessions.

The main presentations are those by the addressees of the statement of objections (and, in merger proceedings, other involved parties).[1028]

Traditionally, the presentations by the addressees of the statement of objections are preceded by a brief presentation by the case team of DG Competition officials responsible for the investigation. The purpose of this presentation is to give, by way of reminder, a summary of the main content of the statement of objections. If, with regard to some objections, the case team were already convinced by the written replies to the statement of objections and had already come to the conclusion that those objections should be dropped, it might be useful for the case team to communicate this conclusion at this point.[1029] Otherwise, the case team should at this point abstain from any comments on

---

[1026] See Articles 6(2) and 13(2) of Regulation 773/2004 and Article 6(2) of Decision 2011/695.

[1027] As to the Commission's discretion in this respect, see Judgments in *Compagnie générale maritime and Others v Commission*, T-86/95, EU:T:2002:50, paragraph 468, in *VBVB and VBBB v Commission*, 43/82 and 63/82, EU:C:1984:9, paragraph 18, and in *Ferriere v Commission*, T-667/19, EU:T:2022:692, paragraph 149.

[1028] Each addressee of the statement of objections (and each other involved party) is entitled to a separate presentation, but, as for the written reply to the statement of objections, two or more of them may also choose to present a joint defence.

[1029] Unless this conclusion had already been validated by the College of Members of the Commission (which would normally not be the case at this stage of the proceedings), it should, however, be made clear that this is only the opinion of the case team.

the written replies to the statement of objections, and limit itself strictly to summarily repeating the main content of the statement of objections.

Complainants and third parties normally make their presentations after the presentations by the addressees of the statement of objections, with at the end a possibility for the addressees of the statement of objections to reply to any hostile presentations.

It is for the Hearing Officer to decide on the order in which the different parties make their presentations, as well as the time allocated for each presentation.[1030]

Article 10(4) of Decision 2011/695 instructs the Hearing Officer to 'ensure that the oral hearing provides addressees of the statement of objections, other involved parties, as well as complainants and interested third persons [. . .] which have been admitted to the oral hearing, with sufficient opportunity to develop their views as to the preliminary findings of the Commission'.

Article 11(1) and (3) of Decision 2011/695 provide that the Hearing Officer may take 'all appropriate measures' for the preparation of the oral hearing. In particular, the Hearing Officer 'may ask for prior written confirmation of the essential contents of the intended statements of persons invited to the hearing', and 'may, after consulting the Director responsible, supply in advance to the persons invited to the hearing a list of questions on which they are invited to make known their views. The Hearing Officer may also indicate to the persons invited to the hearing the focal areas for debate, having regard, in particular, to the facts and issues that the addressees of the statement of objections who have requested an oral hearing want to raise'.[1031]

The General Court has pointed out that 'the mere fact that the Commission imposes a programme for the hearings does not of itself constitute an infringement of the rights of the defence. There can be such an infringement only where the applicants concerned prove that the organisation of the hearings prevented them from attending the hearings relating to objections raised against them or from putting forward orally their arguments against such objections'.[1032]

All addressees of the statement of objections, other involved parties, complainants and interested third persons that have requested or have been admitted to the oral hearing are expected to make a presentation. Such parties are in principle not allowed to attend the hearing as mere observers.[1033]

1030 See Chapter 6 of Decision 2011/695; Article 12(2) even provides that the Hearing Officer 'shall decide [. . .] which persons should be heard on behalf of a party'.

1031 Article 11(2) of Decision 2011/695 adds that, for this purpose, after consulting the director responsible, the Hearing Officer may hold a meeting with the persons invited to the hearing and, where appropriate, the Commission services, in order to prepare for the hearing. For an example of a case in which the Hearing Officer supplied in advance questions to the addressees of a statement of objections, see Final Report of the Hearing Officer in Case COMP/39.793 *EPH and Others* [2012] OJ C316/6, paragraphs 6 and 7.

1032 Judgment in *Cimenteries CBR and Others v Commission*, T-25/95 etc., EU:T:2000:77, paragraph 663; see also paragraph 674 of the same judgment as to the length of the speaking time.

1033 See however above as to other third persons invited by the Commission.

2. Questions

Article 12(3) of Decision 2011/695 provides as follows:

'The Hearing Officer may allow the parties to whom a statement of objections has been addressed, other involved parties, complainants, other persons invited to the hearing, the Commission services and the authorities of the Member States to ask questions during the hearing. To the extent that, exceptionally, a question cannot be answered in whole or in part at the oral hearing, the Hearing Officer may allow the reply to be given in writing within a set time limit. Such written reply shall be distributed to all participants in the oral hearing, unless the Hearing Officer decides otherwise in order to protect the rights of the defence of an addressee of a statement of objections or the business secrets or other confidential information of any person.'[1034]

A first point to be noted is that, while the Hearing Officer may thus allow the different participants at the oral hearing to ask questions, no provision is made for a corresponding obligation to respond to such questions. As a general rule, no participant at the oral hearing is obliged to respond to any question.[1035] Under general principles of good administration, the Commission services may, however, be under an obligation to respond to certain questions.

As to the type of questions that may be admissible, regard should be had to the nature and purpose of the oral hearing. Types of questions that would appear in principle compatible with the nature and purpose of the oral hearing include the following:

- Questions to an addressee of the statement of objections aimed at gaining a better understanding of the content and the strength of that party's written and oral reply to the statement of objections;
- Questions to a complainant aimed at gaining a better understanding of the content and the strength of the complaint, to the extent that the statement of objections relies on the complaint, and of the complainant's views on the statement of objections;
- Questions to interested third persons or other third persons aimed at gaining a better understanding of the content and the strength of their views on the matters covered by the proceedings;
- Questions to addressees of the statement of objection, other involved parties, complainants, interested third persons or other third persons aimed at verifying (their agreement or disagreement with) factual assertions made by another party during the oral hearing;
- Questions to the Commission services aimed at gaining a better understanding of the content of the statement of objections, including questions concerning the choices the Commission has made as to the inclusion or non-inclusion of certain objections, facts or addressees in the statement of objections.

1034 See also above as to the possibility for the Hearing officer to supply questions in advance.

1035 The Commission may, however, following the oral hearing, make use of its powers under Article 18 of Regulation 1/2003 to request information in writing.

Types of questions that are in principle incompatible with the nature and purpose of the oral hearing include the following:

- Question that are unrelated to the statement of objections and the written and oral comments on the statement of objections;
- Questions that extend or reorient the investigation; the Commission can always, following the written and oral replies to the statement of objections, extend or reorient its investigation, but this should be done outside of the oral hearing through use of the Commission's investigative powers, such as requests for information.

F. Some further issues

1. Timing

Article 12(1) of Decision 2011/695 provides that 'after consulting the Director responsible, the Hearing Officer shall determine the date, the duration and the place of the hearing. Where a postponement is requested, the hearing officer shall decide whether or not to allow it.'

Where there are only one or two addressees of the statement of objections, the Hearing Officer may also consult these parties before determining the date of the hearing.[1036]

2. Languages

In antitrust proceedings, participants in the oral hearing may in principle speak in any of the official languages of the EU.[1037]

In practice, simultaneous translation will normally be available from and into English and any other official EU language in which an addressee of the statement of objections has sent its written reply to the statement of objections. Participants who want to use another official EU language at the oral hearing should contact the Hearing Officer sufficiently in advance so that translation can be provided for.[1038]

1036 See Judgment in *Compagnie générale maritime and Others v Commission*, T-86/95, EU:T:2002:50, paragraphs 463 to 466 as to the time to prepare for the oral hearing and as to the issue of certain persons not being able to attend the oral hearing on the determined date; see also Opinion of Advocate General Wahl in *SKW Stahl-Metallurgie v Commission*, C-154/14 P, EU:C:2015:543, paragraph 71: 'The right to be heard is intended to give undertakings the opportunity of being heard, not necessarily of being heard at the time of their best convenience.'

1037 According to Article 1 of Regulation 1 determining the languages to be used by the European Economic Community [1958] OJ 17/385, as last amended by Council Regulation (EU) No 517/2013 [2013] OJ L158/1, 'the official languages and the working languages of the institutions of the Union shall be Bulgarian, Croatian, Czech, Danish, Dutch, English, Estonian, Finnish, French, German, Hungarian, Irish, Italian, Latvian, Lithuanian, Maltese, Polish, Portuguese, Romanian, Slovak, Slovenian, Spanish and Swedish'; with regard to proceedings concerning Article 53 or Article 54 EEA, see also Article 12 of Protocol 23 to the EEA Agreement, as replaced by Decision No 130/2004 of the EEA Joint Committee of 24 September 2004 [2005] OJ L64/57.

1038 See also paragraph 31 of the Notice on Best Practices.

3. Recording

Article 14(8) of Regulation 773/2004 provides as follows:

'The statements made by each person heard shall be recorded. Upon request, the recording of the hearing shall be made available to the persons who attended the hearing. Regard shall also be had to the legitimate interest of the parties in the protection of their business secrets and other confidential information.'[1039]

4. Obligation to provide accurate information

Similar to what the General Court has held with regard to the written reply to a statement of objections,[1040] it would appear that, even if there is no obligation to participate in the oral hearing or to respond to any questions asked during the oral hearing, in light of the general scheme of Regulation 1/2003, the obligation to provide accurate information applies to any statements made at the oral hearing.

5. Use of information obtained at the oral hearing

The oral hearing is not public.[1041]

In the case of antitrust proceedings, information obtained through the oral hearing may only be used for the purpose of judicial or administrative proceedings for the application of Articles 101 and 102 TFEU. Moreover, information that was prepared by other natural or legal persons specifically for the proceedings of the Commission (for instance, other parties' presentations at the oral hearing) or information that the Commission has drawn up and sent to the parties in the course of its proceedings (for instance, the recording of the oral hearing) shall not be used in proceedings before national courts until the Commission has closed its proceedings against all parties under investigation.[1042]

6. New documents

Article 12(2) of Decision 2011/695 empowers the Hearing Officer to decide whether new documents should be admitted during the oral hearing.

1039 The oral submissions of the various parties are recorded in the language used by them, not any translations; see Judgment in *Cimenteries CBR and Others v Commission*, T-25/95 etc., EU:T:2000:77, paragraph 636. If the oral hearing contained a closed session, only the parties that attended the closed session can obtain the recording of that part of the oral hearing.

1040 Judgment in *IBP v Commission*, T-384/06, EU:T:2011:113, paragraph 111.

1041 Article 14(6) of Regulation 773/2004, and recital 20 of Decision 2011/695/EU.

1042 Article 16a(1) and (3) of Regulation 773/2004; see also paragraph 107 of the Notice on Best Practices (adding that, should information disclosed during the oral hearing be used for any other purpose at any point in time with the involvement of outside counsel, the Commission may report the incident to the bar of that counsel, with a view to disciplinary action); see also Judgment of the Eastern New York District Court of 27 August 2010 in *In Re Payment Card Interchange Fee and Merchant Discount Antitrust Litigation* (rejecting a discovery request for a transcript of the oral hearing).

G. After the oral hearing

1. Further written comments

Article 12(4) of Decision 2011/695 provides as follows:

'Where required by the need to ensure the right to be heard, the Hearing Officer may, after consulting the Director responsible, afford the parties concerned, other involved parties, complainants or interested third persons [. . .] the opportunity to submit further written comments after the oral hearing. The Hearing Officer shall fix a date by which such submissions may be made. The Commission shall not be obliged to take into account written comments received after that date.'[1043]

2. Interim report and observations by the Hearing Officer

Article 14 of Decision 2011/695 provides as follows:

'1. The Hearing Officer shall submit an interim report to [the Competition Commissioner] on the hearing and the conclusions he or she draws with regard to the respect for the effective exercise of procedural rights. [. . .]

2. In addition to, and separately from, [this interim report], the Hearing Officer may make observations on the further progress and impartiality of the proceedings. In so doing, the Hearing Officer shall seek to ensure in particular that, in the preparation of draft Commission decisions, due account is taken of all the relevant facts, whether favourable or unfavourable to the parties concerned, including the factual elements relevant for the gravity and duration of any infringement. Such observations may relate to, inter alia, the need for further information, the withdrawal of certain objections, the formulation of further objections or suggestions for further investigative measures pursuant to Chapter V of Regulation (EC) No 1/2003.'

The interim report and the observations of the Hearing Officer are only for internal use by the Commission, and are not communicated to any of the parties to the proceedings.[1044]

3. State of play meeting

The Commission's Notice on best practices for the conduct of antitrust proceedings indicates that after the oral hearing DG Competition will normally offer the addressees of the statement of objections a state of play meeting, in which these parties will be informed of the Commission's or DG Competition's preliminary view on how it intends to pursue the case further.[1045]

1043 See also above as to the possibility exceptionally to allow a question asked at the oral hearing to be replied to in writing after the oral hearing.

1044 See also Judgments in *FMC Foret v Commission*, T-191/06, EU:T:2011:277, paragraph 143, and in *Infineon Technologies v Commission*, T-758/14, EU:T:2016:737, paragraph 112.

1045 Paragraphs 64 and 65 of the Notice on Best Practices; on state of play meetings more generally, see below.

H. State of play meetings and other ways of hearing parties orally

The (formal) oral hearing is not the only way in which the parties may be heard orally in the course of competition proceedings.

The Commission's Notice on best practices for the conduct of antitrust proceedings indicates that DG Competition will offer to the parties against whom it conducts antitrust investigations the possibility to have an exchange of views at several points in time throughout the proceedings during a state of play meeting,[1046] normally chaired by senior management of DG Competition (director or deputy director-general),[1047] except in (non-settlement) cartel cases where this possibility will only be offered once, after the oral hearing.[1048]

State of play meetings are distinct from and complementary to the oral hearing.[1049] They are much more informal in character than the oral hearing, normally do not involve the Hearing Officer, and are normally not attended by complainants or third persons.[1050]

The Commission's Notice on best practices for the conduct of antitrust proceedings indicates that DG Competition may also exceptionally, in order to clarify certain factual points, organise 'triangular' meetings with the parties, possibly involving also complainants or third persons.[1051]

Finally, the Commission's Notice on best practices for the conduct of antitrust proceedings further provides the following as to meetings with the Competition Commissioner or the Director-General:

'If the parties so request, it is normal practice to offer senior officers of the parties subject to the proceedings and the complainant an opportunity to discuss the case with the Director-General for competition, the Deputy Director-General for antitrust, or if appropriate, with the Commissioner responsible for Competition. The senior officers may be accompanied by their legal and/or economic advisors.'[1052]

I. Why ask for an oral hearing?

As explained above, it is for the addressees of a statement of objections to decide whether or not a (formal) oral hearing takes place. This decision no doubt depends on the specificities of each case, and the preferences of the companies concerned and their lawyers.

1046 Paragraphs 60 to 66 of the Notice on Best Practices.

1047 However, in cases involving multiple parties, the meeting may be chaired by the responsible head of unit; paragraph 62 of the Notice on Best Practices.

1048 Paragraph 65 of the Notice on Best Practices; as to settlement cases, see Commission Notice on the conduct of settlement procedures in view of the adoption of Decisions pursuant to Article 7 and Article 23 of Council regulation (EC) No 1/2003 in cartel cases [2008] OJ C167/1, amended [2015] OJ C256/2.

1049 See also Judgment in *Slovak Telekom v Commission*, T-851/14, EU:T:2018:929, paragraph 209.

1050 Paragraph 61 of the Notice on Best Practices also indicates that, 'where several parties are investigated, state of play meetings will be offered to each party separately'.

1051 Paragraphs 67 to 69 of the Notice on Best Practices.

1052 Paragraph 70 of the Notice on Best Practices.

It would nevertheless appear possible to make some general observations as to what factors may make addressees of a statement of objections decide in favour or against requesting an oral hearing, or in what types of cases requesting an oral hearing is likely to make more or less sense. A distinction could be drawn between cartel cases and other antitrust cases.

In cartel cases it usually becomes clear at a relatively early stage of the proceedings, before the sending of the statement of objections, whether or not there is a possibility of the case being conducted under the cartel settlement procedure. Indeed, if the Commission considers that the case may be suitable for settlement, it will normally explore this option with the parties before drafting a statement of objections, and, if the parties are willing to settle, the cartel settlement procedure will be followed. In this case, the parties will waive their right to an oral hearing as part of the settlement conditions.[1053] The cartel cases in which the sending of a statement of objections provides the parties with the option of requesting an oral hearing are thus usually cases in which settlement is no longer an option. The foreseeable outcome of these cases is thus that the Commission will either make a finding of infringement and impose fines or, if it can be convinced by the defence arguments, drop the case (for all or some of the addressees of the statement of objections).

Given the potential magnitude of the fines, and the risks of follow-on actions for damages, an addressee of the statement of objections that sees even only a small chance of convincing the Commission to drop the case against it will be well advised to request an oral hearing, as the hearing gives it an additional chance to set out its defence arguments, and to make them directly to more individuals who may influence the Commission's decision than those likely to read the written reply to the statement of objections. The party may also hope to convince the representatives of the competition authorities of the Member States, who will later give their opinion in the Advisory Committee, or to convince the Hearing Officer, who could recommend to the Competition Commissioner to drop the case against it.

Given that both the potential magnitude of the fines and the risks of follow-on actions for damages depend on the Commission's findings as to the exact duration, scope, intensity, etc. of the cartel, all addressees that see even only a relatively small chance of convincing the Commission on any of these aspects are probably equally well advised to request an oral hearing.

Given that parties are not normally granted access by the Commission to the written replies of the other addressees of the statement of objections,[1054] whereas all parties are heard in a single oral hearing, requesting an oral hearing may also allow those parties that have not coordinated their defence with other addressees of the statement of objections

---

1053 See Commission Notice on the conduct of settlement procedures in view of the adoption of Decisions pursuant to Article 7 and Article 23 of Council regulation (EC) No 1/2003 in cartel cases [2008] OJ C167/1, amended [2015] OJ C256/2; if at some point in the settlement procedure there is no longer agreement, the normal procedure will be followed, and the Commission will draft a normal statement of objections.

1054 See paragraph 103 of the Notice on Best Practices, and Judgment in *Mitsubishi v Commission*, T-133/07, EU:T:2011:345, paragraphs 41 to 44.

to discover the defence arguments of those other parties. This may then allow a party to make at the oral hearing itself and/or later on appeal before the General Court additional arguments which it might otherwise not have been able to make.

Given the potential magnitude of the fines, the General Court's unlimited jurisdiction with regard to fines, and the delaying effect that appeals may have on follow-on actions for damages, it is very often in the interest of those parties that end up being fined by the Commission to bring an appeal before the General Court. As mentioned just above, attending the oral hearing may help parties to find additional arguments which could be used on appeal.

It is thus not surprising that almost invariably parties in non-settlement cartel cases request an oral hearing.

In antitrust cases other than cartel cases, most addressees of a statement of objections also request an oral hearing.

There is, however, a difference with cartel cases in that in non-cartel antitrust cases the fact that a statement of objections has been sent normally does not mean that the option of a settlement is no longer open. Indeed, the parties may contact DG Competition at any time to explore the possibility of a commitment decision pursuant to Article 9 of Regulation 1/2003, including after the sending of a statement of objections.[1055] Requesting an oral hearing does not exclude the possibility of a later commitment decision. In some cases, however, parties that see a good chance of having the case quickly resolved through a commitment decision might prefer not to ask for an oral hearing and to focus instead immediately on commitment discussions, so as to save time and to avoid positions becoming more entrenched. Given its relatively formal character, and the presence of many persons, including possibly complainants and hostile third parties, the oral hearing does not appear a very suitable forum to explore commitment possibilities.

[1055] Paragraphs 118 and 123 of the Notice on Best Practices; on commitment decisions generally, see my papers 'Settlements of EU Antitrust investigations: Commitment Decisions under Article 9 of Regulation No. 1/2003' (2006) 29 *World Competition* 345, and 'Ten years of commitment decisions under Article 9 of Regulation 1/2003: Too much of a good thing?' (New frontiers of antitrust Concurrences Journal 6th International Conference, Paris, 15 June 2015), all also accessible at http://ssrn.com/author=456087.

XIII. Legal Professional Privilege in EU Antitrust Enforcement: Law, Policy and Procedure

This Chapter discusses the law, policy and procedure of legal professional privilege in EU antitrust enforcement. It focuses primarily on the enforcement of Articles 101 and 102 TFEU by the European Commission, but also touches briefly on the enforcement of EU antitrust law by the competition authorities of the EU Member States (addressing in particular the question whether those EU Member States that extend legal professional privilege to in-house lawyers are in breach of EU law), as well as on private enforcement.

A. Introduction and overview

Legal professional privilege is the expression commonly used to describe what the EU Court of Justice has called the 'principle of confidentiality of written communications between lawyer and client'.[1056] As has been pointed out repeatedly,[1057] the expression 'legal professional privilege' is a misnomer, because it is a right of the client, not a privilege of the legal profession. As has been pointed out by the EU Court of Justice, 'the principle of confidentiality does not prevent a lawyer's client from disclosing the written communications between them if it considers that it is in his interest to do so'.[1058]

Legal professional privilege constitutes a limitation on the European Commission's use of coercive powers of investigation under Regulation 1/2003.[1059] Chapter V of this Regulation gives the European Commission a number of powers of investigation which it can use to obtain intelligence and evidence of violations of Articles 101 and 102 TFEU

1056 Judgment in *AM & S Europe v Commission*, 155/79, EU:C:1982:157. In its more recent judgment in *Akzo Nobel Chemicals and Akcros Chemicals v Commission*, C-550/07 P, EU:C:2010:512, the Court of Justice also used the expression 'legal professional privilege'.

1057 See Lord Wilberforce in *Waugh v British Railways Board* [1980] AC 251, at 531; Opinion of Advocate General Warner in *AM & S Europe v Commission*, 155/79, EU:C:1981:19 [1982] ECR 1619 at 1622 and 1633; and Opinion of Advocate General Sir Gordon Slynn in *AM & S Europe v Commission*, 155/79, EU:C:1982:17 [1982] ECR 1642 at 1650.

1058 Judgments in *AM & S Europe v Commission*, 155/79, EU:C:1982:157, paragraph 28, and in *Akzo Nobel Chemicals and Akcros Chemicals v Commission*, T-125/03 and T-253/03, EU:T:2007:287, paragraph 90. See also Order in *Hilti v Commission*, T-30/89, EU:T:1990:27, paragraph 12.
Legal professional privilege does thus not stand in the way of lawyer-client communications being produced voluntarily to the European Commission by the client, for instance in the framework of leniency; see further my papers 'Self-incrimination in EC Antitrust Enforcement: A Legal and Economic Analysis' (2003) 26 *World Competition* 567, and 'Leniency in Antitrust Enforcement: Theory and Practice' (2007) 30 *World Competition* 25, both also accessible at http://ssrn.com/author=456087, and Chapters V and VI of this book.

1059 Council Regulation (EC) No 1/2003 of 16 December 2002 on the implementation of the rules on competition laid down in Articles 81 and 82 of the Treaty [2003] OJ L1/1, last amended by Council Regulation (EC) No 1419/2006 [2006] OJ L269/1. This regulation replaced the earlier Council Regulation No 17 [1962] OJ 13/204 (Special English Edition 1959-62, p. 87).

from companies that are suspected of having committed such violations,[1060] the two main instruments being requests for information (Article 18 of Regulation 1/2003) and inspections (Article 20 of Regulation 1/2003).[1061]

It follows from legal professional privilege, as recognised by the EU Court of Justice since its 1982 judgment in *AM & S Europe v Commission*, that the European Commission cannot use its powers of investigation to compel the disclosure of communications between lawyers and clients, provided that, on the one hand, such communications are made for the purpose and in the interests of the client's rights of defence and, on the other hand, the lawyers are independent lawyers, who are not bound to the client by a relationship of employment, and who are entitled to practise their profession in one of the EU (or EEA) Member States.[1062]

In subsequent judgments, the EU General Court has recognised that internal documents of a company summarising advice received in the exercise of the company's rights of defence from external lawyers are also protected.[1063] Similarly, internal preparatory documents, even if they were not exchanged with a lawyer or were not created for the purpose of being sent physically to a lawyer, are protected if drawn up exclusively for the purpose of seeking legal advice from an external lawyer in the exercise of the rights of defence.[1064] On the other hand, the mere fact that a document has been discussed with an external lawyer is not sufficient to give it protection.[1065]

B. Legal nature, legal basis and rationale

The legal nature, legal basis and rationale of legal professional privilege, as recognised in EU law, were summarised by Advocate General Kokott in paragraphs 47 to 49 of her Opinion in *Akzo Nobel Chemicals and Akcros Chemicals* v *Commission* (with numerous footnotes, omitted here) as follows:[1066]

> '47. *In EU law, the protection of legal professional privilege has the status of a general legal principle in the nature of a fundamental right. This follows, on the one hand, from the principles common to the legal systems of the Member States: legal professional privilege is currently recognised in all*

1060 The powers of investigation can also be used to obtain information from other undertakings or associations of undertakings that may have information relevant for the case; see Commission Notice on best practices for the conduct of proceedings concerning Articles 101 and 102 TFEU [2011] OJ C308/6, paragraph 32.

1061 See further K. Dekeyser, C. Gauer, J. Laitenberger, N. Wahl, W. Wils and L. Prete (eds), *Regulation 1/2003 and EU Antitrust Enforcement – A Systematic Guide* (Wolters Kluwer 2022).

1062 Judgment in *AM & S Europe v Commission*, 155/79, EU:C:1982:157, paragraphs 18 to 27.

1063 Order in *Hilti v Commission*, T-30/89, EU:T:1990:27, paragraph 18.

1064 Judgment in *Akzo Nobel Chemicals and Akcros Chemicals v Commission*, T-125/03 and T-253/03, EU:T:2007:287, paragraph 123.

1065 Judgment in *Akzo Nobel Chemicals and Akcros Chemicals v Commission*, T-125/03 and T-253/03, EU:T:2007:287, paragraph 123.

1066 Opinion of Advocate General Kokott in *Akzo Nobel Chemicals and Akcros Chemicals v Commission*, C-550/07 P, EU:C:2010:229, paragraphs 47 to 49 (numerous footnotes omitted).
For a detailed analysis of the fundamental rights foundation of legal professional privilege, see E. Gippini-Fournier, 'Legal Professional Privilege in Competition Proceedings Before the European Commission: Beyond the Cursory Glance', in B. E. Hawk (ed) *2004 Annual Proceedings of the Fordham Corporate Law Institute – International Antitrust Law and Policy* (Juris Publishing 2005), 587, at 606 to 626.

[28] Member States of the European Union, in some of which its protection is enshrined in case law alone, but in most of which it is provided for at least by statute if not by the constitution itself. On the other hand, the protection of legal professional privilege also derives from Article 8(1) of the ECHR [European Convention on Human Rights] (protection of correspondence) in conjunction with Article 6(1) and (3)(c) of the ECHR (right to a fair trial) as well as from Article 7 of the Charter of Fundamental Rights of the European Union (respect for communications) in conjunction with Article 47(1), second sentence of Article 47(2) and Article 48(2) of that Charter (right to be advised, defended and represented, respect for the rights of the defence).

48. Legal professional privilege serves to protect communications between a client and a lawyer who is independent of that client. On the one hand, it is the essential corollary to the client's rights of defence and, on the other hand, it is based on the specific role of the lawyer as "collaborating in the interests of justice" and as being required to provide, in full independence, and in the overriding interests of justice, such legal assistance as the client needs.

49. Lawyers would be unable to carry out satisfactorily their task of advising, defending and representing their clients, who would in consequence be deprived of the rights conferred on them by Article 6 of the ECHR and by Articles 47 and 48 of the Charter of Fundamental Rights, if lawyers were obliged, in the context of judicial proceedings or the preparation for such proceedings, to cooperate with the authorities by passing them information obtained in the course of related legal consultations.'

C. First cumulative condition: Communications made for the purpose and in the interests of the client's rights of defence

The first of the two cumulative conditions for communications between lawyers and clients to be protected under the *AM & S Europe v Commission* case law is that the exchange with the lawyer must be connected to the client's rights of defence, in that they are 'made for the purposes and in the interests of the client's rights of defence'.[1067]

In the context of the enforcement of Articles 101 and 102 TFEU by the European Commission, this means that the protection covers 'all written communications exchanged after the initiation of the administrative procedure under [Regulation 1/2003] which may lead to a decision on the application of [Articles 101 and 102 TFEU] or to a decision imposing a pecuniary sanction on the undertaking'.[1068]

1067 Judgments in *AM & S Europe v Commission*, 155/79, EU:C:1982:157, paragraphs 21 and 22, and in *Akzo Nobel Chemicals and Akcros Chemicals v Commission*, C-550/07 P, EU:C:2010:512, paragraphs 40 and 41.

1068 Judgment in *AM & S Europe v Commission*, 155/79, EU:C:1982:157, paragraph 23.

It also covers 'earlier written communications which have a relationship to the subject-matter of that procedure'.[1069] In *AM & S Europe v Commission*, the EU Court of Justice accepted on this ground the protection of communications that dated from several years before the initiation of proceedings but that were 'drawn up during the period preceding, and immediately following, the accession of the United Kingdom to the [European Economic] Community, and that [were] principally concerned with how far it might be possible to avoid conflict between the applicant and the Community authorities on the applicant's position, in particular with regard to the Community provisions on competition'.[1070]

Legal advice, for instance given under antitrust compliance programmes, that is general in nature and has no specific connection with the current or future exercise of the rights of defence is not protected.[1071]

Finally, in the *Peridopril (Servier)* case,[1072] the European Commission refused protection to a letter from the external lawyers of Teva (a competitor to Servier) to Servier's external lawyers, found during an inspection at Servier's premises, which warned that Teva would submit an antitrust complaint to the European Commission against Servier, unless an agreement was reached. This letter was in Servier's possession because it had been sent to Servier by Servier's external lawyers, in attachment to an email stating '*Please find enclosed a copy of a letter (confidential) from Teva's Counsel. I suggest we discuss at your earliest convenience*'. Given that the letter originated not from Servier's but from Teva's external lawyers, the letter could not be said to have been prepared for the purpose and in the interests of Servier's rights of defence.[1073] The fact that the letter was attached to an email from Servier's external lawyers did not change the nature of the letter, because the mere fact that a document has been discussed with an external lawyer is not sufficient to give it protection.[1074]

D. Second cumulative condition: Independent (not in-house) lawyers, entitled to practise their profession in an EU (or EEA) Member State

The second of the two cumulative conditions for communications between lawyers and clients to be protected under the *AM & S Europe v Commission* case law is that

---

1069 Judgment in *AM & S Europe v Commission*, 155/79, EU:C:1982:157, paragraph 23.
On the interpretation of the notion of 'relationship with the subject matter of the procedure', see E. Gippini-Fournier, 'Legal Professional Privilege in Competition Proceedings Before the European Commission: Beyond the Cursory Glance', in B. E. Hawk (ed) *2004 Annual Proceedings of the Fordham Corporate Law Institute – International Antitrust Law and Policy* (Juris Publishing 2005), 587, at 625.

1070 Judgment in *AM & S Europe v Commission*, 155/79, EU:C:1982:157, paragraph 34.

1071 Opinion of Advocate General Kokott in *Akzo Nobel Chemicals and Akcros Chemicals v Commission*, C-550/07 P, EU:C:2010:229, paragraph 120; see also Judgment in *Akzo Nobel Chemicals and Akcros Chemicals v Commission*, T-125/03 and T-253/03, EU:T:2007:287, paragraph 127. On antitrust compliance programmes, see my further paper 'Antitrust compliance programmes and optimal antitrust enforcement' (2013) 1 *Journal of Antitrust Enforcement* 52.

1072 Decision C(2010)5044 of 23 July 2010 concerning a claim of legal privilege and/or protection of confidential correspondence between external lawyers in the context of an investigation pursuant to Article 20(4) of Council Regulation (EC) No 1/2003 in Case No COMP/E-1/39.612 – Perindopril (Servier), accessible at http://ec.europa.eu/competition/antitrust/cases/index.html.

1073 Idem, paragraph (15)(i).

1074 Idem, paragraph (15)(ii).

the lawyers are independent lawyers, who are not bound to the client by a relationship of employment, and who are entitled to practise their profession in one of the EU (or EEA) Member States.[1075]

The EU Court of Justice explained in *AM & S Europe v Commission* that 'the requirement as to the position and status as an independent lawyer, which must be fulfilled by the legal advisor from whom the written communications which may be protected emanate, is based on a conception of the lawyer's role as collaborating in the administration of justice by the courts and as being required to provide, in full independence, and in the overriding interests of that cause, such legal assistance as the client needs. [. . .] Such a conception reflects the legal traditions common to the Member States and is also found in the legal order of the [European Union], as is demonstrated by Article [19] of the Protocol on the Statute of the Court of Justice of the [European Union]', according to which only a lawyer authorised to practise before a court of an EU Member State or another State party to the Agreement on the European Economic Area (EEA) may represent or assist a party before the EU Court of Justice and EU General Court.[1076]

The EU Court of Justice added that 'such protection may not be extended beyond those limits, which are determined by the scope of the common rules on the exercise of the legal profession as laid down in Council Directive 77/249/EU [. . .], which is based in its turn on the mutual recognition by all the Member States of the national legal concepts of each of them on this subject'.[1077]

1. The exclusion of in-house lawyers

Following lengthy debate among practitioners and scholars, the EU Court of Justice, following the Opinion of its Advocate General Kokott,[1078] confirmed in *Akzo Nobel Chemicals and Akcros Chemicals v Commission* the exclusion of in-house lawyers from legal professional privilege, even if those in-house lawyers are enrolled with a Bar or Law Society and subject to the corresponding professional ethical obligations.[1079]

This exclusion of all in-house lawyers, even if enrolled with a Bar or Law Society and subject to the corresponding professional ethical obligations, is not discriminatory. Indeed, in-house lawyers are in a fundamentally different position from external lawyers, because of the economic dependence and personal identification of a lawyer in an employment relationship with their undertaking.[1080]

1075 Judgments in *AM & S Europe v Commission*, 155/79, EU:C:1982:157, paragraphs 21 to 26, and in *Akzo Nobel Chemicals and Akcros Chemicals v Commission*, C-550/07 P, EU:C:2010:512, paragraphs 40 to 119.

1076 Judgment in *AM & S Europe v Commission*, 155/79, EU:C:1982:157, paragraph 24.

1077 Judgment in *AM & S Europe v Commission*, 155/79, EU:C:1982:157, paragraph 26.

1078 Opinion of Advocate General Kokott in *Akzo Nobel Chemicals and Akcros Chemicals v Commission*, C-550/07 P, EU:C:2010:229.

1079 Judgment in *Akzo Nobel Chemicals and Akcros Chemicals v Commission*, C-550/07 P, EU:C:2010:512. In-house lawyers, including those that are enrolled with a Bar or Law Society, are similarly excluded from representing parties (other than the EU or EEA Member States and the EU or EEA institutions) before the EU Courts; see Judgment in *Prezes Urzędu Komunikacji Elektronicznej and Republic of Poland v Commission*, C-422/11 P and C-423/11 P, EU:C:2012:553.

1080 Judgment in *Akzo Nobel Chemicals and Akcros Chemicals v Commission*, C-550/07 P, EU:C:2010:512, paragraphs 56 to 58 and Opinion of Advocate General Kokott in *Akzo Nobel Chemicals and Akcros Chemicals v Commission*, C-550/07 P, EU:C:2010:229, paragraphs 83 and 58 to 71.

As explained by Advocate General Kokott:

'There is a structural danger that an enrolled in-house lawyer – even if, as is usually the case, he is himself of good character and has the best intentions – will encounter a conflict of interests between his professional obligations and the aims and wishes of his company.

The susceptibility of an enrolled in-house lawyer to conflicts of interest also makes it difficult for him to raise an effective opposition to any abuses of legal professional privilege. Such abuse may, for example, consist in handing over evidence and information to an undertaking's legal department, under cover of a request for legal advice, for the sole or primary purpose, ultimately, of preventing the competition authorities of gaining access to that evidence and information. At worst, the functional departments of an undertaking may be tempted to misuse the company's internal legal department as a place for storing illegal documents such as cartel agreements and records of meetings between the parties to those cartels and of the modus operandi of a cartel.'[1081]

In EU law, the requirement of independence of the lawyer is thus determined not only positively – by reference to professional ethical obligations – but also negatively – by reference to the absence of an employment relationship.[1082]

What is required for legal professional privilege to apply is that the lawyer is 'structurally, hierarchically and functionally, [. . .] a third party in relation to the undertaking receiving [the] advice'.[1083]

Several attempts have been made to argue that the exclusion of in-house lawyers would somehow be contrary to the European Convention on Human Rights (ECHR).[1084] These arguments were cogently rejected by Advocate General Kokott in *Akzo Nobel Chemicals and Akcros Chemicals v Commission.*[1085] The European Court of Human Rights has not expressed any support for extending legal professional privilege to communications inside a company involving legal advice provided by an in-house lawyer employed by that company.[1086]

1081 Opinion of Advocate General Kokott in *Akzo Nobel Chemicals and Akcros Chemicals v Commission*, C-550/07 P, EU:C:2010:229, paragraphs 149 and 150.

1082 See Opinion of Advocate General Kokott in *Akzo Nobel Chemicals and Akcros Chemicals v Commission*, C-550/07 P, EU:C:2010:229, paragraph 60.

1083 Judgment in *Akzo Nobel Chemicals and Akcros Chemicals v Commission*, T-125/03 and T-253/03, EU:T:2007:287, paragraph 168, confirmed by Judgment in *Akzo Nobel Chemicals and Akcros Chemicals v Commission*, C-550/07 P, EU:C:2010:512, paragraph 50.

1084 On the relationship between the European Convention on Human Rights and EU law, see generally my paper 'EU Antitrust Enforcement Powers and Procedural Rights and Guarantees: The Interplay between EU Law, National Law, the Charter of Fundamental Rights of the EU and the European Convention on Human Rights' (2011) 34 *World Competition* 189, also accessible at http://ssrn.com/author=456087; see also Opinion 2/13 (Accession of the EU to the ECHR) of the EU Court of Justice, EU:C:2014:2454.

1085 Opinion of Advocate General Kokott in *Akzo Nobel Chemicals and Akcros Chemicals v Commission*, C-550/07 P, EU:C:2010:229, in particular paragraphs 47, 141, 148 and 152.

1086 Idem, paragraph 141; see further the judgments of the European Court of Human Rights of 6 December 2012 in *Michaud v France* (Application no 12323/11), of 2 April 2015 in *Vinci Construction and GMT génie civil et services v France* (Applications nos 63629/10 and 60567/10), and of 26 July 2002 in *Meftah and Others v France* (Applications nos 32911/96, 35267/97 and 34595/97), paragraphs 45 to 47.

As I have argued elsewhere,[1087] both the fundamental rights arguments and the instrumental arguments for extending legal professional privilege to in-house lawyers are very weak.

Indeed, it is difficult to see how the possibility to consult in confidence an independent lawyer would be insufficient to guarantee fundamental rights, thereby creating a need to extend legal professional privilege to in-house counsel.[1088] There is a wide choice of independent lawyers companies can turn to, and those companies that can afford to have in-house counsel can also afford to pay an independent lawyer.[1089]

Instrumental arguments, to the effect that extending legal professional privilege to in-house lawyers would lead to better compliance with Articles 101 and 102 TFEU, are not convincing either. These arguments were brought up in the legislative process leading to the adoption of Regulation No 1/2003. Indeed, the Economic and Monetary Committee of the European Parliament initially adopted an amendment providing for the extension of legal professional privilege to in-house counsel,[1090] but this amendment, which was strongly opposed by the European Commission, was subsequently rejected in plenary session of the Parliament by 404 votes against and 69 votes in favour.[1091] The EU Council also declined to include any such extension in Regulation No 1/2003. The European Parliament, EU Council and European Commission thus rejected the arguments that extension of legal professional privilege to in-house counsel would be beneficial for the enforcement of Articles 101 and 102 TFEU.

More generally, neither the economic literature nor the (inevitably anecdotal) empirical evidence support the proposition that legal professional privilege furthers compliance or that enlarging the scope of legal professional privilege leads to more compliance.[1092]

1087 See my papers 'Powers of investigation and Procedural Rights and Guarantees in EU Antitrust Enforcement: The Interplay between European and National Legislation and Case-law' (2006) 29 *World Competition* 3, text accompanied by footnotes 75 to 81, and 'EU Antitrust Enforcement Powers and Procedural Rights and Guarantees: The Interplay between EU Law, National Law, the Charter of Fundamental Rights of the EU and the European Convention on Human Rights' (2011) 34 *World Competition* 189, text accompanied by footnotes 100 and 101; both also accessible at http://ssrn.com/author=456087.

1088 See also Judgment in *Akzo Nobel Chemicals and Akcros Chemicals v Commission*, C-550/07 P, EU:C:2010:512, paragraphs 95 and 96: '[E]ven assuming that the consultation of in-house lawyers employed by the undertaking or group were to be covered by the right to obtain legal advice and representation, that would not exclude the application, were in-house lawyers are involved, of certain restrictions and rules relating to the exercise of the profession without that being regarded as adversely affecting the rights of the defence. Thus, in-house lawyers are not always able to represent their employer before all the national courts, although such rules restrict the possibilities open to potential clients in their choice of the most appropriate legal counsel. It follows from those considerations that any individual who seeks advice from a lawyer must accept the restrictions and conditions applicable to the exercise of that profession. The rules on legal professional privilege form part of those restrictions and conditions'; see also Judgment of the European Court of Human Rights of 26 July 2002 in *Meftah and Others v France* (Applications nos 32911/96, 35267/97 and 34595/97), paragraphs 45 to 47.

1089 In fact extension of legal professional privilege to in-house lawyers might lead to less protection of fundamental rights, in that it could lead large undertakings to use only in-house counsel, thus reducing the availability of independent lawyers on the open market, to the detriment of smaller companies that cannot afford in-house counsel. See also, on legal aid for companies, Judgment in *DEB v Bundesrepublik Deutschland*, C-279/09, EU:C:2010:811.

1090 Amendment No 10 contained in the Evans Report, EP Session document of 21 June 2001, PE 296.005.

1091 Plenary of 6 September 2001, PE 308.749, page 35; see also Opinion of Advocate General Kokott in *Akzo Nobel Chemicals and Akcros Chemicals v Commission*, C-550/07 P, EU:C:2010:229, paragraph 106.

1092 See E. Gippini-Fournier, 'Legal Professional Privilege in Competition Proceedings Before the European Commission: Beyond the Cursory Glance', in B. E. Hawk (ed) *2004 Annual Proceedings of the Fordham Corporate Law Institute – International Antitrust Law and Policy* (Juris Publishing 2005), 587, at 596–606;

Finally, the American model cannot be invoked as an argument for extending legal professional privilege to in-house lawyers under EU law. Indeed, no direct comparison can be drawn with the enforcement system in the USA.

In the EU system, extending legal professional privilege to in-house lawyers would be detrimental to the effectiveness of inspections and thus the possibility of detecting and collecting evidence of cartels and other infringements of Articles 101 and 102 TFEU. Inspections are a crucial instrument in EU antitrust enforcement.[1093] European Commission decisions heavily rely on documentary evidence, which must be collected on the spot and cannot be complemented by summoning witnesses.

Extending legal professional privilege to in-house lawyers would be detrimental to the effectiveness of inspections in two ways. First, it would reduce the universe of the documents that can be found during an inspection that may contain useful evidence of the suspected infringement. More so than legal opinions of in-house lawyers,[1094] the descriptions of facts contained in, and documents attached to, the communications to in-house lawyers from other members of staff regularly contain useful evidence. Secondly, extending legal professional privilege to in-house lawyers would significantly complicate and slow down inspections, as difficult and time-consuming discussions would take place between the inspectors and the company's lawyers to determine which communications with in-house lawyers are privileged. Speed in inspections is often of great importance in practice.

If legal professional privilege were extended to in-house lawyers, it would indeed be difficult to define its precise scope in a way that does not invite abuse. In the US, where in-house lawyers are not as a matter of principle excluded from attorney-client privilege protection, the law appears to be rather uncertain. The problem is that unqualified application of the privilege to communications between all corporate employees and in-house counsel risks

---

L. Kaplow and S. Shavell, 'Legal Advice About Information to Present in Litigation: Its Effects and Social Desirability' (1989) 102 *Harvard Law Review* 565; L. Kaplow and S. Shavell, 'Legal Advice About Acts Already Committed' (1990) 10 *International Review of Law and Economics* 149; S. Shavell, 'Legal Advice', in P. Newman (ed), *New Palgrave Dictionary of Economics and the Law*, vol 2 (1998), 516–520; I. Baum, 'Attorney Corporate Client Privilege: Who Represents the Corporation?' (2007) *Review of Law & Economics*, vol 3, no 1, art 5; and C. E. Parker, R. E. Rosen and V. Lehmann Nielsen, 'The Two Faces of Lawyers: Professional Ethics and Business Compliance With Regulation' (2009) 22 *Georgetown Journal of Legal Ethics* 201.
A piece of anecdotal evidence: it turned out that AM & S Europe continued infringing Article 85 EEC (now Article 101 TFEU) for five years after it received the legal advice at stake in the *AM & S Europe v Commission* case; see European Commission Decision of 6 August 1984 in Case IV/30.350 *Zinc Producer Group* [1984] OJ L220/27.

1093 The success of leniency does not reduce the need for effective inspections; rather to the contrary, effective investigation powers and effective sanctions are preconditions for operating a successful leniency programme; see further my paper 'Leniency in Antitrust Enforcement: Theory and Practice' (2007) 30 *World Competition* 25, also accessible at http://ssrn.com/author=456087, and Chapters V and VI of this book.

1094 As to the legal opinions of in-house lawyers, the European Commission stated in paragraph 37 of its *XXXIInd Report on Competition Policy 2002* (2003) that it 'will in future not consider, pursuant to its guidelines on the method of setting fines, as an aggravating circumstance to be taken into account in determining the amount of a pecuniary penalty to be imposed on a company, the fact that in-house legal advisers had warned the management of the illegality of the conduct forming the subject-matter of the Commission's decision. Such a communication may, however, be used as evidence of the existence of an infringement'. On the European Commission's method of setting fines, see further my paper 'The European Commission's 2006 Guidelines on Antitrust Fines: A Legal and Economic Analysis' (2007) 30 *World Competition* 197, also accessible at http://ssrn.com/author=456087.

leading to zones of silence, through which the corporation could potentially channel all potentially incriminating documents and information. Lower court judgments and academic writing have proposed lots of competing tests to determine the acceptable scope of protection, mostly by limiting who is to be considered as the 'client' to whom communications are confidential (only the board, not other staff, etc.). In *Upjohn*,[1095] the US Supreme Court opted for a case-by-case approach under which each case has to be judged in the light of the rationale of legal privilege protection. This approach arguably leaves a lot of legal uncertainty.

One can easily imagine this borderline problem being much more serious in the case of the European Union, in the absence of a common practice or understanding concerning the role and nature of in-house lawyers in the EU Member States. In the US at least, in-house counsel is a well-established function, present in all (large) corporations.

The US investigation system does not in any event rely to the same extent as that of the EU on on-the-spot inspections to collect documentary evidence. The US enforcement agencies work with discovery orders and witnesses. Disputes on the scope of legal professional privilege are not impinging directly on the powers of the US Department of Justice to gather the necessary evidence. This is partly explained by the extensive investigatory powers at the US Department of Justice's disposal, in particular the power to perform secret recordings by informants of telephone calls and meetings. Furthermore, the basic features of the US system, including criminal sanctions on individuals, grand jury and plea bargaining, give the US Department of Justice a very important leverage to obtain admissions from direct witnesses.[1096]

As legal professional privilege for in-house lawyers has a long-standing tradition in US law, its impact has been factored into the design of the enforcement powers in the US system. The enforcement powers of the European Commission have been designed on the basis of an equally long-standing continental-European tradition of a different treatment of employed and independent lawyers.

2. The exclusion of non-EEA lawyers

The EU Court of Justice made it very clear in *AM & S Europe v Commission* that legal professional privilege only applies to 'any lawyer entitled to practise his profession in one of the [EU or EEA] Member States',[1097] and that 'such protection may not be extended beyond those limits, which are determined by the scope of the common rules on the exercise of the legal profession as laid down in Council Directive 77/249/EU [. . .], which is based in its turn on the mutual recognition by all the Member States of the national legal concepts of each of them on this subject'.[1098]

As the Court pointed out, the same limitation is also reflected in Article 19 of the Protocol on the Statute of the Court of Justice of the European Union, according to which only

1095 *Upjohn Co. v United States*, 449 US 383 (1981).

1096 For a critical assessment of the US system from a defence perspective, see L. W. Jacobs, 'Criminal Enforcement of Antitrust Laws – Problems with the U.S. Model', in B. E. Hawk (ed) *2006 Annual Proceedings of the Fordham Corporate Law Institute – International Antitrust Law and Policy* (Juris Publishing 2007), 25.

1097 Judgment in *AM & S Europe v Commission*, 155/79, EU:C:1982:157, paragraph 25.

1098 Idem, paragraph 26.

a lawyer authorised to practise before a court of an EU Member State or another State party to the Agreement on the European Economic Area (EEA) may represent or assist a party before the EU Court of Justice and EU General Court.[1099]

Advocate General Kokott further explained in *Akzo Nobel Chemicals and Akcros Chemicals v Commission* why 'the inclusion, in addition, of lawyers from third countries would not under any circumstances be justified'[1100]:

'*For, unlike in the relationship between the Member States, in the relationship with third countries there is, generally speaking, no adequate basis for the mutual recognition of legal qualifications and professional ethical obligations to which lawyers are subject in the exercise of their profession. In many cases, it would not even be possible to ensure that the third country in question has a sufficiently established rule-of-law tradition which would enable lawyers to exercise their profession in the independent manner required and thus to perform their role as collaborators in the administration of justice. It cannot be the task of the Commission or the Courts of the European Union to verify, at considerable expense, that this is the case on each occasion by reference to the rules and practices in force in the third country concerned, particularly since there is no guarantee that there will be an efficient system of administrative cooperation with the authorities of the third country on every occasion.*'[1101]

Under EU law, third-country lawyers could thus only be included in legal professional privilege protection on the basis of an international agreement based on mutual recognition of legal qualifications and professional ethical obligations.

In 1984, shortly after the *AM & S Europe v Commission* judgment, the European Commission submitted to the EU Council a recommendation for a Council decision authorising the Commission to open negotiations with a view to the conclusion of such international agreements.[1102] The EU Council never granted any such authorisation, however, and the European Commission withdrew this recommendation as obsolete in 1998.

The Agreement on the European Economic Area, concluded in 1993, led to the extension of EU legal professional privilege to cover lawyers of the EEA/EFTA states (Norway, Iceland and Lichtenstein) under the same conditions as lawyers of the EU Member States.[1103]

From a fundamental rights perspective, the exclusion of third-country lawyers does not appear problematic. Those (relatively rare, and usually large) non-EEA-based companies that are in need of legal assistance in connection with actual or potential EU antitrust enforcement proceedings can no doubt find and afford the services of EU or EEA lawyers.

1099 Idem, paragraph 24; see also Order in *FTA and Others v Council*, T-37/98, EU:T:2000:52, paragraph 25.

1100 Opinion of Advocate General Kokott in *Akzo Nobel Chemicals and Akcros Chemicals v Commission*, C-550/07 P, EU:C:2010:229, paragraph 189.

1101 Idem, paragraph 190.

1102 European Commission, Recommendation of 9 October 1984 for a Council decision authorising the Commission to open negotiations with a view to the conclusion of agreements between the European Economic Community and certain third countries concerning the protection of legal papers in connection with the application of the rules on competition, COM/84/548final; see also European Commission, *Fourteenth Report on Competition Policy 1984* (1985), paragraph 48.

1103 Declaration by the European Community on the rights of lawyers of the EFTA States under Community law, attached to the Agreement on the European Economic Area [1994] OJ L1/567.

E. Internal preparatory documents and internal documents summarising advice from external lawyers

In *Hilti v Commission*, the EU General Court has recognised that internal documents of a company summarising advice received in the exercise of the company's rights of defence from external lawyers are also protected under legal professional privilege.[1104]

In *Akzo Nobel Chemicals and Akcros Chemicals v Commission*, the EU General Court similarly recognised that internal preparatory documents, even if they were not exchanged with a lawyer or were not created for the purpose of being sent physically to a lawyer, are protected if drawn up exclusively for the purpose of seeking legal advice from an external lawyer in the exercise of the rights of defence.[1105]

On the other hand, the mere fact that a document has been discussed with an external lawyer is not sufficient to give it protection.[1106]

Finally, also according to the EU General Court:

'*It must be borne in mind that protection under [legal professional privilege] is an exception to the [European] Commission's powers of investigation, which are essential to enable it to discover, bring to an end and penalise infringements of the competition rules. Such infringements are often concealed and usually very harmful to the proper functioning of the common market. For this reason, the possibility of treating a preparatory document as covered by [legal professional privilege] must be construed restrictively. It is for the undertaking relying on this protection to prove that the documents in question were drawn up with the sole aim of seeking legal advice from a lawyer. This should be unambiguously clear from the content of the documents themselves or the context in which those documents were prepared and found.*'[1107]

Pre-existing documents that are attached to a request for legal advice addressed to an independent lawyer, or to the legal opinion of such a lawyer, are thus not covered by legal professional privilege, unless those pre-existing documents were drawn up with the sole aim of seeking legal advice.

F. Procedure and practice

1. Inspections

Where during an inspection by the European Commission under Article 20 of Regulation 1/2003 a company refuses, on the ground that it is entitled to legal professional privilege, to produce, among the business records demanded by the European Commission, written communications

---

1104 Order in *Hilti v Commission*, T-30/89, EU:T:1990:27, paragraph 18.

1105 Judgment in *Akzo Nobel Chemicals and Akcros Chemicals v Commission*, T-125/03 and T-253/03, EU:T:2007:287, paragraph 123.

1106 Idem, paragraph 123.

1107 Idem, paragraph 124.

between itself and its lawyer, it must provide the Commission's authorised agents with relevant material of such a nature as to demonstrate that the communications fulfil the conditions for being granted legal protection, although it is not bound to reveal the contents of the communications in question.[1108] The company may, in particular, inform the Commission of the author of the document and for whom it was intended, explain the respective duties and responsibilities of each, and refer to the objective and the context in which the document was drawn up. Similarly, it may also mention the context in which the document was found, the way in which it was filed and any related documents.[1109]

The mere fact that a company claims that a document is protected by legal professional privilege is not sufficient to prevent the European Commission from reading that document if the company produces no relevant material of such a kind as to prove that it is actually protected by legal professional privilege.[1110]

In a significant number of cases, a mere cursory look by the Commission officials at the general layout, heading, title or other superficial features of the document will enable them, when deciding whether to put it aside, to confirm the accuracy of the reasons invoked by the company and to determine whether the document at issue is confidential. Nevertheless, on certain occasions, there would be a risk that, even with a cursory look at the document, in spite of the superficial nature of their examination, the Commission officials would gain access to information covered by legal professional privilege. That may be so, in particular, if the confidentiality of the document in question is not clear from external indications.[1111] If the company considers that a cursory look is impossible without revealing the content of one or more specific documents, and the company gives the Commission appropriate reasons for its view, the company is entitled to refuse the Commission officials to take even a cursory look.[1112]

If the Commission considers that the material presented by the company is not of such a nature as to prove that the documents in question are confidential, the Commission officials may place a copy of the document or documents in question in a sealed envelope and then remove it with a view to as subsequent resolution of the dispute. This procedure enables risks of a breach of legal professional privilege to be avoided while at the same time enabling the Commission to retain a certain control over the documents forming the subject matter of the investigation and avoiding the risk that the documents will subsequently disappear or be manipulated.[1113]

The solution of the dispute between the company and the European Commission as to whether the contested document or documents are protected by legal professional privilege cannot be left to an arbitrator or to a Member State authority, but must be sought at the EU level.[1114]

1108 Judgment in *AM & S Europe v Commission*, 155/79, EU:C:1982:157, paragraph 29.

1109 Judgment in *Akzo Nobel Chemicals and Akcros Chemicals v Commission*, T-125/03 and T-253/03, EU:T:2007:287, paragraph 80.

1110 Idem, paragraph 80.

1111 Idem, paragraph 81.

1112 Idem, paragraph 82.

1113 Idem, paragraph 83.

1114 Judgment in *AM & S Europe v Commission*, 155/79, EU:C:1982:157, paragraph 30.

If the European Commission wants to open the sealed envelope and read the contents of the document, it must first adopt a decision rejecting the company's legal professional privilege claim, thus allowing the company concerned to refer the matter to the EU General Court, and to make an application for interim measures seeking suspension of operation of the decision rejecting the legal professional privilege claim.[1115]

Only if the company either does not bring such an application before the EU General Court or after its application has been rejected by the EU Courts (General Court as well as, on a possible further appeal on points of law, Court of Justice) can the European Commission open the sealed envelope and read the contents of the document.[1116]

This procedure being cumbersome and time-consuming, it could be feared that companies may abuse this procedure by making requests, merely as delaying tactics, for protection under legal professional privilege which are clearly unfounded, or by opposing, without objective justification, any cursory look at the documents during an inspection. However, the European Commission has the means to discourage and penalise such conduct. Indeed, such conduct may be penalised under Article 23(1)(c) of Regulation 1/2003 (which provides for fines of up to 1% of the undertaking's total turnover in the preceding business year for producing business records in incomplete form during an inspection or for refusing to submit to an inspection) or be taken into account as aggravating circumstances when calculating any fine imposed for the infringement of Article 101 or 102 TFEU in the course of the investigating of which the inspection took place.[1117]

In practice, the full procedure, with a decision of the European Commission formally rejecting the legal professional privilege claim and subsequent proceedings before the EU Courts, is only very rarely pursued to the end. Often substantial time is, however, spent on discussions between Commission officials and the company's lawyers before the matter is resolved.

2. Requests for information

Disputes concerning legal professional privilege can also arise in the context of requests for information. The procedure follows the same principles as described above for disputes during inspections.

Article 18 of Regulation 1/2003 provides for two types of requests for information: by simple request pursuant to Article 18(2) or by decision pursuant to Article 18(3). While companies are under an obligation to supply, in complete form, information requested

[1115] Judgment in *Akzo Nobel Chemicals and Akcros Chemicals v Commission*, T-125/03 and T-253/03, EU:T:2007:287, paragraphs 85 and 88.

[1116] Idem, paragraphs 86 to 88; and Commission Notice on best practices for the conduct of proceedings concerning Articles 101 and 102 TFEU [2011] OJ C308/6, paragraph 57.

[1117] Judgment in *Akzo Nobel Chemicals and Akcros Chemicals v Commission*, T-125/03 and T-253/03, EU:T:2007:287, paragraph 89. The obligation to submit to an inspection only applies to inspections ordered by decision pursuant to Article 20(4) of Regulation 1/2003, not to inspections by simple authorisation pursuant to Article 20(2) of Regulation 1/2003. However, if the company chooses to submit to an inspection by simple authorisation, the obligation to produce the required business records in complete form applies. In practice, most inspections, including all surprise inspections, conducted by the European Commission are ordered by decision pursuant to Article 20(4).

by decision, there is no obligation to respond to a simple request.[1118] In most cases, the European Commission first sends a simple request pursuant to Article 18(2), and only later, if the company has refused to respond to the simple request, sends a request by decision pursuant to Article 18(3), possibly combined with a decision pursuant to Article 24(1)(d) of Regulation 1/2003 imposing periodic penalty payments to compel compliance with the request for information.

If the company that is the addressee of the request for information claims professional legal privilege with regard to a requested document or documents, it must provide the European Commission with appropriate justification and relevant material to substantiate its claim, while not being bound to disclose the contents of such documents. Redacted versions removing the parts covered by legal professional privilege should be submitted.[1119]

If the Commission is not convinced by the company's arguments, it must adopt a decision rejecting the legal professional privilege claim, thus allowing the company concerned to refer the matter to the EU General Court, and to make an application for interim measures seeking suspension of operation of the decision rejecting the legal professional privilege claim.

As with claims made in the context of inspections, in practice, the full procedure, with a decision of the European Commission formally rejecting the legal professional privilege claim and subsequent proceedings before the EU Courts, is only very rarely pursued to the end. Often substantial time is, however, spent on discussions between Commission officials and the company's lawyers before the matter is resolved.

3. The role of the Hearing Officer

In 2011, the possibility was created for companies to bring disputes about legal professional privilege in antitrust cases before the European Commission's Hearing Officer.[1120]

Article 4(2)(a), read in conjunction with Article 3(7), of Decision 2011/695/EU, provides that, where a company has withheld from the European Commission a document (including where the document has been put in a sealed envelope), claiming that it is covered by legal professional privilege within the meaning of the case law of the EU Courts, the company may, after having raised the matter with the Commission's Directorate-General for Competition, ask the Hearing Officer to examine the claim. The Hearing Officer may only review the matter if the company making the claim consents to the Hearing Officer viewing the information claimed to be covered by legal professional privilege as well as related documents that the Hearing Officer considers necessary for their review. Without revealing the potentially privileged content of the information, the Hearing Officer must communicate to the director responsible in the Directorate-General for Competition and

---

1118 If a company chooses to respond to a simple request pursuant to Article 18(2), it can, however, be fined under Article 23(1)(a) of Regulation 1/2003 for supplying incorrect or misleading information.

1119 Commission Notice on best practices for the conduct of proceedings concerning Articles 101 and 102 TFEU [2011] OJ C308/6, paragraph 52.

1120 Article 4(2)(a) of Decision 2011/695/EU of the President of the European Commission of 13 October 2011 on the function and terms of reference of the hearing officer in certain competition proceedings [2011] OJ L275/29. See further Chapter XI of this book.

to the company concerned their preliminary view, and may take appropriate steps to promote a mutually acceptable resolution. Where no resolution is reached, the Hearing Officer may formulate a reasoned recommendation to the Competition Commissioner,[1121] without revealing the potentially privileged content of the document. The company making the claim is to receive a copy of this recommendation.

The Hearing Officer's recommendation has no binding force.[1122] If, after the intervention of the Hearing Officer, the company maintains its claim, and the European Commission still wants to read and use the document, then the European Commission must do what it would also have to do if the intervention of the Hearing Officer had not been asked, namely, take a decision rejecting the legal professional privilege claim, thus allowing the company concerned to refer the matter to the EU General Court, and to make an application for interim measures seeking suspension of operation of the decision rejecting the legal professional privilege claim.

G. Enforcement of EU antitrust law by the competition authorities of the EU Member States

In most EU Member States, national law provides for legal professional privilege under the same or very similar conditions as under EU law.

It would be contrary to EU law for competition authorities or courts of the EU Member States in cases of enforcement of Articles 101 or 102 TFEU to grant legal professional privilege under more restrictive conditions than those laid down in the case law of the EU Courts.[1123]

Indeed, as mentioned above, in EU law, the protection of legal professional privilege has the status of a general legal principle in the nature of a fundamental right, deriving inter alia from the Charter of Fundamental Rights of the EU. The Charter of Fundamental Rights of the EU is also applicable to the enforcement of Articles 101 or 102 TFEU by the national competition authorities.[1124] The same holds for general principles of EU law. According to the case law of the Court of Justice, 'the requirements flowing from the protection of fundamental rights in the [EU] legal order are also binding on the Member States when they implement [EU] rules'.[1125]

The competition authorities of the EU Member States and the courts of the EU Member States must thus in cases concerning the enforcement of Articles 101 and 102 TFEU

1121 The European Commission is a collegiate body composed of a number of commissioners equal to the number of EU Member States. One of these commissioners has special responsibility for competition ('the Competition Commissioner').

1122 Article 288 TFEU.

1123 See Chapter X of this book.

1124 See Article 51(1) of the Charter ('The provisions of this Charter are addressed [. . .] to the Member States [. . .] when they are implementing Union law.'); Judgments in *Stefano Melloni v Ministerio Fiscal*, C-399/11, EU:C:2013:107, paragraph 60, and in *UBS Europe and Others*, C-358/16, EU:C:2018:715, paragraph 51; and Article 3(1) of the proposed Directive of the European Parliament and of the Council to empower the competition authorities of the Member States to be more effective enforcers and to ensure the proper functioning of the internal market (Provisional agreement resulting from interinstitutional negotiations; European Parliament document PE632.968v01-00 AG\1157771EN.docx of 20 June 2018).

1125 Judgment of 13 April 2000 in Case C-292/97 *Karlsson and Others* [2000] ECR I-2760, para 37.

grant legal professional privilege whenever the conditions laid down in the case law of the EU Courts are fulfilled, even if the conditions for legal professional privilege under national law may not be fulfilled. Companies can directly invoke EU law to ensure their rights in this respect.

More delicate is the question whether EU Member States are allowed to grant legal professional privilege more broadly than under EU law.

This question arises in particular in relation to the few EU Member States, notably Ireland, the Netherlands, Belgium and Portugal, which also grant legal professional privilege protection to exchanges with in-house lawyers.

Under EU law, Member States are under an obligation to ensure the effective and uniform application of Articles 101 and 102 TFEU by their competition authorities.[1126] As explained above, one of the reasons why under EU law legal professional privilege has not been extended to in-house lawyers, even if those in-house lawyers are enrolled with a Bar or Law Society and subject to the corresponding professional ethical obligations, is that such an extension would undermine the effectiveness of the enforcement of Articles 101 and 102 TFEU by the European Commission. There is no sound basis for assuming that the extension of legal professional privilege to in-house lawyers would not similarly affect the effectiveness of the enforcement of Articles 101 and 102 TFEU by the competition authorities of the Member States.

In my view, it follows that those Member States that currently recognise legal professional privilege for in-house lawyers in the context of the enforcement of Articles 101 and 102 TFEU by their national competition authorities are in breach of EU law.

I am not necessarily arguing that the competition authorities or courts of those Member States can directly invoke EU law to deny legal professional privilege to all exchanges with in-house lawyers, as this may offend against the principle of legal certainty, which is a general principle of EU law.[1127] In my view the Member States concerned are, however, under an obligation to enact the necessary legislation to exclude all in-house lawyers from legal professional privilege in cases of enforcement of Articles 101 or 102 TFEU by their national competition authorities.[1128] The European Commission could bring proceedings pursuant to Article 258 TFEU against those Member States that fail to do so.

1126 See Article 35(1) of Regulation 1/2003 and Judgment in *Schenker*, C-681/11, EU:C:2013:404, paragraphs 36, 46 and 49.

1127 See Judgments in *X*, C-60/02, EU:C:2004:10, paragraph 61, and in *Berlusconi*, C-387/02 etc., EU:C:2005:270, paragraph 74.

1128 In Belgium, the extension of legal professional privilege to in-house counsel results from Article 5 of the Law of 1 March 2000, and could thus be reversed by repealing or amending this provision; see Judgment of the Brussels Court of Appeals of 5 March 2013 in Case 2011/MR/3.
It would not appear that in those Member States that extend legal professional privilege to in-house counsel, this extension is in the nature of a constitutional or fundamental right. In any event, according to the case law of the EU Court of Justice, by virtue of the principle of primacy of EU law, which is an essential feature of the EU legal order, rules of national law, even of a constitutional order, cannot be allowed to undermine the effectiveness of EU law, and the application of national standards of protection of fundamental rights cannot compromise the primacy, unity and effectiveness of EU law; see Judgment in *Stefano Melloni v Ministerio Fiscal*, C-399/11, EU:C:2013:107, paragraphs 59 and 60.

H. Private enforcement

Apart from the public enforcement by the European Commission and the competition authorities of the EU Member States, Articles 101 and 102 TFEU are also invoked in litigation between private parties in the courts of the EU Member States (private enforcement).[1129]

Article 5(6) of the EU Damages Directive,[1130] which applies to actions for damages for infringement of Articles 101 or 102 TFEU before the courts of the EU Member States,[1131] provides that 'Member States shall ensure that national courts give full effect to applicable legal professional privilege under [European] Union or national law when ordering the disclosure of evidence'.

This provision leaves open the question what the applicable EU or national law is.[1132]

As to EU law, it is unclear whether or how the *AM & S Europe v Commission* case law, which has its origin in the quasi-criminal context of the enforcement of Articles 101 and 102 TFEU by the European Commission, could be transposed to the context of private enforcement.

A comparison with the *Otto v Postbank* case law,[1133] according to which the privilege against self-incrimination as recognised in the case law of the EU Courts in the context of the enforcement of Articles 101 and 102 TFEU by the European Commission cannot be transposed to private enforcement before the courts of the EU Member States, might suggest that the *AM & S Europe v Commission* case law can similarly not be transposed to private enforcement.[1134]

1129 See Chapter XVII of this book.

1130 Directive 2014/104/EU of the European Parliament and of the Council of 26 November 2014 on certain rules governing actions for damages under national law for infringements of the competition law provisions of the Member States and the European Union [2014] OJ L349/1.

1131 Idem, Articles 1 and 2.

1132 See also F. Wagner-von Papp, 'Access to Evidence and Leniency Materials' (18 February 2016), accessible at http://ssrn.com/abstract=2733973, at pages 49–50.

1133 Judgment in *Otto v Postbank*, C-60/92, EU:C:1993:876, paragraphs 15 to 17.

1134 On the link between legal professional privilege and the privilege against self-incrimination, see E. Gippini-Fournier, 'Legal Professional Privilege in Competition Proceedings Before the European Commission: Beyond the Cursory Glance', in B. E. Hawk (ed) *2004 Annual Proceedings of the Fordham Corporate Law Institute – International Antitrust Law and Policy* (Juris Publishing 2005), 587, at 614–621 and 625.

XIV. Procedural Rights and Obligations of Third Parties in Antitrust Investigations and Proceedings by the European Commission

This chapter provides a systematic overview of the procedural rights and obligations of third parties in investigations and proceedings conducted by the European Commission for the enforcement of Articles 101 and 102 TFEU. Third parties are all natural or legal persons, undertakings and associations of undertakings other than those under investigation. This chapter examines the possibilities for third parties to inform the European Commission about a suspected infringement and to trigger an investigation by the European Commission; the obligations and rights of third parties when responding to requests for information sent to them by the European Commission, when participating in interviews, and when submitting to inspections conducted by the European Commission; the possibilities for third parties to obtain information about pending proceedings and to express their views in them; the rules on the use of languages; and the protection of business secrets and other confidential information, and the restrictions on the use of information obtained by third parties through their participation in the European Commission's proceedings.

A. Who are third parties?

1. Natural or legal persons, undertakings and associations of undertakings other than those under investigation

The third parties considered in this chapter comprise all natural or legal persons, undertakings and associations of undertakings other than those under investigation (and other than the European Commission, which conducts the investigation and proceedings, and the competition authorities of the EU Member States and other authorities with which the European Commission cooperates in its investigations and proceedings).

2. The concept of an undertaking in EU competition law and the need to conduct proceedings against companies or other persons

Article 101 TFEU prohibits 'agreements between undertakings' and 'decisions by associations of undertakings' that may affect trade between EU Member States and restrict competition without redeeming virtue. Article 102 TFEU prohibits any abuse 'by one or more undertakings' of a dominant position within the EU internal market or in a substantial part of it in so far as it may affect trade between EU Member States.

As the EU Court of Justice has pointed out, '[t]he authors of the Treaties [thus] chose to use the concept of an undertaking to designate the perpetrator of an infringement of competition law, who is liable to be punished pursuant to [. . .] Articles 101 TFEU and 102 TFEU, and not the concept of a company or firm or of a legal person'.[1135]

The concept of an undertaking has been defined by the EU Courts and designates an economic unit even if in law that economic unit consists of several legal or natural persons.[1136] For instance, a parent company and one or more subsidiaries that together form a single economic unit constitute a single undertaking for the purposes of Articles 101 and 102 TFEU.

For reasons of enforceability,[1137] the European Commission does not, however, address its decisions (for instance a decision finding an infringement of Article 102 by an undertaking, ordering its termination and/or imposing fines (infringement decision)), to the undertaking concerned, but rather to the legal (or natural)[1138] persons that are responsible for the operation of the undertaking concerned.[1139] For instance, if the undertaking under investigation comprises a parent company and a subsidiary,

---

1135 Judgments of 18 July 2013, *Schindler Holdings and Others v Commission*, C-501/11 P, EU:C:2013:522, paragraph 102, and of 6 October 2021, *Sumal*, C-882/19, EU:C:2021:800, paragraph 39.

1136 Judgments of 18 July 2013, *Schindler Holdings and Others v Commission*, C-501/11 P, EU:C:2013:522, paragraph 103, of 10 September 2009, *Akzo Novel and Others v Commission*, C-97/08 P, EU:C:2009:536, paragraph 55, of 25 November 2020, *Commission v GEA Group*, C-823/18 P, EU:C:2020:955, paragraph 64 and of 6 October 2021, *Sumal*, C-882/19, EU:C:2021:800, paragraphs 41 to 47; see further O. Odudu and D. Bailey, 'The Single Economic Entity Doctrine in EU Competition Law' (2014) 51 *Common Market law Review* 1721; C. Koenig, 'An Economic Analysis of the Single Economic Entity Doctrine in EU Competition Law' (2017) 13 *Journal of Competition Law and Economics* 281, and 'Comparing Parent Company Liability in EU and US Competition Law' (2018) 41 *World Competition* 69; and my papers 'The Undertaking as Subject of E.C. Competition Law and the Imputation of Infringements to Natural and Legal Persons' (2000) 25 *European law Review* 99, and 'Antitrust Compliance Programmes and Optimal Antitrust Enforcement' (2012) 1 *Journal of Antitrust Enforcement* 52, text accompanied by footnotes 22 to 29, also accessible at http://ssrn.com/author=456087.

1137 See Opinion of Advocate General Kokott of 23 April 2009, *Akzo Nobel NV and Others v Commission*, C-97/08 P, EU:C:2009:262, paragraph 37 and footnote 24; and Article 299 TFEU.

1138 If the undertaking concerned were found to consist of an unincorporated business (a single trader, with or without employees, who has not incorporated his or her business, or a professional exercising his or her profession alone and unincorporated, or several natural persons operating a single business without any employment relationship between them and without any form of legal person), the European Commission would necessarily have to address its decision to the natural person or persons operating the business. However, this situation almost never occurs: in practice, proceedings are always conducted against companies or other legal persons. In the *Pre-Insulated Pipes* case, one of the undertakings fined for participation in the cartel was controlled and managed by a natural person, Dr W. H., but the European Commission appears to have made an effort to avoid imposing the fine on him, identifying instead a collection of companies which it held jointly and severally liable for the fine; see recitals 157–160 and Article 3(d) of the Decision of 21 October 1998, *Pre-Insulated Pipe Cartel* [1999] OJ L24/1, and paragraph 105 of the Judgment of 20 March 2002, *HFB and Others v Commission*, T-9/99, EU:T:2002:70, in which the Court found that the European Commission had 'intentionally' not established Dr H.'s liability. See also Judgment of 2 October 2003, *Siderúrgica Aristrain Madrid v Commission*, C-196/99 P, EU:C:2003:529, paragraphs 91 and 101; and see further my paper 'Is Criminalisation of EU Competition Law the Answer?' (2005) 28 *World Competition* 117, also accessible at http://ssrn.com/author=456087.

1139 Judgments of 17 December 1991, *Enichem Anic v Commission*, T-6/89, EU:T:1991:74, paragraph 236; and of 27 March 2014, *Saint-Gobain Glass France and Compagnie de Saint-Gobain v Commission*, T-56/09 and T-73/09, EU:T:2014:160, paragraph 312; and of 12 July 2018, *Silec Cable and General Cable v Commission*, T-438/14, EU:T:2018:447, paragraph 194.

the European Commission may address the infringement decision to the parent company or the subsidiary or both.[1140]

The companies or other persons that are the envisaged addressees of the decision are also the persons that each enjoy the procedural rights that the European Commission must respect before adopting the decision.[1141] For instance, before adopting an infringement decision addressed to a parent company and a subsidiary that are both held liable for the infringement, the European Commission must initiate proceedings against both companies and send a statement of objections to both. Each of these companies has a separate right to have access to the file, make written submissions and request an oral hearing.[1142]

While the investigation in substance concerns the suspected infringement by the **undertaking under investigation**, the European Commission thus conducts its proceedings against the **companies** (or other persons) **under investigation**, being the companies (or other persons) considered responsible for the operation of the undertaking under investigation.[1143]

The undertaking / person distinction is relevant not only on the side of those under investigation, but also on the side of third parties.

Where Regulation 1/2003 grants certain rights to third parties, such as the right to lodge a complaint or the right to be heard as interested third person, it grants these rights to natural or legal persons.[1144]

The concept of an undertaking is, however, also relevant when third parties are the target of the European Commission's powers of investigation. Article 18 of Regulation 1/2003 empowers the European Commission to require 'undertakings and associations of undertakings' to supply information necessary for its investigation, and Article 20 of Regulation 1/2003 empowers the Commission to conduct 'all necessary inspections of undertakings and associations of undertakings'. These powers of investigation can also be used to obtain information from third-party undertakings.[1145] For reasons of enforceability, decisions are, however, addressed to the companies (or other persons) responsible for the operation of the undertaking.[1146]

1140 See Opinion of Advocate General Kokott of 12 January 2012, *Alliance One and Others v Commission*, C-628/10 P and C-14/11 P, EU:C:2012:11, paragraphs 46 to 67; Judgment of 8 July 2004, *JFE Engineering and Others v Commission*, T-67/00 etc., EU:T:2004:221, paragraph 414; Judgment of 9 September 2015, *LG Electronics v Commission*, T-91/13, EU:T:2015:609, paragraphs 64 to 91; and Judgment of 6 October 2021, *Sumal*, C-882/19, EU:C:2021:800, paragraphs 62 and 63.

1141 Judgments of 15 July 2015, *Akzo Nobel NV and Others v Commission*, T-47/10, EU:T:2015:506, paragraph 126, of 10 September 2009, *Akzo Nobel NV and Others v Commission*, C-97/08 P, EU:C:2009:536, paragraph 57, and of 6 October 2021, *Sumal*, C-882/19, EU:C:2021:800, paragraph 56.

1142 In practice, companies belonging to the same undertaking most often exercise their procedural rights jointly, but not always, especially not if they contest that they form a single undertaking. In the European Commission's cartel settlement procedure, companies within the same undertaking must appoint a joint representative; see paragraph 12 of Commission Notice on the conduct of settlement procedures in view of the adoption of decisions pursuant to Article 7 and Article 23 of Council Regulation (EC) No 1/2003 in cartel cases [2008] OJ C167/1.

1143 Where the suspected infringement concerns a decision by an association of undertakings, and the association of undertakings has legal personality, proceedings are usually only conducted against the association of undertakings.

1144 See Articles 7(2) and 27(3) of Regulation 1/2003.

1145 See paragraph 32 of the Notice on Best Practices, Judgment of 5 October 2020, *Intermarché Casino Achats v Commission*, T-254/17, EU:T:2020:459, paragraph 284.

1146 See also Opinion of Advocate General Pitruzzella of 14 July 2022, *Casino, Guichard-Perrachon and Achats Marchandises Casino v Commission*, C-690/20 P, EU:C:2022:579.

3. Who are the undertakings/companies under investigation depends on the scope of the *investigation*

Who are the undertakings/companies under investigation (and hence who are third parties) depends on the scope of the investigation as conducted by the European Commission.

The European Commission has a broad discretion to determine the scope of its investigations.[1147] It may, on grounds of expediency, limit its investigation and proceedings to certain undertakings (for instance, the main participants to a suspected cartel, or those participants for which the evidence is most readily available) or to certain companies responsible for the operation of the undertakings concerned (for instance, only the companies directly involved in the cartel behaviour, or also the ultimate parent companies).[1148] It may also change the scope of the investigation in the course of the investigation, adding or removing companies under investigation.

When exercising this discretion as to the scope of its investigations, the European Commission must, however, use objective criteria, compatible with the principle of equal treatment and the principle of proportionality.[1149]

Whether an undertaking/company is an undertaking/company under investigation or rather a third party in relation to certain proceedings may also depend on whether the European Commission has made a certain factual situation the subject of one or more separate proceedings. The European Commission is entitled both to disjoin and to join proceedings for objective reasons.[1150] For instance, in the *Alrosa and De Beers* case, which concerned the supply of rough diamonds between Alrosa and two subsidiaries of the De Beers group, the European Commission opened two parallel proceedings, one based on Article 101 TFEU, in which it sent a statement of objections to both Alrosa and De Beers, and the other based on Article 102 TFEU, in which it sent a separate statement of objections only to De Beers. Following the Opinion of Advocate General Kokott, the Court of Justice confirmed that, in relation to the proceedings under Article 102 TFEU, Alrosa was a third party. The situation would have been different only if it had transpired that the European Commission had arbitrarily, that is without an objective reason, made a single factual situation the subject of two separate proceedings. However, this was not the case, as it was objectively justified to conduct two separate proceedings in view of their different material legal bases, Article 101 TFEU, on the one hand, and Article 102 TFEU, on the other.[1151]

1147 See further my paper 'Discretion and Prioritisation in Public Antitrust Enforcement, in Particular EU Antitrust Enforcement' (2011) 34 *World Competition* 353, also accessible at http://ssrn.com/author=456078.

1148 See Opinion of Advocate General Kokott of 12 January 2012, *Alliance One and Others v Commission*, C-628/10 P and C-14/11 P, EU:C:2012:11, paragraphs 46–47; Judgment of 8 July 2004, *JFE Engineering and Others v Commission*, T-67/00 etc., EU:T:2004:221, paragraph 414; Judgment of 9 September 2015, *LG Electronics v Commission*, T-91/13, EU:T:2015:609, paragraphs 64 to 91; and Judgment of 6 October 2021, *Sumal*, C-882/19, EU:C:2021:800, paragraphs 62 and 63.

1149 See Opinion of Advocate General Kokott of 12 January 2012, *Alliance One and Others v Commission*, C-628/10 P and C-14/11 P, EU:C:2012:11, paragraphs 48 to 67, and Judgment of 9 December 2020, *Groupe Canal + v Commission*, C-132/19 P, EU:C:2020:1007, paragraphs 94 to 127.

1150 See Judgment of 16 June 2016, *FSL Holdings and Others v Commission*, T-655/11, EU:T:2015:383, paragraphs 56, 57, 131 and 148, and the case law cited therein.

1151 Opinion of Advocate General Kokott of 17 September 2009, *Commission v Alrosa*, C-441/07 P, EU:C:2009:55, paragraphs 174 to 177, and Judgment of 29 July 2010, *Commission v Alrosa*, C-441/07 P, EU:C:2010:3775, paragraphs 88 and 89.

4. How to find out who are the undertakings/companies under investigation

An essential step in any antitrust procedure that advances beyond the preliminary investigation stage is the initiation or opening of proceedings.[1152] In cases other than cartel cases,[1153] the initiation of proceedings usually takes place once the European Commission's initial assessment leads to the conclusion that the case merits further investigation and the scope of the investigation has been sufficiently defined. The initiation of proceedings then signals a commitment on the part of the European Commission to further investigate the case.[1154] In cartel cases, the initiation of proceedings usually takes place later, simultaneously with the adoption of the statement of objections.[1155]

One of the functions of the initiation of proceedings is to identify the companies under investigation.[1156] The decision initiating proceedings is notified to the companies under investigation. In addition, the European Commission's practice is to publish the initiation of proceedings on its website and to issue a press release, unless such publication may harm the investigation.[1157]

If at a later stage of the proceedings, the European Commission considers that the proceedings should be extended to cover more companies, it may take a further decision initiating proceedings also against those additional companies. Again, this decision will be notified to the companies concerned, and may be made public.[1158]

If the European Commission at a later stage of the proceedings concludes that there are no grounds to continue the proceedings with regard to one or more of the companies under investigation, it will close the proceedings in relation to those companies. It will again notify the companies concerned of this decision, and, if the initiation of proceedings had been made public, note the closure on its website and/or issue a press release.[1159]

Already before the initiation of proceedings, companies subject to an investigative measure by the European Commission under Chapter V of Regulation 1/2003, for instance a request

---

1152 Whereas in Article 11(6) of Regulation 1/2003 and in Article 2 of Regulation 773/2004 the term 'initiation of proceedings' is used, the term 'opening of proceedings' is used in paragraphs 17 to 24 of the Notice on Best Practices. An introductory overview of the European Commission's antitrust procedures from start to end is provided in Chapter III. 'Overview of the European Commission's antitrust procedures' below.

1153 For the definition of 'cartels', see Article 2(14) of Directive 2014/104/EU of the European Parliament and the Council of 26 November 2014 on certain rules governing actions for damages under national law for infringements of the competition law provisions of the Member States and of the European Union [2014] OJ L349/1, and recital 2 of Commission Regulation (EU) 2015/1348 of 3 August 2015 amending Regulation (EC) No 773/2004 on the conduct of proceedings by the Commission pursuant to Articles 81 and 82 of the EC Treaty [2015] L208/3.

1154 See paragraphs 17 and 18 of the Notice on Best Practices.

1155 See paragraph 24 of the Notice on Best Practices.

1156 Paragraph 19 of the Notice on Best Practices.

1157 See Article 2(2) of Regulation 773/2004 and paragraphs 20 and 21 of the Notice on Best Practices. Paragraph 20 of the Notice on Best Practices refers to 'the website of the Directorate-General for Competition'. What is meant is the 'Competition Policy' section of the website of the European Commission; see https://ec.europa.eu/competition-policy/index_en.

1158 See paragraph 23 of the Notice on Best Practices.

1159 See paragraphs 76 and 114 of the Notice on Best Practices.

for information pursuant to Article 18 of Regulation 1/2003, have the right to be informed of their procedural status, in particular whether they are themselves subject to an investigation.[1160]

Companies that have been subject to an investigative measure may at any time inquire with the Directorate-General for Competition about the status of the investigation. If such a company considers that it has not been properly informed by the Directorate-General for Competition of its procedural status, it may refer the matter to the Hearing Officer. If the Hearing Officer finds that the company has not been properly informed, the Hearing Officer will take a decision that the Directorate-General for Competition will inform the company of its procedural status.[1161]

B. Overview of the European Commission's antitrust procedures

The antitrust procedures before the European Commission are administrative procedures, in which the Commission, which is an administrative, non-judicial body, acts both as investigator and as first-instance decision-maker.[1162]

Investigations may get started on the basis of a complaint,[1163] information otherwise received from market participants or informants, information received from other authorities,[1164] or obtained by the European Commission through its own monitoring of markets,[1165] or in

---

1160 See Judgments of 8 July 2008, *AC-Treuhand v Commission*, T-99/04, EU:T:2008:256, paragraphs 52 to 59, and Article 4(2)(d) of Decision 2011/695/EU.

1161 See Article 4(2)(d), read in conjunction with Article 3(7), of Decision 2011/695/EU; paragraph 15 of the Notice on Best Practices; and my paper 'The Role of the Hearing Officer in Competition Proceedings before the European Commission' (2012) 35 *World Competition* 431, updated version accessible at http://ssrn.com/author=456078.

1162 The addressees of Commission decisions can subsequently bring an action for annulment against the Commission decision before the EU Courts, thus ensuring the compatibility of the enforcement system with the fundamental right of access to an independent court; see Judgments of 8 December 2011, *Chalkor v Commission*, C-386/10 P, EU:C:2011:815; of 18 July 2013, *Schindler v Commission*, C-501/11 P, EU:C:2013:522; and of 25 October 2018, *Emesa-Trefilería and Industrias Galycas v Commission*, T-406/10, EU:T:2015:499; View of Advocate General Kokott of 13 June 2014, Opinion procedure 2/13 (Accession of the EU to the ECHR), EU:C:2014:2475, paragraphs 146 to 150; Judgment of the European Court of Human Rights of 27 September 2011, *Menarini Diagnostics v Italy* (Application no 43509/08), and Decision of the European Court of Human Rights of 13 March 2012, *Bouygues Telecom v France* (Application no 2324/08); and my papers 'The Combination of the Investigative and Prosecutorial Function and the Adjudicative Function in EC Antitrust Enforcement: A Legal and Economic Analysis' (2004) 27 *World Competition* 201, 'The Increased Level of EU Antitrust Fines, Judicial Review and the ECHR' (2010) 33 *World Competition* 5, and 'The Compatibility with Fundamental Rights of the EU Antitrust Enforcement System in Which the European Commission Acts Both as Investigator and as First-Instance Decision Maker' (2014) 37 *World Competition* 5, all three also accessible at http://ssrn.com/author=456078.

1163 Even when a formal complaint is at the origin of the investigation, the ensuing proceedings are not adversarial proceedings between the complainant and the companies under investigation, but proceedings commenced and conducted by the European Commission, in fulfilment of its task to implement EU competition policy, against the companies investigated; see Judgments of 17 November 1987, *British American Tobacco and Reynolds Industries v Commission*, 142 and 156/84, EU:C:1987:490, paragraphs 19 and 20; of 11 July 2013, *Diamanthandel A. Spira v Commission*, T-108/07 and T-354/08, EU:T:2013:367, paragraph 59; and of 16 December 2020, *Fakro v Commission*, T-515/18, EU:T:2020:620, paragraph 41.

1164 See Article 12 of Regulation 1/2003, and Opinion of Advocate General Kokott of 17 November 2016 and Judgment of 27 April 2017, *FSL Holdings and Others v Commission*, C-469/15, EU:C:2016:884 and EU:C:2017:308.

1165 Such market monitoring can be informal or can take place within the formal framework of a sector inquiry pursuant to Article 17 of Regulation 1/2003.

the context of another investigation,[1166] or, for secret cartels, an application for immunity under the European Commission's Leniency Programme.[1167]

To supplement the initial information thus obtained, the European Commission can make use of the powers of investigation set out in Chapter V of Regulation 1/2003 – namely, requests for information pursuant to Article 18, interviews pursuant to Article 19, and inspections pursuant to Articles 20 and 21 of Regulation 1/2003.[1168]

The investigation or proceedings will ultimately end in one of four possible ways:

- The European Commission may adopt a decision pursuant to Articles 7 and/or Article 23(2) of Regulation 1/2003 finding an infringement of Articles 101 and/or 102 TFEU, ordering its termination and/or imposing fines (**infringement decision**);
- It may accept commitments and make these binding through a decision pursuant to Article 9 of Regulation 1/2003 (**commitment decision**);[1169]
- In exceptional cases where the public interest of the EU so requires,[1170] it may, pursuant to Article 10 of Regulation 1/2003, adopt a declaratory decision finding that Articles 101 and/or 102 TFEU are not applicable to the agreements or practices investigated (**non-infringement decision**);
- It may simply close the investigation or proceedings (**simple closure**).

Before an **infringement decision** can be adopted, the European Commission must take a decision initiating proceedings,[1171] and address a statement of objections to the companies under investigation.[1172] Following the receipt of the statement of objections, the companies under investigation are entitled to access the European Commission's investigation file,[1173] and to respond in writing to the statement of objections within a set time limit.[1174] If they

---

1166 See Judgment of 18 June 2015, *Deutsche Bahn and Others v Commission*, C-583/13 P, EU:C:2015:404, paragraph 59.

1167 See Article 4a of Regulation 773/2004; Commission Notice on Immunity from fines and reduction of fines in cartel cases [2006] OJ C298/11, as amended by Communication from the Commission Amendments to the Commission Notice on Immunity from fines and reduction of fines in cartel cases [2015] OJ C256/1; and my papers 'Leniency in Antitrust Enforcement: Theory and Practice' (2007) 30 *World Competition* 25 and 'The Use of Leniency in EU Cartel Enforcement: An Assessment after Twenty Years' (2016) 39 *World Competition* 327, both also accessible at http://ssrn.com/author=456078.

1168 These investigative measures can be used during all stages of the investigation, from the preliminary investigation before the initiation of proceedings until after the statement of objections and the oral hearing; see Article 2(3) of Regulation 773/2004 and Judgment of 9 April 2019 in *Qualcomm and Qualcomm Europe v Commission*, T-371/17, EU:T:2019:232, paragraphs 67 to 76, confirmed on appeal in Judgment of 28 January 2021 in *Qualcomm and Qualcomm Europe v Commission*, C-466/19 P, EU:C:2021:76, paragraphs 72 and 73.

1169 See my papers 'Settlements of EU Antitrust Investigations: Commitment Decisions under Article 9 of Regulation No. 1/2009' (2006) 29 *World Competition* 345, 'The Use of Settlements in Public Antitrust Enforcement: Objectives and Principles' (2008) 31 *World Competition* 335, and 'Ten Years of Commitment Decisions under Article 9 of Regulation 1/2003: Too Much of a Good Thing?' (2005) *Concurrences* no 3, all three also accessible at http://ssrn.com/author=456078.

1170 See recital 14 of Regulation 1/2003; at the time of writing, no inapplicability decision has been adopted yet.

1171 See Article 2(1) of Regulation 773/2004.

1172 See Article 27(1) of Regulation 1/2003, Article 10 of Regulation 773/2004 and paragraphs 81 to 91 of the Notice on Best Practices.

1173 See Article 27(2) of Regulation 1/2003, Article 15 of Regulation 773/2004, paragraphs 92 to 98 of the Notice on Best Practices, and W. Wils and H. Abbott, 'Access to the File in Competition Proceedings Before the European Commission' (2019) 42 *World Competition* 255, updated version accessible at http://ssrn.com/author=456087.

1174 See Articles 10 and 11 of Regulation 773/2004, and paragraphs 99 to 103 of the Notice on Best Practices.

request so in their written reply to the statement of objections, the companies under investigation are also entitled to develop their arguments further at an oral hearing.[1175] As the investigation progresses and conclusions are drawn from the replies to the statement of objections, the European Commission may adopt supplementary statements of objections, which again trigger for the companies under investigation the rights of access to the file, written reply and oral hearing.[1176] As a final step before adopting the infringement decision, the European Commission must consult the Advisory Committee on Restrictive Practices and Dominant Positions, which is composed of representatives of the competition authorities of the EU Member States.[1177]

In cases of urgency due to the risk of serious and irreparable damage to competition, the European Commission may, already before adopting an infringement decision, on the basis of a prima facie finding of infringement, order interim measures pursuant to Article 8 of Regulation 1/2003 (interim measures decision). Like the adoption of an infringement decision, the adoption of an interim measures decision must be preceded by a decision initiating proceedings,[1178] as well as a statement of objections,[1179] which triggers for the companies under investigation the rights of access to the file,[1180] written reply and oral hearing.[1181] The Advisory Committee must also be consulted.[1182]

Specifically for cartel cases,[1183] the European Commission has created a cartel settlement procedure,[1184] which is an alternative procedure for reaching an infringement decision, which can be used if both the European Commission and the companies under investigation prefer it instead of the normal procedure. Under the cartel settlement procedure, after the initiation of proceedings but before the adoption of a statement of objections, the European Commission and the companies under investigation conduct settlement discussions, culminating in the companies

---

1175 See Article 12 of Regulation 773/2004, paragraphs 106 to 108 of the Notice on Best Practices, and my paper 'The Oral Hearing in Competition Proceedings Before the European Commission' (2012) 35 *World Competition* 397, updated version accessible at http://ssrn.com/author=456087.

1176 See paragraphs 109 to 112 of the Notice on Best Practices.

1177 See Article 14 of Regulation 1/2003.

1178 See Article 2(1) of Regulation 773/2004.

1179 See Article 27(1) of Regulation 1/2003 and Article 10 of Regulation 773/2004.

1180 See Article 27(2) of Regulation 1/2003, and W. Wils and H. Abbott, 'Access to the File in Competition Proceedings Before the European Commission' (2019) 42 *World Competition* 255, updated version accessible at http://ssrn.com/author=456087.

1181 See Articles 10 to 12 of Regulation 773/2004, and Final Report of the Hearing Officer in Case AT.40608 *Broadcom – Interim Measures Procedure* [2021] OJ C81/13.

1182 See Article 14 of Regulation 1/2003.

1183 Also in cases other than cartel cases, the companies under investigation may cooperate with proceedings leading to an infringement decision; see European Commission, Fact Sheet – Cooperation – FAQ (17 December 2018), accessible at https://ec.europa.eu/competition/publications/data/factsheet_guess.pdf. No specific procedural rules for such cooperation cases have been enacted so far.

1184 See Article 10a of Regulation 773/2004, as inserted by Commission Regulation (EC) No 622/2008 of 30 June 2008 amending Regulation (EC) No 773/2004, as regards the conduct of settlement procedures in cartel cases [2008] OJ L171/3; Commission Notice on the conduct of settlement procedures in view of the adoption of decisions pursuant to Article 7 and Article 23 of Council Regulation (EC) No 1/2003 in cartel cases [2008] OJ C167/1, amended by Communication from the Commission – Amendments to the Commission Notice on the conduct of settlement procedures [2015] OJ C256/2; and my paper 'The Use of Settlements in Public Antitrust Enforcement: Objectives and Principles' (2008) 31 *World Competition* 335, also accessible at http://ssrn.com/author=456078.

under investigation making settlement submissions. The statement of objections then mirrors those settlement submissions, and the companies under investigation in their written reply to the statement of objections simply confirm their agreement, and waive their right to an oral hearing. Like for any other infringement decision, as a final step before adopting the infringement decision, the European Commission must consult the Advisory Committee.[1185]

In cases other than secret cartel cases,[1186] the companies under investigation may, at any time during the investigation and proceedings, propose to the European Commission to close the proceedings through a **commitment decision**.[1187] The European Commission is, however, never obliged to close the proceedings through a commitment decision instead of an infringement decision.[1188] If the companies under investigation offer the commitments after the statement of objections or after an interim measures decision, the commitments must meet the concerns expressed in the statement of objections and/or interim measures decision.[1189] If they are offered at an earlier stage of the investigation or proceedings, and the European Commission is willing to close the case through a commitment decision, the European Commission will first adopt a preliminary assessment,[1190] and the commitments offered must meet the concerns expressed in that preliminary assessment. Before adopting the commitment decision, the European Commission must publish a concise summary of the case and the main content of the commitments, inviting observations from interested third parties (market test).[1191] As a final step before adopting the commitment decision, the European Commission must consult the Advisory Committee.[1192] The commitment decision makes the commitments binding, while concluding that there are no longer grounds for action by the European Commission, but without concluding whether or not there has been or still is an infringement.[1193]

Before adopting a **non-infringement decision**, the European Commission must, like before adopting a commitment decision, publish a concise summary of the case and the main content of the proposed course of action, inviting observations from interested third parties (market test),[1194] and consult the Advisory Committee.[1195]

1185 See Article 14 of Regulation 1/2003.

1186 In line with recital 13 of Regulation 1/2003, the European Commission does not adopt commitment decisions in secret cartel cases; see paragraph 116 of the Notice on Best Practices.

1187 See paragraphs 1118 to 128 of the Notice on Best Practices.

1188 See Judgment of 11 July 2007, *Alrosa v Commission*, T-170/06, EU:T:2007:220, paragraph 130.

1189 In other words, the statement of objections and/or interim measures decision qualifies as preliminary assessment within the meaning of Article 9 of Regulation 1/2003; see, by way of examples, Summary of Commission Decision of 29 April 2019 in Case AT.40049 – *Mastercard II* [2019] OJ C300/6 and Summary of Commission Decision of 7 October 2020 in Case AT.40608 – *Broadcom* [2021] OJ C81/9.

1190 If the European Commission had not yet initiated proceedings, it must do so at the latest simultaneously with the adoption of the preliminary assessment; see Article 2(1) of Regulation 773/2004.

1191 See Article 27(4) of Regulation 1/2003 and paragraphs 129 to 133 of the Notice on Best Practices,

1192 See Article 14 of Regulation 1/2003.

1193 See Article 9(1) and recital 13 of Regulation 1/2003.

1194 See Article 27(4) of Regulation 1/2003. If the European Commission had not yet initiated proceedings, it must do so at the latest simultaneously with the publication of the market test notice; see Article 2(1) of Regulation 773/2004.

1195 See Article 14 of Regulation 1/2003.

Finally, at any time during the investigation and proceedings, the European Commission can bring the investigation and proceedings to an end through a **simple closure**. Unless it had not yet contacted the companies under investigation, the European Commission will inform those companies of the closure, and if it had already made public its investigation, it will note the closure on its website and/or issue a press release.[1196]

C. Informing the European Commission about a suspected infringement and triggering an investigation

1. Informing the European Commission about a suspected infringement

a. *Anyone can provide information in any way or form*

Information from citizens and businesses is important in triggering investigations by the European Commission.[1197] The European Commission therefore encourages citizens and businesses to inform it about suspected infringements of Articles 101 and 102 TFEU.[1198]

Any third person can inform the European Commission about a suspected antitrust infringement: consumers, consumer associations, competitors, customers, suppliers, business associations, disgruntled current or former employees, etc.[1199]

The website of the Directorate-General for Competition provides a dedicated email address and telephone number for information about suspected infringements,[1200] but information can also be provided in any other way or form.[1201]

If the information is provided orally, there is no need to follow the formal requirements for interviews pursuant to Article 19 of Regulation 1/2003 and Article 3 of Regulation 773/2004, given that the European Commission has at this preliminary stage not yet started an investigation.[1202]

b. *Informants can remain anonymous*

Informants have the right to remain anonymous if they wish so. Indeed, where the European Commission accepts information supplied on a purely voluntary basis,

---

1196 See paragraphs 76 and 114 of the Notice on Best Practices.

1197 See paragraph 10 of the Notice on Best Practices, and Judgment of 5 October 2020, *Intermarché Casino Achats v Commission*, T-254/17, EU:T:2020:459, paragraph 222.

1198 See paragraph 10 of the Notice on Best Practices, and paragraph 3 of Commission Notice on the handling of complaints by the Commission under Articles 81 and 82 of the EC Treaty [2004] OJ C101/65 ('**Notice on Complaints**').

1199 The undertakings that committed the infringements can also themselves inform the European Commission about their infringements and seek leniency; see Chapter V of this book.

1200 See https://ec.europa.eu/competition-policy/cartels/whistleblower_en.

1201 See paragraph 10 of the Notice on Best Practices, and Judgment of 5 October 2020, *Intermarché Casino Achats v Commission*, T-245/17, EU:T:2020:459, paragraph 206.

1202 See Judgment of 5 October 2020, *Intermarché Casino Achats v Commission*, T-254/17, EU:T:2020:459, paragraphs 193 to 201; pending on appeal *Intermarché Casino Achats v Commission*, C-693/20 P.

accompanied by a request for confidentiality to protect the informant's anonymity, it is in principle bound to comply with such a condition.[1203]

The EU Courts have affirmed that the European Commission's ability to guarantee the anonymity of certain of its sources of information is of crucial importance for the effective enforcement of Articles 101 and 102 TFEU.[1204]

An anonymous whistleblower tool is available on the website of the European Commission.[1205] It is a specifically designed encrypted messaging system that allows two-way communications between informants and the Directorate-General for Competition. The service is run by a specialised external service provider that acts as an intermediary, and which relays only the content of received messages without forwarding any metadata that could be used to identify the informant.[1206]

If the information provided by the informant is subsequently used by the European Commission to justify the opening of an investigation and the conduct of inspections at the premises of the suspected companies, the European Commission will not share with the national competition authorities and courts involved in those inspections any information revealing the identity of the informant, or enabling that identity to be deduced.[1207]

If the information provided by the informant who requested anonymity subsequently leads to the adoption of a statement of objections and an infringement decision against the companies under investigation, the anonymity of the informant will remain protected. The European Commission may use the information provided by the informant as evidence in the statement of objections and the infringement decision, but only if this can be done without revealing the identity of the informant or enabling that identity to be deduced.[1208] Similarly, when granting the companies under investigation access to its investigation file, the European Commission will ensure that the anonymity of the informant remains protected, by denying access to any information that would allow the informant's identity to be deduced.[1209]

1203 See Judgments of 7 November 1985, *Adams v European Commission*, 145/83, EU:C:1985:448, paragraph 34; of 8 July 2004, *Mannesmannröhren-Werke v Commission*, T-44/00, EU:T:2004:218, paragraph 84, confirmed on appeal in Judgment of 25 January 2007, *Salzgitter Mannesmann v European Commission*, C-411/04 P, EU:C:2007:54, paragraph 45; of 8 July 2004, *Dalmine v European Commission*, T-50/00, EU:T:2004:220, paragraph 72, confirmed on appeal in Judgment of 25 January 2007, *Dalmine v European Commission*, C-407/04 P, EU:C:2007:53, paragraph 49; and of 8 July 2008, *BPB v European Commission*, T-53/03, EU:T:2008:254, paragraph 36.

1204 See Judgments of 22 October 2002, *Roquette Frères*, C-94/00, EU:C:2002:603, paragraph 64, and of 5 October 2020, *Intermarché Casino Achats v Commission*, T-245/17, EU:T:2020:459, paragraph 124.

1205 https://ec.europa.eu/competition-policy/cartels/whistleblower_en.

1206 See European Commission Press release IP/17/591 of 16 March 2017 and https://ec.europa.eu/competition-policy/cartels/whistleblower_en.

1207 See Judgment of 22 October 2002, *Roquette Frères*, C-94/00, EU:C:2002:603, paragraphs 62 to 65.

1208 The mere fact that the Commission does not disclose the source of that information does not prevent the Commission from relying on it as evidence, although it might have a bearing on the credibility of that evidence; see Judgments of 25 January 2007, *Dalmine v Commission*, C-407/04 P, EU:C:2007:53, paragraphs 48 to 51; of 8 July 2004, *JFE Engineering and Others v Commission*, T-67/00, T-68/00, T-71/00 and T-78/00, EU:T:2004:221, paragraph 273; and of 8 July 2004, *Mannesmannröhren-Werke v Commission*, T-44/00, EU:T:2004:218, paragraphs 84 to 86.

1209 See W. Wils and A. Abbott, 'Access to the File in Competition Proceedings Before the European Commission' (2019) 42 *World Competition* 255, updated version accessible at http://ssrn.com/author=456087, text accompanied by footnotes 98 to 102. However, see also Judgment of 15 June 2022, *Qualcomm v Commission*, T-235/18, EU:T:2022:358, paragraph 286.

The informant requesting anonymity should, when providing documents, inform the European Commission that it is possible to infer his or her identity as the informant from the documents themselves.[1210]

c. *Informants can strengthen their procedural position by lodging a complaint*

Provided that they fulfil the substantive and procedural requirements set out below, informants can strengthen their procedural position by lodging a complaint.[1211]

Article 7(1) of Regulation 1/2003 provides that the European Commission can find an infringement of Articles 101 or 102 TFEU 'acting on a complaint or on its own initiative'.[1212] The last sentence of Article 27(1) of Regulation 1/2003 provides that 'complainants shall be closely associated with the proceedings'.

It should be noted that the procedural status of complainant has been created by Regulation 1/2003 in relation to its Article 7 (finding of an infringement and ordering its termination).[1213] There is no procedural status of complainant in relation to Article 23 of Regulation 1/2003 (imposition of fines),[1214] or in relation to Article 8 of Regulation 1/2003 (interim measures).[1215]

1210 See, to that effect, Judgment of 7 November 1985, *Adams v European Commission*, 145/83, EU:C:1985:448, paragraphs 53 to 55.

1211 The possibility for third parties to strengthen their procedural position by lodging a complaint is not only available to informants that bring information on a matter which the European Commission is not yet investigating, but is also available to third parties at any point during ongoing investigations and proceedings, until the European Commission has sent its draft final decision to the Advisory Committee; see Judgment of 7 June 2006, *Österreichische Postsparkasse and Bank für Arbeit und Wirtschaft v Commission*, T-213/01 and T-214/01, EU:T:2006:151, paragraphs 90 and 91, 148 to 150, and 160.

1212 Article 29(1) of Regulation 1/2003 similarly provides that the Commission may 'acting on its own initiative or on a complaint' withdraw the benefit of a block exemption regulation in an individual case.

1213 As well as in relation to its Article 29(1) (withdrawal of the benefit of a block exemption regulation in an individual case).
Article 9(2) of Regulation 1/2003 also provides that the Commission may 'upon request or on its own initiative' reopen proceedings previously closed through the adoption of a commitment decision pursuant to Article 9(1) of Decision 1/2003. Such request could be made either by an addressee of the commitment decision or by a third party. For an example of such a request by a third party, see Judgment of 6 February 2014, *Confederación Española de Empresarios de Estaciones de Servicio (CEEES) and Asociación de Gestores de Estaciones de Servicio v Commission*, T-342/11, EU:2014:60.

1214 This point appears to have been overlooked in *Confederación Española de Empresarios de Estaciones de Servicio (CEEES) and Asociación de Gestores de Estaciones de Servicio v Commission*, T-342/11, EU:2014:60, paragraphs 74 to 81. To the extent that the applicants in that case sought the imposition of a fine, they had no procedural status as complainants, and their application for annulment against the Commission's refusal to impose a fine should have been declared inadmissible by the General Court; see, by analogy, Judgment of 9 October 2018, *1&1 Telecom v Commission*, T-43/16, EU:T:2018:660, paragraphs 47 and 48, and Order of 19 February 1997, *Intertronic v Commission*, T-117/96, EU:T:1997:16.

1215 Whereas the Court of Justice's interpretation of Article 3 of Regulation 17 in *Camera Care* as covering also interim measures simultaneously extended the legal status of complainant under Regulation 17 to interim measures (Order of 17 January 1980, *Camera Care v Commission*, 792/79 R, EU:C:1980:18), it is clear from the text of Article 8 of Regulation 1/2003 (compared to the text of its Article 7), as well as from the legislative history of Regulation 1/2003 (Explanatory Memorandum accompanying the Commission's legislative proposal, COM(2000) 582 final of 27.9.2000 at page 18 (explanations relating to Article 8 – Interim measures)) that interim measures can only be adopted at the Commission's own initiative; see also paragraph 80 of the Notice on Complaints, and paragraph 35 of the Final Report of the Hearing Officer in Case AT.40608 *Broadcom – Interim Measures Procedure* [2021] OJ C81/13.

(1) *Substantive and procedural requirements to become a complainant*

According to Article 7(2) of Regulation 1/2003, 'those entitled to lodge a complaint [. . .] are natural or legal persons who can show a legitimate interest and Member States'.[1216]

According to the case law, the requirement to show a legitimate interest means that the natural or legal person (other than an EU Member State) must show that 'his [or her] economic interests have been harmed or are likely to be harmed' as a result of the alleged infringement of Articles 101 or 102 TFEU.[1217]

A person that is a party to a contract that constitutes or is part of the alleged infringement can also lodge a complaint, if that person does not bear significant responsibility for the alleged infringement, particularly where the terms of the contract were imposed on that person by a stronger party against its economic interests.[1218]

Business associations and consumer associations can lodge a complaint if, first, they are entitled to represent the interests of their members and, secondly, the interests of their members have been harmed or are likely to be harmed as a result of the alleged infringement.[1219]

In addition to the substantive requirement of having a legitimate interest, Regulation 773/2004 also imposes a procedural requirement for a complaint to be admissible, namely, the provision of the information required by Form C, set out in the Annex to Regulation 773/2004.[1220]

The European Commission may, however, dispense with this obligation as regards part of the information, including documents required by Form C.[1221]

1216 The procedural rights of the complainant belong to the natural or legal person which lodged the complaint and, if that person no longer exists, its legal successor, but not a mere economic successor; see Final Report of the Hearing Officer in Case COMP/E-1/38.113 – Prokent/Tomra [2008] OJ C219/7.

1217 Judgment of 7 June 2006, *Österreichische Postsparkasse and Bank für Arbeit und Wirtschaft v Commission*, T-213/01 and T-214/01, EU:T:2006:151, paragraphs 114 and 115.
In paragraphs 34 to 38 of its Notice on Complaints, which predates the judgment in *Österreichische Postsparkasse and Bank für Arbeit und Wirtschaft v Commission* (but which has not been amended since; see in this respect Opinion of Advocate General Geelhoed of 27 April 2006, *VW-Audi Forhandlerforenigingen v Skandinavisk Motor*, C-125/05, EU:C:2006:262, paragraph 38), the European Commission has set out an alternative test of 'being directly and adversely affected by the alleged infringement'. Whereas the requirement of being adversely affected is in line with the judgment in *Österreichische Postsparkasse and Bank für Arbeit und Wirtschaft v Commission*, the additional requirement of being directly affected does not appear correct; see also, by analogy, Judgments of 5 June 2014, *Kone and Others*, C-557/12, EU:C:2014:1317, paragraphs 33 and 34; of 12 December 2019, *Otis and Others*, C-435/18, EU:C:2019:1069, paragraphs 27 and 32; and of 12 October 2011, *Association belge des consommateurs test-achats v Commission*, T-224/10, EU:T:2011:588, paragraphs 40 to 44.

1218 See, by analogy, Judgment of 20 September 2001, *Courage and Crehan*, C-453/99, EU:C:2001:465, paragraphs 24 to 34.

1219 See Judgments of 24 January 1995, *Bureau Européen des Médias de l'Industrie Musicale (BEMIM) v Commission*, T-114/92, EU:T:1995:11, paragraphs 28 and 29, and of 18 May 1994, *Bureau Européen des Unions des Consommateurs and National Consumer Council v Commission*, T-37/92, EU:T:1994:54, paragraph 36.

1220 See Article 5 and recitals 6 and 7 of Regulation 773/2004, and Judgment of 19 May 2011, *Ryanair v Commission*, T-423/07, EU:T:2011:226, paragraphs 55 to 59.

1221 Article 5(1), last sentence, of Regulation 773/2004. According to paragraph 31 of the Notice on Complaints, this possibility can in particular play a role in facilitating complaints by consumer associations where they, in the context of an otherwise substantiated complaint, do not have access to specific pieces of information from the sphere of the undertakings complained of.

There is no incompatibility between lodging a complaint and remaining anonymous. As mentioned above, it is clear from the case law of the EU Courts that, where the European Commission accepts information supplied on a purely voluntary basis, accompanied by a request for confidentiality to protect the informant's anonymity, it is in principle bound to comply with such a condition.[1222] Lodging a complaint is always a purely voluntary act, and there is no provision in Regulation 1/2003, Regulation 773/2004 and Form C precluding anonymous complaints.[1223]

Finally, whereas the European Commission has delegated to its Hearing Officer the power to decide on applications to be heard by interested third persons, the Hearing Officer does not have any role in deciding on the admissibility of complaints.[1224]

(2) *Procedural rights of complainants*

Becoming a complainant provides two types of procedural benefits.

First, if the European Commission initiates proceedings and if it subsequently issues a statement of objections relating to a matter covered by the complaint, the complainant must, according to Article 27(4) of Regulation 1/2003, 'be closely associated with the proceedings'.

This does not, however, mean that the proceedings become adversarial proceedings between the complainant and the companies under investigation. Even when a complaint is at the origin of the investigation, the ensuing proceedings are proceedings commenced and conducted by the European Commission, in fulfilment of its task to implement EU competition policy, against the companies under investigation.[1225] It follows that complainants and companies under investigation are not in the same procedural situation, and that the procedural rights of complainants are not as far-reaching as the procedural rights of the companies under investigation. Whereas complainants must be given the opportunity to defend their legitimate interests in the course of the proceedings initiated by the European Commission and therefore be closely associated with them, their procedural rights are not as far-reaching as the rights of the defence of the companies under

---

[1222] See Judgments of 7 November 1985, *Adams v European Commission*, 145/83, EU:C:1985:448, paragraph 34; of 8 July 2004, *Mannesmannröhren-Werke v Commission*, T-44/00, EU:T:2004:218, paragraph 84, confirmed on appeal in Judgment of 25 January 2007, *Salzgitter Mannesmann v European Commission*, C-411/04 P, EU:C:2007:54, paragraph 45; of 8 July 2004, *Dalmine v European Commission*, T-50/00, EU:T:2004:220, paragraph 72, confirmed on appeal in Judgment of 25 January 2007, *Dalmine v European Commission*, C-407/04 P, EU:C:2007:53, paragraph 49; and of 8 July 2008, *BPB v European Commission*, T-53/03, EU:T:2008:254, paragraph 36.

[1223] Not all potential procedural benefits of lodging a complaint may be available to an anonymous complainant, however. As mentioned below, it is not possible to participate anonymously in the oral hearing.

[1224] See Judgment of 7 June 2006, *Österreichische Postsparkasse and Bank für Arbeit und Wirtschaft v Commission*, T-213/01 and T-214/01, EU:T:2006:151, paragraph 132.

[1225] See Judgments of 17 November 1987, *British American Tobacco and Reynolds Industries v Commission*, 142 and 156/84, EU:C:1987:490, paragraphs 19 and 20; of 11 July 2013, *Diamanthandel A. Spira v Commission*, T-108/07 and T-354/08, EU:T:2013:367, paragraph 59; and of 16 December 2020, *Fakro v Commission*, T-515/18, EU:T:2020:620, paragraph 41.
It follows that, if the complainant withdraws its complaint in the course of proceedings started on the basis of that complaint, the European Commission can still continue the proceedings on its own motion; for an example, see Final Report of the Hearing Officer in Case COMP/37.860 *Morgan Stanley Dean Witter/Visa International* [2009] OJ C183/4 at 5.

investigation, and cannot be allowed to interfere with the rights of the defence of the companies under investigation.[1226]

As will be discussed further below, the main manifestations of the complainants' close association with the proceedings are that they are entitled to a copy of the non-confidential version of the statement of objections if a statement of objections is issued on a matter covered by their complaint,[1227] and that they are most likely to be allowed to express their views at the oral hearing of the addressees of the statement of objections if those addressees request such a hearing.[1228]

Secondly, as discussed further below, if the European Commission does not intend to act on the complaint or part of the complaint, including if the European Commission, after having initially acted on the complaint by initiating proceedings and possibly subsequently issuing a statement of objections, later decides no longer to act on the complaint, the complainant is entitled to a reasoned decision rejecting its complaint.

2. No right to trigger an investigation, let alone an infringement decision

a. *The European Commission has a wide discretion to set its enforcement priorities*

Whereas, as mentioned above, anyone can inform the European Commission about a suspected infringement of Articles 101 or 102 TFEU, nobody can compel the European Commission to carry out an investigation, to initiate proceedings, or to continue proceedings up to the stage of a final decision as to the existence or non-existence of the alleged infringement.[1229]

According to the case law of the EU Courts, the European Commission, entrusted by Article 105(1) TFEU with the task of ensuring the application of the principles laid

---

1226 See, to that effect, Judgments of 17 November 1987, *British American Tobacco and Reynolds Industries v Commission*, 142 and 156/84, EU:C:1987:490, paragraphs 19 and 20; of 11 July 2013, *Diamanthandel A. Spira v Commission*, T-108/07 and T-354/08, EU:T:2013:367, paragraph 59; of 26 September 2018, *European Association of Euro-Pharmaceutical Companies (EAEPC) v Commission*, T-574/14, EU:T:2018:605, paragraph 93; and of 16 December 2020, *Fakro v Commission*, T-515/18, EU:T:2020:620, paragraph 41.
In these judgments the term 'right to a fair hearing' is used as shorthand for the more far-reaching procedural rights of the companies under investigation. In the light of the case law on the procedural rights of companies under investigation, the term 'rights of the defence' is arguably the best shorthand; see the excellent discussion and overview in A. Scordamaglia-Toussis, 'An Overview of the Rights of the Defence in EU Antitrust Proceedings', in E. Rousseva (ed), *EU Antitrust Procedure* (Oxford 2020), 337.

1227 See Article 6(1) of Regulation 773/2004. As indicated in Article 6(1), in cases where the cartel settlement procedure applies, complainants are only entitled to written information about the nature and subject matter of the procedure.

1228 See Article 6(2) of Regulation 773/2004.

1229 See Judgments of 18 September 1992, *Automec v Commission*, T-24/90, EU:T:1992:97, paragraphs 75 and 76; of 17 May 2001, *International Express Carriers Conference (IECC) v Commission*, C-449/98 P, EU:C:2001:276, paragraphs 35 to 37; and of 16 December 2020, *Fakro v Commission*, T-515/18, EU:T:2020:620, paragraph 98. The Commission can, however, be required to give a decision if the subject matter of a complaint falls within its exclusive competence, as in the case of the withdrawal in an individual case of the benefit of an exemption regulation; see *Automec v Commission*, as just above, paragraph 75, and Articles 29(1) and (2) of Regulation 1/2003; see further Chapter IV of this book.

down in Articles 101 and 102 TFEU, is responsible for defining and implementing the orientation of EU competition policy. In order to perform that task effectively, the European Commission has a broad discretion to select the cases which it investigates and in which it continues the proceedings up to the stage of a final decision.[1230]

It is not the task of the European Commission to settle individual disputes.[1231] Third parties that consider themselves harmed by an alleged infringement of Articles 101 or 102 TFEU are not dependent on action by the European Commission, as they can bring a private action in the courts of the EU Member States.[1232] Indeed, Article 101(2) TFEU provides that any agreements or decisions prohibited pursuant to Article 101 TFEU shall be automatically void, and the case law has clarified that Article 101(1) and Article 102 TFEU produce direct effects between individuals and create rights for these individuals, and that the national courts whose task it is to apply the provisions of EU law in areas within their jurisdiction must ensure that those rules take full effect and must protect the rights which they confer on individuals, by granting injunctive relief, including interim relief, as well as compensation for harm suffered, under conditions that may not be less favourable than those governing the protection of comparable rights under national law and that ensure the effective protection of the rights conferred by Articles 101(1) and 102 TFEU.[1233]

b. *Complainants are entitled to a reasoned and reviewable decision settling the fate of their complaint*

While complainants, like anyone else, cannot compel the European Commission to carry out an investigation, to initiate proceedings, or to continue proceedings up to the stage of a final decision as to the existence or non-existence of the alleged infringement, complainants have the right to have the fate of their complaint settled within a reasonable time by a decision of the European Commission against which they can bring an action before the EU Courts.[1234]

1230 See Judgments of 14 December 2000, *Masterfood*, C-344/98, EU:C:2000:689, paragraph 46; of 4 March 1999, *Ufex and Others v Commission*, C-119/97 P, EU:C:1999:116, paragraphs 88 and 89; and of 17 May 2001, *International Express Carriers Conference (IECC) v Commission*, C-449/98 P, EU:C:2001:276, paragraphs 35 to 37; see also Judgment of 20 April 1999, *Limburgse Vinyl Maatschappij and Others v Commission*, C-238/99 P etc., EU:C:2002:582, paragraphs 148 to 154 (discretion to take a new decision following annulment of a first decision on purely procedural grounds); see further Chapter IV of this book.

1231 Judgment of 14 February 2001, *Système Européen Promotion (SEP) v Commission*, T-115/99, EU:T:2001:54, paragraph 43.

1232 As already mentioned above, the Commission can, however, be required to give a decision if the subject matter of a complaint falls within its exclusive competence, as in the case of the withdrawal in an individual case of the benefit of an exemption regulation; see Judgment of 18 September 1992, *Automec v Commission*, T-24/90, EU:T:1992:97, paragraph 75, and Articles 29(1) and (2) of Regulation 1/2003.

1233 Judgments of 30 January 1974, *BRT and SABAM*, 127/73, EU:C:1974:6, paragraph 16; of 19 June 1990, *Factortame and Others*, C-213/89, EU:C:1990:257, paragraphs 19 to 21; and of 20 September 2001, *Courage and Crehan*, C-453/99, EU:C:2001:465, paragraphs 19 to 29. Article 1 of Regulation 1/2003 has given direct effect also to Article 101(3) TFEU. See further my paper 'Private Enforcement of EU Antitrust Law and Its Relationship with Public Enforcement: Past, Present and Future' (2017) 40 *World Competition* 3, also accessible at http://ssrn.com/author=456087.

1234 Judgments of 4 March 1999, *Ufex and Others v Commission*, C-119/97 P, EU:C:1999:116, paragraph 86; of 18 March 1997, *Guérin Automobiles v Commission*, C-282/95 P, EU:C:1997:159, paragraphs 36 to 38; of 12 March 2020, *LL-Carpenter v Commission*, T-531/18, EU:T:2020:91, paragraphs 78 to 80; and of 16 December 2020, *Fakro v Commission*, T-515/18, EU:T:2020:620, paragraphs 80 to 124.

The European Commission has indicated that it 'will in principle endeavour to inform complainants of the action that it proposes to take on a complaint within an indicative time frame of four months from the reception of the complaint'.[1235]

If the European Commission already at this stage comes to the preliminary conclusion that it does not intend to act on the complaint, it must start the procedure for rejecting the complaint.

The same procedure for rejecting the complaint must also be followed if the Commission does not immediately reject the complaint but at a later stage of the investigation or proceedings comes to the preliminary conclusion that it does not or no longer intend to adopt a decision pursuant to Article 7 of Regulation 1/2003 finding an infringement and ordering its termination as requested by the complainant.

Before starting the procedure for rejecting the complaint, the European Commission will normally first inform the complainant in a meeting or by phone. The complainant may then decide to withdraw its complaint.[1236]

If the complainant has not withdrawn its complaint, the European Commission must send the complainant a pre-rejection letter pursuant to Article 7 of Regulation 773/2004, informing the complainant of the reasons why it does not intend to act or to continue acting on the complaint, and set a time limit within which the complainant may make know its views in writing.[1237]

The complainant may then request access to the documents on which the European Commission bases its reasoning, or at least non-confidential versions of those documents, as the complainant is not entitled to have access to business secrets or other confidential information belonging to the other parties involved in the proceedings.[1238] This right of access is limited to the documents on which the European Commission's intention to reject the complaint, as set out in the letter pursuant to Article 7 of Regulation 773/2004, is based. It is thus not as far-reaching as the right of access to the entire investigation file afforded to addressees of a statement of objections.[1239]

If the complaint is rejected at a very early stage, merely on the basis of an analysis of the complaint itself, without the European Commission having collected any other

---

1235 Notice on Complaints, paragraph 61, indicating further that, thus, 'subject to the circumstances of the individual case and in particular the possible need to request complementary information from the complainant or third parties, the Commission will in principle inform the complainant within four months whether or not it intends to investigate the case further. The time-limit does not constitute a binding statutory term'.

1236 See paragraphs 139 and 61 of the Notice on Best Practices.

1237 Article 7(1) of Regulation 773/2004.

1238 See Article 8(1) of Regulation 773/2004; Judgments of 17 November 1987, *BAT and Reynolds v Commission*, 142 and 156/84, EU:C:1987:490, paragraph 23, and of 11 July 2013, *Diamanthandel A. Spira v Commission*, T-108/07 and T-354/08, EU:T:2013:367, paragraphs 70 and 71.

1239 See Judgments of 11 July 2013, *Diamanthandel A. Spira v Commission*, T-108/07 and T-354/08, EU:T:2013:367, paragraphs 64 and 65; of 11 January 2017, *Topps Europe v Commission*, T-699/14, EU:T:2017:2, paragraph 30; of 26 September 2018, *European Association of Euro-Pharmaceutical Companies (EAEPC) v Commission*, T-574/14, EU:T:2018:605, paragraph 93; and of 16 December 2020, *Fakro v Commission*, T-515/18, EU:T:2020:620, paragraph 43; and W. Wils and H. Abbott, 'Access to the File in Competition Proceedings Before the European Commission' (2019) 42 *World Competition* 255, updated version accessible at http://ssrn.com/author=456087.

information, the complaint itself may be the only document on which the European Commission's intention to reject the complaint, as set out in the letter pursuant to Article 7 of Regulation 773/2004, is based. In such a case, there are no documents the European Commission needs to give access to.

In other cases, the European Commission's intention to reject the complaint, as set out in the letter pursuant to Article 7 of Regulation 773/2004, may be based on information it has collected from the undertakings targeted by the complaint or from third parties in response to requests for information, or on the response of the undertakings targeted by the complaint if these have been granted the opportunity to comment on a non-confidential version of the complaint.[1240] In such a case, access will be given to a non-confidential version of these responses.[1241]

Where the European Commission's intention to reject the complaint, as set out in the letter pursuant to Article 7 of Regulation 773/2004, is based on the intention to close the proceedings through the adoption of a commitment decision pursuant to Article 9 of Regulation 1/2003 making binding the commitments offered by the companies under investigation that meet the concerns expressed to them in a preliminary assessment, access will be given to a non-confidential version of the preliminary assessment and of the commitments.[1242]

If the complainant considers that it has not been given the access to documents it is entitled to under Article 8 of Regulation 773/2004, the complainant may, after having raised the issue with the Directorate-General for Competition, make a reasoned request to the Hearing Officer, to whom the European Commission has delegated its decisional powers in this respect.[1243]

The time limit within which the complainant may make known its views in writing must be at least four weeks.[1244] If the complainant considers that the time limit is too short, it may request an extension first from the Directorate-General for Competition and, if unsuccessful, from the Hearing Officer, to whom the European Commission has delegated its decisional powers in this respect.[1245]

The complainant is entitled to make known its views in writing, but not at an oral hearing.[1246]

If the complainant fails to make known its views in writing within the time limit set by the European Commission, the complaint is deemed to have been withdrawn.[1247]

1240 See paragraph 71 of the Notice on Best Practices.

1241 See, for instance, Judgment of 11 January 2017, *Topps Europe v Commission*, T-699/14, EU:T:2017:2, paragraphs 30 to 40.

1242 See Final Report of the Hearing Officer in Case AT.39740 Google Search (Shopping) [2018] OJ C9/6, paragraph 6.

1243 Article 3(7) and Article 7(2)(b) and (3) of Decision 2011/695/EU. See, for example, Final Report of the Hearing Officer in Case AT.39740 Google Search (Shopping) [2018] OJ C9/6, paragraph 6.

1244 Article 17(2) of Regulation 773/2004. According to paragraph 139 of the Notice on Best Practices, the time limit will start to run from the date when access has been granted to the main documents on which the European Commission's intention to reject the complaint, as set out in the letter pursuant to Article 7 of Regulation 773/2004, is based.

1245 Article 9(2) of Decision 2011/695/EU; see also paragraph 139 of the Notice on Best Practices.

1246 Judgment of 24 September 1996, *National Association of Licensed Opencast Operators (NALOO) v Commission*, T-57/91, EU:T:1996:125, paragraph 276.

1247 Article 7(3) of Regulation 773/2004.

If the complainant makes known its views within the time limit set by the European Commission, and those written submissions do not lead the European Commission to change its intention not or no longer to act on the complaint, the European Commission must reject the complaint by decision.[1248]

This decision, against which the complainant can bring an action for annulment before the EU General Court, with a possible subsequent appeal on points of law before the EU Court of Justice, must 'state the reasons for [the European Commission's] assessment of whether or not it was appropriate to examine the complaint any further, in a sufficiently precise and detailed manner to enable the [EU Courts] effectively to review the Commission's use of its discretion to define priorities'.[1249]

However, according to settled case law,[1250] 'the review by the Courts of the European Union of the Commission's exercise of its discretion must not lead them to substitute their assessment of [the priorities of EU antitrust enforcement][1251] for that of the European Commission, but focuses on whether the contested decision is based on materially incorrect facts, or is vitiated by an error of law, manifest error of appraisal or misuse of powers'.

In practice, in some cases complainants have been successful in obtaining the annulment of a decision rejecting their complaint.[1252] However, in all the cases where this has happened, the European Commission subsequently adopted a new decision, again rejecting the complaint but now with a better reasoning.[1253] Never has a complainant been successful in making the European Commission change course after an annulment, in the sense that the European Commission would have started acting (again) on the complaint as a result of the annulment. All annulments of decisions rejecting complaints have thus been Pyrrhic victories.[1254]

This state of affairs is not really surprising, given that, as mentioned above, the European Commission has a broad discretion to select the cases which it investigates and in which it continues the proceedings up to the stage of a final decision.

1248 Article 7(2) of Regulation 773/2004.

1249 Judgment of 17 May 2001, *International Express Carriers Conference (IECC) v Commission*, C-450/98 P, EU:C:2001:276, paragraph 54.
While the European Commission must provide reasons why acting (further) on the complaint it is rejecting would not fit within its enforcement priorities, it is not required to set out positively what its enforcement priorities are, given that these may in general be confidential; see Judgment of 12 March 2020, *LL-Carpenter v Commission*, T-531/18, EU:T:2020:91, paragraph 96.

1250 Judgments of 15 December 2010, *Confédération européenne des associations d'horlogers-réparateurs (CEAHR) v Commission*, T-427/08, EU:T:2010:517, paragraph 65; and of 21 January 2015, *easyJet Airline v Commission*, T-355/13, EU:T:2015:36, paragraph 19.

1251 The judgments use the term 'Community interest' or 'European Union interest' as shorthand for (what informs) the priorities of EU antitrust enforcement. However, the use of this term is not mandatory; see Judgment of 17 May 2001, *International Express Carriers Conference (IECC) v Commission*, C-450/98 P, EU:C:2001:276, paragraph 54, and Opinion of Advocate General Ruiz-Jarabo Colomer of 11 January 2001, *International Express Carriers Conference (IECC) v Commission*, C-449/98 P and C-450/98 P, EU:C:2001:7, paragraph 57.

1252 See, for example, Judgment of 17 May 2001, *International Express Carriers Conference (IECC) v Commission*, C-450/98 P, EU:C:2001:276., and Judgment of 9 February 2022, *Sped-Pro v Commission*, T-791/19, EU:T:2022:67.

1253 For an overview of the different grounds for rejecting complaints that have been accepted by the EU Courts, see A. Dawes and E. Rousseva, 'Handling and Rejecting Complaints', in E. Rousseva (ed), *EU Antitrust Procedure* (Oxford 2020), 305, at 320– 331.

1254 See also G.-K. de Bronett, 'Das formelle Verfahren der Komission zwecks Zurückweisung von Antitrust-Beschwerden im Spannungsverhältnis zwischen Politik und Recht' (2015) *Wirtschaft und Wettbewerb* 26.

While this state of affairs should certainly make complainants that have received a decision rejecting their complaint think twice before embarking on an application for annulment, it does not in my view follow that the right of complainants to a reasoned and reviewable decision and the procedure for rejecting complaints do not serve any useful purpose.[1255]

First, while there are no examples of cases where the European Commission changed its orientation following the annulment of a decision rejecting a complaint, there is at least one known example of a case in which such a change happened following the receipt of the complainants' written observations on the pre-rejection letter pursuant to Article 7 of Regulation 773/2004.[1256]

Secondly, the threat of a possible annulment by the EU Courts and the subsequent need to adopt a new decision, with the resulting administrative and reputational costs, has a disciplining effect on the European Commission, thus ensuring that it considers attentively all matters of fact and of law that the complainant brings to its attention and considers all the relevant matters of law and of fact in setting its enforcement priorities in relation to the complaint, as required by the case law.[1257] This, in turn, provides a guarantee to prospective complainants, and may help convince them to lodge complaints that the European Commission would be interested in receiving and acting upon.

Finally, the right of complainants to a reasoned and reviewable decision rejecting their complaint strengthens the European Commission's independence, in that it can help deflect pressure not to act on complaints against politically well-connected targets.[1258]

D. Responding to requests for information, participating in interviews and submitting to inspections

To collect information beyond the initial information triggering the investigation, the European Commission can make use of the powers of investigation set out in Chapter V of Regulation 1/2003, namely, requests for information pursuant to Article 18, interviews pursuant to Article 19, and inspections pursuant to Article 20 of Regulation 1/2003.[1259]

1255 Compare with G.-K. de Bronett, 'Das formelle Verfahren der Komission zwecks Zurückweisung von Antitrust-Beschwerden im Spannungsverhältnis zwischen Politik und Recht' (2015) *Wirtschaft und Wettbewerb* 26, pleading for the abolition of the complaint rejection procedure.

1256 See Final Report of the Hearing Officer in Case AT.39740 Google Search (Shopping) [2018] OJ C9/6, paragraph 7; 'Interview Joaquín Almunia', *Financial Times*, 29 October 2014; and 'How Google ended up "on the wrong side of history"', *Financial Times Weekend*, 18 April/19 April 2015.

1257 See Judgments of 17 May 2001, *International Express Carriers Conference (IECC) v Commission*, C-450/98 P, EU:C:2001:276, paragraph 57; and of 11 July 2013, *Diamanthandel A. Spira v Commission*, T-108/07 and T-354/08, EU:T:2013:367, paragraph 98.

1258 See Chapter III of this book.

1259 These powers of investigation can also be used during sector inquiries pursuant to Article 17 of Regulation 1/2003; see Article 17(2) of Regulation 1/2003 and European Commission Press Release IP/08/49 of 16 January 2008, 'Antitrust: Commission launches sector inquiry into pharmaceuticals with unannounced inspections'.

These powers of investigation can be used during all stages of the investigation, from the preliminary investigation before the initiation of proceedings until after the statement of objections and the oral hearing.[1260]

They can be used to obtain information not only from the undertakings/companies under investigation but also from third parties.[1261]

1. Responding to requests for information

Article 18(1) of Regulation 1/2003 provides that '[i]n order to carry out the duties assigned to it by this Regulation, the Commission may, by simple request or by decision, require undertakings and associations of undertakings to provide all necessary information'.[1262]

Requests for information are regularly sent not only to the undertakings under investigation but also to other undertakings or associations of undertakings that may have information relevant for the case.[1263]

While the European Commission's power to request information concerns undertakings,[1264] requests for information are addressed to one or more of the companies (or other persons) responsible for the operation of the undertaking, for reasons of enforceability.[1265]

Article 18(4) of Regulation 1/2003 provides that the owners of the undertakings or their representatives and, in the case of legal persons, companies or firms, or associations having no legal personality, the persons authorised to represent them by law or by their constitution shall supply the information requested on behalf of the undertaking or the association of undertakings concerned. Lawyers duly authorised to act may supply the information on behalf of their clients. The latter shall remain fully responsible if the information supplied is incomplete, incorrect or misleading.

There are two types of requests for information: **simple requests** pursuant to Article 18(2) and **requests by decision** pursuant to Article 18(3) of Regulation 1/2003.

1260 See Article 2(3) of Regulation 773/2004 and Judgment of 9 April 2019 in *Qualcomm and Qualcomm Europe v Commission*, T-371/17, EU:T:2019:232, paragraphs 67 to 76, confirmed on appeal in Judgment of 28 January 2021 in *Qualcomm and Qualcomm Europe v Commission*, C-466/19 P, EU:C:2021:76, paragraphs 72 and 73.

1261 See paragraph 32 of the Notice on Best Practices and Judgment of 5 October 2020, *Intermarché Casino Achats v Commission*, T-254/17, EU:T:2020:459, paragraph 284.

1262 For a more detailed discussion of requests for information, see M. Kellerbauer and K. Strouvali, 'Requests for Information and Sector Inquiries', in E. Rousseva (ed), *EU Antitrust Procedure* (Oxford 2020), 65.

1263 Paragraph 32 of the Notice on Best Practices.

1264 The European Commission does not have the power to request information from natural or legal persons other than undertakings or associations of undertakings (and other than the governments and competition authorities of the EU Member States); see OECD Global Forum for Competition, 'Requests for Information: Limits and Effectiveness – Contribution from the European Commission' (document DAF/COMP/GF/WD(2018)74 of 24 November 2018), paragraph 5. This contrasts with the competition authorities of the EU Member States, for which this further power is prescribed by the last sentence of Article 8 of Directive (EU) 2019/1 of the European Parliament and of the Council of 11 December 2018 to empower the competition authorities of the Member States to be effective enforcers and to ensure the proper functioning of the internal market [2019] OJ L11/3.

1265 See also Opinion of Advocate General Pitruzzella of 14 July 2022, *Casino, Guichard-Perrachon and Achats Marchandises Casino v Commission*, C-690/20 P, EU:C:2022:579.

Addressees of simple requests for information are under no obligation to respond, but if they choose to respond (as most addressees do, if only to avoid receiving a request by decision), they can be fined up to 1% of their turnover in the preceding business year if they intentionally or negligently supply incorrect or misleading information in response to the request.[1266]

Addressees of requests for information by decision are under an obligation to respond. They can be fined up to 1% of their turnover in the preceding business year if they intentionally or negligently supply incorrect, incomplete or misleading information or do not supply information within the required time limit.[1267] The European Commission can also, either in the decision requesting information or in a subsequent decision, impose periodic penalty payments of up to 5% of the average daily turnover in the preceding business year per day to compel the addressee to supply complete and correct information.[1268]

Both in simple requests for information and in decisions requesting information, the European Commission must state the legal basis and the purpose of the request, specify what information is required and fix the time limit within which the information is to be provided.[1269]

The reasoning of the request must clarify whether the addressee is an undertaking/ company under investigation or a third party.[1270]

Requests for information can be used to request both the handing-over of (copies of) existing **documents** that are detained by or accessible to[1271] the undertakings or associations of undertakings concerned and the provision of **answers to questions**.

The power of the European Commission to request information, and the obligation to provide it if requested by decision, extends to 'all necessary information',[1272] that is, all information for which the European Commission may reasonably suppose that it will help it to determine whether the infringement under investigation has taken place.[1273] In practice, that means that there must be a connection between the

---

1266 See Article 23(1)(a) of Regulation 1/2003.

1267 See Article 23(1)(b) of Regulation 1/2003.

1268 See Articles 18(3) and 24(1)(d) of Regulation 1/2003.

1269 See Article 18(2) and (3) of Regulation 1/2003 and, on the obligation to state specific reasons in decisions requesting information, Judgments of 10 March 2016, *HeidelbergCement v Commission*, C-247/14 P, EU:C:2016:149, paragraph 19, and of 5 October 2020, *Intermarché Casino Achats v Commission*, T-254/17, EU:T:2020:459, paragraph 109.

1270 See Judgment of 5 October 2020, *Intermarché Casino Achats v Commission*, T-254/17, EU:T:2020:459, paragraphs 109 and 131.

1271 See also similarly the second sentence of Article 8 of Directive 2019/1.
According to the case law of the EU Courts, by virtue of a general duty of care, any undertaking or association of undertakings is required to ensure the proper maintenance of records in its books or files of information enabling details of its activities to be retrieved, in order, in particular, to make the necessary evidence available in the event of legal or administrative proceedings; Judgments of 16 June 2011 in *Heineken Nederland and Heineken v Commission*, T-240/07, EU:T:2011:284, paragraph 301, and of 14 March 2014 in *Schwenk Zement v Commission*, T-306/11, EU:T:2014:123, paragraph 83.

1272 Article 18(1) of Regulation 1/2003.

1273 See Judgment of 12 December 1991, *SEP v Commission*, T-39/90, EU:T:1991:71, paragraph 29, upheld on appeal by Judgment of 19 May 1994, *SEP v Commission*, C-36/92 P, EU:C:1994:205, paragraph 21, and Opinion of Advocate General Jacobs of 15 December 1993, *SEP v Commission*, C-36/92 P, EU:C:1993:928, paragraph 21; Judgment of 14 March 2014, *Holcim (Deutschland) and Holcim v Commission*, T-293/11, EU:T:2014:127, paragraph 110; and Opinion of Advocate General Wahl of 15 October 2015, *HeidelbergCement v Commission*, C-247/14 P,EU:C:2015:694, paragraph 85.

information requested by the European Commission and the alleged infringement it investigates.[1274]

There are two exceptions to this broad power to request 'all necessary information'.[1275] These exceptions are primarily relevant for the undertakings under investigation, but may occasionally also be relevant for third parties.

The first exception flows from the privilege against self-incrimination. According to the case law of the EU Court of Justice, whilst the Commission is entitled to compel an undertaking to provide all necessary information concerning such facts as may be known to it and to disclose to it, if necessary, such documents relating thereto as are in its possession, even if the latter may be used to establish, against it or another undertaking, the existence of anti-competitive conduct, the Commission may not compel an undertaking to provide it with answers which might involve an admission on its part of the existence of an infringement which it is incumbent upon the Commission to prove.[1276] The privilege against self-incrimination thus only extends to directly incriminating questions (involving an admission of infringement), not to purely factual questions, nor to the disclosure of documents, and does not amount to a general right to remain silent.[1277]

The privilege against self-incrimination can only be violated in case of compulsion, i.e. only in case of a request for information by decision pursuant to Article 18(3) of Regulation 1/2003, not in case of a simple request pursuant to Article 18(2) of Regulation 1/2003.[1278] It is, however, the Commission's policy to avoid directly incriminating questions also in simple requests for information.[1279]

1274 OECD Global Forum for Competition, 'Requests for Information: Limits and Effectiveness – Contribution from the European Commission' (document DAF/COMP/GF/WD(2018)74 of 24 November 2018), paragraph 8.

1275 There is no exception for business secrets, nor for personal data within the meaning of Article 8(1) of the Charter of Fundamental Rights of the European Union, Article 16(1) TFEU, Regulation (EU) 2016/679 of the European Parliament and of the Council of 27 April 2016 on the protection of natural persons with regard to the processing of personal data and on the free movement of such data (General Data Protection Regulation) [2016] OJ L119/1, and Regulation (EU) 2018/1725 of the European Parliament and of the Council of 23 October 2018 on the protection of natural persons with regard to the processing of personal data by the Union institutions, bodies, offices and agencies and on the free movement of such data [2018] OJ L295/39; see letter from the European Data Protection Supervisor of 22 October 2018 (WW/OL/sn/D (2018) 2422 C 2018-0632), and Order of the President of the General Court of 29 October 2020, *Facebook Ireland v Commission*, T-451/20 R, EU:T:2020:515, paragraphs 54 to 66.

1276 Judgment of 18 October 1989, *Orkem v Commission*, 374/87, EU:C:1989:387, paragraphs 34 and 35, and Judgment of 28 January 2021 in *Qualcomm and Qualcomm Europe v Commission*, C-466/19 P, EU:C:2021:76, paragraphs 142 and 143; see also recital 23 of Regulation 1/2003.

1277 See Judgment of 29 June 2006 in *Commission v SGL Carbon*, C-301/04 P, EU:C:2006:432, Opinion of Advocate General Geelhoed of 19 January 2006, *Commission v SGL Carbon*, C-301/04 P, EU:C:2006:53, and Opinion of Advocate General Pikamäe of 27 October 2020, *DB v Consob*, C-481/19, EU:C:2020:861, paragraphs 97 to 99; see also my papers 'Self-incrimination in EC Antitrust Enforcement: A Legal and Economic Analysis' (2003) 26 *World Competition* 567, 'EU Antitrust Enforcement Powers and Procedural Rights and Guarantees: The Interplay between EU Law, National Law, the Charter of Fundamental Rights of the EU and the European Convention on Human Rights' (2011) 34 *World Competition* 189 at 204–206, and 'Fundamental Procedural Rights and Effective Enforcement of Articles 101 and 102 TFEU in the European Competition Network' (2020) 43 *World Competition* 5 at 31–34, all three also accessible at http://ssrn.com/author=456087.

1278 Judgment of 25 January 2007, *Dalmine v Commission*, C-407/04 P, EU:C:2007:53, paragraphs 31 to 35.

1279 Article 4(2)(b), read in conjunction with Article 3(7), of Decision 2011/695/EU, provides that, where the addressee of a simple request for information pursuant to Article 18(2) of Regulation 1/2003 refuses to reply to a question in such a request invoking the privilege against self-incrimination, as determined by the case law

The second exception concerns legal professional privilege.[1280] According to the case law of the EU Court of Justice, the protection of the confidentiality of certain communications between lawyer and client is an essential corollary to the rights of the defence and serves the important requirement that everyone should be able without restraint to consult a lawyer to obtain independent legal advice.[1281] The communications protected are, however, limited to those between a client and an independent lawyer (not in-house counsel) entitled to practise in one of the EU or EEA Member States.[1282] The protected communications are those made 'for the purpose and in the interests of the client's rights of defence', that is to say which come into existence after the initiation of proceedings or which, although made earlier, 'have a relationship to the subject matter of that procedure'.[1283] Internal documents of an undertaking summarising advice received from independent lawyers are also protected.[1284] Similarly, internal preparatory documents are protected if drawn up exclusively for the purpose of seeking legal advice from an external lawyer in the exercise of the rights of defence.[1285]

As to the **time limit** for responding to the request, paragraph 38 of the Notice on Best Practices provides that addressees are given a reasonable time limit to reply to the request, according to the length and complexity of the request taking into account the requirements of the investigation. In general, this time limit will be at least two

---

of the Court of Justice, it may refer the matter, in due time following the receipt of the request, and after having first raised the issue with the Directorate-General for Competition, to the Hearing Officer. In appropriate cases, and having regard to the need to avoid undue delay in proceedings, the Hearing Officer may make a reasoned recommendation as to whether the privilege against self-incrimination applies and inform the director responsible of the conclusions drawn, to be taken into account in case of any decision taken subsequently pursuant to Article 18(3) of Regulation 1/2003. The addressee of the request shall receive a copy of the reasoned recommendation.

1280 Article 4(2)(a), read in conjunction with Article 3(7), of Decision 2011/695/EU, provides that, where an undertaking or association of undertakings has withheld from the Commission a document, claiming that it is covered by legal professional privilege within the meaning of the case law of the Court of Justice, the undertaking or association of undertakings may, after having raised the matter with the Directorate-General for Competition, ask the Hearing Officer to examine the claim. The Hearing Officer may only review the matter if the undertaking or association of undertakings making the claim consents to the Hearing Officer viewing the information claimed to be covered by legal professional privilege as well as related documents that the Hearing Officer considers necessary for his review. Without revealing the potentially privileged content of the information, the Hearing Officer shall communicate to the director responsible and the undertaking or association of undertakings concerned XXX his XXX Replace with their (gender-neutral) XXX preliminary view, and may take appropriate steps to promote a mutually acceptable resolution. Where no resolution is reached, the Hearing Officer may formulate a reasoned recommendation to the Competition Commissioner, without revealing the potentially privileged content of the document. The party making the claim shall receive a copy of this recommendation. If, after the intervention of the Hearing Officer, the undertaking maintains its claim, and the Commission still wants to read and use the document, then the Commission must do what it would also have to do if the intervention of the Hearing Officer had not been asked, namely, take a decision ordering production of the document or opening the sealed envelope, allowing the undertaking to bring the matter immediately before the General Court through an application for annulment of that decision and an accompanying request for interim relief; see Judgments of 18 May 1982, *AM&S v Commission*, 155/79, EU:C:1982:157, paragraph 32, and of 17 September 2007, *Akzo Nobel v Commission*, T-125/03, EU:T:2007:287, paragraphs 79 and 85.

1281 Judgment of 18 May 1982, *AM&S v Commission*, 155/79, EU:C:1982:157, paragraphs 18 and 23. See further my paper 'Legal Professional Privilege in EU Antitrust Enforcement: Law, Policy & Procedure' (2019) 42 *World Competition* 21, also accessible at http://ssrn.com/author=456087.

1282 Judgments of 18 May 1982, *AM&S v Commission*, 155/79, EU:C:1982:157, and of 14 September 2010, *Akzo Nobel v Commission*, C-550/07 P, EU:C:2010:512.

1283 Judgment of 18 May 1982, *AM&S v Commission*, 155/79, EU:C:1982:157, paragraph 23.

1284 Order of 4 April 1990, *Hilti v Commission*, T-30/89, EU:T:1990:27.

1285 Judgment of 17 September 2007, *Akzo Nobel v Commission*, T-125/03, EU:T:2007:287, paragraph 123.

weeks from the receipt of the request. If from the outset, it is considered that a longer period is required, the time limit to reply to the request will be set accordingly. When the scope of the request is limited, for example if it only covers a short clarification of information previously provided or information readily available to the addressee of the request, the time limit will normally be shorter (one week or less).[1286]

Paragraph 39 of the Notice on Best Practices provides that, if the addressee of a decision requesting information considers that the time limit imposed for its reply is too short, it can make a reasoned request for extension to the Directorate-General for Competition, sufficiently in advance of the expiry of the time limit. If the Directorate-General for Competition considers the request to be justified, additional time will be granted. The Directorate-General for Competition may also agree with the addressee of the request that certain parts of the requested information that are of particular importance or easily available for the addressee will be supplied within a shorter time limit, whereas additional time will be granted for supplying the remaining information.

With regard to request for information by decision, Article 4(2)(c), read in conjunction with Article 3(7), of Decision 2011/695/EU, provides that, if the addressee is unsuccessful in resolving its concerns about the time limit with the Directorate-General for Competition, it may refer the matter to the Hearing Officer, in due time before the expiry of the original time limit set. The Hearing Officer shall decide on whether an extension of the time limit should be granted, taking account of the length and complexity of the request for information and the requirements of the investigation.[1287]

1286 With regard to requests by decision, the EU General Court has held that, because of this threat of a fine, the examination of the appropriateness of the time limit fixed in a decision requesting information is particularly important. That time limit must enable the addressee of the decision not only to provide its reply in practical terms, but also to satisfy itself that the information is complete, correct and not misleading; Judgment of 14 March 2014 in *Schwenk Zement v Commission*, T-306/11, EU:T:2014:123, paragraphs 72 and 73. In the absence of a specific need of the inquiry that warranted the fixing of a particularly short time limit, the imposition of a two-week time limit for a German cement manufacturer to provide information on all contacts, including informal ones, between two of its employees and other manufacturers of cement and related products or their representatives in Germany, over periods of three and seven years, was held to be disproportionate; Judgment of 14 March 2014 in *Schwenk Zement v Commission*, T-306/11, EU:T:2014:123, paragraphs 80 to 92. On the other hand, a time limit of 12 weeks for the provision of a particularly large amount of information, to be provided in a particularly demanding format, was not disproportionate, given the means available to the undertaking concerned because of its economic size; Judgment of 14 March 2014 in *Cemex v Commission*, T-292/11, EU:T:2014:125, paragraphs 132 to 135.

1287 The EU General Court has held that, if the addressee of a decision requesting information fails to request an extension of the time limit, the time limit is deemed to be sufficient; Judgments of 14 May 1998 in *Finnboard v Commission*, T-338/94, EU:T:1998:99, paragraph 54 and of 14 March 2014 in *Cementos Portland Valderrivas v Commission*, T-296/11, EU:T:2014:121, paragraph 95.
The possibility to request first from the Directorate-General for Competition and subsequently from the Hearing Officer an extension of the time limit fixed in a European Commission decision requesting information pursuant to Article 18(3) of Regulation 1/2003 does not alter the time limit for bringing an application for annulment against that Commission decision before the EU General Court. As Article 18(3) of Regulation 1/2003 requires to be indicated in any decision based on that provision, the addressee of a Commission decision requesting information pursuant to Article 18(3) of Regulation 1/2003 can have that decision reviewed by the General Court; see also Judgment in *Schwenk Zement v Commission*, T-306/11, EU:T:2014:123, paragraph 75. According to Article 263 TFEU and Articles 58 and 60 of the Rules of procedure of the General Court ([2015] OJ L105/1), the application for annulment of the Commission decision must be brought within two months and ten days of the notification of the decision to the addressee.

The possibility to request from the Hearing Officer an extension of the time limit for replying to a request for information does not exist for simple requests for information, pursuant to Article 18(2) of Regulation 1/2003. This makes sense, because the addressees of such simple requests for information cannot be fined for not supplying information within the required time limit, only for supplying incorrect or misleading information. Addressees of simple requests for information that consider that the time limit for their reply is too short, and that cannot obtain an extension from the Directorate-General for Competition, can thus not be sanctioned for not replying within the time limit.[1288]

2. Participating in interviews

Article 19(1) of Regulation 1/2003 provides that '[i]n order to carry out the duties assigned to it by this Regulation, the Commission may interview any natural or legal person who consents to be interviewed for the purpose of collecting information relating to the subject-matter of the investigation'.[1289]

Whereas the European Commission can only send requests for information to undertakings or associations of undertakings, any natural or legal person, including in particular any third party, can be an interviewee.

Both the European Commission and the interviewee can take the initiative for the interview, but interviews are always voluntary. The European Commission does not have the power to summon any natural or legal person to an interview.[1290]

Interviews can take place remotely, by telephone or other electronic means, or in person, at the premises of the European Commission or of the interviewee or elsewhere.[1291]

The European Commission must record the interview in full, but it is free to decide on the type of recording.[1292] A copy of the recording must be made available to the interviewee.[1293]

3. Submitting to inspections

Article 20(1) of Regulation 1/2003 provides that '[i]n order to carry out the duties assigned to it by this Regulation, the Commission may conduct all necessary inspections of undertakings and associations of undertakings'.[1294]

1288 The absence of a reply within the time limit may, of course, prompt the Commission to request the information by decision pursuant to Article 18(3) of Regulation 1/2003, in which case Article 4(2)(c) of Decision 2011/695/EU becomes applicable.

1289 For a more detailed discussion of interviews, see A. ter Heegde and E. Rousseva, 'Power to Tak Statements', in E. Rousseva (ed), *EU Antitrust Procedure* (Oxford 2020), 130.

1290 This contrasts with the competition authorities of the EU Member States, for which this further power is prescribed by Article 9 of Directive (EU) 2019/1 of the European Parliament and of the Council of 11 December 2018 to empower the competition authorities of the Member States to be effective enforcers and to ensure the proper functioning of the internal market [2019] OJ L11/3.

1291 See Article 19(2) of Regulation 1/2003 and Article 3(2) of Regulation 773/2004.

1292 Judgment of 6 September 2017, *Intel v Commission*, C-413/14 P, EU:C:2017:632, paragraph 90.

1293 Article 3(3) of Regulation 773/2004.

1294 For a more detailed discussion of inspections, see J. Nuijten, 'Inspections', in E. Rousseva (ed), *EU Antitrust Procedure* (Oxford 2020), 93, and N. Jalabert-Doury, *Competition Inspections under EU Law – A Practitioner's Guide* (Concurrences Books 2020), https://www.concurrences.com/en/all-books/competition-inspections-under-eu-law; see also the Inspection Explanatory Note and the further information available on the website of the European: https://ec.europa.eu/competition-policy/antitrust/procedures/inspections_en.

Article 20(2) of Regulation 1/2003 specifies that the officials and other accompanying persons authorised by the European Commission to conduct the inspection are empowered '(a) to enter any premises, land and means of transport of undertakings and associations of undertakings; (b) to examine the books and other records related to the business, irrespective of the medium on which they are stored; (c) to take or to obtain in any form copies of or extracts from such books or records; (d) to seal any business premises and books or records for the period and to the extent necessary for the inspection; (e) to ask any representative or member of staff of the undertaking or association of undertakings for explanations on facts or documents relating to the subject-matter and purpose of the inspection and to record the answers'.[1295]

Even if much less frequent than requests for information addressed to third parties, inspections of undertakings and associations of undertakings other than those under investigation are possible,[1296] and indeed have happened in some cases.

The European Commission's powers of inspection concern undertakings. Inspection decisions are typically addressed to the parent company 'together with all subsidiaries directly or indirectly controlled by it'.[1297]

Undertakings and associations of undertakings are required to submit to inspections ordered by decision,[1298] and must actively cooperate with it.[1299]

In case of opposition, the authorities of the Member State in whose territory the inspection is to be conducted must afford the necessary assistance to enable the inspection to proceed.[1300] The European Commission can also impose fines of up to 1% of the total turnover in the preceding business year on undertakings that intentionally or negligently refuse to submit to inspections, produce the required books or other records relating to the business in incomplete form or give an incorrect or misleading answer to a question, or when seals are broken.[1301]

1295 While inspections pursuant to Article 20 of Regulation 1/2003 always start at the premises of the undertaking or association of undertakings, they may continue at the European Commission's premises; see Inspection Explanatory Note available on the website of the European Commission's Directorate-General for Competition https://ec.europa.eu/competition-policy/antitrust/procedures/inspections_en and Judgment of 16 July 2020, *Nexans France and Nexans v Commission*, C-606/18 P, EU:C:2020:571, paragraphs 56 to 90.
Article 21 of Regulation 1/2003 provides for the further possibility, under strict conditions, of inspecting any other premises, land and means of transport, including the homes of directors, managers and other members of staff of the undertakings and associations of undertakings concerned.

1296 Judgment of 5 October 2020, *Intermarché Casino Achats v Commission*, T-254/17, EU:T:2020:459, paragraph 284.

1297 J. Nuijten, 'Inspections', in E. Rousseva (ed), *EU Antitrust Procedure* (Oxford 2020), 93 at 97.

1298 Article 20(4) of Regulation 1/2003. Undertakings and associations of undertakings are not obliged to submit to inspections not ordered by decision, but if they agree to such an inspection pursuant to Article 20(3) of Regulation 1/2003, they can be fined up to 1% of their turnover in the preceding business year if they intentionally or negligently produce the required books or other records relating to the business in incomplete form or if they give an incorrect or misleading answer to a question; see Article 23(c) and (d) of Regulation 1/2003.

1299 Judgment of 18 October 1989, *Orkem v Commission*, 374/87, EU:C:1989:387, paragraph 27.

1300 See Article 20(6) to (8) of Regulation 1/2003.

1301 See Article 23(c) to (e) of Regulation 1/2003, and Commission Decision of 30 January 2008, Case COMP/B-1/39.326 *E.ON Energie AG* [2008] OJ C 240/6, confirmed by Judgments of 15 December 2010, *E.ON Energie v Commission*, T-141/08, EU:T:2010:516, and of 22 November 2012, *E.ON Energie*

Legal professional privilege and the privilege against self-incrimination, discussed above with respect to requests for information, similarly limit the European Commission's powers of inspection. The European Commission can neither examine nor copy documents protected by legal professional privilege as defined in the case law of the EU Courts,[1302] nor ask for explanations that would require an admission of infringement.

E. Obtaining information about and expressing one's views in pending proceedings

1. Possibilities available to any third party

a. *Press releases and publications on the website of the European Commission*

As already mentioned above, the European Commission normally publishes the initiation or opening of proceedings on its website and issues a press release. When the European Commission has addressed a statement of objections to the companies under investigation, it also normally publishes a press release setting out the key issues in the statement of objections.[1303]

Even if these press releases and website publications normally do not contain any invitation for third parties to express their views, nothing prevents third parties from doing so, by using the general contact channels indicated on the European Commission's website and referring to the press release and the case number usually mentioned in it.

b. *Market test notice*

As already mentioned above, before adopting a commitment decision or a non-infringement decision, the European Commission must publish in the *Official Journal of the European Union* a notice (market test notice) containing a concise summary of the case and the main content of the commitments or the proposed course of

---

v Commission C-89/11 P, EU:C:2012:738; and Commission Decision of 28 March 2012, Case COMP/39.793 *EPH and others* [2012] OJ C 316/8, confirmed by Judgment of 26 November 2014, *Energetický a průmyslový v Commission*, T-272/12, EU:T:2014:995.

Article 24(1) of Regulation 1/2003 further provides for the imposition of periodic penalty payments to compel submission to an inspection ordered by decision.

1302 See Chapter XIII of this book. Where during an inspection an undertaking claims that a document is protected by legal professional privilege, it must substantiate its claim and, unless this would not be possible without revealing the protected information, allow the Commission officials to have a cursory look at the general layout, heading, title or other superficial features of the document so as to enable them to confirm the accuracy of the claim. In case of disagreement as to whether the document is privileged, the Commission officials may place a copy of the document in a sealed envelope and take it with them; Judgment of 17 September 2007, *Akzo Nobel v Commission*, T-125/03, EU:T:2007:287, paragraphs 80 to 83. The undertaking may then make a request to the Hearing Officer pursuant to Article 4(2)(a) of Decision 2011/695/EU. If no such request is made or the request does not lead to an agreed solution, and the European Commission still wants to read and use the document, then the Commission must take a decision ordering production of the document or opening the sealed envelope, allowing the undertaking to bring the matter immediately before the General Court through an application for annulment of that decision and an accompanying request for interim relief; Judgments of 18 May 1982, *AM&S v Commission*, 155/79, EU:C:1982:157, paragraph 32, and of 17 September 2007, *Akzo Nobel v Commission*, T-125/03, EU:T:2007:287, paragraphs 79 and 85.

1303 Paragraph 91 of the Notice on Best Practices.

action.[1304] The European Commission normally also publishes a parallel press release and may provide further information on its website.[1305]

The market test notice always contains an explicit invitation for third parties to submit observations within a fixed time limit of no less than one month.[1306]

c. *No access to (documents in) the European Commission's investigation file*

While the companies under investigation, once the European Commission has addressed to them a statement of objections, have a right of access to the European Commission's investigation file, third parties do not have any such right.[1307]

Third parties might try to obtain access to documents in the European Commission's investigation file by making a request for public access on the basis of the Regulation (EC) No 1049/2001 (the 'Transparency Regulation'),[1308] but such attempts are unlikely to be successful.

The Transparency Regulation defines the principles, conditions and limits on grounds of public or private interest governing the right of public access to documents held by EU institutions, including the European Commission.

Under the European Commission's detailed internal rules for the application of the Transparency Regulation,[1309] it is open to any natural or legal person to request, on the basis of that regulation, access to documents held by the European Commission.[1310] In accordance with Article 6(1) of the Transparency Regulation, there is no obligation to give reasons for such a request.

The Transparency Regulation does not allow the European Commission the possibility of granting access to a document subject to restrictions on the subsequent use and disclosure of that document.[1311] Documents disclosed under the Transparency Regulation thus enter the public domain.[1312]

1304 Article 27(4) of Regulation 1/2003 and paragraphs 129 to 133 of the Notice on Best Practices.

1305 Paragraph 129 of the Notice on Best Practices.

1306 Article 27(4) of Regulation 1/2003. While the term 'interested third parties' is used in this context, any third parties can submit their observations, not only those who fulfil the requirements to be heard as 'interested third persons' within the meaning of Article 27(3) of Regulation 1/2003, Article 13 of Regulation 773/2004 and Article 5 of Decision 2011/695.

1307 See Opinion of Advocate General Kokott of 17 September 2009, *Commission v Alrosa*, C-441/07 P, EU:C:2009:555, paragraph 182; and Judgment of 11 January 2017, *Topps v Commission*, T-699/14, EU:T:2017:2, paragraph 30; and W. Wils and H. Abbott, 'Access to the File in Competition Proceedings Before the European Commission' (2019) 42 *World Competition* 255, updated version accessible at http://ssrn.com/author=456087, text accompanied by footnotes 33 to 36.

1308 Regulation (EC) No 1049/2001 of the European Parliament and of the Council of 30 May 2001 regarding public access to European Parliament, Council and Commission documents [2001] OJ L145/43.

1309 These detailed rules are set out in an annex to the Commission's rules of procedure that was added by Commission Decision 2001/937/EC, ECSC, Euratom of 5 December 2001 amending its rules of procedure [2001] OJ L345/94.

1310 Articles 2(1) to (3) of the Transparency Regulation, read in conjunction with Article 1 of the annex to the Commission's rules of procedure, mentioned in the footnote just above.

1311 Order of 7 March 2013, *Henkel v Commission*, T-64/12, EU:T:2013:116, paragraph 47.

1312 Judgments of 21 May 2014, *Catinis v Commission*, T-447/11, EU:T:2014:267, paragraph 62; and of 26 April 2016, *Strack v Commission*, T-221/08, EU:T:2016:242, paragraph 128.

Regulation 1/2003, however, contains specific rules regarding access to and the use of documents in the European Commission's investigation file in antitrust proceedings. The Transparency Regulation does not have primacy over either of those regulations. In these circumstances, the EU Courts have recognised that, in relation to such documents, the Commission is entitled to rely on a general presumption that they are not to be disclosed, even in part, on the basis of the Transparency Regulation.[1313]

This does not rule out the possibility for an applicant under the Transparency Regulation to demonstrate that a given document is not covered by that general presumption, or that there exists an overriding public interest justifying the disclosure of the document.[1314] In normal circumstances, however, third parties, who typically want to have access to documents in the European Commission's investigation file because of their private interest in the case, are unlikely to be able to demonstrate this.[1315]

Requests under the Transparency Regulation for access to documents related to the Commission's antitrust proceedings are dealt with in the first instance by the Directorate-General for Competition and in the second instance by the Secretary-General of the European Commission.[1316] The Hearing Officer does not play any role.

2. Third parties can strengthen their procedural position by requesting to be heard as an interested third person

Provided that they fulfil the substantive and procedural requirements set out below, third parties can strengthen their procedural position by requesting to be heard as an interested third person.

a. *Substantive and procedural requirements to be heard as an interested third person*

Article 27(3) of Regulation 1/2003 provides that natural or legal persons who 'show a sufficient interest' have a right to be heard.

Recital 32 of Regulation 1/2003 clarifies what is meant by a third party having 'a sufficient interest', namely, that '[its] interests may be affected by a decision'.

Whereas complainants must show that their economic interests have been harmed or are likely to be harmed as a result of the alleged infringement of Articles 101 or 102 TFEU,

---

1313 Judgment of 7 July 2015, *Axa Versicherung v Commission*, T-677/13, EU:T:2015:473, paragraphs 39, 40, 42 and 94. This presumption applies in relation to proceedings for the application of Article 101 TFEU (Judgment of 27 February 2014, *Commission v EnBW*, C-365/12 P, EU:C:2014:112, paragraphs 92, 93, 101 and 134) and Article 102 TFEU (Judgment of 28 March 2017, *Deutsche Telekom v Commission*, T-210/15, EU:T:2017:224, paragraphs 30 to 32, 43, 44 and 46). The presumption also applies if access to only one document is requested (Judgment of 5 February 2018, *Edeka-Handelsgesellschaft Hessenring v Commission*, T-611/15, EU:T:2018:63, paragraphs 68 to 74).

1314 Judgments of 27 February 2014, *Commission v EnBW*, C-365/12 P, EU:C:2014:112, paragraphs 100 and 117; of 7 July 2015, *Axa Versicherung v Commission*, T-677/13, EU:T:2015:473, paragraph 59; and of 28 March 2017, *Deutsche Telekom v Commission*, T-210/15, EU:T:2017:224, paragraph 62.

1315 See Judgment of 28 March 2017, *Deutsche Telekom v Commission*, T-210/15, EU:T:2017:224, paragraphs 64 to 72.

1316 See Commission's rules of procedure that were added by Commission Decision 2001/937/EC, ECSC, Euratom of 5 December 2001 amending its rules of procedure [2001] OJ L345/94.

interested third persons could either be harmed by the alleged infringement or benefit from it. Their interest in being heard may thus be either against or in support of the companies under investigation.

It would also seem that the sufficient interest does not need to be of an economic nature, even if it most often is.[1317]

The sufficient interest must be defined in the light of the precise conduct that is the subject of the proceedings at stake, and not in the light of abstract legal arguments that go beyond that conduct.[1318] A general interest in the policy choices and legal reasoning that the Commission may develop in a potential decision but not linked to the conduct which is the subject of the proceedings cannot confer a right to be heard.[1319]

Recital 11 of Regulation 773/2004 indicates that consumer associations that apply to be heard should generally be regarded as having a sufficient interest, where the proceedings concern products or services used by the end consumer or products or services that constitute a direct input into such products or services.[1320]

Similarly, business associations have a sufficient interest if their members would individually have a sufficient interest and the association is entitled to represent the interests of its members.[1321]

There is certainly no requirement that the interested third person can provide useful information for the European Commission's proceedings. The 'sufficient interest' relates only to the interests of the third party that requests to be heard.[1322]

Article 5 of Decision 2011/695 empowers the Hearing Officer to decide whether third persons are to be heard, after consulting the director from DG Competition responsible for the case.

1317 See also S. Durande and A. Montesa Lloreda, 'Les droits des tiers dans les procédures concurrences devant la Commission européenne', *Concurrences* no 4-2005, 34, paragraph 42.
Under the EU Merger Regulation (Council Regulation (EC) No 139/2004 of 20 January 2004 on the control of concentrations between undertakings [2004] OJ L24/1), which provides for a very similar right to be heard of third parties that show a sufficient interest, requests to be heard as interested third persons by the International Panel of Experts on Sustainable Food Systems (IPES-Food) in Case M.8084 *Bayer/Monsanto* and by Privacy International in Case M.9660 *Google/Fitbit* have been granted; see Final Report of the Hearing Officer in Case M.8084 *Bayer/Monsanto* [2018] OJ C459/19, paragraph 5, and Final Report of the Hearing Officer in Case M.9660 Google/Fitbit [2021] OJ C194/6.

1318 See, by analogy, Order of the President of the Court of 5 February 2009, *Akzo Nobel Chemicals and Akros Chemicals v Commission*, C-550/07 P, EU:C:2009:60, paragraphs 8 and 9; Order of the President of the Court of 3 April 2014, *Commission v Jorgen Andersen and Others*, C-303/13 P, EU:C:2014:226, paragraph 7; and Order of the Vice-President of the Court of 1 March 2016, *Cousins Material House v Commission*, C-635/15 P, EU:C:2016:166, paragraph 30.

1319 Final Report of the Hearing Officer in Case AT.40208 – *International Skating Union's Eligibility Rules* [2018] OJ C148/7, paragraph 6 and footnote 7.

1320 Final consumers can also individually request to be heard as interested third persons; see Judgment of 7 June 2006, *Österreichische Postsparkasse and Bank für Arbeit und Wirtschaft v Commission*, T-213/01 and T-214/01, EU:T:2006:151, paragraph 114.

1321 See, by analogy, above concerning business associations as complainants.

1322 See, by analogy, Judgment of 7 June 2006, *Österreichische Postsparkasse and Bank für Arbeit und Wirtschaft v Commission*, T-213/01 and T-214/01, EU:T:2006:151, paragraph 163, concerning complainants.
As mentioned below, the contribution that the interested third person can make to the clarification of the relevant facts of the case is, however, one of the factors to be taken into account by the Hearing Officer in deciding whether to admit an interested third person to the oral hearing.

Applications to be heard by interested third persons must be submitted in writing, and explain the applicant's interest in the outcome of the procedure.[1323]

Applications to be heard can be submitted from the date of the initiation of proceedings and until the European Commission consults the Advisory Committee on the basis of a draft decision.[1324]

Where the Hearing Officer considers that an applicant has not shown a sufficient interest to be heard, they must inform the applicant in writing of the reasons thereof, and set a time limit for a further written submission. If the applicant responds within the time limit and the written submission does not lead to a different assessment, the Hearing Officer will take a reasoned decision.[1325]

If the application to be heard is granted, the Hearing Officer must inform the parties to the proceedings as from the initiation of proceedings of the identities of interested third persons to be heard, unless such disclosure would significantly harm a person or undertaking.[1326] In particular, according to the case law of EU Courts, keeping the identity of third parties confidential is justified where there is a risk that an undertaking holding a dominant position in the market might adopt retaliatory measures against competitors, suppliers or customers that have collaborated in the investigation carried out by the Commission.[1327] There is thus no incompatibility between being heard as an interested third person and remaining anonymous.[1328]

On the other hand, nothing prevents interested third persons from making public the fact that their application to be heard has been granted.[1329]

b. *Procedural rights of interested third persons whose application to be heard has been granted*

When the application to be heard of the interested third person has been granted by the Hearing Officer, the European Commission must inform the interested third person in writing of the nature and subject matter of the procedure and must set a time limit within which the interested third person may make known its views in writing.[1330]

1323 Article 5(1) of Decision 2011/695.

1324 See Article 11(6) of Regulation 1/2003, Article 2 of Regulation 773/2004 and paragraphs 17 to 23 of the Notice on Best Practices; Judgment in *Österreichische Postsparkasse and Bank für Arbeit und Wirtschaft v Commission*, T-213/01 and T-214/01, EU:T:2006:151, paragraphs 148 to 151; and, by analogy, W. Wils and H. Abbott, 'Access to the File in Competition Proceedings Before the European Commission' (2019) 42 *World Competition* 255, updated version accessible at http://ssrn.com/author=456087, text accompanied by footnotes 178 to 181.

1325 Article 5(3) of Decision 2011/695.

1326 Article 5(4) of Decision 2011/695; see Article 11(6) of Regulation 1/2003, Article 2 of Regulation 773/2004 and paragraphs 17 to 23 of the Notice on Best Practices.
The companies under investigation have thus no right to be heard on requests by third parties to be heard as interested third person. The companies under investigation cannot either request the Hearing Officer to reverse or reconsider a decision granting the request to be heard of an interested third person.

1327 Judgments in *BPB Industries and British Gypsum v Commission*, C-310/93 P, EU:C:1995:101, paragraphs 26 and 27, and in *General Electric v Commission*, T-210/01, EU:T:2005:456, paragraph 650.

1328 See, similarly above concerning anonymous complainants. Not all potential procedural benefits of being heard as an interested third person may be available to an anonymous interested third person, however. As mentioned below, it is not possible to participate anonymously in the oral hearing.

1329 See, for example, 'BEUC to be involved in EU investigation on Aspen Pharma', *BEUC NEWS*, 27 November 2017, https://www.beuc.eu/press-media/news-events/beuc-be-involved-eu-investigation-aspen-pharma.

1330 Article 13(1) of Regulation 773/2004.

It is for the Directorate-General for Competition to provide the written information on the nature and subject matter of the procedure, and to set the time limit for the interested third person's written comments.

The Directorate-General for Competition has a wide discretion as to how it provides the written information on the nature and subject matter of the procedure. It may do so in the form of a summary document prepared specifically for this purpose. If a statement of objections has been sent, it may also do so by providing the interested third person with a non-confidential version of the statement of objections, but it is not obliged to do so.[1331] If the European Commission has published a detailed press release, which sets out the nature and subject matter of the procedure, the Directorate-General for Competition might simply provide the interested third person with this press release.

If the interested third person considers that it has not been (sufficiently) informed in writing of the nature and subject matter of the procedure, it may, after having first raised the issue with the Directorate-General for Competition, make a reasoned request to the Hearing Officer, who will take a reasoned decision on such request.[1332]

If the interested third person considers that the time limit to make its views known in writing is too short, it may seek an extension, first from the Directorate-General for Competition, and, if unsuccessful, subsequently from the Hearing Officer.[1333]

If the interested third person requests so in its written comments, the Hearing Officer may, 'where appropriate', allow the interested third person to express their views also at the oral hearing of the parties to which a statement of objections has been issued.[1334]

Several points should be noted:

First, interested third persons cannot request an oral hearing. They can only request to be allowed to express their views at the oral hearing of the addressees of the statement of objections, which presupposes that at least one of these addressees has requested an oral hearing.

Second, interested third persons can only request to be allowed to express their views at the oral hearing if they have first requested and been allowed to be heard in writing, and have in their written comments requested the opportunity to participate in the oral hearing.

Third, even if they have made the request in their written comments, interested third persons have no right to participate at the oral hearing. The Hearing Officer has a discretionary power to decide whether or not it is appropriate to admit an interested third person to the oral hearing.[1335] An important consideration which the Hearing Officer

---

1331 Judgment in *Österreichische Postsparkasse and Bank für Arbeit und Wirtschaft v Commission*, T-213/01 and T-214/01, EU:T:2006:151, paragraph 107.
For an example of a case in which the interested third persons received a non-confidential version of the statement of objections, see Final Report of the Hearing Officer in Case COMP/C-3/37.792 – Microsoft [2007] OJ C26/5.

1332 Article 7(2)(b) and (3) juncto Article 3(7) of Decision 2011/695.

1333 Article 9(2) of Decision 2011/695 and paragraph 105 of the Notice on Best Practices.

1334 Article 13(2) of Regulation 773/2004 and Article 6(2) of Decision 2011/695; see further my paper 'The Oral Hearing in Competition Proceedings Before the European Commission' (2012) 35 *World Competition* 397, updated version accessible at http://ssrn.com/author=456087.

1335 See Judgments of 17 January 1984, *VBVB and VBBB v Commission*, 43/82 and 63/82, EU:C:1984:9, paragraph 18, and of 28 February 2002, *Compagnie générale maritime and Others v Commission*, T-86/95, EU:T:2002:50, paragraph 468.

must take into account in making this decision is the contribution that the interested third person can make to the clarification of the relevant facts of the case.[1336] Normally a good indicator for this is the contribution that the interested third person has already made to the Commission's investigation through written comments and responses to requests for information. Practical considerations may also play a role, such as the fact that the interested third person made its request to be heard relatively late, shortly before the oral hearing.[1337]

Fourth, third parties cannot anonymously participate in the oral hearing. Interested third persons that have requested to remain anonymous must thus give up their anonymity if they want to express their views at the oral hearing.[1338]

3. Third parties can further strengthen their procedural position by lodging a complaint

Provided that they fulfil the substantive and procedural requirements for becoming a complainant, third parties can further strengthen their procedural position by lodging a complaint.

The possibility for informants to strengthen their procedural position by lodging a complaint has been discussed above in the section 'Informing the European Commission about a suspected infringement and triggering an investigation'. However, the possibility for third parties to strengthen their procedural position by lodging a complaint is not only available to informants that bring information on a matter which the European Commission is not yet investigating, but also to third parties at any point during ongoing investigations and proceedings, until the European Commission has sent its draft final decision to the Advisory Committee.[1339]

Sometimes a third party that has already made a successful request to be heard as an interested person later lodges a complaint, so as to be benefiting from the stronger procedural position that the status of complainant entails.[1340]

The procedural position of a complainant is indeed in three respects stronger than that of an interested third person:

First, except in cases handled under the cartel settlement procedure, complainants are entitled to a non-confidential version of any statement of objections relating to a matter

1336 See recital 13 of Decision 2011/695.

1337 See Final Report of the Hearing Officer in Case AT.40608 *Broadcom – Interim Measures Procedure* [2021] OJ C81/13, paragraphs 59 and 60, and Final Report of the Hearing Officer in Case AT.40049 *Mastercard II* [2019] OJ C300/3, paragraph 21.

1338 While parties may be assisted at the oral hearing by their lawyers or other qualified persons admitted by the Hearing Officer, they must appear either in person or be represented by a duly authorised agent from among their permanent staff or by legal representatives or representatives authorised by their constitution; see Article 14(4) and (5) of Regulation 773/200, Judgment of 14 July 1972, *Badische Anilin- & Soda-Fabrik v Commission*, 49/69, EU:C:1972:71, paragraph 11, and Chapter XII of this book.

1339 See Judgment of 7 June 2006, *Österreichische Postsparkasse and Bank für Arbeit und Wirtschaft v Commission*, T-213/01 and T-214/01, EU:T:2006:151, paragraphs 90 and 91, 148 to 150, and 160, and Judgment of 2 February 2022, *Polskie Górnictwo Naftowe i Gazownictwo v Commission*, T-616/18, EU:T:2022:43, paragraph 486.

1340 For an example of this, see Final Report of the Hearing Officer in Case COMP/F/38.638 – BR/ESBR [2008] OJ C7/8.

covered by the complaint,[1341] while interested persons are only entitled to written information on the nature and subject matter of the procedure, which, at the discretion of the Directorate-General for Competition, may or may not be given in the form of a non-confidential version of the statement of objections.

Second, because complainants must be 'closely associated with the proceedings',[1342] complainants are most likely to be allowed to express their views at the oral hearing of the addressees of the statement of objections if those addressees request such a hearing. Like for interested third persons, the admission of complainants to be oral hearing requires a request to this effect in the complainants' written comments and is to be granted by the Hearing Officer 'where appropriate'.[1343] Given the complainants' right to be closely associated to the proceedings, their participation in the oral hearing is, however, much less likely to be found inappropriate than that of interested third persons.[1344]

Third, as explained above, if the European Commission later decides no longer to act on the matter covered by the complaint, the complainant is entitled to a reasoned decision rejecting its complaint, must be heard in writing before such a decision is taken through a pre-rejection letter, and has a right of access to non-confidential versions of the documents on which the European Commission's intended rejection of the complaint is based.

F. Use of languages

According to Article 1 of Regulation 1 determining the languages to be used by the European Union,[1345] the official languages of the European Union and the working languages of the European Commission are Bulgarian, Croatian, Czech, Danish, English, Estonian, Finnish, French, German, Greek, Hungarian, Irish, Italian, Latvian, Lithuanian, Maltese, Polish, Portuguese, Romanian, Slovak, Slovenian, Spanish and Swedish.[1346]

According to Article 41(4) of the Charter of Fundamental Rights of the European Union, every person may write to the European Commission in any of the EU official languages selected by the sender, and must have an answer from the European Commission in the same language.[1347]

Third parties can thus inform the European Commission about a suspected infringement, either informally or by lodging a complaint, in any of the EU official languages.[1348] Similarly, third parties can provide comments in response to a market test notice, or request to be heard as an interested third person in any of the EU official languages.

1341 See Article 6(1) of Regulation 773/2004, and recital 5 of Commission Regulation (EC) No 622/2008 of 30 June 2008 [2008] OJ L171/3. In cases handled under the cartel settlement procedure, complainants are, in the same way as interested third persons, only entitled to written information about the nature and subject matter of the procedure.

1342 See Article 27(4) of Regulation 1/2003.

1343 Article 6(2) of Regulation 773/2004 and Article 6(2) of Decision 2011/695.

1344 See also Chapter XII of this book.

1345 Council Regulation No 1 determining the languages to be used by the European Economic Community [1958] OJ 17/385, last amended by Council Regulation (EU) No 517/2013 [2013] OJ L 158/1.

1346 See also Article 55(1) of the Treaty on European Union (EU), and S. Van der Jeught, *EU Language Law* (Europa Law Publishing 2015).

1347 See also Article 20(2)(d) TFEU and Article 2 of Regulation 1.

1348 See also Article 5(3) of Regulation 773/2004, which provides that complaints must be submitted in one of the official languages of the European Union.

All subsequent correspondence from the European Commission to the third party must in principle be in the same language as that initially chosen by the third party. For instance, if the European Commission subsequently wants to reject the complaint, both the pre-rejection letter pursuant to Article 7 of Regulation 773/2004 and the decision rejecting the complaint must in principle be in the same language as the complaint.

According to Article 3 of Regulation 1, documents that the European Commission sends to a person subject to the jurisdiction of a Member State must be drafted in the language of such State. For instance, if the European Commission addresses a request for information to a third party in Sweden, the request must thus in principle be drafted in Swedish.[1349]

A party can however waive its language rights, and agree to receive correspondence from the European Commission in another language.[1350]

According to the case law of the EU Courts, the language rules do not constitute an essential procedural requirement, within the meaning of Article 263 TFEU, the infringement of which necessarily affects the validity of any document addressed by the European Commission to a person in another language. An infringement of the language rules by the European Commission vitiates the procedure only if it gives rise to harmful consequences for that person in the course of the administrative procedure, which can normally be excluded if that person has read and understood the document.[1351]

G. Confidentiality and use of information

1. Protection of confidential information of third parties

Third parties that provide information in the European Commission's antitrust investigations and proceedings are entitled to protection of their business secrets and other confidential information.[1352]

As already mentioned above, where the European Commission accepts information supplied on a purely voluntary basis, accompanied by a request for confidentiality to

---

1349 According to paragraph 28 of the Notice on Best Practices, for simple requests for information, it is standard practice to send the cover letter in the language of the addressee's location or in English (including a reference to Article 3 of Regulation 1) and to attach the questionnaire in English. The addressee is also clearly informed – in the language of the addressee's location – of its right to obtain a translation of the cover letter and/or questionnaire into the language of the addressee's location, as well as the right to reply in that language. This practice allows for more expeditious treatment of information requests, while preserving the rights of addressees.

1350 See paragraph 27 of the Notice on Best Practices.

1351 See Judgments of 9 June 2016, *Compañia Española de Petróleos (CEPSA) v Commission*, C-608/13 P, EU:C:2016:414, paragraphs 36 to 39; of 15 July 1970, *Chemiefarma v Commission*, 41/69, EU:C:1970:71, paragraphs 49 to 53; of 28 November 2019, *Brugg Kabel and Kabelwerke Brugg v Commission*, C-591/18 P, EU:C:2019:1026, paragraphs 24 to 31; of 15 March 2000, *Cimenteries CBR and Others v Commission*, T-25/95, EU:T:2000:77, paragraphs 643 to 645; and of 12 March 2020, *LL-Carpenter v Commission*, T-531/18, EU:T:2020:91, paragraphs 113 to 115.

1352 See Article 339 TFEU, Articles 28 and 27(4) of Regulation 1/2003 and Articles 16(1) and 15(2) of Regulation 773/2004.
On the notions of 'confidential information' and 'business secrets' (the latter being a (not really distinctive) subcategory of the former), see W. Wils and H. Abbott, 'Access to the File in Competition Proceedings Before the European Commission' (2019) 42 *World Competition* 255, updated version accessible at http://ssrn.com/author=456087, text accompanied by footnotes 87 to 115.

protect the informant's anonymity, it is in principle bound to comply with such a condition.[1353] The informant requesting anonymity should, when providing documents, inform the European Commission that it is possible to infer his or her identity as the informant from the documents themselves.[1354]

Also, when the information is not provided on a purely voluntary basis (for instance, in response to a request for information by decision), justified specific fears of reprisals by (dominant) companies under investigation entitle third-party information providers to confidentiality protection.[1355]

More generally, third parties are entitled to protection of their business secrets and any other confidential information that they provide in the course of the European Commission's investigations and proceedings.[1356]

In general,[1357] for given information to be considered as confidential, it is necessary: (i) that it be known only to a limited number of persons; (ii) that the disclosure of that information be liable to cause serious harm to the person who has provided it or to other parties; and (iii) that the interests liable to be harmed by disclosure be objectively worthy of protection.[1358]

1353 See Judgments of 7 November 1985, *Adams v European Commission*, 145/83, EU:C:1985:448, paragraph 34; of 8 July 2004, *Mannesmannröhren-Werke v Commission*, T-44/00, EU:T:2004:218, paragraph 84, confirmed on appeal in Judgment of 25 January 2007, *Salzgitter Mannesmann v European Commission*, C-411/04 P, EU:C:2007:54, paragraph 45; of 8 July 2004, *Dalmine v European Commission*, T-50/00, EU:T:2004:220, paragraph 72, confirmed on appeal in Judgment of 25 January 2007, *Dalmine v European Commission*, C-407/04 P, EU:C:2007:53, paragraph 49; and of 8 July 2008, *BPB v European Commission*, T-53/03, EU:T:2008:254, paragraph 36.

1354 See, to that effect, Judgment of 7 November 1985, *Adams v European Commission*, 145/83, EU:C:1985:448, paragraphs 53 to 55.

1355 See Commission Notice on the rules for access to the Commission file in cases pursuant to Articles 81 and 82 of the EC Treaty, Articles 53, 54 and 57 of the EEA Agreement and Council Regulation (EC) No 139/2004 [2005] OJ C325/7, amended by Communication from the Commission – Amendments to the Commission Notice on rules for access to the Commission file [2015] OJ C256/3, paragraph 19; Judgments of 8 July 2004, *Mannesmannröhren-Werke v Commission*, T-44/00, EU:T:2004:218, paragraph 84, confirmed on appeal in Judgment of 25 January 2007, *Salzgitter Mannesmann v European Commission*, C-411/04 P, EU:C:2007:54, paragraph 45; of 8 July 2004, *Dalmine v European Commission*, T-50/00, EU:T:2004:220, paragraph 72, confirmed on appeal in Judgment of 25 January 2007, *Dalmine v European Commission*, C-407/04 P, EU:C:2007:53, paragraph 49; and of 8 July 2008, *BPB v European Commission*, T-53/03, EU:T:2008:254, paragraph 36; and W. Wils and H. Abbott, 'Access to the File in Competition Proceedings Before the European Commission' (2019) 42 *World Competition* 255, updated version accessible at http://ssrn.com/author=456087, text accompanied by footnotes 98 to 101.

1356 See Article 339 TFEU, Articles 28 and 27(4) of Regulation 1/2003 and Articles 16(1) and 15(2) of Regulation 773/2004.
On the notions of 'confidential information' and 'business secrets' (the latter being a (not really distinctive) subcategory of the former), see W. Wils and H. Abbott, 'Access to the File in Competition Proceedings Before the European Commission' (2019) 42 *World Competition* 255, updated version accessible at http://ssrn.com/author=456087, text accompanied by footnotes 87 to 115.

1357 In addition to this general confidentiality test, confidentiality may also result from specific EU law rules that afford given information specific protection or otherwise preclude, in particular circumstances, the disclosure of that information; see Judgment of 14 March 2017, *Evonik Degussa v Commission*, C-162/15 P, EU:C:2017:205, paragraphs 51, 53 and 55; W. Wils and H. Abbott, 'Access to the File in Competition Proceedings Before the European Commission' (2019) 42 *World Competition* 255, updated version accessible at http://ssrn.com/author=456087, text accompanied by footnotes 103 to 108.

1358 See Judgments of 30 May 2006 in *Bank Austria Creditanstalt v Commission*, T-198/03, EU:T:2006:136, paragraph 71; and of 14 March 2017 in *Evonik Degussa v Commission*, C-162/15 P, EU:C:2017:205, paragraphs 103 and 107; W. Wils and H. Abbott, 'Access to the File in Competition Proceedings Before the European Commission' (2019) 42 *World Competition* 255, updated version accessible at http://ssrn.com/author=456087, text accompanied by footnotes 85 to 102.

When providing their written comments on a non-confidential version of the statement of objections, or on a pre-rejection letter, or on the information they have received on the nature and subject matter of the procedure, as well as when they subsequently submit further information in the course of the same procedure, complainants or interested third persons are under an obligation to clearly identify any material which they consider to be confidential, giving reasons, and to provide a separate non-confidential version by the date set by the European Commission for making their views known.[1359] If undertakings or associations of undertakings fail to comply with this obligation, the European Commission may assume that the documents or statements concerned do not contain confidential information.[1360]

In all other situations in which third parties, at least those that are undertakings or associations of undertakings, provide documents or statements, the European Commission may also require them to identify any material which they consider to be confidential, giving reasons, and to provide a separate non-confidential version within a time limit set by the European Commission.[1361] Again, if they fail to comply with this obligation, the European Commission may assume that the documents or statements concerned do not contain confidential information.[1362]

With the exception of the identity of informants from whom the European Commission has accepted information supplied on a purely voluntary basis, accompanied by a request for confidentiality to protect the informant's anonymity (and the identity of (non-voluntary) information providers with justified specific fears of reprisals by (dominant) companies under investigation), for which confidentiality protection appears absolute,[1363] the protection of confidential information of third parties is not absolute, however.

In particular in the context of access to the file by the companies under investigation to whom the European Commission has addressed a statement of objections,[1364] and as regards confidential information on the investigation file that is capable of having some (exculpatory or inculpatory) evidential value, there is a need to strike a proportionate balance between the protection of confidentiality, on the one hand, and the rights of the defence and the need to ensure efficient application by the European Commission of EU antitrust rules, on the other hand.[1365]

1359 See Article 16(2) of Regulation 773/2004.

1360 Article 16(4) of Regulation 773/2004.

1361 Article 16(3) of Regulation 773/2004.

1362 Article 16(4) of Regulation 773/2004.

1363 See Judgments of 7 November 1985, *Adams v European Commission*, 145/83, EU:C:1985:448, paragraph 34; of 8 July 2004, *Mannesmannröhren-Werke v Commission*, T-44/00, EU:T:2004:218, paragraph 84, confirmed on appeal in Judgment of 25 January 2007, *Salzgitter Mannesmann v European Commission*, C-411/04 P, EU:C:2007:54, paragraph 45; of 8 July 2004, *Dalmine v European Commission*, T-50/00, EU:T:2004:220, paragraph 72, confirmed on appeal in Judgment of 25 January 2007, *Dalmine v European Commission*, C-407/04 P, EU:C:2007:53, paragraph 49; and of 8 July 2008, *BPB v European Commission*, T-53/03, EU:T:2008:254, paragraph 36.

1364 W. Wils and H. Abbott, 'Access to the File in Competition Proceedings Before the European Commission' (2019) 42 *World Competition* 255, updated version accessible at http://ssrn.com/author=456087. On disclosure of information through the publication of the European Commission's final decisions, see Chapter XV of this book.

1365 See the last sentence of Article 27(2) of Regulation 1/2003 and Article 15(3) of Regulation 773/2004; Judgments of 29 June 1995 in *Solvay v Commission*, T-30/91, EU:T:1995:115, paragraph 88; of 20 April 1999 in *Limburgse Vinyl Maatschappij and Others v Commission*, T-305/94 to T-307/94, T-313/94 to T-316/94, T-318/94, T-325/94,

Even if third parties are thus not guaranteed absolute protection of their confidential information, they do, however, benefit from strong procedural safeguards in case the European Commission intends to disclose information for which the third party has claimed confidentiality:

Article 8(1) and (2) of Decision 2011/695/EU provides that, where the Commission intends to disclose information which may constitute a business secret or other confidential information of any undertaking or person, the latter shall be informed in writing of this intention and the reasons thereof by the Directorate-General for Competition. A time limit shall be fixed within which the undertaking or person concerned may submit any written comments. Where the undertaking or person concerned objects to the disclosure of the information it may refer the matter to the Hearing Officer. If the Hearing Officer finds that the information may be disclosed because it does not constitute a business secret or other confidential information or because there is an overriding interest in its disclosure, that finding shall be stated in a reasoned decision which shall be notified to the undertaking or person concerned. The decision shall specify the date after which the information will be disclosed. This date shall not be less than one week from the date of notification.[1366]

Article 8(4) of the Decision 2011/695/EU adds that, where appropriate in order to balance the effective exercise of a party's rights of defence with legitimate interests of confidentiality, the Hearing Officer may decide that parts of the file that are indispensable for the exercise of the party's rights of defence will be made accessible to the party requesting access in a restricted manner, the details of which shall be determined by the Hearing Officer. Recital 16 of Decision 2011/695/EU further explains that such access in a restricted manner may involve, for example, a limitation of the number or category of persons having access, and a limitation of the use of the information being accessed.[1367] The so-called data room procedure is a type of such restricted access.[1368]

The third party the disclosure of whose alleged business secrets or other confidential information the Hearing Officer's decision allows can immediately bring before the EU General Court an action for annulment against the Hearing Officer's decision, as well as a request for suspension or other interim measures.[1369]

T-328/94, T-329/94 and T-335/94, EU:T:1999:80, paragraph 1016; of 14 February 2008 in *Varec*, C-450/06, EU:C:2008:91, paragraph 52; and of 13 September 2018 in *UBS Europe and Others*, C-358/16, EU:C:2018:715, paragraphs 68 and 69; and W. Wils and H. Abbott, 'Access to the File in Competition Proceedings Before the European Commission' (2019) 42 *World Competition* 255, updated version accessible at http://ssrn.com/author=456087, text accompanied by footnotes 117 to 126.

1366 See further Chapter XI of this book.

1367 Such a limitation of the use of the information would be in addition to the generally applicable limitations laid down in Article 16a of Regulation 773/2004.

1368 See paragraphs 97 and 98 of the Notice on Best Practices, and DG Competition Best Practices on the disclosure of information in data rooms in proceedings under Articles 101 and 102 TFEU and under the EU Merger Regulation (2 June 2015), accessible at http://ec.europa.eu/competition/antitrust/legislation/legislation.html.

1369 See Judgment of 24 June 1986 in *AKZO v Commission*, 53/85, EU:C:1986:256, paragraph 29; see also Order of 10 September 2013 in *Commission v Pilkington Group*, C-278/13 P(R), EU:C:2013:558, paragraphs 56 to 58, and Order of 2 April 2019 in *Lantmännen v Commission*, T-79/19 R, EU:T:2019:212.

2. Third parties have no access to business secrets or other confidential information of the undertakings/companies under investigation

Third parties are not allowed to have access to business secrets or other confidential information of the undertakings/companies under investigation.[1370]

Complainants are therefore only entitled to receive a **non-confidential version** of any statement of objections, and the information on the nature and subject matter of the procedure to which interested third persons that have shown a sufficient interest are entitled must be similarly stripped of any business secrets or other confidential information of the undertakings/companies under investigation.

Contrary to what has been mentioned above about the need to balance the protection of third parties' right to confidentiality with the defence rights of the companies under investigation and the need to ensure efficient application by the European Commission of EU antitrust rules, there is no balancing involved here. Business secrets or other confidential information of the undertakings/companies under investigation cannot be disclosed to third parties.[1371]

This asymmetry in the level of protection of business secrets and other confidential information of the undertakings/companies under investigation as compared to those of third parties is justified by the different interests at stake (the rights of the defence of the companies under investigation and the effective enforcement of the EU antitrust rules by the European Commission weighing more heavily than the participation rights of third parties) as well as by the need to avoid 'the unacceptable consequence that an undertaking may be inspired to lodge a complaint with the Commission solely in order to gain access to its competitors' business secrets'.[1372]

3. Restrictions on the use of information obtained by third parties through their participation in the European Commission's proceedings

Article 16a(1) of Regulation 773/2004 provides that any information obtained pursuant to this Regulation can only be used for the purposes of judicial or administrative proceedings for the application of Articles 101 and 102 TFEU.

Article 16a(3) of Regulation 773/2004 further provides that information that was prepared by other natural or legal persons specifically for the European Commission's proceedings and information that the European Commission has drawn up and sent to the parties in the course of its proceedings cannot be used in proceedings before national courts until the European Commission has closed its proceedings against all parties under investigation.

1370 See Article 8(1) and recital 8 of Regulation 773/2004, and Judgments of 17 November 1987, *British American Tobacco and Reynolds Industries v Commission*, 142 and 156/84, EU:C:1987:490, paragraph 21, and of 24 June 1986 in *AKZO v Commission*, 53/85, EU:C:1986:256, paragraph 29. While these provisions and this judgment concern in particular complainants, the same applies *a fortiori* to other third persons, given that complainants are the category of third persons with the most extensive procedural rights; see Judgment of 7 June 2006, *Österreichische Postsparkasse and Bank für Arbeit und Wirtschaft v Commission*, T-213/01 and T-214/01, EU:T:2006:151, paragraph 106.

1371 A different position was taken by the Hearing Officer in one (apparently isolated) case; see Final Report of the Hearing Officer in Case COMP/C-3/37.990 – *Intel* [2009] OJ C227/7, at 9.

1372 Judgment of 24 June 1986 in *AKZO v Commission*, 53/85, EU:C:1986:256, paragraph 28.

XV. Publication of Antitrust Decisions of the European Commission

This chapter deals with the publication by the European Commission of its decisions adopted in the enforcement of the competition rules laid down in Articles 101 and 102 TFEU. It examines the legal basis of such publication and the interests justifying publication; what content of the decision must be published, may be published and cannot be published; the procedure and timing of the publication; and the relationship with public access to documents.

A. Introduction

1. The main types of antitrust decisions of the European Commission

The European Commission's main decisional powers are set out in Articles 7 to 10, 23 and 24 of Regulation 1/2003.[1373] Article 7 empowers the European Commission to adopt decisions finding infringements of Article 101 or 102 TFEU and ordering the termination of such infringements. Article 8 empowers the European Commission to adopt decisions ordering interim measures, Article 9 to adopt decision-making commitments binding, and Article 10 to adopt decisions finding that Article 101 or 102 TFEU is not applicable to an agreement or practice. Articles 23 and 24 empower the European Commission to impose fines and periodic penalty payments by decision.

2. The publication obligation in Article 30 of Regulation 1/2003

Article 30 of Regulation 1/2003 reads as follows:

Article 30

Publication of decisions

'*1. The Commission shall publish the decisions which it takes pursuant to Articles 7 to 10, 23 and 24.*

2. The publication shall state the names of the parties and the main content of the decision, including any penalties imposed. It shall have regard to the legitimate interest of undertakings in the protection of their business secrets.'

1373 Council Regulation (EC) No 1/2003 of 16 December 2002 on the implementation of the rules on competition laid down in Articles 81 and 82 of the Treaty [2003] OJ L1/1, last amended by Council Regulation (EC) No 1419/2006 [2006] OJ L269/1. For a detailed analysis of Regulation 1/2003, see K. Dekeyser, C. Gauer, J. Laitenberger, N. Wahl, W. Wils and L. Prete (eds), *Regulation 1/2003 and EU Antitrust Enforcement – A Systematic Guide* (Wolters Kluwer 2022).

3. The interests justifying publication

The recitals and the legislative history of Regulation 1/2003 do not contain any reasoning as to why the European Commission should publish its antitrust decisions.[1374]

The EU Courts have, however, clarified that the publication by the European Commission of its antitrust decisions serves three interests – namely, the public interest in knowing as fully as possible the reasons behind any action by the European Commission, the interest of the economic operators in knowing the sort of behaviour for which they are liable to be penalised, and the interest of persons harmed by the infringement in being informed about the details thereof so that they may assert their rights against the undertakings punished.[1375]

a. *The public interest in knowing as fully as possible the reasons behind any action by the European Commission*

In mandating the publication by the European Commission of its main antitrust decisions, Article 30 of Regulation 1/2003 reflects the principle laid down in the second subparagraph of Article 1 of the Treaty on European Union (TEU), according to which decisions are to be taken as openly as possible within the European Union.[1376]

b. *The interest of the economic operators in knowing the sort of behaviour for which they are liable to be penalised*

According to the case law of the EU Courts, the supervisory task conferred on the European Commission by Article 105 TFEU in relation to Articles 101 and 102 TFEU 'not only includes the duty to investigate and punish individual infringements but also encompasses the duty to pursue a general policy designed to apply, in competition matters, the principles laid down by the Treaty and to guide the conduct of undertakings in the light of those principles [. . .]. In order that this task may be accomplished, it is essential that economic operators be informed, through the publication of decisions finding infringements and imposing fines, of the conduct that has led the Commission to take punitive action'.[1377]

1374 Regulation 1/2003 does not contain any recital relating to its Article 30, and the Explanatory Memorandum of the European Commission's legislative proposal for what became Regulation 1/2003 (COM(2000)582 final 2000/0243(CNS) of 27 September 2000, at 29) only explains that Article 31 of the proposed regulation, which became Article 30 of Regulation 1/2003, is equivalent to Article 21 of Regulation 17. The latter regulation (Council Regulation No 17 [1962] OJ 13/204 (Special English Edition 1959-62, p 87)) did not contain any recital relating to its Article 21 either.

1375 See Judgment of the General Court of 30 May 2006 in *Bank Austria Creditanstalt v European Commission*, T-198/03, EU:T:2006:136, paragraph 78, and the judgments mentioned in the following footnotes.

1376 Judgments of the General Court of 30 May 2006 in *Bank Austria Creditanstalt v European Commission*, T-198/03, EU:T:2006:136, paragraphs 69 and 78, and of 28 January 2015 in *Akzo Nobel and Others v European Commission*, T-345/12, EU:T:2015:50, paragraph 60.

1377 Judgment of the General Court of 30 May 2006 in *Bank Austria Creditanstalt v European Commission*, T-198/03, EU:T:2006:136, paragraph 57; see also Judgments of the Court of Justice of 28 June 2005 in *Dansk Rørindustri and Others v European Commission*, C-189/02 P, C-202/02 P, C-205/02 P to C-208/02 P and C-213/02 P, EU:C:2005:408, paragraph 170, and of 14 December 2000 in *Masterfoods v HB Ice Cream*, C-344/98, EU:C:2000:689, paragraph 46.
On the role of the European Commission in the enforcement of Articles 101 and 102 TFEU, see further Chapter IV of this book and my paper 'The Judgment of the General Court in *Intel* and the So-Called More Economic Approach to Abuse of Dominance' (2014) 37 *World Competition* 405, also accessible at http://ssrn.com/author=456087.

Publication of the main antitrust decisions of the European Commission, as required by Article 30 of Regulation 1/2003, thus serves not only the private interest of the economic operators in knowing the sort of behaviour for which they are liable to be penalised, but also the public interest of ensuring compliance with Articles 101 and 102 TFEU, which, according to the case law of the EU Courts, are fundamental provisions that are essential for the tasks entrusted to the European Union.[1378]

c. *The interest of persons harmed by the infringement in being informed about the details thereof so that they may assert their rights against the undertakings punished*

Article 101(2) TFEU provides that any agreements or decisions prohibited pursuant to Article 101 TFEU shall be automatically void.

In its case law, the Court of Justice has clarified that Article 101(1) and Article 102 TFEU produce direct effects between individuals and create rights for these individuals, and that the national courts whose task it is to apply the provisions of EU law in areas within their jurisdiction must ensure that those rules take full effect and must protect the rights which they confer on individuals, by granting injunctive relief, including interim relief, as well as compensation for harm suffered, under conditions that may not be less favourable than those governing the protection of comparable rights under national law and that ensure the effective protection of the rights conferred by Articles 101(1) and 102 TFEU.[1379]

It also follows from the case law of the Court of Justice,[1380] as well as from Article 16(1) of Regulation 1/2003, which codified this case law, that when national courts rule under Articles 101 or 102 TFEU on agreements or practices which are already the subject of a European Commission's decision, they cannot take decisions running counter to the decision adopted by the European Commission.

Directive 2014/104[1381] has further encouraged the bringing of actions for damages by persons harmed by infringements of Articles 101 and 102 TFEU established in European Commission decisions.[1382]

Publication of decisions of the European Commission that find infringements of Articles 101 and 102 TFEU, as required by Article 30 of Regulation 1/2003, thus serves

---

1378 See Judgment of the General Court of 7 October 2014 in *Schenker v European Commission*, T-534/11, EU:T:2014:854, paragraphs 80, 81 and 114; Judgment of the Court of Justice of 9 June 1999 in *Eco Swiss*, C-126/97, EU:C:1999:269, paragraph 36; Opinion of Advocate General Geelhoed of 19 January 2006 in *Commission v SGL Carbon*, C-301/04 P, EU:C:2006:53, paragraph 67; and Opinion 2/13 (Accession of the EU to the ECHR) of the Court of Justice of 18 December 2014, EU:C:2014:2454, paragraph 172.

1379 Judgments of the Court of Justice of 30 January 1974 in *BRT and SABAM*, 127/73, EU:C:1974:6, paragraph 16; of 19 June 1990 in *Factortame and Others*, C-213/89, EU:C:1990:257, paragraphs 19 to 21; and of 20 September 2001 in *Courage v Crehan*, C-453/99, EU:C:2001:465, paragraphs 19 to 29. Article 1 of Regulation 1/2003 gave direct effect also to Article 101(3) TFEU.

1380 Judgment of the Court of Justice of 14 December 2000 in *Masterfoods v HB Ice Cream*, C-344/98, EU:C:2000:689, paragraphs 51 and 52.

1381 Directive 2014/104/EU of the European Parliament and of the Council of 26 November 2014 on certain rules governing actions for damages under national law for infringements of the competition law provisions of the Member States and of the European Union [2014] OJ L349/1.

1382 See further Chapter XVII of this book.

the interest of persons harmed by the infringement in being informed about the details thereof so that they may assert their rights against the undertakings found to have committed that infringement.[1383]

4. Other documents to be published together with the decision

Article 14(1) of Regulation 1/2003 provides that, prior to taking any decision under Articles 7 to 10, 23, 24(2) and 29(1),[1384] the European Commission must consult the Advisory Committee on Restrictive Practices and Dominants Positions, which is composed of representatives of the competition authorities of the EU Member States.

Article 14(6) provides as follows:

'Where the Advisory Committee delivers a written opinion, this opinion shall be appended to the draft decision. If the Advisory Committee recommends publication of the opinion, the Commission shall carry out such publication taking into account the legitimate interest of undertakings in the protection of their business secrets.'

For all the decisions requiring prior consultation of the Advisory Committee, Article 16(1) of Decision 2011/695/EU[1385] further requires that the European Commission's Hearing Officer prepare a final report on the respect for the effective exercise of procedural rights throughout the proceedings culminating in the draft decision.[1386]

Article 17(3) of Decision 2011/695/EU provides as follows:

'The Commission shall [. . .] publish the hearing officer's final report in the Official Journal of the European Union, together with the decision, having regard to the legitimate interest of undertakings in the protection of their business secrets.'

1383 Judgments of the General Court of 30 May 2006 in *Bank Austria Creditanstalt v European Commission*, T-198/03, EU:T:2006:136, paragraph 78, and of the Court of Justice of 14 March 2017 in *Evonik Degussa v European Commission*, C-162/15 P, EU:C:2017:205, paragraph 78.
The publication by the European Commission of its decision finding an infringement in particular serves to allow those harmed by the infringement to bring an action before the relevant national court. It is subsequently for the relevant national court before which the action is brought to decide on the way in which further evidence and documents are produced in accordance with the applicable law to resolve the dispute; see Judgment in *Kingdom of the Netherlands v European Commission*, T-380/08, EU:T:2013:480, paragraphs 55 and 82, and Chapter II 'Disclosure of evidence' of Directive 2014/104/EU of the European Parliament and of the Council of 26 November 2014 on certain rules governing actions for damages under national law for infringements of the competition law provisions of the Member States and of the European Union [2014] OJ L349/1.

1384 The list of decisions requiring prior consultation of the Advisory Committee pursuant to Article 14(1) of Regulation 1/2003 is thus mostly but not entirely the same as the list of decisions for which Article 30 prescribes publication. The first difference is that all decisions pursuant to Article 24 (imposition of periodic penalty payments) must be published, whereas the Advisory Committee must only be consulted on draft decisions pursuant to the second paragraph of Article 24 (that is, decisions in which the definitive amount of the periodic penalty payment is fixed at a figure lower than that which would arise under the original decision). The second difference is that the Advisory Committee must also be consulted on draft decisions pursuant to Article 29(1) (withdrawal of the benefit of block exemption regulations in individual cases), whereas Article 30 does not mandate publication of such decisions.

1385 Decision 2011/695/EU of the President of the European Commission of 13 October 2011 on the function and terms of reference of the hearing officer in certain competition proceedings [2011] OJ L275/29.

1386 See further Chapter XI of this book.

5. Publication in the Official Journal and on the European Commission's website

Whereas Article 30 of Regulation 1/2003 does not specify where the European Commission should publish the decisions which it takes pursuant to Articles 7 to 10, 23 and 24 of Regulation 1/2003, it results from Article 17(3) of Decision 2011/695/EU (quoted just above) that such publication must be in the *Official Journal of the European Union*.[1387]

Paragraphs 148 and 149 of the Notice on Best Practices[1388] set out the current practice of the European Commission:

- A non-confidential summary of the decision, (a non-confidential version of) the opinion of the Advisory Committee and (a non-confidential version of) the final report of the Hearing Officer are published in the *Official Journal of the European Union*; and, in addition,
- A non-confidential version of the full text of the decision is published on the website of the European Commission's Directorate-General for Competition in the authentic languages of the decision[1389] as well as in additional languages, if such additional language versions are available[1390].[1391]

1387 At least for those decisions that require prior consultation of the Advisory Committee pursuant to Article 14(1) and hence a final report of the Hearing Officer pursuant to Article 16(1) of Decision 2011/695/EU, which, as explained above, is not the case for decisions pursuant to Article 24(1) of Regulation 1/2003.

1388 Commission notice on best practices for the conduct of proceedings concerning Articles 101 and 102 TFEU [2011] OJ C308/6 ('Notice on Best Practices').
As indicated in its paragraph 7, the Notice on Best Practices does not create any new rights or obligations, nor alter the rights or obligations which arise from the Treaty, Regulation 1/2003, Regulation 773/2004 and the case law of the EU Courts; see Judgment of 19 January 2016 in *Toshiba v Commission*, T-404/12, EU:T:2016:18, paragraph 56.
As reflected in its paragraph 145, the Notice on Best Practices does not cover decisions pursuant to Articles 8 or 10 of Regulation 1/2003.

1389 In line with Regulation 1 (Council Regulation No 1 determining the languages to be used by the European Economic Community [1958] OJ 17/385, last amended by Council Regulation (EU) No 517/2013 [2013] OJ L158/1), the authentic language(s) of the decision is (are) the language(s) of the EU Member State in which the addressee(s) of the decision is (are) based, unless the addressee(s) has (have) given a language waiver accepting to receive the decision in another EU language more convenient to the European Commission (typically English); see paragraphs 25 to 31 of the Notice on Best Practices. If the addressee(s) of the decision is (are) not based in an EU Member State, the authentic language of the decision is typically English; see also Judgment in *Brugg Kabel and Kabelwerke Brugg v European Commission*, C-591/18 P, EU:C:2019:1026, paragraphs 24 to 31.

1390 If English is not an authentic language of the decision, an additional English-language version is typically available.

1391 According to paragraph 36 of the Working Arrangements for the Functioning of the Advisory Committee (Annex to the Communication to the Commission, Working Arrangements for the Functioning of the Advisory Committee on Restrictive Practices and Dominant Positions, C(2019)2310 final, 29 March 2019), the opinion of the Advisory Committee is also published on the website of the Directorate-General for Competition.
According to paragraph 4 of the document 'Guidance on the preparation of public versions of Commission Decisions adopted under Articles 7 to 10, 23 and 24 of Regulation 1/2003', made available on 4 June 2015 on the website of the European Commission's Directorate-General for Competition at https://ec.europa.eu/competition/antitrust/guidance_on_preparation_of_public_versions_antitrust_04062015.pdf, all the documents published in the *Official Journal of the European Union* are also made available on the website of the European Commission's Directorate-General for Competition.

This practice of only publishing a non-confidential summary of the decision in the *Official Journal of the European Union* is in conformity with Article 30 of Regulation 1/2003 and Article 17(3) of Decision 2011/695/EU, on condition that the summary contains the names of the parties and the main content of the decision, including any penalties imposed, as required by Article 30(2) of Regulation 1/2003.[1392]

The justification for this practice of only publishing a non-confidential summary of the decision in the *Official Journal of the European Union* is that it saves translation costs, given that the *Official Journal of the European Union* appears in the 24 official languages of the EU.[1393]

The practice of publishing a non-confidential version of the full decision only in the languages available is compatible with the principle of equal treatment and with the linguistic regime of the European Union.[1394]

6. Publication of other types of decisions

While Article 30 of Regulation 1/2003 mandates publication of decisions taken pursuant to Articles 7 to 10, 23 and 24 of Regulation 1/2003, neither Regulation 1/2003 nor its Implementing Regulation 773/2004[1395] contain any provision either mandating or prohibiting the publication of other decisions taken pursuant to Regulation 1/2003 and/or Regulation 773/2004.

As mentioned above, according to the second subparagraph of Article 1 TEU, decisions are to be taken as openly as possible within the European Union. According to the case law of the EU Courts, it follows from this principle that, 'in the absence of provisions explicitly ordering or prohibiting publication, the power of the institutions to make acts which they adopt public is the rule'.[1396]

In paragraph 150 of the Notice on Best Practices, the European Commission has indicated that it 'intends to make public on its website decisions rejecting complaints (pursuant to Article 7 of the Implementing Regulation [773/2004]) or a summary thereof. [. . .] Other types of decisions may also be published in appropriate cases.'

1392 On the other hand, in the light of the principle that decisions are taken as openly as possible, Article 30(2) of Regulation 1/2003 does not limit the European Commission's power to publish a non-confidential version of the full text of its decision, if, resources permitting, it considers it appropriate to do so; see Judgments of the General Court of 30 May 2006 in *Bank Austria Creditanstalt v European Commission*, T-198/03, EU:T:2006:136, paragraph 76, and of 28 January 2015 in *Akzo Nobel and Others v European Commission*, T-345/12, EU:T:2015:50, paragraph 60.

1393 See Judgment of the General Court of 30 May 2006 in *Bank Austria Creditanstalt v European Commission*, T-198/03, EU:T:2006:136, paragraph 76.

1394 See Judgment of the General Court of 30 May 2006 in *Bank Austria Creditanstalt v European Commission*, T-198/03, EU:T:2006:136, paragraphs 102 and 103.

1395 Commission Regulation (EC) No 773/2004 of 7 April 2004 relating to the conduct of proceedings by the Commission pursuant to Articles 81 and 82 of the EC Treaty [2004] OJ L123/18, last amended by Commission Regulation (EU) 2015/1348 of 3 August 2015 amending Regulation (EC) No 773/2004 relating to the conduct of proceedings by the Commission pursuant to Articles 81 and 82 of the EC Treaty [2015] OJ L208/3.

1396 See Judgments of the General Court of 30 May 2006 in *Bank Austria Creditanstalt v European Commission*, T-198/03, EU:T:2006:136, paragraphs 69 and 87, and of 28 January 2015 in *Akzo Nobel and Others v European Commission*, T-345/12, EU:T:2015:50, paragraph 76.

B. What content of the decision must be published, may be published and cannot be published?

1. Overview

According to the first sentence of Article 30(2) of Regulation 1/2003, the publication of the decision must include 'the names of the parties and the main content of the decision, including any penalties imposed'.

As mentioned above, according to the second subparagraph of Article 1 TEU, decisions are to be taken as openly as possible within the European Union. According to the case law of the EU Courts, it follows from this principle that, 'in the absence of provisions explicitly ordering or prohibiting publication, the power of the institutions to make acts which they adopt public is the rule'.[1397]

The European Commission thus has a wide discretion: it is free to publish not only the main content of the decision, but also other content of the decision, or indeed the full text of the decision.[1398]

However, the important limitation to this discretion is that the European Commission cannot publish 'information falling under the protection of professional secrecy'.[1399] The obligation 'not to disclose information of the kind covered by the obligation of professional secrecy' is laid down in Article 339 TFEU, and is reflected in the second sentence of Article 30(2) of Regulation 1/2003 as well as in Article 28(2) of Regulation 1/2003 and Article 16(1) of Regulation 773/2004.[1400]

2. Information covered by the obligation of professional secrecy

Whereas the second sentence of Article 30(2) of Regulation 1/2003 only mentions that the European Commission 'shall have regard to the legitimate interest of undertakings in the protection of business secrets', it is clear from the case law of the EU Courts that the concept of 'information covered by the obligation of professional secrecy' includes

---

1397 See Judgment in *Bank Austria Creditanstalt v European Commission*, T-198/03, EU:T:2006:136, paragraph 69, and of 28 January 2015 in *Akzo Nobel and Others v European Commission*, T-345/12, EU:T:2015:50, paragraph 76.

1398 Judgments of the General Court of 28 January 2015 in *Evonik Degussa v European Commission*, T-341/12, EU:T:2015:51, paragraphs 155, 156 and 161, and of 28 January 2015 in *Akzo Nobel and Others v European Commission*, T-345/12, EU:T:2015:50, paragraphs 123, 124 and 128.

1399 Judgments in *Bank Austria Creditanstalt v European Commission*, T-198/03, EU:T:2006:136, paragraphs 69 and 88, and of 28 January 2015 in *Akzo Nobel and Others v European Commission*, T-345/12, EU:T:2015:50, paragraph 123.

1400 Judgments of the General Court of 30 May 2006 in *Bank Austria Creditanstalt v European Commission*, T-198/03, EU:T:2006:136, paragraph 71; of 12 October 2007 in *Pergan Hilfsstoffe für industrielle Prozesse v European Commission*, T-474/04, EU:T:2007:306, paragraph 62; of 28 January 2015 in *Akzo Nobel and Others v European Commission*, T-345/12, EU:T:2015:50, paragraph 61; and of 28 January 2015 in *Evonik Degussa v European Commission*, T-341/12, EU:T:2015:51, paragraphs 78 to 81.
Whereas the wording of Article 339 TFEU and of Article 28(2) of Regulation 1/2003 only refers to the officials and other servants of the European Commission, it is clear from the case law of the EU Courts that the European Commission itself is also subject to the obligation of professional secrecy; see also W. Wils and H. Abbott, 'Access to the File in Competition Proceedings before the European Commission' (2019) 42 *World Competition* 255, updated version accessible at http://ssrn.com/author=456087 (text accompanying) footnote 77.

not only business secrets (that is, commercially sensitive information)[1401] but also other confidential information.[1402]

There appears to be no practical need to distinguish between business secrets and other confidential information.[1403]

According to the case law of the EU Courts, **generally**,[1404] three cumulative conditions must be satisfied for information to be confidential and hence covered by the obligation of professional secrecy:

- First, the information 'must be known only to a limited number of persons';
- Second, it must be 'information whose disclosure is liable to cause serious harm to the person who has provided it or to third parties';
- Third, 'the interests liable to be harmed by disclosure must be worthy of protection. The assessment as to the confidentiality of a piece of information requires, in this regard, the individual legitimate interests opposing disclosure of the information to be weighed against the public interest that the activities of the [European Union] institutions take place as openly as possible'.[1405]

These three cumulative conditions of this general confidentiality test will be examined in more detail further below.

In addition to the threefold general confidentiality test, information may also fall under the protection of professional secrecy because of other EU law rules (including primary and secondary law as well as general principles) that (i) afford such information 'specific protection'[1406] or (ii) otherwise preclude, in particular circumstances, the disclosure of that information[1407].

1401 Opinion of Advocate General Szpunar of 29 July 2016 in *Evonik Degussa v European Commission*, C-162/15 P, EU:C:2016:587, paragraph 41.

1402 Judgments of the Court of Justice of 7 November 1985 in *Adams v European Commission*, 145/83, EU:C:1985:448, paragraph 34; and of the General Court of 18 September 1996 in *Postbank v European Commission*, T-353/94, EU:T:1996:119; of 12 October 2007 in *Pergan Hilfsstoffe für industrielle Prozesse v European Commission*, T-474/04, EU:T:2007:306, paragraph 63; and of 15 July 2015 in *Pilkington Group v European Commission*, T-462/12, EU:T:2015:508, paragraph 45.

1403 See W. Wils and H. Abbott, 'Access to the File in Competition Proceedings before the European Commission' (2019) 42 *World Competition* 255, updated version accessible at http://ssrn.com/author=456087, text accompanied by footnotes 77 to 84.

1404 See Judgment of the General Court of 12 October 2007 in *Pergan Hilfsstoffe für industrielle Prozesse v European Commission*, T-474/04, EU:T:2007:306, paragraph 65.

1405 Judgments of the General Court of 30 May 2006 in *Bank Austria Creditanstalt v European Commission*, T-198/03, EU:T:2006:136, paragraph 71; and of 12 October 2007 in *Pergan Hilfsstoffe für industrielle Prozesse v European Commission*, T-474/04, EU:T:2007:306, paragraph 65; and of the Court of Justice of 14 March 2017 in *Evonik Degussa v European Commission*, C-162/15 P, EU:C:2017:205, paragraph 107.

1406 See Judgments of the General Court of 30 May 2006 in *Bank Austria Creditanstalt v Commission*, T-198/03, EU:T:2006:136, paragraphs 32 to 35; and of 12 October 2007 in *Pergan Hilfsstoffe für industrielle Prozesse v Commission*, T-474/04, EU:T:2007:306, paragraphs 64 and 75; as well as Judgment of the Court of Justice of 14 March 2017 in *Evonik Degussa v Commission*, C-162/15 P, EU:C:2017:205, paragraphs 51 and 55.
Examples include Article 4 of Directive (EU) 2016/943 of the European Parliament and of the Council of 8 June 2016 on the protection of undisclosed know-how and business information (trade secrets) against their unlawful acquisition, use and disclosure [2016] OJ L157/1; and Article 16(1) of Directive (EU) 2019/1937 of the European Parliament and of the Council of 23 October 2019 on the protection of persons who report breaches of Union law [2019] OJ L305/17. See also below for the example of personal data.

1407 See, to that effect, Judgment of the Court of Justice of 14 March 2017 in *Evonik Degussa v Commission*, C-162/15 P, EU:C:2017:205, paragraphs 51, 53 and 55. See also below for examples of legitimate expectations and equal treatment.

Finally, two general points should be noted:

- '[T]he burden of proof [. . .], in respect of confidential treatment, is borne by the person requesting such treatment';[1408] and
- '[Any] request for confidentiality must be assessed on its own merits. Thus, reasoning based exclusively on analogy cannot suffice.'[1409]

3. The three cumulative conditions of the general confidentiality test

a. *Known only to a limited number of persons*

As mentioned above, the first of the three cumulative conditions of the general confidentiality test is that the information 'must be known only to a limited number of persons'.

This first condition is typically fulfilled if the information is not known outside the company from which the European Commission obtained the information.

It is certainly not fulfilled if the information is available to the general public, or is capable of being inferred from publicly available information.

Moreover, confidentiality has to be assessed in relation to the circles that normally deal with the kind of information concerned.[1410] If the information is only of relevance to specialised circles, the condition is not fulfilled if the information is already available to specialists or capable of being inferred by them.[1411]

On this ground, the General Court in *Pilkington* confirmed that information on prices which the applicant had agreed with its customers and on quantities supplied was not known only to a limited number of persons, because the applicant itself had communicated this information to the other participants in the cartel.[1412]

On the other hand, the fact that information may have been available to other parties as part of the access to the file during the European Commission's administrative procedure does not as such prevent that information from being known only to a limited number of persons.[1413]

1408 Judgment of the General Court of 28 January 2015 in *Evonik Degussa v European Commission*, T-341/12, EU:T:2015:51, paragraph 92.

1409 Order of the President of the General Court of 25 October 2018 in *JPMorgan Chase and Others v European Commission*, T-420/18 R, EU:T:2018:724, paragraph 74.

1410 Judgment of the General Court of 15 July 2015 in *Pilkington Group v European Commission*, T-462/12, EU:T:2015:508, paragraph 63.

1411 Judgment of the General Court of 15 July 2015 in *Pilkington Group v European Commission*, T-462/12, EU:T:2015:508, paragraphs 56, 57 and 60; see also, by analogy, Order of the President of the Second Chamber of the General Court of 27 September 2017 in *Yich United Steel Corp. v European Commission*, T-607/15, EU:T:2017:698, paragraph 18.

1412 Judgment of the General Court of 15 July 2015 in *Pilkington Group v European Commission*, T-462/12, EU:T:2015:508, paragraphs 60, 61, 65 and 66.

1413 Judgments of the General Court of 28 January 2015 in *Akzo Nobel and Others v European Commission*, T-345/12, EU:T:2015:50, paragraphs 66 to 68, and in *Evonik Degussa v European Commission*, T-341/12, EU:T:2015:51, paragraphs 95 to 97.

b. *Disclosure is liable to cause serious harm*

As mentioned above, the second of the three cumulative conditions of the general confidentiality test is that it must be 'information whose disclosure is liable to cause serious harm to the person who has provided it or to third parties'.

As also mentioned above, 'the burden of proof [. . .], in respect of confidential treatment, is borne by the person requesting such treatment',[1414] and '[any] request for confidentiality must be assessed on its own merits. Thus, reasoning based exclusively on analogy cannot suffice'.[1415]

The most common example of information that may fulfil this second condition is commercially sensitive information (business secrets) such as technical and/or financial information relating to an undertaking's know-how, margin calculations and price structure, production secrets and processes, supply sources, quantities produced and sold, market shares, customers and distributors lists, marketing plans, cost and methods of assessing costs, and sales strategy.[1416]

Disclosure of such commercially sensitive information may cause serious harm, to the extent that such information could be exploited by competitors or other market participants in the course of normal competition.[1417]

The extent to which disclosure of such information will cause serious and irreparable harm depends on a combination of factors, such as, inter alia, how significant the information is in commercial terms for the undertaking providing the information and its usefulness for other market participants.[1418]

It is further important to consider how recent the information is. The case law of the EU Courts has developed a rebuttable presumption in this respect: '[I]nformation which was secret or confidential, but which is at least five years old, must as a rule, on account of the passage of time, be considered historical and therefore as having lost its secret or confidential nature unless, exceptionally, the party relying on that nature shows that, despite its age, that information still constitutes essential elements of its commercial position or that of interested third parties.'[1419]

1414 Judgment of the General Court of 28 January 2015 in *Evonik Degussa v European Commission*, T-341/12, EU:T:2015:51, paragraph 92.

1415 Order of the President of the General Court of 25 October 2018 in *JPMorgan Chase and Others v European Commission*, T-420/18 R, EU:T:2018:724, paragraph 74.

1416 See paragraph 10 of the 'Guidance on the preparation of public versions of Commission Decisions adopted under Articles 7 to 10, 23 and 24 of Regulation 1/2003', made available on 4 June 2015 on the website of the European Commission's Directorate-General for Competition https://ec.europa.eu/competition/antitrust/guidance_on_preparation_of_public_versions_antitrust_04062015.pdf.

1417 See Order of the President of the General Court of 25 October 2018 in *Crédit agricole and Crédit agricole Corporate and Investment Bank v European Commission*, T-419/18 R, EU:T:2018:726, paragraph 48.

1418 See Order of the Vice-President of the Court of Justice of 10 September 2013 in *European Commission v Pilkington Group*, C-278/13 P(R), EU:C:2013:558, paragraph 42.

1419 Judgments of the Court of Justice of 14 March 2017 in *Evonik Degussa v European Commission*, C-162/15 P, EU:C:2017:205, paragraph 64, and of 19 June 2018 in *Bundesanstalt für Finanzdienstleistungsaufsicht v Ewald Baumeister*, C-15/16, EU:C:2018:464, paragraphs 54 and 56; and Opinion of Advocate General Szpunar of 21 July 2016 in *Evonik Degussa v European Commission*, C-162/15 P, EU:C:2016:587, paragraphs 131 to 134.

Any rebuttal of this presumption must be duly substantiated. Thus, the mere claim that the information is 'current' or 'indicative' of the applicant's current activity is not sufficient.[1420]

Sometimes it is the combination of given information and the identity of its provider that is particularly sensitive. Like in the context of access to the file,[1421] information providers' specific fears of reprisals or of other negative consequences of providing certain information to the European Commission may lead the European Commission to accord confidential treatment to: the identity of its provider; information that would reveal that identity[1422]; the substantive information provided; or to a combination of these types of information.[1423] Where the European Commission accepts information supplied on a purely voluntary basis, accompanied by a request for confidentiality in order to protect the informant's anonymity, it is in principle bound to comply with such a condition.[1424]

c. *Interests worthy of protection*

As mentioned above, the third of the three cumulative conditions of the general confidentiality test is that 'the interests liable to be harmed by disclosure must be worthy of protection. The assessment as to the confidentiality of a piece of information requires, in this regard, the individual legitimate interests opposing disclosure of the information to be weighed against the public interest that the activities of the [European Union] institutions take place as openly as possible'.

1420 See Order of the President of the General Court of 25 October 2018 in *JPMorgan Chase and Others v European Commission*, T-420/18 R, EU:T:2018:724, paragraph 87.

1421 See Commission Notice on the rules for access to the Commission file in cases pursuant to Articles 81 and 82 of the EC Treaty, Articles 53, 54 and 57 of the EEA Agreement and Council Regulation (EC) No 139/2004 [2005] OJ C325/7, amended by Communication from the Commission – Amendments to the Commission Notice on rules for access to the Commission file [2015] OJ C256/3, paragraph 19; and W. Wils and H. Abbott, 'Access to the File in Competition Proceedings before the European Commission' (2019) 42 *World Competition* 255, updated version accessible at http://ssrn.com/author=456087, text accompanied by footnotes 98 to 102.

1422 This might mean that information provided by others to the Commission must also be treated as confidential, even if the providers concerned did not request such treatment; see Judgments of the General Court of 28 April 1999 in *Endemol Entertainment v European Commission*, T-221/95, EU:T:1999:85, paragraph 70; and of 25 October 2002 in *Tetra Laval v European Commission*, T-5/02, EU:T:2002:264, paragraphs 99 to 101.

1423 See to that effect, Judgments the Court of Justice of 7 November 1985 in *Adams v European Commission*, 145/83, EU:C:1985:448, paragraphs 34, 35 and 37; of the General Court of 1 April 1993 in *BPB Industries and British Gypsum v European Commission*, T-65/89, EU:T:1993:31, paragraph 33, confirmed on appeal in Judgment of the Court of Justice of 6 April 1995 in *BPB Industries and British Gypsum v European Commission*, C-310/93 P, EU:C:1995:101, paragraphs 26 and 27; and Judgment of the Court of Justice of 22 October 2002 in *Roquette Frères*, C-94/00, EU:C:2002:603, paragraphs 62 to 66; of the General Court of 25 October 2002 in *Tetra Laval v European Commission*, T-5/02, EU:T:2002:264, paragraphs 98, 105 and 107; of 18 June 2008 in *Michelin v European Commission*, T-203/01, EU:T:2003:250, paragraphs 124 and 125; of 14 December 2005 in *General Electric v European Commission*, T-210/01, EU:T:2005:456, paragraphs 630, 650, 653, 663 and 666; and of 8 July 2008 in *BPB v European Commission*, T-53/03, EU:T:2008:254, paragraph 36.

1424 See Judgments of the Court of Justice of 7 November 1985 in *Adams v European Commission*, 145/83, EU:C:1985:448, paragraph 34; of the General Court of 8 July 2004 in *Mannesmannröhren-Werke v Commission*, T-44/00, EU:T:2004:218, paragraph 84, confirmed on appeal in Judgment of the Court of Justice of 25 January 2007 in *Salzgitter Mannesmann v European Commission*, C-411/04 P, EU:C:2007:54, paragraph 45; of the General Court of 8 July 2004 in *Dalmine v European Commission*, T-50/00, EU:T:2004:220, paragraph 72, confirmed on appeal in Judgment of the Court of Justice of 25 January 2007 in *Dalmine v European Commission*, C-407/04 P, EU:C:2007:53, paragraph 49; and of the General Court of 8 July 2008 in *BPB v European Commission*, T-53/03, EU:T:2008:254, paragraph 36.

This third condition thus in fact consists of two parts: *first*, the interests liable to be harmed must be worthy of protection (legitimate), and, *secondly*, even if this is the case, the legitimate interests opposing disclosure must be weighed against the interests justifying publication.[1425]

Addressees of decisions in which the European Commission found an infringement of Articles 101 and/or 102 TFEU have often tried to prevent the publication of the details of the infringement, as described in the decision, on the ground that the publication of such details would damage their reputation, affect their position in business relationships, and/or facilitate actions for damages by those who consider themselves harmed by the infringement.

Such claims for confidential treatment are most unlikely to succeed. Indeed, the EU Courts have made it very clear that 'the interest of an undertaking which the Commission has fined for an infringement of competition law in the details of the offending conduct of which it is accused not being disclosed to the public does not in principle warrant any particular protection, given the public interest in knowing as fully as possible the reasons behind any Commission action, the interest of the economic operators in knowing the sort of behaviour for which they are liable to be penalised and the interest of persons harmed by the infringement in being informed of the details thereof so that they may, where appropriate, assert their rights against the undertakings punished, and in view of the fact that the undertaking which has been fined may seek judicial review of such a decision'.[1426]

Invocation of the right to protection of private life guaranteed in Article 7 of the EU Charter of Fundamental Rights and in Article 8 of the European Convention on Human Rights (ECHR) does not alter this conclusion, since 'a person cannot, according to the well-established case law of the European Court of Human Rights, rely on Article 8 of the ECHR in order to complain of a loss of reputation which is the foreseeable consequence of his own actions, such as the commission of a criminal offence'.[1427]

Whether an interest is legitimate or worthy of protection may depend on who relies on it. Thus, whereas the European Commission itself may decide not to publish certain information in order to protect its investigations and the effectiveness of its enforcement of Articles 101 and 102 TFEU, private parties cannot claim confidentiality protection for information on the ground that its publication would harm the European Commission's investigations or the effectiveness of its enforcement of Articles 101 and 102 TFEU.[1428]

1425 See Judgment of the General Court of 28 January 2015 in *Akzo Nobel and Others v European Commission*, T-345/12, EU:T:2015:50, paragraph 79.

1426 Judgment of the General Court of 28 January 2015 in *Evonik Degussa v European Commission*, T-341/12, EU:T:2015:51, paragraph 107, referring to earlier judgments, and confirmed on appeal by Judgment of the Court of Justice of 14 March 2017 in *Evonik Degussa v European Commission*, C-162/15 P, EU:C:2017:205; see also Judgment of the General Court of 15 July 2015 in *Pilkington Group v European Commission*, T-462/12, EU:T:2015:508, paragraphs 67 to 71, and Article 5(5) of Directive 2014/14.

1427 Judgment of the General Court of 28 January 2015 in *Evonik Degussa v European Commission*, T-341/12, EU:T:2015:51, paragraph 125, referring to judgments of the European Court of Human Rights, and confirmed on appeal by Judgment of the Court of Justice of 14 March 2017 in *Evonik Degussa v European Commission*, C-162/15 P, EU:C:2017:205, paragraph 117.

1428 See Judgments of the General Court of 28 January 2015 in *Evonik Degussa v European Commission*, T-341/12, EU:T:2015:51, paragraphs 112 to 120, and of the Court of Justice of 14 March 2017 in *Evonik Degussa v European Commission*, C-162/15 P, EU:C:2017:205, paragraph 101.

Even if the interest or interests liable to be harmed by disclosure are worthy of protection, it is also required that those interests are not outweighed by the interests justifying publication. As explained above, the latter interests include the public interest in knowing as fully as possible the reasons behind any action by the European Commission, the interest of the economic operators in knowing the sort of behaviour for which they are liable to be penalised (and the corresponding public interest of ensuring compliance with Articles 101 and 102 TFEU), and the interest of persons harmed by the infringement in being informed about the details thereof so that they may assert their rights against the undertakings found to have committed that infringement.

The outcome of this weighing up of interests may be affected by the extent to which (the party claiming confidentiality protection has substantiated that) disclosure of the information concerned will cause serious harm. The extent to which disclosure of information is liable to cause serious harm may depend in turn on a combination of factors, such as, in the case of commercially sensitive information, how significant the information is in commercial terms for the undertaking providing the information and its usefulness for other market participants in the course of normal competition.[1429] On the other side, the balance may also be affected by the extent to which the piece of information is important for a proper understanding of the reasoning contained in the decision.

Finally, as already mentioned above, '[each] request for confidentiality must be assessed on its own merits',[1430] which means that the outcome of the weighing up of the competing interests may be different for each piece of information for which confidentiality protection is claimed.[1431]

4. Personal data

Article 16(1) TFEU and Article 8(1) of the EU Charter of Fundamental Rights provide that natural persons have the right to the protection of personal data concerning them.[1432]

The rules relating to the protection of natural persons with regard to the processing of personal data by the European Commission have been laid down in Regulation 2018/1725.[1433]

1429 See Order of the Vice-President of the Court of Justice of 10 September 2013 in *European Commission v Pilkington Group*, C-278/13 P(R), EU:C:2013:558, paragraph 42, and Order of the President of the General Court of 25 October 2018 in *Crédit agricole and Crédit agricole Corporate and Investment Bank v European Commission*, T-419/18 R, EU:T:2018:726, paragraph 48.

1430 Order of the President of the General Court of 25 October 2018 in *JPMorgan Chase and Others v European Commission*, T-420/18 R, EU:T:2018:724, paragraph 74, adding that thus, 'reasoning based exclusively on analogy cannot suffice'.

1431 See, by analogy, Order of the President of the Second Chamber of the General Court of 27 September 2017 in *Changmao Biochemical Engineering Co. v European Commission*, T-741/16, EU:T:2017:700, paragraph 20.

1432 The case law has clarified that companies have standing to seek protection of this right on behalf of their employees; see Judgment of the General Court of 15 July 2015 in *Pilkington Group v European Commission*, T-462/12, EU:T:2015:508, paragraph 81, reversing the opposite position earlier expressed in Judgment of the General Court of 30 May 2006 in *Bank Austria Creditanstalt v European Commission*, T-198/03, EU:T:2006:136, paragraphs 95 and 96; see also Judgment of the General Court of 5 October 2020 in *Les Mousquetaires and ITM Entreprises v European Commission*, EU:T:2020:460, paragraph 32.

1433 Regulation (EU) 2018/1725 of the European Parliament and of the Council of 23 October 2018 on the protection of natural persons with regard to the processing of personal data by the Union institutions, bodies, offices and agencies and on the free movement of such data, and repealing Regulation (EC) No 45/2001 and Decision No 1247/2002/EC [2018] OJ L313/39.

Article 3(1) of Regulation 2018/1725 defines 'personal data' as any information relating to an identified or identifiable natural person, and the definition of 'processing' in Article 3(3) covers disclosure by publication.

Under Article 5(1)(a) and (b) and (2) of Regulation 2018/1725, the processing of personal data by the European Commission is lawful if it is necessary for the performance of a task carried out in the public interest or in the exercise of official authority vested in the European Commission or necessary for compliance with a legal obligation, and the basis for the processing is laid down in EU law. Also under the 'data minimisation' principle laid down in Article 4(1)(c) of Regulation 2018/1725, personal data shall be limited to what is necessary in relation to the purposes for which they are processed.

As explained above, Article 30 of Regulation 1/2003, Article 1 TEU and the corresponding case law of the EU Courts provide the legal basis for the publication by the European Commission of its antitrust decisions. The question is thus to what extent the inclusion of personal data is necessary for such publication.

Inclusion of personal data in the published decision would most obviously be necessary if a natural person were the addressee, or one of the addressees, of the decision, as Article 30(2) of Regulation 1/2003 requires that the publication shall state the names of the parties.[1434] However, this situation almost never occurs: in practice decisions are always addressed to companies or other legal persons.[1435]

Even if the addressees of the decision are companies or other legal persons, the decision is likely to contain information allowing the identification of natural persons. Indeed, given the obligation for the European Commission to adequately reason its decisions

---

1434 The antitrust prohibitions contained in Articles 101 and 102 TFEU are addressed to undertakings and associations of undertakings. The concept of undertaking in that context must be understood as designating an economic unit, even if in law that economic unit consists of several persons, natural or legal; see Judgments of the Court of Justice of 10 September 2009 in *Akzo Nobel and Others v European Commission*, C-97/08 P, EU:C:2009:536, paragraphs 54 and 55 and of 18 July 2013 in *Schindler Holding and Others v European Commission*, C-501/11 P, EU:C:2013:522, paragraph 102.
However, decisions by the European Commission ordering termination of infringements or imposing fines can only be addressed to persons, not least because such decisions must be enforced; see Opinion of Advocate General Kokott of 23 April 2009 in *Akzo Nobel NV and Others v European Commission*, C-97/08 P, EU:C:2009:262, paragraph 37, and Article 299 TFEU. The European Commission therefore addresses its decisions to the person or persons to whom the conduct of the undertaking can be imputed, typically a parent company and one or more of its subsidiaries.
If the undertaking infringing Articles 101 or 102 TFEU were found to consist of an unincorporated business (a single trader, with or without employees, who has not incorporated her business, or a professional exercising her profession alone and unincorporated, or several natural persons operating a single business without any employment relationship between them and without any form of legal person), the European Commission would necessarily have to address its decision to the natural person or persons operating the business.

1435 In the *Pre-Insulated Pipes* case, one of the undertakings fined for participation in the cartel was controlled and managed by a natural person, Dr W. H., but the European Commission appears to have made an effort to avoid imposing the fine on him, identifying instead a collection of companies which it held jointly and severally liable for the fine; see recitals 157–160 and Article 3(d) of the Decision of the European Commission of 21 October 1998, *Pre-Insulated Pipe Cartel* [1999] OJ L24/1, and paragraph 105 of the Judgment of the General Court of 20 March 2002 in *HFB and Others v European Commission*, T-9/99, EU:T:2002:70, in which the General Court found that the European Commission had 'intentionally' not established Dr H.'s liability. See also Judgment of the Court of Justice of 2 October 2003 in *Siderúrgica Aristrain Madrid v European Commission*, C-196/99 P, EU:C:2003:529, paragraphs 91 and 101.

finding an infringement of Articles 101 or 102 TFEU,[1436] such decisions may mention the names of representatives or employees of the companies concerned or at least contain information allowing the identification of such individuals.[1437]

For the purposes of the publication of the decision, however, the inclusion of the names of representatives or employees of the companies concerned is, in most cases, not necessary. The general policy of the European Commission is therefore to remove such names from the published decision, and to replace them with a more general description, for instance by referring to 'Mr X' or 'one of the company's representatives'.[1438] In some cases, though, the inclusion of a natural person's specific function within the company may be necessary for the proper understanding of the published decision.[1439]

In any event, as has been recognised in the case law, 'where the Commission publishes a decision addressed to an undertaking which has taken part with its competitors in a cartel, the customers of the undertaking concerned will necessarily deduce that some of that undertaking's employees were parties to the discussions under investigation and/or concluded the agreements under investigation. It is equally inevitable that those same customers will assume that the employees concerned are those responsible for commercial relations with them. The customers will make those deductions even if the Commission publishes an extremely summary version of its decision, containing solely the names of the addressees, a reference to the products concerned and a general description of the infringement. Consequently, the applicant cannot request that references to its customers be omitted from the published version of the [. . .] decision on the ground that those customers would be able to deduce the names of the natural persons who took part in the anticompetitive arrangements'.[1440]

5. Information obtained through the European Commission's leniency programme; the protection of the effectiveness of the leniency programme and the facilitation of follow-on actions for damages

The European Commission has a leniency programme, under which it grants immunity from fines, or a reduction in fines, to participants in a secret cartel that cooperate with

1436 See Article 296 TFEU and Article 41(1)(c) of the EU Charter of Fundamental Rights.

1437 See Order of the President of the General Court of 8 June 2009 in *Z v European Commission*, T-173/09 R, EU:T:2009:180, paragraphs 25 and 26.

1438 See Order of the President of the General Court of 8 June 2009 in *Z v European Commission*, T-173/09 R, EU:T:2009:180, paragraphs 19 and 20; paragraph 22(a) of the 'Guidance on the preparation of public versions of Commission Decisions adopted under Articles 7 to 10, 23 and 24 of Regulation 1/2003', made available on 4 June 2015 on the website of the European Commission's Directorate-General for Competition https://ec.europa.eu/competition/antitrust/guidance_on_preparation_of_public_versions_antitrust_04062015.pdf; and A. ter Heegde and K. Todorova-Milanova, 'Publication of Antitrust Decisions and Other Documents', in E. Rousseva (ed), *EU Antitrust Procedure* (Oxford 2020), paragraph 17.32.
If it thus becomes impossible to identify a specific individual, there is obviously no problem anymore of protection of personal data; see Order of the President of the General Court of 25 October 2018 in *JPMorgan Chase and Others v European Commission*, T-420/18 R, EU:T:2018:724, paragraph 81.

1439 See also A. ter Heegde and K. Todorova-Milanova, 'Publication of Antitrust Decisions and Other Documents', in E. Rousseva (ed), *EU Antitrust Procedure* (Oxford 2020), paragraph 17.32.

1440 Judgment of the General Court of 15 July 2015 in *Pilkington Group v European Commission*, T-462/12, EU:T:2015:508, paragraph 82.

its investigations by providing information about the cartel.[1441] The current version of this leniency programme is set out in the 2006 Leniency Notice.[1442]

In order to obtain immunity from fines, the immunity applicant must, among other conditions, provide the European Commission with a leniency corporate statement,[1443] which must include, in so far as it is known to the applicant at the time of the submission, a detailed description of the cartel arrangement, as well as with other evidence relating to the alleged cartel in possession of the applicant or available to it at the time of the submission, including in particular any evidence contemporaneous to the infringement.[1444]

In order to obtain a reduction in fines, the leniency applicant must, among other conditions, provide the European Commission with evidence which represents significant added value compared to the evidence already in the European Commission's possession.[1445] The provision of such evidence may or may not include the provision of a leniency corporate statement.

The decisions of the European Commission in cartel cases often rely to a significant extent on information obtained through the leniency programme, and thus often extensively refer to, and quote from, both leniency corporate statements and other documents provided by leniency applicants.

The 2006 Leniency Notice, Regulation 773/2004 and Directive 2014/104 provide for special protection against the disclosure of leniency corporate statements (as opposed to other documents provided by leniency applicants).[1446]

This special protection against disclosure of leniency corporate statements does, however, as a rule not apply to the publication by the European Commission of its own decision, even if such decision contains information obtained from leniency corporate statements, because the publication of the European Commission's decision discloses only that decision, and the information contained in it, without involving the disclosure of any leniency corporate statement nor of any other document provided to the European Commission under the leniency programme.[1447]

1441 See Chapter V of this book.

1442 Commission Notice on Immunity from fines and reduction of fines in cartel cases [2006] OJ C298/11, as amended by Communication from the Commission Amendments to the Commission Notice on Immunity from fines and reduction of fines in cartel cases [2015] OJ C256/1 ('2006 Leniency Notice').

1443 The term 'leniency corporate statement' is defined in Article 4a of Commission Regulation (EC) No 773/2004 of 7 April 2004 relating to the conduct of proceedings by the Commission pursuant to Articles 81 and 82 of the EC Treaty [2004] OJ L123/18, as amended by Commission Regulation (EU) 2015/1348 of 3 August 2015 [2015] OJ L208/3, as a 'voluntary presentation of [the undertaking's] knowledge of a secret cartel and [its] role therein, which may also be in the form of voluntary presentations of the knowledge of former or current employees or representatives of the undertaking', 'drawn up specifically for submission to the Commission with a view to obtaining immunity from or reduction of fines under the Commission's leniency programme'.

1444 Points 9 and 11 of the 2006 Leniency Notice.

1445 Point 24 of the 2006 Leniency Notice.

1446 Points 33, 35, 35a, and 40 of the 2006 Leniency Notice; Articles 4a(3), 15(1b) and 16a(2) of Regulation 773/2004; and Article 2(16) and (17) and Articles 6(6)(a) and 7(1) of Directive 2014/104.

1447 See, to that effect, Judgments of the General Court of 28 January 2015 in *Evonik Degussa v European Commission*, T-341/12, EU:T:2015:51, paragraph 93, and of the Court of Justice of 14 March 2017 in *Evonik Degussa v European Commission*, C-162/15 P, EU:C:2017:205, paragraphs 89 to 97.

The only leniency-related confidentiality protection that can be invoked by leniency applicants in the context of the publication of decisions of the European Commission, concerns the publication of verbatim quotations from leniency corporate statements, which is not permitted.[1448]

For information in a decision to qualify as a verbatim quotation from a leniency corporate statement, and hence to be confidential and covered by the obligation of professional secrecy, two cumulative conditions must be fulfilled: first, the information must be taken word for word from a leniency corporate statement (verbatim), and, secondly, the way in which the information is presented in the decision must be such that the source of the information can be identified (quotation).[1449]

Where a decision contains such a verbatim quotation, the European Commission can thus fulfil its obligation not to publish the verbatim quotation either by redacting the verbatim information from the decision to be published, or by making other redactions which have the effect that the source of the verbatim information can no longer be identified, or through some combination of both.

Apart from the exception for verbatim quotations, addressees of cartel decisions that have submitted information as leniency applicants do not have any right to prevent the European Commission from publishing the full content of its decision on the ground that the decision contains information obtained through the leniency programme.[1450]

In the exercise of its discretion to publish only the main content of the decision or also other content of the decision, the European Commission itself may decide to redact from the published version of its cartel decisions not only verbatim quotations but also other information, so as to (further) protect the effectiveness of its leniency programme.

Whereas the European Commission is free to do so, private parties, however, cannot rely on the need to protect the effectiveness of the leniency programme to seek confidentiality protection.[1451]

Whereas the European Commission is free, in the exercise of its discretion, to redact from the published version of its cartel decisions not only verbatim quotations but also other information, so as to (further) protect the effectiveness of its leniency programme,

---

1448 See Judgment of the Court of Justice of 14 March 2017 in *Evonik Degussa v European Commission*, C-162/15 P, EU:C:2017:205, paragraphs 87, 97, 109 and 110; see also the sixth and seventh sentences of recital 26 of Directive 2014/104.

1449 See, to that effect, Judgment of the Court of Justice of 14 March 2017 in *Evonik Degussa v European Commission*, C-162/15 P, EU:C:2017:205, paragraph 109, and Opinion of Advocate General Szpunar of 21 July 2016 in *Evonik Degussa v European Commission*, C-162/15 P, EU:C:2016:587, paragraphs 123 to 125.

1450 See, to that effect, Judgments of the General Court of 28 January 2015 in *Evonik Degussa v European Commission*, T-341/12, EU:T:2015:51, paragraphs 68 to 175, and of 15 July 2015 in *AGC Glass Europe and Others v European Commission*, T-465/12, EU:T:2015:505, paragraphs 62 to 73, and of the Court of Justice of 14 March 2017 in *Evonik Degussa v European Commission*, C-162/15 P, EU:C:2017:205, paragraphs 72 to 120, and of 26 July 2017 in *AGC Glass Europe and Others v European Commission*, C-517/15 P, EU:C:2017:598, paragraphs 66 to 89.

1451 See Judgments of the General Court of 28 January 2015 in *Evonik Degussa v European Commission*, T-341/12, EU:T:2015:51, paragraphs 112 to 120, and of the Court of Justice of 14 March 2017 in *Evonik Degussa v European Commission*, C-162/15 P, EU:C:2017:205, paragraph 101.

it is equally free only to redact verbatim quotations, so as to facilitate follow-on actions for damages. This discretion is not affected in any way by the fact that access to other leniency information than (leniency corporate statements and) verbatim quotations could also be granted by the national courts dealing with the follow-on actions for damages.[1452]

Again, it is for the European Commission, and the European Commission alone, to weigh up, in the circumstances of the case, the effectiveness of its leniency programme, on the one hand, and the interest of the public and economic operators in being aware of the content of its decision in order to protect their rights, on the other.[1453]

Finally, the European Commission is also free to alter over time its policy and practice in this respect, including through successive publications of the same decision, if after having first published a version of its decision containing less information it later decides to publish a second version containing more information.[1454]

6. The right to judicial review, the presumption of innocence, and the particular circumstances of the Pergan Judgment

Pursuant to the fourth subparagraph of Article 263 TFEU, Article 256(1) TFEU and Article 47 of the EU Charter of Fundamental Rights, addressees of antitrust decisions of the European Commission have the right to bring an action for annulment of the decision before the General Court, as well as a subsequent appeal on points of law only before the Court of Justice.

Article 278 TFEU provides that actions brought before the EU Courts do not have suspensory effect. However, in the course of an action for annulment or of an appeal pending before it, both EU Courts can order interim measures pursuant to Articles 278 and/or 279 TFEU.

It is clear from the case law of EU Courts that the judicial review of the decision, on the one hand, and the publication of that decision, on the other hand, are two quite separate things.

If an addressee of a decision wants to question the legality of the decision, this can only be done through an action for annulment against the decision (including a subsequent appeal). The publication procedure does not serve to correct any illegalities that may affect the decision itself.[1455]

1452 See, to that effect, Judgment of the General Court of 15 July 2015 in *Pilkington Group v European Commission*, T-462/12, EU:T:2015:508, paragraph 88.

1453 See Judgments of the General Court of 28 January 2015 in *Evonik Degussa v European Commission*, T-341/12, EU:T:2015:51, paragraphs 119, and of the Court of Justice of 14 March 2017 in *Evonik Degussa v European Commission*, C-162/15 P, EU:C:2017:205, paragraph 101.

1454 See, to that effect, Judgments of the General Court of 28 January 2015 in *Evonik Degussa v European Commission*, T-341/12, EU:T:2015:51, paragraphs 151 to 163, of 15 July 2015 in *Pilkington Group v European Commission*, T-462/12, EU:T:2015:508, paragraphs 75 to 78, and of the Court of Justice of 14 March 2017 in *Evonik Degussa v European Commission*, C-162/15 P, EU:C:2017:205, paragraph 101. On the (historically evolving) relationship between leniency and private enforcement more generally, see further Chapters V, XVII and XVIII of this book.

1455 See, to that effect, Judgment of the General Court of 12 October 2007 in *Pergan Hilfsstoffe für industrielle Prozesse v European Commission*, T-474/04, EU:T:2007:306, paragraph 66.

Furthermore, given that actions before the EU Courts do not have suspensory effect, and that decisions of the European Commission are presumed to be valid unless and until they have been declared void by the EU Courts, the fact that an addressee of the decision has brought before the General Court an action for annulment of the decision (including a subsequent appeal before the Court of Justice) that is still pending does not in any way prevent the publication of the decision, unless the General Court or Court of Justice were to have ordered, by way of interim measures in the course of the action for annulment of the decision (including a subsequent appeal before the Court of Justice), that the decision cannot be published. Neither the fundamental right of access to a court nor the presumption of innocence leads to a different conclusion.[1456]

The Pergan Judgment of the General Court[1457] concerned a very particular case, in which the European Commission had found, and insisted that it had found, in its Organic Peroxides Cartel Decision[1458] that Pergan had infringed Article 101 TFEU by participating in the cartel,[1459] and had included in the recitals of the Organic Peroxides Cartel Decision extensive language to that effect,[1460] but had made it impossible for Pergan to bring an application for annulment against that decision because it had not included Pergan in the operative part of the decision.[1461]

In those very particular circumstances, the General Court held that the normal balance of interests (under which the public interest in knowing as fully as possible the reasons behind any action by the European Commission, the interest of the economic operators in knowing the sort of behaviour for which they are liable to be penalised and the interest of persons harmed by the infringement in being informed about the details thereof so that they may assert their rights against the undertakings punished outweigh the interest of the undertaking found to have infringed the competition rules in the non-disclosure to the public of the details of its infringement)[1462] did not apply.[1463] On

---

1456 See, to that effect, Order of the President of the General Court of 23 November 2017 in *Nexans France and Nexans v European Commission*, T-423/17 R, EU:T:2017:835, paragraphs 70 to 78, confirmed by Order of the Vice-President of the Court of Justice of 12 June 2018 in *Nexans France and Nexans v European Commission*, C-65/18 P(R), EU:C:2018:426; Order of the President of the General Court of 25 October 2018 in *JPMorgan Chase and Others v European Commission*, T-420/18 R, EU:T:2018:724, paragraphs 29 to 51; Order of the President of the General Court of 25 October 2018 in *Crédit agricole and Crédit agricole Corporate and Investment Bank v European Commission*, T-419/18 R, EU:T:2018:726, paragraphs 33 to 67; and Order of the Vice-President of the Court of Justice of 21 March 2019 in *Crédit agricole and Crédit agricole Corporate and Investment Bank v European Commission*, C-4/19 P(R), EU:C:2019:229, paragraphs 32 to 42; as well as Judgment of the General Court of 8 July 2020 in *VQ v European Central Bank*, T-203/18, EU:T:2020:313, paragraphs 122 and 124.

1457 Judgment of the General Court of 12 October 2007 in *Pergan Hilfsstoffe für industrielle Prozesse v European Commission*, T-474/04, EU:T:2007:306 ('Pergan Judgment').

1458 Commission Decision of 10 December 2003 relating to a proceeding under Article 81 of the EC Treaty and Article 53 of the EEA Agreement – Case COMP/E-2/37.857 Organic Peroxide, non-confidential version (redacted following the *Pergan* Judgment) accessible at https://ec.europa.eu/competition/antitrust/cases/index.html.

1459 See Pergan Judgment, paragraphs 72 and 73, as well as paragraph 19 (mentioning that, in a letter of 28 June 2004 informing Pergan of the intention to publish the decision, the European Commission 'stated that in that decision, the Commission had concluded that the applicant had committed an infringement of [Article 101 TFEU]').

1460 See Pergan Judgment, paragraph 12.

1461 See Pergan Judgment, paragraphs 11 and 19.

1462 See Pergan Judgment, paragraph 72.

1463 Pergan Judgment, paragraph 73.

the contrary, in those circumstances, Pergan's interest in the respect for its fundamental right to the presumption of innocence (under which every person is presumed to be innocent until her guilt has been established according to law) weighed against the publication of the recitals in the Organic Peroxides Cartel Decision describing Pergan's participation in the infringement, and this interest was not outweighed by any interest justifying publication.[1464]

Following the Pergan Judgment, addressees of antitrust decisions of the European Commission have tried to extend the logic of the Pergan Judgment to situations other than the very particular circumstances of the Pergan Judgment. It is, however, far from clear that the Pergan Judgment can be extended to any situation other than the very particular circumstances of that case.

Indeed, as the vice-president of the Court of Justice has pointed out:

> 'it does not in any way follow from the judgment of 12 October 2007, *Pergan Hilfsstoffe für industrielle Prozesse v Commission* (T-474/04, EU:T:2007:306) that the General Court established a general principle according to which the Commission can publish findings on, or in particular make any allusion to the liability of, a person only if that person has been able to enjoy all the usual guarantees accorded for the exercise of the rights of the defence.
>
> In that regard, it is necessary to note the particular circumstances in the case giving rise to that judgment, in which the Commission had published a decision in which it concluded that an undertaking had participated in an infringement of EU competition law without mentioning that participation in the operative part of that decision. Accordingly, the undertaking concerned did not have standing to bring proceedings against the Commission's decision and, consequently, was entirely unable to contest the substance of the findings referring to an infraction concerning it set out in the grounds of that decision.'[1465]

For instance, it is quite common that the recitals of cartel decisions of the European Commission include factual descriptions of behaviour outside the temporal, geographic or product scope for which an infringement is found in the operative part of the decision.

The case law has consistently recognised (both before and after the Pergan Judgment) that the inclusion of such factual descriptions in the recitals of the decision is legitimate, as they explain the factual and historical context of the infringement as found in the operative part of the decision.[1466]

1464 Pergan Judgment, paragraphs 75 to 80.

1465 See Order of the Vice-President of the Court of Justice of 21 March 2019 in *JPMorgan Chase and Others v European Commission*, C-1/19 P(R), EU:C:2019:230, paragraphs 23 and 24.

1466 Judgments of the General Court of 30 May 2006 in *Bank Austria Creditanstalt v European Commission*, T-198/03, EU:T:2006:136, paragraphs 81 to 91, and of 22 March 2012 in *Slovak Telekom v European Commission*, T-458/09 and T-171/10, EU:T:2012:145, paragraphs 50 and 51; and Orders of the President of the General Court of 25 October 2018 in *JPMorgan Chase and Others v European Commission*, T-420/18 R, EU:T:2018:724, paragraph 36, and in *Crédit agricole and Crédit agricole Corporate and Investment Bank v European Commission*, T-419/18 R, EU:T:2018:726, paragraph 37.

Addressees of antitrust decisions of the European Commission have argued in a number of cases that it would follow from the Pergan Judgment that such factual descriptions of behaviour outside the temporal, geographic or product scope of the finding of infringement in the operative part of the decision must be redacted from the published version of the decision, because applications for annulment of a decision can only be directed against the operative part of the decision and the recitals constituting necessary support for the operative part.[1467] In some cases, such arguments have also been accepted.[1468]

Such extensive application of the Pergan Judgment beyond the particular circumstances of that case appears mistaken, however.[1469] Indeed, the inclusion in the recitals of a decision of factual descriptions of behaviour outside the temporal, geographic or product scope of the finding of infringement in the operative part of the decision does not amount to a finding or an allusion of liability, and hence cannot constitute a violation of the presumption of innocence. On the contrary, their exclusion from the finding of infringement in the operative part makes it precisely clear that such factual descriptions are **not** findings of, or allusions to, liability, but merely provide factual context.[1470] The fact that the addressees of the decision can only bring an application for annulment against the operative part of the decision and the recitals constituting necessary support for the operative part does not preclude publication, because the presumption of innocence does not require the possibility of bringing an action for annulment against recitals that constitute neither a finding of liability nor an allusion to liability.[1471]

1467 See Judgment of the General Court of 17 September 1992 in *Nederlandse Bankiersvereniging and Nederlandse Vereniging van Banken v European Commission*, T-138/89, EU:T:1992:95, paragraph 31.

1468 See, for instance, Judgment of the Court of Appeal of England and Wales of 14 October 2015 in *Air Canada and Others v Emerald Supplies Limited and Others* [2015] EWCA Civ 1024, paragraphs 57, 58 and 69.

1469 See Order of the President of the General Court of 25 October 2018 in *Crédit agricole and Crédit agricole Corporate and Investment Bank v European Commission*, T-419/18 R, EU:T:2018:726, paragraphs 40 to 44 and 61 to 68, confirmed on appeal by Order of the Vice-President of the Court of Justice of 21 March 2019 in *Crédit agricole and Crédit agricole Corporate and Investment Bank v European Commission*, C-4/19 P(R), EU:C:2019:229, paragraphs 14 to 23; see also Order of the President of the General Court of 25 October 2018 in *JPMorgan Chase and Others v European Commission*, T-420/18 R, EU:T:2018:724, paragraphs 54 to 59, confirmed on appeal by Order of the Vice-President of the Court of Justice of 21 March 2019 in *JPMorgan Chase and Others v European Commission*, C-1/19 P(R), EU:C:2019:230.

1470 See in particular Order of the President of the General Court of 25 October 2018 in *Crédit agricole and Crédit agricole Corporate and Investment Bank v European Commission*, T-419/18 R, EU:T:2018:726, paragraph 65, confirmed on appeal by Order of the Vice-President of the Court of Justice of 21 March 2019 in *Crédit agricole and Crédit agricole Corporate and Investment Bank v European Commission*, C-4/19 P(R), EU:C:2019:229, paragraph 20.

1471 The fact that the recitals are not necessary support for the operative part of the decision also means that those recitals are not covered by the binding effect that the decision of the European Commission has in follow-on actions for damages before national courts pursuant to the *Masterfoods* case law and Article 16(1) of Regulation 1/2003; see Explanatory Memorandum of the European Commission's legislative proposal for what became Regulation 1/2003, COM(2000)582 final 2000/0243(CNS) of 27 September 2000, at 24 ('The potential for conflict depends on the operative part of the Commission decision and the facts on which it is based.'); Judgment of the United Kingdom Competition Appeal Tribunal of 4 March 2020 in *Royal Mail Group v DAF Trucks and Others* [2020] CAT 7; and, by analogy, sixth sentence of recital 34 of Directive 2014/104/EU of the European Parliament and of the Council of 26 November 2014 on certain rules governing actions for damages under national law for infringements of the competition law provisions of the Member States and of the European Union [2014] OJ L349/1 ('The effect of the finding should, however, cover only the nature of the infringement and its material, personal, temporal and territorial scope as determined by the competition authority [. . .].').

As explained above, the situation in the Pergan Judgment was very different indeed.[1472] In that case, the European Commission had found, and insisted that it had found, in its Organic Peroxides Cartel Decision[1473] that Pergan had infringed Article 101 TFEU by participating in the cartel,[1474] and had included in the recitals of the Organic Peroxides Cartel Decision extensive language to that effect,[1475] but had made it impossible for Pergan to bring an application for annulment against that decision by not including Pergan in the operative part of the decision.

7. Legitimate expectations

According to the case law of the EU Courts, the principle of legitimate expectations is a fundamental principle of EU law. Any person whom an institution of the European Union has led to entertain legitimate expectations may rely on the principle of legitimate expectations, if that individual has been given precise, unconditional and consistent assurances, from authorised, reliable sources.[1476]

However, companies cannot have a legitimate expectation that an existing situation that is capable of being altered within the limits of the discretionary power of the European Commission will be maintained.[1477]

As explained above, except for information that is confidential and hence covered by the obligation of professional secrecy, the European Commission has a wide discretion: it is free to publish not only the main content of the decision, but also other content of the decision, or indeed the full text of the decision.

It follows that, for information that is not confidential, undertakings cannot rely on the principle of legitimate expectations when the European Commission changes its practice and publishes more information than previously.[1478]

1472 See also Order of the President of the General Court of 25 October 2018 in *Crédit agricole and Crédit agricole Corporate and Investment Bank v European Commission*, T-419/18 R, EU:T:2018:726, paragraphs 37 and 63; Order of the President of the General Court of 25 October 2018 in *JPMorgan Chase and Others v European Commission*, T-420/18 R, EU:T:2018:724, paragraph 57; Order of the Vice-President of the Court of Justice of 21 March 2019 in *Crédit agricole and Crédit agricole Corporate and Investment Bank v European Commission*, C-4/19 P(R), EU:C:2019:229, paragraphs 18 and 21; and Order of the Vice-President of the Court of Justice of 21 March 2019 in *JPMorgan Chase and Others v European Commission*, C-1/19 P(R), EU:C:2019:230, paragraphs 23 and 24.

1473 Commission Decision of 10 December 2003 relating to a proceeding under Article 81 of the EC Treaty and Article 53 of the EEA Agreement – Case COMP/E-2/37.857 Organic Peroxide, non-confidential version (redacted following the *Pergan* Judgment) accessible at https://ec.europa.eu/competition/antitrust/cases/index.html.

1474 See Pergan Judgment, paragraphs 19 (finding that, in a letter of 28 June 2004 informing Pergan of the intention to publish the decision, the European Commission had 'stated that in that decision, the Commission had concluded that the applicant had committed an infringement of [Article 101 TFEU]') 72 and 73.

1475 See Pergan Judgment, paragraph 12.

1476 See Judgment of the General Court of 29 April 2004 in *Tokai Carbon and Others v European Commission*, T-236/01, EU:T:2004:118, paragraph 152, and the case law referred to therein.

1477 See Judgment of the General Court of 28 January 2015 in *Evonik Degussa v European Commission*, T-341/12, EU:T:2015:51, paragraph 153, and the case law referred to therein.

1478 See Judgments of the General Court of 28 January 2015 in *Evonik Degussa v European Commission*, T-341/12, EU:T:2015:51, paragraphs 151 to 164, and of 15 July 2015 in *Pilkington Group v European Commission*, T-462/12, EU:T:2015:508, paragraphs 75 to 78.

8. Equal treatment

The principle of equal treatment or principle of non-discrimination is a general principle of EU law, which requires that comparable situations must not be treated differently and different situations must not be treated alike unless such treatment is objectively justified.[1479]

The comparability of different situations must be assessed with regard to all the elements which characterise them. Those elements must, in particular, be determined and assessed in the light of the subject matter and purpose of the EU act which makes the distinction in question. The principles and objectives of the field to which the act relates must also be taken into account.[1480]

As to the publication of antitrust decisions of the European Commission, as explained above, except for information that is confidential and hence covered by the obligation of professional secrecy, the European Commission has a wide discretion: it is free to publish not only the main content of the decision, but also other content of the decision, or indeed the full text of the decision.

It follows that, for information that is not confidential, undertakings cannot rely on the principle of equal treatment to stop the European Commission from changing its practice and publishing more information than under its previous practice.[1481]

C. Procedure and timing

Following the adoption by the European Commission of a decision the publication of which is required under Article 30 of Regulation 1/2003, the European Commission, through its Directorate-General for Competition, will, pursuant to Article 16(3) of Regulation 773/2004, require the addressees of that decision, within a set time limit, to

(a) Identify any part of the decision, the summary of the decision, the opinion of the Advisory Committee and the final report of the Hearing Officer which they claim to be confidential and to substantiate each claim for confidentiality;

(b) Provide a non-confidential version of the decision, in which the confidential passages are deleted; and

(c) Provide a concise description of each piece of deleted information.[1482]

1479 See Judgment of the Court of Justice of 19 December 2019 in *HK v European Commission*, C-460/18 P, EU:C:2019:1119, paragraph 66.

1480 See Judgment of the Court of Justice of 19 December 2019 in *HK v European Commission*, C-460/18 P, EU:C:2019:1119, paragraph 67.

1481 See Judgments of the General Court of 15 July 2015 in *Pilkington Group v European Commission*, T-462/12, EU:T:2015:508, paragraphs 75 to 77, and of 28 January 2015 in *Evonik Degussa v European Commission*, T-341/12, EU:T:2015:51, paragraph 164.

1482 According to Article 16(4) of Regulation 773/2004, failure to comply with such a request within the set time limit allows the European Commission to assume that the decision does not contain any confidential information of the addressee concerned.
See also paragraphs 17 to 19 and 23 and 24 of the 'Guidance on the preparation of public versions of Commission Decisions adopted under Articles 7 to 10, 23 and 24 of Regulation 1/2003', made available on 4 June 2015 on the website of the European Commission's Directorate-General for Competition https://ec.europa.eu/competition/antitrust/guidance_on_preparation_of_public_versions_antitrust_04062015.pdf.

If no agreement can be reached between the interested person and the Directorate-General for Competition as to which parts of the decision are confidential,[1483] the Directorate-General for Competition will, pursuant to Article 8(1) to (3) of Decision 2011/695/EU, set a time limit within which the interested person can, through a reasoned request,[1484] refer the matter to the European Commission's Hearing Officer for decision.[1485]

The Hearing Officer is only empowered to decide to the extent that there is disagreement between the interested person and the Directorate-General for Competition. If the Directorate-General for Competition agrees with the interested person that certain information in the decision should not be published (either because it considers that the information is confidential, or in the exercise of the European Commission's discretion not to publish information the publication of which is not mandatory under Article 30(2) of Regulation 1/2003), that position is final.[1486]

The Hearing Officer's competence covers any objection based on a ground, arising from rules or principles of EU law, relied on by the interested person in order to claim protection of the confidentiality of the contested information,[1487] as well as whether there is an overriding interest in its disclosure.[1488]

If the Hearing Officer agrees with the interested person that the contested information is confidential and that there is no overriding interest in its publication, the Hearing Officer's decision is final.

If the Hearing Officer considers that the information is not confidential or that there is an overriding interest in its publication, the Hearing Officer will adopt on behalf of the European Commission a reasoned decision, which will be notified to the interested person, and which must specify the date after which the information may be published, which must be at least one week from the date of notification.[1489]

1483 See Article 3(7) of Decision 2011/695/EU of the President of the European Commission of 13 October 2011 on the function and terms of reference of the hearing officer in certain competition proceedings [2011] OJ L275/29.

1484 As mentioned above, 'the burden of proof [. . .], in respect of confidential treatment, is borne by the person requesting such treatment' (Judgment of the General Court of 28 January 2015 in *Evonik Degussa v European Commission*, T-341/12, EU:T:2015:51, paragraph 92) and '[any] request for confidentiality must be assessed on its own merits. Thus, reasoning based exclusively on analogy cannot suffice' (Order of the President of the General Court of 25 October 2018 in *JPMorgan Chase and Others v European Commission*, T-420/18 R, EU:T:2018:724, paragraph 74).

1485 See Chapter XI of this book.

1486 Judgment of the General Court of 15 July 2015 in *Pilkington Group v European Commission*, T-462/12, EU:T:2015:508, paragraphs 30 to 34.

1487 See Judgments of the Court of Justice of 14 March 2017 in *Evonik Degussa v Commission*, C-162/15 P, EU:C:2017:205, paragraphs 40 to 56, and of 26 July 2017 in *AGC Glass Europe and Others v Commission*, C-517/15 P, EU:C:2017:598, paragraphs 51 to 59.

1488 Article 8(2) of Decision 2011/695/EU.

1489 Article 8(2) of Decision 2011/695/EU.
Whereas the date to be specified in the decision of the Hearing Officer after which the publication can take place must thus be at least one week from the date of notification, it does not necessarily follow from Article 263 TFEU, or from Article 47 of the EU Charter of Fundamental Rights, that the date must be after the normal time limit of two months and ten days for bringing an action for annulment before the General Court; see, to that effect, Judgment of the General Court of 8 July 2020 in *VQ v European Central Bank*, T-203/18, EU:T:2020:313, paragraphs 102 to 106 and 112 to 124.

The interested person can then, pursuant to Article 263 TFEU, bring before the General Court an application for annulment of this decision adopted by the Hearing Officer on behalf of the European Commission. Article 278 TFEU provides that actions brought before the EU Courts do not have suspensory effect, but the interested person can, in addition to the application for annulment, request from the General Court a suspension of that decision or other interim measures pursuant to Articles 278 and 279 TFEU, with the possibility of a subsequent appeal before the Court of Justice.[1490]

Given the above procedure, 'it should be acknowledged that producing a non-confidential version of a Commission competition decision can take a certain amount of time'.[1491] The European Commission must, however, endeavour to publish its decisions 'in the shortest time possible and, in any event, within a reasonable time frame which must be established on the basis of the specific circumstances of each case. In that regard, it is necessary to take into consideration the [. . .] number of requests for confidentiality submitted by the undertakings concerned and the technical and legal complexity of those requests'.[1492]

Unless the confidentiality claims cover the entire decision, the European Commission should not wait until all the requests for confidentiality submitted by the undertakings concerned have been finally settled, but should rather already publish a provisional version of the decision excluding all information for which confidentiality has been requested.[1493]

D. Relationship with public access to documents under Regulation 1049/2001

As mentioned above, in mandating the publication by the European Commission of its main antitrust decisions, Article 30 of Regulation 1/2003 reflects the principle laid down in the second subparagraph of Article 1 TEU, according to which decisions are to be taken as openly as possible within the European Union.[1494]

1490 See, for example, Order of the President of the General Court of 23 November 2017 in *Nexans France and Nexans v European Commission*, T-423/17 R, EU:T:2017:835, Order of the Vice-President of the Court of Justice of 12 June 2018 in *Nexans France and Nexans v European Commission*, C-65/18 P(R), EU:C:2018:426; Order of the President of the General Court of 25 October 2018 in *Crédit agricole and Crédit agricole Corporate and Investment Bank v European Commission*, T-419/18 R, EU:T:2018:726, and Order of the Vice-President of the Court of Justice of 21 March 2019 in *Crédit agricole and Crédit agricole Corporate and Investment Bank v European Commission*, C-4/19 P(R), EU:C:2019:229; and Order of the President of the General Court of 25 October 2018 in *JPMorgan Chase and Others v European Commission*, T-420/18 R, EU:T:2018:724, and Order of the Vice-President of the Court of Justice of 21 March 2019 in *JPMorgan Chase and Others v European Commission*, C-1/19 P(R), EU:C:2019:230.

1491 Judgment of the General Court of 7 October 2014 in *Schenker v European Commission*, T-534/11, EU:T:2014:854, paragraph 129.

1492 Judgment of the General Court of 7 October 2014 in *Schenker v European Commission*, T-534/11, EU:T:2014:854, paragraph 130.

1493 See Judgment of the General Court of 7 October 2014 in *Schenker v European Commission*, T-534/11, EU:T:2014:854, paragraphs 136 to 141; paragraph 149 of the Notice on Best Practices; and paragraph 36 of the Working Arrangements for the Functioning of the Advisory Committee (Annex to the Communication to the Commission, Working Arrangements for the Functioning of the Advisory Committee on Restrictive Practices and Dominant Positions, C(2019)2310 final, 29 March 2019).

1494 Judgments of the General Court of 30 May 2006 in *Bank Austria Creditanstalt v European Commission*, T-198/03, EU:T:2006:136, paragraphs 69 and 78, and of 28 January 2015 in *Akzo Nobel and Others v European Commission*, T-345/12, EU:T:2015:50, paragraph 60.

This principle of openness, repeated in Article 15 TFEU, also constitutes the basis for the right of any citizen of the European Union, and any natural or legal person residing or having its registered office in an EU Member State, to have a right of access to documents of the institutions of the European Union.[1495] The detailed rules for the exercise of this right of public access have been laid down in Regulation 1049/2001.[1496]

Regulation 1049/2001 could also be used to seek access to antitrust decisions of the European Commission.

While there are some links between, on the one hand, publication of antitrust decisions pursuant to Article 30 of Regulation 1/2003, and, on the other hand, requests for public access to such decisions pursuant to Regulation 1049/2001, there are also clear differences.

A first link is that, if a document has been published, a request for public access to that document can be answered by providing the publication references.[1497]

A second link is that the time limits laid down in Regulation 1049/2001 are part of the reason why, as mentioned above, the European Commission must endeavour to publish its decisions in the shortest time possible and, in any event, within a reasonable time, and why, unless the confidentiality claims cover the entire decision, the European Commission should not wait until all the requests for confidentiality submitted by the undertakings concerned have been finally settled, but rather already publish a provisional version of the decision excluding all information for which confidentiality has been requested.[1498]

A first difference is that the case law of the EU Courts formulated on the basis of Regulation 1049/2001, according to which there is a general presumption capable of justifying the refusal to disclose documents in a file relating to a proceeding under Article 101 or 102 TFEU,[1499] cannot be transposed to publication of decisions pursuant to Article 30 of Regulation 1/2003, because such publication reflects not only the general principle of openness, but also specific considerations concerning the effectiveness of the application of EU competition law.[1500]

1495 Article 15(3) TFEU and Article 42 of the EU Charter of Fundamental Rights.

1496 Regulation (EC) No 1049/2001 of the European Parliament and of the Council of 30 May 2001 regarding public access to European Parliament, Council and Commission documents [2001] OJ L145/43.

1497 See Article 7 of the Detailed rules for the application of Regulation (EC) No 1049/2001 of the European Parliament and of the Council of 30 May 2001 regarding public access to European Parliament, Council and Commission documents, Annex to Commission Decision of 5 December 2001 amending its rules of procedure [2001] OJ L345/94.

1498 See Judgment of the General Court of 7 October 2014 in *Schenker v European Commission*, T-534/11, EU:T:2014:854, paragraphs 130 to 141.

1499 See Judgments of the Court of Justice of 27 February 2014 in *Commission v EnBW*, C-365/12 P, EU:C:2014:112, paragraphs 92, 93, 101 and 134, and of the General Court of 7 July 2015 in *Axa Versicherung v Commission*, T-677/13, EU:T:2015:473, paragraphs 39, 40, 42 and 94, of 28 March 2017 in *Deutsche Telekom v Commission*, T-210/15, EU:T:2017:224, paragraphs 30 to 32, 43, 44 and 46, and of 5 February 2018 in *Edeka-Handelsgesellschaft Hessenring v Commission*, T-611/15, EU:T:2018:63, paragraphs 68 to 74.

1500 See Judgment of the Court of Justice of 14 March 2017 in *Evonik Degussa v European Commission*, C-162/15 P, EU:C:2017:205, paragraphs 77 to 79.

A second difference is that, while, as mentioned above, for the publication of its decisions pursuant to Article 30 of Regulation 1/2003, the European Commission has delegated to its Hearing Officer the power to decide, subject to judicial review, on any objection based on a ground, arising from rules or principles of EU law, relied on by the interested person in order to claim protection of the confidentiality of the contested information, as well as whether there is an overriding interest in its disclosure, the Hearing Officer does not have any role in the application of Regulation 1049/2001.[1501]

[1501] See Detailed rules for the application of Regulation (EC) No 1049/2001 of the European Parliament and of the Council of 30 May 2001 regarding public access to European Parliament, Council and Commission documents, Annex to Commission Decision of 5 December 2001 amending its rules of procedure [2001] OJ L345/94, and Chapter XI of this book.

XVI. Re-adoption by the European Commission of Cartel Decisions Annulled on Procedural Grounds by the EU Courts

This chapter deals with the re-adoption by the European Commission of decisions imposing fines on undertakings found to have participated in cartels in violation of Article 101 TFEU (cartel decisions) following the annulment of those decisions by the EU Courts (General Court and Court of Justice) on procedural grounds. It gives an overview of cases in which such re-adoption has taken place and analyses the applicable legal principles and policy considerations.

A. Introduction: Commission decisions and their review by the EU Courts

The European Commission's main decisional powers are set out in Articles 7 and 23 of Regulation 1/2003.[1502] Article 7 empowers the European Commission to adopt decisions finding infringements of Article 101 TFEU and ordering the termination of such infringements. In cases concerning cartels, decisions pursuant to Article 7 are invariably combined with a decision pursuant to Article 23(2)(a), which empowers the Commission to impose fines to penalise the infringement found.

The procedural rules governing the Commission's administrative proceedings leading to cartel decisions are laid down in the EU Treaties and Charter of Fundamental Rights, Council Regulation 1,[1503] Council Regulation 1/2003, Commission Regulation 773/2004,[1504] various Commission notices or guidelines, and the case law of the EU Courts.[1505]

1502 Council Regulation (EC) No 1/2003 of 16 December 2002 on the implementation of the rules on competition laid down in Articles 81 and 82 of the Treaty [2003] OJ L1/1, last amended by Council Regulation (EC) No 1419/2006 [2006] OJ L269/1. For a detailed analysis of Regulation 1/2003, see K. Dekeyser, C. Gauer, J. Laitenberger, N. Wahl, W. Wils and L. Prete (eds), *Regulation 1/2003 and EU Antitrust Enforcement – A Systematic Guide* (Wolters Kluwer 2022).

1503 Council Regulation No 1 determining the languages to be used by the European Economic Community [1958] OJ 17/385 (Special English Edition 1952-58, p 59), last amended by Council Regulation (EU) No 517/2013 [2013] OJ L363/1.

1504 Commission Regulation (EC) No 773/2004 of 7 April 2004 relating to the conduct of proceedings by the Commission pursuant to Articles 81 and 82 of the EC Treaty [2004] OJ L123/18.

1505 See further E. Rousseva (ed), *EU Antitrust Procedure* (Oxford UP 2020) and L. Ortiz Blanco (ed), *EU Competition Procedure* (4th ed, Oxford UP 2021), and my papers 'EU Antitrust Enforcement Powers and Procedural Rights and Guarantees: The Interplay between EU Law, National Law, the Charter of Fundamental Rights of the EU and the European Convention On Human Rights' (2011) 34 *World Competition* 189, 5, also accessible at http://ssrn.com/author=456087, and Chapter X of this book.

Pursuant to Article 263 TFEU, the addressees of decisions adopted by the European Commission can bring an action for annulment of the decision before the EU Courts, more precisely before the General Court, with the possibility of a further appeal only on points of law before the Court of Justice.[1506]

According to the case law, 'the scope of judicial review provided for in Article 263 TFEU extends to all the elements of Commission decisions relating to proceedings applying Article 101 TFEU [. . .] which are subject to in-depth review by the General Court, in law and in fact, in the light of the pleas raised by the appellants [. . .] and taking into account all the evidence submitted by the latter, whether that evidence be presented prior to or after the decision taken, whether it was submitted previously in the context of the administrative procedure or, for the first time, in the context of the proceedings before the General Court, in so far as that evidence is relevant to the review of the legality of the Commission decision'.[1507]

One of the grounds for annulment listed in Article 263 TFEU is 'infringement of an essential procedural requirement'.[1508] Not every procedural irregularity thus constitutes a ground for annulment.[1509] A procedural irregularity in the administrative proceedings resulting in the Commission's decision will constitute a ground for the annulment of that decision 'only if the Court of Justice or the General Court finds that in the absence of the irregularity in question the contested [decision] might have been substantially different, that the irregularity makes judicial review impossible, or that, on account of the irregularity that it contains, the [decision] in question breaches a fundamental institutional rule'.[1510]

According to the case law, 'the EU Courts cannot, in the context of the review of legality referred to in Article 263 TFEU, substitute their own reasoning for that of [the Commission]'.[1511] If the application for annulment is well founded, the Court can thus

---

1506 See further K. Lenaerts, I. Maselis and K. Gutman, *EU Procedural Law* (Oxford UP 2014) and C. Naômé, *Appeals Before the Court of Justice of the European Union* (Oxford UP 2018), my paper 'The Increased Level of EU Antitrust Fines, Judicial review and the ECHR' (2010) 33 *World Competition* 5, also accessible at http://ssrn.com/author=456087, and Chapter IX of this book.

1507 Judgment in *Galp Energía España and Others v Commission*, C-603/13 P, EU:C:2016:38, at para 71.

1508 According to J. Schwartze, 'Judicial Review of European Administrative Procedure' (2004) 68 *Law and Contemporary Problems* 85 at 97, 'procedural infringements can hardly be classified as essential or unessential: what is meant, instead, is the essential or unessential infringement of the same provision'.

1509 A similar distinction between procedural irregularities that can or that cannot affect the substantive outcome can also be found in Article 58 of the Statute of the Court of Justice of the European Union, which limits appeals against judgments of the General Court on the ground of breaches of procedure before that court to breaches of procedure which adversely affect the interests of the appellant, and in Article 4(2) of Protocol No 7 to the European Convention on Human Rights, which allows for the reopening of criminal cases following a final acquittal or conviction where there has been a fundamental defect in the previous proceedings, which could affect the outcome of the case.

1510 K. Lenaerts, I. Maselis and K. Gutman, *EU Procedural Law* (Oxford UP 2014), at 371, with multiple references to judgments of the Court of Justice. See also Opinion of Advocate General Emiliou of 12 May 2022, *HSBC Holdings and Others v Commission*, C-883/19 P, EU:C:2022:384;paragraphs 38 to 62 Judgment in *Intel v Commission*, C-413/14 P, EU:C:2017:632, paragraphs 94 to 102; Judgment in *NKT Verwaltung and NKT v Commission*, C-607/18 P, EU:C:2020:385, paragraphs 56 and 57; Judgment of 12 January 2023, *HSBC Holdings and Others v Commission*, C-883/19 P, EU:C:2023:11, paragraphs 95 and 96

1511 Judgment in *Galp Energía España and Others v Commission*, C-603/13 P, EU:C:2016:38, paragraph 73.

not correct the Commission's decision, but must declare it void, as required by Article 264 TFEU, to the extent that the action is well founded.[1512] It is then for the Commission to draw the necessary consequences, as required by Article 266 TFEU.

An important exception to this impossibility for the Court to correct the Commission's decision concerns the determination of the amount of the fine. According to the case law:

'The review of legality is supplemented by the unlimited jurisdiction which the Courts of the European Union [are] afforded by [. . .] Article 31 of Regulation No 1/2003, in accordance with Article 261 TFEU. That jurisdiction empowers the Courts, in addition to carrying out a mere review of the lawfulness of the penalty, to substitute their own appraisal for the Commission's and, consequently, to cancel, reduce or increase the fine or penalty payment imposed.'[1513]

However, 'the scope of that unlimited jurisdiction is strictly limited, unlike the review of legality provided for in Article 263 TFEU, to determining the amount of the fine'.[1514]

B. Overview of re-adoption cases

By the end of 2020, the European Commission had re-adopted annulled cartel decisions in eleven cases:

1. PVC

The first re-adoption took place in July 1994 in the *PVC* case. The Commission had adopted an initial decision in December 1988, fining fourteen PVC producers for their participation in a cartel.[1515] In so far as it concerned twelve of these fourteen undertakings,[1516] this initial decision was annulled by the Court of Justice in June 1994 for infringement of an essential procedural requirement within the meaning of Article 173 EEC (now Article 263 TFEU) on the ground that the Commission had failed to carry out the authentication of its decision in accordance with the Commission's own Rules of Procedure.[1517] Six weeks after this annulment, without taking any further procedural steps, the Commission adopted the new decision, identical to the initial decision but now duly authenticated, addressed to the twelve undertakings for whom the first decision had been annulled.[1518] The twelve undertakings brought actions for annulment against the re-adopted decision, contesting in particular on various grounds the legality of such

---

1512 See Judgments in *Commission v Verhuizingen Coppens*, C-441/11 P, EU:C:2012:778, paragraphs 34 to 54, and in *Soliver v Commission*, T-68/09, EU:T:2014:867, paragraphs 107 to 113.

1513 Judgment in *Chalkor v Commission*, C-386/10 P, EU:C:2011:815, paragraph 63.

1514 Judgment in *Galp Energía España and Others v Commission*, C-603/13 P, EU:C:2016:38, paragraph 76.

1515 Commission Decision 89/190/EEC of 21 December 1988 relating to a proceeding pursuant to Article 85 of the EEC Treaty (IV/31.865 – *PVC*) [1989] OJ L74/1.

1516 One of the undertakings did not bring an application for annulment of the first decision, and another undertaking's application was declared inadmissible by the General Court as it was time-barred. For these two undertakings, the initial decision thus became final; see Judgment in *Commission v AssiDomän and Others*, C-310/97 P, EU:C:1999:407.

1517 Judgment in *Commission v BASF and Others*, C-137/92 P, EU:C:1994:247.

1518 Commission Decision 94/599/EC of 27 July 1994 relating to a proceeding pursuant to Article 85 of the EC Treaty (IV/31.865 – *PVC*) [1994] OJ L239/14. See also European Commission Press release IP/94/732 of 27 July 1994.

re-adoption. These actions were ultimately rejected by the Court of Justice in the *PVC II* Judgment of October 2002, the leading judgment on re-adoption of antitrust decisions.[1519]

2. Soda ash

The Commission re-adopted in December 2000 three decisions in the *Soda ash* cases. In December 1990, the Commission had adopted four decisions, imposing fines on Solvay and ICI for an infringement of Article 85 EEC, on Solvay and a German undertaking for another infringement of Article 85 EEC, on Solvay for an infringement of Article 86 EEC, and on ICI for an infringement of Article 86 EEC.[1520] Upon applications for annulment brought by Solvay and ICI, the General Court annulled in June 1995 the third and fourth decisions, as well as the second decision in so far as it concerned Solvay, on the same ground as the annulments of the initial decision in *PVC*, namely failure of authentication of the decisions.[1521] These annulments were confirmed on appeal by the Court of Justice in April 2000.[1522] Eight months later, without taking any further procedural steps, the Commission re-adopted the third and fourth decisions, as well as the second decision in so far as it concerned Solvay.[1523] Solvay brought applications for annulment against the two re-adopted decisions concerning it. After the General Court had upheld these two re-adopted decisions in December 2009,[1524] the Court of Justice annulled these decisions in October 2011, on the ground of infringement of the rights of the defence, in that Solvay had not been granted full access to the file during the administrative proceedings preceding both the initial and the re-adopted decisions.[1525] The Commission did not subsequently

---

1519 Judgment in *Limburgse Vinyl Maatschappij and Others v Commission*, C-238/99 P etc., EU:C:2002:582 ('*PVC II* Judgment'), confirming the Judgment of the General Court in *Limburgse Vinyl Maatschappij and Others v Commission*, T-305/94 etc., EU:T:1999:80.

1520 Commission Decision 91/297/EEC of 19 December 1990 relating to a proceeding under Article 85 of the EEC Treaty (IV/33.133–A: *Soda – Solvay, ICI*; OJ 1991 L 152/1), Commission Decision 91/298/EEC of 19 December 1990 relating to a proceeding under Article 85 of the EEC Treaty (IV/33.133-B: *Soda – Solvay, CFK*; OJ 1991 L 152/16), Commission Decision 91/299/EEC of 19 December 1990 relating to a proceeding under Article 86 of the EEC Treaty (IV/33.133 – *C: Soda – Solvay*; OJ 1991 L 152/21), and Commission Decision 91/300/EEC of 19 December 1990 relating to a proceeding under Article 86 of the EEC Treaty (IV/33.133–D: *Soda – ICI*; OJ 1991 L 152/40).

1521 Judgments in *Solvay v Commission*, T-32/91, EU:T:1995:117, in *ICI v Commission*, T-37/91, EU:T:1995:119, and in *Solvay v Commission*, T-31/91, EU:T:1995:116. The first decision was also annulled, but on a different ground, namely, infringement of the rights of the defence in that Solvay and ICI had not been granted full access to the file during the administrative procedure; see Judgments in *Solvay v Commission*, T-30/91, EU:T:1995:115 and in *ICI v Commission*, T-36/91, EU:T:1995:118. The German undertaking did not bring an action for annulment against the second decision, which thus became final in so far as it concerns that undertaking.

1522 Judgments in *Commission v ICI*, C-286/95 P, EU:C:2000:188, and in *Commission v Solvay*, C-287/95 P and C-288/95 P, EU:C:2000:189.

1523 Commission Decision 2003/6/EC of 13 December 2000 relating to a proceeding pursuant to Article 82 of the EC Treaty (Case COMP/33.133–C: *Soda ash – Solvay*; OJ 2003 L 10/10), Commission Decision 2003/7/EC of 13 December 2000 relating to a proceeding pursuant to Article 82 of the EC Treaty (Case COMP/33.133–D: *Soda ash – ICI*; OJ 2003 L 10/33) and Commission Decision 2003/5/EC of 13 December 2000 relating to a proceeding under Article 81 of the EC Treaty (COMP/33.133–B: *Soda ash – Solvay, CFK*; OJ 2003 L 10/1). See also European Commission Press release IP/00/1449 of 13 December 2000.

1524 Judgments in *Solvay v Commission*, T-57/01, EU:T:2009:519, and in *Solvay v Commission*, T-58/01, EU:T:2009:520. The General Court only slightly reduced the amounts of the fines.

1525 Judgments in *Solvay v Commission*, C-109/10 P, EU:C:2011:686, and in *Solvay v Commission*, C-110/10 P, EU:C:2011:687.

attempt to re-adopt a second time these twice annulled decisions. While the judgments of the Court of Justice in *Soda ash* do not dwell on the question of the re-adoption of decisions, the opinions of Advocate General Kokott are of interest in particular on the compatibility of re-adoptions with the fundamental right to have a matter adjudicated within a reasonable duration.[1526]

3. Steel beams (Arbed/Arcelor)

The Commission re-adopted in November 2006 a decision concerning one of the undertakings in the *Steel beams* case. In February 1994, the Commission had imposed fines on fourteen producers and distributors of steel beams for infringements of Article 65 ECSC, including a fine of ECU 11,200,000 on Arbed SA.[1527] Upon an action for annulment brought by Arbed SA, the General Court in March 1999 partially annulled the decision, on the ground that Arbed's participation in one of the infringements had not been established, and, in the exercise of its unlimited jurisdiction, fixed the amount of the fine at EUR 10,000,000.[1528] Upon appeal brought by Arbed SA, the Court of Justice in October 2003 annulled the entire decision in so far as it concerned Arbed SA, on the ground of violation of the rights of the defence, in that the statement of objections had not been addressed to Arbed SA but rather to its daughter company TradeArbed SA and had not indicated that a fine would be imposed on Arbed SA.[1529] Following this annulment, the Commission re-opened its proceedings as regards Arbed SA. It sent in March 2006 a statement of objections to Arcelor Luxembourg SA, the legal successor of Arbed SA, and two other Arcelor companies. In their responses to this statement of objections, the Arcelor companies did not contest the infringement as upheld by the General Court. The new decision imposed on the Arcelor companies the same fine of EUR 10,000,000 as fixed by the General Court.[1530] The Arcelor companies did not bring an application for annulment against this re-adopted decision.

4. Alloy surcharge (ThyssenKrupp)

The Commission re-adopted in December 2006 a decision concerning one of the undertakings in the *Alloy surcharge* case. In January 1998, the Commission had adopted an initial decision imposing fines on six stainless steel producers, including ThyssenKrupp Stainless, for an infringement of Article 65 ECSC.[1531] Upon an application for annulment brought by ThyssenKrupp Stainless, the General Court partially annulled the initial decision in so far as it held ThyssenKrupp Stainless responsible for the participation

---

1526 Opinions of Advocate General Kokott in *Solvay v Commission*, C-109/10 P, EU:C:2011:256, and in *Solvay v Commission*, C-110/10 P, EU:C:2011:257.

1527 Commission Decision 94/215/ECSC of 16 February 1994 relating to a proceeding pursuant to Article 65 of the ECSC Treaty concerning agreements and concerted practices engaged in by European producers of beams [1994] OJ L116/1. See also European Commission Press release IP/94/134 of 16 February 1994.

1528 Judgment in *Arbed SA v Commission*, T-137/94, EU:T:1999:46.

1529 Judgment in *Arbed SA v Commission*, C-176/99 P, EU:C:2003:524.

1530 Commission Decision of 8 November 2006 relating to a procedure under Article 65 of the ECSC Treaty in Case COMP/C.38.907 – *Steel beams* [2008] OJ C235/4. See also European Commission Press release IP/06/1527 of 8 November 2006.

1531 Commission Decision 98/247/ECSC of 21 January 1998 relating to a proceeding pursuant to Article 65 of the ECSC Treaty (Case IV.350814 – *Alloy surcharge*) [1998] OJ L100/55. See also European Commission Press release IP/98/70 of 21 January 1998.

of Thyssen Stahl in the cartel infringement, on the ground of violation of the rights of the defence, because the statement of objections preceding the initial decision had not indicated that ThyssenKrupp Stainless would also be held liable for Thyssen Stahl's participation in the cartel. The General Court furthermore, in the exercise of its unlimited jurisdiction, reduced by 20% (the remainder of) the fine imposed on ThyssenKrupp Stainless because of its cooperation with the Commission's investigation.[1532] Following this partial annulment, the Commission sent in April 2006 a new statement of objections to ThyssenKrupp Stainless and, after ThyssenKrupp Stainless had responded in writing and at an oral hearing, adopted in December 2006 a new decision, fining ThyssenKrupp Stainless for Thyssen Stahl's participation in the cartel. In this new decision, the Commission applied a 20% fine reduction identical to the reduction which the General Court had granted for the other part of ThyssenKrupp Stainless's fine.[1533] The application for annulment brought against this new decision was rejected by the EU Courts.[1534]

5. Reinforcing bars

The *Reinforcing bars* case is unique in that it has led to two successive re-adoptions, in September 2009 and in July 2019. In December 2002, the Commission had adopted an initial decision imposing fines on eight undertakings for taking part in a concrete reinforcing bar cartel in Italy, in violation of Article 65 ECSC.[1535] Upon applications for annulment by the eight undertakings, the General Court annulled in October 2007 this initial decision because the legal basis used in it, namely Article 65 ECSC, was no longer in force at the time of its adoption.[1536] Following this annulment, the Commission adopted in September 2009 a new, second decision, largely identical to the initial decision, but now with Articles 7 and 23(2) of Regulation 1/2003 as legal basis.[1537] All eight undertakings brought again applications for annulment against this second

---

1532 Judgment in *Krupp Thyssen Stainless and Acciai Speciali Terni v Commission*, T-45/98 and T-47/98, EU:T:2001:288, confirmed on appeal by Judgment in *ThyssenKrupp v Commission*, C-65/02 P and C-73/02 P, EU:C:2005:454.

1533 Commission Decision of 20 December 2006 relating to a procedure under Article 65 of the ECSC Treaty (Case COMP/F/39.234 – *Alloy surcharge – re-adoption*) [2007] OJ L182/31. See also European Commission Press release IP/06/1851 of 20 December 2006.

1534 Judgment in *ThyssenKrupp Stainless v Commission*, T-24/07, EU:T:2009:236, confirmed on appeal by Judgment in *ThyssenKrupp Nirosta v Commission*, C-352/09 P, EU:C:2011:191.

1535 Commission Decision 2006/894/EC of 17 December 2002 relating to a proceeding under Article 65 of the ECSC Treaty against Alfa Acciai SpA, Feralpi Siderurgica SpA, Ferriere Nord SpA, IRO Industrie Riunite Odolesi SpA, Leali SpA, Acciaierie e Ferriere Leali Luigi SpA in liquidazione (in liquidation), Lucchini SpA, Siderpotenza SpA, Riva Acciaio SpA, Valsabbia Investimenti SpA, Ferriera Valsabbia SpA and the association of undertakings Federacciai (Federazione delle Imprese Siderurgiche Italiane) (Case C.37.956 – *Reinforcing bars*) [2006] OJ L353/1. See also European Commission Press release IP/02/1908 of 17 December 2002.

1536 Judgments in *SP, Leali, Acciaierie e Ferriere Leali Luigi, IRO, Lucchini, Ferriera Valsabbia, Valsabbia Investimenti* and *Alfa Acciai v Commission*, T-27/03, T-46/03, T-58/03, T-79/03, T-80/03, T-97/03 and T-98/03, EU:T:2007:317; *Riva Acciaio v Commission*, T-45/03, EU:T:2007:318; *Feralpi Siderurgica v Commission*, T-77/03, EU:T:2007:319; *Ferriere Nord v Commission*, T-94/03, EU:T:2007:320. The ECSC Treaty was signed in 1952 for a duration of 50 years and expired on 23 July 2002.

1537 Commission Decision C(2009)7492 final of 30 September 2009 relating to an infringement of Article 65 of the ECSC Treaty (COMP/37.956 – *Reinforcing bars, re-adoption*), as modified by Commission Decision C(2009) 9912 final of 8 December 2009 relating to a proceeding under Article 65 of the ECSC Treaty (Case COMP/37.956 – *Reinforcing bars, re-adoption*) [2011] OJ C98/16. See also European Commission Press release IP/09/1389 of 30 September 2009.

decision before the General Court, which in December 2014 upheld the second decision, with only small fine reductions for two undertakings.[1538] Five of the eight undertakings brought a further appeal to the Court of Justice, which in September 2017 annulled the second decision in so far as it concerned those five undertakings, on the ground of infringement of an essential procedural requirement flowing from Regulation 773/2004, in that no oral hearing had been held on the substance of the case to which the competition authorities of the Member States had been invited.[1539] Following this second annulment, and after a new oral hearing in April 2018, to which the competition authorities of the Member States were invited,[1540] the Commission adopted in July 2019 a new, third decision re-imposing fines on the five undertakings for whom the second decision had been annulled.[1541] The new fines are, however, significantly lower than the fines imposed in the first and second decisions. Indeed, in recognition of the long duration of the overall proceedings before the Commission and the Courts, the Commission reduced the fines by 50%. The Commission also copied the two small fine reductions granted by the General Court. Finally, as one of the undertakings was, in the meantime, in liquidation, and had no longer any turnover, its fine was set at zero, in application of Article 23(2), second subparagraph, of Regulation 1/2003, which limits fines to 10% of the overall turnover of the undertaking concerned in the business year preceding the Commission's decision. The four undertakings on whom an above-zero fine was imposed have brought applications for annulment of this third decision. Following the rejection of these applications of annulment by the General Court in November 2022,[1542] three of the undertakings further appealed to the Court of Justice.[1543]

1538 Judgments in *Leali* and *Acciaierie e Ferriere Leali Luigi v Commission*, T-489/09, T-490/09 and T-56/10, EU:T:2014:1039; *IRO v Commission*, T-69/10, EU:T:2014:1030; *Feralpi v Commission*, T-70/10, EU:T:2014:1031; *Riva Fire v Commission*, T-83/10, EU:T:2014:1034; *Alfa Acciai v Commission*, T-85/10, EU:T:2014:1037; *Ferriere Nord v Commission*, T-90/10, EU:T:2014:1035; *Lucchini v Commission*, T-91/10, EU:T:2014:1033; *Ferriera Valsabbia* and *Valsabbia Investimenti v Commission*, T-92/10, EU:T:2014:1032. The General Court granted a 3% fine reduction to Riva Fire and a 6% fine reduction to Ferriere Nord.

1539 Judgments in *Feralpi Holding v Commission*, C-85/15 P, EU:C:2017:709; *Ferriera Valsabbia SpA and Others*, C-86/15 P and C-87/15 P, EU:C:2017:717; *Ferriere Nord v Commission*, C-88/15 P, EU:C:2017:716; *Riva Fire v Commission*, C-89/15 P, EU:C:2017:713. Indeed, the competition authorities of the Member States had not been invited to participate in the first oral hearing of 13 June 2002, which concerned the substance of the case and which took place before the expiry of the ECSC Treaty. Such participation was not provided for in the ECSC Treaty, under which the Commission had exclusive competence to apply the competition rules. They were invited to the second oral hearing of 30 September 2002, but that oral hearing dealt only with the legal consequences of the expiry of the ECSC Treaty for the continuation of the proceedings. On the oral hearing in Commission competition proceedings, see Chapter XII of this book.

1540 While the invitation of the competition authorities of the Member States constitutes an essential procedural requirement, there is no obligation for the competition authorities of the Member States to attend the oral hearing; see Judgment in *Servier v Commission*, T-691/14, EU:T:2018:922, paragraph 163.

1541 Commission Decision of 4 July 2019 relating to a proceeding under Article 65 of the ECSC Treaty (Case AT.37956) [2020] OJ C312/13. See also Final Report of the Hearing Officer, Case AT.37956 – *Reinforcing bars* [2020] OJ C312/7, and European Commission Daily News 04/07/2019.

1542 Judgments in *Ferriera Valsabbia and Valsabbia Investimenti v Commission*, T-655/19, EU:T:2022:689, in *Alfa Acciai v Commission*, T-656/19, EU:T:2022:690, in *Feralpi v Commission*, T-657/19, EU:T:2022:691, and in *Ferriere Nord v Commission*, T-667/19, EU:T:2022:692.

1543 Cases C-29/23 P *Ferriera Valsabbia and Valsabbia Investimenti v Commission*, C-30/23 P *Alfa Acciai v Commission*, and C-31/23 P *Ferriere Nord v Commission*, currently pending

6. Carbonless paper (Bolloré)

The Commission readopted in June 2010 a decision concerning one of the undertakings in the *Carbonless paper* case. In December 2001, the Commission had imposed fines on 11 undertakings for an infringement of Article 81 EC in the carbonless paper sector, including a fine of EUR 22.68 million on Bolloré.[1544] Upon the application for annulment before the General Court and the subsequent appeal before the Court of Justice brought by Bolloré, the Court of Justice in September 2009 annulled this initial decision in so far as it concerned Bolloré, on the ground of violation of the rights of the defence, in that the initial decision held Bolloré liable both for its own direct participation in the cartel and, as parent company, for the participation of one of its subsidiaries in the cartel, whereas the statement of objections preceding the initial decision had only mentioned Bolloré's liability as parent company.[1545] Following this annulment, the Commission sent in December 2009 a new statement of objections to Bolloré, now also covering its direct participation in the cartel. After Bolloré had responded to the statement of objections in writing and at an oral hearing, the Commission adopted in June 2010 a new decision addressed to Bolloré, finding the same infringement as in the initial decision but imposing a slightly lower fine of EUR 21.26 million, in recognition of Bolloré's cooperation in that Bolloré during the re-adoption proceedings no longer contested the participation of its subsidiary in the cartel.[1546] Bolloré's application for annulment against this new decision was rejected by the Courts.[1547]

7. Gas insulated switchgear (Mitsubishi and Toshiba)

The Commission re-adopted in June 2012 a decision concerning two of the undertakings in the *Gas insulated switchgear* case. In January 2007, the Commission had imposed fines on eleven European and Japanese undertakings for their participation in a cartel for gas insulated switchgear projects, in violation of Article 81 EC, including a fine of EUR 113,925,000 on Mitsubishi, a fine of EUR 86,250,000 on Toshiba, and a fine of EUR 4,650,000 on Mitsubishi and Toshiba jointly and severally.[1548] Upon applications for annulment by Mitsubishi and by Toshiba, the General Court in July 2011 confirmed the finding of the infringement of Article 81 EC but annulled the fines imposed on those two undertakings, on the ground of infringement of the principle of equal treatment, in that the Commission had used a different reference year for the calculation of the fines imposed on the Japanese undertakings than the one used for the calculation of the fines imposed on the European producers. The General Court did not use its unlimited jurisdiction to set

---

1544 Commission Decision 2004/337/EC of 20 December 2001 relating to a proceeding pursuant to Article 81 of the EC Treaty and Article 53 of the EEA Agreement (Case COMP/E-1/36.212 – *Carbonless paper*) [2004] OJ L115/1.

1545 Judgment in *Papierfabrik August Koehler, Bolloré and Divipa v Commission*, C-322/07 P, C-327/07 P and C-338/07 P, EU:C:2009:500, paragraphs 34 to 48.

1546 Commission Decision of 23 June 2010 relating to a proceeding under Article 101 TFEU and Article 53 EEA (Case COMP/36.212) [2011] OJ C138/21. See also Final Report of the Hearing Officer [2011] OJ C138/19, and European Commission Press release IP/10/788 of 23 June 2010.

1547 Judgment in *Bolloré v Commission*, T-372/10, EU:T:2012:325, confirmed on appeal by Judgment in *Bolloré v Commission*, C-414/12 P, EU:C:2014:301.

1548 Commission Decision of 24 January 2007 relating to a proceeding under Article 81 EC and Article 53 EEA (Case COMP/38.899 – *Gas Insulated Switchgear*) [2008] OJ C5/7. See also European Commission Press release IP/07/80 of 24 January 2007.

new fines.[1549] Following these annulments, the Commission sent in February 2012 letters to Mitsubishi and to Toshiba expressing its intention to re-impose fines and setting out the parameters of the new calculation. After having received Mitsubishi's and Toshiba's written comments, the Commission adopted in June 2012 a new decision imposing a fine of EUR 74,817,000 on Mitsubishi, a fine of EUR 56,793,000 on Toshiba (both lower than the initial fines), and a fine of EUR 4,650,000 on Mitsubishi and Toshiba jointly and severally (identical to the initial fine).[1550] Mitsubishi's and Toshiba's applications for annulment against this new decision were rejected by the EU Courts.[1551] The Courts rejected in particular Toshiba's plea that the Commission should have sent a new statement of objections before imposing the new fine.[1552]

8. Heat stabilisers (GEA and Akzo)

The Commission re-adopted in June 2016 two decisions concerning two of the undertakings in the *Heat stabilisers* case. In November 2009, the Commission had imposed fines on eleven undertakings, including GEA and Akzo, for participation in one or two cartel infringements in violation of Article 81 EC relating to two categories of heat stabilisers.[1553] GEA and Akzo both brought applications for annulment of this initial decision. The General Court rejected GEA's application,[1554] and, in the exercise of its unlimited jurisdiction, reduced the fines imposed on Akzo by 1%.[1555] In the initial decision, another company, ACW, was held jointly and severally liable with GEA for part of the fines imposed on GEA. Similarly, another company, Elementis, was held jointly and severally liable with Akzo for part of the fines imposed on Akzo. In February 2010, the Commission adopted a decision amending the initial decision, reducing the amount of the fines for which ACW was held jointly and severally liable with GEA, because the higher amount in the initial decision exceeded the ceiling of 10% of ACW's turnover in the business year preceding the initial decision, in violation of Article 23(2) of Regulation 1/2003.[1556] In June 2011, the Commission adopted a second decision amending the initial decision, removing the joint and several liability of Elementis

---

1549 Judgments in *Toshiba v Commission*, T-113/07, EU:T:2011:343, paragraphs 280 to 297, and in *Mitsubishi v Commission*, T-133/07, EU:T:2011:345, paragraphs 264 to 280. The appeals brought by Toshiba and Mitsubishi against these judgments of the General Court, in so far as these judgments confirmed the finding of infringement of Article 81 EC, were rejected by the Court of Justice by Judgment in *Siemens AG and Others v Commission*, C-239/11 P, C-489/11 P and C-498/11 P, EU:C:2013:866.

1550 Commission Decision of 27 June 2012 amending Decision C(2006)6762 final of 24 January 2007 relating to a proceeding under Article 81 EC (now Article 101 TFEU) and Article 53 EEA to the extent that it was addressed to Mitsubishi Electric Corporation and Toshiba Corporation (Case COMP/39.966 – *Gas Insulated Switchgear – Fines*) [2013] OJ C70/12. See also European Commission Press release IP/12/705 of 27 June 2012.

1551 Judgment in *Mitsubishi v Commission*, T-409/12, EU:T:2016:17, and Judgment in *Toshiba v Commission*, T-404/12, EU:T:2016:18, confirmed on appeal by Judgment in *Toshiba v Commission*, C-180/16 P, EU:C:2017:520/559.

1552 Judgment in *Toshiba v Commission*, T-404/12, EU:T:2016:18, paragraphs 37 to 87, confirmed on appeal by Judgment in *Toshiba v Commission*, C-180/16 P, EU:C:2017:520/559, paragraphs 21 to 34.

1553 Commission Decision of 11 November 2009 relating to a proceeding under Article 81 EC and Article 53 EEA (Case COMP/38.589 – *Heat Stabilisers*) [2010] OJ C307/9. See also European Commission Press release IP/09/1695 of 11 November 2009.

1554 Judgment in *GEA Group v Commission*, T-45/10, EU:T:2015:507.

1555 Judgment in *Akzo Nobel and Others v Commission*, T-47/10, EU:T:2015:506, paragraphs 329 and 330, confirmed on appeal by Judgment in *Akzo Nobel and Others v Commission*, C-516/15 P, EU:C:2017:314.

1556 Commission Decision C(2010) 727 of 8 February 2010 modifying Decision C(2009) 8682 final of 11 November 2009 relating to a proceeding under Article 81 EC and Article 53 EEA (Case COMP/38.589 – *Heat Stabilisers*).

for parts of the fines imposed on Akzo, on the ground that the Commission's powers to impose fines on Elementis had been time-barred at the time of the initial decision.[1557] Upon applications for annulment brought by GEA and Akzo respectively, the General Court in July 2015 annulled the two decisions amending the initial decision, on the ground of violation of the right to be heard, in that GEA had not been heard before the adoption of the first amending decision and Akzo had only been granted a few days to provide its views on the second amending decision.[1558] Following these two annulments, and after having heard GEA and Akzo in writing, the Commission in June 2006 adopted two new decisions amending the initial decision, identical to the two annulled amending decisions, while also taking into account the 1% fine reduction that the General Court had granted to Akzo.[1559] GEA brought an application for annulment against the first of these new amending decisions, which, following a first judgment of the General Court in October 2018 that was annulled by the Court of Justice in November 2020,[1560] was rejected by the General Court in January 2023.[1561]

9. Airfreight

The Commission re-adopted in March 2017 a decision in the *Airfreight* case. In November 2010, the Commission had adopted an initial decision imposing fines for an infringement of Article 101 TFEU, Article 53 EEA and Article 8 of the EU/Switzerland Agreement on Air Transport committed by twelve air cargo carriers.[1562] All but one of the air cargo carriers brought an application for annulment of this initial decision. In December 2015, the General Court held that the initial decision was vitiated by a defective statement of reasons. Depending on the forms of order sought before the General Court, that vice entailed the annulment in full or in part in respect of the various parties that had challenged the initial decision.[1563] Following these annulments, and after having heard the parties concerned on its intention to adopt a new decision, the Commission adopted in March 2017 a new decision in respect of the parties for whom the initial decision had been

---

1557 Commission Decision of 30 June 2011 modifying Decision C(2009) 8682 final of 11 November 2009 relating to a proceeding under Article 81 EC and Article 53 EEA (Case COMP/38.589 – *Heat Stabilisers*). That the Commission powers had been time-barred had become apparent following the interpretation of Article 25(6) of Regulation 1/2003 in the Judgment of 29 March 2011 in *ArcelorMittal v Commission* and *Commission v ArcelorMittal*, C-201/09 P and C-216/09 P, EU:C:2011:190.

1558 Judgments in *GEA v Commission*, T-189/10, EU:T:2015:504, and in *Akzo v Commission*, T-485/11, EU:T:2015:517.

1559 Commission Decisions C(2016) 3920 and C(2016) 3933 of 29 June 2016 modifying Decision C(2009) 8682 final of 11 November 2009 relating to a proceeding under Article 81 EC and Article 53 EEA (Case COMP/38.589 – *Heat Stabilisers*). See also European Commission Daily News 29/06/2016.

1560 Judgments in *GEA v Commission*, T-640/16, EU:T:2018:700 and C-823/18 P, EU:C:2020:955.

1561 Judgment in *GEA v Commission*, T-640/16 RENV, EU:T:2023:18.

1562 Commission Decision of 9 November 2010 relating to a proceeding under Article 101 TFEU, Article 53 EEA and Article 8 of the Agreement between the European Community and the Swiss Confederation on air transport (Case C.39258 – *Airfreight*) [2014] OJ C371/11. See also European Commission Press release IP/10/1487 of 9 November 2010.

1563 Judgments in *Air Canada v Commission* (T-9/11, EU:T:2015:994); *Koninklijke Luchtvaart Maatschappij v Commission* (T-28/11, EU:T:2015:995); *Japan Airlines v Commission* (T-36/11, EU:T:2015:992); *Cathay Pacific v Commission* (T-38/11, EU:T:2015:985); *Cargolux Airlines v Commission* (T-39/11, EU:T:2015:991); *Latam Airlines Group and Lan Cargo v Commission* (T-40/11, EU:T:2015:986); *Singapore Airlines and Singapore Airlines Cargo v Commission* (T-43/11, EU:T:2015:989); *Deutsche Lufthansa and Others v Commission* (T-46/11, EU:T:2015:987); *British Airways v Commission* (T-48/11, EU:T:2015:988); *SAS Cargo Group and Others v Commission* (T-56/11, EU:T:2015:990); *Air France-KLM v Commission* (T-62/11, EU:T:2015:996); *Air France v Commission* (T-63/11, EU:T:2015:993); and *Martinair Holland v Commission* (T-67/11, EU:T:2015:984).

annulled.[1564] For one of the air carriers, Martinair, the fine imposed by the new decision is lower than the initial fine, in application of Article 23(2), second subparagraph, of Regulation 1/2003, which limits fines to 10% of the overall turnover of the undertaking concerned in the business year preceding the Commission's decision, as Martinair's turnover was lower in 2016 than in 2009.[1565] On the other hand, for those air carriers for whom the fine had been capped at 10% of their turnover in the initial decision but whose turnover had since increased, the Commission did not impose a higher fine in the new decision but rather imposed the same fine as in the initial decision.[1566] Applications for annulment against this new decision were ruled upon by the General Court in March 2022.[1567] Several further appeals have been brought before the Court of Justice.

10. Envelopes (Printeos/Tompla)

The Commission re-adopted in June 2017 a decision concerning one of the undertakings in the *Envelopes* case. In December 2014, the Commission had imposed fines on five envelopes producers. Under the Commission's cartel settlement procedure,[1568] all five undertakings had recognised their liability for the infringement, and received a 10% fine reduction on this ground.[1569] One of the five undertakings, Printeos/Tompla, brought an action against this initial decision before the General Court, seeking annulment only of the fine, not of the finding of infringement. In December 2016, the General Court annulled the fine imposed on Printeos/Tompla, on the ground of failure to state adequate reasons as to the relative amounts of the fines imposed on the five undertakings.[1570] Following this annulment, and after having heard Printeos/Tompla on its intention to adopt a new decision, the Commission adopted in June 2017 a new decision, re-imposing the same fine on Printeos/Tompla, with additional reasoning.[1571] Printeos/Tompla's application for annulment of this new, second

---

1564 Commission Decision of 17 March 2017 relating to a proceeding under Article 101 TFEU, Article 53 EEA and Article 8 of the Agreement between the European Community and the Swiss Confederation on air transport (Case AT.39258 – *Airfreight*) [2017] OJ C188/14. See also Final Report of the Hearing Officer, *Airfreight (re-adoption)* (AT.39258) [2017] OJ C188/10, and European Commission Press release IP/17/661 of 17 March 2017.

1565 European Commission Press release IP/17/661 of 17 March 2017.

1566 Commission Decision of 17 March 2017 relating to a proceeding under Article 101 TFEU, Article 53 EEA and Article 8 of the Agreement between the European Community and the Swiss Confederation on air transport (Case AT.39258 – *Airfreight*) [2017] OJ C188/14, paragraph 27 of the summary. See also Final Report of the Hearing Officer, *Airfreight (re-adoption)* (AT.39258) [2017] OJ C188/10, paragraph 21.

1567 See Court of Justice Press Release No 53/22 (30 March 2022), 'Cartel on the airfreight market: the General Court rules on actions brought by multiple airlines'.

1568 See Article 10a of Regulation 773/2004, as inserted by Commission Regulation (EC) No 622/2008 of 30 June 2008 amending Regulation (EC) No 773/2004, as regards the conduct of settlement procedures in cartel cases [2008] OJ L171/3; Commission Notice on the conduct of settlement procedures in view of the adoption of decisions pursuant to Article 7 and Article 23 of Council Regulation (EC) No 1/2003 in cartel cases [2008] OJ C167/1, amended by Communication from the Commission – Amendments to the Commission Notice on the conduct of settlement procedures [2015] OJ C256/2; and my paper 'The Use of Settlements in Public Antitrust Enforcement: Objectives and Principles' (2008) 31 *World Competition* 335, also accessible at http://ssrn.com/author=456078.

1569 Commission Decision of 10 December 2014 relating to a proceeding under Article 101 TFEU and Article 53 EEA (Case AT.39780 – *Envelopes*) [2015] OJ C74/5. See also European Commission Press release IP/14/2583 of 11 December 2014.

1570 Judgment in *Printeos v Commission*, T-95/15, EU:T:2016:722.

1571 Commission Decision of 16 June 2017 amending Decision C(2014)9295 final relating to a proceeding under Article 101 TFEU and Article 53 EEA (Case AT.39780 – *Envelopes*) [2018] OJ C39/10. See also Final Report of the Hearing Officer, Envelopes (re-imposition of a fine) (AT.39780) [2018] OJ C39/9, and European Commission Daily News 16/06/2017.

decision was rejected by the General Court.[1572] Following the initial decision, and while its application for annulment was pending before the General Court, Printeos/Tompla had in March 2015 provisionally paid the fine. Following the annulment of the initial fine, the Commission repaid in February 2017 the fine, while rejecting Printeos/Tompla's claim for payment of interest. Upon an action brought by Printeos/Tompla against this refusal to pay interest, the General Court and the Court of Justice in February 2019 and January 2021 ordered the Commission to pay Printeos/Tompla default interest calculated from the day of the provisional payment at a standard rate.[1573]

11. Retail food packaging (CCPL/Coopbox)

The Commission re-adopted in December 2020 a decision concerning one of the undertakings in the *Retail food packaging* case. In June 2015, the Commission had imposed fines on ten undertakings for cartels in the retail food packaging sector, including fines of EUR 33,694,000 on CCPL/Coopbox for participation in three cartels.[1574] In July 2019, the General Court annulled this initial decision in so far as it imposed these fines on CCPL/Coopbox, on the ground of insufficient reasoning as to the percentage of reduction of the fine on account of inability to pay.[1575] Following this annulment, and after having heard CCPL/Coopbox on the new fine calculation, the Commission adopted in December 2020 a new decision, imposing new fines of EUR 9,441,000 on CCPL/Coopbox. The much lower amount of the new fine results from the application of Article 23(2), second subparagraph, of Regulation 1/2003, which limits fines to 10% of the overall turnover of the undertaking concerned in the business year preceding the Commission's decision, as CCPL/Coopbox's turnover in 2019 was much lower than in 2014.[1576] An application for annulment of this new decision was dismissed by the General Court in December 2022.[1577]

C. Analysis

1. A natural consequence of Articles 263, 264 and 266 TFEU...

The phenomenon of re-adoption by the European Commission of decisions annulled by the EU Courts is, at first analysis, a natural consequence of Articles 263, 264 and 266 TFEU. As already mentioned above, the EU Courts cannot, in the context of the review of legality under Article 263 TFEU, substitute their own reasoning for that of

---

1572 Judgment in *Printeos v Commission*, T-466/17, EU:T:2019:671. While the defect was not sufficient to lead again to an annulment, the General Court did, however, criticise the reasoning of the amount of the fine in the second decision, and on this ground exceptionally condemned the Commission to the costs, in application of Article 135 of the Rules of Procedure of the General Court; see paragraphs 175 to 177 of the judgment.

1573 Judgments in *Printeos v Commission*, T-201/17, EU:T:2019:81 and in *Commission v Printeos*, C-301/19 P, EU:C:2021:39.

1574 Commission Decision of 24 June 2015 relating to a proceeding under Article 101 TFEU and Article 53 EEA (Case AT.39563 – *Retail food packaging*) [2015] OJ C402/8. See also European Commission Press release IP/15/5253 of 24 June 2015.

1575 Judgment in *CCPL and Coopbox v Commission*, T-522/15, EU:T:2019:500.

1576 See 'Antitrust: Commission re-adopts decision and fines CCPL €9.44 million for its participation in retail food packaging cartels', European Commission Daily News 17/12/2020.

1577 Judgment in *CCPL and Others v Commission*, T-130/21, EU:T:2022:778.

the Commission.[1578] If an application for annulment is well founded, the Court can thus not correct the Commission's decision, but must declare it void, as required by Article 264 TFEU, to the extent that the action is well founded.[1579] It is then for the Commission to draw the necessary consequences, as required by Article 266 TFEU.

Furthermore, according to well-established case law, annulment of a decision does not necessarily affect the preparatory acts, and the procedure for replacing an annulled decision may, in principle, be resumed at the very point at which the illegality occurred.[1580]

In the *PVC* and *Soda ash* cases, in which the illegality consisted in the failure to authenticate the decision in accordance with the Commission's own Rules of Procedure, the Commission could thus, without taking any further procedural steps, literally 're-adopt' its decision, with proper authentication.[1581]

In those cases where the illegality occurred at an earlier stage, what the Commission did was not simply 're-adopt' the initial decision, but rather resume its administrative proceedings at the point where the illegality occurred. For instance in the *Steel beams (Arbed/Arcelor)*, *Alloy surcharge (ThyssenKrupp)* and *Carbonless paper (Bolloré)* cases, where the illegality had occurred at the point of the statement of objections, the Commission resumed its proceedings with a new statement of objections. The fact that the term 're-adoption' is commonly used to describe such resumption of the proceedings should not deflect from the reality of what happens.[1582]

2. …but also a matter of discretion

While the Commission may, in principle, following an annulment, resume its proceedings at the point where the illegality occurred, with a view to adopting a new decision, it is, however, under no obligation to do so.

Indeed, according to well-established case law, in order to perform effectively its task of ensuring application of the principles laid down in Articles 101 TFEU, the Commission has a broad discretion to select the cases which it investigates and in which it continues the proceedings up to the stage of a final decision.[1583]

Following the annulment of its initial decision, the Commission has thus also, in principle, a discretion whether or not to resume proceedings and whether or not to adopt a new decision.[1584]

1578 Judgment in *Galp Energía España and Others v Commission*, C-603/13 P, EU:C:2016:38, paragraph 73.

1579 See Judgments in *Commission v Verhuizingen Coppens*, C-441/11 P, EU:C:2012:778, paragraphs 34 to 54, and in *Soliver v Commission*, T-68/09, EU:T:2014:867, paragraphs 107 to 113.

1580 Judgments in *Spain v Commission*, C-415/96, EU:C:1998:533, paragraphs 31 and 32; in *Limburgse Vinyl Maatschappij and Others v Commission*, C-238/99 P etc., EU:C:2002:582 ('*PVC II* Judgment'), paragraph 73; and in *Solvay v Commission*, C-109/10 P, EU:C:2011:686, paragraphs 66 to 68.

1581 See Judgment in *Limburgse Vinyl Maatschappij and Others v Commission*, C-238/99 P etc., EU:C:2002:582 ('*PVC II* Judgment'), paragraph 75.

1582 See also Judgment in *Bolloré v Commission*, T-372/10, EU:T:2012:325, paragraphs 74 to 77.

1583 Judgments in *Masterfoods*, C-344/98, EU:C:2000:689, paragraph 46; in *Ufex and Others v Commission*, C-199/97 P, EU:C:1999:116, paragraphs 88 and 89; and in *IECC v Commission*, C-449/98 P, EU:C:2001:276, paragraphs 35 to 37. See further Chapter IV of this book.

1584 Judgment in *Limburgse Vinyl Maatschappij and Others v Commission*, T-305/94 etc., EU:T:1999:80, paragraphs 148 to 154.

In its press statements on the occasion of the adoption of new decisions following the annulment of the initial decision, the Commission has stated that 'the Commission will correct any procedural mistake made so that companies rest assured that they will not escape cartel fines for procedural reasons',[1585] that 'the decision confirms that the Commission will not let cartels go unpunished' because 'cartels are illegal and cause consumers and businesses to suffer',[1586] or that 'the re-adoption of this decision is based on the public interest in pursuing an effective and deterrent enforcement against cartels'.[1587]

In this respect, the General Court has held that 'the Commission's assertion that it is determined that the members of anti-competitive cartels should not escape, on procedural grounds, the penalties applicable under EU law, is not a manifestation of bias but merely the assertion of a clear intention, wholly consistent with the task entrusted to the Commission, of making good, on a case-by-case basis, the procedural irregularities found, in order not to undermine the effectiveness of EU competition law'.[1588]

However, the Commission has not always resumed proceedings in cases where it could in principle do so. As already mentioned above, the Commission did not attempt to re-adopt a second time the twice annulled decisions in *Soda ash.*

3. The principle of ne bis in idem

The main limitation on the possibility to re-adopt a decision or resume proceedings after the annulment of an initial decision results from the principle of *ne bis in idem.*[1589] This general principle of EU law is enshrined in Article 50 of the Charter of Fundamental Rights of the European Union, which reads as follows:

'*No one shall be liable to be tried or punished again in criminal proceedings for an offence for which he or she has already been finally acquitted or convicted within the Union in accordance with the law.*'

According to the explanations to the Charter, to which according to Article 6(1) TEU due regard must be given, this provision 'corresponds to Article 4 of Protocol No 7 to the ECHR, but its scope is extended to European Union level between the Courts of the Member States'.[1590]

Article 4 of Protocol No 7 to the Convention for the Protection of Human Rights and Fundamental Rights (ECHR) reads as follows:

> '*1. No one shall be liable to be tried or punished again in criminal proceedings under the jurisdiction of the same State for an offence for which he has already been finally acquitted or convicted in accordance with the law and penal procedure of that State.*

1585 European Commission Press release IP/06/1851 of 20 December 2006, concerning the *Alloy surcharge (ThyssenKrupp)* case; see similarly European Commission Press release IP/09/1389 of 30 September 2009, concerning the first re-adoption in the *Reinforcing bars* case.

1586 European Commission Press release IP/17/661 of 17 March 2017, concerning the *Airfreight* case.

1587 European Commission Daily News 04/07/2019, concerning the second re-adoption in the *Reinforcing bars* case.

1588 See Judgment in *Bolloré v Commission*, T-372/10, EU:T:2012:325, paragraph 73.

1589 See further my paper 'The Principle of *Ne Bis In Idem* in EC Antitrust Enforcement: A Legal and Economic Analysis' (2003) 26 *World Competition* 131, also accessible at http://ssrn.com/author=456087, and S. Frisch, '*Ne bis in idem* under an optimal antitrust enforcement framework' (2023) 24 *ERA Forum.*

1590 Explanations relating to the Charter of Fundamental Rights [2007] OJ C303/17 at 34.

2. *The provisions of the preceding paragraph shall not prevent the reopening of the case in accordance with the law and penal procedure of the State concerned, if there is evidence of new or newly discovered facts, or if there has been a fundamental defect in the previous proceedings, which could affect the outcome of the case.'*

As the Court of Justice held in the *PVC II* Judgment, the principle of *ne bis in idem* thus

'precludes, in competition matters, an undertaking from being found guilty or proceedings from being brought against it a second time on the grounds of anti-competitive conduct in respect of which it has been penalised or declared non liable by a previous unappealable decision. [. . .]

On the other hand, it does not in itself preclude the resumption of proceedings in respect of the same anti-competitive conduct where the first decision was annulled for procedural reasons without any ruling having been given on the substance of the facts alleged, since the annulment decision cannot in such circumstances be regarded as an "acquittal" within the meaning given to that expression in penal matters. In such a case, the penalties imposed by the new decision are not added to those imposed by the annulled decision but replace them'.[1591]

The Commission can thus not resume proceedings and adopt a new decision if the initial decision has been annulled on substantive grounds, in that the EU Courts found that the Commission had failed to establish, in law or in fact, the alleged infringement of Article 101 TFEU in the initial decision.[1592]

Resumption of proceedings and adoption of a new decision is also precluded by the principle of *ne bis in idem* if the EU Courts have annulled the fine, including for procedural reasons, but have then exercised their unlimited jurisdiction under Article 261 TFEU to set a new amount of the fine. Indeed, once the EU Courts have actually exercised their unlimited jurisdiction, the Commission definitively loses its power.[1593]

The *Butadiene rubber (Eni/Polimeri/Versalis)* case provides an illustration of this last point. In November 2006, the Commission had imposed fines on five undertakings for an infringement of Article 81 EC and Article 53 EEA, including a fine of EUR 272,250,000 on Eni/Polimeri/Versalis.[1594] The latter fine included a 50% increase of the basic amount of the fine on account of recidivism.[1595] In July 2011, the General Court confirmed the finding of infringement but annulled the initial decision in so far as it imposed the fine on Eni/Polimeri/Versalis, on the ground that the Commission had not provided sufficient detailed and precise evidence in the initial decision that the same 'undertaking'

1591 Judgments in *Spain v Commission*, C-415/96, EU:C:1998:533, paragraphs 31 and 32; in *Limburgse Vinyl Maatschappij and Others v Commission*, C-238/99 P etc., EU:C:2002:582 ('*PVC II* Judgment'), paragraphs 59 and 62.

1592 For a dissenting view, see P. A. Biolan, 'Reopening EU Competition Investigations After Judicial Annulment; Beyond Procedural Errors' (2017) 8 *Journal of European Competition Law & Practice* 83.

1593 Judgments in *Spain v Commission*, C-415/96, EU:C:1998:533, paragraphs 31 and 32; in *Limburgse Vinyl Maatschappij and Others v Commission*, C-238/99 P etc., EU:C:2002:582 ('*PVC II* Judgment'), paragraph 693.

1594 Commission Decision of 29 November 2006 relating to a proceeding under Article 81 EC and Article 53 EEA (Case COMP/F/38.638 – *BR/ESBR*) [2008] OJ C7/11. See also European Commission Press release IP/06/1647 of 29 November 2006.

1595 See further Chapter VIII of this book.

within the meaning of Article 81 EC had repeatedly infringed the cartel prohibition. In the exercise of its unlimited jurisdiction, the General Court set the amount the fine at EUR 181,500,000.[1596] In March 2013, the Commission sent a new statement of objections to Eni/Polimeri/Versalis with a view to re-imposing the 50% uplift for recidivism,[1597] in apparent breach of the principle of *ne bis in idem*. Eni/Polimer/Versalis immediately brought actions before the General Court to stop this re-opening of proceedings. The Commission later withdrew the new statement of objections and closed the case, with the result that the actions before the General Court became without object.[1598]

4. Prescription

In some cases, resumption of proceedings and adoption of a new decision following the annulment of the initial decision may be impossible because of prescription.

Article 25 of Regulation 1/2003 lays down the limitation periods for the imposition of fines.

It follows from Article 25(1)(b), (2) and (5) that the limitation period for imposing fines for an infringement of Article 101 TFEU expires at the latest ten years after the infringement ceases. This time limit is extended by the time during which the decision of the Commission is the subject of proceedings pending before the EU Courts.

The length of the proceedings before the EU Courts against the initial decision does thus not affect the possibility for the Commission to re-open proceedings and adopt a second decision after the annulment of the initial decision.[1599]

However, if the initial decision had been adopted close to the end of the limitation period, not enough time may remain after the annulment to adopt a new decision, in particular in cases where the illegality occurred at a relatively early stage of the proceedings, for instance at the stage of the statement of objections, and many procedural steps thus need to be taken before a new decision can be adopted.

5. The fundamental right to have a matter adjudicated within a reasonable duration

Undertakings targeted by cartel investigations have a fundamental right to have their case dealt with within a reasonable time, a right recognised in the case law of the Court of Justice as a general principle of European Union law and enshrined in Article 41(1) and the second paragraph of Article 47 of the Charter of Fundamental Rights.

1596 Judgments in *Eni v Commission*, T-39/07, EU:T:2011:356, and in *Polimeri Europa v Commission*, T-59/07, EU:T:2011:361. The appeals brought by Eni and Versalis against these judgments of the General Court were rejected by the Court of Justice by Judgments in *Eni v Commission*, C-508/11 P, EU:C:2013:289 and in *Versalis v Commission*, C-511/11 P, EU:C:2013:386.

1597 See European Commission Press release IP/13/179 of 1 March 2013, 'Antitrust: Commission sends second statement of objections to ENI and Versalis in synthetic rubber cartel after General Court judgment'.

1598 See Orders of the General Court of 7 March 2014 in *Eni v Commission*, T-240/12 and T-211/13 [2014] OJ C135/46, and in *Versalis v Commission*, T-241/12 and T-210/13 [2014] OJ C135/47.

1599 As the Court of Justice pointed out in the Judgments in *Spain v Commission*, C-415/96, EU:C:1998:533, paragraphs 31 and 32; and in *Limburgse Vinyl Maatschappij and Others v Commission*, C-238/99 P etc., EU:C:2002:582 ('*PVC II* Judgment'), paragraph 151, the suspension of the limitation period while court proceedings are pending 'merely protects the Commission from the effects of the annulment for a period the duration of which is not attributable to it'.

The Court of Justice has held that the reasonableness of the duration of proceedings must be appraised in the light of the circumstances specific to each case and, in particular, the importance of the case for the parties concerned, its complexity and the conduct of the parties and of the competent authorities, the list of relevant criteria not being exhaustive.[1600] It follows that the fact that the limitation period for the imposition of penalties as laid down in Article 25 of Regulation 1/2003 has not yet expired is not decisive.[1601]

The unreasonableness of the duration of the proceedings can result not only from the excessive duration of one or several individual stages of the proceedings but also from the overall length of the administrative and judicial proceedings taken together.[1602] In some re-adoption cases, the absolute length of the proceedings, taking into account all stages of the administrative and judicial proceedings, becomes particularly long.

The *Reinforcing bars* case, for instance, started with inspections by the Commission between October and December 2000. By the time the Commission adopted its third decision in July 2019, more than 18 years had already passed. Given that in the judgments of September 2017, the Court of Justice has not dealt with a number of grounds of appeal raised against the judgments of the General Court to the extent that the latter judgments confirmed the Commission's second decision, it could be expected that at least some of the undertakings concerned will exercise their right to have the third Commission decision again reviewed by the General Court and the Court of Justice. Assuming that this third round of judicial review will put a definitive end to the administrative and judicial proceedings, it is foreseeable that 22 or 23 years could easily have passed by then.[1603] There is undeniably a real risk in this case that the Court of Justice may consider that the overall duration of the proceedings, including the two stages before the General Court following the Commission's first and second decisions, is unreasonably long.[1604] The question then arises whether this should have precluded the Commission from adopting a third decision.

1600 See Opinion of Advocate General Kokott in *Solvay v Commission*, C-109/10 P, EU:C:2011:256, paragraph 237, and the case law referred to therein, and Final Report of the Hearing Officer, Case AT.37956 – *Reinforcing bars* [2020] OJ C312/06, paragraph 14.

1601 See Opinion of Advocate General Kokott in *Solvay v Commission*, C-109/10 P, EU:C:2011:256, paragraph 347, and Final Report of the Hearing Officer, Case AT.37956 – *Reinforcing bars* [2020] OJ C312/06, paragraph 15.

1602 See Opinion of Advocate General Kokott in *Solvay v Commission*, C-109/10 P, EU:C:2011:256, paragraphs 238 and 239, and Final Report of the Hearing Officer, Case AT.37956 – *Reinforcing bars* [2020] OJ C312/06, paragraph 16. It cannot be argued that the Commission should only assess the duration of its own proceedings. Article 41(1) and the second paragraph of Article 47 of the Charter of Fundamental Rights are but two expressions of the same fundamental right of the parties to have their case done with within a reasonable time. From the point of view of the undertakings concerned, all that matters is when their 'affair' is finally adjudicated upon by an impartial authority; see Opinion of Advocate General Kokott in *Solvay v Commission*, C-109/10 P, EU:C:2011:256, paragraph 240, and Final Report of the Hearing Officer, Case AT.37956 – *Reinforcing bars* [2020] OJ C312/06, paragraph 17. The Commission cannot absolve itself from all responsibility for the overall duration of the proceedings, including the judicial stages, because the compatibility with fundamental rights of the system in which the Commission acts both as investigator and first-instance decision-maker in antitrust cases is dependent on the parties having the possibility to have the Commission's decisions reviewed by the EU Courts; see Judgment in *Schindler v Commission*, C-501/11 P, EU:C:2013:522, paragraph 34, and Final Report of the Hearing Officer, Case AT.37956 – *Reinforcing bars* [2020] OJ C312/06, paragraph 18; see further Chapter IX of this book.

1603 See Final Report of the Hearing Officer, Case AT.37956 – *Reinforcing bars* [2020] OJ C312/06, paragraph 13.

1604 Final Report of the Hearing Officer, Case AT.37956 – *Reinforcing bars* [2020] OJ C312/06, paragraph 19.

According to the European Court of Human Rights, a failure to adjudicate within a reasonable time must, as a procedural irregularity constituting the breach of a fundamental right, give rise to an entitlement of the party concerned to an effective remedy granting it appropriate relief.[1605]

The Court of Justice has often been confronted with the question what remedy the General Court or the Court of Justice itself should grant if the General Court or the Court of Justice finds that the administrative and/or judicial proceedings in an antitrust case have been unreasonably long. The Court of Justice has consistently held that the General Court or the Court of Justice can only annul a Commission decision finding an infringement of Articles 101 or 102 TFEU and imposing fines for such an infringement if it has been proven that the unreasonable duration of the administrative and/or judicial proceedings has adversely affected the ability of the undertakings concerned to defend themselves in the administrative and/or judicial proceedings. Abstract and imprecise claims by the undertakings concerned that their rights of the defence were breached are not sufficient.[1606] What must be proven is a concrete adverse effect on the undertaking's ability to defend itself, for instance in that the individuals within the undertaking that would be able to provide exculpatory explanations of the evidence in the Commission's file were no longer alive or available at the time the undertaking was granted belated access to the Commission's file, whereas those individuals would have been available if the access to the file had not been belated.[1607]

In the absence of a proven concrete adverse effect on the undertaking's ability to defend itself, the Court of Justice has always held that the General Court or the Court of Justice could only grant financial compensation. Whereas older case law considered that this compensation could be granted by the General Court or the Court of Justice in the form of a reduction of the fine applied by the Court in the exercise of its unlimited jurisdiction within the meaning of Article 261 TFEU,[1608] the more recent case law considers that the appropriate remedy is for the undertaking concerned to bring a separate action for damages under Article 268 TFEU in conjunction with the second paragraph of Article 340 TFEU.[1609]

This case law concerns the remedy the General Court or the Court of Justice should grant if the General Court or the Court of Justice finds that the administrative and/or judicial proceedings in an antitrust case have been unreasonably long, whereas the question the

---

1605 See Judgment in *Kudla v Poland*, Application 30210/96, paragraphs 150–156; see also Judgment in *Groupe Gascogne v Commission*, C-58/12 P, EU:C:2013:770, paragraph 72, and Final Report of the Hearing Officer, Case AT.37956 – *Reinforcing bars* [2020] OJ C312/06, paragraph 20.

1606 See Judgment in *Nederlandse Federatieve Vereniging voor de Groothandel op Elektrotechnisch Gebied v Commission*, C-105/04 P, EU:C:2006:592, paragraphs 42 and 43; Opinion of Advocate General Kokott in *Solvay v Commission*, C-109/10 P, EU:C:2011:256, paragraphs 250 to 262; and Final Report of the Hearing Officer, Case AT.37956 – *Reinforcing bars* [2020] OJ C312/06, paragraphs 21 and 22.

1607 See Judgment in *Nederlandse Federatieve Vereniging voor de Groothandel op Elektrotechnisch Gebied v Commission*, C-105/04 P, EU:C:2006:592, paragraphs 56 and 49; Opinion of Advocate General Kokott in *Solvay v Commission*, C-109/10 P, EU:C:2011:256, paragraphs 312 to 320; and Final Report of the Hearing Officer, Case AT.37956 – *Reinforcing bars* [2020] OJ C312/06, paragraph 23; see also Judgment in *Xellia Pharmaceuticals and Aplpharma v Commission*, T-471/13, EU:T:2016:460, paragraphs 357 to 371.

1608 Judgment in *Baustahlgewebe v Commission*, C-185/95 P, EU:C:1998:608, paragraph 48.

1609 Judgments in *Der Grüne Punkt – Duales System Deutschland v Commission*, C-385/07 P, EU:C:2009:456, paragraph 195; *Groupe Gascogne v Commission*, C-58/12 P, EU:C:2013:770, paragraphs 81–83; *Bolloré v Commission*, C-414/12 P, EU:C:2014:301, paragraph 106; and *CEPSA v Commission*, C-608/13 P, EU:C:2016:414, paragraph 71.

Commission was confronted with in the *Reinforcing bars* case was the different question whether it should continue proceedings and adopt a new, third decision, which, with the ensuing judicial review, to which the undertakings are fully entitled, would easily prolong the already very long proceedings by another four or five years.[1610] An essential difference is that the Commission is under no obligation to resume proceedings after an annulment on procedural grounds of an earlier decision finding an antitrust infringement and imposing fines, nor under any obligation to continue such resumed proceedings until the adoption of a new decision.[1611]

The undertakings concerned by the *Reinforcing bars* case argued that, in a situation where there is a real risk that the Court of Justice may consider that the overall duration of the proceedings is already unreasonably long, the Commission would necessarily lose all discretion and would automatically be obliged to discontinue the proceedings.[1612] This view appears wrong in that it puts too one-sidedly all weight on the need to protect the undertakings' rights under the Charter of Fundamental Rights to have their case dealt with within a reasonable time, while neglecting entirely the importance of the implementation of the EU competition rules, which is a fundamental aim of the EU Treaties.[1613]

The correct position rather appears to be that, in such a situation, the Commission is under an obligation, in the exercise of its discretion whether or not to resume proceedings and to continue such proceedings up to the adoption of a new decision finding an antitrust infringement and imposing fines, to consider and give due weight to the possible breach of the undertakings' fundamental right to have their case dealt with within a reasonable time that has already occurred as well as to the further impact of its decision on the protection of the undertakings' fundamental right. This means that, before adopting a new decision, the Commission must examine, taking into account all the circumstances of the case, whether the contribution that the adoption of such a new decision makes to the attainment of the aim of the implementation of the EU competition rules would not be outweighed by the impact of this course of action on the protection of the undertakings' rights under the Charter of Fundamental Rights. If the outcome of the balancing exercise is that the contribution that the adoption of a new decision makes to the attainment of the aim of the implementation of the EU competition rules outweighs the impact of this course of action on the respect for the undertakings' fundamental right under the Charter, the Commission can adopt such a third decision. To remedy the possible breach of the undertakings' fundamental right, the Commission must then, in my view, grant a reduction in the amount of the fines. The size of the reduction must reflect the specificities of the case, including the fact that the excessive duration as a result of the annulment of earlier decisions is not attributable to the conduct of the undertakings.[1614]

1610 See Final Report of the Hearing Officer, Case AT.37956 – *Reinforcing bars* [2020] OJ C312/06, paragraph 28.

1611 See Final Report of the Hearing Officer, Case AT.37956 – *Reinforcing bars* [2020] OJ C312/06, paragraphs 29 and 30.

1612 See Final Report of the Hearing Officer, Case AT.37956 – *Reinforcing bars* [2020] OJ C312/06, paragraph 31.

1613 See Opinion 2/13 (Accession of the EU to the ECHR) of the Court of Justice, EU:C:2014:2454, paragraph 172; Opinion of Advocate General Kokott in *Solvay v Commission*, C-109/10 P, EU:C:2011:256, paragraph 328; and Final Report of the Hearing Officer, Case AT.37956 – *Reinforcing bars* [2020] OJ C312/06, paragraph 31.

1614 See Final Report of the Hearing Officer, Case AT.37956 – *Reinforcing bars* [2020] OJ C312/06, paragraphs 32 to 34.

A similar approach has been taken by the Commission in the *Reinforcing bars* case. As explained in the summary of the third decision adopted in July 2019:

'In the present case, the Commission's discretion to adopt a decision must be exercised by weighing up the public interest in obtaining effective enforcement of the competition rules against the interest of the addressees in obtaining the fullest possible remedy for the alleged infringement of their fundamental rights owing to the lengthy duration of the proceedings.

The outcome of the Commission weighing up the respective interests shows that, in the present case, the adoption of a decision imposing fines will avoid impunity of the parties by ensuring a deterrent effect and consistent and effective application of the competition rules. At the same time, the specific circumstances of this case were taken into consideration by the Commission for the purposes of setting the fines applicable to the addressees of the Decision. The addressees will therefore be able to benefit from an appropriate reduction of the fines otherwise applicable, in order to mitigate the potential consequences of procedural errors committed by the Commission.

[. . .] the Commission concludes that a reduction of the fines of 50% as an extraordinary attenuating circumstance may be granted in order to mitigate the negative consequences for the addressees of this Decision arising from the lengthy duration of the proceedings.'[1615]

6. Further legal and policy considerations

On various occasions,[1616] concerns have been expressed about the EU law and practice concerning re-adoption of cartel fining decisions following annulments for procedural reasons: What is the point of judicial review if, following an annulment, the same decision can be re-adopted? What incentives remain for the Commission to respect the procedural rules? And is this EU law and practice compatible with the case law of the European Court of Human Rights?

Such questioning could be enlarged to cover also the EU (case) law according to which not all procedural irregularities constitute grounds for annulment but only those in the absence of which the contested decision might have been substantially different (sometimes referred to in the literature as the 'harmless error principle').[1617] According to the Court of Justice, '[t]hat rule makes good sense since it would be a manifestly disproportionate and wrong result if a decision correct as to its content were to be struck down

---

1615 Commission Decision of 4 July 2019 relating to a proceeding under Article 65 of the ECSC Treaty (Case AT.37956) [2020] OJ C312/13, paragraphs 24, 25 and 45 of the summary.

1616 See, for instance, the panel discussion 'And so what? Procedural violations in EU Competition Law' at the 4th Chillin' Competition Conference (Brussels, 28 November 2018; https://chillingcompetition.com/), and L. Idot, *Europe*, 2012, comm. 330, 'Reprise d'une décision annulée en matière de cartels', and *Europe*, 2014, comm. 305, 'Reprise d'une décision annulée et délai raisonnable'.

1617 See Judgments in *Infineon Technologies v Commission*, C-99/17 P, EU:C:2018:773, paragraphs 77 and 78, and in *ICF v Commission*, C-467/13 P, EU:C:2004:2274, paragraphs 26 to 29; Opinion of Advocate General Wahl in *SKW Metallurgie v Commission*, C-154/14 P, EU:C:2015:543; H. P. Nehl, *Principles of Administrative Procedure in EC Law* (Hart Publishing 1999) at 97; and E. Barbier de la Serre, '*UPS/TNT*: Taking the Right to be Heard Seriously' (2017) 8 *Journal of European Competition Law & Practice* 502.

owing to a flaw in the procedure leading to its adoption which, however, had no effect on the content of the decision'.[1618]

Both the 'harmless error principle' and the possibility of re-adoption of decisions annulled on procedural grounds reflect a predominantly instrumental conception of procedural rules. The underlying idea is that procedural rules predominantly exist to ensure the correctness of the substantive outcomes.[1619]

The EU law on re-adoption of cartel fining decisions annulled on procedural grounds appears fully compatible with the European Convention on Human Rights and the case law of the European Court of Human Rights.[1620]

As already apparent from the above analysis on the principle of *ne bis in idem*, Article 4(1) of Protocol No 7 ECHR limits the prohibition of a second procedure or second punishment to the situation where the defendant 'has already been finally acquitted or convicted in accordance with the law and penal procedure of that State'. As clarified by the *PVC II* judgment, this is not the case for a European Commission cartel fining decision that has been annulled by the EU Courts on procedural grounds, and without the EU Courts having exercised their unlimited jurisdiction. Moreover, Article 4(2) of Protocol No 7 ECHR provides that the prohibition of a second procedure or second punishment 'shall not prevent the reopening of the case in accordance with the law and penal procedure of the State concerned, [. . .] if there has been a fundamental defect in the previous proceedings, which could affect the outcome of the case'.

In the same spirit, the European Court of Human Rights has a 'settled case-law to the effect that when the applicant has suffered an infringement of his rights guaranteed by Article 6 of the Convention, he should, as far as possible, be put in the position in which he would have been had the requirements of that provision not been disregarded, and that the most appropriate form of redress would, in principle, be the reopening of proceedings'.[1621]

Fears about the lack of incentives for the Commission to respect procedural rules do not appear justified either. As an institution charged with guarding EU law,[1622] the Commission is naturally inclined to respect procedural rules. It has also created in its internal organisation the function of Hearing Officer for competition proceedings, whose

---

1618 Judgment in *Hercules v Commission*, C-51/92 P, EU:C:1999:357, paragraph 68.

1619 See P. Craig, *EU Administrative Law* (3rd edition, Oxford UP 2018) at 361–362; Opinion of Advocate General Ruiz-Jarabo Colomer in *Aalborg, Portland and Others v Commission*, C-204/00 P, EU:C:2003:85, paragraph 30 ('In short, defects in the procedure do not have a life of their own in isolation from the substance of the case.'); H. P. Nehl, *Principles of Administrative Procedure in EC Law* (Hart Publishing 1999) at 98, footnote 254 (referring to the German concept of *dienende Funktion* ('serving function') of administrative procedure); E. Barbier de la Serre, 'Procedural Justice in the European Community Case-law concerning the Rights of the Defence: Essentialist and Instrumental Trends' (2006) 12 *European Public Law* 225; and Chapter X of this book.

1620 The 'harmless error principle' also appears perfectly in line with the case law of the European Court of Human Rights; see, for instance, Judgment of 15 February 2007 in *Verdú Verdú v Spain*, Application no 43432/02, paragraphs 27 and 28.

1621 Judgment of 23 October 2018 in Case of *Produkcija Plus storitveno podjete D. A.o. v Slovenia*, Application no 47072/15, paragraph 65.

1622 See Article 17(1) TEU.

general mission is to safeguard the effective exercise of procedural rights throughout competition proceedings before the Commission.[1623]

In any event, even in those cases where the Commission can subsequently resume its proceedings and adopt a new decision, the annulment of the initial decision is never without cost for the Commission. First, annulments on procedural grounds cause reputational damage. Secondly, when annulling the initial decision, the EU Courts invariably condemn the Commission to the costs of the court proceedings.[1624] Third, reopening proceedings and adopting a new decision consumes administrative resources. Finally, when, following an annulment, the Commission reimburses a provisionally paid fine, it must pay default interest calculated from the day of the provisional payment at a standard rate. Indeed, in its judgment confirming this obligation, the Court of Justice specifically mentioned its incentive effect:

'[T]*he obligation, in the event of annulment of a decision entailing the provisional payment of an amount such as a fine imposed for infringement of competition rules, to repay the amount paid together with default interest calculated from the date of payment of that amount is an incentive for the institution concerned to pay particular attention when adopting such decisions, which may entail an obligation for an individual to pay a considerable amount immediately.*'[1625]

As to the incentives for addressees of cartel fining decisions to raise procedural pleas before the EU Courts, there is no indication that such pleas have been raised less frequently since the *PVC II* judgment of October 2002, which made the possibility of re-adoptions fully clear. Furthermore, as discussed above, the Commission cannot always resume proceedings after an annulment on procedural grounds,[1626] and has not always done so in cases where it could in principle have resumed proceedings.[1627] Finally, when re-adoption has happened, the newly imposed fines have in several cases been lower than the initial fines,[1628] while they have never exceeded the initial fines.[1629]

1623 See Chapter XI of this book.

1624 As already mentioned above, in the *Envelopes (Printeos/Tompla)* case, the General Court even condemned the Commission again to the costs when rejecting the application for annulment brought against the second decision.

1625 Judgment in *Commission v Printeos*, C-301/19 P, EU:C:2021:39, paragraph 86.

1626 See, in particular, the example of the *Butadiene rubber (Eni/Polimeri/Versalis)* case above, and the issue of prescription discussed above.

1627 See the example of the *Soda ash* case above.

1628 See the *Reinforcing Bars, Carbonless paper (Bolloré), Gas insulated switchgear (Mitsubishi and Toshiba)* and *Retail food packaging (CCPL/Coopbox)* cases above.

1629 See the *Airfreight* case above on the asymmetric application of a cap of 10% of turnover in the last business year preceding the (re-)adoption of the decision.

XVII. Private Enforcement of EU Antitrust Law and its Relationship with Public Enforcement: Past, Present and Future

This chapter contains a history of private enforcement of EU antitrust law and its relationship with public enforcement, from the 1957 EEC Treaty over Regulation 17 and Regulation 1/2003 until Directive 2014/104 and the current outlook.

A. Introduction

Private enforcement refers to the use of Articles 101 and 102 TFEU in litigation between private parties in the courts of the EU Member States,[1630] as opposed to **public enforcement**, the latter referring to proceedings conducted or brought by competition authorities (either the European Commission or the competition authorities of the EU Member States), including such proceedings that are triggered by complaints from private parties to such authorities.

Three types of private enforcement can be distinguished,[1631] corresponding to three ways in which Articles 101 and 102 TFEU can be invoked in litigation between private parties:

- Articles 101 and 102 TFEU may be used as a 'shield', that is **as a defence** against a contractual claim for performance or for damages because of non-performance or against some other claim, for instance in an intellectual property infringement action;
- Articles 101 and 102 TFEU may be used offensively, as a 'sword', as a basis for **claims for injunctive relief, including interim relief**;
- Articles 101 and 102 TFEU may be used offensively, as a 'sword', as a basis for **claims for damages.**[1632]

1630 Private enforcement actions can equally be brought by public bodies that, as buyers of goods or services, suffer harm as a result of an antitrust infringement. For instance, the European Commission, as a purchaser of elevators for its office buildings, has brought an action for damages against some companies involved in the elevators and escalators cartel; see judgment in *Europese Gemeenschap v Otis*, C-199/11, EU:C:2012:684. Private enforcement of Articles 101 and 102 TFEU could also take place in foreign courts or before arbitration panels that have jurisdiction to hear the case.

1631 See F. G. Jacobs and T. Deisenhofer, 'Procedural Aspects of the Effective Private Enforcement of EC Competition Rules: A Community Perspective', in C.-D. Ehlermann and I. Atanasiu (eds), *European Competition Law Annual 2001: Effective Private Enforcement of EC Antitrust Law* (Hart Publishing 2003), 187 at 189, and my paper 'Should Private Antitrust Enforcement Be Encouraged in Europe?' (2003) 26 *World Competition* 473, also accessible at http://ssrn.com/author=456087, at footnotes 2 to 13.

1632 Article 2(5) of Directive 2014/104/EU of the European Parliament and of the Council of 26 November 2014 on certain rules governing actions for damages under national law for infringements of the competition law provisions of the Member States of the European Union [2014] OJ L349/1, defines 'claim for damages' as 'a claim for compensation for harm caused by an infringement of competition law'.

Private actions may be brought concerning alleged infringements that neither are nor have been the object of public enforcement proceedings (**stand-alone actions**).

Private actions may also run in parallel with or follow upon public enforcement proceedings concerning the same alleged infringement. The two most common types of such links between private actions and public enforcement proceedings appear to be the following:

- **Claims for interim relief pending public enforcement proceedings**: A private party may bring a complaint concerning an alleged antitrust infringement before a competition authority and, while the authority is investigating the complaint or once the authority has opened proceedings with a view to adopting a prohibition decision, the complainant may in a private action request interim relief pending the outcome of the public enforcement proceedings.
  For instance, in the *Dutch Crane-Hire* case, the complainant, whose complaint against certain rules of two Dutch associations of crane-hire firms triggered the European Commission's investigation under Article 101 TFEU, sought and indeed obtained, once the European Commission had sent a statement of objections, an injunction in a private action in the Dutch courts against the two associations, suspending the application of the contested rules until the European Commission had adopted a decision on the matter.[1633]
- **Follow-on actions for damages**: After a competition authority has concluded its proceedings with the finding of an infringement of Article 101 or Article 102 TFEU, private parties may bring an action for damages in national court against the undertakings found to have committed the infringement so as to obtain compensation for the damage suffered as a result of that infringement.

Actions for damages that do not directly rely on a finding of infringement made in public enforcement proceedings are considered to be **stand-alone actions for damages**. Such stand-alone actions may, however, be related in a less direct way with public enforcement proceedings. For instance, in the first stand-alone damages case heard by the UK Competition Appeal Tribunal, the supermarket Sainsbury's was awarded 68.6 million pounds in damages from MasterCard resulting from the multilateral interchange fee (MIF) as set and applied by MasterCard for transactions in the UK (UK MIF) as from December 2006.[1634] Sainsbury's could not rely on any public enforcement decision covering the same MIF and the same time period, but its private action had been preceded by a decision of the European Commission, confirmed by the EU General Court and Court of Justice, finding an infringement of Article 101 TFEU in relation to MasterCard's MIF for cross-border transactions between EEA countries (intra-EEA MIF) during the December 1992–December 2007 period.[1635]

1633 See Commission Decision of 29 November 1995 relating to a proceeding pursuant to Article 85 of the EC Treaty (IV/34.179, 34.202, 216 – *Stichting Certificatie Kraanverhuurbedrijf and the Federatie van Nederlandse Kraanverhuurbedrijven*) [1995] OJ L312/79, paragraph 13. For another example of a similar situation, see Judgment in *Postbank v Commission*, T-353/94, EU:T:1996:119. The frequency of this type of cases depends, of course, on the availability, in law and in practice, of interim measures granted by the competition authority investigating the main case.

1634 Judgment of 14 July 2016 in *Sainsbury's v MasterCard* [2016] CAT 11.

1635 Idem, at paragraphs 14 to 16 and 20 to 26 and Annex 2; European Commission Decision of 19 December 2007 in Case COMP/34.579 *MasterCard* [2009] OJ C264/8; and Judgments in *MasterCard v European Commission*, T-111/08, EU:T:2012:260, and C-382/12, EU:C:2014:2201.

B. Before Regulation 1/2003

1. The Treaty provisions

The provisions on antitrust initially laid down in Articles 85 to 89 of the 1957 Treaty establishing the European Economic Community have remained essentially unchanged through the successive Treaty changes, and are currently contained in Articles 101 to 105 TFEU.[1636] In the remainder of this chapter, I will use the current Article numbers and Treaty name, even when referring to times when earlier versions were in force.

In these Treaty provisions, the focus is clearly on public enforcement.

Article 105(1) TFEU provides that the European Commission 'shall ensure the application of the principles laid down in Articles 101 and 102',[1637] and that it must act 'in cooperation with the competent authorities in the Member States'.

Article 103 TFEU provides that the Council adopt implementing regulations, and lists a number of issues that these implementing regulations should cover in particular, including 'provision for fines and periodic penalty payments', 'detailed rules for the application of Article 101(3), taking into account the need to ensure effective supervision on the one hand, and to simplify administration to the greatest extent possible on the other', and a definition of 'the respective functions of the Commission and of the Court of Justice'.

For a transitional period, until the implementing regulations adopted by the Council pursuant to Article 103 TFEU have entered into force, Article 104 TFEU entrusts the authorities of the Member States with applying Articles 101 and 102.

The only reference to private enforcement is contained in Article 101(2) TFEU, which provides that 'any agreements or decisions prohibited pursuant to this Article shall be automatically void'. This points to the first of the three types of private enforcement identified above, more specifically to the use of Article 101 TFEU as a defence in contractual litigation.

The text of the Treaty provisions is silent on other types of private enforcement (private actions for injunctive relief and for damages, as well as the use of Article 102 TFEU as a defence in private litigation), as well as on the relationship between public and private enforcement.

2. Regulation 17

In 1962 the Council adopted, pursuant to Article 103 TFEU, Regulation 17, the first regulation implementing Articles 101 and 102 TFEU,[1638] which has governed the application of Articles 101 and 102 TFEU until it was replaced by Regulation 1/2003 on 1 May 2004.

1636 The main change has been the addition, through the 2007 Lisbon Treaty, of the third paragraph of Article 105 TFEU, which confirms the Council's and Commission's respective powers with regard to block exemption regulations, as already recognised in practice since the 1960s.

1637 As the General Court has pointed out in its judgment in *Automec v European Commission*, T-24/90, EU:T:1992:97, paragraph 74, Article 105(1) TFEU constitutes the specific expression in the antitrust area of the general supervisory role conferred on the European Commission by Article 17(1) TEU.

1638 Council Regulation No 17 [1962] OJ 13/204 (Special English Edition 1959-62, p 87).

Regulation 17 focused exclusively on public enforcement.

The European Commission was given exclusive competence to apply Article 101(3) TFEU through exemption decisions, and the grant of such decisions was made dependent on the agreement having been notified by the parties to the European Commission.[1639]

The European Commission was empowered to find infringements of Articles 101 and 102 TFEU and to order their termination, either on its own initiative or upon complaints from the EU Member States or from private parties showing a legitimate interest, as well as to impose fines and periodic penalty payments.[1640]

Regulation 17 also recognised the competence of the competition authorities of the EU Member States to apply Articles 101(1) and 102 TFEU, but provided that they lost their competence to deal with a specific case once the European Commission had initiated proceedings in that case.[1641]

In the memorandum accompanying its proposal for what became Regulation 17, the European Commission had mentioned, when discussing fines and periodic penalty payments, that in addition to these penalties may be added the publicity of the decision and the risks inherent in the nullity of the agreement and in claims for damages that third parties might raise.[1642] Neither the Commission nor the Council did, however, see fit to include any reference to private enforcement in the articles or recitals of Regulation 17.

3. The case law of the EU Court of Justice

In a series of cases, starting relatively soon after the entry into force of the Treaty in 1958, the EU Court of Justice was called upon to clarify the possibility of private enforcement of Articles 101 and 102 TFEU as well as the relationship between public and private enforcement. Indeed, the very first case reaching the Court of Justice through the preliminary reference mechanism from a national court concerned a dispute between private parties before the Dutch civil courts in which Article 101 TFEU was invoked as a defence.[1643]

In its case law, the Court of Justice progressively clarified that Article 101(1) and Article 102 TFEU produce direct effects between individuals and create rights for these individuals, and that the national courts whose task it is to apply the provisions of EU law in areas within their jurisdiction must ensure that those rules take full effect and must protect the rights which they confer on individuals, by granting injunctive relief, including interim relief, as well as compensation for harm suffered, under conditions that may not be less favourable than those governing the protection of comparable rights under national law and that ensure the effective protection of the rights conferred by Articles 101(1) and 102 TFEU.[1644]

1639 Articles 4 to 9(1) of Regulation 17.

1640 Articles 3 and 15 of Regulation 17.

1641 Article 9(3) Regulation 17.

1642 *Premier règlement d'application des articles 85 et 86 du Traité (Proposition de la Commission au Conseil)* (1960), at 3.

1643 *De Geus v Bosch and Van Rijn*, 13/61, EU:C:1962:11.

1644 Judgments in *BRT and SABAM*, 127/73, EU:C:1974:25, in *Factortame and Others*, C-213/89, EU:C:1990:257, and in *Courage v Crehan*, C-453/99, EU:C:2001:465.

As to the relationship between public and private enforcement, the case law has emphasised the primary role of the European Commission, and thus of public enforcement, as resulting from Article 105 TFEU and Regulation 17, and the correspondingly supplemental role of private enforcement. In particular:

- Under the 'provisional validity' doctrine, the Court of Justice effectively prohibited private enforcement of Article 101 TFEU in relation to agreements that predated Regulation 17 and had been notified to the European Commission under that regulation until they had been the subject of a decision by the European Commission rejecting the request for an exemption under Article 101(3) TFEU.[1645]
- As to complaints brought by private parties before the European Commission, the case law has clarified that, unlike civil courts, whose task is to safeguard the individual rights of private persons in their relations *inter se*, the European Commission as an administrative authority must act in the public interest; that, consequently, the European Commission is entitled to refer to the EU interest in order to determine the degree of priority to be applied to the various cases brought to its notice; and that, where it finds insufficient EU interest and the national courts can protect the complainant's rights, it may refer the complainant to the national courts.[1646]
- As to the relationship between the European Commission and national courts in those instances where they share competence, the Court of Justice held in *Masterfoods* that national courts must, when ruling on agreements or practices that may subsequently be the subject of a decision by the European Commission, avoid giving decisions that could conflict with a decision contemplated by the European Commission in the implementation of Articles 101(1) and 102 and Article 101(3) TFEU; that when national courts rule on agreements or practices that are already the subject of a European Commission's decision they cannot take decisions running counter to that of the European Commission, even if the latter's decision conflicts with a prior decision given by a national court; and, conversely, that the European Commission cannot be bound by a decision given by a national court in the application of Articles 101(1) and 102 TFEU, and that the European Commission is entitled to adopt at any time individual decisions under Articles 101 and 102 TFEU, even where an agreement or practice has already been the subject of a decision by a national court and the decision contemplated by the European Commission conflicts with that national court's decision.[1647]

4. The practice of private enforcement before Regulation 1/2003

Looking at the practice of EU antitrust enforcement before Regulation 1/2003, it is clear that public enforcement, mainly by the European Commission, played the central role. Private enforcement played, however, a supplementary role.

1645 Judgments in *De Geus v Bosch and Van Rijn*, 13/61, EU:C:1962:11, in *Brasserie de Haecht v Wilkin*, 48/72, EU:C:1973:11, and in *KVBBB v Free Record Shop*, C-39/96, EU:C:1997:214.

1646 Judgments in *Automec v European Commission*, T-24/90, EU:T:1992:97, paragraphs 85 to 94, and in *Ufex and Others v European Commission*, C-119/97 P, EU:C:1999:116, paragraph 88.

1647 Judgment in *Masterfoods and HB*, C-344/98, EU:C:2000:689, paragraphs 51, 52 and 48.

It is notoriously difficult to obtain precise figures about private enforcement. Commercial disputes are routinely settled, often before they reach the courts. Many of the cases that reach the courts are settled before they reach final judgments. Even those cases that reach final judgment are not necessarily reported.

On the basis of the available evidence,[1648] it would appear that, in the last years before the replacement of Regulation 17 by Regulation 1/2003 on 1 May 2004, Articles 101 and 102 TFEU were invoked in at least several dozen private cases per year.

Private enforcement appears to have been particularly well established in Germany and in the Netherlands, but also substantial in Belgium, the United Kingdom, Austria, Italy, France and Spain.

Most of the cases involved the use of Articles 101 and 102 TFEU as a defence or their offensive use to obtain injunctive relief, sometimes combined with an additional claim for damages. These cases were mostly stand-alone cases, and mostly concerned either vertical agreements or abuse of dominance.

C. Regulation 1/2003

1. Abolition of the notification system and accompanying changes

As from 1 May 2014, Regulation 17 was replaced by Regulation 1/2003.[1649]

The main change consisted in the abolition of the centralised notification and authorisation system for Article 101(3) TFEU and its replacement by a directly applicable exception system.

Both the competition authorities of the Member States and the national courts are thus empowered to apply not only Articles 101(1) and 102 TFEU, but the whole of Articles 101 and 102 TFEU.[1650]

Whereas Regulation 17 did not mention national courts, their role is explicitly recognised in Regulation 1/2003, recital 7 of which reads as follows:

'National courts have an essential part to play in applying the [EU] competition rules. When deciding disputes between private individuals, they protect the subjective rights

---

1648 See in particular B. Rodger, *Competition Law Comparative Private Enforcement and Collective Redress across the EU* (Wolters Kluwer 2014), Part I, Chapters 3 and 4; U. Böge and K. Ost, 'Up and Running, or is it? Private enforcement – the Situation in Germany and Policy Perspectives' (2006) *European Competition Law Review* 197 at 197; J. Temple Lang, 'Foreword', in C. A. Jones, *Private Enforcement of Antitrust Law in the EU, UK and USA* (Oxford UP 1999), at ix; and B. J. Rodger, 'Private enforcement of competition law, the hidden story: competition litigation settlements in the United Kingdom, 2000–2005' (2008) *European Competition Law Review* 96.

1649 Council Regulation (EC) No 1/2003 of 16 December 2002 on the implementation of the rules on competition laid down in Articles 81 and 82 of the Treaty [2003] OJ L1/1. See further Chapter I of this book.

1650 The power to withdraw the benefit of exemption regulations in individual cases remains, however, reserved for the European Commission and, within certain limits, the competition authorities of the Member States; see Article 29 of Regulation 1/2003.

under [EU] law, for example by awarding damages to the victims of infringements. The role of national courts here complements that of the competition authorities of the Member States. They should therefore be allowed to apply [Articles 101 and 102 TFEU] in full.'

In order to avoid that the abolition of the European Commission's monopoly to apply Article 101(3) TFEU would lead to a renationalisation of competition policy, Article 3 of Regulation 1/2003 obliges both the competition authorities of the Member States and national courts to apply also Articles 101 or 102 TFEU whenever they apply national competition law to agreements or practices that fall within the scope of Articles 101 or 102 TFEU, and precludes the application of national competition laws that are stricter than Article 101 TFEU to agreements falling within the scope of Article 101 TFEU.[1651]

2. Relationship between private and public enforcement

Regulation 1/2003 contains four provisions concerning the relationship between private enforcement and public enforcement, two of which codify previous case law of the Court of Justice and two of which were new:

- Article 16(1) codifies the *Masterfoods* case law, mentioned above,[1652] confirming that, when national courts rule on agreements or practices under Articles 101 or 102 TFEU which are already the subject of a European Commission's decision, they cannot take decisions running counter to the decision adopted by the Commission; and that they must also avoid giving decisions which would conflict with a decision contemplated by the Commission in proceedings it has initiated;
- Article 15(1) provides that, in proceedings for the application of Articles 101 or 102 TFEU, national courts may ask the European Commission to transmit to them information in its possession or its opinion on questions concerning the application of the EU antitrust rules. This provision also reflects previous case law;[1653]
- Article 15(3) provides that the competition authorities of the Member States, acting on their own initiative, may submit observations to the national courts of their Member State on issues relating to the application of Articles 101 or 102 TFEU, and that, where the coherent application of Article 101 or 102 TFEU so requires, the European Commission may similarly intervene as *amicus curiae* in cases before courts of the Member States.

  Whereas the case law predating Regulation 1/2003 only concerned the relationship between the European Commission and national courts, this provision also empowers, even primarily, the competition authorities of the Member States in relation to their national courts. This reflects the fact that under Regulation 1/2003, most of the public enforcement of Articles 101 and 102 TFEU is done by the national competition authorities, in close cooperation with the European Commission and with each other inside the European Competition Network.[1654]

1651 See Chapters I and II of this book.

1652 Judgment in *Masterfoods and HB*, C-344/98, EU:C:2000:689.

1653 See Orders in *Zwartveld*, C-2/88, EU:C:1990:315 and EU:C:1990:440, and Judgment in *Netherlands and Van der Wal v European Commission*, C-174/98 P and C-189/98 P, EU:C:2000:1, paragraph 25.

1654 See Article 11(1) and recital 15 of Regulation 1/2003; Commission Notice on cooperation within the Network of Competition Authorities [2004] OJ C101/43; and Chapter I of this book.

- Finally, Article 15(2) provides that Member States shall forward to the European Commission a copy of any written judgment of national courts deciding on the application of Article 101 or 102 TFEU.
  This information could possibly lead the European Commission to make use of its power under Article 15(3) to intervene as *amicus curiae* if the case reaches a higher national court on appeal, or to initiate itself proceedings, as allowed under the *Masterfoods* case law.

3. The impact of Regulation 1/2003 on the practice of private enforcement

The main effect of Regulation 1/2003 has been in the sphere of public enforcement.

Indeed, the empowerment of national competition authorities to apply Article 101(3) TFEU, the obligation under Article 3 of Regulation 1/2003 to apply also Articles 101 and 102 TFEU whenever national competition law is applied to agreements or practices falling within the scope of Articles 101 and 102 TFEU, and the close cooperation between the European Commission and the national competition authorities within the European Competition Network have quickly led to a major increase in the public enforcement of Articles 101 and 102 TFEU by the national competition authorities.[1655]

This large increase in public enforcement of Articles 101 and 102 TFEU at the level of the EU Member States has also very substantially increased the role of the national courts that act as competition authorities (in those (relatively few) Member States in which the national competition authority does not adopt decisions finding infringements of Articles 101 or 102 TFEU and imposing fines, but rather brings the case before a national court that acts as first-instance decision-maker) as well as (in all Member States) the role of the (higher) national courts that act as review courts before which appeals or applications for judicial review against the decisions of national competition authorities can be brought.

As to the impact of Regulation 1/2003 on private enforcement, three effects can be distinguished:

- The first effect concerns the defensive use of Article 101 TFEU in contractual litigation. Regulation 1/2003 has brought to an end the phenomenon of agreements falling under Article 101(1) TFEU and fulfilling the conditions of Article 101(3) TFEU but not covered by a block exemption regulation being unenforceable simply because they had not been notified to the European Commission. In all situations where in a contractual dispute before a national court the defendant invokes Article 101(2) TFEU, the claimant can now fully rely on Article 101(3) TFEU and the national court can itself decide on the matter.
  This change is likely to have caused a reduction in the number of cases in which Article 101 TFEU is invoked as a defence in contractual litigation. From the perspective of the optimal enforcement of Article 101 TFEU, this reduction does not, however, constitute a loss, as the enforcement of the substantive rule laid down in Article 101 TFEU, namely the prohibition on restrictive agreements without

---

1655 See the figures in Chapter I of this book, showing that the national competition authorities have become, in quantitative terms, the primary public enforcers of Articles 101 and 102 TFEU, adopting 90% of all decisions.

redeeming virtue, cannot possibly be served by rendering agreements that do not violate this prohibition unenforceable.[1656]

- The second effect concerns the offensive use of Article 101 TFEU, in particular in actions for injunctive relief. The abolition of the European Commission's exclusive competence to apply Article 101(3) TFEU removed the possibility for defendants to delay the national court procedure, in particular in cases where injunctive relief is sought, by notifying the agreement to the European Commission.
  This change is likely to have caused an increase in private actions seeking injunctive relief.
- The third effect concerns all types of private enforcement (defensive use, actions for injunctive relief and actions for damages) of both Article 101 and Article 102 TFEU. As a result of the obligation under Article 3 of Regulation 1/2003 for national courts to apply also Articles 101 and 102 TFEU when applying national competition law to agreements or practices falling within the scope of Articles 101 and 102 TFEU, in a number of cases in which before Regulation 1/2003 only national competition law would have been applied Articles 101 or 102 TFEU will now be applied.

The available evidence appears to confirm the above analysis, showing a decrease in the use of EU antitrust law as a defence relative to its offensive use to obtain injunctive relief in the years following the entry into application of Regulation 1/2003 compared to the preceding years,[1657] as well as an overall increase (though not a dramatic one) in the private enforcement of Articles 101 and 102 TFEU.

As to the relationship between public and private enforcement, the overall picture appears to have remained largely the same in the first years following the entry into application of Regulation 1/2003 as before Regulation 1/2003:

Public enforcement still played the central role in the application of Articles 101 and 102 TFEU, indeed even more than before, as the increased involvement of the national competition authorities, working together with the European Commission in the European Competition Network, led to a major increase in public enforcement.[1658]

Private enforcement still played a supplementary role. Most of the private cases still involved the use of Articles 101 and 102 TFEU as a defence or their offensive use to obtain injunctive relief, sometimes combined with an additional claim for damages. These cases were still mostly stand-alone cases, and mostly concerned either vertical agreements or abuse of dominance.

D. A brief flirtation with the American model

1. Private enforcement in the USA

In marked contrast with the situation in Europe (and indeed in the rest of the world), private actions for damages and, to a much lesser extent, for injunctive relief, based

---

1656 See my book *Principles of European Antitrust Enforcement* (Hart 2005), section 1.1.4.1.1.

1657 See B. Rodger, *Competition Law Comparative Private Enforcement and Collective Redress across the EU* (Wolters Kluwer, 2014), Part I, Chapters 3 and 4, in particular Chapter 4, at footnote 28.

1658 See Chapter I of this book.

on the antitrust provisions of the Sherman and Clayton Acts, are very common in the United States. Indeed, 95% of antitrust cases in the United States are private actions.[1659]

Already in 1890, Section 7 of the Sherman Act, since replaced by Section 4 of the Clayton Act, provided for private enforcement of the antitrust laws. Section 4 of the Clayton Act currently provides that 'any person who shall be injured in his business or property by reason of anything forbidden in the antitrust laws may sue therefor in [a] district court of the United States [. . .], and shall recover threefold damages by him sustained, and the cost of suit, including a reasonable attorney's fee'.[1660]

This provision thus not only creates the possibility to bring actions for damages, but specifically encourages such actions by providing in addition for treble damages and, as an exception to the normal American rule that each party bears its own costs, irrespective of whether the suit is successful, provides for a right for the successful plaintiff to recover its costs, including expert fees, and attorney's fees.[1661]

The provision of treble damages and the asymmetric cost rule reflect a **conception of private actions for damages as an instrument of deterrence and punishment.**[1662]

This conception of private actions for damages as an instrument of deterrence rather than compensation is also apparent in the case law of the US Supreme Court, which excludes the passing-on defence in actions brought by direct purchasers and denies standing to indirect purchasers.[1663]

This American conception of private actions for damages as an instrument of deterrence and punishment can be understood in the light of the specific history of US antitrust enforcement.[1664]

While the 1890 Sherman Act made antitrust violations misdemeanours, punishable by fines and imprisonment, no budgetary appropriation was made for public enforcement.[1665]

1659 H. Hovenkamp, *The Antitrust Enterprise: Principle and Execution* (Harvard University Press 2005), at 58.

1660 § 4 Clayton Act, 15 USC § 15.

1661 The cost rule is asymmetric, in that the successful defendant cannot claim recovery of its costs from the plaintiff. In Europe, cost rules are a matter of national law. The normal rule in most Member States is the symmetrical rule that the successful litigant (plaintiff or defendant) can recover costs from the other party.

1662 See my paper 'The Relationship between Public Antitrust Enforcement and Private Actions for Damages' (2009) 32 *World Competition* 3, also accessible at http://ssrn.com/author=456087, at footnotes 62 to 73.

1663 *Hanover Shoe v United Shoe Machinery*, 392 US 481 (1968) and *Illinois Brick v Illinois*, 431 US 720 (1977). A number of states allow, however, for indirect purchasers to sue under state law. In *California v ARC America*, 490 US 93 (1989), the US Supreme Court held that such state laws are not pre-empted by Section 4 of the Clayton Act. See further US Antitrust Modernization Commission, *Report and Recommendations* (April 2007), Chapter II.B 'Indirect Purchaser Litigation', and the literature referred to therein.

1664 Also, as has been pointed out by Sir Francis Jacobs, 'Civil Enforcement of EEC Antitrust Law' (1984) 82 *Michigan Law Review* 1364 at 1371: '[T]he observer detects in the United States a powerful ideological influence that favors private enforcement rather than action through the public authorities'; see more generally R. A. Kagan, *Adversarial Legalism – The American Way of Law* (Harvard University Press 2001).

1665 See D. I. Baker, 'Revisiting History – What Have We Learned About Private Antitrust Enforcement That We Would Recommend To Others?' (2004) 16 *Loyola Consumer Law* Review 379 at 382. The idea of treble damages came from the now repealed English Statute of Monopolies of 1623, 21 Jac. I, c. 3 (1623), *repealed*, S.L. (Repeals) (1969). Outside the antitrust area, other historical examples exist in Europe of multiple damages, including in ancient Roman law, but these examples always appear to correspond to time periods or situations where public enforcement was non-existent or weak; see also D. Waelbroeck and D. Slater, 'The Commission's Green Paper on Private Enforcement: 'Americanization' of EC Competition Law Enforcement?', in C.-D. Ehlermann and I. Atanasiu (eds), *European Competition Law Annual 2006: Enforcement of Prohibition*

Private treble damages actions were thus a **substitute for public enforcement**. Also later, when criminal enforcement by the Department of Justice had started, potential fines were until 1974 limited to USD 50,000, thus leaving a deterrence gap to be filled by follow-on treble damages actions.[1666] Still today, while the Department of Justice has statutory authority to prosecute all violations of Sections 1 and 2 of the Sherman Act criminally, the scope of criminal enforcement has in fact been narrowed over time to 'hard-core' price-fixing, bid-rigging or market allocation cartels.[1667] For other antitrust violations, US public enforcement is in practice limited to prospective injunctive relief, leaving a deterrence gap to be filled by follow-on treble damages actions.[1668]

The public antitrust enforcement of Articles 101 and 102 TFEU does not suffer from similar deficiencies. Indeed, the European Commission and the competition authorities of the EU Member States, working together in the European Competition Network, have a large capacity to deter and punish infringements of Articles 101 and 102 TFEU by imposing fines on the companies that commit such infringements.[1669] There would thus not appear to be any need to import into Europe the specifically American conception of private actions for damages as an instrument of deterrence and punishment.

2. The inherent superiority of public enforcement for deterrence and punishment

More fundamentally, as far as deterrence and punishment are concerned, public antitrust enforcement is inherently superior to private actions for damages.[1670]

---

of Cartels (Hart Publishing 2007), 425 at 427–428. In the case of the English Parliament's Statute of Monopolies of 1623, the King's favourites were the likely targets of enforcement under the statute, and public enforcement could thus not be relied on; see D. Baker, as above.

1666 See S. Calkins, 'An Enforcement Official's Reflections on Antitrust Class Actions' (1997) 39 *Arizona Law Review* 413, at 427–430 and 440. In 1974, US Congress reclassified Sherman Act violations as felonies, and the maximum fines have since been substantially increased; see Antitrust Procedures and Penalties Act, Pub L No 93–528, § 3, 88 Stat 1706, 1708 (1974) (raising the maximum fine to USD 1 million), Antitrust Amendments Act of 1990, Pub L No 101–588, § 4, 104 Stat 2879, 2880 (1990) (raising the maximum fine to USD 10 million), and Antitrust Criminal Penalty Enhancement and Reform Act of 2004, HR 1086 (raising the maximum fine to USD 100 million).

1667 See US Antitrust Modernization Commission, *Report and Recommendations* (April 2007), at 296–297 (and footnote 19).

1668 See US Antitrust Modernization Commission, *Report and Recommendations* (April 2007), Chapter III.C 'Government Civil Monetary Remedies'; OECD, *Remedies and Sanctions in Abuse of Dominance Cases*, DAF/COMP(2006)19 (15 May 2007); S. Calkins, 'Civil Monetary Remedies Available to Federal Antitrust Enforcers' (2006) 40 *University of San Francisco Law Review* 567; H. First, 'The Case for Antitrust Civil Penalties', NYU Law & Economics Working Paper no 08–38 (August 2008); and section 6.3.4.5 of my book *Efficiency and Justice in European Antitrust Enforcement* (Hart Publishing 2008). In a few cases, the Federal Trade Commission has used its power to seek disgorgement of unlawful profits; see S 13(G) of the FTC Act and *FTC v Mylan Labs Inc*, 62 F Suppl 2d 25, 36 (DCC 1999), and US Antitrust Modernization Commission, *Report and Recommendations* (April 2007).

1669 The public enforcement of Articles 101 and 102 TFEU has undoubtedly suffered from other kinds of deficiencies, and in my view still suffers today in the cartel area from a too exclusive focus on monetary penalties on undertakings and a lack of punishment for individuals, including imprisonment; see my paper 'Is Criminalization of EU Competition Law the Answer?' (2005) 28 *World Competition* 117, also accessible at http://ssrn.com/author=456087, and chapter 6 of my book *Efficiency and Justice in European Antitrust Enforcement* (Hart Publishing 2008) and F. Wagner-von Papp, 'Individual sanctions for competition law infringements: Pros, cons and challenges – Introduction', *Concurrences* no 2-2016, 14. This problem cannot, however, be solved by developing private actions for damages as an instrument of deterrence.

1670 See my paper 'Should Private Antitrust Enforcement Be Encouraged in Europe?' (2003) 26 *World Competition* 473, also accessible at http://ssrn.com/author=456087; Chapter 4 of my book *Principles of European*

Follow-on actions for damages do have some additional deterrent effect in that the damages add a cost to the fines or other penalties imposed in the preceding public enforcement. However, if additional monetary penalties were indeed required for optimal deterrence, these could be provided for in an administratively much cheaper and more reliable way by increasing the fines imposed in the public enforcement proceeding.[1671]

Stand-alone actions for damages can contribute to deterrence, but public enforcement appears superior for at least two reasons.[1672]

First, public enforcement, through its reliance on state power, benefits from more effective investigative and sanctioning powers. Competition authorities are generally better at discovering and proving antitrust infringements than private parties, because the authorities have wider investigative powers, allowing them to collect not only the information detained by the victims of the infringements, but also by the infringers and any other source. This advantage for public enforcement exists even in the US, where private plaintiffs benefit from liberal discovery rules.[1673]

Public enforcement is also superior because more effective sanctions are available and because the level of the sanctions can be better controlled. As to the type of sanctions available, private actions for damages can only lead to the imposition of monetary sanctions in the form of damages. Public enforcement allows not only for the imposition of monetary sanctions in the form of fines, but also other types of sanctions, such as director disqualifications and prison sanctions. As I have argued in detail elsewhere,[1674]

Antitrust Enforcement (Hart publishing 2005); and W. Möschel, 'Should Private Enforcement of Competition Law Be Strengthened?', in D. Schmidtchen, M. Albert and S. Voigt (eds), *The More Economic Approach to European Competition Law*, Conferences on New Political Economy 24 (Mohr Siebeck 2007), 101.

1671 See also M. Handler, 'The Shift from Substantive to Procedural Innovations in Antitrust Suits- The Twenty-Third Annual Antitrust Review' (1971) 71 *Columbia Law Review* 1 at 9.

1672 A third reason is that private actions for damages appear more costly than public enforcement. Indeed, in private actions for damages many resources have to be spent in the determination and allocation of the damages, more than those which would be spent in the setting of the sanction in public enforcement; see K. G. Elzinga and W. Breit, *The Antitrust Penalties: A Study in Law and Economics* (Yale University Press 1976), at 95. Public enforcement may also generally be cheaper because of the higher degree of specialisation of the actors involved and the generally lower cost of administrative procedures compared to civil litigation; see also W. Möschel, 'Should Private Enforcement of Competition Law Be Strengthened?', in D. Schmidtchen, M. Albert and S. Voigt (eds), *The More Economic Approach to European Competition Law*, Conferences on New Political Economy 24 (Mohr Siebeck 2007), 101, at 106.

1673 K. G. Elzinga and W. Breit, *The Antitrust Penalties: A Study in Law and Economics* (Yale University Press 1976) at 142–143. American-style discovery appears undesirable because of its high cost and the risk of discovery being abused to obtain competitors' business secrets; see F. G. Jacobs and T. Deisenhofer, 'Procedural Aspects of the Effective Private Enforcement of EC Competition Rules: A Community Perspective', in C.-D. Ehlermann and I. Atanasiu (eds), *European Competition Law Annual 2001: Effective Private Enforcement of EC Antitrust Law* (Hart Publishing 2003), 187, J. H. Langbein, 'The German Advantage in Civil Procedure' (1985) 52 *University of Chicago Law Review* 823, and F. Wagner-von Papp, 'Access to Evidence and Leniency Materials' (18 February 2016), accessible at http://ssrn.com/abstract=2733973. In Europe, private plaintiffs have additional difficulties in gathering evidence on a transnational basis in several Member States, whereas the European Commission's investigatory powers cover the whole of the European Union, and national competition authorities are able to obtain the help of their colleagues from other Member States within the European Competition Network set up under Regulation No 1/2003; see my paper 'Powers of Investigation and Procedural Rights and Guarantees in EU Antitrust Enforcement: The Interplay between European and National Legislation and Case-law' (2006) 29 *World Competition* 3, also accessible at http://ssrn.com/author=456087, and chapter 1 of my book *Efficiency and Justice in European Antitrust Enforcement* (Hart 2008).

1674 See Chapter 8 of my book *The Optimal Enforcement of EC Antitrust Law* (Kluwer Law International, 2002); my paper 'Is Criminalization of EU Competition Law the Answer?' (2005) 28 *World Competition* 117, also accessible at http://ssrn.com/author=456087; and chapter 6 of my book *Efficiency and Justice in European*

effective deterrence of cartels requires a combination of monetary sanctions on companies and individual penalties, in particular imprisonment.

As to the level of the monetary sanctions (fines or damages), public enforcement has the additional advantage of allowing better control in setting the optimal amount of the sanction. In principle, the amount of monetary sanctions should exceed the expected gain from the violation multiplied by the inverse of the probability of a monetary sanction being effectively imposed.[1675] Calculating the optimal amount of the sanction is always difficult in practice, but with public enforcement at least one can attempt to target the optimal amount.[1676] When the sanction consists of damages awarded as a result of private litigation, it becomes virtually impossible to target the optimal amount. Indeed, damages will be calculated not by reference to the offender's gain, but by reference to the losses which those plaintiffs who happen to bring claims manage to prove. Furthermore, single damage awards fail to incorporate the necessary multiplier inversely reflecting the probability of detection and punishment.[1677]

Secondly, private actions for damages are inevitably driven by the private gains and expenses of the parties concerned. These private interests will often diverge from the general interest. Cases that should be brought to clarify the law and generate deterrence in the general interest may never arise through private litigation, because no private party has a sufficient interest to bring an action, or because cases are settled without any clarification of the law.[1678] Conversely, private plaintiffs will try to obtain interpretations of the law that are to their financial or commercial benefit, irrespective of their general merit, or to win cases in which they have large financial or commercial stakes, irrespective of the merit

---

Antitrust Enforcement (Hart 2008); see also F. Wagner-von Papp, 'Individual sanctions for competition law infringements: Pros, cons and challenges – Introduction', *Concurrences* no 2-2016, 14, and OECD, *Sanctions in Antitrust Cases*, DAF/COMP/GF(2016)6 (14 October 2016).

1675 See my paper 'Optimal Antitrust Fines: Theory and Practice' (2006) 29 *World Competition* 183, also accessible at http://ssrn.com/author=456087, at footnotes 31 to 69, and section 3.2.1 of my book *Efficiency and Justice in European Antitrust Enforcement* (Hart 2008).

1676 See my paper 'Optimal Antitrust Fines: Theory and Practice' (2006) 29 *World Competition* 183, also accessible at http://ssrn.com/author=456087, at footnotes 105 to 114; my paper 'The European Commission's 2006 Guidelines on Antitrust Fines: A Legal and Economic Analysis' (2007) 30 *World Competition* 197, also accessible at http://ssrn.com/author=456087, at footnotes 51 to 63 and 76 to 86; and sections 3.4, 4.3.2 and 4.4.3 of my book *Efficiency and Justice in European Antitrust Enforcement* (Hart 2008).

1677 The trebling of damages in the US could be considered as trying to address this problem, but it does so in a very crude way. Indeed, there is no reason to assume that trebling is the right multiplication, and it is certain that the multiplier should be variable, reflecting the fact that some types of antitrust violations are difficult to hide, thus necessitating a low multiplier or even no multiplier at all, whereas other types are easily concealable, thus requiring a high multiplier; see F. H. Easterbrook, 'Detrebling Antitrust Damages' (1985) 28 *Journal of Law & Economics* 445 at 454–457, and R. A. Posner, *Antitrust Law*, 2nd edition (University of Chicago Press 2001), at 272.

1678 The general problem is that there are significant externalities in private actions for damages, and that deterrence and punishment and clarification of the law are public goods; see generally S. Shavell, 'The Fundamental Divergence between the Private and the Social Motive to Use the Legal System' (1997) 26 *Journal of Legal Studies* 575. Specifically on settlements, see F. G. Jacobs and T. Deisenhofer, 'Procedural Aspects of the Effective Private Enforcement of EC Competition Rules', in C.-D. Ehlermann and I. Atanasiu (eds), *European Competition Law Annual 2001: Effective Private Enforcement of EC Competition Law* (Hart Publishing 2003), 187–227, at 196: '[I]t must be remembered that settlements are based on considerations of convenience and not necessarily on considerations of legality. And they are rarely published. Thus, settlements cannot contribute to the clarification and a better understanding of the competition rules to the same extent as judgments'; on the use of settlements in public enforcement, see Chapter VI of this book.

of the interpretation of the law on which the case is won. As Judge Posner has observed in relation to the US experience:

'*Students of the antitrust laws have been appalled by the wild and woolly antitrust suits that the private bar has brought – and won. It is felt that many of these would not have been brought by a public agency and that, in short, the influence of the private action on the development of antitrust doctrine has been on the whole a pernicious one. The concern is not limited to the class action.*'[1679]

Competition authorities are not perfect. They can, and occasionally do, make mistakes. But at least they try, or can be led (by the public scrutiny their behaviour is subjected to and by the finite budgets they are allocated), to decide on case selection and priority setting with a view to maximising respect for the antitrust prohibitions, while minimising the costs of antitrust enforcement.[1680] The same cannot be said about private plaintiffs. Indeed, there is no reason whatsoever why they would care about optimal enforcement. The only consideration driving private enforcement is the private gains and expenses of the different potential plaintiffs. This leads to at least three problems: inadequate investment, unmeritorious suits and undesirable settlements. The problem of inadequate investment results from the fact that, for many of the most meritorious antitrust enforcement actions, the social benefit of successfully bringing the action far exceeds the damages award a potential private plaintiff can hope for. Private plaintiffs thus have insufficient incentives to invest in detecting and litigating meritorious cases.[1681] The problem of unmeritorious actions results primarily from the difficulty in drawing the borderline between anticompetitive and procompetitive behaviour, especially in cases of alleged exclusionary practices, combined with the fact that competitor plaintiffs have as much or arguably even more of an incentive to bring actions against strong legitimate competition by their rivals as against anticompetitive behaviour.[1682] In the US, the problem of unmeritorious actions has been identified as a major problem by many observers.[1683] Just as private cost/

1679 R. A. Posner, *Antitrust Law*, 2nd edition (University of Chicago Press 2001), at 275.

1680 See, with regard to the US antitrust agencies, W. H. Page, 'Antitrust Damages and Economic Efficiency: An Approach to Antitrust Injury' (1980) 47 *University of Chicago Law Review* 467 at 503 ('Although there are some random, even perverse, elements in the criteria for case selection by the Department of Justice and the Federal Trade Commission, those organizations have no clear incentive to bring anticompetitive cases, and seem to consider the efficiency consequences of their enforcement policies'), R. A. Posner, *Antitrust Law*, 2nd edition (University of Chicago Press 2001), at 275–276 ('The tight budget constraint has forced the agencies to be selective in their choice of cases. Although they might select the silliest cases to bring, there is no reason in theory why they should and no evidence that they do') and K. G. Elzinga and W. Breit, *The Antitrust Penalties: A Study in Law and Economics* (Yale University Press 1976) at 141.

1681 See generally S. Shavell, 'The Fundamental Divergence between the Private and the Social Motive to Use the Legal System' (1997) 26 *Journal of Legal Studies* 575, and further my paper 'Should Private Antitrust Enforcement Be Encouraged in Europe?' (2003) 26 *World Competition* 473, also accessible at http://ssrn.com/author=456087, at 482–483, and section 4.3.2 of my book *Principles of European Antitrust Enforcement* (Hart 2005).

1682 The reason why the incentive appears even stronger is that anticompetitive behaviour tends toward raising prices, which also benefits competitors, whereas legitimate competitive behaviour reduces the price level.

1683 See i.a. E. A. Snyder and T. E. Kauper, 'Misuse of the Antitrust Laws: The Competitor Plaintiff' (1991) 90 *Michigan Law Review* 551, S. C. Salop and L. J. White, 'Economic Analysis of Private Antitrust Litigation' (1986) 74 *Georgetown Law Journal* 1001, W. J. Baumol and J. A. Ordover, 'Use of Antitrust to Subvert Competition' (1985) 28 *Journal of Law & Economics* 247, R. A. Posner, *Antitrust Law*, 2nd edition (University of Chicago Press 2001), at 275, R. P. McAfee and N. Vakkur, 'The Strategic Abuse of the Antitrust Laws' (2004) 1 *Journal of Strategic Management Education* 3, and R. P. McAfee, H. M. Mialon and S. H. Mialon, 'Private Antitrust Litigation: Procompetitive or Anticompetitive?', in V. Ghosal and J. Stennek (eds), *The Political Economy of Antitrust* (Elsevier 2007), 453.

benefit calculations drive the bringing of suits, they also determine their eventual settlement. Settlements may be desirable in that they save administrative cost, but the private incentive to settle risks again fundamentally diverging from the general interest.[1684]

Finally, the fact that competition authorities may not detect and punish all antitrust violations does not justify the conclusion that private actions for damages would be needed to fill a deterrence gap. It is in all likelihood not in the general interest that all antitrust violations are prosecuted. Indeed, antitrust enforcement always has a cost.[1685] How much antitrust enforcement is desirable depends, of course, on how much value society attaches to the avoidance of antitrust violations, but that value is certainly not infinite, given the multitude of other societal concerns. Moreover, effective deterrence does not require that each and every violation is detected and punished, but rather that the expected penalty, which is a function both of the probability of detection and punishment and of the size of the penalties imposed, exceeds the expected gains of antitrust infringements.[1686] In any event, if there is a need to increase the existing level of deterrence and punishment, this should be done by strengthening public enforcement, which, for the reasons explained above, is the superior instrument as far as the objective of deterrence and punishment is concerned.[1687]

3. The 2005 Green Paper on damages actions

In December 2005, the European Commission published a Green Paper,[1688] in which it put forward for discussion a number of possible measures to facilitate damage claims for breach of EU antitrust law.

This Green Paper was to a significant extent infused with the American conception of private actions for damages as an instrument of deterrence and a potential replacement for public enforcement.[1689]

1684 See K. Roach and M. J. Trebilcock, 'Private enforcement of Competition Laws' (1996) 34 *Osgoode Hall Law Journal* 461, at 488. A Brussels-based private antitrust lawyer once told me the story of one of his clients who, upon having received legal advice that its dominant competitor was acting in violation of Article 102 TFEU, had used this legal opinion to negotiate a market-sharing agreement with the dominant competitor. See also D. Wilsher, 'The Public Aspects of Private Enforcement in EC Law: Some Constitutional and Administrative Challenges of a Damages Culture' (2006) 3 *The Competition Law* Review 27 at 35; and leading article 'MS.dosh settlement – Microsoft's pay-offs show why regulators are necessary', *Financial Times*, 26 November 2004, 12; J. Kay, 'Antitrust concerns are not so easily dismissed', *Financial Times*, 30 November 2004, 13; B. Groom, European Comment, 'Microsoft's Brussels trouble not over yet', *Financial Times*, 10 November 2004, 16 ('It is a comfort that competition policy in Europe is pursued largely by public authorities rather than through private lawsuits. Rival companies can be bought off, but the [European] Commission's role is to safeguard consumers.'); and A. Murray, 'A Microsoft Foe Quits the Battle, With Check in Hand', *Wall Street Journal Europe*, 7 December 2004; on the use of settlements in public enforcement, see Chapter VI of this book.

1685 See G. J. Stigler, 'The Optimum Enforcement of Laws' (1970) 78 *Journal of Political Economy* 526 and K. G. Elzinga and W. Breit, *The Antitrust Penalties: A Study in Law and Economics* (Yale University Press 1976) at 9–15.

1686 See further my paper 'Optimal Antitrust Fines: Theory and Practice' (2006) 29 *World Competition* 183, also accessible at http://ssrn.com/author=456087, and chapter 3 of my book *Efficiency and Justice in European Antitrust Enforcement* (Hart 2008).

1687 See further my paper 'Should Private Antitrust Enforcement Be Encouraged in Europe?' (2003) 26 *World Competition* 473, also accessible at http://ssrn.com/author=456087, at 485–486, and section 4.4.2 of my book *Principles of European Antitrust Enforcement* (Hart 2005).

1688 European Commission, Green Paper on Damages actions for breach of EC antitrust rules, COM(2005)672 of 19 December 2005.

1689 See also D. Waelbroeck and D. Slater, 'The Commission's Green Paper on Private Enforcement: 'Americanization' of EC Competition Law Enforcement?', in C.-D. Ehlermann and I. Atanasiu (eds), *European Competition Law Annual 2006: Enforcement of Prohibition of Cartels* (Hart Publishing 2007), 425.

Indeed, the Green Paper started out by stating that 'public and private enforcement [. . .] serve the same aims: to deter anti-competitive practices forbidden by antitrust law [. . .]'.[1690] Shortly after the publication of the Green Paper, the then Director General of the European Commission's Directorate General for Competition further explained that 'compensation of victims should not be seen as an end in itself, but part of an overall strategy to enhance deterrence'.[1691]

Among the possible measures put up for discussion in the Green Paper figured the introduction of double damages for cartel infringements and the exclusion of the passing-on defence, clearly inspired by the American example.[1692]

These proposals were not well received, and the European Commission subsequently abandoned the American approach in the 2008 White Paper and in the 2013 legislative proposal and recommendation on collective redress, discussed hereafter.

4. The American model rejected: The 2008 White Paper and the 2013 legislative proposal and Recommendation on collective redress

In April 2008, the European Commission published a **White Paper** on damages actions for breach of the EU antitrust rules,[1693] which contained proposed measures focussing on the compensation function of private actions for damages (rather than the deterrence function) and the preservation of strong public enforcement.

Indeed, the White Paper set out its objectives as follows:

'The primary objective [. . .] is to improve the legal conditions for victims to exercise their right under the Treaty to reparation of all damage suffered as a result of a breach of the EC antitrust rules. Full compensation is, therefore, the first and foremost guiding principle. [. . .] Another important guiding principle of the Commission's policy is to preserve strong public enforcement of [Articles 101 and 102 TFEU] by the Commission and the competition authorities of the Member States. Accordingly, the measures put forward in this White Paper are designed to create an effective system of private enforcement by means of damages actions that complements, but does not replace or jeopardise, public enforcement.'[1694]

In June 2013, the European Commission adopted a **proposal for a Directive** of the European Parliament and of the Council on actions for damages.[1695]

1690 Idem, at 3.

1691 OECD, *Private Remedies*, DAF/COMP(2006)34 of 11 January 2008, at 271.

1692 Green Paper, at 7 and 8.

1693 European Commission, White Paper on Damages actions for breach of the EC antitrust rules, COM(2008)165 of 2 April 2008.

1694 Idem, at 3.

1695 European Commission, Proposal for a Directive of the European Parliament and of the Council on certain rules governing actions for damages under national law for infringements of the competition law provisions of the Member States and of the European Union, COM(2013)404 of 11 June 2013.

According to its Explanatory Memorandum, the proposal sought:

'*to ensure the effective enforcement of EU competition rules by*

(i) *optimising the interaction between the public and private enforcement of competition law; and*

(ii) *ensuring that victims of infringements of the EU competition rules can obtain full compensation for the harm they suffered.*'[1696]

As is apparent from the Explanatory Memorandum,[1697] the first of these two objectives concerned in particular the protection of the competition authorities' leniency programmes.[1698] Following the 2011 judgment of the Court of Justice in *Pfleiderer*,[1699] it was feared that, in the absence of EU legislation, uncertainty about the possible disclosure of leniency documents in follow-on damages actions might discourage cartel participants from applying for leniency to the competition authorities.

The accompanying press release explained more generally that the proposal 'fully takes into account the key role played by competition authorities (at EU or national level) to investigate, find and sanction infringements. Contrary to the US system, the proposal does not seek to leave the punishment and deterrence to private litigation'.[1700]

Simultaneously with the proposal for a Directive on antitrust damages actions, the European Commission also adopted a **Recommendation on collective redress**.[1701]

This Recommendation is not limited to damages actions for infringements of Articles 101 and 102 TFEU. It covers both injunctive and compensatory collective redress, and concerns violations of all rights granted under EU law, including in particular consumer rights.

With respect to compensatory collective redress, it recommends that the claimant party should be formed on the basis of express consent of the natural or legal persons claiming to have been harmed ('opt-in' principle), that contingency fees should not be permitted, and that punitive damages should be prohibited.[1702]

In a press memorandum accompanying this Recommendation, it was further explained that 'the European approach to collective redress clearly rejects the US-style system of "class actions"'.[1703]

1696 Idem, at 2–3.

1697 Idem, at 3.

1698 See Chapters V and XVIII of this book.

1699 Judgment in *Pfleiderer*, C-360/09, EU:C:2011:389.

1700 European Commission, Press release IP/13/525 at 2.

1701 Commission Recommendation of 11 June 2013 on common principles for injunctive and compensatory collective redress mechanisms in the Member States concerning violations of rights granted under Union law [2013] OJ L201/60. This Recommendation was accompanied by a Communication from the Commission to the European Parliament, the Council, the European Economic and Social Committee and the Committee of the Regions, 'Towards a European Horizontal Framework for Collective Redress', COM(2013)401 of 11.

1702 Commission Recommendation of 11 June 2013 on common principles for injunctive and compensatory collective redress mechanisms in the Member States concerning violations of rights granted under Union law [2013] OJ L201/60, paragraphs 21, 30 and 31.

1703 European Commission, MEMO Frequently Asked Questions: European Commission recommends collective redress principles to Member States, MEMO/13/530, at 2.

E. Directive 2014/104 on actions for damages

Following the European Commission's 2013 legislative proposal, the European Parliament and the Council of the European Union adopted Directive 2014/104 (hereafter also: 'the Directive') in November 2014.[1704] According to its Article 21, EU Member States shall bring into force the laws, regulations and administrative provisions necessary to comply with this Directive by 27 December 2016.

1. Subject matter and scope

As apparent from its Article 1 and Article 2(1) and (3), the Directive covers actions for damages relating not only to infringements of Articles 101 and 102 TFEU but also to parallel infringements of similar provisions of national competition law.[1705]

The Directive covers only actions for damages, not other forms of private enforcement. This could simply be understood as a result of path dependency, given that the 2005 Green Paper and the 2008 White Paper also only concerned actions for damages. It has been pointed out, however, that this exclusive focus on damages actions, and in particular the exclusion of actions for injunctive relief, has never been properly explained.[1706]

2. Full compensation but no punishment

Reflecting the case law of the Court of Justice,[1707] Article 3(1) and (2) of the Directive confirms that any natural or legal person who has suffered harm caused by an infringement of antitrust law is entitled to full compensation of that harm, covering compensation for actual loss and for loss of profit, plus the payment of interest.

Article 3(3) adds that full compensation 'shall not lead to overcompensation, whether by means of punitive, multiple or other types of damages'.

1704 Directive 2014/104/EU of the European Parliament and of the Council of 26 November 2014 on certain rules governing actions for damages under national law for infringements of the competition law provisions of the Member States and of the European Union [2014] OJ L349/1. Among the many commentaries on this Directive, see in particular P. Van Nuffel, Institutional Report – Private enforcement of EU competition law, XXVII FIDE Congress (Budapest, 18–21 May 2016); as well as H. Schweitzer, 'Die neue Richtlinie für wettbewerbsrechtliche Schadenersatzklage' (2014) *Neue Zeitschrift für Kartellrecht* 335; P. Roth, 'Too much or too little? The EU initiatives to promote private redress', in *Antitrust between EU law and National law / Antitrust fra diritto Nazionale e diritto dell'Unione Europea* (Bruylant 2015) 51; and F. Wagner-von Papp, 'Access to Evidence and Leniency Materials' (18 February 2016), accessible at http://ssrn.com/abstract=2733973.

1705 This broader scope allowed the adoption of the Directive on the joint legal bases of Articles 103 and 114 TFEU and hence the use of the ordinary legislative procedure rather than the special legislative procedure foreseen in Article 103 TFEU, under which the European Parliament would merely have been consulted.

1706 See F. G. Wilman, 'The End of the Absence? The growing body of EU legislation on private enforcement and the main remedies it provides for' (2016) 53 *Common Market Law Review* 887 at 911–912, and C. Cauffman, 'Injunctions at the request of third parties in EU competition law' (2010) 17 *Maastricht Journal of European and Comparative Law* 58 at 58–60; see also P. C. Müller-Graf, General Report - Private enforcement of EU competition law, XXVII FIDE Congress (Budapest, 18–21 May 2016), at 91–94. At the time of the 2005 Green Paper, the focus on damages actions could be understood as resulting from the comparison with the American model.

1707 See Judgment in *Manfredi*, C-295/04 to 298/04, EU:C:2006:461.

In its 2007 judgment in *Devenish, etc. v Vitamin cartellists*,[1708] the English High Court already held that the principle of *ne bis in idem*,[1709] which is a fundamental principle of EU law, precludes the award of exemplary or punitive damages in an action for damages following a fining decision by the European Commission, even if the fine has been commuted to zero as a result of the application of the European Commission's Leniency Notice.[1710] The English High Court added that the award of such damages is also precluded by Article 16 of Regulation 1/2003. The principle of *ne bis in idem* would appear to preclude equally the award of exemplary or punitive damages in an action for damages following a decision of a competition authority of an EU Member State under Articles 101 or 102 EU.[1711]

In the light of the *Masterfoods* judgment of the EU Court of Justice, according to which the European Commission, because of the role assigned to it by the Treaty in the application of Articles 101 and 102 TFEU, is 'entitled to adopt at any time individual decisions under [Articles 101 and 102 TFEU], even where the agreement of the practice has already been the subject of a decision by a national court and the decision contemplated by the Commission conflicts with that national court's decision',[1712] it could be argued that the award of punitive damages in stand-alone actions under Articles 101 and 102 TFEU was also already precluded before the Directive, as this would prevent the European Commission from later imposing fines for the same infringement without breaching the principle of *ne bis in idem.*[1713]

3. Passing-on of overcharges

In line with the Directive's general focus on compensation and the rejection of the American conception of private actions for damages as an instrument of deterrence and punishment, Articles 12 to 14 of the Directive provide that defendants must be able to invoke the passing-on defence, that indirect purchasers also have a right to full compensation, and that at any level of the supply chain overcompensation must be avoided.

4. Joint and several liability

Article 11(1) and the first sentence of Article 11(5) of the Directive provide that, as a general rule, undertakings which have infringed Articles 101 or 102 TFEU or the

---

1708 *Devenish etc. v Sanofi-Aventis etc.* [2007] EWHC 2394 (Ch), 19 October 2007 (Mr Justice Lewison). The High Court also held that restitutionary remedies are not available in cartel damages actions, compensatory damages being an adequate and appropriate remedy. On the issue of restitutionary remedies, the judgment was appealed, and was confirmed by the Court of Appeal in *Devenish v Sanofi-Aventis etc.* [2008] EWCA Civ 1086, 14 October 2008.

1709 See generally my article 'The Principle of *Ne Bis in Idem* in EC Antitrust Enforcement: A Legal and Economic Analysis' (2003) 26 *World Competition* 131, also accessible at http://ssrn.com/author=456087, and chapter 3 of my book *Principles of European Antitrust Enforcement* (Hart 2005).

1710 See also the judgment of the EU General Court in *Archer Daniels Midland v Commission*, Case T-59/02, EU:T:2006:272, paragraphs 349–352.

1711 In its Judgment in *Manfredi*, C-295/04 to 298/04, EU:C:2006:461, the EU Court of Justice held that the principle of effectiveness does not require punitive damages. The *ne bis in idem* issue was not raised in this case.

1712 Judgment in *Masterfoods and HB*, C-344/98, EU:C:2000:689, paragraph 48.

1713 See my paper 'The Relationship between Public Antitrust Enforcement and Private Actions for Damages' (2009) 32 *World Competition* 3, also accessible at http://ssrn.com/author=456087, at 21–22.

corresponding provisions of national competition law through joint behaviour are jointly and severally liable for the harm caused by the infringement. Injured parties have the right to require full compensation from any infringer. The infringer may, however, recover a contribution from the other infringers, the amount of which shall be determined in the light of their respective responsibility for the harm caused by the infringement.

These general provisions essentially confirm the law as it already existed under the national laws of the (then) EU Member States.[1714] They also confirm another difference with the law in the USA, which provides for joint and several liability but does not allow for contribution.[1715] This difference further illustrates the broader difference between American law on antitrust damages actions, which focuses on deterrence, and EU law, which focuses on compensation.

The Directive provides, however, also for three exceptions to the general rules on joint and several liability:

i) An undertaking or person that has been granted immunity from fines by a competition authority under a leniency programme (**immunity recipient**) is only joint and severally liable to its direct or indirect purchasers or providers, and to other injured parties only where full compensation cannot be obtained from the other undertakings that were involved in the same infringement. The amount of contribution which other infringers can recover from the immunity recipient shall also not exceed the amount of the harm it caused to its own direct or indirect purchasers or providers.[1716]
Recital 38 provides the following reasoning for this exception in favour of immunity recipients:
'*Undertakings which cooperate with competition authorities under a leniency programme play a key role in exposing secret cartel infringements and in bringing them to an end, thereby often mitigating the harm which could have been caused had the infringement continued. It is therefore appropriate to make provision for undertakings which have received immunity from fines from a competition authority under a leniency programme to be protected from undue exposure to damages claims, bearing in mind that the decision of the competition authority finding the infringement may become final for the immunity recipient before it becomes final for other undertakings which have not received immunity, thus potentially making the immunity recipient the preferential target of litigation. It is therefore appropriate that the immunity recipient be relieved in principle from joint and several liability for the entire harm and that any contribution it must make vis-à-vis co-infringers not exceed the amount of the harm caused to its own direct or indirect purchasers or, in the case of a buying cartel, its direct or indirect providers.*'

1714 See for instance N. Dunleavy, 'Contribution among Antitrust Defendants in English Law' (2009) 30 *European Competition Law Review* 22.

1715 See J. Angland, 'Joint and Several Liability, Contribution, and Claim Reduction' (2008), accessible at http://ssrn.com/abstract=1528007, and M. Hviid and A. Medvedev, 'The Role of Contribution among Defendants in Private Antitrust Litigation' (2010) 30 *International Review of Law & Economics* 306.

1716 Article 11(4), second sentence of Article 11(5) and Article 2(19) of the Directive. See further Chapter XVIII of this book.

ii) Small or medium-sized enterprises (SMEs) as defined in European Commission Recommendation 2003/361/EC[1717] are only liable for their own direct and indirect purchasers if their market share in the relevant market was below 5% at any time during the infringement and the application of the normal rules of joint and several liability would irretrievably jeopardise their economic viability and cause their assets to lose all their value. The exception does not, however, apply if the SME has led the infringement or has coerced other undertakings to participate therein, or if the SME has previously been found to have infringed Articles 101 or 102 TFEU or the corresponding provisions of national competition law.[1718]

Somewhat surprisingly,[1719] no reasoning for this exception can be found in the recitals of the Directive. The exception did not figure in the European Commission's legislative proposal, so no reasoning can be found there either. This second exception for SMEs has been the subject of strong criticism,[1720] also by the delegations of three Member States at the time of the adoption of the Directive by the Council of the European Union.[1721]

As explained hereafter, a possible justification for this second exception for SMEs is that it limits a negative side effect of the first exception for immunity recipients.[1722]

Already before the Directive, there were grounds for concern about the impact on the market structure of the imposition of high fines in cartel cases in which immunity is granted to the largest competitor in the market.

Indeed, as Advocate General Geelhoed has pointed out, 'in the event of a collective infringement like a cartel as opposed to an infringement by a single offender, the [European] Commission must also consider the subsequent effects of the fines and take into account the size of a given company. [. . .] The example [. . .] is a cartel consisting of one big player and several small players. The big player cooperated with the Commission and receives immunity under the Leniency Notice. In such cases very high fines could have put the smaller players out of business, in which case the Commission's intervention would have resulted in a monopoly'.[1723]

As I have shown elsewhere,[1724] it appears that in 46% of the cartel cases in which the European Commission granted immunity in the past ten years the immunity recipient was the cartel participant with the highest turnover

1717 European Commission Recommendation 2003/361/EC concerning the definition of micro, small and medium-sized enterprises [2003] OJ L124/36.

1718 Article 11 (3) and (4) of the Directive.

1719 See Article 296 TFEU.

1720 See H. Schweitzer, 'Die neue Richtlinie für wettbewerbsrechtliche Schadenersatzklage' (2014) *Neue Zeitschrift für Kartellrecht* 335, at 344.

1721 See Council of the European Union, Statement by the Polish, Slovenian and German delegations, 14680/14 ADD 1 (3 November 2014).

1722 See also Chapter XVIII of this book.

1723 Opinion in *Showa Denko v Commission*, C-289/04 P, EU:C:2006:52, paragraph 61 and footnote 16; see also my paper 'Optimal Antitrust Fines: Theory and Practice' (2006) 29 *World Competition* 183, also accessible at http://ssrn.com/author=456087, at footnotes 94 to 96.

1724 See Table 4 of my paper 'The Use of Leniency in EU Cartel Enforcement: An Assessment after Twenty Years' (2016) 39 *World Competition* 327, both also accessible at http://ssrn.com/author=456078.

in the market affected by the cartel, whereas on average there were seven participants per cartel, and the undertaking with the highest turnover should thus have been the immunity recipient in only 15% of the cases if there had been no correlation between being the undertaking with the largest turnover and being the immunity recipient.[1725]

On the reassuring side, it should be pointed out that, whereas in 46% of the cases the immunity recipient has the largest turnover affected by the cartel, in many of these cases the other cartel participants are also large companies that cannot easily be fined out of business. Moreover, and most importantly, the European Commission has a policy of capping fines so as to avoid undertakings going out of business because of a fine. Indeed, in addition to the 10% of total turnover cap laid down in Article 23(2) of Regulation 1/2003, the European Commission reduces fines on the ground of inability to pay.[1726] On the other hand, in the absence of perfect capital markets, high fines can have a negative effect on the competitiveness of smaller companies, even below the level of inability to pay, and may thus negatively affect the market structure.[1727] Damages awards, or the combination of fines and damages awards, can have the same negative effects on the market structure. The Directive's exception for immunity recipients from full joint and several liability increases the risk of such negative effects. The second exception for SMEs mitigates this negative side effect of the exception for immunity recipients. To the extent that SMEs have more difficulty accessing finance than larger enterprises, the focus on SMEs appears cogent.[1728]

iii) A third exception to the general rules on joint and several liability concerns the situation where an injured party has reached a **consensual settlement** with one of the co-infringers. Article 19(2) and (3) of the Directive provide that non-settling co-infringers shall not be permitted to recover contribution for the remaining claim from the settling co-infringer,[1729] except where the non-settling co-infringers cannot pay the damages that correspond to the remaining claim

---

1725 Given that under the European Commission's Fining Guidelines (Guidelines on the method of setting fines imposed pursuant to Article 23(2)(a) of Regulation No 1/2003 [2006] OJ C210/2) fines are calculated as a percentage of each undertaking's turnover in the goods or services affected by the cartel, this result should not come as a surprise: The undertakings with the largest affected turnover can expect the highest fine, and hence have the most to gain from applying for leniency.

1726 See paragraph 35 of the 2006 Fining Guidelines, Commission Document SEC(2010)737, 'Inability to pay under paragraph 35 of the 2006 Fining Guidelines and payment conditions pre-and post-decision finding an infringement and imposing fines' (June 2010), available at the Register of Commission documents, http://ec.europa.eu/transparency/regdoc/registre.cfm?CL=en; and paragraph 87 of the European Commission's Notice on best practices for the conduct of proceedings concerning Articles 101 and 102 TFEU [2011] OJ C308/6.

1727 See my paper 'Optimal Antitrust Fines: Theory and Practice' (2006) 29 *World Competition* 183, also accessible at http://ssrn.com/author=456087, at footnotes 67 to 71.

1728 See European Commission, 'An action plan to improve access to finance for SMEs', Communication from the Commission to the Council, to the European Parliament, to the Committee of the Regions, and to the Social and Economic Committee, COM(2011)870 of 7 December 2011.

1729 Article 19(1) of the Directive provides that, following a consensual settlement, the claim of the settling injured party is reduced by the settling co-infringer's share of the harm that the antitrust infringement inflicted upon the injured party.

of the settling injured party. The latter possibility may, however, be expressly excluded under the terms of the consensual settlement.

5. Binding effect of public enforcement decisions

Article 9 of the Directive provides that an infringement of Articles 101 or 102 TFEU or of corresponding provisions of national competition law found by a final decision of a national competition authority or by a court reviewing the decision of the national competition authority must be deemed to be irrefutably established for the purposes of an action for damages brought before a court in the same EU Member State. Where the action for damages is brought in another EU Member State, the finding of infringement must constitute at least prima facie evidence.

As mentioned above, the binding effect of a finding of infringement by the European Commission in follow-on actions for damages in the national courts of all EU Member States already flows from Article 16 of Regulation 1/2003 and the *Masterfoods* case law of the Court of Justice.

As explained in recital 34 of the Directive, the binding effect in follow-on actions for damages of a finding of infringement made in public enforcement proceedings 'cover[s] only the nature of the infringement and its material, personal, temporal and territorial scope as determined by the competition authority or review court in the exercise of its jurisdiction'.[1730]

Specifically for cartel infringements,[1731] Article 17(2) of the Directive adds a rebuttable presumption that cartel infringements cause harm.

6. Disclosure of evidence

Article 5 of the Directive provides that, upon request of claimant who has presented a reasoned justification containing reasonably available facts and evidence sufficient to support the plausibility of its claim for damages, national courts must be able to order the defendant or a third party to disclose relevant evidence which lies in their control. The disclosure of evidence must be limited to that which is proportionate. Disclosure of evidence containing confidential information must be possible where relevant to the action for damages, but such information must be effectively protected. Those from whom disclosure is sought must have an opportunity to be heard before the national court orders disclosure.[1732]

In damages actions relating to an antitrust infringement that is or has been the object of public enforcement proceedings, the competition authority's file is an obvious location for potentially relevant evidence. Competition authorities are thus an obvious addressee of disclosure orders. However, competition authorities have limited resources, and these resources should primarily be devoted to their core task of detecting and prosecuting

---

1730 See also the judgment of the English House of Lords in *Inntrepreneur Pub Company (CPC) et al v Crehan* [2006] UKHL 38.

1731 As defined in Article 2(14) of the Directive.

1732 See further the detailed and enlightening analysis in F. Wagner-von Papp, 'Access to Evidence and Leniency Materials' (18 February 2016), accessible at http://ssrn.com/abstract=2733973.

infringements.[1733] For this reason, Article 6(10) of the Directive provides that national courts may request the disclosure from a competition authority of information in its file only where no party or third party is reasonably able to provide that evidence.

7. Protection of leniency statements and settlement submissions

Article 6(6) of the Directive provides that national courts can never order any party or third party (including competition authorities) to disclose leniency statements or settlement submissions.[1734]

Article 7(1) of the Directive adds that leniency statements and settlement submissions cannot be used in actions for damages if they have been obtained solely through access to the file of a competition authority.

Leniency statements are defined in Article 2(16) of the Directive as oral or written presentations voluntarily provided by, or on behalf of, an undertaking or a natural person to a competition authority or a record thereof, describing the knowledge of that undertaking or natural person of a cartel and describing its role therein, which presentations were drawn up specifically for submission to the competition authority with a view to obtaining immunity or a reduction of fines under a leniency programme, not including pre-existing information.[1735]

Settlement submissions are defined in Article 2(18) of the Directive as voluntary presentations by, or on behalf of, an undertaking to a competition authority describing the undertaking's acknowledgement of, or its renunciation to dispute, its participation in an infringement of Articles 101 or 102 TFEU or corresponding provisions under national law and its responsibility for that infringement, which were drawn up specifically to enable the competition authority to apply a simplified or expedited procedure.

Recital 26 of the Directive adds that the protection of leniency statements and settlement submissions 'should also apply to verbatim quotations from leniency statements or settlement submissions in other documents'.[1736]

1733 See my paper 'The Relationship between Public Antitrust Enforcement and Private Actions for Damages' (2009) 32 *World Competition* 3, also accessible at http://ssrn.com/author=456087.

1734 See further Chapters V, VI and XVIII of this book.

1735 Article 2(14) of the Directive defines 'cartel' as 'an agreement or concerted practice between two or more competitors aimed at coordinating their competitive behaviour on the market or influencing the relevant parameters of competition through practices such as, but not limited to, the fixing or coordination of purchase or selling prices or other trading conditions, including in relation to intellectual property rights, the allocation of production or sales quota, the sharing of markets and customers, including bid-rigging, restrictions of imports or exports or anti-competitive actions against other competitors'.
Article 2(15) of the Directive defines 'leniency programme' as 'a programme concerning Article 101 TFEU or a corresponding provision under national law on the basis of which a participant in a secret cartel, independently of the other undertakings involved in the cartel, cooperates with an investigation of the competition authority, by voluntarily providing presentations regarding that participant's knowledge of, and role in, the cartel in return for which that participant receives, by decision or by discontinuation of proceedings, immunity from, or a reduction in, fines for its involvement in the cartel'.
Article 2(17) of the Directive defines 'pre-existing information' as 'evidence that exists irrespective of the proceedings of a competition authority, whether or not such information is in the file of a competition authority'.

1736 See further Opinion of Advocate General Szpunar in *Evonik Degussa v European Commission*, C-162/15 P, EU:C:2016:587, paragraphs 115 to 129.

Recitals 26 and 27 contain the following justification for the protection of leniency statements and settlement submissions:

'Leniency programmes and settlement submissions are important tools for the public enforcement of Union competition law as they contribute to the detection and efficient prosecution of, and the imposition of penalties for, the most serious infringements of competition law. Furthermore, as many decisions of authorities in cartel cases are based on a leniency application, and damages actions in cartel cases generally follow on from these decisions, leniency programmes are also important for the effectiveness of actions for damages in cartel cases. Undertakings might be deterred from cooperating with competition authorities under leniency programmes and settlement procedures if self-incriminating statements such as leniency statements and settlement submissions, which are produced for the sole purpose of cooperating with the competition authorities, were to be disclosed. Such disclosure would pose a risk of exposing cooperating undertakings or their managing staff to civil or criminal liability under conditions worse than those of co-infringers not cooperating with the competition authorities. To ensure undertakings' continued willingness to approach competition authorities voluntarily with leniency statements or settlement submissions, such documents should be exempted from the disclosure of evidence. [. . .]

The rules in this Directive on the disclosure of documents other than leniency statements or settlement submissions ensure that injured parties retain sufficient alternative means by which to obtain access to the relevant evidence that they need in order to prepare their actions for damages.'

As I have argued elsewhere,[1737] denying damages claimants access to leniency statements appears fully justified. There is indeed an important difference between, on the one hand, leniency statements, and, on the other hand, most other documents in the competition authority's file, including other (pre-existing) documents submitted as part of a leniency application: The leniency statement would not have existed (and could thus never have been obtained by the competition authority, either through the use of its compulsory investigation powers or from an informer or any other source, nor ever have been obtained by the damages claimant, through discovery or any other means), but for the cartel participant's voluntary act of making a leniency application, thereby facilitating the discovery and punishment of the cartel by the competition authority, as well as subsequent follow-on actions for damages. In such a situation, it does not appear unfair to deny damages claimants the right to obtain or use the leniency statement, whereas allowing such use risks deterring cartel participants from making leniency applications.

A similar reasoning justifies the protection of settlement submissions: unlike most other documents in the competition authority's file, the settlement submission would not have existed (and could thus never have been obtained by the competition authority, either through the use of its compulsory investigation powers or from an informer or any other

---

1737 See my paper 'The Relationship between Public Antitrust Enforcement and Private Actions for Damages' (2009) 32 *World Competition* 3, also accessible at http://ssrn.com/author=456087, at footnote 95; see also OECD Secretariat, *Relationship between public and private antitrust enforcement*, DAF/COMP/WP3(2015)14 of 15 June 2015, paragraph 63.

source, nor ever have been obtained by the damages claimant, through discovery or any other means), but for the infringer's voluntary act of acknowledging to the competition authority its participation in and responsibility for the infringement, thereby allowing the competition authority to save time and resources, which may allow the competition authority to reach sooner a final decision in the case at hand, thus allowing also sooner follow-on actions for damages, as well as to redirect resources to detecting and punishing more other infringements, or to do so more quickly, again also possibly allowing for more and earlier follow-on actions for damages in those other cases. In such a situation, it does not appear unfair to deny damages claimants the right to obtain or use the settlement submission, whereas allowing such use risks deterring infringers from making settlement submissions to the competition authorities.

The question has been raised whether the apparently absolute protection of leniency statements and settlement submissions established by Articles 6(6) and 7(1) of the Directive is compatible with the EU Treaties, which, according to the case law of the Court of Justice, grant victims of infringements of Articles 101 or 102 TFEU a right to compensation, and require the effective protection of this right.[1738]

The case law of the Court of Justice would indeed appear to imply that, in a situation where, in order to ensure effective protection of the right to compensation enjoyed by a claimant, it would be necessary for the claimant to be able to use a leniency statement or settlement submission, there should be a possibility for a weighing-up and reconciliation on a case-by-case basis of the respective interests in favour and against protection of the leniency statement or settlement submission.

I do not think that this poses a major problem, for two reasons.

First, the situation in which, in order to ensure effective protection of the right to compensation enjoyed by a claimant, it would be necessary for the claimant to be able to use a leniency statement or settlement submission, is highly unlikely to arise, as there are all kinds of other documents that can be used, including in particular the competition authority's final decision.[1739]

Secondly, as far as leniency statements and settlement submissions in the European Commission's files are concerned, Articles 6(6) and 7(1) of the Directive do not really establish an absolute protection against the use of such leniency statements or settlement submissions, because they concern only two of the avenues through which access to such leniency statements or settlement submissions could possibly be obtained, namely *primo* disclosure orders by national courts and *secundo* access to the file in the course of the competition authority's antitrust enforcement proceedings.

[1738] See H. Schweitzer, 'Die neue Richtlinie für wettbewerbsrechtliche Schadenersatzklage' (2014) *Neue Zeitschrift für Kartellrecht* 335, at 341–343, and judgments in *BRT and SABAM* and in *Courage v Crehan*, C-453/99, EU:C:2001:465, in Judgment in *Pfleiderer*, C-360/09, EU:C:2011:389, in *Donau Chemie and Others*, C-536/11, EU:C:2013:366 and in *European Commission v EnBW Energie Baden-Württemberg*, C-365/12 P, EU:C:2014:112; see also judgment in *AXA Versicherung v European Commission*, T-677/13, EU:T:2015:473, paragraph 133.

[1739] See also *European Commission v EnBW Energie Baden-Württemberg*, C-365/12 P, EU:C:2014:112, paragraph 106, and the first sentence of recital 27 of the Directive, and A. Howard, 'Disclosure of Infringement Decisions in Competition Damages Proceedings: How the UK Courts Are Leading the Way Ahead of the Damages Directive' (2015) 6 *Journal of Competition Law & Practice* 256.

Another avenue, which is unaffected by the Directive, is *tertio* requests from national courts to the European Commission under Article 15(1) of Regulation 1/2003.[1740]

If ever the situation were to arise in which a national court considers that, in order to ensure effective protection of the right to compensation enjoyed by a claimant, it would be necessary for the claimant to be able to use a leniency statement or settlement submission in the European Commission's files, the national court could make a request to the European Commission to transmit this document pursuant to Article 15(1) of Regulation 1/2003 and the *Zwartveld* case law on which this provision is based.[1741] The European Commission may then have to weigh up in the specific case the respective interests in favour and against transmitting the document. If the European Commission decides against transmitting the document, this decision could be submitted to the EU Courts for judicial review either through a preliminary reference by the national court pursuant to Article 267 TFEU or through an application for annulment brought by the claimant pursuant to Article 263 TFEU.

8. Temporary protection of information from public enforcement proceedings

Article 6(5) of the Directive provides that, until the competition authority has closed its proceedings, national courts cannot order disclosure of (a) information that was prepared by a natural or legal person specifically for the proceedings of a competition authority and (b) information that the competition authority has drawn up and sent to the parties in the course of its proceedings.

Article 7(2) of the Directive adds that, until the competition authority has closed its proceedings, such information cannot be used in actions for damages if it has been obtained solely through access to the file of a competition authority.

Recital 25 of the Directive explains these provisions as follows:

'An exemption should apply in respect of any disclosure that, if granted, would unduly interfere with an ongoing investigation by a competition authority concerning an infringement of Union or national competition law. Information that was prepared by a competition authority in the course of its proceedings for the enforcement of Union or national competition law or sent to the parties to those proceedings (such as a "Statement of

---

1740 However, see also the European Commission's Notice on the cooperation between the Commission and the courts of the EU Member States in the application of Articles 81 and 82 EC [2004] OJ C101/54, as amended by Communication from the Commission – Amendments to the Commission Notice on the cooperation between the Commission and the courts of the EU Member States in the application of Articles 81 and 82 EC [2015] OJ C256/5, paragraphs 26 and 26a.
A fourth possible avenue, equally unaffected by the Directive (see Article 6(2) of the Directive and Judgment in *Axa Versicherung v Commission*, T-677/13, EU:T:2015:473, paragraph 135), is requests from claimants to the European Commission under Regulation (EC) No 1049/2001 of the European Parliament and of the Council of 30 May 2001 regarding public access to European Parliament, Council and Commission documents [2001] OJ L145/43; see Judgment in *European Commission v EnBW Energie Baden-Württemberg*, C-365/12 P, EU:C:2014:112. This avenue is, however, fundamentally unsuited for this purpose, because Regulation 1049/2001 concerns public access, irrespective of the purpose for which access is sought, and hence does not allow for the proper weighing of the claimant's specific private right to compensation.

1741 Orders in *Zwartveld*, C-2/88, EU:C:1990:315 and EU:C:1990:440, and Judgment in *Netherlands and Van der Wal v European Commission*, C-174/98 P and C-189/98 P, EU:C:2000:1, paragraph 25.

Objections") or prepared by a party thereto (such as replies to requests for information of the competition authority or witness statements) should therefore be disclosable in actions for damages only after the competition authority has closed its proceedings, for instance by adopting a decision under Article 5 or under Chapter III of Regulation (EC) No 1/2003, with the exception of decisions on interim measures.'

The practical effect of this temporary protection of information from public enforcement proceedings is to discourage actions for damages that run in parallel with public enforcement proceedings, and to encourage instead follow-on actions that only take place after the closure of the competition authority's proceedings.

Waiting until after the closure of the public enforcement proceedings should not be too problematic for damages claimants, because Article 10(4) of the Directive provides for the suspension of limitation periods during public enforcement proceedings and until one year after the termination of those proceedings. In addition, if the public enforcement proceedings terminate with an infringement decision, the damages claimants will be able to rely on this decision.

Following the adoption of the Directive, the European Commission in 2015 amended Regulation 773/2004,[1742] its implementing regulation of Regulation 1/2003, so as to reflect the provisions of the Directive.[1743] Article 16a(3) of Regulation 773/2004, as amended, provides that, until the European Commission has closed its proceedings against all parties under investigation, (a) information that was prepared by a natural or legal person specifically for the proceedings of a competition authority and (b) information that the competition authority has drawn up and sent to the parties in the course of its proceedings obtained pursuant to Regulation 773/2004 'shall not be used in proceedings before national courts'. This temporary protection goes beyond the Directive in that it is not limited to actions for damages. It thus appears to cover also, for instance, the situation where a complainant in the European Commission's proceedings, who has obtained a copy of the statement of objections pursuant to Article 6(1) of Regulation 773/2004, wanted to use this statement of objections to seek interim relief in a national court. As mentioned above, this has happened in several cases in the past.[1744] Moreover, the possibility of obtaining interim relief in national court during a European Commission investigation appears more important under Regulation 1/2003 than it was under Regulation 17, given that Article 8 of Regulation 1/2003 has abolished the procedural status of complainants with respect to the adoption of interim measures by the European Commission itself.[1745]

1742 Commission Regulation (EC) No 773/2004 of 7 April 2004 relating to the conduct of proceedings by the Commission pursuant to Articles 81 and 82 of the EC Treaty [2004] OJ L123/18. This regulation is based on Article 33 of Regulation 1/2003, which enables the Commission to adopt implementing provisions for that regulation.

1743 Commission Regulation (EU) 2015/1348 of 3 August 2015 amending Regulation (EC) No 773/2004 relating to the conduct of proceedings by the Commission pursuant to Articles 81 and 82 of the EC Treaty [2015] OJ L208/3. For the same purpose, the European Commission also amended four of its procedural notices; see OJ C256 of 5 August 2015.

1744 See Commission Decision of 29 November 1995 relating to a proceeding pursuant to Article 85 of the EC Treaty (IV/34.179, 34.202, 216 – *Stichting Certificatie Kraanverhuurbedrijf and the Federatie van Nederlandse Kraanverhuurbedrijven*) [1995] OJ L312/79, paragraph 13, and Judgment in *Postbank v Commission*, T-353/94, EU:T:1996:119..

1745 See A. Nordsjo, 'Regulation 1/2003: Power of the Commission to Adopt Interim Measures' (2006) *European Competition Law Review* 299.

However, Article 16a of Regulation 773/2004, as amended, does not affect Article 15(1) of Regulation 1/2003 and the *Zwartveld* case law on which the latter provision is based.[1746] The national court before which the complainant seeks interim relief could thus still ask the European Commission to transmit to it the statement of objections pursuant to Article 15(1) of Regulation 1/2003.

9. Encouragement of consensual dispute resolution

Recital 48 of the Directive reads as follows:

'*Achieving a "once-and-for-all" settlement for defendants is desirable in order to reduce uncertainty for infringers and injured parties. Therefore, infringers and injured parties should be encouraged to agree on compensating for the harm caused by a competition law infringement through consensual dispute resolution mechanisms, such as out-of-court settlements (including those where a judge can declare a settlement binding), arbitration, mediation and conciliation. [. . .].*'

The Directive contains three provisions that indeed facilitate consensual dispute resolution:

- Article 18(1) and (2) of the Directive provide that the limitation period for bringing an action for damages is suspended for the duration of any consensual dispute resolution process and that national courts seized of an action for damages may suspend their proceedings for up to two years where the parties thereto are involved in consensual dispute resolution;
- As already mentioned above, Article 19(2) and (3) of the Directive protect settling co-infringers against having to pay contribution to non-settling co-infringers; and
- Article 18(3) provides that a competition authority may consider compensation paid as a result of a consensual settlement and prior to its decision imposing a fine to be a mitigating factor.

10. The impact of Directive 2014/104 on the practice of private enforcement

As mentioned above, both under Regulation 17 and in the first years following the entry into application of Regulation 1/2003, most of the private enforcement of EU antitrust law involved the use of Articles 101 and 102 TFEU as a defence or their offensive use to obtain injunctive relief, sometimes combined with an additional claim for damages. These cases were mostly stand-alone cases, and mostly concerned either vertical agreements or abuse of dominance.

The principal intended and likely effect of Directive 2014/104 on the practice of private enforcement is an increase in the number of (purely compensatory) follow-on actions for damages. Significant change as to the frequency of stand-alone actions for damages was not intended by the legislator and is most unlikely to result from the Directive.[1747]

1746 Orders in *Zwartveld*, C-2/88, EU:C:1990:315 and EU:C:1990:440, and Judgment in *Netherlands and Van der Wal v European Commission*, C-174/98 P and C-189/98 P, EU:C:2000:1, paragraph 25.

1747 See P. Van Nuffel, Institutional Report – Private enforcement of EU competition law, XXVII FIDE Congress (Budapest, 18–21 May 2016), at 239, and P. Roth, 'Too much or too little? The EU initiatives to promote private redress', in *Antitrust between EU law and National law / Antitrust fra diritto Nazionale e diritto dell'Unione Europea* (Bruylant 2015) 51, at 52; see also above as to the rejection of the American conception of private actions for damages as an instrument of deterrence and punishment.

To some extent the intended effect of Directive 2014/104 appears to have already materialised before the Directive becomes applicable on 27 December 2016. Indeed, it appears that already since 2005 there has been in several EU Member States a marked increase in the number of follow-on actions for damages.[1748] In part this increase may be the result of increased awareness as a result of (the discussions surrounding) the European Commission's 2005 Green Paper, 2008 White Paper and 2013 legislative proposal.[1749]

In the last few years, in Germany, the Netherlands and the UK, practically every infringement decision of the European Commission or of the national competition authority already appears to have triggered follow-on actions for damages.[1750] Directive 2014/104 may lead to a similar development in the other EU Member States.

F. Outlook

Directive 2014/104 has brought to an end a decade-long discussion about the role of private actions, or at least private actions for damages, in the enforcement of Articles 101 and 102 TFEU. The American conception of private actions for damages as an instrument for deterrence and punishment, and thus a substitute for public enforcement, has been clearly rejected. Instead, the central role of public enforcement, by the European Commission and the national competition authorities, working together in the European Competition Network, has been reaffirmed, with private actions for damages performing a supplementary, purely compensatory role.

This basic orientation is most unlikely to change in the foreseeable future. It is not unlikely, however, that discussion will continue or will emerge on various more specific issues concerning the interaction between public and private enforcement. The following could be mentioned in particular:[1751]

1. Voluntary compensation as a ground for reducing fines

As the OECD Secretariat has pointed out:

'An emerging issue in the interplay between public and private enforcement is how and to what extent should courts or competition authorities pro-actively support and encourage out-of-court settlements with the victims (or opt-in/opt-out collective settlements) and voluntary redress/compensations of the victims within the administrative proceeding. The rationale for encouraging a voluntary redress scheme or consensual dispute resolution

---

1748 See B. Rodger, *Competition Law Comparative Private Enforcement and Collective Redress across the EU* (Wolters Kluwer, 2014), Part I, Chapters 3 and 4, in particular Chapter 4, at footnote 28.

1749 In part the increase may also be a consequence of legislative initiatives at the national level, some of which may have reflected competition between jurisdictions to attract legal business; see C.-D. Ehlermann, 'Foreword', in A. P. Komninos, *EC Private Antitrust Enforcement – Decentralised Application of EC Competition Law by National Courts* (Hart Publishing 2008), at x.

1750 See P. C. Müller-Graf, General Report - Private enforcement of EU competition law, XXVII FIDE Congress (Budapest, 18–21 May 2016), at 94.

1751 See also, on the relationship between private enforcement and the so-called more economic approach, U. Böge and K. Ost, 'Up and Running, or is it? Private enforcement – the Situation in Germany and Policy Perspectives' (2006) *European Competition Law Review* 197, at 203–205, and my paper 'The Judgment of the EU General Court in *Intel* and the So-Called More Economic Approach to Abuse of Dominance' (2014) 37 *World Competition* 405, also accessible at http://ssrn.com/author=456087, at footnotes 84 to 89.

systems is related to the costs and uncertainty of litigation. Competition-related damage claims can be particularly costly, time-consuming and more complex than other civil actions. Alternative dispute resolution (or consensual dispute resolution) mechanisms allow victims to settle cases quickly and easily on a voluntary basis'.[1752]

As mentioned above, Article 18(3) of Directive 2014/104 provides that a competition authority may consider compensation paid as a result of a consensual settlement and prior to its decision imposing a fine to be a mitigating factor.

It has been argued that the European Commission should take inspiration from this provision in Directive 2014/14 to amend its own Fining Guidelines, which do not list compensation paid as a mitigation factor,[1753] and that it should develop a practice of granting fine reductions on this ground, so as to contribute to a harmonised approach within the European Competition Network.[1754]

In two cases in 1998 and 2002, *Pre-Insulated Pipes Cartel* and *Nintendo*, the European Commission granted reductions of the fines imposed on respectively ABB and Nintendo for violations of Article 101 TFEU in recognition of the fact that ABB had paid 'substantial compensation to Powerpipe and its previous owner' and that Nintendo had 'offered substantial financial compensation to third parties identified in the Statement of Objections as having suffered financial harm as a result of [Nintendo]'s violation'.[1755] The European Commission has refused to grant such reductions in other cases, and the EU General Court has confirmed that the European Commission is under no obligation to grant such reductions.[1756]

2. The cumulative financial impact of fines and damages

Article 20(1) of Directive 2014/104 provides that the European Commission shall review the Directive and shall submit a report thereon to the European Parliament and the Council by 27 December 2020.

Article 20(2)(a) of the Directive specifies that this report shall in particular include information on 'the possible impact of financial constraints flowing from the payment of fines imposed by a competition authority for an infringement of competition law on the possibility for injured parties to obtain full compensation for the harm caused by that infringement of competition law'.

As already mentioned above, in cartel cases in which the largest competitor receives immunity under the competition authority's leniency programme – a relatively frequent

---

1752 OECD Secretariat, *Relationship between public and private antitrust enforcement*, DAF/COMP/WP3(2015)14 of 15 June 2015, paragraph 70.

1753 European Commission, Guidelines on the method of setting fines imposed pursuant to Article 23(2)(a) of Regulation No 1/2003 [2006] OJ C210/2, paragraph 29. It should be noted, however, that the list of mitigating circumstances in this paragraph 29 is not exhaustive, as is apparent from the wording 'such as'.

1754 C. Prieto, 'Incitations aux réparations spontanées dans le cadre du *public enforcement*', *Concurrences* no 2-2016, paragraph 19.

1755 Decision of 21 October 1998, *Pre-Insulated Pipes Cartel* [1999] OJ L24/1, recital 172, and Decision of 30 October 2002, *Nintendo* [2003] OJ L255/33, recitals 440 and 441.

1756 Judgment of 27 September 2006 in *Archer Daniels Midland v Commission*, Case T-59/02, EU:T:2006:272, paragraphs 349 to 355.

occurrence – the cumulative financial impact of fines and damages may also negatively affect the market structure.[1757]

This raises the broader question whether the EU antitrust enforcement system is not too exclusively focused on monetary penalties on undertakings, as opposed to a combination of such penalties and sanctions on individuals.[1758]

3. The continued attractiveness of leniency programmes

This issue is discussed in the next and final chapter of this book.

1757 See further also S. Davies, P. L. Ormosi and M. Graffenberger, 'Mergers after cartels: How markets react to cartel breakdown', University of East Anglia Centre for Competition Policy (CCP) Working Paper 14-1 (20 March 2014).

1758 See my paper 'Is Criminalization of EU Competition Law the Answer?' (2005) 28 *World Competition* 117, also accessible at http://ssrn.com/author=456087, and chapter 6 of my book *Efficiency and Justice in European Antitrust Enforcement* (Hart Publishing 2008) and F. Wagner-von Papp, 'Individual sanctions for competition law infringements: Pros, cons and challenges – Introduction', *Concurrences* no 2-2016, 14, and OECD, *Sanctions in Antitrust Cases*, DAF/COMP/GF(2016)6 (14 October 2016).

XVIII. Should the Damages Directive Be Revised to Grant Companies That Have Received Immunity from Fines under the Competition Authorities' Leniency Programmes Also Immunity from Damages?

Following various proposals in the academic literature, and in the light of the observed decrease in the number of leniency applications received by European competition authorities in the period 2015–2020, the German Monopolies Commission (Monopolkommission) proposed in 2022 to amend the Damages Directive 2014/104 so as to immunise companies that have received immunity under the competition authorities' leniency programmes from follow-on actions for damages.

This final chapter analyses the development of follow-on actions for damages, discusses the question what number of leniency applications would be optimal, takes a closer look at the figures, examines the possible and likely causes of the observed evolution of the number of leniency applications, and argues that it would be unwise to grant immunity recipients full protection from damages, because this would be unjust, would harm public anti-cartel enforcement and would increase market concentration.

A. Follow-on actions for damages and the Damages Directive 2014/104

1. Development over time

While the possibility of private enforcement of Article 101 TFEU predates the use of leniency by the European Commission and the national competition authorities, the current practice of follow-on actions for damages in cartel cases developed much more recently.

As already mentioned in Chapter XVII of this book, in a series of cases, starting relatively soon after the entry into force of the EEC Treaty in 1958, the EU Court of Justice was called upon to clarify the possibility of private enforcement of Articles 101 and 102 TFEU as well as the relationship between public and private enforcement. Indeed, the very first case reaching the Court of Justice through the preliminary reference mechanism from a national court concerned a dispute between private parties before the Dutch civil courts in which Article 101 TFEU was invoked as a defence.[1759]

[1759] *De Geus v Bosch and Van Rijn*, 13/61, EU:C:1962:11.

In its case law, the Court of Justice progressively clarified that Articles 101 and 102 TFEU produce direct effects between individuals and create rights for these individuals, and that the national courts whose task it is to apply the provisions of EU law in areas within their jurisdiction must ensure that those rules take full effect and must protect the rights which they confer on individuals, by granting injunctive relief, including interim relief, as well as compensation for harm suffered, under conditions that may not be less favourable than those governing the protection of comparable rights under national law and that ensure the effective protection of the rights conferred by Articles 101 and 102 TFEU.[1760]

It is notoriously difficult to obtain precise figures about private enforcement. Commercial disputes are routinely settled, often before they reach the courts. Many of the cases that reach the courts are settled before they reach final judgments. Even those cases that reach final judgment are not necessarily reported.

On the basis of the available evidence,[1761] it would appear that, at the turn from the 20th to the 21st century, Articles 101 and 102 TFEU were invoked in at least several dozen private cases per year. Most of the cases involved the use of Articles 101 and 102 TFEU as a defence or their offensive use to obtain injunctive relief, sometimes combined with an additional claim for damages. These cases were mostly stand-alone cases, and mostly concerned either vertical agreements or abuse of dominance. There is little or no evidence of follow-on actions for damages in cartel cases at that time.

The current practice of follow-on actions for damages in cartel cases emerged in the wake of the ***Courage and Crehan* judgment** of the EU Court of Justice in 2001,[1762] and the subsequent policy initiatives by the European Commission.

In *Courage and Crehan*, the Court of Justice held that '[t]he full effectiveness of [Article 101 TFEU] and, in particular, the practical effect of the prohibition laid down in [Article 101(1)] would be put at risk if it were not open to any individual to claim damages for loss caused to him by a contract or by conduct liable to restrict or distort competition. Indeed, the existence of such a right strengthens the working of the [EU] competition rules and discourages agreements or practices, which are frequently covert, which are liable to restrict or distort competition. From that point of view, actions for damages before the national courts can make a significant contribution to the maintenance of effective competition in the [European Union]'.[1763] The Court of Justice has repeated

---

1760 Judgments in *BRT and SABAM*, 127/73, EU:C:1974:25, in *Factortame and Others*, C-213/89, EU:C:1990:257, and in *Courage v Crehan*, C-453/99, EU:C:2001:465.

1761 See in particular B. Rodger, *Competition Law Comparative Private Enforcement and Collective Redress across the EU* (Wolters Kluwer, 2014), Part I, Chapters 3 and 4; U. Böge and K. Ost, 'Up and Running, or is it? Private enforcement–the Situation in Germany and Policy Perspectives' (2006) *European Competition Law Review* 197 at 197; J. Temple Lang, 'Foreword', in C. A. Jones, *Private Enforcement of Antitrust Law in the EU, UK and USA* (Oxford UP 1999), at ix; and B. J. Rodger, 'Private enforcement of competition law, the hidden story: competition litigation settlements in the United Kingdom, 2000–2005' (2008) *European Competition Law Review* 96.

1762 *Courage v Crehan*, C-453/99, EU:C:2001:465.

1763 Judgment in *Courage v Crehan*, C-453/99, EU:C:2001:465, paragraphs 26 and 27. In later judgments, the Court of Justice has clarified that the 'any individual' who can claim damages for the loss caused to her by the restrictive agreement or practice includes victims of umbrella pricing (that is, undertakings not party to the cartel, having regard to the practices of the cartel, setting their prices higher than would otherwise have been

these statements in many subsequent judgments, including in its Grand Chamber judgment in *Sumal*, in which it stated that, 'just as is the case for the implementation of the EU competition rules by public authorities (public enforcement), actions for damages for infringement of those rules (private enforcement) are an integral part of the system for enforcement of those rules, which are intended to punish anticompetitive behaviour on the part of undertakings and to deter them from engaging in such conduct'.[1764]

Following the *Courage and Crehan* judgment, the European Commission took a series of initiatives to attract attention to the possibility of bringing actions for damages, including in particular follow-on actions in cartel cases, and to encourage and facilitate the bringing of such actions.

In 2004, the European Commission published a **study** on the conditions for bringing actions for damages in the then 25 EU Member States, and how such actions might be facilitated.[1765] In 2005, the European Commission published a **Green Paper**,[1766] in which it put forward for discussion a number of possible measures to facilitate damage claims for breach of EU antitrust law. In 2008, the European Commission published a **White Paper** on damages actions for breach of the EU antitrust rules,[1767] and in 2013, the European Commission adopted a **proposal** for a Directive of the European Parliament and of the Council on actions for damages.[1768]

The *Courage and Crehan* judgment and the subsequent policy initiatives by the European Commission raised the awareness of the possibility of bringing actions for damages, in particular follow-on actions in cartel cases, and the interest on the part of victims and lawyers to bring such actions. Several EU Member States have also already taken legislative initiatives to facilitate the bringing of such actions, reflecting to some extent competition between jurisdictions to attract this emerging legal business.[1769]

---

expected under competitive conditions); see Judgment in *Kone and Others*, C-557/12, EU:C:2014:1317) as well as a public body which granted loans on favourable terms in order to acquire assets subject to the cartel (Judgment in *Otis and Others*, C-435/18, EU:C:2019:1069).

1764 Judgment in *Sumal*, C-882/19, EU:C:2021:800, paragraph 37. Two comments could be made on the quoted paragraph: First, in the French version of the judgment (French being the internal working language of the Court of Justice), the verb used is '*réprimer*', which would arguably be better reflected in English by 'to combat' than 'to punish'. Secondly, while the Court of Justice in this paragraph appears to reduce the broader concept of 'private enforcement' to 'actions for damages' only, it has since confirmed, in paragraphs 52 and 53 of its judgment in *Repsol Comercial de Productos Ptrolíféros*, C-25/21, EU:C:2023:298, that actions for declaration of nullity equally contribute to ensuring the full effectiveness of Article 101 TFEU.

1765 European Commission, Directorate-General for Competition, Study on the conditions of claims for damages in case of infringement of EC competition rules: comparative and economics reports, 2004.

1766 European Commission, Green Paper on Damages actions for breach of EC antitrust rules, COM(2005)672 of 19 December 2005.

1767 European Commission, White Paper on Damages actions for breach of the EC antitrust rules, COM(2008)165 of 2 April 2008.

1768 European Commission, Proposal for a Directive of the European Parliament and of the Council on certain rules governing actions for damages under national law for infringements of the competition law provisions of the Member States and of the European Union, COM(2013) 404 of 11 June 2013.

1769 See C.-D. Ehlermann, 'Foreword', in A. P. Komninos, *EC Private Antitrust Enforcement–Decentralised Application of EC Competition Law by National Courts* (Hart Publishing 2008), at x.

As a result, since 2005 a marked increase in the number of follow-on actions for damages could be observed in several EU Member States.[1770] By the time the European Commission's proposal finally led to the adoption by the European Parliament and the Council of the **Competition Damages Directive 2014/104**,[1771] in Germany, the Netherlands and the UK (then still an EU Member State), practically every infringement decision of the European Commission or of the national competition authority already appears to have triggered follow-on actions for damages.[1772]

2. The Competition Damages Directive

Directive 2014/104 applies to all damages actions for violation of EU competition law and of national competition law applied in parallel with EU competition law,[1773] without any reference to a distinction between 'stand-alone' and 'follow-on' actions, but many of its provisions appear to address primarily or exclusively follow-on actions for damages.[1774]

According to its Article 1, Directive 2014/104 pursues two objectives: first, ensuring that victims of competition law infringements can effectively exercise their right to full compensation,[1775] and, secondly, 'coordinating' public enforcement and private actions for damages.

In pursuit of the first objective, Directive 2014/104 contains in particular provisions on disclosure of evidence in damages actions before national courts (Article 5), on the binding effect of decisions of national competition authorities in follow-on actions for damages (Article 9), on limitation periods (Article 10) and on quantification of harm (Article 17).

The second objective of 'coordinating' public enforcement and private actions for damages reflected the desire to protect the existing public enforcement mechanisms, in particular the competition authorities' leniency programmes, from possible adverse consequences from increased private enforcement.[1776]

1770 See B. Rodger, *Competition Law Comparative Private Enforcement and Collective Redress across the EU* (Wolters Kluwer, 2014), Part I, Chapters 3 and 4, and my paper 'Private Enforcement of EU Antitrust Law and its Relationship with Public Enforcement: Past, Present and Future' (2017) 40 *World Competition* 3, also accessible at http://ssrn.com/author=456087, text accompanied by footnotes 151 to 153.

1771 Directive 2014/104/EU of the European Parliament and of the Council of 26 November 2014 on certain rules governing actions for damages under national law for infringements of the competition law provisions of the Member States and of the European Union [2014] OJ L349/1 ('EU Damages Directive').

1772 See P. C. Müller-Graf, General Report – Private enforcement of EU competition law, XXVII FIDE Congress (Budapest, 18–21 May 2016), at 94.

1773 Articles 1 and 2(1) and (3) of Directive 2014/104/EU.

1774 See Opinion of Advocate General Pitruzzella in *Repsol Comercial de Productos Petrolíferos*, C-25/21, EU:C:2022:659, paragraphs 44 and 45; P; Van Nuffel, Institutional Report – Private enforcement of EU competition law, XXVII FIDE Congress (Budapest, 18–21 May 2016), at 239; and P. Roth, 'Too much or too little? The EU initiatives to promote private redress', in *Antitrust between EU law and National law / Antitrust fra diritto Nazionale e diritto dell'Unione Europea* (Bruylant 2015) 51 at 52.

1775 According to Article 3(3) of Directive 2014/104/EU, 'full compensation under this Directive shall not lead to overcompensation whether by means of punitive, multiple or other types of damages'. While the European Commission had flirted with the American model of multiple damages in its 2005 Green Paper, this model was firmly rejected in the 2008 White Paper, the 2013 legislative proposal, and finally Directive 2014/104/EU itself; see further Chapter XVII of this book.

1776 See F. G. Wilman, 'The End of the Absence? The growing body of EU legislation on private enforcementand the main remedies it provides for' (2016) 53 *Common Market Law Review* 887 at 906.

Directive 2014/104 contains two measures to protect the leniency programmes of the European Commission and the national competition authorities:

First, Articles 6(6) and 7(1) of Directive 2014/104 **prohibit the disclosure and the use in evidence of leniency statements and settlement submissions** in damages actions in national courts.[1777]

'Leniency statement' is defined in Article 2(16) of the Directive as 'an oral or written presentation voluntarily provided by, or on behalf of, an undertaking or a natural person to a competition authority or a record thereof, describing the knowledge of that undertaking or natural person of a cartel and describing its role therein, which presentation was drawn up specifically for submission to the competition authority with a view to obtaining immunity or a reduction of fines under a leniency programme, not including pre-existing information', the latter being defined in Article 2(17) as 'evidence that exists irrespective of the proceedings of a competition authority, whether or not such information is in the file of a competition authority'.

'Settlement submission' is defined in Article 2(18) of the Directive as 'a voluntary presentation by, or on behalf of, an undertaking to a competition authority describing the undertaking's acknowledgement of, or its renunciation to dispute, its participation in an infringement of competition law and its responsibility for that infringement of competition law, which was drawn up specifically to enable the competition authority to apply a simplified or expedited procedure'.

The justification for this protection of leniency statements and settlement submissions against disclosure and use in evidence is set out as follows in recital 26 of Directive 2014/104:

'*Leniency programmes and settlement procedures are important tools for the public enforcement of Union competition law as they contribute to the detection and efficient prosecution of, and the imposition of penalties for, the most serious infringements of competition law. Furthermore, as many decisions of competition authorities in cartel cases are based on a leniency application, and damages actions in cartel cases generally follow on from those decisions, leniency programmes are also important for the effectiveness of actions for damages in cartel cases. Undertakings might be deterred from cooperating with competition authorities under leniency programmes and settlement procedures if self-incriminating statements such as leniency statements and settlement submissions, which are produced for the sole purpose of cooperating with the competition authorities, were to be disclosed. Such disclosure would pose a risk of exposing cooperating undertakings or their managing staff to civil or criminal liability under conditions worse than those of co-infringers not cooperating with the competition authorities. To ensure undertakings' continued willingness to approach competition authorities voluntarily with*

[1777] These provisions have been complemented by further provisions limiting the disclosure through access to the competition authorities' files and the use of leniency statements and settlement submissions laid down in Articles 15(1b) and 16a(2) of Commission Regulation (EC) No 773/2004 relating to the conduct of proceedings by the Commission pursuant to Articles 81 and 82 of the EC Treaty, as amended by Commission Regulation (EU) 2015/1348 of 3 August 2015 [2015] OJ L208/3, and in Article 31 (3) and (4) of Directive (EU) 2019/1.

leniency statements or settlement submissions, such documents should be exempted from the disclosure of evidence. That exemption should also apply to verbatim quotations from leniency statements or settlement submissions included in other documents. Those limitations on the disclosure of evidence should not prevent competition authorities from publishing their decisions in accordance with the applicable Union or national law. In order to ensure that that exemption does not unduly interfere with injured parties' rights to compensation, it should be limited to those voluntary and self-incriminating leniency statements and settlement submissions.'

As a second measure to protect the competition authorities' leniency programmes against potential adverse effects from follow-on actions for damages, Article 11(4) and (5), second sentence, of Directive 2014/104 **partially exempts immunity recipients from joint and several liability**.

Under Directive 2014/104, the general rule for cartels and other joint competition law infringements is joint and several liability, with contribution between joint infringers. Article 11(1) of the Directive thus provides that 'undertakings which have infringed competition law through joint behaviour are jointly and severally liable for the harm caused by the infringement of competition law; with the effect that each of those undertakings is bound to compensate for the harm in full, and the injured party has the right to require full compensation from any of them until he has been fully compensated', and Article 11(5), first sentence, provides that 'an infringer may recover a contribution from any other infringer, the amount of which shall be determined in the light of their relative responsibility for the harm caused by the infringement of competition law'.[1778]

In derogation from this general rule, Article 11(4) of Directive 2014/104 provides that an immunity recipient is jointly and severally liable to its own direct and indirect purchasers and providers, but to other injured parties only where full compensation cannot be obtained from the other infringers. Similarly, Article 11(5), second sentence, provides that 'the amount of contribution of an infringer which has been granted immunity from fines under a leniency programme shall not exceed the amount of the harm it caused to its own direct or indirect purchasers or providers'.[1779]

The justification for this partial exemption of the immunity recipient from joint and several liability is set out as follows in recital 38 of Directive 2014/104:

'*Undertakings which cooperate with competition authorities under a leniency programme play a key role in exposing secret cartel infringements and in bringing them to an end, thereby often mitigating the harm which could have been caused had the infringement*

1778 These general provisions essentially confirm the law as it already existed under the national laws of the (then) EU Member States; see for instance N. Dunleavy, 'Contribution among Antitrust Defendants in English Law' (2009) 30 *European Competition Law Review* 22. They also confirm another difference with the law in the USA, which provides for joint and several liability but does not allow for contribution; see J. Angland, 'Joint and Several Liability, Contribution, and Claim Reduction' (2008), accessible at http://ssrn.com/abstract=1528007, and M. Hviid and A. Medvedev, 'The Role of Contribution among Defendants in Private Antitrust Litigation' (2010) 30 *International Review of Law & Economics* 306.

1779 Article 11(6) adds that, 'to the extent the infringement of competition law caused harm to injured parties other than the direct or indirect purchasers or providers of the infringers, the amount of any contribution from an immunity recipient to other infringers shall be determined in the light of its relative responsibility for that harm'.

continued. It is therefore appropriate to make provision for undertakings which have received immunity from fines from a competition authority under a leniency programme to be protected from undue exposure to damages claims, bearing in mind that the decision of the competition authority finding the infringement may become final for the immunity recipient before it becomes final for other undertakings which have not received immunity, thus potentially making the immunity recipient the preferential target of litigation. [. . .]'.

Being a directive rather than a regulation,[1780] Directive 2014/104 is not directly applicable. It rather obliges the EU Member States to bring into force the laws or regulations necessary to comply with its provisions. Article 21(1) of Directive 2014/104 set 27 December 2016 as the deadline for this transposition into national law.

Moreover, as regards the temporal application of Directive 2014/104, that directive contains in its Article 22 a special provision which explicitly states the conditions for the temporal application of its provisions, distinguishing between, on the one hand, substantive provisions, and, on the other hand, non-substantive or procedural provisions.[1781]

Under Article 22(1) of Directive 2014/104, Member States had to ensure that the national measures adopted in order to comply with substantive provisions of that directive do not apply retroactively. Under Article 22(2), Member States had to ensure that any national measures adopted in order to comply with the non-substantive provisions of that directive do not apply to actions for damages of which a national court was seized prior to 26 December 2014.[1782]

For example, the binding effect of decisions of national competition authorities finding an infringement on follow-on actions for damages, as provided for in Article 9(1) of Directive 2014/104, constitutes a substantive provision, and thus only applies to decisions of national competition authorities that have become final after the entry into force of the relevant national law transposing Directive 2014/104 or after the expiry of the transposition deadline on 27 December 2016.[1783]

The partial exemption of immunity recipients from joint and several liability, as provided for in Article 11(4) and (5) of Directive 2014/104, undoubtedly also constitutes a substantive provision, and appears thus limited to cartel cases where both the infringement and the immunity application took place after the entry into force of the relevant national law transposing Directive 2014/104 or after the expiry of the transposition deadline on 27 December 2016.[1784] As a result, the partial exemption of immunity recipients from joint

---

1780 See Article 288 TFEU.

1781 See Judgments in *Cogeco Communications*, C-637/17, EU:C:2019:263, paragraph 25, and in *PACCAR and Others*, C-163/21, EU:C:2022:863, paragraph 27.

1782 The Member States thus enjoyed a measure of discretion in deciding, when transposing Directive 2014/104/EU, whether the national rules intended to transpose the directive's non-substantive provisions would apply to actions for damages brought after 26 December 2014 but before the date of transposition of that directive or, at the latest, before the expiry of the period prescribed for its transposition (27 December 2016); see Judgment in *Cogeco Communications*, C-637/17, EU:C:2019:263, paragraph 28.

1783 Judgment in *Repsol Comercial de Productos Ptrolíféros*, C-25/21, EU:C:2023:298, paragraphs 33 to 46.

1784 See, by analogy, Judgments in *Repsol Comercial de Productos Ptrolíféros*, C-25/21, EU:C:2023:298, paragraphs 33 to 46, and in *Volvo and DAF Trucks*, C-267/20, EU:C:2022:494, as well as the currently pending Case C-605/21, *Heureka Group*.

and several liability, as provided for in Article 11(4) and (5) of Directive 2014/104, does not appear to have had any practical application in follow-on actions for damages yet.

While the provisions of Directive 2014/104 are thus only slowly reaching practical application, the number of follow-on actions for damages appears to have continued increasing in the meantime.[1785]

In particular, the European Commission's decision in the Trucks Cartel case, adopted on 19 July 2016 and summarily published on 6 April 2017,[1786] has given rise to a very large number of follow-on actions for damages in several Member States, resulting in more than 3,000 first-instance judgments and more than 1,000 judgments by appeal courts in Spain alone.[1787]

B. The proposal of the German Monopolkommission to grant immunity recipients full protection from damages actions

1. Various academic proposals

Already at the time of adoption of Directive 2014/104, the partial exemption of immunity recipients from joint and several liability, as laid down in Article 11(4) and (5) of Directive 2014/104, was criticised by some observers as an inadequate way to address potential negative effects of follow-on actions for damages on the competition authorities' leniency programmes.

Most notably, Christian Kersting argued already in 2014, on the one hand, that the limitation of the immunity recipient's joint and several liability to its own direct and indirect purchasers and providers is problematic, because it puts a significant burden on the exercise of the other injured parties' right to compensation,[1788] and, on the other

---

1785 While business-to-business damages litigation has strongly developed, actions brought by or on behalf of consumers have been much rarer; see M. Sousa Ferro, 'Consumer Antitrust Private Enforcement in Europe' (2022) 13 *Journal of European Competition Law & Practice* 578, and BEUC (The European Consumer Organisation)'s Response to the public consultation in relation to the evaluation of Regulation 1/2003 (6 October 2022), accessible at https://ec.europa.eu/info/law/better-regulation/have-your-say/initiatives/13431-EU-antitrust-procedural-rules-evaluation/F3347442_en. For a rare example of two cases brought by consumers, see Order in *Deutsche Bank*, C-198/22 and C-199/22, EU:C:2023:166. While, through its Article 52, the Digital Markets Act (Regulation (EU) 2022/1925 of the European Parliament and of the Council of 14 September 2022 on contestable and fair markets in the digital sector [2022] OJ L261/1) has been added to Annex I to Directive (EU) 2020/1828 of the European Parliament and of the Council of 25 November 2020 on representative actions for the protection of the collective interests of consumers ([2020] OJ L409/1), Articles 101 and 102 TFEU currently remain absent from this Annex.

1786 Summary of Commission Decision of 19 July 2016 relating to a proceeding under Article 101 of the Treaty on the Functioning of the European Union and Article 53 of the EEA Agreement (Case AT.39824–Trucks) [2017] OJ C108/6.

1787 See F. Marcos, 'Trucks Cartel Damages Claims: Thousand and Odd Judgments Issued by Spanish Appeal Courts' (2023) *Zeitschrift für Europäisches Privatrecht* 178.

1788 C. Kersting, 'Removing the Tension Between Public and Private Enforcement: Disclosure and Privileges for Successful Leniency Applicants' (2014) 5 *Journal of European Competition Law & Practice* 2 at 4. Professor Kersting also suggested that this limitation of the external liability in relation to the injured parties might be contrary to Article 101 TFEU, as interpreted by the Court of Justice. As has been pointed out by other authors, however,

hand, that immunity recipients should be privileged much further by allowing them to claim full compensation for all damages paid to injured parties from the other cartel members. This rule could even be extended to leniency applicants who receive a partial reduction of the fine by correspondingly decreasing, in relation to their co-infringers, their share of the damages to be paid to the victims.[1789]

Most radically, Philipp Kirst and Roger Van den Bergh have argued that the immunity recipient should receive full immunity from damages, also in relation to the injured parties, and that all further leniency recipients should also receive immunity from damages in proportion to the fine reduction received.[1790] In yet another variation, Paolo Buccirossi, Catarina Marvão and Giancarlo Spagnolo have argued that only the immunity recipient should receive full immunity from damages, without any need to limit the civil liability of other leniency recipients.[1791]

2. Private practitioners raise the alarm

In 2018, Johan Ysewyn and Siobhan Kahmann attracted attention to 'a worrying reality for anti-cartel enforcement by the European Commission – and possibly national competition authorities within the EU: the noticeable decrease of the number of immunity applications over the last several years, and the resulting impact on the Commission's ability to detect cartels'.[1792] Among the reasons for the decline in the number of immunity applications, they highlighted 'the major game changer: private damages; Whereas in the past, damages claims used to be virtually non-existent in the EU, over recent years they have become the new reality, especially in the business-to-business area'.[1793]

Ysewyn and Kahmann further indicated that, instead of making an immunity application, companies and their lawyers 'are looking for other ways to protect their interests. One way is to make sure that once the company's participation in the cartel stops, a file is "ready to go" in case the authorities open an investigation so as to benefit at least from a 50% fine reduction as the first-in leniency applicant, without benefiting from full immunity. In practice this means that they are playing the "waiting game" in order for the five-year statute of limitation period to expire'.[1794]

---

the EU legislator should enjoy broad discretion on how and by what instruments public and private enforcement are to be coordinated, as long as the right of the injured person to claim damages is not abrogated or restricted in an unreasonable way; see J.-U. Franck, 'Striking a balance of power between the Court of Justice and the EU legislature: the law on competition damages actions as a paradigm' (2018) 43 *European Law Review* 837, and W.-H. Roth, '*Courage* and Directive 2014/104/EU' (2022) 59 *Common Market Law Review* 61.

1789 C. Kersting, 'Removing the Tension Between Public and Private Enforcement: Disclosure and Privileges for Successful Leniency Applicants' (2014) 5 *Journal of European Competition Law & Practice* 2 at 4.

1790 P. Kirst and R. Van den Bergh, 'The European Directive on Damages Actions: A Missed Opportunity to Reconcile Compensation of Victims and Leniency Incentives (2016) 12 *Journal of Competition Law & Economics* 1. The argument has subsequently been repeated and expanded by Philipp Kirst in Part III (Chapter 6) of his book *The Impact of the Damages Directive on the Enforcement of EU Competition Law* (Edward Elgar, 2021); see also my review of this book in (2023) 60 *Common Market Law Review* 610.

1791 P. Buccirossi, C. Marvão and G. Spagnolo, 'Leniency and Damages: Where Is the Conflict?' (2020) 49 *Journal of Legal Studies* 335; a draft of this paper was already available on SSRN in 2015.

1792 J. Ysewyn and S. Kahmann, 'The decline and fall of the leniency programme in Europe', *Concurrences* no 1-2018, 44–50 at 44.

1793 Idem, at 56.

1794 Idem, at 58. Such ready but not sent leniency applications are sometimes referred to as 'cupboard applications'.

3. Positions of the German authorities

The German Federal Competition Authority (Bundeskartellamt) being one of the national competition authorities noticing a marked decline in the number of leniency applications it received, its president, Andreas Mundt, argued on several occasions in 2021 and 2022 that thought should be given to immunising immunity recipients from follow-on damages.[1795]

In its Competition Policy Agenda until 2025, published on 21 February 2022, the German Federal Ministry for Economic Affairs and Climate Action (BMWK) indicated that 'we want to strengthen cartel prosecution through an initiative to better protect immunity recipients and reform the EU Competition Damages Directive'.[1796]

Given that the European Commission has the exclusive competence to make a legislative proposal to amend or replace Directive 2014/104,[1797] this should be understood as an invitation to the European Commission to make such a proposal, or at least, as a preparatory step, to start the review of this Directive. Indeed, Article 20(1) of Directive 2014/104 provides that the Commission shall review this Directive and shall present a report thereon, if appropriate accompanied by a legislative proposal, to the European Parliament and the Council by 27 December 2020. The Commission respected this deadline in that it submitted a report on 14 December 2020,[1798] but it indicated in this report that, given the implementation deadline and the non-retroactivity of the substantive provisions of Directive 2014/104, it was too early to carry out a meaningful evaluation of this Directive. The Commission did, however, indicate that it 'plans to evaluate the Directive and report on such evaluation once sufficient experience from the application of the rules of the Directive has accumulated'.[1799]

4. The proposal of the German Monopolkommission

On 5 July 2022, in its XXIV Biennial Report, the German Monopolies Commission (Monopolkommission) made a specific proposal to amend Directive 2014/104 so as to immunise immunity recipients from follow-on damages.[1800]

The Monopolkommission started by observing the decline in the number of leniency applications received by the Bundeskartellamt since 2014. Between 2005 and 2013, the

---

1795 See 'Cartel whistleblowers may need protection from damages actions, Bundeskartellamt chief says' (*MLex*, 14 September 2021); 'Warum Kartellamtschef Mundt das Kronzeugenprogramm ausweiten will' (*Handelsblatt*, 10 January 2022); and 'European leniency programs must consider reform, Germany's Mundt says' (*MLex*, 8 April 2022).

1796 Bundes ministerium für Wirtschaft und Klimaschutz, Wettbewerbspolitische Agenda des BMWK bis 2025 (21.02.2022), accessible at https://www.bmwk.de/Redaktion/DE/Downloads/0-9/10-punkte-papier-wettbewerbsrecht.pdf?__blob=publicationFile&v=8, at page 5.

1797 See Article 17(2) TEU and Articles 103(1), 114(1) and 289(1) TFEU.

1798 European Commission, Staff Working Paper on the implementation of Directive 2014/104/EU of the European Parliament and of the Council of 26 November 2014 on certain rules governing actions for damages under national law for infringements of the competition law provisions of the Member States and of the European Union, SWD(2020) 338 final of 14.12.2020; see also Press release 'Antitrust: Commission publishes report on implementation of Damages Directive', IP/20/2413 of 14 December 2020.

1799 Idem, at 3.

1800 Monopolkommission, Wettbewerb 2022, XXIV. Haupgutachten gemäβ § 44 Abs. 1 Satz 1 GWB (5.7.2022), Section 2.5, pages 161–173.

annual number of leniency applications had steadily increased from 13 in 2005 to 41 in 2013. Between 2014 and 2020, the number of leniency applications steadily decreased from 41 to 11 per year.[1801]

The Monopolkommission also referred to the figures published by the OECD in its Competition Trends 2022, which show, for the period 2015 to 2020, a 70.5% decline in leniency applications in Europe, as well as 68.5% decline in the Americas and also a decline in the Asia-Pacific region.[1802]

The Monopolkommission then discusses the possible explanations for this decline, mentioning in particular Directive 2014/104 and its transposition in German law as the possible cause highlighted by the Bundeskartellamt.[1803] In the light of the simultaneous decline in the number of leniency applications outside Europe, where there has been no similar change regarding follow-on actions for damages, the Monopolkommission concludes, however, that it is unlikely that Directive 2014/104 and its transposition in German law are the main cause of the decline in the number of leniency applications received by the Bundeskartellamt.[1804]

The Monopolkommission nevertheless proceeded to propose, in order to optimise the use of leniency,[1805] that the immunity recipient should be fully exempted from liability for damages, unless full compensation cannot be obtained from the other infringers,[1806] and unless the immunity recipient enjoys a dominant position,[1807] and on condition that the immunity recipient makes its leniency statements available to the injured parties.[1808]

C. What is the optimal number of leniency applications and what explains the observed evolution of the number of leniency applications?

1. The optimal level of anti-cartel enforcement and the optimal balance between leniency and ex officio investigations

Before considering the observed evolution of the number of leniency applications, and the possible and likely causes for that evolution, it is useful first to reflect on what would constitute the **optimal number of leniency applications**.

Obviously, the perspective to be taken should be the societal perspective of optimal anti-cartel enforcement, not the private interest of the antitrust industry.[1809] From the perspective of the lawyers handling leniency applications, more leniency applications mean more billable hours. From the perspective of competition authorities, leniency applications provide, compared to the more arduous work of *ex officio* investigations, an

---

1801 Idem, at 164.

1802 OECD, Competition Trends 2022, at 46.

1803 Monopolkommission, Wettbewerb 2022, XXIV. Haupgutachten gemäß § 44 Abs. 1 Satz 1 GWB (5.7.2022), at 165–166.

1804 Idem, at 166.

1805 Idem, at 167.

1806 Idem, at 170.

1807 Idem, at 170–171.

1808 Idem, at 172.

1809 See generally R. B. Reich, 'The Antitrust Industry' (1980) 68 *The Georgetown Law Journal* 1053.

easier route to decisions, the performance of competition authorities often being measured by the number of decisions they adopt.[1810] Taken to the absurd extreme, the optimum for the antitrust industry would be a leniency policy that grants not only the first cartel participant requesting leniency but also all further cooperating cartel participants full immunity and/or generous rebates from both fines and damages. This might lead to many leniency applications, and a high output by competition authorities, but at the price of low deterrence and many cartels. From the societal perspective of optimal anti-cartel enforcement, the primary objective should be to reduce the incidence of cartels rather than let cartels form and detect them afterwards.[1811]

On the other hand, total deterrence of cartels, and of other antitrust violations, while much beloved and regularly achieved in economic models, is neither achievable nor desirable in the real world.[1812] The reasons for this are both economic and psychological.

The economic reason is that the enforcement measures to prevent violations are normally not without cost. Detecting, prosecuting and punishing violations has a significant administrative cost, which includes both the cost borne by the public sector (cost of competition authorities and courts) and the cost borne by the businesses and individuals concerned (cost of lawyers and experts, management time). Apart from administrative costs, the pursuit of deterrence could also have undesirable side effects. For instance, errors or the risk of errors in the imposition of sanctions could lead to lawful and economically desirable conduct being deterred. Given the existence of these costs, it is unlikely to be optimal to pursue full prevention of antitrust violations. Depending, on the one hand, on the cost of achieving different degrees of prevention, and, on the other hand, on how much value society attaches to the avoidance of antitrust violations, the optimum will be to pursue a certain degree of prevention, which in all likelihood will be less than 100%.[1813]

The psychological reason is that people tend to rely disproportionately on those incidents that can easily be brought to mind, because they are recent, happened close to them, or were well publicised (availability bias).[1814] This phenomenon has several implications for the use of fines to deter antitrust violations. First, it confirms the importance for competition authorities to give maximum publicity to the cases in which they successfully

---

1810 Including, I must admit, by me; see Chapter I of this book.

1811 See W. E. Kovacic, 'A Case for Capping the Dosage: Leniency and Competition Authority Governance', in C. Beaton-Wells and C. Tran (eds), *Anti-Cartel Enforcement in a Contemporary Age–Leniency Religion* (Hart Publishing 2015), 123 at 130 and R. Alimonti, S. Kümmel and T. Nau, 'The interplay between leniency programmes and private enforcement: the economist perspective on recent policy proposals' (2022) 21 *Competition Law Journal* 170 at 171.

1812 See my papers 'Optimal Antitrust Fines: Theory and Practice' (2006) 29 *World Competition* 183, text accompanied by footnotes 26 and 27 and 56 and 57, also accessible at http://ssrn.com/author=456087, and Chapter VIII of this book.

1813 See generally, with regard to deterrence, G. J. Stigler, 'The Optimum Enforcement of Laws' (1970) 78 *Journal of Political Economy* 526 and K. G. Elzinga and W. Breit, *The Antitrust Penalties: A Study in Law and Economics* (Yale UP 1976) at 9–15.

1814 See R. B. Korobkin and T. S. Ulen, 'Law and Behavioral Science: Removing the Rationality Assumption from Law and Economics' (2000) 88 *California Law Review* 1051, at 1085–1090 and A. Tversky and D. Kahneman, 'Availability: A Heuristic for Judging Frequency and Probability', in D. Kahneman, P. Slovic and A. Tversky (eds), *Judgment under Uncertainty: Heuristics and Biases* (Cambridge UP 1982), 163.

discover and punish violations, in particular the cases with the highest fines. Secondly, it implies that it will never be possible to achieve complete deterrence. Indeed, even if the competition authorities managed at some point in time to detect so many violations and to impose such high fines that all companies will be deterred from committing new violations, this situation will not last, given that the urge to restrict competition will not disappear,[1815] and that over time the memory of those successful prosecutions will fade,[1816] with the result that violations will thus again be committed. In the meantime, competition authorities risk, however, having lost enforcement experience and capabilities, which would be costly and time-consuming to build up again.

Specifically concerning leniency, it is also important to keep in mind that **leniency is not a substitute but a complement to other methods of collecting intelligence and evidence of cartel infringements.**[1817] Indeed, leniency will work well if the cartel participants concerned perceive a risk that the competition authorities will detect and establish the cartel infringement without recourse to leniency. The risk could be a specific one, where the competition authority is already collecting or receiving information of the cartel infringement by other means (or is believed to be doing so, or to be doing so in the near future) or a more general one, where a competition authority, as a result of many other recent cases of successful detection and prosecution, is believed to be good at it. If leniency policies are well designed in that immunity is only granted to the first co-conspirator to come forward, and reductions in penalties are linked to the timing of the cooperation as compared to the other co-conspirators, cartel participants may decide to cooperate out of fear that a co-conspirator may do so before them.[1818] Such a 'race to cooperate' may amplify the positive effects of leniency, but again such a race is most likely to start if there is a risk that the competition authorities will detect and establish the antitrust violation without recourse to leniency, or at least a belief by at least one

---

1815 See also W. Eucken 'The Competitive Order and Its Implementation' (Autumn 2006) 2 *Competition Policy International* 219 (English translation of 'Die Wettbewerbsordnung und ihre Verwirklichung' (1949) 2 *Ordo–Jahrbuch für die Ordnung von Wirtschaft und Gesellschaft* 1), at 222 ('There is an omnipresent, strong and irrepressible urge to eliminate competition and to acquire a monopolistic position.'); S. Wilks and I. Bartle, 'The Unanticipated Consequences of Creating Independent Competition Agencies' (January 2002) 25 *Western European Politics* 148 at 152 ('Since abuse of market power is endemic in every market economy and is indeed a major component in the competitive strategies of most large companies, the elimination of anti-competitive practices (rather like the elimination of racial intolerance) is an impossible goal. Yet, as with racial equality, it is essential for governments to confirm support for free competition.'); and D. D. Sokol, 'Antitrust in 2025: Cartels, Agency Effectiveness, and a Return to Back to the Future' (December 2010) 2 *CPI Antitrust Journal*, electronic copy available at http://ssrn.com/abstract=1733246, at 2 ('In many cases the same industries are recidivists because, as a new generation retires, the next generation relearns how to coordinate with competitors. This illustrates the social norm within society and within the industry.').

1816 See K. Mehta, 'Cartel detection probability and the rate of cartel enforcement', July 2021, https://www.researchgate.net/publication/353224163_Cartel_detection_probability_and_the_rate_of_cartel_enforcement, at 6 ('In fact the most relevant risk factor for firms and their legal advisors is likely to be in terms of a sustained high number of annual cartel prohibitions. Such a deterrence indicator implies that the authority's cartel case pipeline must equal a multiple of annual decisions to sustain a high annual rate of decisions.')

1817 See my paper 'Leniency in Antitrust Enforcement: Theory and Practice' (2007) 30 *World Competition* 25, also accessible at http://ssrn.com/author=456087, Chapter V of this book, and OECD Policy Roundtable: Ex-officio cartel investigations and the use of screens to detect cartels, DAF/COMP/(2013)27, 7 July 2014.

1818 See also M. Bigoni, S. O. Fridolfsson, C. Le Coq and G. Spagnolo, 'Trust, Leniency and Deterrence' (2014), available at http://ssrn.com/abstract=2469778.

of the conspirators that at least one of the other co-conspirators may believe that there is such a risk.[1819]

A leniency policy will thus work well if the antitrust enforcement authority concerned has first built up a sufficient level of credibility as to its capacity to detect and punish cartel infringements on its own. As the statistics in Table 1 above show, the European Commission already had a good track record in detecting and punishing cartels by the time it introduced its leniency programme in 1996. Without this track record, the leniency programme could not have achieved the same rapid success.

For authorities that have managed to build up sufficient credibility, and subsequently operate a successful leniency programme, there may be a risk in relying too much on this success. If for a prolonged period they do not detect and prosecute any case anymore other than through leniency, they may lose their capacity to do so, or at least cartelists may start doubting their continued capacity to do so. If this were to happen, the success of their leniency programmes would risk coming to an end.[1820]

2. A closer look at the figures

Turning now to the **observed evolution of the number of leniency applications in Europe**, whereas the Monopolkommission referred to what were at the time the most recent available figures, being those in the OECD Competition Trends 2022, showing a 70.5% decline in the number of leniency applications in Europe in the period 2015 to 2020, more recent figures indicate that, at least in the case of the European Commission, the downward trend has already been reversed. Indeed, at a Concurrences event on 24 January 2023, Maria Jaspers, Director for Cartels at the European Commission's Directorate-General for Competition, revealed that the European Commission has received in 2022 twice as many leniency applications as in 2021, and three times as many as in 2020, adding that this increase 'might partly be due to the fact that we had last year also visibly stepped up our *ex officio* (on our own initiative) activities in order to generate cases outside the leniency programme'.[1821] This reversal appears to concern not only the European Commission. Indeed, according to the latest OECD figures, while the number of leniency applications continued declining in 2021 in other parts of the world, in Europe the number of leniency applications was 32% higher in 2021 than in 2020.[1822]

It should also be noted that other national competition authorities than the German Bundeskartellamt do not necessarily have the same experience or problem perception. For example, Margarida Matos Rosa, the outgoing president of the Portuguese Competition

1819 See my paper 'Leniency in Antitrust Enforcement: Theory and Practice' (2007) 30 *World Competition* 25, also accessible at http://ssrn.com/author=456087, at footnotes 91 to 94; and OECD Policy Roundtable, *Ex officio cartel investigations and the use of screens to detect cartels* (2013), available at http://www.oecd.org/daf/competition/exofficio-cartel-investigation-2013.pdf.

1820 See my paper 'Leniency in Antitrust Enforcement: Theory and Practice' (2007) 30 *World Competition* 25, also accessible at http://ssrn.com/author=456087, at footnotes 131 and 132, Chapter V of this book; and OECD, Competition Trends 2022, at 38.

1821 Concurrences, Global Cartel Enforcement Trends Webinar, 24 January 2023, https://www.concurrences.com/en/events/global-cartel-enforcement-trends-webinar-110012, page 5 of the transcript; see also MLex, 'Cartel leniency applications to EU regulator on the rise again, senior enforcer says', 24 January 2023.

1822 OECD, Competition Trends 2023, at 19.

Authority, indicated on 28 April 2023 that the Portuguese Competition Authority is 'really happy with the number of tip-offs and leniency requests that came through because they also spanned a lot of different markets. Last year we received eight full leniency requests. I want to believe that that is related to our strong enforcement over the years. As long as strong enforcement is present, it is a deterrent to companies but also means there is a higher probability of being detected. I think firms weigh what the costs may be for them if they are detected with the private enforcement costs. They make their decision taking both into account'.[1823]

3. The question then arises as to what could be the possible and likely reasons behind the significant decrease in the number of leniency applications in Europe between 2015 and 2020, the recent reversal of this trend, and the divergent experiences of national competition authorities. Possible and likely explanations of the observed evolution of the number of leniency applications

a. *Fewer cartels*

The first possible and likely explanation is a **decline in the number of cartels.**[1824] While the number of cartels cannot be directly observed, there are several reasons why such a decline is likely.

Primo, as visible in Table 3 in Chapter V of this book, in the period 2001–2015, the European Commission found and punished a high number of cartels, in significant part due to the success of its leniency policy. Indeed, the comparison between the figures for the 1996–2000 period and the figures for the 2001–2005 period shows that the number of cartel decisions tripled following the introduction of the leniency programme. As already mentioned above, there can be no doubt that this tripling of the number of cartel decisions has significantly increased deterrence. Similar increases in anti-cartel enforcement by several national competition authorities have, of course, added to this effect.

Secundo, as mentioned above, since 2005 there has been a significant increase in the number of follow-on actions for damages. The perspective of having to pay not only fines but also follow-on damages and corresponding legal costs obviously adds to deterrence.[1825]

Tertio, and not unrelatedly, in the last two decades many companies have also invested in more and better antitrust compliance.[1826] While the limitations of compliance programmes

---

1823 Global Competition Review (GCR), 'Margarida Matos Rosa: the exit interview', 28 April 2023, https://globalcompetitionreview.com/article/margarida-matos-rosa-the-exit-interview.

1824 See also D. Zimmer, 'Geht dem Bundeskartellamt die Arbeit aus?' *Wirtschaft und Wettbewerb (WuW)*, Nr. 4/2022, page 181.

1825 See also Monopolkommission, Wettbewerb 2022, XXIV. Haupgutachten gemäß § 44 Abs. 1 Satz 1 GWB (5.7.2022), at 166.

1826 See T. Makatsch and R. Bäuerle, 'Kronzeugenschutz und Kartellschadenersatz: Stimmt die Balance noch?, *Wirtschaft und Wettbewerb (WuW)*, Nr. 10/2022, page 529, at 532.

should not be ignored,[1827] it is difficult to believe that the spread of compliance programmes would have had no impact. The likely impact of the introduction of good compliance programmes is that, during a first period, more applications for leniency are made, as cartels are discovered, brought to an end and reported, and, afterwards, fewer leniency applications, because of fewer cartels. The observed increase in the number of leniency applications until 2014, and the subsequent decrease, would appear to fit this expected impact.

Quarto, in reaction to the introduction of leniency programmes and the increased anti-cartel enforcement, companies may have found other ways than cartels to achieve the same or similar anti-competitive results, in particular mergers and the acquisition of minority shareholdings.[1828]

b. *The evolution of the number of ex officio cartel investigations*

The second possible and likely explanation for the observed evolution of the number of leniency applications is the **evolution of the number of *ex officio* cartel investigations**, that is, investigations started otherwise than through leniency.

As explained above, leniency is not a substitute but a complement to other methods of collecting intelligence and evidence of cartel infringements, and competition authorities take a risk in relying too much on the success of their leniency programmes. If for a prolonged period they do not detect and prosecute any case anymore other than through leniency, they may lose their capacity to do so, or at least cartelists may start doubting their continued capacity to do so. If this were to happen, the success of their leniency programmes would risk coming to an end.

As is visible from Table 7 in Chapter V of this book and immediately below, which shows the number of European Commission decisions concerning cartels that were not detected through leniency, this scenario may have become true in the case of the European Commission.

Table 7: Decisions following ***ex officio*** *cartel investigations*

Period	Number of decisions following *ex officio* cartel investigations
1986–1990	9
1991–1995	8
1996–2000	9
2001–2005	15
2006–2010	9
2011–2015	4
2016–2020	0

1827 See Chapter VII of this book.

1828 See K. Hüschelrath and F. Smuda, 'Do Cartel Breakdowns Induce Mergers? Evidence from EC Cartel Cases' (2012) 9 *European Competition Journal* 7, and S. Heim, K. Hüschelrath, U. Laitenberger and Y. Spiegel, 'The Anticompetitive Effect of Minority Share Acquisitions: Evidence from the Introduction of National Leniency Programs' (2022) 14 *American Economic Journal: Microeconomics* 366.

Whereas in the 2001–2005 and 2006–2010 periods there were still many decisions concerning cartels that had not been detected through leniency, there were only four such decisions in the 2011–2015 period, the most recent of these being the December 2014 decision concerning the *Envelopes* cartel, which was detected thanks to information received from an informant.[1829] In the 2016–2020 period, there were none.[1830]

Beyond the case of the European Commission, the figures in the OECD Competition Trends 2002 indicate a decline in *ex officio* cartel investigations in the period 2015–2020 in Europe, the Americas and the Asia-Pacific region,[1831] coinciding with the decline in leniency applications.

While some *ex officio* investigations have started with information obtained from other authorities or gleaned from the specialised press, informants have always been the main source of information allowing the detection of cartels other than through leniency.[1832]

In the last few years, the Cartel Directorate of the European Commission's Directorate-General for Competition has again invested in developing its capacity to detect cartels other than through leniency,[1833] with some visible first results.[1834] As already mentioned above, this may explain the increase in leniency applications in the most recent years. The divergent experiences of different national competition authorities in terms of continued success of their leniency programmes may similarly be explained by their different track records in terms of *ex officio* enforcement.

1829 Decision of 10 December 2014 in Case AT.39780 *Envelopes*, Summary publication in [2015] OJ C74/5.

1830 In 2022, the European Commission adopted a decision following an *ex* officio cartel investigation that had been started by the German Federal Competition Authority (Bundeskartellamt), which transferred the case to the European Commission; see Decision of 12 July 2022 in Case AT.405220 *Metal packaging*, Summary publication in [2023] OJ C57/5.

1831 OECD, Competition Trends 2022, at 38.

1832 See also M. E. Stucke, 'Leniency, Whistle-Blowing and the Individual: Should We Create Another Race to the Competition Agency?', in C. Beaton-Wells and C. Tran (eds), *Anti-Cartel Enforcement in a Contemporary Age Leniency Religion* (Hart 2015), 209. Whereas it has often been suggested (not always disinterestedly) that econometric tools could be used to detect cartels, the experience with such tools has not been good, with some limited exceptions in public procurement markets; see OECD Competition Policy Roundtable Background Note, *Data Screening Tools for Competition Investigations* (2022), https://www.oecd.org/daf/competition/data-screening-tools-in-competition-investigations-2022.pdf. In the United States, the Department of Justice Antitrust Division has in the past employed several methods for cartel screening and found that those methods did not produce solid leads for cartel investigations; see OECD Policy Roundtable, *Ex officio cartel investigations and the use of screens to detect cartels* (2013), http://www.oecd.org/daf/competition/exofficio-cartel-investigation-2013.pdf, at 38, footnote 129. Similarly, the European Commission's attempt to use economic data analysis in the *Cement* cartel investigation has delivered no results, while consuming a huge amount of resources; see information on the opening and closure of proceedings in Case 39520 *Cement and related products* on the European Commission's website http://ec.europa.eu/competition/antitrust/cases/index.html; Opinion of Advocate General Wahl in *HeidelbergCement v Commission*, C-247/14 P, EU:C:2015:694; and Judgment in *HeidelbergCement v Commission*, C-247/14 P, EU:C:2016:149.

1833 To better attract informants, the European Commission created in 2017 an anonymous whistle-blower tool. This is a specifically designed encrypted messaging system that allows two-way communications between informants and the European Commission's Directorate-General for Competition. The service is run by a specialised external service provider that acts as an intermediary, and which relays only the content of received messages without forwarding any metadata that could be used to identify the informant; see European Commission Press release IP/17/591 of 16 March 2017 and https://ec.europa.eu/competition-policy/cartels/whistleblower_en.

1834 See MLex, 'Flagrance cartel probe started on enforcers' own initiative, senior EU official says', 31 March 2023, and MLex, 'Quality of anonymous tip-offs is on the rise, EU's McCallum says', 26 May 2023.

c. *Uncertainty about follow-on actions for damages*

If the **fear of follow-on actions for damages** may be the third possible explanation for the observed evolution of the number of leniency applications, its relevance may very well be merely transitional, as well as derivative of the insufficient *ex officio* enforcement explanation.

One could indeed believe that, when MAN made its immunity application to the European Commission in 2010, it may not have anticipated the flood of follow-on actions for damages that the European Commission's 2016 decision in the Trucks Cartel case has given rise to, and that it might have been discouraged from making its immunity application if it had foreseen this.

The uncertainty and complexity of the Trucks Cartel follow-on litigation may, however, be a symptom of the still relatively new development of follow-on damages litigation in Europe. Over time, and thanks to the litigation in cases like the Trucks Cartel case, uncertainty about follow-on damages liability will be reduced, and liability for follow-on damages will become a predictable factor that can be more easily integrated into a company's decision to apply for leniency.[1835]

In any event, the more decisive element would appear to be the threat of *ex officio* enforcement. If the risk of the cartel being detected otherwise than through leniency is sufficiently high, it will always make sense to apply for leniency, irrespective of the size and uncertainty of the follow-on damages liability.

D. Three (sets of) reasons why it would be unwise to grant immunity recipients full protection from damages

In any event, granting immunity recipients full protection from follow-on actions for damages would be most unwise, for three sets of reasons: it would create injustice, weaken public anti-cartel enforcement, and (further) increase market concentration.

1. Injustice

Granting immunity recipients full protection from damages would constitute an extreme departure from centuries-old common European legal and moral standards.

Corrective justice is a foundational principle of private law. It received its classical formulation in Aristotle's treatment of justice in *Nicomachean Ethics*, Book V.[1836]

Corrective justice deals with voluntary and involuntary transactions (contracts and torts) and focuses on whether one party has committed and the other has suffered a transactional injustice. It aims at 'the maintenance and restoration of the notional equality with which

---

1835 As to the phenomenon of 'cupboard applications' described by J. Ysewyn and S. Kahmann, 'The decline and fall of the leniency programme in Europe', *Concurrences* no 1-2018, 44, at 58, one could think about amending Article 25(1)(b) of Regulation 1/2003 to prolong the limitation period.

1836 Aristotle, *Nicomachean Ethics*, V, 2–5, 1130a14-1133b28.

the parties enter the transaction. This equality consists in persons' having what lawfully belongs to them. Injustice occurs when, relative to this baseline, one party realises a gain and the other a corresponding loss. The law corrects this injustice when it re-establishes the initial equality by depriving one party of the gain and restoring it to the other party'.[1837]

Corrective justice is thus concerned not only with ensuring that the injured party receives full compensation, but also with ensuring that the party that caused the injury pays.[1838]

This dual aspect is also reflected in the case law of the Court of Justice, according to which Article 101 TFEU entails not only the victim's right to compensation but also the infringing undertakings' corresponding obligation to provide compensation for the damage caused.[1839]

While the idea and the practice of public enforcement authorities granting immunity from punishment or a reduced penalty in exchange for cooperation to help convict co-conspirators is probably as old as criminal prosecution,[1840] this has always been distinguished from the private law obligation to make reparation, which is governed by the principle of corrective justice, and which can only be waived by the injured party.

As John Locke wrote in 1690 in his *Second Treatise of Government*:

'*From these two distinct rights (the one of punishing the crime, for restraint and preventing the like offence, which right of punishing is in everybody, the other of taking reparation, which belongs only to the injured party) comes it to pass that the magistrate, who by being magistrate hath the common right of punishing put into his hands, can often, where the public good demands not the execution of the law, remit the punishment of criminal offences by his own authority, but yet cannot remit the satisfaction due to any private man for the damage he has received. That he who hath suffered the damage has a right to demand in his own name, and he alone can remit.*'[1841]

Fully exempting immunity recipients from the obligation to provide compensation, even to their own direct and indirect purchasers and providers, would constitute an extreme and entirely unprecedented departure from the common principle of corrective justice.

Also in the USA, immunity recipients remain liable for (single – that is, compensatory, non-punitive) damages to their own direct and indirect purchasers and providers.[1842] Indeed, using best efforts to make restitution to injured parties and to remediate the harm

---

1837 E. J. Weinrib, 'Corrective Justice in a Nutshell' (2002) 52 *University of Toronto Law Journal* 349 at 349.

1838 See also D. A. Crane, 'Why Leniency does not Undermine Compensation', in C. Beaton-Wells and C. Tran (eds), *Anti-Cartel Enforcement in a Contemporary Age–Leniency Religion* (Hart Publishing 2015), 263 at 268.

1839 Judgment in *Skanska Industrial Solutions*, C-724/17, EU:C:2019:204, paragraphs 28 to 32, referring to the Opinion of Advocate General Wahl in *Skanska Industrial Solutions*, C-724/17, EU:C:2019:100, paragraphs 60 to 62.

1840 See N. K. Katyal, 'Conspiracy Theory' (2003) 112 *Yale Law Journal* 1307, at 1330–1331, referring to practices in English law going back to the early 12th century, as well as in early American law.

1841 J. Locke, *The Second Treatise on Civil Government* (1690), Chapter II, paragraph 11.

1842 Antitrust Criminal Penalty Enhancement and Reform Act of 2004, Pub. L. 108-237, §§ 201–214, 118 Stat. 661 (June 22, 2004), 15 USC § 1 note (2004 Act), § 213. See also D. A. Crane, 'Why Leniency does not Undermine Compensation', in C. Beaton-Wells and C. Tran (eds), *Anti-Cartel Enforcement in a Contemporary Age–Leniency Religion* (Hart Publishing 2015), 263 at 267.

caused by the illegal activity is even a condition for obtaining leniency from the US Department of Justice.[1843] The essence of the principle of corrective justice remains thus respected in the same way as under Directive 2014/104.[1844]

The injustice of fully exempting the immunity recipient from damages is aggravated by the fact that the immunity recipient is often among the cartel participants with the highest turnovers, or indeed the single highest turnover, in the market affected by the cartel.

The injustice of fully exempting the immunity recipient from damages is not only problematic as such, but also risks undermining the effectiveness of anti-cartel enforcement.

Indeed, corporate managers are not necessarily just maximisers of profits for themselves and their principals. They may feel a moral responsibility to live within the law whether or not they are likely to be caught, and this normative commitment could trump their interest calculus. The public punishment of those who violate the antitrust prohibitions has thus not only a deterrent effect, in that it helps create a credible threat of punishment for those who would be willing to commit violations on the basis of a profit calculation, but also moral effects, in that it sends a message to the spontaneously law-abiding, reinforcing their moral commitment to the rules.[1845]

For people to have such moral commitment to the law, however, it is important that the law and its enforcement are perceived to be fair.[1846] The injustice of fully exempting the immunity recipient from damages may similarly affect the willingness of potential complainants and informants to help the competition authorities. As explained above, informants are particularly important for *ex officio* cartel enforcement, which in turn is important for the continued success of leniency programmes.

2. Harm to public anti-cartel enforcement

Perversely, fully exempting immunity applicants from damages would weaken public anti-cartel enforcement because it would reduce the evidentiary value of the immunity applicant's leniency statements and discourage leniency applications by potential second-in and third-in applicants.

1843 US Department of Justice, Antitrust Division Leniency Policy and Procedures (4 April 2022), included in DOJ Justice Manual, Criminal Antitrust Enforcement, https://www.justice.gov/atr/page/file/1490246/download, 7-3.310, and 7-3.320, point 5.

1844 Article 3(3) of Directive 2014/104/EU prohibits 'overcompensation, whether by means of punitive, multiple or other types of damages'.

1845 See C. D. Stone, 'Sentencing the corporation' (1991) 71 *Boston University Law Review* 383 at 389; J. Adenaes, 'The Moral or Educative Influence of Criminal Law' (1971) 27 *Journal of Social Issues* 17, and 'General prevention revisited: research and policy implications' (1975) 66 *Journal of Criminal Law & Criminology* 338, at 341–343; K. G. Dau-Schmidt, 'An Economic Analysis of the Criminal Law as a Preference-Shaping Policy' (1990) *Duke Law Journal* 1, C.R. Sunstein, 'On the Expressive Function of the Law' (1996) 144 *University of Pennsylvania Law Review* 2021, D.M. Kahan, 'Social Influence, Social Meaning, and Deterrence' (1997) 83 *Virginia Law Review* 349, N. K. Katyal, 'Deterrence's Difficulty' (1997) 95 *Michigan Law Review* 2385, G. E. Lynch, 'The Role of Criminal Law in Policing Corporate Misconduct' (1997) 60 *Law and Contemporary Problems* 23, D. M. Kahan, 'Social Meaning and the Economic Analysis of Crime' (1998) 27 *Journal of Legal Studies* 609, and K. G. Dau-Schmidt, 'Preference shaping by the law', in P. Newman (ed), *The New Palgrave Dictionary of Economics and the Law* (Macmillan 1998) 84.

1846 See T. R. Tyler, *Why People Obey the Law* (Yale UP 1990), as well as the literature listed in the footnote immediately above.

One of the consequences of the use of leniency programmes and the increased anti-cartel enforcement it has enabled, and of the increased compliance activity, is that written evidence of cartels is increasingly rare, as cartelists are increasingly careful to avoid creating such evidence.[1847]

In order to be able to establish the cartel infringement and impose fines that will be upheld by the courts upon appeal, the competition authorities thus need to rely to a large extent on the leniency statements provided by the immunity applicant. This raises the important question what the evidentiary value of such statements is.

According to the case law of the Court of Justice, 'statements which run counter to the interests of the declarant must in principle be regarded as particularly reliable evidence. [. . .] a statement made by a company admitting the existence of an infringement by that company entails considerable legal and economic risks, including, inter alia, the risk of actions for damages being brought before the national courts, in the context of which the Commission's establishment of a company's infringement may be invoked. [. . .] Nonetheless, statements made by the undertakings concerned in the context of an application for leniency pursuant to the Leniency Notice must be assessed with caution and, in general, cannot be regarded as particularly reliable evidence if they have not been corroborated by other evidence'.[1848]

To obtain the required corroborating evidence, competition authorities most often need the help of second-in or further leniency applicants.[1849]

Granting full immunity from damages to the immunity applicant would in two ways undermine the ability of competition authorities to collect the legally required evidence to prove the cartel infringement.

First, it would reduce the evidentiary value of the leniency statements of the immunity applicant. As mentioned above, the fact that leniency applicants are liable for damages is precisely an important factor which has allowed the courts to admit leniency statements as reliable evidence. In the absence of follow-on liability for damages, it could legitimately be feared that immunity applicants would make unreliable leniency statements, exaggerating the scope and effects of the cartel, with the intention of harming their competitors.[1850]

1847 See L. M. Marx and C. Mezzetti, 'Effects of leniency on concealment effort by colluding firms' (2014) 2 *Journal of Antitrust Enforcement* 305, and R. Polley, 'Is the Continued Success of Leniency in Cartel Cases in Danger? Somme Comments from a Private Practitioner's Perspective', *CPI Antitrust Chronicle*, September 2015, at 3.

1848 Judgment in *Campine and Campine Recycling v Commission*, T-240/17, EU:T:2019:778, paragraphs 119 to 121; see also Judgments in *Siemens and Others v Commission*, C-239/11 P, C-489/11 P and C-498/11 P, EU:C:2013:866, paragraphs 140–141; *Dole Food and Dole Germany v Commission*, T-588/08, EU:T:2013:130, paragraph 94; *FSL and Others v Commission*, T-655/11, EU:T:2015:383, paragraph 152; and *Huhtamäki and Huhtamaki Flexible Packaging Germany v Commission*, T-530/15, EU:T:2019:498, paragraph 55

1849 See also K. Mehta, 'Cartel detection probability and the rate of cartel enforcement', July 2021, https://www.researchgate.net/publication/353224163_Cartel_detection_probability_and_the_rate_of_cartel_enforcement, at 8 ('Some theoretical models also assume the extreme scenario that solely an immunity applicant is necessary: successful cartel infringement cases, on the contrary, have overwhelmingly depended on critical corroborative evidence from a limited number of applicants for reductions of fines, particularly from those cartel members also with significant market shares, so as to enable the prohibition decision to withstand the inevitable judicial review.')

1850 See also P. Kirst and R. Van den Bergh, 'The European Directive on Damages Actions: A Missed Opportunity to Reconcile Compensation of Victims and Leniency Incentives (2016) 12 *Journal of Competition Law & Economics* 1, at 20: 'The higher the damages that other cartel members face after the revelation of the cartel, the higher will be the competitive advantage for the immunity recipient.'

The reduced evidentiary value of the leniency statements of the immunity applicant would increase the need for corroborating evidence provided by second-in or further leniency applications.

However, the second harmful effect of granting full immunity from damages to the immunity applicant would precisely be that potential second-in and further leniency applicants would be less willing to come forward, because they would bear an increased burden of civil liability, whereas without their leniency application the competition authority might not be able to prove the infringement.[1851]

3. Increased market concentration

Scholars have in recent years expressed concern about increased market concentration.[1852]

The *ex post* impact of anti-cartel enforcement on market structure is a relevant consideration in designing optimal fining, leniency and damages policies.[1853]

Imagine by way of illustration that a cartel, which has been functioning very profitably for many years, is discovered in some local market, on which five companies with comparable market shares are active, four of which are not active in other markets and have limited financial reserves, whereas the fifth is a subsidiary of a large, financially strong, international group. All five companies have been equally active in the cartel, and none has cooperated with the competition authority's investigation. If one were to focus exclusively on deterrence, one would advocate in such a case the imposition of high fines on all five cartel participants. The risk, however, is that this could lead to the elimination of the four smaller competitors and the domination of the market by the fifth, stronger company.

In a variation on the same example, it could also be that the fifth, stronger company is the one which disclosed the existence of the cartel to the competition authority, and for that reason qualifies for immunity from fines. This was roughly the situation with the Luxembourg Brewers Cartel, which the European Commission fined in 2001.[1854]

As Advocate General Geelhoed has pointed out, 'in the event of a collective infringement like a cartel as opposed to an infringement by a single offender, the [European] Commission must also consider the subsequent effects of the fines and take into account the size of a given company. [. . .] The example [. . .] is a cartel consisting of one big player and several small players. The big player cooperated with the Commission and receives immunity under the Leniency Notice. In such cases very high fines could have

---

1851 See also MLex, 'Leniency review shouldn't overlook victims' rights to damages, EU's Vestager says', 9 September 2022, quoting European Commission Executive Vice-President Margrethe Vestager: 'What would that do to the incentives of Number 2 and Number 3 from coming in [to cooperate with investigators]. Very often they have very important evidence.'

1852 See G. Koltay, S. Lorincz and T. Valletti, 'Concentration and Competition: Evidence from Europe and Implications for Policy, CESifo Working Paper Nr. 9640, March 2020.

1853 See my paper 'Optimal Antitrust Fines: Theory and Practice' (2006) 29 *World Competition* 183, also accessible at http://ssrn.com/author=456087, text accompanied by footnotes 95 and 96.

1854 See European Commission Decision of 5 December 2001 in Case COMP/37.800/F3 *Luxembourg Brewers*, [2002] OJ L253/21, and Judgment in *Brasserie Nationale and Others v Commission*, Joined Cases T-49/02 to T-51/02, EU:T:2005:298.

put the smaller players out of business, in which case the Commission's intervention would have resulted in a monopoly'.[1855]

As I demonstrated in an earlier paper,[1856] on the basis of a sample containing all the cartel decisions adopted by the European Commission in the 2006–2015 period in which immunity was granted, and as summarised in Table 6 in Chapter V of this book and immediately below, it appears that in 46% of the cases the immunity recipient was the cartel participant with the highest turnover in the market affected by the cartel, whereas on average there were 7 participants per cartel, and the undertaking with the highest turnover should thus have been the immunity recipient in only 15% of the cases if there had been no correlation between being the undertaking with the largest turnover and being the immunity recipient.

Table 6: Immunity recipients with the highest turnover in the affected market

Period	2006–2015
Number of immunity recipients	46
Number of immunity recipients with the highest turnover in the market affected by the cartel	21 = 46%
Total number of undertakings involved	316
Average number of undertakings per cartel	7

Given that under the European Commission's 2006 Fining Guidelines the fines are calculated as a percentage of each undertaking's turnover in the goods or services affected by the cartel, the above result should not come as a surprise: The undertakings with the largest affected turnover can expect the highest fine, and hence have the most to gain from applying for leniency.

This problem of the potential negative *ex post* effect of anti-cartel enforcement on market structure would become acute if the immunity recipient were to be also granted immunity from damages. As long as the immunity recipient only receives immunity from fines, the problem can be managed by the competition authority's imposing not too high fines on the smaller cartel members.[1857] If the immunity recipient were to receive also immunity from fines, the problem would become unmanageable.

The German Monopolkommission proposes to solve this problem by not granting immunity from damages to immunity recipients that enjoy a dominant position.[1858]

1855 Opinion in *Showa Denko v Commission*, C-289/04 P, EU:C:2006:52, paragraph 61 and footnote 16.

1856 See my paper 'The Use of Leniency in EU Cartel Enforcement: An Assessment After Twenty Years' (2016) 39 *World Competition* 327, also accessible at http://ssrn.com/author=456087, Table 4 and full list of cases in the annex.

1857 This is what the European Commission did in the *Luxembourg Brewers* case; see European Commission Decision of 5 December 2001 in Case COMP/37.800/F3 *Luxembourg Brewers* [2002] OJ L253/21, and Judgment in *Brasserie Nationale and Others v Commission*, T-49/02 to T-51/02, EU:T:2005:298.

1858 Monopolkommission, Wettbewerb 2022, XXIV. Haupgutachten gemäβ § 44 Abs. 1 Satz 1 GWB (5.7.2022), at 170–171.

This proposed solution is, however, far from adequate. Leaving aside the important practical question of who would at what point in time in which procedural setting have to discharge the evidentiary burden of proving the existence or absence of a dominant position, cartels that encompass a dominant company are unlikely to exist in the real world.[1859]

In preparation for earlier papers, I have examined all cartel decisions adopted by the European Commission since 1986:[1860] not a single one appeared to comprise a dominant undertaking at the time of the cartel infringement or at the time of the European Commission's decision.

This should not come as a surprise, since a dominant undertaking is, by definition, an undertaking that enjoys 'a position of economic strength [. . .] which enables it to prevent effective competition being maintained on the relevant market by affording it the power to behave to an appreciable extent independently of its competitors, customers and ultimately of its consumers'.[1861] In other words, dominant companies are companies that do not need cartels to reach anti-competitive outcomes, as they can reach such outcomes through unilateral behaviour.

As illustrated by the example of the Luxembourg Brewers Cartel mentioned above, the problem is not with cartels encompassing a dominant company – which are unlikely to exist – but with immunity recipients becoming dominant as a result of the detection and punishment of the cartel and the follow-on damages litigation, as well as, below the point of dominance, competitors being weakened, and market structures becoming more concentrated.

1859 See also R. Alimonti, S. Kümmel and T. Nau, 'The interplay between leniency programmes and private enforcement: the economist perspective on recent policy proposals' (2022) 21 *Competition Law Journal* 170 at 178.

1860 See the lists of decisions in the annexes to my papers 'The Use of Leniency in EU Cartel Enforcement: An Assessment After Twenty Years' (2016) 39 *World Competition* 327 and 'Regulation 1/2003: An Assessment After Twenty Years' (2023) 46 *World Competition* 3, both also accessible at http://ssrn.com/author=456087.

1861 Judgment in *United Brands v Commission*, 27/76, EU:C:1978:22, paragraph 65.

TABLE OF CASES

European Court of Human Rights

EUROPEAN UNION

Court of Justice

General Court (Court of First Instance)

Advocate General Opinions

European Ombudsman

European Commission

Hearing Officer Final Reports

EFTA Court

NATIONAL COURTS

Belgium

Germany

Greece

Portugal

United Kingdom

United States

INDEX

E

H

I

R

S

U

V

Concurrences Review

Concurrences is a print and online quarterly peer reviewed journal dedicated to EU and national competitions laws. It has been launched in 2004 as the flagship of the Institute of Competition Law in order to provide a forum for academics, practitioners and enforcers. Concurrences' influence and expertise has garnered contributions or interviews with such figures as Christine Lagarde, Bill Kovacic, Emmanuel Macron, Antonin Scalia and Magrethe Vestager.

CONTENTS

More than 15,000 articles, print and/or online. Quarterly issues provide current coverage with contributions from the EU or national or foreign countries thanks to more than 2,500 authors in Europe and abroad.

FORMAT

In order to balance academic contributions with opinions or legal practice notes, Concurrences provides its insight and analysis in a number of formats:

- Forewords: Opinions by leading academics or enforcers
- Interviews: Interviews of antitrust experts
- On-Topics: 4 to 6 short papers on hot issues
- Law & Economics: Short papers written by economists for a legal audience
- Articles: Long academic papers
- Case Summaries: Case commentary on EU and French case law
- Legal Practice: Short papers for in-house counsels
- International: Medium size papers on international policies
- Books Review: Summaries of recent antitrust books
- Articles Review: Summaries of leading articles published in 45 antitrust journals

BOARDS

The Scientific Committee is headed by Laurence Idot, Professor at Panthéon Assas University. The International Committee is headed by Frederic Jenny, OECD Competition Comitteee Chairman. Boards members include Douglas Ginsburg, Benoît Cœuré, Howard Shelanski, Richard Whish, Wouter Wils, Joshua Wright, etc.

ONLINE VERSION

Concurrences website provides all articles published since its inception, in addition to selected articles published online only in the electronic supplement.

WRITE FOR CONCURRENCES

Concurrences welcome spontaneous contributions. Except in rare circumstances, the journal accepts only unpublished articles, whatever the form and nature of the contribution. The Editorial Board checks the form of the proposals, and then submits these to the Scientific Committee. Selection of the papers is conditional to a peer review by at least two members of the Committee. Within a month, the Committee assesses whether the draft article can be published and notifies the author.

www.ingramcontent.com/pod-product-compliance
Ingram Content Group UK Ltd.
Pitfield, Milton Keynes, MK11 3LW, UK
UKHW020222290926
15470UKWH00001B/329

9 781939 007650